Islam in the Modern World

Edited by Jeffrey T. Kenney
and Ebrahim Moosa

Routledge
Taylor & Francis Group

LONDON AND NEW YORK

First published in 2014
by Routledge
2 Park Square, Milton Park, Abingdon, Oxon OX14 4RN

Simultaneously published in the USA and Canada
by Routledge
711 Third Avenue, New York, NY 10017

Routledge is an imprint of the Taylor & Francis Group, an informa business

British Library Cataloguing in Publication Data
A catalogue record for this book is available from the British Library

Library of Congress Cataloging in Publication Data
Islam in the modern world / edited by Jeffrey T. Kenney and Ebrahim Moosa.
p. cm. -- (Religions in the modern world)
Includes bibliographical references and index.
1. Islam--21st century. 2. Islam--20th century. I. Kenney,
Jeffrey T. (Jeffrey Thomas), 1954- II. Moosa, Ebrahim.
BP161.3.I739 2013
297--dc23
2013002611

ISBN: 978-0-415-78085-8 (hbk)
ISBN: 978-0-415-78086-5 (pbk)
ISBN: 978-0-203-73634-0 (ebk)

Typeset in Gentium
By Saxon Graphics Ltd, Derby

MIX
Paper from
responsible sources
FSC
www.fsc.org FSC® C013604

Printed and bound by CPI Group (UK) Ltd, Croydon, CR0 4YY

To our students ... past, present, and future

Contents

Part III: Case studies of tradition and change

Illustrations

Tables

Maps

Contributors

Muhamad Ali, PhD is an Assistant Professor in Islamic Studies in the Department of Religious Studies at the University of California, Riverside, USA. He teaches Islam in Southeast Asia, topics in modern Islam, and approaches to Islam in religious studies. He is a graduate of the Department of Islamic and Middle Eastern Studies, Edinburgh University, UK, and the University of Hawaii at Manoa, USA. He has published two books: *Multicultural-Pluralist Theology* (2003) and *Bridging Islam and the West: An Indonesian View* (2009), along with many articles, including "Islamic Liberalism in Southeast Asia" (2012). His current project is a history of religious pluralism in Indonesia.

Jonathan Brown is a Professor of Islamic Studies in the School of Foreign Service at Georgetown University in Washington, DC, USA. His book publications include *The Canonization of al-Bukhari and Muslim: The Formation and Function of the Sunni Hadith Canon* (2007), *Hadith: Muhammad's Legacy in the Medieval and Modern World* (2009) and *Muhammad: A Very Short Introduction* (2011). He has published articles in the fields of hadith, Islamic law, Sufism, Arabic lexical theory and pre-Islamic poetry and is the editor in chief of the *Oxford Encyclopedia of Islamic Law*.

Gary R. Bunt is Reader in Islamic Studies in the Department of Theology, Religious Studies and Islamic Studies at the University of Wales Trinity Saint David, UK. He directs the university's MA Islamic Studies (by distance learning). Dr Bunt's primary research focus is on Islam in cyberspace, and his books include *iMuslims: Rewiring the House of Islam* (2009), *Islam in the Digital Age* (2003) and *Virtually Islamic* (2000). A related research website and blog can be found at www.virtuallyislamic.com.

Anthony R. Byrd is a PhD candidate in the Graduate Division of Religion at Emory University, USA. In addition to work on contemporary Islamic theology and political liberalism, his research focuses on philosophy and theology in the classical tradition surrounding issues of reason and evil, moral psychology, and models of the self in Islamic thought.

Carl W. Ernst is William R. Kenan, Jr., Distinguished Professor of Religious Studies at the University of North Carolina at Chapel Hill, USA. He is a specialist in Islamic studies, with a focus on West and South Asia. His published research, based on the study of Arabic, Persian, and Urdu, has been mainly devoted to general and critical issues of Islamic studies, pre-modern and contemporary Sufism, and Indo-Muslim culture. His most recent book is *How to Read the Qur'an: A New Guide, with Select Translations* (2011).

Marcia Hermansen is Director of the Islamic World Studies programme at Loyola University Chicago, USA, where she teaches courses in Islamic studies and religious studies in the Theology Department. She received her PhD from the University of Chicago in Arabic and Islamic Studies. Her books include *Muslima Theology: The Voices of Muslim Women Theologians* (forthcoming), *Shah Wali Allah's Treatises on Islamic Law* (2010) and *The Conclusive Argument from God*, a study and translation (from Arabic) of Shah Wali Allah of Delhi's *Hujjat Allah al-Baligha* (1996). She was an associate editor of the *Macmillan Encyclopedia of Islam and the Muslim World* (2003). Dr Hermansen has contributed numerous academic articles in the fields of Islamic thought, Sufism, Islam and Muslims in South Asia, Muslims in America, and women and gender in Islam.

Tiffany A. Hodge is completing her PhD at Emory University, USA, in the West and South Asian Religions (WSAR) programme. During the academic year 2012–13, she will serve as a visiting professor in Vanderbilt University's Religion department. A Fulbright scholar and Charlotte Newcombe dissertation fellow, Hodge conducted her dissertation fieldwork in rural Bangladesh on religious authority and dispute resolution.

Mohsen Kadivar has been a Visiting Research Professor of Islamic Studies in the Department of Religion at Duke University, USA, since 2009. An Iranian dissident who was jailed for speaking out against the authoritarianism of the Iranian regime, Kadivar has published widely on theology and philosophy. He is an outspoken critic of Iranian-style Islamic theocracy. For more details see http://kadivar.com.

Jeffrey T. Kenney is Professor of Religious Studies and University Professor at DePauw University, USA, where he teaches courses in comparative religions and Islamic studies. His research focuses on modern Islamic thought in Egypt and the greater Middle East, with a special interest in political religion, radicalism, Islamism, modernization, and secularization. His publications on these subjects have appeared in journals, books, and encyclopedias.

Ahmet T. Kuru is Associate Professor of Political Science at San Diego State University, USA, and formerly postdoctoral scholar at Columbia University, USA. He is the co-editor (with Alfred Stepan) of *Democracy, Islam, and Secularism in Turkey* (2012). Kuru is the author of *Secularism and State Policies toward Religion: The United States, France, and Turkey* (2009), which received the Distinguished Book Award from the Society for the Scientific Study of Religion. His articles have been published in *World Politics*, *Comparative Politics*, and *Political Science Quarterly*. Kuru is the Chair of the American Political Science Association's Religion and Politics Section.

Bruce B. Lawrence is an Emeritus Professor of Religion at Duke University, USA. The Marcus Family Professor of Islamic Studies, he also served as the inaugural director of the Duke Islamic Studies Center. He has authored, co-authored, edited or co-edited 16 books, many of which have won prizes, while also sparking debates in and beyond the academy. His research focuses on Islam in all phases and all disciplines, with special attention to institutional Islam in Asia, Indo-Persian Sufism, the religious masks of violence, and contemporary Islam as both Abrahamic faith and religious ideology.

Robert D. Lee has taught political science at Colorado College, USA, since 1971. His interest in Islam developed from dissertation research on Algeria in the colonial period and then from an interest in contemporary Muslim intellectuals and their efforts to reinterpret the past.

Richard C. Martin (PhD, Near Eastern Studies at New York University, 1975) is Professor Emeritus of Islamic Studies and History of Religions at Emory University, USA. He is the author of several articles and books on Islam, and coauthor of *Defenders of Reason in Islam: Mu`tazilism from Medieval School to Modern Symbol* (1997); and editor in chief of *The Encyclopedia of Islam and the Muslim World* (2004). He has served on several editorial boards and is past president of the American Research Center in Egypt.

Namrata Mitra is a graduate student in the philosophy and literature programme at Purdue University, USA. She is currently completing her dissertation titled *Nationalism Haunted by Evil: Representations of 1947 Partition*. Her research interests include social and political philosophy, postcolonial literature and theory, and transnational feminism.

Valentine M. Moghadam is Professor of Sociology and Director of the International Affairs Program at Northeastern University in Boston, USA, which she joined in January 2012. Among her many publications, Professor Moghadam is author of *Modernizing Women: Gender and Social Change in the Middle East* (first published 1993; second edition 2003; updated third edition expected in 2013); *Women, Work and Economic Reform in the Middle East and North Africa* (1998); *Globalizing Women: Transnational*

Feminist Networks (2005), which won the American Political Science Association's Victoria Schuck award for best book on women and politics for 2005; and *Globalization and Social Movements: Islamism, Feminism, and the Global Justice Movement* (2009, updated second edition fall 2012). She has edited seven books, most recently *Making Globalization Work for Women: The Role of Social Rights and Trade Union Leadership* (2011). With Professor Massoud Karshenas, she is co-editor of *Social Policy in the Middle East: Economic, Political, and Gender Dynamics* (2005).

Kathleen M. Moore is Professor of Religious Studies at the University of California Santa Barbara, USA. Her publications concern Muslims in the United States and their encounters with the American legal system, including *The Unfamiliar Abode: Islamic Law in the United States and Britain* (2010).

Ebrahim Moosa is Professor of Religion and Islamic Studies in the Department of Religion at Duke University, USA. He has published on modern Islamic ethics and Islamic law with a comparative perspective on developments in the Middle East and South Asia. His book *Ghazali and the Poetics of Imagination* (2005) won a prize at the American Academy of Religion and he was named Carnegie scholar in 2005 in order to pursue research on south Asian *madrasas*.

Jørgen S. Nielsen is Professor and Director of the Centre for European Islamic Thought in the Faculty of Theology at the University of Copenhagen, Denmark. Since 1978 his research has focused on Islam in Europe, and he is the author of *Muslims in Western Europe* (3rd edn, 2004).

Mark Sedgwick is Professor of Arab and Islamic Studies at Aarhus University in Denmark. He previously taught Arab history for many years at the American University in Cairo, Egypt. He is the author of *Islam & Muslims: A Guide to Diverse Experience in a Modern World* (2006) and of books on Sufism and on Islamic modernism. He also works on Islam in Europe and on terrorism and counter-radicalization.

William Shepard is Retired Associate Professor of Religious Studies at the University of Canterbury in New Zealand, where he taught from 1978 to 1998. Prior to that he taught at Cornell College in Iowa, USA. His PhD is from Harvard University. His main research interest has been modern Islamic ideological thought, on which he has published a number of articles, and several translations of Sayyid Qutb's writings, including *Sayyid Qutb and Islamic Activism* (1996), a full translation of Qutb's *Social Justice in Islam*. He has also published a textbook, *Introducing Islam* (2009; e-book version, JBL Online).

Abdulkader Tayob (PhD, Temple University, 1989) currently holds a research chair at the University of Cape Town in South Africa (Islam, African publics and religious values). He has published a number of books, edited books, and numerous articles and book chapters on the study of religion, Islam in Africa and modern Islamic thought. His most recent books are *Religion in Modern Islamic Discourse* (2009) and *Schools and Education in Europe and South Africa* (2011), edited with Inga Niehaus and Wolfram Weiße.

Malika Zeghal is the Prince Alwaleed Bin Talal Professor in Contemporary Islamic Thought and Life at Harvard University, USA. She studies religion through the lens of Islam and power. She is particularly interested in Islamist movements and in religious institutions in the Muslim world, with special focus on the Middle East and North Africa in the postcolonial period and on Muslim diasporas in North America and Western Europe. She has more general interests in the circulation and role of religious ideologies in situations of conflict and/or dialogue. She has published a study of central religious institutions in Egypt, *Gardiens de l'Islam* (1996), and a volume on Islam and politics in Morocco, *Islamism in Morocco: Religion, Authoritarianism, and Electoral Politics* (2008), which won the French Voices-Pen American Center Award. She is currently working on a book on states, secularity, and Islam in the contemporary Arab world, forthcoming at Princeton University Press.

Acknowledgements

A project such as this accumulates many debts. The editors owe special thanks to the contributors for their hard work and patience. Any success the book achieves rests firmly on the strength of their splendid chapters. Anonymous readers, at various stages, provided useful insights into improving both style and content.

Sam Kigar, Alex McKinley, and Hunter Bandy—three talented Duke University graduate students—prepared the index. Andrew Miller at DePauw University provided early research assistance.

At Routledge, we wish to thank Lesley Riddle for inviting us to take on the project and nurturing it in its infancy, Katherine Ong and Jillian D'Urso for their efforts during the rebellious teenage years, and Stacey Carter for ensuring a mature final product.

We apologize in advance if we have overlooked anyone.

*I*ntroduction

Jeffrey T. Kenney and
Ebrahim Moosa

Modernity and the study of Islam

This book is about the role and place of Islam in modern Muslim societies. It covers a historical period that begins around 1800 and continues to the present day. Much of the analysis, however, focuses on developments that date from the mid-twentieth century. An edited work, with a range of contributors from different academic fields of study, the book lacks an overarching theory of modernity or Islam's relation to it. But modernity and modernization are at the heart of each chapter, and a few words about their meaning and impact will set the stage for what is to come. Modernity can be understood simply as a period of time during which a series of dramatic social, economic, and cultural transformations took place. The period, however, is not the same for every region and people around the world. In Europe, where modernity and the benefits that flowed from it first emerged, the transformations began, more or less, in the seventeenth century. In the Muslim world, as noted above, the story began later. Modernization constitutes the processes by which societies and peoples become modern. Being modern is often associated with being aware, or self-conscious, of the changes that are occurring in society and of actively engaging with these changes. The condition of being modern, then, as one scholar has noted, is "an attempt by modern men and women to become subjects as well as objects of modernization, to get a grip on the modern world and make themselves at home in it" (Berman 1988: 5).

In theory, the fact that Muslim societies were latecomers to the experience of modernity and the process of modernization need not impact the way in which Islam is studied and understood. After all, if one views modernization as a series of technological and economic developments, "there is no such thing as a 'modern society' plain and simple; there are only societies more or less advanced in a continuum of modernization" (Berger et al 1974: 9). In practice, however, the latecomer status of Muslim societies has created an interpretive dilemma with broad implications. Put simply, Europe's path to modernization established a model that other peoples were expected to follow, and this expectation was reinforced by Europe's power and sense of purpose.

European modernity brought in its wake advancements in science, technology, and bureaucratic organization that transformed the region into the center of global power and trade. As a result, Europe brought much of the rest of the world into its sphere of influence. A clear demonstration of this influence was the imperialist expansion of European nations (into Latin American, Asia, Africa, and the Middle East), during the eighteenth and nineteenth centuries, and the colonial systems that followed. Colonialism reinforced the dominance of Europe by exploiting the resources, both human and natural, of territorial possessions, imposing foreign control of local economies and governments, and establishing new social and cultural patterns that disrupted traditional life. Thus the "developed" center integrated the "developing" periphery into a subordinate role. There are, to be sure, exceptions to this global assessment, which is derived from world systems theory. But the exceptions do not undermine the historical rule: that for much of the modern period, the West (initially Europe and then the United States too) has set the pace for modernity and modernization, and others have followed.

Not surprisingly, Muslims found it difficult to "get a grip on" and "make themselves at home in" a modern world that was seemingly made by and for the advantage of others. Thus being modern for Muslims meant, at least in part, being self-conscious about their lack of control over global modernity, and about the search for a way to be modern without being (or becoming) Western. For this reason, the process of modernization in Muslim societies—related to industry, state bureaucracy, education, and social and legal reform—was accompanied by a steady stream of cultural assertions, of claims that the modernizing changes taking place in Muslim societies were fully compatible with Islamic tradition and Muslim identity. Islamizing modernity and modernization addressed two pressing concerns: First, it breathed new life into Islamic culture(s) threatened by Western influence and invasion. Second, it legitimized the changes that Muslims societies needed to undergo if they were to develop and become competitive in the new world system.

Of course, modernization discourse, Islamic culture-talk, should not be confused with structural and institutional modernization. But these two should not be separated either, for how people think and talk about change provides insight into how they have integrated change into their identity, making it part of who they are. This is particularly important to keep in mind for students of modern Islam and Muslim societies. Because most Muslims, contrary to some Western critics, embraced modernity and the opportunities that it entailed, and because they did so by thinking and talking about modernity in Islamic terms, modern identity and Muslim identity were often fused in public discourse and popular opinion. Thus the study of modern Islam brings one in contact with a range of issues, institutions, and developments that some might otherwise understand as secular or removed from religion. This is evident in the ongoing discussions/debates that have taken place in Muslim societies. Assertions of Islamic culture and Muslim identity were not simply a once-and-done phenomenon, something that occurred in the aftermath of contact with the West and the initial impulse to modernize. Instead, these assertions have come in waves as Muslims and Muslim societies encountered new challenges in domestic, regional, and international contexts.

The waves of assertion started in the nineteenth century, continued throughout the twentieth and into the twenty-first. Early responses to the West and colonialism gave way to concerns about independence, national identity, and the state of Israel. And once formed, Muslim-majority nation-states took up issues such as public education, women's rights, the legal system, and religion-state relations. Conflicts, both regional and international, played a significant role in spurring debates about Muslim identity, and the list of conflicts provides dramatic evidence of the tensions that have fractured Muslim societies: Arab-Israeli Wars (1948, 1967, 1973), India-Pakistan Wars (1947, 1965, 1971), Iranian Revolution (1979), Soviet invasion of Afghanistan (1979), Persian Gulf

War (1990-91), collapse of the Soviet Union (1991), attacks of 9/11, the US-led invasion of Afghanistan (2001), the Iraq war or Gulf War II (2003), and the ongoing war on terror. These major conflicts were also interspersed with other events—some might call them pseudo-events because their importance was exaggerated beyond their immediate context—that became occasions to debate identity differences between Muslims and Westerners, Islam and the West: publication of Salman Rushdie's reputedly sacrilegious novel *The Satanic Verses* (1988), followed by the religious edict of Ayatollah Ruhollah Khomeini, Iran's supreme leader, calling for Rushdie's death (1989); controversy over cartoon-depictions of the Prophet Muhammad in a Danish newspaper (2005); headscarf ban in France (2010); and the Qur'an-burning incident by a Florida pastor (2011, 2012).

Taken together, this event history, which is certainly not comprehensive, demonstrates that the meaning of modernity for Muslims has unfolded across time—an experiential reality not particular to Muslims but important for understanding the shifting nature of the subject "Islam in the modern world." It also highlights the interdependent nature of identity formation in a modern, globalizing environment. For peoples everywhere now tend to know who they are through their interaction with and understanding of others.

Structure of the volume

While Islam in the modern world is the subject of this work, Islam will be approached, to borrow a biological classification, as a species within a larger genus, religion. Islam may have unique characteristics that set it apart from, say, Christianity and Hinduism, but these three religions also share a family resemblance and thus have much in common. Modernity brought in its wake transformations in science, technology, education, politics, and economics, along with related shifts in thinking about family, gender, sexuality, and the distinction between public and private life. As a result of these changes, religions as traditional institutions have witnessed dramatic challenges to their authority, knowledge claims, and sphere of influence in society. The challenges were even greater for those traditions whose cultural dominance lay outside the West, where modernity and the material benefits that flowed from it first emerged.

This comparative religions approach is reflected in the planning of the volume, which compensates for its lack of a clear-cut narrative about modern Islam by offering, instead, a framework of study rooted in a set of goals. The goals are threefold:

1   to show the multiple ways Muslims have engaged with modernity;
2   to ground this engagement in the interplay between socio-historical circumstances and interpretations of Islamic tradition and identity;
3   to provide as complex and culturally diverse a portrait of the lived Muslim experience as possible.

These goals are reflected throughout the chapters, which have been structured to provide an analytic framework for studying the operation of religions in modern societies. The three framing structures are "Traditions and transformations," "Themes and trends," and "Case studies."

Traditions and transformations

This section highlights the connections between traditional Islamic institutions and practices and their modern interpretations and reinventions. It uses six major elements of the tradition—ones often found in introduction to Islam textbooks— that emerged during the formative period of Islam (dated, typically, CE 600–1100) and that have come to be understood as central to Islamic belief, practice and communal identity: scripture (Brown, Chapter 1), ethics and law (Moosa, Chapter 2), governance and government (Lee, Chapter 3), theologies (Byrd and Martin, Chapter 4), Sufi piety and devotion (Ernst, Chapter 5), and education (Zeghal, Chapter 6).

　Just how important are these traditional elements for those seeking to understand modern Islam and modern Muslim societies? This may seem a strange question given the importance of the past for any religion and religious community. But it helps raise a point about the tension at the heart of the tradition-versus-change dynamic. Viewed one way, societies depend upon tradition to establish norms of behavior and thinking, and to ensure continuity and stability across generations. When Muslims say, "This is the way we do things in Islam" or "This is what Muslims believe," they are communicating something essential about what holds them together as Muslims. There are, to be sure, disagreements among Muslims about aspects of faith and practice, and about the way ongoing intellectual, behavioral, and institutional patterns relate to modern developments. But disagreements still revolve around traditional patterns of meaning that have been inherited from the past. As Edward Shils has noted, "Human beings cannot survive without traditions even though they are so frequently dissatisfied with their traditions" (1981: 322).

　Dissatisfaction with traditions often arises in the very context that calls into question their importance: change. And the change brought about by modernity, with its heightened attention to the self, subjectivity, and new forms of knowledge, creates particular challenges for traditional ways of doing and thinking about things:

> The routinisation of daily life has no intrinsic connection with the past at all, save in so far as what 'was done before' happens to coincide with what can be defended in a principled way in the light of incoming knowledge. To sanction a practice because it is traditional will not do; tradition can be justified, but only in the light of knowledge which is not itself authenticated by tradition .... For justified tradition

is tradition in sham clothing and receives its identity only from the reflexivity of the modern.

(Giddens 1990: 38)

Here the modern is what provides tradition with meaning; without the modern, tradition would have nothing to mirror its relevance and thus fade away. But how far can one push this insight? For example, the notion that the Qur'an derives its meaning and significance solely because of the modern circumstances that inspire its (re-) interpretation would sound absurd to believing Muslims, for whom the Qur'an is Allah's eternal message resonating throughout history, true for all time. Still, it provides an important counterpoint for students of Islam, students of religions, as they try to make sense of Muslim assertions of Islamic tradition in modern contexts.

Themes and trends

No matter how extensive the knowledge base of traditional sacred sources, no matter how insightful they are about the human condition, new situations arise that push Muslim thought and action in new directions. Muslims societies are constantly encountering developments in science and technology, politics, trade, social attitudes, and cultural expression; and these developments impact, positively or negatively, a range of social actors: states, institutions, groups, families, and individuals. The first section of this volume explores the dynamic of tradition-versus-change through the lens of the elemental categories that shaped the tradition in the classical period. Despite their centrality to Muslim traditions and identities, these traditional elements provide only one vantage point of understanding, and they do not capture the depth and breadth of the modern Muslim experience. Indeed, because these elements are rooted in an Islamic frame of reference, they can limit the potential to see Muslim modernity as part of a larger global modernity. This section takes up six thematic trends that have (re-)shaped life in Muslim societies, and around the world: women and gender (Moghadam and Mitra, Chapter 7), cyberspace (Bunt, Chapter 8), globalization (Lawrence, Chapter 9), militant movements (Shepard, Chapter 10), secularization (Kenney, Chapter 11), and popular culture (Sedgwick, Chapter 12).

Each of these trends is part of a larger pattern of global events; each also has particular resonances within Muslim societies. The trends allow for an exploration of similarities and differences both between Muslim societies and others, and within Muslim societies themselves. Not all Muslim societies, for example, have responded in the same way to calls for women's rights; not all have experienced the same challenge of religious militancy; not all have adopted the same attitude toward secularization and the idea of the secular. Muslim societies, then, are not monolithic. This may seem an obvious point, but it is one worth making since the tendency among many in the

West is to think of the Muslim world as an undifferentiated whole. A parallel insight to consider is that not all non-Muslim societies, with special reference to Western ones, have evolved in the same manner regarding women's rights, religious militancy, and secularization. Avoiding overgeneralizations about Muslim societies will ensure a clearer understanding of how Islam does and does not operate in the modern world.

Case studies

This section presents a number of focused studies of living Islam across a range of Muslim societies and cultures. The analytic categories adopted in the first two sections of the volume can have the unintended consequence of communicating a deconstructed view of Islamic tradition and Muslim life. In reality, Muslims experience and understand their tradition in a holistic and integrated way. So, while modernity may have made Muslims more self-conscious about issues of identity and authenticity, that does not mean they wake up every morning alienated from their societies and tradition. In fact, the everyday life of Muslims, like the everyday life of most people, is grounded in particular places, with particular sets of concerns and understandings of the way life should be lived. This is not to discount the importance of the beliefs and commitments that bind Muslims around the world or the notion of all Muslims living together in a community of believers (*umma*). Nor is it to suggest that the impact of globalization is not real. Rather, the emphasis on place situates the idea of the greater Muslim community and globalization in the culturally diverse contexts in which they are encountered.

   The case studies in this section offer overviews of country-specific developments in Turkey (Kuru, Chapter 14), Iran (Kadivar, Chapter 16), and the United States (Moore, Chapter 17); regional trends in Europe (Nielsen, Chapter 15), Southeast Asia (Ali, Chapter 19), and Africa (Tayob, Chapter 20); an ethnographic meditation on women and Islamic law in Bangladesh (Hodge, Chapter 18); and the phenomenon of media preachers (Hermansen, Chapter 13). Taken together, they shed light on the variety of Islams that emerge when the analytic focus shifts from the macro to the micro.

The current moment

Events after January 2011, when the Tunisian, Egyptian, and Yemeni autocratic leaders were deposed by public protests and social upheaval, signal a new watershed moment in modern Muslim history. It is not only a significant moment for an ethnically and religiously diverse modern Middle East but the uprisings serve as a beacon for other Muslim societies in the region and beyond. Dramatic social change in Muslim majority societies has once again surprised observers as it did during the events of 1979 in Iran. The momentum for change spawned by the information and cyber revolutions in more than one way served as a catalyst for the transformations in progress in select Arabic-speaking Muslim majority countries. Whether the current stage is called late modernity or post-modernity, what is clear is that it nevertheless remains pregnant with life-altering possibilities. Few people predicted that longstanding despotic regimes armed by world powers would crumble at the feet of people's power in the way that the Arab Spring demonstrated.

Distinctive of the current moment is the mixed nature of the narratives that fueled the fires of revolt. The uprisings began peacefully as civil protests and yet they were met with state brutality. In Tunisia, Egypt, Yemen, and Bahrain the uprisings remained relatively peaceful with only the regimes using force. In other places, such as Libya, Syria, and in Yemen, part of the opposition took up arms against the regime with higher levels of turmoil and instability. Whether societies in the Muslim world will beat their swords to ploughshares remain to be seen since the uprisings for all purposes will for some time remain a work-in-progress. What is significant is the realization that the best *modus operandi* for change is to embrace peaceful and reasoned protest and minimize political violence. Groups that once advocated and then renounced violence in pursuit of social change such as the Muslim Brotherhood in Egypt are now in power. But the Brotherhood had some time ago recognized the tactical deficits of political violence while the Renaissance Party in power in Tunisia had never adopted violence as a strategy. Yet in several Muslim majority countries political violence is still rife with few signs of its abatement. Most observers are curious to find clues that a different and more hopeful political culture in Muslim majority countries will finally win out.

The role of religion in social change remains ambivalent and unpredictable. Even though religion was not prominent during the uprisings, Islamists nevertheless succeeded to power in both Tunisia and Egypt. Yet, Muslim communities remain divided about the place of religion in their political futures. Pessimists about religion point to the tenacious religious despotism in Iran, the destructive military-religious dictatorship in the Sudan or the suffocating religiously backed monarchies in the Gulf. Optimists about religion present Turkey as a much admired political model of Islamic secularism. Islamic parties that once struggled to survive in Turkey are viewed as the saviors and the rejuvenators of post-modern Turkey. And some of the leaders of Tunisia's Islamic political parties have declared the Turkish political experiment with political Islam to be a model worthy of emulation. Tunisian Islamic parties have preferred a governance option that is inclusive of parties adhering to secular ideologies, a lesson that its counterparts in Egypt have yet to learn.

Whether these changes foreshadow a less theocratic form of religion in the Muslim public sphere remain to be seen. Less despotism and state-controlled religion seem to appeal to large sections of the modern Muslim world. Yet, for now at least, the public sphere is not without a very active form of religion. And a broad spectrum of theorists has for some time cautioned against viewing the sacred and the secular as irreconcilable absolutes. All indicators show that the propensity in Muslim majority countries is not to pose religion in antithetical terms to the secular. Rather, some have advocated a "theo-ethical equilibrium" where the integration between a religious outlook and secularly grounded moral or political principles are viewed as a feasible option in many societies, including Muslim societies (Madan 2006: 21–22).

In the past observers had noted the arrival of technological modernity in Muslim societies. But there was always a question as to how cultural modernity navigated Muslim societies. There is no doubt that cultural modernity has made an impact but it is hard to quantify. So a significant question in the form of a query for the future is whether the aesthetic of modernity/post-modernity has made any gains in Muslim societies? Has it been theorized and conceptually named in terms of the autonomy of the aesthetic? In other words, has a full-blown ideology of the modern been conceptualized that differentiates modern practice from that which preceded it? Clearly, in some Muslim majority countries, such as Indonesia, Iran, and parts of the Arab Middle East where the uprisings succeeded, the political aesthetics have changed. Politics is about the feelings of people and their fear for the tyrants has disappeared (Moosa 2011). Whether those positive feelings of taking control of one's destiny will grow and translate into other spheres of life remains to be seen.

Yet compared to a half-century earlier, things have changed. Into the first decade of the twenty-first century, the substance of Muslim cultural and political thought, as well as the approaches to the study of Muslim societies, looks very different from an earlier epoch. The diversity of approaches to the study of Muslim thought and societies, to which this volume attests, casts a complex analytical lens on Muslim practices in modernity. This will hopefully be a continuous trend that will be refined over time and deepen our understanding of Muslim societies in the modern period and beyond.

References

Berger, Peter, Brigitte Berger, and Hansfried Kellner (1974) *The Homeless Mind: Modernization and Consciousness*, New York: Vintage Books.

Berman, Marshall (1988) *All That Is Solid Melts Into Air: The Experience of Modernity*, New York: Penguin Books.

Giddens, Anthony (1990) *The Consequences of Modernity*, Stanford, CA: Stanford University Press.

Madan, T.N. (2006) *Images of the World: Essays on Religion, Secularism, and Culture*, New Delhi: Oxford Collected Essays; New York: Oxford University Press.

Moosa, E. (2011) "Aesthetics and Transcendence in the Arab Uprisings," *Middle East Law and Governance*, 3: 2–1 171–80.

Shils, Edward (1981) *Tradition*, Chicago: University of Chicago Press.

Part I

Traditions and transformations

1

Scripture in the modern Muslim world: the Quran and Hadith

Jonathan Brown

Introduction: modernity and the global challenge to scripture

Jews, Christians and Muslims all believe in sacred scriptures, books that claim in some way to be the inspired word of God and truth itself. These scriptures tell stories of the past, often predict events of the future and instruct man on the nature of faith and morality. Beyond the pages of these books, however, lies the reality of the outside world. Today, our understanding of this reality makes powerful claims about what can and cannot have happened in the past, about the nature of the cosmos and about what is fair or moral. What happens when the sacred book and the world seem to contradict one another? Which one convinces us, and how do we maintain belief in scripture or reconcile its message with the outside world when a conflict arises? This, in a nutshell, is the problem of scripture in the modern world.

For Western civilization, this tension between the truth of scripture and the reality of the world came into sharp contrast with the emergence of modernity in the eighteenth century, and this challenge has spread globally as modernity has gradually transformed new regions. For Muslims, the challenge to scripture was imposed from the outside with the coming of European colonialism and the sudden economic, political and social changes that it introduced. For Muslims, the problem of scripture in the modern world has thus presented itself not only with a jarring abruptness but also in the context of foreign cultural and political domination. Muslim debates over scripture and how it should be read in recent history have thus swirled around the contending themes of "tradition," "modernity," "the West," reform and cultural authenticity.

The pre-modern heritage of scripture in Islam

Islamic thought is a universe in which precedent and tradition carry tremendous weight. As such, understanding how Muslims approach scripture today must take into account how they understood it in the pre-modern period. Islam holds that God revealed two bodies of knowledge to the Prophet Muhammad. The first, the foundational scripture, was the revealed book of the Quran, the direct words of God sent down to Muhammad via the angel Gabriel. The second was Muhammad's authoritative precedent, his Sunna, the divinely inspired lifestyle and teachings that explained and implemented the Quran's message.

The Quran was not revealed all at one time. Muslims believe that God sent it down piecemeal over the 23 years of Muhammad's prophetic career, often to address the needs or questions of the Muslim community. After the Prophet's death in 632, the Quran was compiled and eventually promulgated around 650 in an official edition by a committee of learned Muslims appointed by the caliph Uthman, the third leader to succeed Muhammad. Although there are some variations in pronunciation and occasionally some minor differences over wording, the Quran as compiled by Uthman is and has been the Quran known and used by Muslims worldwide.

Unlike the Quran, the Sunna of Muhammad was not originally compiled in book form. Muhammad's followers understood his Sunna as the totality of his words, deeds, attitudes and approaches to questions of faith, lifestyle and law. As the Muslim community spread throughout the Middle East, different schools of thought appeared with contrasting ideas of how best to understand the Sunna. One group, known later as the Partisans of Tradition, believed that the Sunna should be known primarily through individual reports, called Hadiths, describing in detail the Prophet's words and deeds. Another group, later known as the Partisans of Reason, believed that, while Hadiths were important, the Sunna is best known through the living tradition of practice and problem-solving inherited from Muhammad's followers.

The Partisans of Reason had important concerns. Unlike the Quran, which was compiled soon after the Prophet's death and was agreed upon by all Muslims, the Hadiths were not written down systematically for a century. It was not long before Hadiths began appearing in the thousands. Some were clearly forgeries made up by the various sides in the severe political and sectarian rifts that opened up within the Muslim community in the century after Muhammad died. Although the Partisans of Reason were happy to act on Hadiths if they were well-known and authentic, they preferred their deductions based on the Quran and the rulings of the early Muslim community to uncertain Hadiths. The Partisans of Tradition, however, felt that Muslims had to stick closely to the revealed teachings of Muhammad in order to preserve the true and untainted message of Islam. They developed a method of sorting through Hadiths in order to sift the forged from the authentic ones. This method centered on demanding a chain of transmission (*isnad*) for each Hadith, then evaluating whether each person in this chain was reliable, whether he or she had really heard it from the supposed source, and how well corroborated the report was. Beginning in the late 700s, followers of this school of thought compiled the Hadiths of which they approved into written collections. For Sunni Muslims, six collections produced in the ninth century became particularly authoritative. The most famous are the *Sahihayn* (The Two Authentic Books) of al-Bukhari (d. 870) and Muslim (d. 875). In Imami Shiism, four books became the authoritative references.

The Quran and the Sunna provided the basis of Islamic law and theology. This was true for both Sunni and Shiite Muslims, although they differed greatly on how the Sunna should be understood. For Sunnis it was through Hadiths and the derivation of law by the Ulama, or Muslim scholars. For Shiites it was through the teachings of the Imams, or descendants of the Prophet who inherited his infallible understanding of God's message and whose teachings were then built on by Shiite Ulama.

In Sunni Islam, Hadiths would become the major source of Islamic law and dogma. The Quran contained only a small amount of information about Islam's ritual and law—even the famous five daily prayers are not specified in it. Important elements of Islamic dogma, such as the existence of an Antichrist and the second coming of Jesus,

Figure 1.1 Muslim pilgrims visiting Muhammad's tomb in Medina follow the tradition of saying "Peace be upon you" to him. Courtesy of Jonathan Brown.

also are only explicitly known from Hadiths. For Sunnis, Hadiths could add to, explain and even overrule Quranic verses (since the Prophet might change a ruling over time or simply explain a Quranic verse in a way that changed its evident meaning).

Another pillar of Sunni interpretive activity was the concept of *ijma'*, or consensus. Sunni scholars believed that, since the Prophet had said in a Hadith that "My community will never agree in error," if the Ulama came to a consensus on a particular stance then that stance was known with as much force and certainty as the word of God itself. Consensus has been crucial for Sunni law and dogma. The requirement for Muslim women to cover their hair, for example, is not explicitly mentioned in the Quran and only appears in unreliable Hadiths. But it is agreed upon by the Ulama, so it has long been considered established law.

Submission to Hadiths was a central tenet of Sunni Islam. Even if a Hadith seemed implausible or seemed to contradict the Quran, if the chain of transmission was authentic, Sunni scholars would accept it. Another school of theology that emerged as a competitor to Sunni Islam in the eighth and ninth centuries, however, was far more skeptical. Known as Mutazilism, this school would not accept a Hadith if it contradicted reason or compromised what they understood to be the Quranic vision of Islam. For example, Sunnis and Mutazilites disagreed vehemently about a Hadith in which the Prophet tells that during the last third of the night God descends to the lowest heavens to answer the prayers of believers. Mutazilites objected that if God moves then God must have a body, and that is unacceptable anthropomorphism. Sunnis maintained that man has no right to question the Prophet's pronouncements. In another Hadith that Sunnis upheld, the Prophet tells his followers that if a fly lands in their drink, they should submerge the fly fully and then take it out and drink. The Prophet explains that if there is disease on one wing of the fly, on the other is the cure. Mutazilites rejected this because they doubted that Muhammad could know such things.

It may seem that I am spending too much time on Hadiths. What about the Quran in classical Islamic thought? The Quran was the touchstone of all Muslim piety and doctrine, but it was always understood through the Sunna (however Sunnis, Shiites and groups within these two sects might define it). Early on, Sunni Muslims declared that it is the Sunna that rules over the Quran, not the Quran that rules over the Sunna. The Mutazilite school of theology disagreed. It believed that only the historical certainty of the Quran should be the basis for Islamic beliefs, but this school was eclipsed by Sunni Islam in the ninth century.

Even the way that the Quran was read and understood was often dictated by the Sunna and the circumstances of the Prophet's life. Muslim scholars did not read Quranic verses in a vacuum or assume that their meaning was independent of context. They relied on identifying the "occasions of revelation (*asbab al-nuzul*)", or the situations in which and the causes for which Quranic verses were revealed. They also asserted that verses of the Quran revealed later in the Prophet's career could overrule or adjust instructions given in earlier verses, a phenomenon known as abrogation (*naskh*).

In one sense, this attention to context and development was essential. Many Quranic verses only make sense when taken in the context of specific circumstances, debates or battles of the Prophet's life. For example, the context of revelation alerted Muslim scholars that the verse "Fighting has been prescribed for you though it be hateful to you" (Quran 2:216) was only directed at the Prophet and his companions at a certain point in their conflict with the Meccans. It was not a general commandment to fight for all time. Other verses of the Quran clearly mark a chronological development in Islam's teachings—such as a series of verses that first merely discourage drinking wine but then later prohibit it.

Because there were sometimes many Hadiths and reports about when and why a Quranic verse was revealed, Muslim scholars often came to different conclusions about what verses of the Quran meant. For example, one verse states "There is no compulsion in religion" (Quran 2:25). Some medieval Muslim scholars held that this verse was revealed by God to the Prophet as a general principle: people had to be free to choose their beliefs. Others believed that the verse was revealed as a response to a particular episode during the Prophet's life, in which a Muslim family's child decided to become Jewish. In this interpretation, the verse was only a commentary on this one case; it was not an order for Muslims to respect people's freedom of religion in general. Another group of scholars held that this verse had been superseded by a later verse ordering the Muslims to fight the unbelievers. The challenge of looking at the varied Hadiths, "occasions of revelation" and instances of *naskh* led Muslim scholars to write huge Quranic commentaries. Known as *tafsir*, this was a popular genre of Muslim scholarship.

The meaning of the Quran was also strongly influenced by Muslim scholars' intensive study of the Arabic language. Like the circumstances of revelation, the meaning of Arabic words at the time of the Prophet controlled interpretation of the Quran. Muslim scholars believed that language, especially Arabic, was divinely bestowed upon mankind, and the meaning of Quranic words was thus firm and decreed. Once a Muslim scholar had studied the language and occasions of revelations of a verse, the meaning of the verse was set.

Setting the stage for modern Islamic thought

Modern Islamic thought has been formed by two main forces, one internal to the Muslim community and one external. Modernity, which we discussed briefly above, is an economic, political, social and intellectual transformation that began in Britain and Western Europe and has been transforming the globe ever since. For Muslims from Constantinople to Delhi, modernity did not emerge organically within their own societies as it did in Europe. It was imposed through European colonialism. The force of

British, Dutch and French arms brought many of the Muslim peoples of India, Southeast Asia and North Africa under European rule by the early 1800s. Muslims, long confident in the might of their armies and their station as the adherents of God's true religion, were faced with the overwhelming technological and economic superiority of non-believers. The order and advancement of European societies was undeniable, and Muslims were faced with the daunting question "If we are following God's true religion, why are we behind? Is it due to a flaw in Islam or to some failing in how we Muslims understand and practice our religion?" Answering these questions, Muslims had to decide, if they had strayed from the true understanding of Islam, how much should modernity and the ways of the West be taken into account in charting a course back to greatness? Muslim scholars and intellectuals have pondered these questions until today.

The second major influence has been internal and emerged totally separate from interactions with Europe. In the mid-1700s, in areas such as central Arabia and India that had previously been marginal in the Muslim world, powerful movements of revival and reform appeared. Although distinct from one another, these movements shared a common idea that the Muslim community had lost touch with the untainted, theologically pure Islam of the Prophet and the early Muslim community. The cultural influences of the Greek and Persian worlds had adulterated Muslim thought with an obsession with formal logic and mysticism. Rigid schools of law and Sufi brotherhoods had become fossilized churches in a religion that should erect no barrier between man and God and should be based on a loyalty to the Quran and Sunna alone. Some of these revival movements were scholarly, like that of the Indian scholar Shah Wali Allah (d. 1762) of Delhi, while others added a military dimension, like the Wahhabi movement of Arabia.

Modern Muslim schools of thought on scripture

The most helpful way to examine modern Islamic thought is to divide it into four major schools. Although in some cases this means imposing our own categories on Muslim intellectuals, this allows us to help identify the distinguishing features of different schools of thought and understand how they relate to one another. The four groups that we will examine we will call (1) Islamic modernists, (2) modernist Salafis, (3) traditionalist Salafis and (4) late Sunni traditionalists respectively.

Islamic modernists

For one camp of modern Muslim thinkers, it is the intellectual currents of Europe and the expectations of modernity that govern their conception of how Islam should be understood and how Islamic scripture should be read. This school of thought advocates radical breaks with how scripture and Islam as a whole were understood by Muslims before the twentieth century. These Muslim intellectuals are generally influenced deeply by European post-modernist philosophers and literary theorists, advocating completely novel visions of how Muslims should conceive of their religion.

Islamic modernists' most influential work came in critiquing the corpus of Hadiths. Beginning in the second half of the nineteenth century, some Muslim intellectuals concluded that the Hadith tradition was not at all a reliable representation of Muhammad's message. A few of these thinkers went so far as to reject altogether the authoritativeness of the Prophet's precedent.

One of the most influential intellectual movements in the Muslim world in the twentieth century was the *Ahl-e Quran*, the "People of the Quran," also known as the "Quran-only" movement, which emerged and flourished in South Asia. This approach to Hadiths and the Quran built on the work of Chiragh Ali (d. 1895), an Indian who worked in the civil service of the local ruler of Hyderabad. Ali rejected all sources of Islamic law and dogma except the Quran and called for a reinterpretation of Islamic law based on the ideals of humanism (such as rationalism, science and non-religiously-based ethics). If the Quran did not provide any comprehensive vision of law or dogma, that was no problem; Ali claimed that Muslims had always been supposed to revise their law in accordance with the needs of the times. As part of his radical reforms, Ali rejected consensus as a type of proof.

Ali was profoundly influenced by European scholars who had studied Islam and produced profound criticism of Hadiths. Like their critical reading of the Bible, scholars from Germany and Hungary had examined the Hadith corpus and concluded that much of the material that Muslims believed was authentic, such as Muhammad's predictions about the future or his statements about which Muslims were rightly guided, was in fact made up by early Muslims promoting their respective agendas. Ali bought into many of these criticisms, and saw Hadiths such as the above-mentioned report about the fly to be embarrassments that defamed the true face of Islam. For him, abandoning Hadiths was necessary for saving the rest of Islam's message.

The Quran-only movement was formally inaugurated by the Indian Muslim intellectuals Abdallah Chakralawi (d. 1930) and Ahmad Din Amritsari (d. 1936) in the early twentieth century. Amritsari had been a student at a missionary school, and his readings in Hadiths led him to conclude that many of them were shockingly foul and patently false. Other Indian Quran-only scholars attacked the transmission-based method of Hadith criticism carried out by early Sunnis. They considered it silly and ineffective, since this method did not consider heavily enough the actual contents of the Hadith as an indication of its authenticity. The Indian intellectual Mistri Muhammad Ramadan (d. 1940) abandoned the idea of trying to extrapolate the details of Islamic law from the Quran. The holy book readily provided all the legal information Muslims needed, he argued, and anything omitted or left ambiguous was intentional—God had left humans free to use their reason in order to adapt to new times.

Although the Quran-only movement flourished in India, it flared only briefly in the Arab world. In a 1906 issue of the famous Islamic reformist journal *al-Manar* (The Lighthouse), the Egyptian physician Muhammad Tawfiq Sidqi (d. 1920) wrote an article entitled "Islam is the Quran Alone" in which he argued that Islam was never meant to be derived from anything other than the Quran. How, Sidqi asked, could God ever allow His religion to depend on a source as dubious as Hadiths? What has been understood as the Sunna was never intended to be a permanently binding source of law. It was only for the first generation of Muslims. After them, Muslims were expected to adapt their law to circumstance according to the principles laid out in the Quran.

Hadiths were patently unreliable in Sidqi's opinion, with the possible exception of those very few that were so widely transmitted that their authenticity was sure. Hadith criticism had begun too late to catch many of the forgeries, and as a result many reports attributed to the Prophet were actually *israiliyyat*, or stories from Jewish lore attributed to Muhammad (Juynboll 1969: 28–30). As a doctor, Sidqi devoted special attention to Hadiths that he considered incompatible with the realities of modern medicine, such as the above-mentioned Hadith of the fly. Sidqi's writings, however, proved too controversial and he quickly recanted his ideas.

By far the most influential modernist critique of the Hadith tradition came from the Egyptian Mahmud Abu Rayya (d. 1970), who wrote a scathing work entitled "Lights on the Muhammadan Sunna (*Adwa' ʿal al-sunna al-muhammadiyya*)" (1958). In this book, Abu Rayya argued that only the Quran, reason and unquestionably reliable, and massively transmitted Hadiths were originally meant to be the basis of Islam. Like Sidqi, Abu Rayya was convinced that many supposedly authentic Hadiths were actually Jewish lore that had been attributed to Muhammad. Such reports included the unacceptably anthropomorphic Hadith that "God created Adam in His image" and the bizarre report that Moses knocked out the eye of the angel of death when he came to take his soul.

Islamic modernism and its Quran-only trend have thrived among Western Muslim scholars. Although they have not always upheld explicit Quran-only positions, many have ignored Hadiths in their discussions of Islamic law and dogma, as is the case with the American Amina Wadud's revaluation of the traditional Islamic view of gender. The Quran-only movement has continued among some Turkish intellectuals, such as Edip Yuksel and his colleagues, who have published the *Reformist Quran*, an English translation and explanation of the holy book written without consulting Hadiths.

We should also note a modernist who has proven extremely adept at arguing for radical reform of how Hadiths are viewed. In her work *Women and Islam*, the French-educated Moroccan social scientist Fatema Mernissi states her intent to "disinter" the original message of Islam "from the centuries of oblivion that have managed to obscure it" (Mernissi 1987: 77). Mernissi argues that, in general, classical Muslim scholarship functioned as a tool of the social and political elite, indulging "the desire of male politicians to manipulate the sacred" (Mernissi 1987: 43). In order to prove this, she examines early Muslims who transmitted Hadiths from the Prophet that Mernissi considers misogynist and unbefitting Muhammad. One of the Prophet's followers narrated a Hadith, considered authentic by Sunni scholars, in which the Prophet says "A community that entrusts its affairs to a woman will not flourish." Effectively engaging in historical psychoanalysis, Mernissi uses the work of classical Muslim scholars to argue such Hadiths were forged by misguided early Muslims who indulged misogynist beliefs.

A unique modernist vision for the proper treatment of Hadiths came from the Pakistani intellectual Fazlur Rahman (d. 1988), who in 1968 was forced to flee his country due to controversies about his writings and eventually settled in as a professor at the University of Chicago. Rahman accepted Western criticisms that Hadiths were historically unreliable and acknowledged that most Hadiths were not actually said by the Prophet. Rahman, however, did not consider this an act of intentional deception on the part of those who forged these Hadiths. The early Muslims who put their own legal or doctrinal rulings in the mouth of their Prophet never considered themselves to be historians, but rather to be living implementers of the Prophet's Sunna. Although many of the details of the Sunna were thus fabricated, the *concept* of the Sunna was authentic. It was not detailed case law, but rather an umbrella of behavioral norms and an interpretive process by which Muslims could adapt their law to changing circumstances. This had been the practice of the Partisans of Reason, who had employed the legal reasoning learned from Muhammad, the original exemplar of Islam, to elaborate law in new situations. This was also why so many early Hadiths were actually "forgeries"—these early jurists had phrased the conclusions they reached using the interpretive process of the Sunna in the words of Muhammad. Consensus (*ijma'*) was the acknowledgment of the community that a newly developed part of the Sunna was authoritative.

Unfortunately, Rahman continues, setting down Hadiths in authoritative collections turned the dynamic Sunna into a petrified and unchanging set of rules. Rahman states that Hadiths need to be reexamined critically according to historical criticism in order to determine if they were really part of the original Sunna, "whose very life blood was free and progressive interpretation" (Rahman 1965: 40). Once this is determined, modern Muslims can pick up with new interpretation where the classical Muslim scholars left off when the Sunna was frozen in the ninth century.

Of the four schools of thought we are discussing here, only the Islamic modernists advanced novel and revolutionary understandings of how the Quran should be read. For the other three schools, the Word of God was simply too sacrosanct to bear much critical review. As with Hadiths, Rahman made a seminal contribution to debates about how Muslims should understand the Quran. He offered a fundamental criticism of how Muslim religious scholars had read the holy book. It should not be read atomistically, with each verse interpreted separately and chained in by its "occasions of revelation," its meaning frozen in time. The "occasions of revelation," Rahman objects, are often unclear, and one frequently finds contradictory reports. It is the Quran itself that is the best source for understanding its intended meaning, not Hadiths. Today Muslims must understand the intent *behind* Quranic verses and the commands they issue. The Quran was revealed at various moments in the Prophet's career to address specific historical realities. What modern Muslims must do is undertake a "double movement" in which they first identify the moral reason or ethical goal behind a Quranic verse and then see how that intent and goal should be realized in the present day. Muslims treat the Quran criminally when they insist on literally implementing its rulings, since so much has changed socially and economically since the Prophet's time. The basic message of the Quran was "socioeconomic justice and essential human egalitarianism," so Muslims should not stress the details, for example, of Quranic laws on how much a woman should inherit. Rather, Muslims should realize that the Quran was pursuing social justice by offering the right of inheritance to women who did not enjoy it in pre-Islamic Arabia (Rahman 1982: 18–19).

One of Rahman's most remarkable realizations was the way that language inherently delimits the power of revelation. The Quran may have come from God, but, once it was spoken by Muhammad, it was constrained by human language. For traditional Muslim scholars this was not a problem. Arabic was the eternal language revealed by God to man and preserved by punctilious Muslim scholarship. For Islamic modernists, however, deeply influenced by European post-modernist philosophy, this changed the picture completely. European philosophers such as Michel Foucault, Jacques Derrida and Hans-Georg Gadamer stressed how language is fluid and how meaning is created by the interaction of speaker and audience, text and reader. Texts have no fixed meaning, since the very meaning of words themselves are unstable and constantly recreated in the dialogic relationship between word and object, text and context.

This approach has been taken by up the Syrian intellectual Muhammad Shahrur. An engineer by training, Shahrur sees himself as an independent thinker working outside the ranks of the traditional Ulama, trying to free the Quran from their fossilized grasp. He rejects the atomistic assumptions of the Ulama and proposes approaching the Quran anew. Putting forth his approach in his controversial 1990 book *al-Quran wa'l-Kitab* (The Quran and the Book), Shahrur sees a fundamental division between the eternal, unchanging divine message and the human, changing, particular understanding of that message. Arguing that Muslims had never properly understood the way the Quran refers to itself, Shahrur argues that the Quran is the eternal message, while the "Book" (*kitab*) that the Quran often refers to, and which has always been assumed to be a synonym for the Quran itself, is really the changing temporal understanding. This human understanding changes as science and knowledge advance. Thus the form of the Quran, God's actual words, is eternal and unchanging, but because our perspective always shifts and because the meaning of language changes with context, the content of these words is actually changing (Christmann 2004: 267–68).

The literary and post-modern approach to the Quran was also adopted by the late Egyptian literary scholar Nasr Hamid Abu Zayd (d. 2010), at one time a literature professor at Cairo University. Like Shahrur basing his reading of the Quran on post-modern literary theory, Abu Zayd sees the Quran as divine but as irrefutably prisoner to the conventions of human language. Because language itself is not fixed and constantly develops, the Quran is not a fixed, rigid message but rather a continuing conversation between God and man. Its core message remains the same and its values can be applied in every era, but its specific rules and references cannot be fixed in their meaning according to the classical understanding of Muslim scholars.

It is important to note that neither Shahrur nor Abu Zayd have popular Muslim audiences. Their work has proven extremely controversial in the Muslim world. Abu Zayd was actually declared an apostate by leading scholars of Cairo's al-Azhar University after a 1996 trial, and he lived the rest of his life in exile in the Netherlands. Rahman's work resonated among educated Pakistanis and Indian Muslims, but his greatest influence was as a Western academic writing for a non-Muslim audience.

Modernist Salafis

The Salafi movement was the name that many of the adherents of this school of thought derived from the *Salaf*, or the pious early generations of Muslims, from whose example these reformists hoped to reconstitute Islam's original purity. To a large extent, the eighteenth-century movements of revival and reform were all Salafi in their approach. For them, the early Muslim community represented their hopes for the future. It was powerful, dynamic, and preceded what many reformists viewed as the superstitions, blind loyalty to tradition and the havoc wreaked on medieval Islam by foreign cultural accretions such as Greek logic and Persian mysticism. In terms of their thought, by the mid-1800s these Salafi movements had split into two main branches, which we will call the modernist and traditionalist Salafi groups. These two branches interacted with and affected one another, for both shared a common vision of recapturing the early Islam of the *Salaf*. But they proposed different means and had opposing attitudes towards modernity.

The modernist Salafi trend has been the most influential and vigorous of the modern Muslim schools of thought. Nonetheless, it was essentially a response to modernity. Its proponents looked back into history at the pure Arab Islam of the Prophet's time, but what they recreated by drawing unsystematically from the rich tradition of Islamic civilization was an Islam tailored to fit the modern world. Arguably the most influential modernist Salafi was the Indian Sir Sayyid Ahmad Khan (d. 1898).

Khan believed that only by reconciling with modernity and Western (British) rule could Islam survive. In 1868 he adopted a Western lifestyle, and in 1875 he successfully founded the Anglo-Muhammadan Oriental College at Aligarh in India, the most successful center of reformist Islamic education (Ahmad 1967: 31).

Khan authored numerous books, including a commentary on the Bible and a *tafsir* commentary on the Quran. Like the earlier Indian revivalist Shah Wali Allah, Khan rejected many of the institutions of medieval Islam. He also infused his works with distinctly modern notions, such as an acceptance of Darwinian evolution and the position that nothing in the Quran can be interpreted as contradicting the laws of nature (Ahmad 1967: 43, 46; Ahmad and von Grunebaum 1970: 34). He also rejected claims of *ijma'* as convincing proof in scholarly discourse.

In the 1860s, Khan first encountered European scholars' criticism of the reliability of Hadiths. He accepted many of their critiques. He acknowledged, for example, that classical Muslim scholars had not taken the contents of Hadiths sufficiently into account when determining their authenticity and that the historical lag in writing down Hadiths had resulted in copious forgeries, many concocted to sanctify and glorify Muhammad.

To overcome this challenge of forged and backward Hadiths, Khan proposed reexamining the Hadith corpus using a new method of criticism he drew from the Partisans of Reason and the Mutazilites as well as from Western historical criticism. Any Hadith incompatible with modern reason, belittling to the Prophet or contradicting the Quran must be rejected (Ahmad 1967: 49ff.). He added that Hadiths should be screened to see if they describe miracles that could not be reasonably believed or historical events that could not have happened.

Ultimately, defending Islam against infectious Western skepticism was Khan's real goal. Although he admitted many Western criticisms of Hadiths, he also understood that Hadiths were essential for defending the basic Islamic worldview. Khan's concern for protecting religion from modernity even led him to defend the Bible against European critics. Against claims that the global flood of Noah was impossible and not born out in the historical record, Khan countered that the flood had really occurred but had been restricted to one locale (Troll 1978: 111).

While Khan was writing in India, Egypt witnessed a simultaneous efflorescence of the modernist Salafi movement. In fact, the most influential participants in Islamic thought in the late nineteenth- and early twentieth-century Arab world were the Egyptian Salafi Muhammad ʿAbduh (d. 1905) and his Syrian student Rashid Rida (d. 1935). ʿAbduh was educated at the storied al-Azhar Mosque but was drawn into reformist intellectual circles and spent several years in France and Lebanon. Eventually, after Egypt came under British rule, ʿAbduh was appointed as the chief mufti of Egypt.

Although ʿAbduh never dealt with the issue of Hadiths in a systematic way, he upheld the orthodox stance that the Sunna is the second major source of law and dogma in Islam. However, he accepted that the traditional methods of Hadith criticism were insufficient and that the Hadith corpus must be reexamined critically. In theory, he states, disobeying what is known to have been the Sunna of the Prophet is anathema. This holds true, however, for "a few only of the Hadiths," namely those that were so widely transmitted from the Prophet that no one doubted their reliability. In the case of Hadiths that fell short of this mark, whoever felt comfortable with them could believe them, but no one could be forced to believe in them or be declared an unbeliever for rejecting them. ʿAbduh was also very skeptical about Hadiths predicting the future, the end of the world or *israiliyyat*, and accepted very few such reports as authentic.

ʿAbduh's senior student Rashid Rida proved his chief acolyte, and his journal *al-Manar* (The Lighthouse) was the main forum for reformist writings. Rida dealt with Hadiths in much more detail than his teacher. Like ʿAbduh, he argued that the Quran is the true basis of Islam and that only well-known Hadiths can really be relied upon. He equated widely transmitted, well-known Hadiths with the "practical," living Sunna that all Muslims know, such as prayer, pilgrimage rituals and a few of the Prophet's sayings. Like his teacher ʿAbduh, Rida called for Hadiths to be reexamined with more attention given to analyzing the contents of the Hadith and whether it accorded with the Quran and modern science. In the case of the Hadith of the fly, for example, Rida noted its clash with modern medicine.

The Egyptian modernist Salafi Mahmud Shaltut (d. 1963), the influential head of al-Azhar University, and the popular Azhar scholar and author Muhammad al-Ghazali (d. 1996) followed in Rida's footsteps. Both upheld that Muslims cannot be declared unbelievers for rejecting any article of faith that is derived from Hadiths not widely known and acknowledged as authentic. For example, Shaltut broke with a centuries-old tenet of Sunni belief, saying that Muslims did not have to believe that Jesus would return at the end of time. He argued that, since this belief was based on a handful of Hadiths, it was not obligatory for faith. Like ʿAbduh, al-Ghazali returned to some Mutazilite ideas to minimize the role of Hadiths. He affirms the predominance of the Quran, saying, "We believe that the Quran is the basis, and the Sunna is built on it."

Modernist Salafis have not advocated the radical new approaches to the Quran that we saw with Islamic modernists, but they have made the holy book the centerpiece of their understanding of Islam. For them, Hadiths and the complex bodies of law developed in medieval Islam distracted Muslims from the inspiring and catalyzing message of the Quran. Although they could not escape the importance of Hadiths as a necessary context for many Quranic verses, modernist Salafis have called Muslims to read the Quran closely and comprehensively, focusing on its themes and not the isolated meanings of individual verses. As Muhammad ʿAbduh said, the Quran is "its own best commentary." One famous female scholar of Egypt, Aisha ʿAbd al-Rahman (d. 1999), argued the same in her many writings on the Quran and Muhammad.

Modernist Salafis have sought to bring the Quran into dialogue with the realities and challenges of the modern world so that Muslims might derive direct guidance from it. ʿAbduh's and Rida's scattered discourses on the Quran were published in *al-Manar* in the Arab world. In South Asia, this application of the Quran was best exemplified by the huge Urdu-language translation and extensive commentary on the holy book produced by Abul Kalam Azad (d. 1958), an Indian Muslim involved in the independence movement against the British and later the Minister of Education in India after independence (he is the Muslim disciple of Gandhi in that 1982 film). Steeped in medieval Islamic philosophy as well as reformist ideas and Western thought, Azad's *Tarjuman-e Quran* is a profound mediation on the Quran's message to modern man. In Egypt, Shaltut wrote several books on the Quran designed to revive Muslim connection with the holy book and breaking with the traditional verse-by-verse commentary of pre-modern Islam. His student, Muhammad al-Ghazali, also focused on renewing and reviving *tafsir*. In his 1992 *tafsir*, al-Ghazali tries to show the core themes focused on by each chapter of the Quran, demonstrating the chapter's coherent unity.

Some intellectuals have brought the Quran to bear on issues of social and political justice. Perhaps the most famous of all the *tafsir* works in the modern period, and certainly the most widely read in the Arab world, is *In the Shade of the Quran* by the Egyptian political dissident and Muslim Brotherhood member Sayyid Qutb (d. 1966). Although he began as a secular literary critic, Qutb later embraced Islam and pushed for an Islamic revival in Egyptian social and political life. Imprisoned by the Egyptian government for ten years, Qutb penned his fantastically powerful *In the Shade of the Quran* as a personal, narrative reading of the Quran. Breaking away from Hadiths and the context of verses, Qutb's work engages the Quran directly, reveling in its aesthetic world and drawing out spiritual nourishment and visions of social and political justice. The early verses of the Quran, revealed in Mecca, Qutb saw as its universal ethical and theological message. Later verses revealed in Medina contained Islam's political message.

An Iranian Shiite contemporary of Qutb also embodied the message of social justice and liberation theology in his many writings on the Quran. Although he wrote no comprehensive commentary on the Quran, the Marxist-inspired writer Ali Shariati (d. 1977) infused his writings with references to the holy book. Influenced by Frantz Fanon's pleas on behalf of the oppressed "wretched of the earth," Shariati writes, "the Quran begins in the name of God and ends in the name of the people" (referring to the opening verse of "In the name of God, the most gracious, the most merciful," and the last line of the last chapter) (Cragg 2008: 76, 85).

Perhaps the only Quran commentary that can compete with Qutb's *Shade* in popularity in the Arab world is the *tafsir* of the beloved Egyptian preacher Muhammad Mitwalli al-Sharawi (d. 1998). Compiled from transcripts of the lessons he delivered in mosques (aired and re-aired on TV), this *tafsir* brings the Quran into intimate contact with the realities and hardships of modern Egyptian life. Al-Sharawi spoke in Egyptian colloquial Arabic, reading through verses of the Quran and then translating them into the world of the listener and interpreting how the holy book addressed modern needs.

Traditionalist Salafis

What we have termed traditionalist Salafism is the direct descendent of the early modern movements of revival and reform. The most persistent and most politically active traditionalist Salafi movement was founded by Muhammad Ibn ʿAbd al-Wahhab (d. 1792) in the mid-eighteenth century in central Arabia, expanding through its alliance with the Saud family and eventually becoming the predominant religious movement on the Arabian Peninsula. A second center of traditional Salafism, this one academic, appeared in the Yemeni city of Sanaa in the same period. A third school developed in Damascus in the second half of the nineteenth century around revivalist Hadith scholars Jamal al-Din al-Qasimi (d. 1914) and Tahir al-Jaza'iri (d. 1920). In India, some of the devotees of Shah Wali Allah's revivalist scholarship formed their own strict Traditionalist Salafi school, dubbed the *Ahl-e Hadith* (The People of Hadith).

Unlike modernists and modernist Salafis, traditionalist Salafis have no concern for the pressures of modernity. They believe that if Muslims return to the authentic Sunna of the Prophet as preserved in the Hadith corpus, the Muslim world will once again enjoy God's favor regardless of any perceived superiority boasted by the West today. Traditionalist Salafis consider the other schools of thought discussed so far in this chapter to be misguided by Western influence. At worst they are infidels or heretics, at best "imitators of the West."

The most illustrative example of traditionalist Salafis is Muhammad Nasir al-Din al-Albani (d. 1999), an Albanian whose family immigrated to Syria. Growing up in Damascus, al-Albani was deeply affected by the writings of Rashid Rida. He began to speak out against what he saw as heretical innovations in every area of Syrian religious life and penned many works attempting to reorient social and religious practices to the pure Sunna of Muhammad as communicated by Hadiths.

Like the other reform movements, traditionalist Salafis like al-Albani have aimed at reviving Islam's original purity and greatness by clearing away the dross of later cultural accretions. Unlike modernist Salafis, who drew eclectically on Mutazilism and modern rationalism, they have struggled literally to revive the Prophet's Sunna through a narrow focus on Hadiths. Like their modernist Salafi counterparts, traditionalist Salafis identify the causes of the Muslim community straying from true Islam as excessive loyalty to the medieval schools of Islamic law instead of a reverence for the Quran and Sunna, an indulgence in speculative theology and popular Sufi practices such as visiting the graves of saints.

To cure these ills, traditionalist Salafis have not merely engaged in the study of Hadiths, they have tried to cultivate its most critically rigorous spirit. They demand that only the most reliable Hadiths be used in Islamic thought, breaking with the practice of the classical Muslim scholars, who would accept unreliable Hadiths on issues that they saw as marginal. Al-Albani thus published numerous books dividing the Hadiths contained in classical Sunni Hadith collections into sound and unreliable Hadiths. The Indian Salafi Hadith scholar Shibli Numani (d. 1916), an associate of Ahmad Khan, compiled a new biography of Muhammad that purged reports transmitted by early Muslim historians that Hadith critics had considered unreliable.

When it comes to the Quran, traditionalist Salafis avow the same dominant role for Hadiths as we found in pre-modern Islam. They do not concur with the modernist reemphasis on the Quran as the ultimate arbiter in matters of faith and law. Like the early Partisans of Hadith, al-Albani asserts that in both law and dogma "we cannot distinguish between God and His Prophet." It is thus perfectly acceptable to derive articles of faith from any Hadith as long as it had a reliable chain of transmission—they did not limit themselves to massively transmitted Hadiths like modernist Salafis. Like the early Partisans of Hadith, traditionalist Salafis place complete faith in the classical science of Hadith criticism, so they reject calls by reformers to reexamine Hadiths in the light of modern science and ethics.

Late Sunni traditionalists

All the approaches to understanding Islam in the modern period that we have discussed so far have advocated the rejection of significant components of Sunni Islam as it existed in the medieval world through the 1600s. Conversely, what we can call late Sunni traditionalism argues that it is precisely these institutions that are essential for properly living as a Muslim today. In other words, closely following one of the accepted Sunni schools of law, believing in the medieval schools of theology (heavily influenced by Greek logic) and participating in a Sufi brotherhood provides modern Muslims with all the legal, spiritual and theological tools they need to succeed. Properly understood and correctly combined, these classical institutions allow Muslims to answer all the challenges of modernity. Advocates of late Sunni traditionalism generally refer to their school of thought as "Traditional Islam" or "Sunnism in its authentic form." Prominent representatives of this school include the Grand Mufti of Egypt from 2003–2013, Ali Gomaa.

Late Sunni traditionalism mitigates the stipulations of Islamic law that seem incompatible with modernity by drawing on the collective diversity of the four Sunni legal schools and the rich intellectual heritage of Sunni legal theory. Although engaging in interest-bearing commercial transactions is generally prohibited in Islamic law, a minority opinion in one Sunni school of law allows Muslims to take and pay interest if living in a non-Muslim country. A principle of late Sunni legal theory, "Let he who is afflicted with some need take the permissive ruling," permits a Muslim to act on this minority ruling. As a result of this methodology, late Sunni traditionalism produces a manifestation of Islam that adapts to many of the stringencies of the modern world while remaining grounded in "authentic" Islamic tradition.

Just as traditionalist Salafis have resurrected the approach of the Partisans of Hadith, late Sunni traditionalists have revived the methods of the Partisans of Reason jurists. Late Sunni traditionalists subordinate Hadiths to the interpretive traditions of the Sunni schools of law and Sunni legal theory. They affirm their total confidence in the classical method of Hadith criticism. They also, however, entrust jurists, not Hadith scholars, with the ultimate authority in determining the authenticity and implication of a Hadith. One maxim often used describes Hadith scholars as pharmacists and legal scholars as doctors; the first group produces medicines but does not know how to use them, the second knows how to use the drugs to cure patients.

For late Sunni traditionalists, it is the continuous heritage of Islamic legal scholars since medieval times, not some disconnected return to the Hadiths, that provides the true understanding of scripture in the modern world. This approach allows these scholars to circumvent Hadiths that are problematic today. Ali Gomaa admits that numerous Hadiths, considered authentic by medieval Muslim scholars, exist that command Muslims to kill Muslim apostates. Such Hadiths include "Whoever changes their religion [from Islam], kill them." But Gomaa argues that neither the Prophet nor the early caliphs actually implemented these rulings when individuals left Islam. This means that these Hadiths conceive of apostasy as really meaning treason to the Muslim state, not a person's individual choice of belief.

Late Sunni traditionalists consider themselves a direct continuity of pre-modern Islam, and as such they do not introduce revolutionary readings of the Quran. Like all Muslim scholars, they consider the Quran and Sunna to be the revealed sources of truth. But they subordinate all scripture to the interpretive methods and historical tradition of Muslim legal scholars.

Conclusion

The role of scripture in Muslim life today is rich, important and somewhat paradoxical. The Quran is omnipresent in the Muslim world: a boatman on the Niger River recites the holy book from memory as he ferries his passengers, though he cannot understand Arabic; many taxicabs in Egypt have their radios tuned to a 24-hour Quran recitation station; and Quranic verses in stunningly beautiful calligraphy adorn the walls and ceilings of large and small mosques from Morocco to Malaysia. Yet most of Islamic dogma and practice comes not from the Quran but from the Hadiths and the legal thought of the Ulama. Although the person and memory of the Prophet Muhammad are as revered as the Quran in the Muslim world, the actual scriptural corpus of the Hadiths is little known compared to the Quran.

Figure 1.2 Quranic verse used in state public art in Tehran commemorating those who died in the Iran-Iraq War. It states that the martyrs remain alive with their Lord. Courtesy of Jonathan Brown.

For most Christians and Jews in the urban centers of the West, scripture no longer holds the mystery or authority of divine word. Although for more orthodox Jews and Evangelical Christians the Bible is still considered the literal word of God (we have to remember that in South Africa, for example, two-thirds of the population affirms this belief) (*Economist*, February 12, 2011: 55), Biblical scholars and even many clerics have accepted that the messages of Christianity and Judaism must be understood without a strong belief in the divine status of scripture. In the Islamic world, however, the truth-value of scripture still reigns. Many Muslim scholars, both radical reformists and traditional scholars who feel that tradition may need review, have critiqued the historical reliability and the authority of Hadiths. The Quran, however, has retained its close association with revealed truth and is considered the intact word of God. Certainly, Muslim scholars and intellectuals have debated how the Quran should be interpreted, but no Muslim scholar of any note has questioned its status as preserved revelation. When secularist intellectuals such as Abu Zayd have suggested that, although it may have originated with God, the Quran is inherently subject to the tensions of human language, they have met with hostile audiences. Modernists such as Abu Zayd and Fatema Mernissi have found that their social-scientific and literary criticisms have resonated amongst intellectual circles in the Muslim world and in the West, but almost nowhere else.

Summary

- Medieval Muslim scholars read the Quran through the prism of the Hadiths and the Prophet's life. This seemed necessary because the Quran was revealed in the context of particular historical events.
- Unlike the Quran, the Hadiths were of debatable historical authenticity, and Muslim scholars disagreed about which ones truly represented the Prophet's message.
- In the modern period, many Muslim scholars have proposed prioritizing the Quran over the traditional prism of Hadiths, in part because of debates over the authenticity of Hadiths.
- Modern science and lifestyle have presented a new challenge to the worldview prescribed in the Hadiths.
- Modern, Western approaches to history, scripture and even language have posed unprecedented challenges to assumptions about the Quran and Hadiths, but these challenges are largely immaterial to most of the world's Muslims.

Discussion points

- If the Quran is historically reliable but Hadiths are debatable, why would Muslims allow the Hadiths to define the Quran's meaning? Have modern Muslim scholars challenged this?
- How much do you think modern science and/or moralities should influence the way we interpret scripture?
- Of the four modern Muslim approaches to scripture, are any of them truly free from modern influence? What would the Muslim scholars who uphold these positions say?
- Which of the approaches to scripture discussed above makes the most sense to you? Why?

Further reading

For more on how the Quran has been interpreted in the Muslim world in recent times, see Massimo Campanini's short but concise *The Quran: Modern Muslim Interpretations* (New York: Routledge, 2011). The next step would be to look at the collection of essays in *Modern Muslim Intellectuals and the Qur'an* (ed. Suha Taji-Farouki, Oxford: Oxford University Press, 2006). For an overall look at the Quran and how it has been understood and handed down by Muslims throughout history, see Ingrid Mattson's *The Story of the Qur'an* (Oxford: Blackwell, 2008) and Anna Gade's *The Qur'an: An Introduction* (Oxford: Oneworld, 2010). To compare modern Muslim approaches to the Quran with the pre-modern, flip through the translation of the classic *Tafsir al-Jalalayn*, a product of fifteenth-century Ulama (trans. Feras Hamza. Louisville, KY: Fons Vitae, 2008).

For more on Hadiths in both the pre-modern and modern Muslim traditions, see Jonathan Brown's *Hadith: Muhammad's Legacy in the Medieval and Modern World* (Oxford: Oneworld, 2009). Daniel Brown's *Rethinking Tradition in Modern Islamic Thought* (Cambridge: Cambridge University Press, 1996) is also very helpful.

References

Ahmad, Aziz (1967) *Islamic Modernism in India and Pakistan,* London: Oxford University Press.

Ahmad, Aziz and G.E. von Grunebaum (eds) (1970) *Muslim Self-Statement in India and Pakistan 1857–1968*, Wiesbaden, Germany: Otto Harrossovitz.

Christmann, Andreas (2004) "'The Form is Permanent, but the Content Moves': The Qur'anic text and its Interpretation(s) in Mohamad Shahrour's *al-Kitab wa al-Qur'an*," in Suha Taji-Farouki (ed.) *Modern Muslim Intellectuals and the Qur'an*, Oxford: Oxford University Press.

Cragg, Kenneth (2008) *The Pen and the Faith: Eight Modern Muslim Writers and the Quran*, New York: Routledge.

Juynboll, G.H.A. (1969) *The Authenticity of the Tradition Literature: Discussions in Modern Egypt*, Leiden: Brill.

Mernissi, Fatema (1987) *Women and Islam*, trans. Mary Joe Lakeland, Oxford: Basil Blackwell.

Rahman, Fazlur (1965) *Islamic Methodology in History*, Karachi: Central Institute for Islamic Research.

—— (1982) *Islam and Modernity*, Chicago: University of Chicago Press.

Troll, Christian (1978) *Sayyid Ahmad Khan: A Reinterpretation of Muslim Theology*, New Delhi: Vikas Press.

Ethical landscape: laws, norms, and morality

Ebrahim Moosa[1]

Outline

- Muslim ethics is an amalgam of differentiated discourses merging duty-based rules of *fiqh* (deontological theory), virtue ethics (*akhlāq* and *adab*) and utilitarian approaches (*maṣlaḥa* and *maqāṣid*). A single practice might involve an aspect of each of these discourses.
- Ethics is fused into the lived world of Muslims; tradition and modernity are intertwined.
- Contests between canonical interpretations of Islam and new scriptural readings generate dynamism in debate.
- Epistemology is at the heart of Muslim ethical deliberation.
- Laypersons often flout the ethical rulings but find solace in personal redemptive readings of the tradition.

Introduction

Muslim ethical thinking in the twenty-first century must be rendered in diverse and sometimes discontinuous and conflicting ways. Once the 'modern' was imagined as selected rootstock of 'tradition.' But such facile metaphors are no longer convincing. It is now impossible to untwist the 'modern' from longstanding indigenous 'traditions' of Islamdom. The Muslim ethical landscape is the confluence of multiple traditions—modern and pre-modern, local and transnational—and is better thought of as rootstalks or kudzu that shoots out roots and leaves from any point in the organism (May 2005).[2]

Muslim ethics is essentially about claims and duties between humans. Yet these claims rely on a combined commitment to God, an obligation to reason, and the need to obtain the greatest good. In other words, it is about how others make claims on us and how we reciprocate to others and to God (Nagel 1986: 164).[3] An ensemble of discourses constitutes Muslim ethics. These discourses span the categories known as "Islamic law," "Sharīʿa" and "fiqh." Duty-based ethics in syncopation with virtue ethics (*adab* and *akhlāq*) and utilitarian forms of moral reasoning cumulatively seek to advance the good. While ethics in Islam do take the form of both embedded and abstract reason, the theistic shadow remains a permanent one. Drawing from this rich discursive source, Muslims partake of teachings, practices and dispositions of an ethical, moral and spiritual valence.

This chapter addresses five themes: the everyday, the global, the family, sex and intimacy, and innovation in Muslim ethics. Ethics is part of the everyday lives of Muslims in local contexts, just as it is part of a global and transnational conversation. Ethics impact the family in a variety of ways, from marriage to sexuality. Through innovation in methodology contemporary Muslim ethicists have been able to find some solutions to challenging issues; but they view it as a work in progress. Crucially important to Muslims is that progress in the realm of the ethical is also part of the story of Muslim civilization that many faithful around the world seek to advance.

Everyday life

Kaukab, a Muslim woman of Pakistani origin, is one of the characters in Nadeem Aslam's *Maps for Lost Lovers*. It is midmorning, in an unnamed English city, and she is already preparing the evening's meal of bitter gourd. She starts her chores with the Arabic words, "I begin this action with the name of Allah." As she fastidiously sets out to clean the rice, she also listens to the music of the Nusrat Fateh Ali Khan, the late Pakistani rock star of Muslim spiritual music in the Urdu language called qawwali. Aslam writes in Kaukab's voice: "Nusrat Fateh Ali Khan's voice, singing Allah's praises, fills the air from the cassette player on the refrigerator." "Nusrat is gone," we hear Kaukab reminiscing, "leaving his songs behind, the way when a snail dies its shell remains" (Aslam 2004: 290).

Ruminating over her purchases for dinner and the imported cassettes from Pakistan, Kaukab dwells on the music. Something she was taught or heard from Muslim clerics pricks her conscience. "Islam is said to forbid music, Kaukab remembers as she marinades the chicken breasts with natural yoghurt... but she has always reminded herself that when the holy Prophet Muhammad, peace be upon him, had migrated to Medina, the girls there had welcomed him by playing the duff drums and singing tala`al-badru ʿalayna, which is Arabic for 'The white moon has risen above us'" (Aslam 2004: 290).

This scene lyrically and accurately portrays an everyday scene of Muslim ethical life. It limns several aspects of modern Muslim ethical life by bringing into light the culture of right conduct (*adab*), intentionality (*niyya*) and the ambivalence of the ethical. Kaukab appears to be well-informed. Thrown into the complex and insoluble problems of Muslim ethics, she finds resolution without going to a Muslim cleric for advice or reading self-help manuals on ethics such as *The Lawful and the Prohibited in Islam* (Qaraḍāwī 1982).

The scene begins simply, powerfully, and exactly like any number of activities in the life of a Muslim—from the most mundane activities to the most sacred—with a benediction, called the *basmala* or *bismillah*. The *basmala* stands in for a long Arabic expression, "In the name of Allah the Most Gracious, the Dispenser of Grace." From childhood Kaukab, like millions of others, was taught that every good deed ought to begin with the *basmala*, and was lacking in blessedness without it. Now in adulthood, it is an ingrained habit and she almost instinctively begins the preparation of food, viewed as a divine gift, with the name of God.

In her practice, God's name connects Kaukab's mundane act to a deeper meaning: a reality higher, greater and beyond her. Her invocation points to her religious conscience. She brings into vision her pious intention and enacts what Islam's premier exemplar, the Prophet Muhammad, had encouraged all his followers to frequently do: always check one's intention at the beginning, middle and end of an act. Sincerity of intent, to do things selflessly in order to earn the love and grace of God, is all that matters.

"All actions are measured by their intentions," the Prophet Muhammad famously said. Intentions signify the kinds of connections Kaukab makes in her mind. How does she make meaning out of the ordinary? For this housewife, cooking is a service to her family. At the same time, this act connects her to something infinitely complex and beyond her comprehension: God. It is the frame of mind and the way one conducts oneself—cognitively and physically—that forms the all-important network of the ethical. Establishing the right relationship with things is what Muslim writers of the past called *adab*, a code of proper conduct that matures with civility and culture, and that finds its beginning on the inside of a human being. The early writers imagined that conduct radiated from the heart into the limbs and into one's external performance. Today, we might describe acts of conscience or mind to occur in simultaneity with the movements of one's body, joining intention and action into one seamless move.

In any ethical practice what counts is not whether the mind or the body initiated an action, but this: how many profound connections does an individual's intention and action make with the world? Connections are all-important, irrespective of whether they are made when doing mundane tasks in the intimate world of domesticity, in the public realm of politics or when flying out into the far reaches of space. In short: actions are consequential. This is precisely what the pre-partition poet-philosopher Muhammad Iqbal, a highly revered figure in Pakistan, the country of Kaukab's birth, so insightfully explained. For people who struggle to understand what makes an act secular or sacred, Iqbal has a profound answer. "An act is temporal or profane," Iqbal writes, "if it is done in a spirit of detachment from the infinite complexity of life behind it; it is spiritual if it is inspired by that complexity" (Iqbal and Sheikh 1999: 122). Crucially, Iqbal urges us to think about the *complexity* of life behind an act. Kaukab fills the rote preparation of the evening meal with a heightened awareness of the intricate life behind her daily mundane acts.

One shoot of Muslim ethics resembles the 'must do' and 'must not do' (duties) features of some ethical systems. Moral philosophers call this deontological ethics. In Islam these duty-based moral rules are divided into two types. The first type involves the duty to *perform* acts (commission). Muslims, for example, are required to perform five prayers a day, to fast in the month of Ramadan, to annually pay religious-taxes and to undertake the pilgrimage once in a lifetime, if one can afford it. The Arabic terms for duty are *farḍ* or *wājib*. Failing to adhere to these rules can result in an earthly and/or otherworldly penalty. Of course, in a freedom-obsessed world, the mere mention of 'duty' might sound odd. But in many cultures, including many Muslim cultures, duty is not antithetical to freedom. Performing a duty can itself be a profound act. One of the characters in Vikram Chandra's *Sacred Games* insightfully declares, "Love is duty, duty is love" (Chandra 2006: 934).

A second type of rules requires the believer to scrupulously *avoid* or *refrain* from performing certain specified acts. These are called prohibitions (*muḥarramāt or ḥarām*). Hence, a Muslim is duty-bound to avoid eating certain foods and drinking alcoholic drinks, and to abstain from adultery, stealing, murder, violence, lying, dishonesty, backbiting, gossip, negligence, disobedience to parents, cruelty to humans and animals, among other things. In both doing and avoiding certain acts, an individual Muslim is performing the work of *dīn*, namely, acts by which an individual Muslim can attain salvation in the afterlife. Muslims believe that disobeying God's rules amounts to a sin and can result in suffering in the hereafter. But divine grace and compassion can also result in forgiveness followed by bliss in Eden.

Yet, music is the medium that best reveals Kaukab's complex thoughts. While she enjoys the inspiring spiritual music of Nusrat, the proscription of music by Muslim clerics confounds and troubles her. Kaukab's passing thought that *"Islam is said to forbid music ..."* stems from this duty-based moral thinking that requires Muslims to refrain from listening to music. This is the view of religious experts who interpret the teachings of the Qur'an and the statements of the Prophet Muhammad in this duty-based system of ethical thinking, called *fiqh*. *Fiqh* literally means "to understand." The folk who are expert in this literature are called the jurists (*fuqahā*) and the learned (*ʿulamā*).

Revelation, also called the Sharī ʿa, is the source material or raw data that the jurists and scholars interpret. Literally, the word Sharī ʿa means "a path to water." Both the Qur'an and the traditions (*ḥadīth*) of the Prophet Muhammad comprise the source teachings of revelation. But as revelation, Sharī ʿa is always in need of rigorous interpretation. Its meanings and purposes have to be explained and therefore require the skills of experts. Often, Muslims refer to the interpretation of the rules in a shorthand manner as "Sharīʿa." Technically, the correct name would be *fiqh*, namely, the understanding of the revelation.

So, in the view of *fiqh*-experts the ban on music in Islam is a watertight one. In their view it is firmly supported by a centuries-old consensus (*ijmā*), which is binding in its authority. However, a vocal minority of contemporary scholars contests the validity of this consensus-based opinion. The permissibility or impermissibility of listening to music in Islam, they argue, was debated from multiple angles since early Islam.

Firstly, Muslim mystics over the centuries favored listening to uplifting music that transported them to levels of spiritual ecstasy. Secondly, past Muslim authorities unanimously permitted the use of percussion instruments employed during festivals and celebrations. However, these same scholars disallowed music made by string and wind instruments. Why? Because, in their view, statements attributed to the Prophet Muhammad disclosed the impermissible use of such instruments. As the debate continues, some scholars dispute the evidence as unreliable and as insufficiently compelling to ban music made by string and wind instruments.

Even though Muslims encounter music in their daily lives there remains a great deal of unease on the permissibility of music in practice. Several decades ago, the prominent Shaykh Yusuf al-Qaraḍāwī, a Qatar-based scholar, ruled music to be permissible. In his view music promotes cheer, relaxation and dignity, as part of a Sharīʿa-compliant form of entertainment. Qaraḍāwī came under considerable criticism from other religious scholars who charged that he flouted the canonical tradition and bent the rules of interpretation (Bin Mūsá 1428/2007). However, he countered by arguing that when issuing legal opinions (*fatwās*), his own interpretative method, Qaraḍāwī said, was to make things easy for people. This motive, he argued, was endorsed by the Prophet Muhammad himself, who said: "Make things easy, and do not make things difficult; give good news and do not alienate people."

Qaraḍāwī's critics are unforgiving; they accuse him of bowdlerizing the tradition and for completely subverting the golden rules of interpretation that Muslim scholars adhered to for centuries (Bin Mūsá 1428/2007). Qaraḍāwī rebuts their charges, stating that the evidence on music is not as clear-cut as his critics pretend it to be. Opinions, in his view, are shaped by the kind of intellectual effort (*ijtihād*) one invests in order to understand the evidence. Qaraḍāwī also takes comfort in the fact that, according to Muslim tradition, good faith efforts to adjudicate in matters of the Sharīʿa still deserve reward in the eyes of God, even if those rulings prove to be incorrect, ultimately.

Kaukab and Qaraḍāwī both find music acceptable but they arrive at this decision by very different paths. Qaraḍāwī does rigorous scholarly work to sift and strain the evidence in order to find the correct answer. Kaukab uses different tools, namely analogy and intuition. Stories she heard as a child of the Prophet Muhammad's arrival in Medina, the city that became his new home after he migrated from the dangers of Mecca, was one source. If the Prophet himself was welcomed by festive drumbeats and song, then Nusrat's lyrics of earthly and divine love accompanied by a full ensemble of instruments could not, in her view, possibly amount to a sin. But something unsaid seems to also inform her decision: conscience. Did Kaukab continue to listen to music because she found solace in a prophetic teaching? The one that said: "Ask your heart! [literally, *istafti qalbak*—Ask your heart for a *fatwā*] even though the expert jurists (*muftūn*, sing. *muftī*) have issued their verdict on this matter." And so the disagreement about the lawfulness of music and other issues continue to be debated by both laypersons like Kaukab or among the community of experts in the *fatwā*-literature. Both groups, laypersons and experts continually update the Muslim tradition, which the next example will further amplify.

Global debates

In 1965 a *fatwā*, an ethical-legal opinion, arrived in South Africa from India. A prominent Muslim businessman of Indian ancestry, Mr. A.M. Moola solicited the ruling from a visiting Indian Muslim religious figure during the latter's visit to Durban in 1964. The businessman's query was the following: Could a Muslim businessman like himself participate in interest-bearing transactions with banks and corporations? Interest or usury, known as *ribā*, is prohibited by Islam's ethical teachings. The Qur'an issues stern warnings of damnation for those who participate in interest-bearing transactions. Surely, these admonitions must have dogged Mr. Moola's conscience because, as members of a minority religious community in a society dominated by Christians and other African faiths, interest for Muslim businessmen like him was unavoidable. At the time, there were no non-interest-bearing Sharī 'a-compliant alternatives for finance as there are today in the global multibillion-dollar Islamic finance and banking industry.

Mr Moola's question was put to the Dār al-Iftā, the Department of Fatwās of the renowned Muslim seminary in India, known as Dār al-ʿUlūm Deoband, some 100km from Delhi, the Indian capital. Deoband is an institution where advanced Islamic education is imparted in order to train students in orthodox Islamic teachings. The study of Islamic law or *fiqh* is one of the main subjects taught in South Asia's madrasas and the rule-based ethical method is the primary narrative of this brand of Islam. Departments of Fatwās are found at nearly all madrasas, big and small. In the Middle East, the renowned al-Azhar University is a major authoritative resource for *fatwās*. In Muslim majority countries, the religious affairs ministries also appoint specialized *fatwā*-issuing councils or a state-appointed Grand Muftī. Millions of queries are put to these councils and institutions annually. Nowadays, online services are sought-after outlets where e-*fatwās* are solicited.

Figure 2.1 Islamic banking in Malaysia, 2010. Courtesy of Bloomberg/Getty Images.

The other feature of the Deoband school is that it is rigorous in issuing its ethical and juridical verdicts almost exclusively according to the Hanafī law school. What is the Hanafī law school? If Islam has two major theological divisions between the Sunnī and Shīʿa doctrines, then each sect also has super-specialist interpreters of ethical and juridical teachings. These specialists are renowned for their ability to articulate rules of interpretation—*ijtihād*—at a meta-level. In other words, they devised a theory of interpretation (a hermeneutic) that gained a following among their students. For this reason these experts were hailed as master-jurists (*mujtahid* pl. *mujtahidūn*). Each founder's hermeneutical paradigm, known in Arabic as a *madhhab*, became a franchise with the help of dedicated students and admirers, and spread to different geographical regions of the Muslim world. These paradigms of interpretation developed scholarly expertise and generated canonical texts and opinions. Today they are known as the Muslim law schools. Named after their founders, most Sunnīs follow the Hanafī, Mālikī, Shāfiʿī, Hanbalī law schools. The Shīʿa adhere to either the Jaʿfarī, Zaydī or Ismāʿīlī schools. Laypersons and even specialists in ethical and legal matters often commit themselves to the authority (*taqlīd*) of these schools and their opinions. However, there is also a growing trend that disavows obedience to the canonical authorities of these schools. This trend insists that Muslims are obliged to directly access the meaning of the scriptures in imitation of the practice of the pious ancestors, known as the *salaf*. This trend has become known as the *salafīs*, some of whom have grown in notoriety.

The Hanafī school and some of their adherents today adhere to old-style doctrines developed when Islam was a pre-modern empire. Under Islamic imperial rule, the world was politically divided into at least two kinds of political territories: (1) territories inhabited by people of other faiths or no faith, but who negotiated political treaties with the Islamic empire and (2) territories that had no such treaties. Those territories with no political treaty also had no agreement of mutual recognition and were *potentially* at war with the Islamic realm. The Muslim constitutional jurists designated "no-treaty" territories as the "jurisdiction of war" (*dār al-ḥarb*).

In order to assist the Muslim minority in South Africa, the experts (*muftīs*) at Deoband consulted their sourcebooks. They found a precedent that could help the Muslims of South Africa in the question of commercial interest. The Hanafī law school, they argued, permitted interest-bearing transactions to take place between Muslim traders and people of other faiths, provided they were in a region that qualified as a "jurisdiction of war." Since Muslims were a minority in South Africa, the region approximated the ancient definition of a "jurisdiction of war." On this reasoning, the experts at Deoband ruled that Muslims in South Africa were exempt from the ban on participating in interest-bearing transactions. As the authors of the *fatwā* wrote: "... and the application of rulings with regard to dealings in interest [*sūdī kārobār*] between Muslims and non-Muslims would also be applicable" (Mehtar 1965: 8–9).

The Deoband scholars hoped that they had provided a way out for South African Muslims in order that they might economically thrive with the use of this exemption. Due to their unfamiliarity with the South African context, they could not have predicted the Muslim reaction to their ruling. A well-meaning *fatwā* became a source for controversy among Muslims in South Africa (Makki 1966: 2–12; Abed 1966: 13–19; Anonymous 1966: 2–8).

At least two kinds of Muslim audiences reacted to the *fatwā*. The first audience was secular educated Muslims. They sensed that the *fatwā* peddled antiquarian ideas marked by an outdated political theology of empire. To boot, it designated South Africa as a "jurisdiction of war." This group was acutely alert to the treacherous political challenges Muslims as a religious minority faced in apartheid South Africa. These secular Muslims were caught between combating legislated racism on the one hand, and aspiring to attain the political franchise for all South Africans in a democratic future on the other. The *fatwā*, in their view, could distort the self-image of Muslims as a minority, if the territory in which they wished to live was framed as theologically hostile to Islam. Under apartheid, political hostility was directed against all people of color, not so much against religion. The *fatwā* resembled a kind of apartheid mentality itself by allocating to each territory a different political status and for creating legal exceptions for Muslim practice. The spokesperson for this group, Professor Fatima Meer, complained that the *fatwā* entrenched the minority status of Muslims, made simplistic distinctions between Muslims and people of other faiths and implied that the vast majority was an entity with which Muslims were at war (Meer 1966: 12). Such ethical teachings, she argued, could prejudice the well-being of South African Muslims and jeopardize their prospects of being part of a free democratic majority.

The second audience that responded to the *fatwā* was the Muslim religious scholars. Among them was the Council of Theologians (Jamiatul Ulama of Transvaal) seated in a province now known as Gauteng. This council is a standard-bearer of the Deoband school in South Africa. On this occasion, the council strongly dissented from the Indian *fatwā*. Muftī Ebrahim Sanjalvi (d. 1983) was the chief spokesperson of this organization. Exemplifying intra-Muslim diversity, a *muftī* based in South Africa voiced his scholarly disagreement with a group of *muftīs* in India, even though they belonged to the same Deobandi theological fraternity.

Sanjalvi said he doubted whether South Africa could be neatly classified as a "jurisdiction of war" (Sanjalvi 1966). While there were some features confirming that designation, there were also other characteristics that suggested it was a "jurisdiction of safety" (*dār al-amān*), another category of classical Islamic law. But Muftī Sanjalvi's main thread of reasoning was the following: the prohibition of interest was explicitly and unambiguously mentioned in the Qur'an. For this reason alone, he stated, it was not permissible for Muslims to partake in interest-bearing transactions; neither in trade with fellow Muslims, nor for that matter, in their transactions with non-Muslims. With this counter-*fatwā*, the South African affiliates of the Deoband school distanced themselves from what they deemed to be the ill-informed response of the parent institution in India.

Several important things can be learnt about Muslim ethics from this episode. The first lesson is that there are diverse forms of ethical reasoning among Muslims and even within a single scholarly fraternity. The second is that different forms of reason are operative within Muslim ethics. The Indian Deobandis proposed a form of reasoning embedded in the canonical tradition of the Hanafī school to which they were utterly committed. The Indian *fatwā* tried its best to find a precedent that could work, but the antique precedent they found was neither legible nor intelligible to Muslim audiences in the twentieth century. The remedy they offered was out of place. Furthermore, the *fatwā* misread the context of South Africa where political realities and the aspirations of the Muslim community offered very different desiderata to what the *fatwā* provided.

The third lesson is that even scholars aligned to the authority (*taqlīd*) of the canonical law schools occasionally mix and match their interpretative strategies. The South African Deobandi leader, Mufti Sanjalvi, ignored the canonical opinion and resorted to *ijtihād*, independent investigation. He countered the canonical teachings with a fresh reading of the scriptural sources. Since the 1960s it has become increasingly noticeable that followers of the law schools, like Sanjalvi and Qaraḍāwī, adopt a mixture of interpretive strategies, combining scriptural reasoning in conjunction with the canonical reasoning of the law schools.

The fourth lesson is context. A qualified and brilliant scholar might know the rules of Muslim ethics, but fail to grasp the context where his opinions will be applied. In all ethical deliberations, knowing the context is often far more important than knowing the rules. The Indian Deoband *fatwā* backfired because the *muftīs* on the subcontinent were unaware of the complex political and religious terrain of South Africa.

Mechanically applying *fatwās* from a bygone age in new contexts frequently miscarries. The most infamous case is the *fatwā* which Ayatollah Ruhullah Khomeini issued against the British-Indian author of *The Satanic Verses*, Salman Rushdie, for making blasphemous comments about the Prophet Muhammad and his family. Khomeini stated the death penalty which Islamic law prescribed for anyone found guilty of satirizing the Prophet. The opinion issued by the head of the Iranian state ignored the modern context of international law, disrupted global international relations, and created a furor around freedom of speech. In a cyber-age of *e-fatwās* the consideration of context is immensely important. In the next *fatwā*, again context, place and purpose become all-important considerations.

The family

Local conditions often become a catalyst for a change in ethical thinking. Take as an example the case of married female Muslim converts in Europe and North America.

Even though they have converted to Islam, their marriages to unconverted spouses are thriving and they do not see the need to end their perfectly good marriages. Their husbands do not object to their conversion to Islam. But the duty-based rules of Muslim law and ethics raise questions about such marriages. How?

The general Islamic marriage law allows Muslim men to marry spouses belonging to the Jewish or Christian faiths. However, Muslim women cannot marry men belonging to other faiths. Under the existing *fiqh* rules, if a wife converts while her husband does not, then the Muslim wife's marriage contract contravenes the rules and therefore the marriage must be terminated and the parties be separated.

Religious authorities are not always very clear as to the reasoning underpinning this rule. Authorities often assume that husbands determine the religion of the family. A non-Muslim husband they fear might coerce her to abandon Islam and become an apostate. Other scholars say that the husband will raise the children in his faith, depriving the wife of raising her offspring as Muslims. So what should these converted women do? Should they end their marriages, according to the established rules? Is that even tenable? Or is there another solution?

This question was put to the Dublin-based European Council of Fatwā and Research (ECFR). The ECFR is by design based in a Muslim-friendly European capital. Its European character also facilitates travel of international experts for consultations that might otherwise prove difficult in other capitals given immigration and travel restrictions. This council is headed by distinguished scholars like Yusuf al-Qaraḍāwī and Faisal al-Mawlawī, among others. After many meetings, the ECFR deliberated on this real-life (*nāzila* pl. *nawāzil*), not hypothetical, case. Such a case is in part resolved by making reference to older ethical and juridical literature and, if necessary, reinterpreting this for the present. The ECFR ruled that it was not necessary for European convert Muslim women to end their marriages. In other words, contrary to the established rule, their conversion did not impact their marriage contracts from an Islamic ethical and legal perspective. Needless to say, this ruling has sparked a great deal of controversy and serious disagreement among Muslim scholars the world over. How did these ECFR experts set aside the established rule and the unbroken practice for centuries?

Firstly, the ECFR scholars argued that what appeared to be a consensus preventing Muslim women from remaining married to non-Muslim men was a not a consensus. Normally, the authority of a precedent based on consensus is even stronger than an explicit text of scripture. Why? In terms of the rules of interpretation, a text of scripture is open to multiple interpretations, whereas a consensus decision is held to be less ambiguous. The ECFR undermined the older consensus position by using the writings of a noted fourteenth-century Ḥanbalī scholar, Ibn al-Qayyim al-Jawzīyya to validate their opinion.

Secondly, the ECFR gave a different interpretation to Qur'anic verse 60:10, which was alleged to have banned the marriages of Muslim women to non-Muslim men. The relevant portion of the verse reads: "... believing women are no longer lawful to their un-believing husbands, and nor are the non-believing husbands any longer lawful to them" (Qur'an 60:10).[4] But a crucial piece of historical information casts this verse in a very different light and repositions the hermeneutical framework. The verse dealt with women who fled their pagan husbands in Mecca and arrived in Medina as converted Muslims. Why did they flee to Medina? Their pagan husbands coerced them to abandon their Islamic faith. It was in this context that the Qur'an counseled separation between a Muslim wife and her non-Muslim husband. But the ECFR also found other precedents to support its ruling. So when husbands did not object to the faith of their Muslim wives then matters were different. A case in point was the Prophet Muhammad's own daughter Zaynab. She was married to a non-Muslim Meccan, named Abū al-ʿĀṣ. The difference of his faith did not affect their marriage since he also visited her in Medina (Ḥaṣwah 2009: 134). The senior companion ʿAlī b. Abī Ṭālib also ruled that the marriage contract was intact if a non-Muslim husband lived in the domicile of the Muslim wife.

Thirdly, what really drove the ECFR's thinking were two doctrines with older histories but in modern Muslim usage both were frequently used. The first doctrine is that all rules of the Sharīʿa, especially those dealing with social transactions, serve explicit and implicit notions of public interest (maṣlaḥa). The second doctrine is that the Sharīʿa aimed to preserve certain purposes. Medieval Muslim jurists have counted these "purposes of the Sharīʿa" (maqāṣid al-Sharīʿa) as numbering five. The goal of the Sharīʿa is to preserve religion, life, reason, wealth and paternity, an idea that is nowadays glossed as the preservation of the family.

For many traditional scholars, the ECFR's views sounded radical. Female sex with a spouse from another faith is viewed as crossing certain boundaries of propriety. Anxiety over female sexuality is culturally often more highly prized for reasons that anthropologists and sociologists have amply explored. But in patriarchal Muslim societies female conduct is viewed as an index of the moral order, if not moral health, of the society, irrespective of the detrimental corruption men might unleash on society.

Sexuality and intimacy

Female and male sexual conduct is what the Egyptian writer Alaa al-Aswany insightfully explores in his novel Chicago. He not only predicts the fall of the authoritarian president of his country but in one of many subplots of the book, he explores different forms of human frailty (al-Aswany 2008). Intimacy and human sexuality is enigmatic for its beauty, its freight of anxiety and also its capacity to diminish. Despite the abundance of rules and self-discipline, ultimately human desire wins out, often with unpredictable outcomes.

In the city of Chicago, two Egyptian medical students are pursuing PhDs in histology. Tariq Haseeb, a nerd-like character gets excellent grades in college but lacks social skills and masturbates compulsively. His sexual attraction for a fellow Egyptian from Tanta changes everything for him. Shaymaa Muhammadi, like him, is a qualified physician. Wearing a veil in her mid-thirties, she is deeply devout and unmarried. Her father reluctantly consented to her studies abroad since he preferred to find her an appropriate spouse.

Tariq and Shaymaa's mutual attraction soon leads to physical and erotic encounters. She allows him access to her body but they do not engage in vaginal sex, a domain mutually agreed to be the "red line," a boundary only to be enjoyed after marriage. Aswany sensitively describes their encounters.

> He didn't dare take off her dress but they embraced closely and their muscles contracted in instinctive successive thrusts until they both crossed the gate of pleasure together.

But soon Shaymaa, overcome with guilt, sobs and regrets her deed.

> "How I despise myself!"
> "I love you," he whispered, kissing her hands.
> "I am now an immoral woman!"
> "Who said that?"
> "I've fallen!" ... She looked at him from behind her tears and said, "You couldn't respect me now after what I've done with you."
> "You're my wife: how could I not respect you?"
> "I am not your wife."
> "Aren't we going to get married?"
> "Yes, but right now I am forbidden to you."
> "We haven't committed fornication, Shaymaa. And there are noble hadiths, all authentic, all unanimous, in stating that God Almighty forgives trespasses that do not amount to fornication of those He wills. We love each other and intend to be lawfully wedded, God willing. And God the merciful forgives us."
>
> *(al-Aswany 2008: 219-220)*

For several months they continue to seek each other's company until one day Shaymaa announces to him that she is pregnant.

> "Now do you know the catastrophe, Tariq? I am pregnant in sin, Tariq. In sin."...
> "You're mistaken."
> "What do you mean?"
> "You couldn't be pregnant."
> "I did the test twice."

"I assure you it is impossible."

She looked at him shrewishly and said, "You are a doctor and you know very well what happened is possible." It seemed the red line had been compromised.

(al-Aswany 2008: 301)

Mortified by the circumstances of her pregnancy, Shaymaa proposes a "shot gun" marriage in order to cover-up their transgression. But Tariq balks at the prospect of marrying without the consent of his family. Unplanned fatherhood coupled with his faltering grades and fear of failure causes Tariq to predictably retreat. The next time we see Shaymaa in the novel again is when she makes her way through screaming anti-abortion protesters to reach the clinic where she plans to have an abortion. From the opposite side of the street the protestors yell:

"Ruthless murderer!"

"Are you Muslim?"

"Does your God allow the killing of children?"

(al-Aswany 2008: 338-9)

Shaymaa eventually has the abortion and when she awakes after the procedure she surprisingly finds an exhausted Tariq at her side.

With refreshing candor Aswany presents to us what millions experience in human relations. Into her mid-thirties Shaymaa had internalized the virtue of sexual abstinence. Sex, according to the duty-based morality advocates, is only permissible within marriage. Outside of marriage sex is a sin. Violations of Islam's sexual rules in societies where Sharīʿa is enforced are in theory punishable with severe penalties, ranging from flogging to the death penalty. But prosecution for this offence has a high bar. Proof of a sexual offence is almost impossible for it requires at least four people to testify that they had witnessed the sexual encounter. Unlawful sex conducted in private, where the law has no reach, is only an offense against God and has to be expiated by repentance.

But Shaymaa's guilt and shame induced low self-esteem. This psychological trauma is common to male and female experiences in many cultures. Shaymaa's moral formation and discipline (*akhlāq*) was designed around sexual restraint not experimentation. Very early in her life, Shaymaa was taught that to follow the Sharīʿa meant to internalize the most virtuous character (Ḥilmī 2004: 7). At home and school she was taught right conduct (*adab*) that constitutes those basic values of truthfulness, honesty, fairness, compassion, love, altruism, respect and honor for others and their property, among other values essential for humans to flourish. The purpose of virtue ethics in Islam is to train one's sensibility, in order to intuitively do the right thing when there are no rules to guide one.

The story is about paradox: how humans respect certain boundaries within their frailties. The sinfulness of sex outside wedlock is so deeply ingrained in each of Tariq and Shaymaa's consciousnesses that they retrofit their transgressions in sex. In order not to commit the ultimate sin they physically avoid sexual intercourse. Therefore Tariq can confidently reassure Shaymaa that technically they had not committed the sin of fornication, called *zinā*. On the other hand Tariq mentions nothing of his practice of masturbation. At least one view in Muslim ethics thinks of it as a healthy form of sexual gratification while the majority deems it to be abominable. Many Muslim ethicists and religious counselors would have encouraged Tariq to rather continue with masturbation instead of despoiling the ethical formation of his female friend. But even if Tariq did receive the counseling would it have convinced him to desist?

Zinā is deemed a major sin in Islam. In magnitude of offence, it joins the list of sins alongside murder and disobedience to one's parents. Shaymaa is especially wracked by guilt because she understands the gravity of the offence through her moral formation. The God of the Qur'an is all-seeing and all-knowing, whose presence instills in his servants the awareness to behave correctly. Concerned that she feels dishonored by their semi-sexual encounters, Tariq consoles Shaymaa with words to let her know that he intends to marry her in order to redeem the offence. He uses a narrative of piety coupled with his knowledge of the technical aspects of duty-based morality. He skillfully marshals his information to work around his guilt. Playing the role of a pastor he offers Shaymaa solace by saying that divine compassion invites forgiveness for them. How? By the standards of his own private morality he stresses that the absence of vaginal sex meant that they did not commit *zinā*. They both know a good amount of Islamic theology to take comfort in the knowledge that God's mercy surpasses His wrath and that the doors for divine pardon are always open.

When a very brave and veiled Shaymaa terminates her pregnancy she breaks all stereotypes. It is not expected that a pious Muslim woman would even contemplate abortion, let alone agree to termination. What this episode shows is that Muslim women, like men, are bearers of different stripes of morality and ethical orientations. We do not know for how many months Shaymaa was pregnant. But in the duty-based version of Sharīʿa rules there is room for the justifiable termination of pregnancy within a fourth-month period from the date of conception. Is pregnancy conceived outside of wedlock a justifiable reason for the termination of a pregnancy? Given the shame and diminished social status that Shaymaa would suffer in Egyptian society if she gave birth to a child outside wedlock, some Muslim ethicists would justify her decision to terminate her pregnancy (al-Laknawī 1417/1996: 325). There might be others who would demur and possibly recommend that she deliver the child and then give it up for adoption, an option that she did not choose in America (Moosa 1992).

The Islamic position on abortion and other related issues have altered with the advances in biotechnology and new investigative procedures. The traditional, pre-modern Muslim position allows justifiable termination within four months of conception; but this position has been challenged. Now that sonograms and other types of instrumentation show forms of life in a fetus at the very early stages of a pregnancy, some Muslim ethicists have adopted a more conservative position on abortion, recommending termination only when the mother's life is threatened (Brockopp 2003).

Debates centered on technology, science and bioethics pose some of the greatest challenges to inherited notions of Muslim ethics. Biotechnology has cast a molecular gaze on life, even as it enables the reverse engineering of life (Rose 2007: 83). The technological age is primarily concerned with intervention and its goal is to rewrite and transform life. With the aid of technology, our understanding of the good life (*bios*) is radically altered by our growing knowledge of the living and vital processes of animal life (*zoë*) of which we are part. Biotechnology, in turn, has rewritten the older script of science and medicine. Instead of description and diagnosis, medicine is now capable of highlighting one's susceptibility to disease and calculates one's predisposition to the empire of risk. The future of life will be measured in terms of risk, in what some have described as the emergence of a thoroughgoing promissory culture. In dealing with these new frontiers of ethics, Muslim thinkers, like all other religious traditions, are desperately trying to remain current in order to provide the best guidance to their communities in uncharted waters (Moosa 2012). Finding the right tools and instruments to evaluate the challenges requires innovation in method, an effort already underway and the topic of the next section.

Innovation

Innovation in methodology via the doctrine of public interest and purpose-oriented teachings caused a gradual shift in modern Muslim ethical thinking. With this approach, contemporary Muslim ethicists are able to question the inherited cultural logic embedded in the ethical rules. They can also reassign and link the ethical values to new cultural contexts with the help of this innovation. One of the biggest challenges in modern Muslim ethics has been the question of gender. The older duty-based ethics advanced patriarchal values that were injurious to the welfare of women. Now, under the guidance of new readings of the Sharīʿa, Muslim ethicists have slowly begun to espouse gender equality and fairness.

Most notable in this approach has been the way the historical tradition has been reread and reinterpreted. Debates in the present always make reference to readings and teachings in the past. By listening carefully to the multiple voices in the past, many contemporary ethicists draw on some of the earlier interpretative soundings to assist them in a bid to give new meanings to practices in the present. Authenticity and continuity in tradition is highly valued and therefore new readings are viewed as important. Yet resistance to this new approach in Muslim ethics has not been uncommon. Muslim orthodoxy, represented by the ʿulamā, frequently rail at the outcomes of this kind of thinking. They fear that utilitarianism will become rife and would gradually supplant the carefully constructed, centuries-old hermeneutical system of the canonical schools of Islamic law.

Bear in mind that methodological innovation in law and ethics was prompted by a political analysis of the balance sheet of Muslim gains and losses in the modern period. Some Muslim reformers and thinkers in the nineteenth century believed that Western colonization of Muslim lands and setbacks to Muslim power had been caused by a lack of innovation in knowledge, together with a moribund tradition. A once vibrant faith's spirit of rational theology, they thought, was erased by creeping superstition that dulled Islam's spirit of progress and rendered it ineffective.

Why and how? Muslim thinkers and laypersons alike, analysts claimed, became slavishly obedient to dogma and authority (taqlīd). Obedience to authority was identified as the main culprit and "cause of intellectual stagnation" in ethical thought (Colloquium 1953: 60). For many Muslim reformers this state of affairs epitomized the "decline of Islam" thesis, one that later twentieth-century scholars criticized as an inaccurate portrayal of affairs (Schulze 1995).

The cure, many a Muslim thinker proposed, was ijtihād. If ijtihād in early centuries meant the scholarly license to propose a new interpretative paradigm, then modern Muslim thinkers, many proponents reasoned, should also be able to engage in "independent thinking." In reality, rhetoric surpassed the actual practice of ijtihād. (Ijtihād was always permitted in Shīʿa thought but even in that tradition it had seen better days.) The monumental task of recontextualizing the interpretation of Muslim sources and doctrines to match the new realities was hardly broached. And ijtihād remained a rallying cry for mobilization, without a convincing intellectual roadmap. Despite its deficiencies, the call for ijtihād did introduce some changes in Muslim attitudes that impacted ethical and moral thinking.

Advocates of ijtihād hoped to curb the authoritarianism of Muslim clerical orthodoxy (ulamā). While such a move was intended to unshackle the minds of lay Muslims from an uncritical adherence to tradition, it also turned out to be a double-edged sword. Lay Muslims were urged to seek out fresh inspiration from the Qur'an and the prophetic tradition in the successful manner that their pious ancestors (salaf) did. Hence the rise of a trend called salafism that wished to invoke the primitive spirit of tradition. This invitation to reach for new interpretations had one failing. It did not provide for a coherent framework to interpret the Qur'an and the hadith. The outcome was the oversimplification of tradition.

However, Muslim laypersons were the greatest beneficiaries of this new scripture-centered activism that was popularized by a variety of brands of salafism. Modern and professionally educated Muslim men and women—doctors, engineers, lawyers, economists and scientists—all availed themselves of this freedom to pronounce on matters of law and ethics. They often provided common sense and face-value interpretations of the Qur'an and a limited number of prophetic traditions. This ranged from the authoritarian Wahhabi thread from Saudi Arabia to the more tolerant and piety-oriented *salafism* of the Levant, South and East Asia. But a whole range of other actors—from educated Muslims, political and cultural activists to militants and terrorists—found a license in this "do-it-yourself" brand of Islam. Unfettered use of *ijtihād* proved to be lethal in the hands of militants and violent extremists. Militants mixed a hodgepodge of religious narratives into a combustible political rhetoric in response to grievances and victimization that many Muslims experienced at the hands of ruthless Euro-American powers and their equally ruthless proxies. In this way militants succeeded in beguiling unsuspecting audiences with their eloquence in order to justify their nihilistic acts of violence. The former leader of al-Qaida, Osama bin Laden was a veritable poster boy for this brand of militancy when he issued a pseudo *fatwā*—a scholarly opinion—declaring war on his political adversaries, the United States and its allies. In doing so, bin Laden single-handedly rewrote the contemporary Muslim ethical tradition and replaced it with his earth shaking violence as a teaching for his followers. The repudiation of his views from more credible voices in Muslim ethical circles was often belated, unheard and ineffective.

Conclusion

The take home from this chapter is that the practice and theory of Muslim ethics is diverse in its outcome. It depends on methods, approaches, temperaments and contexts. The pre-modern ethical models are attractive for their coherence but their utility for a very different world is questionable.

The premier challenge for practitioners of modern Muslim ethics is one of epistemology. How does knowledge of the present shape an ethics of Muslims today so that it comports to and synchronizes with their lived experiences? Time and space continue to change as our technologies shrink both. Along with this, the social and lived ethical imaginary of Muslims continues to evolve. Muslims espouse new ideals that are embedded in science and technology and enmeshed in capitalist political systems that are driven by the nation-state and fueled by the ideals of equality, democracy, human rights and globalization. Needless to say, liberal capitalism and its ideals are not uniformly welcomed in the Muslim world. To deal with these complexities, innovation in Muslim ethics would have to accelerate at a much more rapid rate than thus far experienced. A search for a new ethics might have to go beyond the reading of texts and involve a fairly sophisticated study and understanding of the social context in which Muslims find themselves.

Summary

- Deliberation in modern Muslim ethics is no longer the exclusive terrain of Muslim traditional clerics and scholars, even though they play a major role.
- Interpretation centers around debates about epistemology and the latter is central to all debates on Muslim ethics.
- Ethical debates frequently occur in counterpoint or are contrapuntal. Voices from the past frequently converse with voices in the present.

Discussion points

- Is "Muslim ethics" a neologism? Do Muslims use other terms to refer to ethical sources? Name them.
- Can you explain on what grounds music is forbidden in Islam? How do those who favor music justify their argument?
- What were the two most effective methods thus far for innovation in method in Muslim ethics?
- Discuss the importance and role of *fatwās* in Muslim ethical deliberation.
- How much does context matter in discussions of Muslim ethics? Discuss the feature of counterpoint in Muslim ethical discussion. Is this a practice unique to Islam or do other traditions engage in the same strategy?

Further reading

Ali, Kecia (2006) *Sexual Ethics and Islam: Feminist Reflections on Qur'an, Hadith, and Jurisprudence*, Oxford: Oneworld.
Brockopp, Jonathan E. (ed.) (2003) *Islamic Ethics of Life: Abortion, War, and Euthanasia*, Columbia, SC: University of South Carolina Press.
Kadri, Sadakat (2012) *Heaven on Earth: A Journey through Shari'a Law from the Deserts of Ancient Arabia to the Streets of the Modern Muslim World*, New York: Farrar, Straus and Giroux.
Moosa, Ebrahim. "Muslim Ethics and Biotechnology," in James W. Haag, Gregory R. Peterson and Michael L. Spezio (eds) *The Routledge Companion to Religion and Science*, New York: Routledge, 455–65.
Sajoo, Amyn B. (2004) *Muslim Ethics: Emerging Vistas*, London and New York: I.B. Tauris.

References

Abed, Ismail (1966) "A Refutation of the Deobandi Fatwa on Interest and Usury," *The Muslim Digest*, February.
Anonymous (1966) "Moolla and Mullahs Break Silence," *The Muslim Digest*, April.
al-Aswany, Alaa (2008) *Chicago: A Novel*, trans. Farouk Abdel Wahab, London: Fourth Estate.

al-Laknawī, ʿAbd al-Ḥayy (1417AH/1996) "Sharḥ ʿAllāma ʿAbd Al-Ḥayy," *Hidāya*, Vol. 4. Karachi: Idāra-t al-Qurʾān wa al- ʿulūm al-islāmīya.

Aslam, Nadeem (2004) *Maps for Lost Lovers,* London: Faber and Faber.

Bin Mūsá, ʿAbd Allāh Ramaḍān (2007) *Al-Radd ʿAlā Al-Qaraḍāwī Wa Al-Judayʿ.* Dahūk, al- ʿIrāq: al-Atharīya li al-Turāth.

Brockopp, Jonathan E. (ed.) (2003) *Islamic Ethics of Life: Abortion, War, and Euthanasia,* Columbia, SC: University of South Carolina Press.

Chandra, Vikram (2006) *Sacred Games.* Harper: New York, 2006.

Colloquium on Islamic Culture in its Relation to the Contemporary World (1953) *Colloquium on Islamic Culture in Its Relation to the Contemporary World,* Princeton: Princeton University Press.

Ḥaṣwah, Māhir Ḥusayn (2009) *Fiqh Al-WāQiʿ Wa-Atharuhu Fī Al-IjtihāD,* Herndon, VA: al-Maʿhad al-ʿĀlamī lil-Fikr al-Islāmī.

Ḥilmī, Muṣṭafā (1424/2004) *Al-Akhlāq Bayna Al-Falāsifa Wa ʿulamāʾ Al-Islām,* Beirut: Dār al-Kutub al-ʿIlmīya.

Iqbal, Muhammad and M. Saeed Sheikh (eds) (1999) *Reconstruction of Religious Thought in Islam,* 4th edn, Lahore: Institute of Islamic Culture.

Makki, Mohammed (1966) "Deoband Ulamas Declare South Africa a Darul Harb," *The Muslim Digest,* February: 2–12

May, Todd (2005) *Gilles Deleuze: An Introduction,* Cambridge and New York: Cambridge University Press.

Meer, Fatima (1966) *Interest and Dar-ul-Harb in Islam: A Preliminary Analysis of the Fatwa on Riba of the Muftees of Dar-ul-Uloom, Deoband,* Durban: Indian Views Press.

Mehtar, M.A. (trans.) (1965) "An Important Fatwa Permitting Free and Full Participation by Muslims in the Economic Development and the use of Banking and Financial Institutions in a Country like South Africa by the Muftees of Darul Uloom Deoband," pamphlet.

Moosa, Ebrahim (1992) "'The Child Belongs to the Bed': Illegitimacy and Islamic Law," in Sandra Burman and Eleanor Preston-White (eds) *Questionable Issue: Illegitimacy in South Africa,* Cape Town: Oxford University Press, 1992: 171–84.

—— (2012) "Muslim Ethics and Biotechnology," in James W. Haag, Gregory R. Peterson and Michael L. Spezio (eds) *The Routledge Companion to Religion and Science,* New York: Routledge, 455–65.

Nagel, Thomas (1986) *The View from Nowhere,* New York and Oxford: Oxford University Press.

Qaraḍāwī, Yūsuf (1982) *The Lawful and the Prohibited in Islam - Al-Halal Wal-Haram Fil Islam,* Ḥalāl Wa-Al-Ḥarām Fī Al-Islām, Indianapolis, IN: American Trust Publications.

Rose, Nikolas S. (2007) *The Politics of Life Itself: Biomedicine, Power, and Subjectivity in the Twenty-First Century,* Princeton: Princeton University Press.

Sachedina, Abdulaziz Abdulhussein (2009) *Islamic Biomedical Ethics: Principles and Application,* Oxford and New York: Oxford University Press.

Sanjalvi, Muftī Ebrahim, Jamiatul Ulama of Transvaal, pamphlet "Darul Harb and Riba," dated 10 Zul Qadah 1385/March 3, 1966.

Schulze, Reinhard (1995) "How Medieval Is Islam? Muslim Intellectual and Modernity," trans. Laila Friese, in Jochen Hippler and Andrea Lueg (eds) *The Next Threat: Western Perceptions of Islam,* Boulder, CO: Pluto Press with Transnational Institute.

Notes

1   I would like to thank Sam Kigar, Ali Mian, Bruce Lawrence and Leela Prasad for their feedback and suggestions of earlier drafts of this essay. All errors are mine exclusively.

2   I am indebted to Deleuze and Gauttari for the concept of the rhizome.

3   This definition is inspired by the work of Thomas Nagel (1986: 164).

4   The full verse is: "Oh you who have attained to faith! Whenever believing women come to you, leaving the domain of evil, question them, although God is fully aware of their faith; and if you determined that they are indeed believers, then do not send them back to the deniers of the truth. These believing women are no longer lawful to their un-believing husbands, and nor are the non-believing husbands any longer lawful to them …. And do not hold on to the marriage-tie with women who deny the truth" (Qur'an 60:10). The context of this verse requires some explanation. In the early years of Islam when there were hostilities between the Prophet Muhammad at Medina and his pagan foes in Mecca, some married women in Mecca converted to Islam and sought refuge in Medina. Since there was also a political treaty between Medina and Mecca to return any Meccans who went over to the Muslim side without the permission of their guardians, the Meccans were insisting that these converted Meccan women be returned. When the Prophet explained that married women did not fall under the guardianship clause of the treaty, the matter was resolved by compensating the Meccan husbands for the dower they spent on their now Muslim wives. Effectively the marriages were annulled. According to the verse the Prophet first had to interview the refugee Meccan women to verify that they did not leave their husbands under the false pretext of faith when in fact the underlying reasons were more mundane such as marital strife or to be near other family members. Therefore, the Qur'an's instruction to the Prophet that he should interview the women in order to ascertain their motives.

Governance
and
government

Robert D. Lee

Outline

- Muslim states, like non-Muslim states, face challenges of governance that cause them to invoke religion in one of three ways.
  - Mostly commonly Muslim states assert their allegiance to religious law.
  - Some Muslim states claim special religious status for their leadership.
  - Most Muslim-majority governments portray themselves as representative of the religious community or communities.
- There is no single pattern in the way Muslim nation-states use Islam. There is no single model of Islamic government.
- National history and politics better explain the relationship between religion and politics in a given Muslim country than can any blanket assertion about the nature of Islam.

The challenges of governance

Governments everywhere use religion for political purposes, and where governments rely most heavily on religion, opponents tend to formulate dissent in religious terms. Political actors everywhere seek to augment their power by clothing themselves in rectitude and portraying their projects as consistent with God's will. Governments everywhere establish limits and rules for the functioning of religious organizations, and everywhere governments seek some control over education, which was once the responsibility of religious authorities. Some states have sought to separate religion from politics, while others have proclaimed the need to unify the two, but no state has fully achieved either of those elusive objectives.

States in which Muslims constitute the majority of inhabitants do not differ in kind from other states, although they may differ in some degree by the way they structure the relationship between religion and politics. One study reports Muslim states involve themselves more deeply in religious affairs than governments where other religions predominate. It is difficult to determine whether this involvement results from the nature of the religion or from the circumstances of Muslim states, which tend to be poorer, newer and more recently subject to colonialism than the average. The same study shows that Muslim states show somewhat fewer signs of separation between religion and politics than the average (Fox 2008: 80).

Muslim states have developed many types and qualities of government. States such as Turkey and Indonesia have taken enormous strides toward becoming full-fledged liberal democracies. A number of states in the Middle East and North Africa persist as monarchies. Two or three states, including Iran, have sought specifically to define themselves as "Islamic." Pakistanis have long debated whether they inhabit an "Islamic" state or simply a state that is Muslim by virtue of its origins, its population and its volition. Many Muslim states are republics that espouse a will to become liberal and democratic, but fall well short of that ideal in the estimation of citizens and observers. Such authoritarian governments often invoke Islam to bolster legitimacy.

When Muslim states call upon religion, they do so in one of three basic ways. First, and most commonly, they seek to demonstrate that their laws reflect religious norms. For some states those norms apply most notably to family law—marriage, divorce and property rights. Separate religious courts handle these issues in some countries. Other countries insist that some version of Sharia, a concept of Islamic law derived from the Quran and the Sunna of the Prophet, constitutes the foundation for all or some of their legislation. Special bodies, such as the Council of Guardians in Iran, may be entrusted with reviewing legislation to ensure its conformity with their interpretation of Sharia. Governments generally support and control the training of religious scholars (ulama), who define the religious law and shape public debate. If a government permits, lay persons may enter that debate and even criticize the government for its "deviation" from religious norms. Governments relying heavily on religious law to legitimate their actions unintentionally invite opposition from groups based in a religious perspective.

Second, leadership that claims relationship to divinity can provide religious cover for government actions. Some governments invoke genealogy. For example, the Jordanian and the Moroccan monarchies trace family history to the clan of the Prophet. Jordan and Morocco are mainstream (Sunni or Sunnite) Muslim countries, where genealogy has normally mattered much less than in the minority (Shii or Shiite) version of the religion, which is attached to the memory of Ali, cousin and son-in-law of the Prophet. The Shia regard Ali and his descendants as "designated imams" entitled to rule over the community. The Ayatollah Khomeini, founder of the Islamic Republic, did not claim to be an imam in the line of Ali, but he did design a constitution in which the most distinguished jurist of his generation would serve as a substitute for the last designated imam, who is believed to have been in hiding since 874. In both Sunnism and Shiism there exist mystical strains that honor "holy men" who have special contact with God. Such holy men, called shaykhs (shuyukh, sheiks), pass their wisdom to disciples, who over the centuries have formed many powerful religious associations (brotherhoods) or orders. Political leadership in Nigeria, the Sudan, Senegal and elsewhere has often depended on such organizations, themselves products of genealogy.

The Saudi leadership defines itself more by its role in Islam than by its genealogy. As defender of the Holy Places, Mecca and Medina, where Islam emerged in the seventh century, the king assumes a role defined by geography. Similarly the Great Leader of modern Iran, elected by a committee of clerics, actually rules by virtue of his role rather than by genealogy, although the country invokes the exemplary leadership of Ali and his descendants much more frequently than Sunni countries evoke the memory of Muhammad as a political leader. Sunnis have never had a clear theory of leadership. While the word "khalifa" (caliph) suggests a unique office, it is not clear that the title was used for half a century after the Prophet's death, and then, when it did come into use, it seemed to differ little from ordinary kingship. Over the centuries the predominant form of both Sunni and Shii leadership has been hereditary monarchy.

The third way in which modern states and politicians seek to justify themselves in religious terms is to claim solidarity with the Muslim community. Most ideally, government represents the community of all believers. Early Islamic leaders took the title "commander of the faithful" or "commander of the believers." Fred Donner argues that the community of believers may have included Christians and Jews in the early years, before boundaries began to sharpen (Donner 2010). Under Umayyad rule (roughly 660 to 750) it was still possible to imagine Muslims as one single community, although the Khwarij (Kharijites) had already taken their distance. They abandoned the Caliph Ali in his battle with the governor of Damascus, because they thought Ali,

Figure 3.1 A common Arabic inscription on a wall in rural Morocco: *God, King, Country*. Found throughout the country, it symbolizes the links between rulership, people and God. Courtesy of Lauren Kenney.

the fourth successor to Muhammad as the leader of the Muslims, had already betrayed the community by agreeing to arbitrate the dispute. The followers of Ali gradually came to see themselves as a separate community, which became known as the Shia, and then the Shia splintered into still other communities. It became impossible to speak of a single Muslim community.

In the modern world a further splintering of the community has occurred along the lines of nation-states. Osama bin Laden may have imagined that he spoke for all Muslims, but most statesmen and politicians make much more modest claims. They see themselves and their organizations as representative of Moroccan, Malay, Pakistani or Indonesian Muslims, or some subset thereof. Their power lies in their ability to speak for a community, which is at least partially defined by religion. The Muslim Brotherhood, for example, defines itself by not simply religion but a set of political objectives. National leaders may see themselves as speaking for all citizens or for all Muslim citizens, but other politicians and organizations may challenge their claims. The great Tunisian historian of the fourteenth century, Ibn Khaldun, saw "group feeling" as the key to political power and stability; he thought bedouins naturally possessed a group feeling that permitted them to seize power and establish dynasties in North Africa (Ibn Khaldun 1967). In the era of modern nation-states, where boundaries seldom follow any "natural" lines—ethnic or religious—group feeling must be constructed. Religion is often one of the foundations.

Each of these political uses of religion gives rise to controversy and conflict in the modern era. Muslim statesmen use one or all of these tools to shore up power and legitimacy but they also struggle to explain why their use is proper and why their opponents who call upon the same tools to challenge regimes misuse them. It is one thing to say, as the Saudis do, that the Sharia is the only source of legislation in that country. But it is increasingly clear that not even the Wahhabi religious scholars (ulama), long partners of the Saud family in the governance of that country, fully agree on what the Sharia is and what it means for the modern age. (The Wahhabis trace their doctrine to an eighteenth-century theologian, Muhammad ibn Abd al-Wahhab.) The most serious opposition to Saudi rule has come from ulama persuaded that the monarchy has permitted erosion of legal and moral principles. The Wahhabi interpretation of the Sharia may be less severe than that imposed on Afghanistan by the Taliban, using amputation and executions to slow the spread of universal education and socializing between the sexes, but the Wahhabi interpretation differs markedly from what Turks or Indonesians understand when they use the word "Sharia."

Appeal to religious law

The Saudi ulama, with the backing of the monarchy, seek to prevent open consideration of the most fundamental issue: what is the Sharia? How did that concept take shape in Islamic history? Is it a concept that remains flexible? Who has a right to interpret and reinterpret its meaning in the twenty-first century context? These are pressing questions almost everywhere in the Muslim world. Sharia is now a contested term. Not even the Egyptian government, which has never shared Saudi views of the Sharia, has been willing to countenance free discussion of this issue. Professor Nasir Abu Zayd, who explored such issues at the University of Cairo, found himself accused of apostasy and forcibly divorced from his Muslim wife in an Egyptian court. Those Muslim intellectuals who have pressed hardest for *ijtihad*—adaptation of the Sharia to modern circumstances through a process of interpretation—have often been forced into exile or have chosen to develop their ideas in Europe or America. Fazlur Rahman left Pakistan for the United States. Mohammed Arkoun made his career in France, partly because his native Algeria remained unsympathetic to his ideas. Abu Zayd left Egypt to teach in the Netherlands. Tariq Ramadan, whose grandfather founded the Muslim Brotherhood in Egypt, flourishes as an Islamic liberal in Europe.

Mustafa Kemal Atatürk, the founder of the modern Turkish state, "solved" the Sharia problem in the 1920s by abolishing it together with the system of religious courts that sustained it. Of course, abolishing a religious concept such as Sharia—which is not a stone tablet one can smash, a single manuscript one can burn—does not erase the concept from memory or negate its influence. Survey research shows that modern Turks think they know what the Sharia is, and many say they believe in its implementation, but few associate the Sharia with curbs on political or individual liberties (Toprak 2005: 170). On the contrary, many Turks have supported the current government in insisting that civil liberty means that one should be free to practice religion as one wishes, even if that means a woman covering her head in a public place. Nearly a century after Atatürk "abolished" the Sharia, debate about it is still as sharp in Turkey as elsewhere.

Why have so few Muslim states been willing to permit full-scale discussion of Islamic law? Why do so many regimes impose strict curbs on academic freedom? One answer is that many Muslim governments are relatively young and weak. Most emerged from some version of imperial domination, where religion served as an important element of nationalist identity in the struggle for independence. Newly independent regimes struggled to establish national unity in countries that were anything but united in religion or ethnicity; they sought to control any source of challenge, whether from the universities or the religious establishment. Rulers looked to religious officials (ulama) to articulate an understanding of Islam as a fixed, unchanging truth. These officials acquired a stake in the truth they articulated and propagated. Rulers helped enforce the Truth, and the ulama, often on the public payroll, supported rulers in return. Despite the Arab Spring, authoritarianism remains the norm in the Muslim world, and authoritarian regimes generally prefer certainty and permanence over doubt, critique and change. Even rulers with apparently secular inclinations often tend to accept the traditional thinking of the ulama.

A second reason Muslim states tend to embrace the concept of an unchanging Sharia, whether harsh and narrow or broad and more tolerant, is that they have done so to defend themselves against the challenge of Islamist groups. The first such group, the Muslim Brotherhood in Egypt, emerged in 1928 under the leadership of Hasan al-Banna, who lacked formal theological training. Banna's objective was to put Islam back in the center of Egyptian life and culture, reinforcing its sense of national identity and bolstering its resistance to British colonial rule. Setting a pattern for most Islamist organizations that have followed in its path, the Brotherhood advocated rigorous implementation of the Sharia. By definition, Islamist organizations invoke Islam for political purposes. Their claim depends heavily on the idea that "Islam is the answer." An Islamic state would be one that implements the Sharia, and Islamists start from a conviction that the Sharia is knowable, known and fixed. Even the authoritarian governments of the Muslim world have found themselves seeking to accommodate the Islamists, which means affirming commitment to the Sharia as a concept, even though that concept is ill-defined.

Islamist pressure has caused some Muslim governments to pull back on fundamental liberties and rights that once seem guaranteed. In Iran, Islamists took power after the revolution of 1979 and set out to restrict practices they deemed immoral. They imposed restrictions on women's dress and activities and on some religious minorities (especially Bahais). The Taliban takeover in Afghanistan, after the Soviet invasion and subsequent withdrawal from that country, represented drastic change as well. More subtle changes have occurred in some countries where Islamist movements have asserted their strength.

Religious leadership

Leadership that depends upon a whiff of the divine may be less important than the Sharia in legitimating Muslim nation-states but such leadership has nonetheless been important in some countries. In the nineteenth century, Sudan arose against its British and Egyptian rulers on the shoulders of a man who claimed to be the mahdi, a prophetic figure who created an autonomous Islamic state. The British and the French took him down, but his successor and a rival from the Khatmiya Sufi order continued to dominate Sudanese politics for half a century. Iran is the only place where a distinguished member of the ulama, the Ayatollah Khomeini, has engineered a revolution and seized the reins of government. Although he never claimed to be the Hidden Imam in the Shiite tradition, Khomeini nonetheless permitted himself to be called "Imam Khomeini," and parlayed his religious pre-eminence into leadership of his country for a full decade after the revolution. Khomeini's religious credentials and personal charisma generated veneration and sanctity for the regime. The founder of modern Saudi Arabia, Abd al-Aziz ibn Abd al-Rahman Al-Saud, was also called imam, although that term has a different connotation in a Sunni country than it does in Shii Iran. The long time leader of Northern Nigeria, Ahmadu Bello, held a religious title as the Sardauna of Sokoto.

Figure 3.2 Ayatollah Khomeini. Courtesy of iStockphoto.

Formal religious titles and credentials may matter less than a perceived spirituality. The late King of Morocco, Hassan II, acquired a reputation for saintliness, baraka, as a result of his multiple escapes from assassination. The king, who typically presided over Friday prayers, called himself "commander of the faithful," as did some of the earliest successors to the Prophet, but he accrued additional religious prestige as he dodged bullets and miraculously escaped attempted *coups d'état*. Mere survival attested to his baraka. Anwar al-Sadat of Egypt sought to portray himself as a good Muslim, the "believer President," one who spoke in a mosque almost every Friday. Breaking with the policies of his predecessor, Gamal abd al-Nasir, who had banned the Brotherhood and executed its radical ideologue, Sayyid Qutb, Sadat liberated the leaders of the Muslim Brotherhood at the beginning of his presidency. Yet abd al-Nasir died a normal death and enjoyed a reputation as a good Muslim, while Sadat was assassinated by a group that regarded him as a traitor to Islam, for his lifestyle and his actions.

Religious community: Ulama, Sufis, Islamists

Formal leadership roles and personal piety do not suffice to legitimate rule in modern Muslim countries. Commitment to follow the Sharia may not be sufficient, either, unless a government can impose its understanding of Sharia and manage an interpretation that incorporates the necessary adaptation to contemporary circumstances. Every Muslim government needs the support of the community to establish a reputation for piety and to implement laws consistent with Muslim values. Winning and holding that support has become vital for every government, authoritarian or democratic. In most Muslim polities the religious scholars, the ulama, have been key intermediaries between governing authorities and local populations. In some areas, organizations led by mystics (Sufi orders) have also been pillars of effective governance by virtue of their hierarchical character and their broad, popular support. Almost everywhere a third form of religious organization has emerged in the modern era to challenge both ulama and Sufis and assert a new, voluntary, politicized form of religious community. Such organizations have sometimes been labeled "fundamentalist," or are lumped together in a category called "political Islam." They are most frequently called "Islamist" organizations. The Muslim Brotherhood, created in Egypt in 1928, remains the model.

Ulama

The architects of Islamic law working in the ninth and tenth centuries put great emphasis on the consensus of the community as a route to establishing the right path. One of the early lawyers, al-Shafii (d. 820), cited a *hadith* in which Muhammad is quoted as saying: "My community will never agree upon error." It seems unlikely that al-Shafii thought that all Muslims would agree on a certain interpretation. Most likely he took the effective "community" to be the scholars responsible for interpreting the written texts of Islam and deriving a legal system from them. The struggle between rulers and scholars in the Abbasid period (750–1250) ended in a victory for the ulama, who insisted upon fashioning a law based on hadith texts and established interpretations. The caliph Mamun, who ruled from 813 to 833 in Baghdad, capital of the Abbasid Empire, favored more flexible legal interpretation that would have facilitated fresh legislation and enhanced the power of the caliph. The ulama depended upon the ruler for law enforcement, but the ruler could not legislate without the approval of the scholars, whose consensus defined the path of virtue.

Modern governments have been more successful than Mamun in commanding the support of the ulama. From the medieval period the power and autonomy of the ulama depended not just on their prestige and expertise but also on their financial independence. Believers gave wealth, usually in the form of land, for the support of the religious establishment. With the income from these lands (s. *waqf*, pl. *awqaf*), which were protected from taxation, and with the support of ordinary believers, ulama were able to sustain a set of elementary and secondary schools, a network of mosques and, of course, themselves and their families. In many parts of the Muslim world, government fell into the hands of military elites, many of them foreign to the countries they were ruling, often quite disconnected from local populations. The ulama, usually of local origin and education, were the vital link with the community at large. When Napoleon Bonaparte and his French army invaded Egypt in 1798, a very thin stratum of Ottoman officials fled the country; a Mamluk military elite, itself of Turkish origin, failed to defend the country against the intruders, and Napoleon found himself treating with members of the local ulama in hopes of gaining the cooperation, if not the friendship, of the local community.

Modern governments have reduced the power of the ulama by confiscating *waqf* lands and putting them under state administration, turning ulama into employees of the state, establishing state supervision of mosques, and transferring the responsibility for education (even religious education) from the ulama to the state. The process started sooner in some countries than in others. It proceeded more quickly and more completely in some states, more slowly and more partially in others, but some version of that process has affected every Muslim-dominated nation-state. Domination of the community of believers has meant, first and foremost, curbing and directing the community of scholars that has long been the driving force of Islam. Conquest by outside powers tended to accelerate the process.

In Sunni Islam, there is no hierarchy of ulama. While certain mosques and universities such as al-Azhar in Cairo enjoy international reputations and draw scholars from around the world, Egyptian ulama do not necessarily command the obedience of colleagues elsewhere. The lack of international hierarchy facilitates government takeover of religious institutions at the national level in predominantly Sunni contexts. In contrast, in Shii Islam, and especially the Twelver Shii (Imami) community of Iraq and Iran, there exists a hierarchy of clerics that governments have sought without much success to subvert. (Twelvers believe that Ali was the first of twelve designated imams, the twelfth of whom has been hidden since the ninth century.) The ulama maintained some autonomy and independent power in Iran throughout the twentieth century, an autonomy and power that enabled some of them under the leadership of the Ayatollah Khomeini to mount a revolution against the Shah in 1978–79. By their support, the Iranian public validated the ulama as representatives of the community and accepted Khomeini's idea of establishing an Islamic state.

Sufis

In both the Sunni and the Shii communities, governments had difficulty dealing with another form of religious community, the Sufi brotherhoods. Drawing upon ancient mystical traditions of India and Persia, Sufis represented on the one hand a response to the legalism of mainstream Islam and on the other hand an appeal to a kind of spirituality that preceded and surpassed Islam itself. The great Sufis established a tradition of self-denial and inner virtue that focused not upon this world but on the love, beauty and compassion of a world beyond. Sufi poetry, dance and music seems far removed from politics, but great Sufi masters generated followers, and followers constituted organizations that continue to command the loyalties of hundreds, thousands or even millions of believers. Some of these organizations, often referred to as brotherhoods, came to have an influence on modern politics. Some mystics commanded only small, local followings and came to be honored as saints after their death. Others achieved such prominence that their names became attached to a spiritual path (*tariq*) they had pursued. Hence, the proliferation of brotherhoods such as the Naqshbandiya, the Tijaniya and the Rahmaniya.

Mustafa Kemal Atatürk abolished all such brotherhoods after taking power in the new Turkey, which emerged at the collapse of the Ottoman Empire in 1918. He turned their meeting places into museums, and at the same time he made ulama employees of the state, took control of all mosques and put education under state supervision. In theory, the state dominated all aspects of religion, but the Sufi organizations, dependent on personal loyalties of disciple to master, simply went underground. A Sufi disciple learns from his shaykh and then goes on to train another circle of disciples. These personal loyalties survived and the brotherhoods reappeared in Turkey once the government eased up on legal restrictions in the 1950s.

Mainstream Islam resisted Sufism in the beginning but then came to acknowledge its role. Sufis carried Islam into the far reaches of central Asia, into India, and into many parts of Africa. Although Sufis turned out to be the most successful missionaries of Islam, reform movements such as Wahhabism, prevalent in Saudi Arabia, accuse Sufism of hedonism, polytheism, violation of the legal tradition and more. Independent governments of North Africa have supported reform movements against local saint cultures and Sufi brotherhoods, partly because French colonial authorities managed to woo support from populist forms of Islam against the more threatening versions they associated with the ulama. Because the French often favored the Sufis, independent governments were determined to oppose or even eradicate them. Reformist Islamist movements tended to be hostile to the Sufi orders as well. But violent Islamist attacks on governments in places such as Algeria tipped the balance again and caused these governments, now charged with being insufficiently religious, to cultivate the support of folk Islam and, closely related, the Sufi brotherhoods (Scheele 2007). In some countries Sufis have not been a factor in politics, but politicians in countries such as Senegal and Nigeria cannot afford to ignore the power of the Sufi brotherhoods.

Islamists

A century ago a government might have thought it commanded the Muslim community if it controlled the ulama and maintained the support and favor of the leading brotherhoods. But the Islamist organizations that emerged in the twentieth century do not fit neatly into either of these categories. Hasan al-Banna called his creation, the Muslim Brotherhood, "a Salafiyya [reformist] message, a Sunni way, a Sufi truth, a political organization, an athletic group, a cultural-educational union, an economy [sic] company and a social idea" (Mitchell 1993: 14). He resembled a Sufi shaykh in his style, but the organization drew civil servants and teachers to an enterprise that was dedicated to self-improvement and community enhancement. He invoked Islam in the name of Egyptian authenticity and nationalism. Without immediately challenging the political realm, Banna nonetheless drew a following that provoked government suspicion and hostility. Similar organizations emerged in Turkey and Pakistan.

These organizations proposed a new definition of religious community. The relevant community was no longer the ulama or the members of a Sufi brotherhood, nor was it the community of all believers. Rather, the community was those who voluntarily joined a modern association to achieve common purposes in the name of Islam. The Islamist groups were participatory organizations appealing to mass constituencies on the basis of action not belief. Even though they arose in countries that were by no means democratic, these organizations recognized that the basis of politics was shifting. Educated, informed, energetic individuals could affect political outcomes by thinking, writing, propagandizing, agitating, organizing and fighting. Those who joined were "true Muslims," Muslims willing to act out their beliefs.

These Islamist organizations have challenged the claim of governments to represent the Muslim community. Some have offered violent challenge. Others dare the government to let them compete in fair elections. Still others labor primarily in the social and economic realm, building up support and finances as well as influence for the future. Often these organizations provide education, medical services and charitable activities that governments themselves aim to supply but often fail to do so adequately. Islamist associations and organizations may thus effectively assist governments in their efforts to satisfy public needs and demands, even though their success and strength may also be interpreted as government weakness. Muslim governments thus find themselves with a difficult decision about how to treat these organizations.

The decision is easiest when Islamism takes its most radical, violent form. Car bombings, suicide attacks, assaults on tourists or police officers—violent efforts to debilitate or discredit a government have generally drawn a forceful government response. Egypt, Saudi Arabia, Algeria, Syria, Indonesia, Tajikistan, Morocco and Tunisia all have unleashed fierce repression in response to Islamist violence. The Algerian struggle marked the entire decade of the 1990s but finally ended in government victory. In unleashing the military and police forces against Islamists, governments must take care to show that they are not waging a war on Islam or against ordinary, law-abiding Muslims. Often governments have made certain concessions to non-violent Islamist demands—tighter enforcement of dress codes, greater authority for religious courts, modification of family law—in an effort to undercut popular support for Islamic radicalism. They have chosen to Islamize society in an effort to undercut the agenda of Islamist radicals.

Governments face more difficult decisions about whether Islamist organizations should be permitted to function freely outside of the political sphere and, especially, whether they should be accorded the right to form political parties and participate in a democratic process. The two questions are not entirely separate. Some academic specialists have argued that Islamist organizations can contribute to the creation of a civil society. By organizing Quran study groups they contribute to female literacy. By coordinating volunteers they draw people into active roles in the service of the community. Through sponsorship of publications and media outlets they contribute not just to the knowledge of Islam but also to awareness of the outside world, developments in science, and a sense of national as well as Muslim identity. None of these activities can be conducted, however, without a government's permission or at least its benign neglect. Governments reluctant to democratize may also be reluctant to permit the development of a civil society. While a strong civil society may be a prerequisite for democracy, there was little evidence from the Muslim world that civic organizations, whether Islamist or not, could outfox a determined, authoritarian government and force it into democratization, at least until the events of the Arab Spring of 2011 (Bayat 2007).

The attitude of the Egyptian government toward the Muslim Brotherhood illustrates the sort of ambivalence toward Islamist organizations that many governments feel. Gamal abd al-Nasir outlawed the Brotherhood and put its leaders in prison on the charge that the Brotherhood had tried to assassinate him. When Anwar al-Sadat became president in 1970, he liberated the leadership and inaugurated a policy of tolerating the Brotherhood without legalizing it, on condition it separate itself from any terrorist activities. The government harassed the organization without banning it until 2011, when it acquired legality for the first time since the 1950s. The government actually subsidized some institutions and programs managed by the Brotherhood, but until the uprising of 2011 it also prohibited the organization from becoming a political party and competing directly in elections. Nonetheless, by running individuals on the lists of other parties, the Brotherhood managed to elect members of the People's Assembly. Under Sadat and his successor Hosni Mubarak, the regime dominated the People's Assembly through the National Democratic Party, which always won elections with a crushing majority. Thus the government both cultivated the Muslim Brotherhood and blocked its path to power. Was the Brotherhood a part of the system or the primary opponent of Egyptian authoritarianism? Would the victory of the Brotherhood in free and fair elections solidify the democratization of the country or merely open the way to a new form of authoritarianism? Does the Egyptian military, dominant in Egyptian politics ever since 1952, regard the Islamists as a threat or an ally against the dispersed and less organized voices demanding reform of Egyptian government?

In two countries, Turkey and Indonesia, Islamist organizations have moved directly into the political realm and contributed to democratization. For years the followers of Mustafa Kemal Ataturk, known as Kemalists, succeeded in denying Islamists the right to form and maintain political parties. The constitution prevented political parties from appealing to religious interests. On that ground, the courts outlawed one Islamist party after another until finally an Islamist politician and former mayor of Istanbul, Recep Tayyip Erdoğan, managed to form a party that pulled the Islamist constituency into a broadly based conservative coalition and won a majority in the Turkish Parliament in 2002. After 30 years of effort the Islamist movement won a share of power and brought a certain rural, religious, more traditional Turkey into broad support for Turkish democracy that had been lacking in the years dominated by the Kemalists and other secular parties. Turkish democracy acquired increased legitimacy, and the Erdoğan government demonstrated an unprecedented degree of strength and stability.

Something similar happened in Indonesia. On the one hand, President Sukarno (1945–1967) rejected the efforts of Islamist political parties to challenge secularizing policies, but to everyone's great surprise his successor, President Suharto (1967–1998), permitted and even encouraged Muslim cultural revival. These actions have opened the way for Islamists to support the system and even participate in government. Islamists now seek representation and influence via a number of political parties; the government has embraced commitment to Islam as a religion without relinquishing the principles of Pancasila, a broad, tolerant Indonesian ideology first formulated by Sukarno. Liberalization has advanced hand in hand with Islamization.

In other countries leaders have continued to insist that Islamists who claim to be democrats cannot be trusted. If they were to win elections, they would change the rules and implement an undemocratic form of Islamic rule, such as that of Iran or of Sudan. In Algeria, a sudden decision to democratize taken by President Chadli Bendjedid led to rapid growth of an Islamist party, the Front Islamique du Salut (FIS). Victorious in the first round of legislative elections, the FIS threatened to sweep the second round and win control of Parliament. Instead, the military stepped in, set aside President Bendjedid and launched a campaign of repression that turned into civil war in the 1990s. Islamists blamed the army for the violence that enveloped the country, and the military, eventually successful in restoring order, blamed Islamist militants for the catastrophe. The Algerian example caused the neighboring states of Morocco and Tunisia to be severe in repressing every sign of Islamist militancy. The leader of the Islamist movement in Tunisia, Rachid al-Ghannouchi, professed strong commitments to democracy but the regime banned his movement and forced him into exile. The Tunisian leader, Ben Ali, built mosques and printed fancy copies of the Quran but kept Islamists in jail. Mosques closed after prayer to prevent use for political meetings. Demonstrations that began with a simple act of self-immolation in the rural South caused Ben Ali to flee the country in early 2011. The subsequent return of al-Ghannouchi and his party's success in free elections created both fear of Islamist takeover and hope that there, as in Turkey and Indonesia, Islamist participation in the political process would help solidify a fledgling democracy.

The dilemma then for the governments of predominately Muslim states is that they almost all feel the need to represent the community of believers. This has never been easy, as shown by the defections from the third caliph Uthman and the civil war (656–661) that began when his successor, Ali, sought to maintain his hold on the caliphate despite opposition from Muawiyya of the Umayyad family. The community of believers has been fractured ever since, and the creation of nation-states in the nineteenth and twentieth centuries accentuated the problem. With only a few exceptions, mere loyalty to a dynastic family was no longer a sufficient adhesive. Implementation of the law itself depended on national actions, and national actions presumed the effectiveness of a national community. To enhance feelings of community, these nation-states turned to Islam but found themselves facing a challenge in plurality: ulama, Sufi brotherhoods, local holy men and Islamist associations claimed to speak for the Muslim community within national boundaries and even beyond. The Muslim community was not one but several, and the more governments sought to respond to its multiple demands and needs, the more they often alienated religious minorities. Nationalism without Islam appeared weak and inauthentic; nationalism tightly bound to Islam veered toward intolerant exclusivism.

Variation in national response

Muslim states have responded differently to the challenge of governance. From full application of a rigidly defined Sharia to vague invocation of Islamic law as an inspiration for positive legislation, from traditional identification of rulers with religious power and insight to modern notions of leadership based in popular choice, and from state insistence on a single official version of Islam to acknowledgment and accommodation of pluralism—the range of response is enormous. Muslim states could scarcely be more different in the way they use Islam. Three sets of factors partially explain this variation. First is the early history of Islam in the country, the conditions it encountered, the nature and pace of conversion. Second is the impact, if any, of imperialism and colonialism. Third is the timing of independence.

It is easier to describe the resulting variety of states than to create a theory that would incorporate these three factors. For example, suppose we assume only two values for the first factor, whether (1) an area underwent direct conquest by the Arabs or (2) whether Islam arrived via merchants and missionaries. Suppose we assume three values on the second factor: (1) no imperial involvement; (2) indirect involvement; and (3) direct foreign control in the nineteenth and twentieth centuries. Suppose we arbitrarily permit three categories on the third factor, measured by when contemporary borders were established: (1) pre World War I; (2) between the wars; (3) post World War II. Those somewhat simplistic decisions produce eighteen (2 x 3 x 3) categories, which may help explain diversity but do not provide much guidance in figuring out why Islam is more politicized in some states than others, or why certain states elect more repressive policies than others, or why some Muslim states have embarked on serious efforts to democratize while others have not. Categories do not necessarily produce theory.

Saudi Arabia necessarily ends up in a category by itself. The presence on its territory of the holy cities of Mecca and Medina and its role in the birth of Islam make religion an integral part of its identity. The identification of the Saud family with the Wahhabi movement since the eighteenth century sets it apart as well. The Wahhabis propounded an eccentric, anti-Sufi, exclusivist version of Islam that became the norm in Arabia, thanks to the power of the Saud family, which managed to escape direct European domination. Less exposed to Western pressures and ideas than most surrounding countries, and ultimately endowed with extravagant wealth, the Saudis managed to maintain antiquated versions of religion and government without much challenge until the 1970s. For the moment they seem to have succeeded in repressing opposition from both liberal and radical Islamists.

The most populous Muslim state in the world, Indonesia, is far removed from the birthplace of the religion. Arab traders and Sufi missionaries brought the religion to that part of the world, where indigenous populations were of very different ethnic and cultural backgrounds. Islamic practices absorbed local customs; pluralism characterized Indonesian Islam from the beginning, in great contrast with Saudi Arabia. While scholars maintained contact with the Middle East, climate, geography and Dutch colonial domination imparted a spin to Indonesian politics that sets it apart from Saudi Arabia. Both the history of Islam in the country and the impact of colonialism are crucial in accounting for Indonesian Islam.

The Muslim republics of Central Asia, once a part of the Soviet Union, further illustrate the diversity of Muslim states. There the imperial power sought to suppress Islam (and all religion) in the name of Marxist theory. Religious revival in that region acquired an anti-imperial twist. Independence came only after the collapse of the Soviet Union. The early Arab conquests reached only some of these states, including Turkmenistan, Uzbekistan and Tajikistan, and it is in these states that Islam plays a more important role in contemporary politics than in Kazakhstan or Kyrgyzstan. The dominance of Persian-speakers in Tajikistan sets it apart from the other republics, which are dominated by Turkish speakers, as are Azerbaijan and Turkey itself. These states constitute an important subset of Muslim states but they are perhaps less similar than different.

The distinctiveness of Turkey among these states stems from its role as the core region of the Ottoman Empire (1300–1918) and as a country that recreated itself as a nation-state in the aftermath of World War I. It fought off European domination, escaped Soviet rule, and defined itself against Islam and the Ottomans, only to find itself now, in the early years of the twenty-first century, acknowledging its debt to the Muslim tradition. Its membership in NATO, its determination to join Europe, its will to liberalize and democratize even while it accommodates Islamist demands—these factors and others make it impossible to lump Turkey with its Arab neighbors, with its Turkish-speaking cousins in the Caucasus region and Central Asia, or with the former Ottoman territories of Europe and North Africa. In short, Turkey is a case apart.

Many in the West have generalized about the Muslim world on the basis of what they have seen of (or read about) Iran, but Iran does not equate with any other Muslim country. Conquered early by the Arabs, it underwent conversion to Islam over a period of centuries but never sacrificed Persian for Arabic as the common language of the country. While Persian speakers became essential as intellectuals, scientists, and bureaucrats in the Abbasid caliphate (850–1250), which was centered in Baghdad, a minority version of Islam, Shiism, became the state ideology in Iran with the accession of the Safavid family to the Persian throne in 1500. While Twelver Shia also constitute a majority in Iraq, Iran is the only Muslim country consistently governed by Shia in the modern period. It underwent heavy imperial influence but largely escaped direct occupation. Yet negative reaction to foreign interference helps explain the revolution of 1979 that put Iran in a category by itself. The current constitution of the Islamic Republic of Iran does not resemble the constitution of any other Muslim state, past or present. The formal structure of its government combines European notions of constitutionalism and democracy with institutions designed to ensure that all government policies will conform to Islamic law.

These examples suggest a pattern. Every country dominated by Muslims is unique. Each faces the challenges of governance described in this chapter but confronts those challenges with different cultural baggage, different resources and different ideas. Egypt is unique by virtue of its existence as an entity since ancient times. It bears the imprint of the Pharaohs, early Christianity, Arabism, Islam and European imperialism. Algeria is unique by virtue of a revolution against French rule, which had sought to turn Islam to its own purposes. Senegal is unique in the importance played by Sufi brotherhoods in the politics of the country. Malaysia is unique because the state has used Islamic revival as a means of advancing the economic and political interests of the Malays against other ethnic interests, primarily Chinese. No two states are alike.

Because the states differ so significantly in their geography and their history, it is natural that they employ Islam to different degrees and for different political purposes. They identify with Islam in a variety of ways, ranging from the universal to the particular. They draw on Islam as a source of ideological and legal inspiration to different extents. They create and regulate institutions such as courts, schools, mosques and religious associations to fit their cultures and needs, and they attempt to respond to and reshape the local political cultures, which necessarily reflect Islamic belief and practice.

Conclusion

Muslim governance differs significantly by virtue of history and geography and also by virtue of choices made by individual nation-states. It is impossible to attribute these differences to a single phenomenon called Islam. If Islam directly accounted for the way Muslim peoples are governed, there could scarcely be so much variation over space and time. Muslim nation-states find Islam more or less useful in a variety of ways: to strengthen national identity, to reinforce the legitimacy of policy choices, and to maintain or modify political attitudes. They choose to employ religion in different ways, writing it into the constitution, appointing and controlling its official agents, controlling how it is taught, deciding how and to what extent it affects the legal system. Opposition forces find Islam useful, too; they respond to government policies, and governments must shape policies in response to opposition pressures. Some governments seek to repress Islamist oppositions, and others placate Islamists without caving in to them. Islamists have won full power in a few states, at least temporarily—Afghanistan, Sudan, Pakistan and Iran are the principal examples.

At the death of the Prophet in 632, traditional accounts suggest Muslims were confused about how the community should be governed. No one could claim to be another Prophet. The decisions taken by a small band of followers and disciples proved decisive in the short run, and then came civil war and the establishment of one kingdom, the Umayyad, and then another governed by the Abbasid dynasty. Each of these changes produced new arrangements in Muslim governance. Today it is nation-states that establish those arrangements. They are the principal loci of political power in the Muslim world, and, as has always been the case, it is political power that decides how religion will or will not be employed in the process of governance. Politics shapes religion more decisively than religion shapes politics.

Summary

- All governments rely on religion in some fashion; governments in Muslim-majority countries may differ from others in the ways they invoke religion.
- Governments of Muslim-majority countries must take account of religious law; they often rely on leadership claiming religious credentials; and they often rely on mainstream religious leadership and/or Sufi brotherhoods for support.
- Islamist organizations have arisen to challenge the notion that either the official hierarchy (ulama) or the Sufi brotherhoods adequately represent the Muslim community. They have sought to further politicize Islam.
- There is no single pattern of governance in Muslim-majority states. Nation-states have encountered Islam at different times and in different ways. They have been subject to different forms and degrees of colonial and imperial influence, and they have acceded to independence at very different moments.
- Islam as a set of beliefs related to the Quran cannot account for the diverse ways in which Muslim countries are governed.
- Patterns of governance reflect national histories more than they reflect texts or political theory.

Discussion points

- To what extent are Muslim-majority states distinct from other countries in the way in which they use religion for political purposes?
- Why does the Sharia figure so centrally in the debates about what constitutes an Islamic state?
- How should governments deal with Islamist organizations, such as the Muslim Brotherhood, who claim to be the "true Muslims" and who want an "Islamic state?"
- Why is it that a number of Muslim countries, led by Turkey and Indonesia, have moved toward democratic practice, while others resist democratization and its implications for Islam?
- Europeans and Americans have tended to see Islam as an obstacle to democratic governance. Does the argument of this chapter support or oppose that tendency?

Further reading

Eickelman, Dale and James Piscatori (1996) *Muslim Politics,* Princeton: Princeton University Press.

The authors help one understand how Islam has become entangled in the language of politics in a broad spectrum of countries. No one authority effectively speaks for Islam in any single country, much less in the Muslim world as a whole.

Lee, Robert D. (2009) *Religion and Politics in the Middle East,* Boulder, CO: Westview Press.

The study compares the relationship between religion and politics in a Jewish state with the relationship in three Muslim states: Turkey, Iran and Egypt. The differences between Jewish and Muslim states may not be greater than the differences among the three Muslim states.

Norris, Pippa and Ronald Inglehart (2004) *Sacred and Secular: Religion and Politics Worldwide,* Cambridge: Cambridge University Press.

Based on survey research done in a number of Muslim and non-Muslim countries, the book demonstrates broad support for democratic political objectives but sharp divisions over rights of women and gays. The authors argue that the trend is toward secularization, despite apparent worldwide revival of religious influence.

Hefner, Robert W. (2000) *Civil Islam: Muslims and Democratization in Indonesia,* Princeton: Princeton University Press.

Hefner describes the impact of Islamist groups on politics in Indonesia and the transition toward democratic politics in a national atmosphere very different from that of the Middle East and North Africa.

White, Jenny (2002) *Islamist Mobilization in Turkey: A Study in Vernacular Politics,* Seattle: University of Washington Press.

A highly readable and thoughtful account of Islamist political success in a suburb of Istanbul, this book helps explain the subsequent success of the Erdoğan government at the national level. Together the White and Hefner volumes demonstrate a central theme of this chapter: that one must be cautious in generalizing about governance in the Muslim world.

Mottahedeh, Roy (2001) *The Mantle of the Prophet: Religion and Politics in Iran,* New York: I.B. Tauris.

Mottahedeh's book is an accessible and insightful study of religious education and the clerical class in revolutionary Iran. It has become a classic.

References

Bayat, Asef (2007) *Making Islam Democratic: Social Movements and the Post-Islamist Turn,* Stanford, CA: Stanford University Press.

Donner, Fred M. (2010) *Muhammad and the Believers: At the Origins of Islam,* Cambridge, MA: Harvard University Press.

Fox, Jonathan (2008) *A World Survey of Religion and the State*, Cambridge: Cambridge University Press.

Haghayeghi, Mehrdad (1995) *Islam and Politics in Central Asia,* New York: St. Martin's Press.

Ibn Khaldun (1967) *The Muqaddimah*, trans. Franz Rosenthal, Princeton, NJ: Princeton University Press.

Mitchell, Richard P. (1993) *The Society of Muslim Brothers,* New York: Oxford University Press.

Scheele, Judith (2007) "Recycling Baraka: Knowledge, Politics, and Religion in Contemporary Algeria," *Comparative Studies in Society and History*, 49(2): 304–28.

Toprak, Binnaz (2005) "Islam and Democracy in Turkey," *Turkish Studies*, 6(2): 167–86.

From Isfahan to the internet: Islamic theology in the global village

Anthony R. Byrd and
Richard C. Martin

Foundations of modern Islamic theology

Theology is a branch of knowledge and discursive practice derived from two Greek terms, *theos* and *logos*. In combination they literally mean "speaking/reasoning about God," and more broadly refer to discourse on problems in religious understanding. It names an intellectual religious discipline that Christianity, Judaism, and Islam (the Abrahamic religions) pursued in separate but parallel traditions that have occasionally interacted with each other since Late Antiquity. Theology has both an inward and outward direction. Inwardly it serves to construct and defend a particular interpretation or understanding of religion shared by a group or movement within a religious tradition. Outwardly it functions to defend particular teachings against critics of the tradition. Much of what has just been said about early Islamic theology applied also to Jewish, and particularly Christian, theology within their respective communities. The purpose of this chapter is to describe the central problems of Islamic theology and to consider the work of some of the theologians who have debated these issues over the past two centuries and the schools of thought they represented. In order to do so, it is necessary to consider the beginnings of theological debate and speculation during the early centuries of Islam.

That Muslim theologians have been among the liveliest public intellectuals throughout Islamic history is demonstrated in this ninth-century passage from a work by the extremely witty literary critic and polymath, Abu 'Uthman 'Amr ibn Bahr al-Basri, known as al-Jahiz, "the bug-eyed." Commenting on how theologians, by the very nature of what they do, attract far more controversy than other religious scholars, such as jurists, Quran scholars, *hadith* compilers, and the like, Jahiz says:

> There is another field which is unknown to the common people and throws the mob into confusion. Yet whenever a question arises in this field, they jump into the discussion oblivious of their own incompetence and of the true nature of their disability... . If a scholar stands up in the main street or the market place and discusses grammar and poetry, or discourses on the law, astronomy, mathematics, medicine, geometry or the crafts, only specialists will gather round and dispute with him. But let him say so much as a word about predestination, or mention the knowledge and will, or human capacity to create one's own acts, or consider whether or not God created unbelief, and there will be no fool of a porter, no down-and-out wretch, no tongue-tied idiot, or ignorant blockhead who will not stop and contribute his own two cents.
>
> *(adapted from Pellat 1969: 79)*

Who were the theologians that Jahiz and others tussled with?

The classical Islamic term for theology is *kalam*, which literally means "talking," but has the technical meaning of dialectical reasoning and debate about such central problems as the nature of God, prophecy, religious duties, social morality, and establishing a just society. Surviving *kalam* texts from early and medieval Islam generally took the following form; a proposition or thesis was stated, often in the form of a question, such as: What is the fate of believers who disobey the commands of God as stated in the Quran, the divine revelation? Is such a one still a Muslim? Must he or she be punished here and now by the community (known as the *umma*), or only by God in the Final Judgment? These were pressing questions for the first generations of Muslims as they sought to conceptualize a *Muslim* identity among the much larger non-Muslim populations of Syria, Iraq, and Iran over which Muslim armies and rulers rapidly established rule.

Kalam propositions were clarified and positions or doctrines were crafted through a dialectical process of statements and objections, by critics or presumed critics, which then were answered, citing the Quran, the remembered sayings or *hadith* of the Prophet Muhammad, the teachings of a noted teacher in the past, and logical argument. Theological reasoning and the study to become proficient in it was called *'ilm al-kalam*, the science or study of *kalam*. The process of such reasoning bears the imprint of actual dialectical argumentation that took place in lectures and in debates between contending scholars. Biographies of Muslim scholars from the early period indicate that many intellectuals studied dialectical theology, along with Islamic law, the Quran and its interpretation, the prophetic *hadith*, and Arabic grammar and lexicography—even if they did not go on to become master teachers of *kalam*. In modern times, the printing press, universities, the internet, and blogging are among the new ways in which Muslims participate in theological discussion and debate.

One of the earliest Muslim theological writings to survive is a defense of free will in the practice of religion. The text describes an exchange that took place around the year 700 CE between the ruler, Caliph 'Abd al-Malik, and the pious theologian and mystic, Hasan al-Basri. The caliph had written to the popular theologian requesting an explanation of the latter's claim that human acts are not predestined by God but rather products of human free will. Hasan al-Basri was reputed to be teaching that human behavior must be based on human free will; otherwise, how could humans be held accountable for their actions on the Day of Judgment? What was at stake in the caliph's question was whether the Umayyad caliphs, who had ruled from Damascus, Syria, for the past 40 years, and of whom 'Abd al-Malik was one of the most powerful and influential, did so by divine determination or by human choice and power to act on one's choice. If the latter, as Hasan al-Basri's reply seemed to indicate, then caliphs, like all humans, would be responsible on the Day of Judgment for abuses of office and violations of Islamic teachings and codes of ethics and piety. This would not have been an answer that 'Abd al-Malik would have wanted to hear. The Caliph preferred to believe that his office and official conduct, some of which was controversial and unpopular, was necessary and foreordained by God.

This story from eighth-century Islam illustrates several problems that are also addressed by contemporary Muslim theologians. One is the principle of *speaking truth to power*; that is, bringing religious and ethical values to bear on the behavior and deeds of all humans, even presidents and other leaders of Islamic states. Like Hasan al-Basri, Muslim intellectuals today apply theological criticism to the major problems of the day, such as what kinds of government can and should Muslims live under? When are war and violent coercion justified? How are Muslims to understand permissible gender relations and sexual identity in the world of the twenty-first century? How should believers relate to non-Muslims when Muslims are in the majority (as in Saudi Arabia) and when they are in the minority (as in America)? Surprisingly perhaps, these kinds of issues are not as modern as they might seem. Muslim intellectuals have generally tackled these problems by consulting the Quran and *sunna* (example) of the Prophet, and the arguments advanced by Muslim theologians and philosophers in pre-modern Islam. Nonetheless, globalization, the internet, cable television, and the dislocations caused by colonialism in the twentieth century and international warfare in Muslim lands in the twenty-first century have radically changed the context in which theological inquiry and criticism are framed and pursued. In this chapter we will consider some of the major problems facing Muslim theologians today and some of the chief practitioners of modern Islamic theology in a variety of national and regional contexts.

In pre-modern Islam, jurisprudence (*fiqh*) exercised considerable influence on Islamic societies under the caliphate and the sultanates that ruled from Spain to Central and South Asia. It was the *muftis* who specialized in one of the several schools of law, who interpreted the practical and legal consequences of Islamic law for the private sector of society (divorces, inheritance, questions of proper acts of worship, etc.), while the *qadis* appointed by sultans, amirs and other heads of state settled conflicts and problems on behalf of the state or public sector, working within the framework of the foundational source of the *shari'a*. Theological problems such as those mentioned above generated contending schools of thought, such as the Mu'tazila and Ash'ariyya, but in pre-modern times theology did not serve the public and state interests that Islamic law did. The modern context has changed the framing of much of modern Muslim theological discourse.

The circle of students who studied with Hasan al-Basri (his name refers to the southern Iraqi city of Basra) some 70 years after the death of the Prophet Muhammad were a major source for the pursuit of theological reasoning in the coming generations. Those who studied and practiced '*ilm al-kalam* were known as *mutakallimun*, dialectical theologians. The students of *kalam* in Hasan al-Basri's time began to diverge and develop contending interpretations of some fundamental understandings of what being Muslim required in one's relation to God (*Allah*), to other Muslims, and to non-Muslims. The development of Islamic jurisprudence (*fiqh*) in the same period from such foundational sources as the Quran and the *hadith*, as well as established regional custom, was regarded by rulers and ruled alike as essential to establishing and maintaining a just and stable Muslim society. The theologians, most of whom also studied jurisprudence, pushed deeper into the intellectual foundations of Islam to determine the nature of the authority of the Quran and the Prophet's exemplary teachings, his *sunna*. They asked such questions as: How do we know that the Quran is what it claims to be? What warrants belief that the Prophet Muhammad really was a prophet with authority equal to and indeed surpassing and finalizing that of earlier prophets? How do we conceive of God—does He possess the same attributes as humans, such as speaking and seeing like human beings? Under what kind of government and which kind of religious authority should Muslims live, if indeed they have a choice?

By the beginning of the ninth century, the two major schools of theology mentioned above were forming in Iraqi cities such as Basra and Baghdad and further east in Iran and Central Asia. They represented two very different ways of intellectualizing and interpreting Islamic religious doctrine. One took its name from the fact that disputes within the circle of Hasan al-Basri caused some students 'to withdraw' (*i'tizal*) to form a separate school, the Mu'tazilites. By the tenth century, the Mu'tazilites had many grand teachers (*shaykhs*) in Iraq, Iran, and elsewhere. They were generally known to base human understanding of the meaning of the Quran and the Prophet's teachings on human reason and intellect. In ethics they refined Hasan al-Basri's position that humans respond to God's commands with free will, which makes a certain sense of divine reward and punishment on Judgment Day. Most of them also argued that although the Quran was the authoritative Word of God, it was separate from the eternal God and thus was created in human space and time.

The latter issue about the created Quran drew a strong reaction from other theologians who shared with the larger Muslim population a much more pious sense of the Quran as the eternal Word of God, uncreated, and having no creaturely imperfection. Indeed, this newer but increasingly more popular school of theology also placed reason and the intellect in the service of understanding revelation, but subservient to its claims; hence, the advocates of this trend denied that reason could be the judge of revelation. Their understanding of God's absolute transcendental power led them to advance a theory of predestination. Abu al-Hasan al-Ash'ari (d. 936), who was a prize student of one of the leading Mu'tazilite shaykhs in the early tenth century, eventually challenged many of the Mu'tazilite teachings in favor of those just described. In the ensuing generations, large numbers of theologians adopted and further developed al-Ash'ari's critique of Mu'tazilism and his more conservative construction of Islamic doctrine. Since the eleventh century, the Ash'arite school has predominated among Sunni Muslims, who account for the vast majority of Muslims living today, while Mu'tazilite theology has been preserved primarily among some Shiite theologians and more progressive Sunni intellectuals.

By the end of the eleventh century, the great theologian and jurist, Abu Hamid al-Ghazali (d. 1111) represented a trend away from theology by dialectical disputation of discrete points of doctrine to more Aristotelian forms of logical argument. The rise of the *madrasa* form of advanced learning in the religious sciences placed Islamic law and jurisprudence at the center of higher education in the late medieval and early modern periods. As a result, by the nineteenth century, Islamic theology more broadly was loosened from the tight school traditions of the Ash'arites and Mu'tazilites to find a voice, or voices, in the Islamic responses to European colonialism, modernity, and secularism. In the modern context, some Muslim intellectuals have discovered in the problems the Mu'tazilites and Ash'arites debated (as opposed to their methods of disputing) some relevance for Islamic theological analyses of contemporary issues facing Muslims today.

Nineteenth-century theology: Afghani and 'Abduh

The emergence of modern theologies in the Islamic world in the nineteenth century was structured by events in the eighteenth century that were marked by interactions with the West and the experience of imperialism and subsequent colonial rule. Thus a persistent theme in modern Islamic theology has been a tapestry of responses, including adaptation, rejection, and reform, to Western ideas and influence, and in particular the problems of politics and state power. Ideas evolved in the context of Western imperial economic and military power, administered within the framework of colonial rule of Muslim lands in North Africa, the Middle East, South and Southeast Asia. In the eighteenth century, Islam itself became in some Muslim intellectual circles a basis for the assertion of an authentically indigenous identity. This was in opposition to a more modernist attempt to adapt Islamic teachings to the changing social and political conditions of Islamic lands. However, it must be kept in mind that the political and theological reform and revival movements that emerged in the eighteenth and nineteenth centuries were not entirely a product of interaction with the modernizing West; authentic Islamic movements seeking reform through intra-Islamic criticism were already emerging in the Muslim world in the eighteenth century and helped to shape the character of modern Islamic theologies. A prime example is the puritanical Wahhabi reform movement, which in recent decades has been associated with anti-Western theological teachings. It arose, however, as an indigenous movement in the Arabian Peninsula, at first quite removed from interactions with the West.

In the nineteenth century, the most important contributions to Islamic theology emerged from the reform efforts of Jamal al-Din al-Afghani (1839–97) and his most important student, Muhammad 'Abduh (1849–1905). The relationship between the Western powers and the Muslim world changed from one of adaptation and cooperation in the eighteenth century to one of dominance and subjugation in the nineteenth. As Muslim intellectuals began to react to European dominance, many thinkers advanced a more pronounced reliance on Islamic principles as a defense against Western influence. Theology was, and continues to be, central to this task. Afghani was a leading figure in the intellectual defense of Islam. He traveled and taught in Iran and Egypt, but also in Europe, and he advocated a program of Islamic reform and Muslim solidarity while also vigorously asserting the theoretical compatibility of Islam with modern science and reason. While his work was not strictly theological in nature but aimed rather at political reform, his Egyptian student Muhammad 'Abduh, trained in the traditional Islamic sciences at al-Azhar University in Cairo, emerged as the fountainhead of Islamic theology in Arab lands in the modern period. His theological reflections were developed during a period of overt political activism, influenced by Afghani, which drew Egyptian intellectuals and workers into a movement of national opposition to the European powers. In Egypt this opposition took the form of the Urabi Rebellion (1879–82). 'Abduh's efforts to generate public support for the Urabi movement led to his exile in Lebanon. However, by 1882 'Abduh seemed to have accepted the reality of the British military-economic occupation and was able to return to Cairo. In 1899 he was appointed Grand Mufti of Egypt, the head of the religious court system. In this latter part of his career, 'Abduh focused his efforts on the integration of Islamic and modern ideas and the implementation of his revivalist agenda through a succession of public offices.

'Abduh's thought was bounded by his context: he was an intellectual and religious reformer in late nineteenth-century British-controlled Egypt and his theology was structured by his responses to the intellectual and practical problems of his day. However, he was also working within a tradition of thought informed by the early history of Islamic theology and the theological puzzles of the Ash'arites and Mu'tazilites. A case in point is the doctrine of 'destiny and fate' (al-qada wa al-qadar), a topic of furious theological debate in the classical period that touched on such issues as the freedom of the will, God's foreknowledge of events, and the role of reason. This set of topics re-emerges in modern Islamic theology in a new register and with a new salience. European detractors of Islam in 'Abduh's time and since have used the Islamic doctrine of predestination implied by "destiny and fate" to argue for a pervasive fatalism that explains the "backwardness" of Muslim societies in economics, military power, and morals. In 'Abduh's time, this perceived fatalism and backwardness was used to justify colonial rule. 'Abduh published an essay on the topic in 1884 in a journal he founded that subsequently became widely read by Muslim intellectuals. The essay helps to clarify both the nexus of his political and theological agenda as well as the connections between classical and modern Islamic theology. Much of 'Abduh's essay is taken up with demonstrating the falsity of Islam's detractors; he argues that it is the very doctrine of destiny and fate that accounts for the historical success of Muslims, whose rule spread from the Pyrenees that separate Spain and France to the Great Wall of China, despite their small numbers and lack of familiarity with different climes or variations in geography. They brought kings under their sway and brought low the Caesars and the Khusrows [of Persia] in a period of less than 80 years. Surely this must be counted among the greatest of all paranormal events and miracles!

('Abduh and al-Afghani 1980 [1884])

It is perhaps worth pointing out that the perception of an irrational Muslim fatalism as a cause of asymmetrical political and military power between the West and the Muslim world is as current today as it was when 'Abduh felt called to refute it in the 1880s.

Connected to 'Abduh's defense of the doctrine of destiny and fate is a defense of Ash'arite theology on the topic of predestination and moral responsibility, conceived as the "acquisition" (*kasb*) from God of acts by the human agent. He argues that the doctrine of "destiny and fate" implies an element of choice called "acquisition," and that this element of choice is responsible for reward or punishment in the afterlife and is the basis of juridical responsibility and political action in this life. 'Abduh's thought as it appears in his major theological work, *The Theology of Unity*, makes his filiations with the classical theological tradition clear. In a manner of expression deeply reminiscent of classical *kalam* discourse, 'Abduh says of God that "none of his deeds proceed from Him of necessity as He essentially is" ('Abduh 2004 [1897]: 57), confirming God's absolute omnipotence. In the same passage, he also inveighs that "one school of opinion even went so far in putting God under necessity that the student might suspect from their claims that they were reckoning Him under obligation and liability." This is a clear rejection of the Mu'tazilite doctrine concerning God's moral obligation to perform only good acts. Persistent misunderstandings over 'Abduh's Mu'tazilite sympathies can, however, also be drawn from the text; he does give a high place to reason, particularly in the determining of moral value. The elements of both Ash'arite and Mu'tazilite theology in 'Abduh's thought can be understood as having led to a divergence of conservative and liberal Muslim theology in the twentieth century, both of whom trace their respective genealogies to 'Abduh's ideas.

In his scholarly theological work and public career, 'Abduh sought to conceptualize how Islam could provide a basis for modern society and to provide a reinterpretation of Islam with reference to what he saw as its essentials, but in light of modern circumstance. 'Abduh saw his role thus:

First, to liberate thought from the shackles of *taqlid* [tradition], and understand religion as it was understood by the elders of the community before dissension appeared; to return, in the acquisition of religious knowledge, to its first sources, and to weigh them in the scales of human reason, which God has created in order to prevent excess or adulteration in religion, so that God's wisdom may be fulfilled and the order of the human world preserved; and to prove that, seen in this light, religion must be accounted a friend to science, pushing man to investigate the secrets of existence, summoning him to respect established truths, and to depend on them in his moral life and conduct.

(Hourani 1983: 170–71)

In the above mission statement we can see several of the themes that were to have a profound and lasting influence on the shape of Islamic theologies in the modern period. 'Abduh's rejection of *taqlid*, which he understood as blind adherence to tradition, sought to dislodge the weight of centuries of religious authority in the fields of law and theology that had accumulated throughout the medieval and early modern periods. This impulse was linked to the revival of *ijtihad*, or independent reasoning in law and theology, and it opened a path to the reinterpretation of the *sunna* in light of modern conditions. 'Abduh's call to return to the original sources of Islamic authority and the paradigmatic example of the early Muslim community, the *salaf*, reflect his understanding of the ideal society. This society, for 'Abduh, was one that willingly submits to God's commands and interprets them rationally in light of a concern for the general welfare (*maslaha*) of society. The society that actively obeys God's commands is the virtuous society, but it is also the prosperous and secure society, for the actions that are pleasing to God are also those that ensure stability and progress. For 'Abduh, this society had already existed in the "golden age" of Islam, and it is to this paradigmatic time, in which Islam was free and secure in its essentials and, importantly, unbounded by the subsequent tradition, that society must return in spirit.

Muhammad 'Abduh was the leading Muslim intellectual of his day and his influence in subsequent generations extended far beyond the boundaries of Egypt or even the traditional Muslim world. His influence can be seen to some degree in all the twentieth-century theologies discussed below. As such, his legacy is a complex one. His desire to return to the original sources and reliance on the symbol of the *salaf* is later picked up and expanded by more "fundamentalist" or Islamist impulses in the tradition. The vindication of reason as a source of moral and religious knowledge is a theme picked up most forcefully by more liberal reformers who argue in Islamic terms on behalf of political liberalism and religious pluralism. The call for independent judgment and the abandonment of blind adherence to past authority (*taqlid*) is a trend that has been adopted by most (if not all) modern theologies in the Islamic tradition. Beyond the Arabic-speaking Middle East, Muslim intellectuals elsewhere, especially South Asia, were grappling with some of the same issues that concerned Muhammad 'Abduh and his interlocutors.

"Islam is the answer": Islamist theologies in the twentieth century

'Abduh's most prolific disciple, Muhammad Rashid Rida (1865–1935), became the leading figure in the years following 'Abduh's death of a movement that pursued some of 'Abduh's ideas in an increasingly Islamist direction. Rida was a Syrian who came to Cairo to study with 'Abduh and began publishing the journal *The Beacon* (*al-Manar*) in 1898. *Al-Manar* went on to become a leading source of reformist Muslim ideas and its influence, and that of 'Abduh and Rida, was felt from the Straits of Gibraltar to the South China Sea. However, while 'Abduh seemed to envision the *salaf* as extending from Muhammad through the classical period, Rida imagined the *salaf* strictly as the generation of Muhammad and his companions. Rida vigorously advocated framing modern Islam on the basis of this original community's pure and essential Islam: hence the name of his school, the Salafiyya.

The Salafiyya under Rida's leadership gradually moved to a more radical rejection of the emerging Islamic Westernizers and secularists, and following the First World War, Rida gave increasing support to the arch-conservative Wahhabi revival in the Arabian peninsula and interpreted Sunnism in the mode of the strictest Sunni school of law, the Hanbaliyya. Seeing the influence of Western ideas and nationalism in particular as a threat to Islamic identity and Muslim solidarity, Rida and the Salafiyya advocated a return to the pan-Islamism of the caliphate, the only condition under which the full application of Islamic law in society was, in their view, possible. Rida wedded a strict adherence to the *salaf* with a rejection of more mystical elements of the Islamic tradition, a profound respect for the Arabic language, and an activism (the original sense of *jihad*) that he saw as uniting the essence of Islam with modern civilization. The emphasis on activism was to have particular salience in the thought of later Islamist or fundamentalist theologies.

In areas directly affected by the increasing influence of European imperialism, Islamist theologies developed further, but now in the context of concrete organizations rather than in small intellectual circles gathered around a leading thinker. The legitimacy and appeal of these movements was predicated on both the failure of secularizing and modernist movements to resolve the problems of Muslim societies and on the persistent influence of Islam in social life. Two movements were dominant in this development in the Arabic-speaking Middle East, the Wahhabi movement in Arabia and the Muslim Brotherhood in Egypt: only the latter of which will be dealt with in any detail here.

The Muslim Brotherhood was established by Hasan al-Banna (1906–49), a former schoolteacher who came to fear the erosion of Islamic values in the challenge of modernization and secularism and who felt the strength of Islamic society could only be restored by a return to its sources, the Quran and *sunna*. The Muslim Brotherhood was both a revivalist movement with its origin in the ideas of Afghani, 'Abduh, and Rida, but also a concrete response to political conditions in Egypt and the wider Arab East in the post-World War I period, including the failure of efforts at social reform by liberal nationalists and the oppression of Palestine. The acme of intellectual production during the mid-twentieth century for the Brotherhood was the theology advanced by Sayyid Qutb (1906–66) in a number of works, the most widely read of which is his *Ma'alim fi al-Tariq* (*Signs along the Road*, or simply *Milestones*), published in 1964, only two years before his execution by the Egyptian government.

Qutb's theology is at heart a political theology that centers on the theological role of *shari'a*. Qutb saw all societies as *jahaliyya* societies, ignorant and morally debased by Western ideologies (nationalism, liberalism, socialism) and a lack of authentic Islamic belief and practice. The oppression and moral malaise of modern societies rests in their failure to submit to God's authority. In the place of these false ideologies, Qutb offers Islam as the answer. Like Rida, Qutb envisioned the *salaf* as the ideal Islamic community. Qutb argues that it was not until the early religious community under Muhammad became a political community in Medina that the *shari'a* could begin to dictate religious and social mores. Thus, Qutb draws the conclusion that one can only "organize [oneself] according to the Divine Law (*al-shari'a*)" when one's "practical life" has taken a "permanent form," which means, for Qutb, an "autonomous state" that can stand behind "enforcement" of the *shari'a* (Qutb n.d.: 34). Like other modern "fundamentalist" theologies, Qutb collapses religious and political identity; there is no Muslim religious community without a Muslim political community. And the penultimate characteristic of the Muslim religio-political community is the institution of the *shari'a*: "The basis of the message is that one should accept the *shari'a* without any question and reject all other laws in any shape or form. This is Islam. There is no other meaning of Islam" (Qutb n.d.: 36).

Qutb argues that Islam, which now specifically means acceptance of the *shari'a*, intends to abolish injustice and promote freedom from servitude to others, understood as submission to any man-made law. This is an extremely activist stance more in line with the revivalism of Rashid Rida than with Afghani and 'Abduh, particularly as it is embedded in his discussion of jihad, the divine command to remake the world with the goal of ensuring justice. The only reliable method for ensuring justice is to rely exclusively on the *shari'a*, which Qutb conceived as the embodiment of the divine will, coextensive with the Quran itself. The only reliable source of moral reasoning is revelation. This position is not unique in Islamicate civilization: it is the standard position of the dominant Ash'arite theological school of Sunni Islam. Qutb's conflation of the *shari'a* with the modern concept of state law was more broadly modern, a product of the postcolonial engagement of Muslim societies with the vestiges of colonial legal systems. His theological conflation of the *shari'a* and Quran was a product of his own more radical thought.

The crux of Qutb's theology of the *shari'a* is the claim that obedience to the *shari'a* is more fundamental than even belief in God—submission to the *shari'a* is Islam itself.

> This obedience to the shari'a of God is necessary for the sake of this harmony, even more necessary than the establishment of the Islamic belief, as no individual or group of individuals can be truly Muslim until they wholly submit to God alone in the manner taught by the Messenger of God ... thus testifying *by their actions* that there is no deity except God and that Muhammad is God's Messenger.
>
> *(Qutb n.d.: 89)*

Islamic belief is only meaningful in the context of obedience to the *shari'a*, and the *shahada* (the testimony that "there is no God but Allah" and "Muhammad is His Messenger") only has content insofar as it is illustrated in the act of obedience to the *shari'a*. The *shari'a* is logically prior to belief and implementing the *shari'a* is temporally prior to creating believing Muslims, that is, one learns what it means to be a believing Muslim by obeying the *shari'a*. Qutb's theology is pushing back against an Enlightenment epistemology that would make religious belief but one choice among many and so expresses the need for a vanguard that can accumulate political power and enforce the *shari'a*. Islam in Qutb's theology is less religion in the usual sense and more analogous to culture or civilization: in fact, Qutb posits only two types of civilization, *jahaliyya* (sub-Islamic ignorance) and Islam, and only the latter is real civilization in any meaningful sense; *jahaliyya* civilization denies the sovereignty of God and appeals to man's animalistic nature. The center of Qutb's theology rests on the *shari'a* as the locus of a political community and religious authority. Therefore, any system of government that is not based explicitly on the *shari'a*, as defined by Qutb, is not only not binding on a Muslim citizen, but requires political action to challenge it.

Shi'a theologies of revival and reform

A brand of Islamist reform, similar in style to that of Qutb but grounded in the particularities of the cultural, political, and religious situation of twentieth-century Iran, produced perhaps the most well-known image of Islam in the American popular imagination in the later decades of the twentieth century, that of the bearded and glowering figure of Ayatollah Ruhollah Khomeini (1902–89). The formation of the Islamic Republic of Iran in 1979 brought to power a militant but traditional Iranian fundamentalism, the chief representative of which was Khomeini, the supreme leader of the new republic.

Khomeini's brand of theology is comparable to the traditional ideological program of Islamist or fundamentalist programs of reform that had been emerging in various

Muslim communities up to this point in the twentieth century, and included opposition to vice (gambling, alcohol), implementation of Islamic law by the state, Quran inspired punishments for crime, and opposition to modernization of the role of women in society. Khomeini's political theology was intolerant of religious minorities and political opposition and argued that the *fuqaha* (jurists) had been vested with authority from God to establish a government in accord with Islamic principles, narrowly conceived as they were by the clerics, many of whom themselves were becoming increasingly narrow-minded and authoritarian.

The most prominent thinker to have directly opposed the fundamentalism and intolerance of the Islamic Republic under the ulama's rule has been the Iranian philosopher and theologian Abdolkarim Soroush. Soroush was originally a strong supporter of the 1979 revolution, but has since developed a rigorous critique of its brand of Islam and state power. Soroush received a traditional Islamic theological education in Iran as well as university training in the hard sciences before completing his education in London, first in chemistry and then the philosophy of science. His work has increasingly turned to issues in the philosophy of religion and ethics, and he is one of the world's leading authorities on the medieval Muslim poets Rumi and Hafez. Soroush's critique of the Iranian regime and his call for progressive reform in the Islamic tradition on such issues as human rights, the role of reason, and democracy is grounded in a set of theological and philosophical positions, many of which are discussed at length in his collection of essays *Reason, Freedom, and Democracy in Islam* (2000). Soroush recognizes the efforts of religious revivalists of the distant past (al-Ghazali [d. 1111], Rumi [d. 1273]), and more recent nineteenth- and twentieth-century thinkers ('Abduh, Rida, and Muhammad Iqbal in South Asia), and sees himself as a contributor to this tradition of religious reform. However, he also understands that the failure of these religious reformers lay in their lack of an adequate epistemological theory to support and structure their respective theologies. Influenced by his training in the philosophy of science and the sociology of knowledge, Soroush grounds his epistemology and the hope of genuine reform in a distinction between religion and religious knowledge. Religion is eternal, transcendent, and beyond complete human apprehension, while religious knowledge is a variety of human knowledge and thus incomplete, insufficient, and culture-bound.

> That which remains constant is religion [*din*]; that which undergoes change is religious knowledge and insight [*marifa-e dini*]. Religion has not faltered in articulating its objectives and its explanations of good and evil; the defect is in the human being's understanding of religion's intents. Religion is in no need of reconstruction and completion. Religious knowledge and insight that is human and incomplete, however, is in constant need of reconstruction. Religion is free from cultures and unblemished by the artifacts of human minds, but religious

knowledge is, without a shadow of a doubt, subject to such influences. Revivalists are not lawgivers [*sharian*] but exegetes [*sharihan*].

(*Soroush 2000: 31*)

Elsewhere Soroush develops this theory in terms of the essentials and accidentals of religion, the latter being those elements—culture, language, historical time, geographic location—in which a religion begins or is practiced, and a further distinction between personal knowledge of religion and religious knowledge. The former is one's own comprehension of religion that, however pure or beautiful or fulfilling, is not religion itself. Nor is subjective experience religious knowledge, which Soroush sees as "a branch of human knowledge that has a collective and dynamic identity and that remains viable through the constant exchange, competition, and cooperation of scholars." Religious knowledge relies on error as much as truth in a constant and dynamic process of negotiation with culture. Religious knowledge "changes, evolves, contracts, expands, waxes, and wanes. It is temporal and in constant commerce with other realms of human culture" (Soroush 2000: 34). Religious knowledge, the accidentals that build up and seek to describe religion itself, is analogous to other branches of human knowledge such as science or political theory and so is contested and cumulative, subject to expansion and contraction based on historical circumstance and so, like science, amenable to vigorous debate, correction, and progress.

This epistemological modesty is the background for Soroush's robust defense of democracy, rationality, and religious tolerance. He is critical of the lack of sufficient rational premises in contemporary Muslim theological and legal discourse and of the role reason is given in religious discourse generally:

> The role of rationality in the arena of religion has, thus far, been that of a timid and discreet servant of understanding and defense of religion. However, defense and affirmation cannot be complete without critique and analysis. The enterprise of rationality is an all-or-nothing project. One may not employ reason to attest to the truth of one's opinions, without leaving the door open to its fault-finding critique. The attempt to enjoy the sweet affirmation of reason without tasting its bitter reproach is pure self-delusion.
>
> (*Soroush 2000: 154*)

Rationality extends beyond the defense and critique of religious knowledge by generating debates and standards in other fields of human knowledge by which religious knowledge can appropriately be judged. For Soroush, issues such as justice and human rights are an extra-religious discourse belonging to philosophy in general; traditional religious teachings on matters of collective importance, such as the equality of women and freedom of religion, must be held to a rational standard of objective truth, dialogically determined, and the rectitude of acts demonstrated rationally and philosophically. One may detect in Soroush's approach an openness to a rationalistic style of theological discourse pioneered by the Mu'tazila in the early centuries of Islam. Indeed, in many of his more recent writings he has invoked the rationalist example of the Mu'tazila.

Islamic theology and Muslim minorities

It is estimated that today roughly one-fifth, some 317 million, of all Muslims worldwide live as minorities in non-Muslim states (Pew 2009), and this has generated very real and interesting theological puzzles for minority Muslim populations in the West and elsewhere regarding Islamic identity, Islamic modes of dress, commerce, family life, political participation, and citizenship in liberal societies. Traditional Islamic jurisprudence raises questions about the permissibility of Muslims living under non-Muslim rule, engaging in practices of social cooperation that form bonds of allegiance and solidarity with non-Muslims, and aiding in the well-being of non-Muslim polities. Islamic theologies have begun to emerge that seek to reconcile Muslim minority status with the dictates of revelation and the methods of reimagining the body of Islamic tradition on these issues. Tariq Ramadan is perhaps the most well-known theologian in the West to deal extensively with these issues. Ramadan lives and writes in Europe, primarily in French and English, but also in Arabic. By family background and training in the Islamic religious sciences at the famed al-Azhar University in Cairo, Ramadan came of age intellectually in the conservative Ash'arite theological interpretation of Islam. However, in working out what this meant for Muslims living in the West and for Europeans and Americans seeking to understand Islam, Ramadan, like Soroush, seems to have introduced elements of Mu'tazilite theological and ethical reasoning.

Born in Switzerland in 1962, Ramadan is a scion of the founders of the Muslim Brotherhood in Egypt. His grandfather was Hasan al-Banna, the founder of the Brotherhood, and his father was exiled from Egypt by President Gamal Abdel Nasser; Nasser had repressed the Muslim Brothers for their theological criticism of the Nasser government. Ramadan's work as both an academic and public intellectual has been informed by his experience as both a Muslim and a European, and he writes principally for an audience of Western Muslims (primarily second- and third-generation university-educated youths) and other Muslims who read Western languages in an effort to encourage the development of an authentic European Islam. The thrust of Ramadan's work has been to encourage European Muslims to re-approach the Quran and *sunna* in light of their European context, establishing a European Muslim identity that is based on the essential sources rather than a simple and unreflective opposition to the West (Ramadan 1999, 2004, 2009).

Figure 4.1 Tariq Ramadan. Courtesy of AFP/Getty Images.

The challenge posed to Muslims requires them to become reacquainted with not only the authoritative sources of Quran and *sunna*, but also with the history and use of the Islamic sciences, such as law, theology, and Sufism, which provide methodologies for applying Revelation to the contemporary situation of Muslims living in the West:

> For Muslims living in Europe, it is of the greatest importance not only to know what these sciences actually are – and how they are interconnected – but, more deeply, to be able to re-read the Islamic Message with its original life force and acquire a global vision of the fields, studies and means at their disposal so that they can face their current situation.
>
> *(Ramadan 1999: 42)*

In this sense, Ramadan's project is traditionalist as well as rationalist; he is seeking to balance the uniqueness of the Quranic Revelation with the importance and utility of using reason to interpret the sources and apply their ethical imperatives to lived moral experience. His theological work attempts to separate jurisprudence (*usul al-fiqh*) from the interpretations of a more strident form of traditionalism that understands the Islamic theological and juridical frame as fixed and immutable.

Ramadan sees the Islamic sciences not as a set of transcendent and binding rulings (as did Qutb), but rather as a dynamic method of allowing the Islamic message to engage with the contemporary context.

The theme of an Islamic frame of reference in a dynamic relationship to reason is articulated more fully in Ramadan's 2004 work, *Western Muslims and the Future of Islam*. Here Ramadan continues the project of his previous works by more fully elaborating on what he sees as the universal values inherent in Revelation, their elucidation through the Islamic sciences in reference to contemporary realities, and their relevance to issues of identity and coexistence for European Muslims. Ramadan also begins to argue more forcefully for the role Western Muslims must play on the global stage for the resuscitation of the Islamic tradition. It is Western Muslims, because of their historical situation on the threshold of two traditions, two worlds, who have the freedom and responsibility to reimagine the tradition, playing out the distinction between the universality of the Islamic message and contemporary non-Muslim cultural contexts (Ramadan 2004).

Humankind is distinguished from the rest of creation in Ramadan's theology by intelligence and free will; this of course parallels the Mu'tazilite position on free will, defended in opposition to the traditionalist Hanbalite and Ash'arite predestinarians. Parallel to the freedom of the will is an original and natural faith that already and immediately has knowledge of *tawhid*, God's oneness.

> The human being is, essentially, responsible; awareness of *tawhid* invites humanity to set out on the quest along the divine path (*sabil Allah*), to control, in the midst of the fluctuations of life, the contradictions within its being, its weaknesses, and its deficiencies.
>
> *(Ramadan 2004: 14-15)*

Through human freedom and an innate religious knowledge, God calls all men to take responsibility for their moral performance. The determining factor in an act's moral assessment, given the situation in which is actually occurs, is the moral intention of the agent.

There is no opposition between faith—intrinsic to all human beings and required to access these private movements of the soul—and the intellect (*aql*), which provides a pre-existing framework for interpreting and implementing revelation.

> The quest for the Transcendent cannot be undertaken without the mind. There is absolutely no contradiction here between the realm of faith and the realm of reason. On the contrary, the spark of faith, born in the original testimony, needs intellect to confirm that testimony and to be capable of being faithful to the original covenant. The realm of faith necessarily calls on intellect, which, by accepting the

two types of Revelation [Quran and *hadith*], allows faith to be confirmed, deepened, and rooted and to grow to fullness in the heart and human consciousness.

(Ramadan 2004: 14–15)

Ramadan's emphasis on the intellect as a valid source of moral knowledge in the absence of scriptural proscription and his moral psychology that gives prime place to freedom, responsibility, emotion, and private revelation is best viewed in light of the history of Islamic ethical discourse—a tradition which is generally opposed by the type of strict traditionalism evidenced by the piety-minded *hadith* folk. Historically, the unifying link between the ethical rationalism of the medieval Mu'tazila and "soft rationalism" of Tariq Ramadan is their similarity in context. Both are primarily responding to a situation of religious and cultural diversity, and so both are attempting to address the questions of communal identity and coexistence in a complex and changing pluralist society. In both, these questions take place within the ethical sphere and show a concern for recognizing the universality of moral principle while simultaneously securing the uniqueness of the Muslim Revelation as a frame of reference for moral reasoning.

Feminist theologies: Islamist and liberal reformist

The role of women in Islamic societies has been a salient one in the modern period, and here too pre-modern theological discourse has been resurrected and reinterpreted for modern use. Islamic feminists have generally challenged traditional male-dominated discourses about women, such as the teachings of the Muslim Brotherhood and Sayyid Qutb, in one of two ways: by challenging either male dominant interpretations of the Quran or the *shari'a*, that is, through scriptural reinterpretation, or through interrogating the premises of traditional jurisprudence. Much of the theological debate among Muslim feminists has centered on reinterpreting the Quran and the sharia as sources for constructing positions and theories of the normative role of women in society. The general feminist move has been to challenge the preponderant male-oriented understanding and social ethos of the submissive role of women, and the debate has centered on traditional school interpretations as the sites where traditional male-oriented *epistemes* or ways of reasoning may be challenged. One strategy that has emerged recently among progressive and modernist Muslim feminists has been to appeal to the rationalist ethics of the Mu'tazila. Other Muslim feminist thinkers have sought to construct theological responses to modernity in keeping with the Islamist agendas of movements such as the Muslim Brotherhood and the more radical theology of Sayyid Qutb.

Are Islamist and more liberal feminist theologians able to reach across the theological divide and engage each other? Margot Badran is among those scholars writing on feminism in Islam who has concluded that the chance for productive conversation between Islamist feminists and other Islamic feminists is unlikely. In *Feminism in Islam: Secular and Religious Convergences* (2009), she follows others in distinguishing between Western and Islamic feminisms, which are less radical. She characterizes the latter as inherently religious, between Muslim *secular* feminisms on the one side, and *Islamist* feminisms on the other. In Badran's view, secular feminism in Islam developed over a century ago and is

> located within the context of a secular territorial nation-state composed of equal citizens, irrespective of religious affiliation and a state protective of religion while not organized officially around religion. ... Islamic feminism, by contrast, burst [recently] on the global scene as a new discourse or interpretation of Islam grounded in *ijtihad,* or independent investigation of the Qur'an and other religious texts.
>
> *(Badran 2009: 2–3)*

Badran's thesis is, as her title implies, that these two forms of Muslim feminism, secular and Islamic, are not "hermetically sealed" and are in occasional dialogue and often converge with each other. The third type of feminism in contemporary Islam, however, *absolutist* Islamic feminists (Badran calls them "Islamist feminists"), "promote political Islam and its patriarchal version of religion," and choose not to be in dialogue with the other two groups. In this section we will review some expressions of Muslim feminist theologies. We will begin with recently articulated Islamist feminist theologies embedded in several prominent social movements; a subsequent section will focus on more liberal feminist theologies and their filiations with other modernist strands of theology.

Saba Mahmood's ethnographic work on an urban woman's mosque movement in Cairo has challenged liberal notions of agency posited by feminist scholarship and has complicated how we conceive modern Islamic theology. Feminist theorists, she argues in *Politics of Piety* (2005), have not adequately responded to the increased participation of women from a variety of social classes in the Islamic revival, since their support would appear to contravene their interests. In the movement Mahmood describes, women gather together in the mosque (a space usually dominated by men) to study Islamic texts, traditions, and bodily practices aimed towards the cultivation of what Mahmood calls, reminiscent of the revival of Aristotelian virtue ethics, "the ideal virtuous self." The relationships between the women's mosque movement as a transnational phenomenon, feminism, and the Islamic theological tradition are not easy to categorize. For instance, the participants in Mahmood's ethnographic work (and many prominent Islamic women preachers elsewhere) reject the term "feminist" as an accurate characterization of who they are or what they do. Although they promote agendas that feminists would claim, such as women's education and place in the public arena, they also concentrate on cultivating values such as submission and obedience, which run contrary to the modernist impetus of the types of feminist thinking familiar in Europe, for example. Furthermore, many of the women in the mosque movement would not consider themselves (or be considered) *theologians* in the traditional sense of the word, however, they do engage in extensive theological reasoning and reflect the types of theological concerns characteristic of modern Islam. The movement they are supporting and shaping, they claim, is a response to the way in which Islam has been divorced from the routines and decisions of daily life, a process they call "Westernization" or "secularization." To remedy this relegation of Islam to a set of abstract concepts divorced from the everyday, the women in the mosque movement aim to cultivate and learn the bodily aptitudes, virtues, and desires that would reinstate Islam as the guiding force behind action, habit, and thought. In addition to a correct practice of the pillars of the faith, their concern is to restore pious living to all aspects of life, and as one participant put it, *tahqiq al-taqwa*, the realization of piety (Mahmood 2005: 50).

Al-Huda International, an organization with centers in Pakistan and Canada, provides Islamic education and social welfare programs for women and is considered part of the women's mosque movement. It has attracted the active participation of a large group of middle and upper class urban women in Pakistan, although it has successfully expanded to other sectors of society, and promotes what many would consider a very conservative practice of Islam. Among Muslim feminists it is controversial. Khanum Shaikh cites theologian Riffat Hassan's critique of Farhat Hashmi's (Al-Huda's founder) philosophy as an Islamic version of Laura Bush's "compassionate conservatism" and also notes that in the perception of others she is propagating "Wahhabi Islam," the puritanical and fundamentalist interpretation of Islam that arose in Arabia in the eighteenth century (Shaikh 2010: 178–79). Among the practices cited as extreme by Al-Huda's critics are the students' choices in modest dress (notably *hijab,* the *abaya*—Hashmi herself covers all of her face except her eyes), the rejection of music and "popular" Islam, and the abstention from certain rituals occurring in communal celebrations. In her book on the movement, *Transforming Faith* (2009), Sadaf Ahmed explores the motivations and practices of women who have been drawn to Al-Huda and engaged with Islam through its teachings. As Ahmed writes, "all of these practices go against the dominant cultural norms of the society these women are part of, and it is therefore not uncommon to hear them jeered as 'extremists,' 'fundos,' or 'ninjas'" (Ahmed 2009: 3). However, none of these controversial aspects is a goal in itself, and in fact, the students are not required to follow any of these precepts at home or during lessons, although many adapt at least some of these modes of dress. Those students who undergo significant transformations are encouraged and admired by teachers and peers, and become an example for others.

Al-Huda seeks through its pedagogy to develop character, self-confidence, and moral agency in its students grounded in knowledge of the Quran and *sunna* and its application in their roles as wives, sisters, and mothers. Lectures and tapes in Urdu and English cover topics such as Quranic translation and commentary, the authentic Islamic acceptability of certain festivals (Valentine's day, the birthday of the Prophet, etc.), the use of images and photos in Islam, music and Islam, and they also provide instruction on behavior and proper dress. Al-Huda's methods are intended to help students become pious individuals capable of negotiating Islamic principles in the specific circumstances of their everyday lives in a variety of ways. These methods also encourage students to become teachers and share what they have learned and how they have learned it. Al-Huda and cognate Islamist feminists stress a physical and performative goal of theology alongside its more traditional intellectual goal. Farhat Hashmi, like Mahmood's interlocutors, does not consider herself a feminist. The engagement of these women with the tradition and each other generates a form of moral agency and theological reasoning that challenges our understandings of Islamic feminism as opposing normative social roles.

Some Muslim scholars have sought to engage, or at least resist, the claims of Margot Badran referred to above that *Islamist* feminism is to be considered *the* Islamic feminism by exploring other medieval theological modes of contesting different understandings of Quran and *sunna*. We will consider these theologians under the category liberal-reformist. For some, the ninth-century Mu'tazili approach to framing and disputing differences can be read as an approach to theology that is at once rationalist in epistemology, liberal in ethics, and open to dialogue with other schools of thought within Islam as well as with non-Muslim traditions. Khaled Abou El Fadl has recently investigated the relevance of medieval theological debates to the question of Quran and *sunna* and the status of women, and he has done so with a sophisticated historical analysis that bears witness to the early Islamic disputations. He has concluded that Mu'tazili positions hold the most relevance for moderate Muslims like himself, although his reference to the Mu'tazila in the 1990s was guarded and often in footnotes, and it was not until after September 11, 2001 that he declared himself to be a follower of the Mu'tazili school, a position that has caused considerable blowback, especially from conservative Sunni Islamists.

Abou El Fadl's discussion of the Mu'tazila is important because his historical and ethical analysis of the early sects and schools of thought makes greater sense of the conflicts among different theological and ideological discourse communities today. In a passage that is strikingly consistent with the Mu'tazili linguistic theory of the Created Quran (*khalq al-quran*), he asserts that when God expresses himself in the Quran, the *kalam Allah*, he does so perfectly with respect to himself as divine speaker, but insofar as he does so in a human language with its creaturely imperfections, human knowledge of God is imperfect and not absolute (Abou El Fadl 2001: 128). He adds:

> I am not arguing that the [jurists'] search for the Divine Will should be abandoned; I am arguing the text does not embody the full Divine Will and does not embody

the full authorial intent either. The text embodies indicators to the Divine Will and to the authorial intent as well.

In addition to following indicators in the text, the interpreter applies her own reasoning powers and moral sensibilities, sometimes even when the resulting judgments seem to contradict the text. Here, Abou El Fadl is making the classic Mu'tazili argument from their debate with the Ash'ariyya, and the Hanbaliyya. The Mu'tazilites, in concert with Socrates in the Euthyphro, believed that God reveals divine commands and prohibitions that can be known *a priori* to be good. It follows, then, that moral reasoning is independent of the text but must be applied to the text. What happens when, as Abou El Fadl puts it:

> A person can read a text that seems to go against everything that he or she believes about God ... and [one] might even exclaim, "This cannot be from God, the God that I know!" What does one do in such a case? The appropriate response is to exercise what I have called a *conscientious-pause* ... I argue that as long as a person has exhausted all the possible avenues towards resolving the conflict, Islamic theology requires that a person abide by the dictates of his or her conscience.
>
> *(ibid: 93–94)*

Here Abou El Fadl is referring to the Muslim subject as free, based on divinely granted reasoning powers (*'aql*) to interrogate the text rationally. Between the text and the believing Muslim (*mu'min*) is the act or process of reasoning that is inherently theological. This is true regardless of whether or not such reasoning is expressed in formal scholastic theological terms or the kinds of theological reasoning applied to problems within the Muslim *umma* today, which have very noticeable echoes from the early sectarian disputes and the rise of schools of *kalam*.

Like Abou El Fadl, Amina Wadud also directly or indirectly expresses Mu'tazili insights in staking out a Muslim feminist position in *Inside the Gender Jihad* (2006). Wadud wanted, as a progressive Muslim feminist intellectual, to think through such problems as women's justice and the basis of Muslim participation in global human rights from a distinctly Islamic point of view: "I concluded early in my search that one way to resolve my questions about gender was to direct myself to *Islamic theology* rather than Muslim social contexts or commentary, present or historical" (Wadud 2006: 187). The Mu'tazili theologian's independent moral reasoning as interpreter of Quran and *sunna* (that is, the teachings must make rational moral sense consistent with the overall message of the Quran) comes to bear upon the passage that Islamic feminists have had the most difficult time accepting literally or reinterpreting more positively, Quran 4:34:

Men are in charge of women by [right of] what Allah has given one over the other and what they spend [for maintenance] from their wealth. So righteous women are devoutly obedient, guarding in [the husband's] absence what Allah would have them guard. But those [wives] from whom you fear arrogance – [first] advise them; [then if they persist], forsake them in bed; and [finally], strike them. But if they obey you [once more], seek no means against them. Indeed, Allah is ever Exalted and Grand.

Wadud speaks forthrightly on the moral difficulty this well-known verse causes her as a Muslim woman:

Even though I have tried through different methods, there is no getting around this one, even though I have tried for two decades. I simply do not and cannot condone permission for a man to "scourge" a woman or apply *any kind* of strike to a woman … . This also has implications in implementing the *hudud* (penal code) ordinances. This verse, and the literal implementation of *hudud*, both imply an ethical standard of human actions that are archaic and barbarian at this time in history. They are unjust in the way that human beings have come to understand justice, and hence unacceptable to universal notions of human dignity.
　　I have had what Khaled Abou El Fadl calls a "conscientious pause" regarding the application of the *hudud* ordinances and the verse on wife beating.

(Wadud 2006: 200)

Wadud, like most other modern Muslim theologians who raid the archives of the classical tradition, does not resort to deploying the medieval dialectical methods of *kalam*. She nonetheless argues a position reminiscent of Mu'tazili theological ethics, which places upon the believing Muslim the need to make rational, moral sense of revelation and the divine commands and prohibitions.
　　Ziba Mir-Hosseini has referenced early Islamic theology directly in her writings on feminine justice. She writes as an ethnographer as well as a Shiite Muslim feminist activist in the wake of the Iranian Revolution, in which context she has become a strong advocate for gender justice. She poses the problem:

Muslim jurists claim, and all Muslims believe, that justice and equality are intrinsic values and cardinal principles in Islam and the *shari'a*. If this is the case, in a state that claims to be guided by the *shari'a*, why are justice and equality not reflected that regulate gender relations and the rights of men and women. Why do Islamic jurisprudential texts … treat women as second-class citizens and place them under men's domination.

(Mir-Hosseini 2006: 629)

She bases her argument for gender equality on the distinction between *shari'a* and *fiqh*, a distinction that claims, "while the *shari'a* [comprising Quran and *sunna*] is sacred, universal and eternal, *fiqh* is human and—like any other system of jurisprudence—subject to change." Islamic religious and legal thinking go astray when jurists and other Muslim intellectuals conflate their juristic interpretations (*fiqh*) with *shari'a*, that is, regard their *interpretation* of the *shari'a* to *be* the *shari'a*. Thus Mir-Hosseini contends that faulty or patriarchal interpretations of the *shari'a* must be challenged at the level of *fiqh*.

Mir-Hosseini, however, also references the medieval Mu'tazili/Ash'ari theological disputations as an *Islamic* context for understanding contemporary conflicts between Revolutionary Iranian Islamists and modernists. Citing both Soroush and Abou El Fadl, Mir-Hosseini argues that the problem of advancing an Islamic theology of human justice, including gender justice, is to be found in the tenth- and eleventh-century *kalam* disputation between the Ash'arites and the Mu'tazilites.

> The dominant *Ash'ari* school holds that our notion of justice is contingent on religious texts; whatever [the texts] say is just and not open to question. The *Mu'tazili* school, on the other hand, argues that the value of justice exists independent of religious texts; our sense and definition of justice is shaped by sources outside religion, is innate, and has a rational basis. I adhere to the second position, as developed by Abdolkarim Soroush
>
> (Mir-Hosseini 2006: 633)

We may conclude then that some contemporary feminist appeals have found the rationalism and ethical humanism of the medieval Mu'tazilite theologians amenable to their own understanding of the *shari'a* and for their own ethical responsibility for establishing a just society. These "neo-Mu'tazilites" operate as individual scholars who participate in common liberal theological conversation through conferences, professional societies, and their writings. They do not attempt to challenge their Islamist opponents (or each other) with the dialectical methods of disputation that dominated discourse in the ninth to eleventh centuries, nor do they attempt to revive the scholastic categories of the medieval *mutakallimun*. However, they do attach importance to reviving *Mu'tazili* theological ideas in the form of a modern *Islamic* discourse that, even though its ancestors lost to Ash'arism as the main Sunni school of theology, by its rationalism and potential for liberalism and progressivism makes it an alternative "Islamic" form of reasoning.

Postscript: modern Islamic theology in the global village

We close this chapter by emphasizing a couple of themes that have run throughout the discussion above. It is clear by now that "Islamic theology" does not denote a unified concept, nor does "modern" necessarily indicate adherence to the project of 'modernity,' understood as the institution of constitutionalism, democracy, the free market, civil equality, and consumerism, among other things (Asad 2003). This is partly historical and partly demographic; there is no central, orthodox body of doctrine that applies across the Islamic tradition universally. There are practices that are common to almost all Muslims, such as praying at appointed times in the direction of the Ka'ba in Mecca and going on the Hajj pilgrimage to Mecca. Most Muslims also believe the Quran is the revealed word of God, and they greatly revere the Prophet Muhammad and regard his example as something to be followed. Theology generates problems that its various proponents believe are worth disputing over. This chapter has focused on two schools of theology, the Ash'arites and Mu'tazilites, the former being the most conservative and the most followed by Sunni Muslims today, while the latter has drawn supporters from both Sunni and Shi'i Muslims in pre-modern and modern times

Modernity has presented new opportunities and contexts in which Islamic theological expression and debate are taking place. The internet is a main source of broadcasting Islamic (and anti-Islamic) religious and theological ideas at the popular level. Television has also played an important role, as evidenced by the ratings and longevity of Egyptian theologian Yusuf al-Qaradawi's program, *Sharia and Life* (*al-shari'a wa-l-hayat*). At the professional institutional level are modern universities in Muslim countries and in the West, most of which now have faculties in religious studies and theology. Muslim scholars are finding increasing opportunities in Europe and the Americas to teach courses on Islam, often in departments that combine Sunni, Shi'i, and secular Muslim intellectuals with non-Muslim theologians and historians of religion. This "globalization" of theological discourse is having an impact on growing numbers of students with very diverse national, ethnic, and religious backgrounds, as well as on books, professional journals, popular publications, and on professional organizations of scholars who teach about religion.

As this book goes to press, Abdolkarim Soroush, the Shiite Iranian philosopher discussed above, is teaching courses on Islamic thought as a visiting professor at an American university, giving guest lectures at several others, and preparing to discuss Islamic thought at an annual meeting of a professional society of scholars of the Middle East. Hasan Hanafi, a Sunni professor of philosophy at Cairo University, has gathered around him a faculty and group of students who have applied postmodern criticism and critical theory to problems in Islamic thought. Hanafi also has lectured in Europe and the United States and frequently attends international conferences on modern thought at conferences in Asia, Africa, Europe and the Americas. Like Soroush, Hanafi has been the subject of numerous doctoral dissertations and scholarly books around the world. Like so much else in our world, Islamic theology has gone global. The categories "Shi'i" and "Sunni" are really heritage markers, not theological identifications, for a growing number of Muslim theologians today, particularly among liberal and progressive Muslim thinkers. In the global village in which we now live, Islamic theology, judged by its practitioners, is still very relevant and now much more accessible to the educated reader, Muslim *and* non-Muslim, than at any time in the past.

Summary

- Many modern theologians have looked to the classical tradition for inspiration, even as they reimagine the tradition of Islamic theology in approaching problems and circumstances unique to the modern experience.
- These problems have included political and moral autonomy, civil equality, human rights, and religious identity in a secular world order.
- Islamic theology does not denote a unified concept, and we can expect the "globalization" of theological discourse to act as a centrifugal force in articulating Islamic principles in the future.

Discussion points

- What is the classical term for "theology" in the Islamic tradition, and what distinctive meaning does it have in the Muslim context?
- How would you characterize the relationship between Islamic theology in the pre-modern and in the modern period? Are the same issues discussed in the same ways?
- Discuss the impact colonialism and the advent of the modern nation-state has had on the content of modern theology in the Muslim world.
- Would you consider the women participants in organizations such as Al-Huda International feminists? Theologians?
- Discuss some differences between the Mu'tazilite and Ash'arite schools of theology as presented in the chapter. Why have certain modern Muslim theologians sought to revitalize Mu'tazili thought?

Further reading

Euben, Roxanne L. and Muhammad Qasim Zaman (eds.) (2009) *Princeton Readings in Islamist Thought: Texts and Contexts from al-Banna to Bin Laden*, Princeton and Oxford: Princeton University Press.

This edited volume is an excellent resource for those who wish to dig deeper into the twentieth-century intellectual history of Islamist theologies. Includes translations and commentaries on important Islamist works, including Ayatollah Khomeini and Hasan al-Banna.

Fakhry, Majid (1997) *A Short Introduction to Islamic Philosophy, Theology and Mysticism*, Oxford: Oneworld.

As the title indicates, Fakhry's useful study offers a readable introduction to the intellectual traditions of Islam.

Martin, Richard C. and Mark R. Woodward with Dwi S. Atmaja (1997) *Defenders of Reason In Islam: Mu'tazilism from Medieval School to Modern Symbol*, Oxford: Oneworld.

This useful guide to Islamic theology, focusing on Mu'tazilism, juxtaposes a classical theological text with contemporary Muslim thinkers, highlighting the filiations between the two traditions.

Sachedina, Abdulaziz (2001) *The Islamic Roots of Democratic Pluralism*, Oxford: Oneworld.

This seminal text is by one of the most prolific liberal-democratic reformers in the Iranian tradition of Islamic theology. Topics include the twentieth-century history of Islamic reform, reason and rationality in Islam, democracy, and religious pluralism.

References

'Abduh, Muhammad (2004 [1897]) *The Theology of Unity*, trans. and ed. Ishaq Musa'ad and Kenneth Cragg, Kuala Lumpur: Islamic Book Trust.

'Abduh, Muhammad and Jamal al-Din al-Afghani (1980 [1884]) "Destiny and Fate (*al-Qada' wa al-Qadar*)," in *al-'Urwa al-Wuthqa*, No. 7, 1884. Published Edition: Beirut: Dar al-Kitab al-'Arabi, 1980, pp. 89–98. Unpublished translation by Vincent J. Cornell, Emory University.

Abou El Fadl, Khaled (2001) *Speaking in God's Name: Islamic Law, Authority, and Women*, Oxford: Oneworld.

Ahmed, Sadaf (2009) *Transforming Faith: The Story of Al-Huda and Islamic Revivalism among Urban Pakistani Women*, Syracuse, NY: Syracuse University Press.

Asad, Talal (2003) *Formations of the Secular: Christianity, Islam, Modernity*, Stanford, CA: Stanford University Press.

Badran, Margot (2009) *Feminism in Islam: Secular and Religious Convergences*, Oxford: Oneworld.

Hourani, Albert (1983) *Arabic Thought in the Liberal Age, 1789-1939*, Cambridge: Cambridge University Press.

Mahmood, Saba (2005) *Politics of Piety: The Islamic Revival and the Feminist Subject*, Princeton, NJ: Princeton University Press.

Mir-Hosseini, Ziba (2006) "Muslim Women's Quest for Equality: Between Islamic Law and Feminism," *Critical Inquiry*, 32,(4): 629–45.

Pew Forum on Religion and Public Life (2009) "Mapping the Global Muslim Population: A Report on the Size and Distribution of the World's Muslim Population," Pew Research Center, http://pewforum.org/docs/?DocID=454.

Pellat, Charles (ed.) (1969) *The Life and World of Jahiz*, trans. D.M. Hawke, London: Routledge and Kegan Paul Ltd.

Qutb, Sayyid (1964) *Milestones*, Damascus: Dar al-Ilm.

Ramadan, Tariq (1999) *To Be A European Muslim*, London: The Islamic Foundation.

—— (2004) *Western Muslims and the Future of Islam*, Oxford: Oxford University Press.

—— (2009) *Radical Reform: Islamic Ethics and Liberation*, Oxford: Oxford University Press.

Shaikh, Khanum (2010) "New Expressions of Religiosity: Al-Huda International and the Expansion of Islamic Education for Pakistani Muslim Women," in Zayn R. Kassam (ed.) *Women and Islam*, Santa Barbara, CA: Praeger.

Soroush, Abdolkarim (2000) *Reason, Freedom, and Democracy in Islam: Essential Writings of Abdolkarim Soroush*, trans. and ed. Mahmoud Sadri and Ahamd Sadri, Oxford: Oxford University Press.

Wadud, Amina (2006) *Inside the Gender Jihad: Women's Reform in Islam*, Oxford: Oneworld.

5 Piety and devotion

Carl W. Ernst

Spiritual intermediaries

The personal dimension of piety and devotion towards God and his representatives has played a major role throughout the history of Islam. Initially, and perennially since then, this focus on the personal side of religion has been concentrated on the Prophet Muhammad as the representative of God *par excellence*. The logic of this approach can be understood fairly easily, once one takes into account what has been called "the paradox of monotheism." That is, if God is an infinite being, the creator of the universe, who is beyond human comprehension, how can we mortals have any knowledge or contact with him? The answer is that there must be a messenger, a human like us, who brings news and tidings from God to humanity. Such messengers are known in the Abrahamic traditions as prophets, though they certainly have their analogues in other religions. While some modern-day reformists are content to regard these messengers as the equivalent of postmen, it is understandable that prophets have often taken on major significance as the specially chosen vehicles of divine communication and the elite of humanity. The mystery of how they are selected by God, and for what distinct qualities, is the subject of considerable speculation. The point is that a prophet, particularly the one whom Muslims regard as the last prophet that God has sent to humanity (that is, Muhammad), fulfills a vital role as the intermediary between God and humanity.

The need for a spiritual intermediary should be stressed particularly today, when a predominant Protestant attitude assumes that God is infinitely transcendent and all humans are equally remote from divinity. In pre-modern Islam (and pre-modern Christianity, for that matter), it was, on the contrary, common to suppose that God must be manifest through one or more human intermediaries. The visualization of that possibility in terms of the Prophet Muhammad was made possible for generations of Muslims by a remarkable series of biographies, poems, and lovingly detailed narrations that discussed every conceivable attribute of his life and, indeed, every aspect of his physical appearance. Many of these narrations highlighted the story of the ascension of the Prophet into Paradise where he entered the presence of God. Moreover, mystics speculated that the Prophet Muhammad was no ordinary mortal, but the first being created by God, a primordial light from which the rest of the universe was manifested. In addition, he was regarded as possessing a unique ability to intercede with a merciful God on behalf of sinful humanity. So for many Muslims, the key to salvation had to include a close relationship with the Prophet Muhammad.

Obviously, the intimate connection that was possible with the Prophet Muhammad during his lifetime was severed by his death, and that event was unquestionably a crisis for the early Muslim community for a number of reasons. Was the agreement between the Arab tribes and Muhammad now canceled? Was he to be replaced by another prophet? Or was some other arrangement to be worked out to provide divine guidance? In reality, there were many solutions proposed for this critical situation, including the continuation of prophetic charisma through the Prophet's nephew and son-in-law, 'Ali, and his descendants—known to history as the Shi'i Imams. That particular development of Islamic thought, known as Shi'ism, stressed the need for a living representative of God on earth at any given time. In the best-known variant of this tradition there were 12 principal Imams, who both by their physical relationship to the Prophet Muhammad and their intrinsic spiritual quality were the bearers of a divine authority and knowledge that humanity desperately needed. Like the Prophet, they were viewed by their devotees as receptacles of the light of guidance, despite the hostility of a world of darkness and ignorance. The disappearance of the twelfth Imam in the late ninth century set the stage for messianic expectations of his triumphal return as one of the signs of Judgment Day.

While the history of Islamic sectarianism is beyond the scope of this essay, the development of Islamic piety and devotion through Sufism clearly calls upon the central authority of the Prophet Muhammad, and the need for an ongoing series of human representatives for future generations. The development of the concept of sainthood in Sufism also draws upon the vocabulary of the authority of the Imams in Shi'ism. The point is that, for much of the later Islamic tradition, linkage with the Prophet Muhammad through a chain of Sufi masters was the way in which many Muslims received authoritative teachings and connected to their spiritual source by ritual and pious devotion.

Sufism defined and in history

The term "Sufism" is obviously a European coinage, as one of the "isms" catalogued by European thinkers. "Sufi" is probably derived from the Arabic word *suf* or "wool," designating the garment of ascetics who refused to wear fine silks, but when people called Sufis began to appear in Muslim societies a couple of hundred years after the time of the Prophet Muhammad, the name began to imply religious attitudes of more emphatic piety than usual. Sufis developed a vocabulary for the inner spiritual life, emphasizing the performance of the normal Islamic rituals but with a deeper dimension, often including "extra credit" prayers late at night, and other intensive practices. Sufi leaders from the area around Baghdad, many of whom had roots in the artisan classes, meditated intensively on the Qur'an and developed complex philosophical understandings of prophecy and the nature of God. The ideas of the Baghdad Sufis found residence in eastern Persia, where parallel spiritual traditions had been developed by sages who speculated on cosmic realities as well as "self-blamers" who were critical of the hypocritical religious establishment. Ultimately, the concept of "becoming a Sufi" (*tasawwuf*, which we normally translate as Sufism) took root throughout Muslim societies from Spain to India. While the term "Sufism" has often been translated as "Islamic mysticism," that may be too limited a term, because of the notions of private spiritual experience and even occultism that are often associated with mysticism. It may be more useful to consider Sufism as a tradition of ethical and spiritual ideals that has been embodied in Muslim societies.

The institutionalization of Sufism rested upon two major factors: the master-disciple relationship, and the support of political authorities as well as the masses. While the early Sufi movement had been relatively informal, with personal relationships characterized by considerable spontaneity, the growth of the pedagogy of Sufism led to the establishment of large networks of disciples and a highly developed hierarchical concept of spiritual teaching. By the twelfth or thirteenth century of the common era, major Sufi teachers in the central Islamic lands became the foci of spiritual paths or chains of transmission (often named after those masters) that delivered Sufi practices to immense audiences. Thus, 'Abd al-Qadir al-Jilani became known as the founder of the Qadiriyya Sufi order, a tradition which is found in practically every Muslim country from Morocco to Sri Lanka. Likewise, the Sufi orders known as the Chishtiyya, Suhrawardiyya, and Naqshbandiyya emerged from the teachings of particular masters, often to be found in a particular region and with a particular set of practice characteristics. The Chishtis, for example, were known for their use of music in their devotional practices, while the Naqshbandis shunned such activities as emotional excess. With the expansion of empires such as the Mughals and the Ottomans, the Sufi orders received considerable royal patronage in the form of land endowments, and their physical presence was quite visible in the form of majestic tombs of saints as well as lodges or convents housing large numbers of Sufi devotees, sometimes known as dervishes. For many Muslims, the Sufi saints were accepted as local intercessors, who could, through their connection to the Prophet Muhammad, help the individual have access to divine grace. It is also worth pointing out that Sufi shrines, and the festivals that they sponsored, were also open to women's participation in ways that other sites of Muslim religious practice were not. Up till the end of the eighteenth century, it is safe to say that the majority of Muslim societies included Sufi Islam as a major trajectory for channeling religious devotion and piety, both for elite Sufis as well as ordinary believers. It should not be forgotten that each of the Sufi orders claimed an unbroken transmission of spiritual authority that ultimately went back to the Prophet Muhammad, and therefore to God himself.

In terms of spiritual practices, Sufi teachers emphasized intensive meditation on the inner meanings of the Qur'an and reverence for the Prophet Muhammad as the bearer of the revelation, and indeed as the noblest of humanity. Meditation upon the names of God (known as *dhikr* or recollection) sought to connect with the vast creative energies residing in the divine qualities, by silent or vocal repetition of the 99 divine names. Psychological exploration of the spiritual path was articulated in the form of itineraries or maps of the numerous "states" and "stations" traversed by the soul from its initial repentance to its ultimate union with God. The role of the spiritual master was crucial, since it presumed the insightful diagnosis of the spiritual needs of the disciple. Elite followers of Sufi teachers received intensive training that required lengthy periods of seclusion in order to recite litanies of prayer as well as rigorous self-examination. On a more popular level, poems and stories regarding the prophets and the saints were widely circulated and performed, providing ritual occasions for connecting to those who were closest to God. The burial sites of notable saints were considered to be full of divine blessings, and pilgrimage to these shrines became a widespread practice throughout Muslim societies. The articulation of Sufi institutions was always defined in local terms, focused on the very concrete tombs of Sufi saints, and expressed through particular lineages of masters and disciples that sometimes overlapped with family descent.

Criticisms of Sufism

Major changes begin to take place in Muslim societies, beginning in Arabia in the late eighteenth century, when leaders of the Wahhabi movement targeted Sufi and Shi'i shrines as centers of economic and religious authority that (in their view) had too long monopolized Muslim spirituality and social life. The rhetoric of the Wahhabis was quite clear: any religious site that gave extraordinary respect to a human being was nothing better than an idol temple, and the centuries of traditional practice that had grown up around Sufi shrines were only a new form of paganism. The program of reform engendered by this movement included iconoclastic gestures such as attacks on the Shi'i shrines of Iraq in the early 1800s, as well as the destruction of the monumental tombs of the Prophet Muhammad's family in Medina in 1925. As far as Sufism was concerned, one of the effects of this reformist tendency was an internal critique directed at practices such as pilgrimage to saints' tombs, celebration of the Prophet Muhammad's birthday, and the performance of musical rituals, all of which were condemned as heretical innovations that had no place in authentic Islam. The fact that these practices had been performed for centuries in numerous locations around the world made no difference. As in the Protestant Reformation, there was a wholesale rejection of tradition in the name of a return to the purified practices of the original religious foundation. Thus, members of the Chishti Sufi order who were involved in the creation of the Deoband seminary in northern India in the late nineteenth century wrote extensively about what they considered proper religious practice—and this did not include things such as visiting tombs, listening to ecstatic music, or making what were considered to be exaggerated gestures of respect either to the Prophet Muhammad or to any of the Sufi luminaries who were regarded as saints.

It is striking that some of the most important Muslim reformist movements of the twentieth century were led by thinkers who had been nurtured in Sufi circles. Such was the case with Abu al-'Ala' Maudoodi, founder of the Jama'at-i Islami in Pakistan, as well as Hasan al-Banna, organizer of the Muslim Brotherhood in Egypt. In both cases, these leaders preserved authoritarian tendencies associated with the role of Sufi masters, while eliminating most of the spiritual practices that had been the stock in trade of the Sufi orders. By creating mass movements that were aimed at empowering individual Muslims to have a direct relationship with God as defined by reformist discourse, these new critics of Sufism identified the mediating role of the Sufi saints as a heresy that had to be eliminated. In short, for the first time in more than 1,000 years, a significant group of Muslims rejected Sufism as un-Islamic. In retrospect, this critique is not altogether surprising. Sufi establishments had become more or less feudalistic concerns based on income from land rents combined with hereditary aristocracy. The growth of literacy in Muslim societies, which was encouraged by the introduction of printing in the nineteenth century, introduced new options for individual religious identity that did not require the permission of the local Sufi master or his representative. The tension between these models of religious authority produced predictable conflicts. When the new secular models of European education were introduced, skepticism about medieval superstition and miracle-mongering furnished new ammunition to attack the claims of Sufism.

European Orientalist views of Sufism

Another factor in the modern debate about Sufism was undoubtedly European scholarship about Islam, which is commonly known as Orientalism (or the science of knowing the East). In part because of longstanding prejudices against Islam, the earliest Orientalist writings about Sufism in the 1790s combine a mixture of admiration for Sufi poetry and spirituality with the conviction that it must have come from somewhere else besides Islam. Therefore, these European scholars assumed that Sufism was either part of some generic Oriental mysticism that was more or less Hindu or Buddhist in origin, or else that Sufis had borrowed all their ideas from Christian monks or Greek philosophers. There were also racial theories that attributed mysticism to the genius of the Aryan race (that is, Iranians and Indians rather than Arabs), since anti-Semitic views ruled out any possibility of philosophical and cultural creativity among Arabs and Jews. Negative perspectives on Islam were also reinforced by Christian missionaries, who argued forcefully (although without much success) that Islam was a false religion and that Muslims should simply convert to Christianity. These conclusions were introduced at the very beginning of the modern European study of Islam, so that in Orientalist circles it was considered to be indisputable that Sufism had nothing to do with Islam. The publication of Orientalist scholarship in translation necessarily had some impact in Muslim societies, even when its conclusions were rejected. For when the terms of debate were laid down by Orientalists (or missionaries), even the defenders of Islamic culture ended up using the same concepts and ideas introduced by their opponents, and in the process they sometimes ended up internalizing some of the mentality of the Europeans. In any case, it seems to be more than a remarkable coincidence that Muslim reformists began to denounce Sufism as un-Islamic at precisely the same time as Orientalists affirmed the same position; despite the fact that the reformists detested Sufism while the Orientalists admired it, both agreed on its non-Islamic character.

Sufism and colonialism

With the extension of European imperialism in the nineteenth century, which included the conquest of nearly all major Muslim societies, Sufi orders played an ambiguous role. In some cases, Sufi leaders who possessed major landholdings cooperated with the new French, British, Italian, or Russian authorities and maintained their privileges under colonial rule. In other situations, Sufis coming from marginal backgrounds raised revolts against European invasions, and in these situations Sufis provided some of the only significant Muslim resistance to colonial conquest—as one sees in the cases of 'Abd al-Qadir in Algeria, Shaykh Shamil in the Caucasus, or even in the messianic movement of the Sudanese Mahdi. As a result, colonial authorities maintained extensive security dossiers on Sufi groups, which they regarded as consisting of charismatic leaders with formidable armed followings.

Distinctive local histories of Sufism

In any event, the advent of colonial rulers and their postcolonial sequel meant that Sufi orders and their extensive possessions would come under the scrutiny and control of the modern nation-state. This was an event of significant proportions. While statistics are not generally available for pre-modern periods, one striking example is Istanbul prior to the First World War, where roughly one out of four men was an active resident of a Sufi lodge (Kreiser 1992: 49). Although earlier empires had certainly attempted to control the Sufi shrines and orders, the modern nation-state possessed much greater resources to do so, and the extensive financial donations that could be expected at major shrines were a definite incentive for state intervention. In this way, Sufism was now subject not only to ideological attack but also to bureaucratic regulation. In Egypt, governmental control took the form of a Council of Sufi Orders (*turuq*) that attempted to regulate all Sufi devotional activities, although some of the largest orders were not even officially recognized. Likewise, in Pakistan the Ministry of Charitable Trusts has been the official means of controlling major Sufi shrines and their income.

In some cases, the collision of state power with the residual resources of Sufi orders was cataclysmic. In 1925, the secular Turkish state abolished the Sufi orders and closed all their lodges (in part because of an abortive military revolt headed by a Sufi leader). The Saudi Arabian authorities have similarly denied space and recognition to Sufi orders. And the Iranian revolution of 1978–79 empowered a regime that was deeply unsympathetic to institutional Sufism, which could easily have formed a competitive spiritual alternative. Accordingly, Sufi groups in Iran (all of which in modern times have necessarily taken on a Shi'i identity) have been alternately repressed and marginalized. This anti-Sufi policy continues an emphasis found in Iran ever since the Safavid dynasty imposed Shi'ism as the state religion in the sixteenth century; this resulted in the rejection of institutional Sufism along with the tolerance of private philosophical mysticism. It is, ironically, in secular Turkey that Sufism has thrived most vigorously, in part because of the encouragement of the performances of the Whirling Dervishes as a tourist phenomenon, but also because of the survival of the Sufi orders in the form of non-governmental organizations and quasi-political groups. The current Turkish government of Prime Minister Erdoğan is often described as not only Islamist (that is, sympathetic to the influence of Islam on the political order) but also as deeply in tune with Sufi piety.

At the risk of generalization, it might be said that urban populations in Arab countries have turned their backs on Sufism more resolutely than other Muslims. While there are still major festivals that take place at Sufi shrines in Arab lands, such as the tomb of Ahmad al-Badawi in Tanta (near Cairo), which attracts more than a million devotees, such events are viewed with suspicion both by reformist Muslims and by secular modernists; both groups are equally convinced that these festivals are primarily attended by uneducated lower-class folk who are the victims of medieval superstition. It is probably still the case that the rural population is much more likely to accept the authority of Sufi saints than are the educated urban elite. Indeed, the high percentage of rural population in countries like Pakistan (where it is least 67 percent) may be one reason why Sufism is still so popular there. Most remarkable, perhaps, is the situation in Senegal, where it is estimated that 90 percent of the population is attached to one or another of Sufi orders that rule the country. The most popular shrine in Senegal, the tomb of Ahmadou Bamba (1853–1927) in Tuba, attracts two million pilgrims on the anniversary of his death. Each of these cases has to be treated individually in terms of recent national history.

Colonial rulers and their postcolonial successors have come to different arrangements with Sufi groups, either completely repressing them (as in Turkey, to a lesser extent in Iran, or even more ruthlessly in the former Soviet republics) or coming to some accommodation that is mutually advantageous. Ironically, the Soviet extermination of religion in Soviet Central Asia has been so successful that many people can no longer recall what Islam was actually like. This has created a situation in which entrepreneurial post-Soviet elites have attempted to create "New Age" styles of Sufism that would be safely distinct from the convenient threat of jihadist terrorism.

In Malaysia, Sufi orders exist, but keep a very low profile because of the highly conservative nature of state-sponsored Islam. In contrast, nominally secular Indonesia witnesses a remarkable spectrum of spiritual opportunities linked to Sufi traditions, some of which are offered on regular television shows. Meanwhile, in Hindu-dominated India, Sufism is often treated as a universal humanism that has only the merest connection with Islam. There, it is indeed a badge of honor that the majority of pilgrims to the shrines of Sufi saints such as Mu'in al-Din Chishti in Ajmer (typically over one million at the annual festival) are non-Muslims, whose devotion is even more remarkable testimony to the authenticity of the saints.

Globalization and Sufism

But for the phenomenon of globalization in relation to Sufism, we must look instead, not to the traditional homelands of Sufism in the countries of Asia and Africa, but to the representation of Sufism in Europe and America; this example will help clarify how similar processes are also functioning in traditionally Muslim countries. The most striking recent representation of Sufism has been the spectacular popularity of the poetry of the great Persian Sufi Jalaluddin Rumi, whose verse in modern English translation is said to be the best-selling poetry in America. Through the efforts of gifted American poets such as Robert Bly and Coleman Barks (followed by a host of less talented imitators), these new versions of Rumi have attracted the attention of some of the luminaries of American culture, ranging from journalist Bill Moyers to popular entertainers and actors such as Debra Winger, Martin Sheen, and even Madonna. What is remarkable about these poems is the way that they present Rumi as an ecumenical figure who transcends any religion; both Islamic origins and Persian poetic conventions are downplayed, and the erotic and humorous aspects of his verse are emphasized. In any case, what is striking is the way in which Rumi has become the touchstone for modern rethinking of identity in a non-authoritarian mode.

A parallel phenomenon is the widespread production and distribution of sound recordings of Sufi music, in a variety of formats ranging from sober and academic ethnomusicology to exuberant world-music recordings and fusion dance hits. The wildly popular crossover success of Pakistani vocalist Nusrat Fateh Ali Khan, who has appeared on numerous Hollywood film scores, is a powerful testimony to the broad appeal of this particular tradition of Sufi music, based on the qawwali performance associated mainly with the Chishti order. The Pakistani-American rock group Junoon is likewise determined to make the Punjabi lyrics of Sufi poet Bulleh Shah the basis for a message of liberation that can appeal to youth worldwide. Similar tendencies can be seen in Senegal, where the well-established Mouride Sufi brotherhood has had a powerful impact on music and popular culture over the past century. The influence of this Sufi tradition appears in musicians such as Youssou N'dour, who has an enormous following in Europe, particularly in France. Devotional performance of the Arabic and Wolof poems of Mouride founder Ahmadou Bamba is featured on fusion recordings made in Canada by Musa Dieng Kala.

Both the print and audio dissemination of cultural products associated with Sufism illustrate a process that has been taking place in Muslim societies for at least a century and a half, which consists of the use of new technologies to publicize the previously esoteric teachings of Sufism; this process may be called "the publication of the secret." The introduction of print and lithography technology made possible the distribution of Sufi teachings on a scale far beyond what manuscript production could attain. As has been noted in the case of Ibn 'Arabi's Arabic works, when they first emerged into print in the late nineteenth century, suddenly a work that had been represented by at most 100 manuscripts (and those difficult of access) was easily available at a corner bookstore in 1,000 copies. Evidence is still far from complete, but indications are that in the principal locations for the introduction of printing technology on a mass basis in the nineteenth century (Cairo, Istanbul, Tehran, and Delhi), the main patrons of publication, aside from governments, were Sufi orders (Ernst 2011: chapter 7; Ernst and Lawrence 2002: chapters 6 and 7). Another striking instance of the newly specialized situation of Sufism is the way Sufi leaders could focus on marketing to their disciples through the publication of Sufi periodicals, a topic that is only beginning to be explored, but which is well attested in the Ottoman regions, in Egypt, and in South Asia. To this one can add lithographic printing (both color and black and white) for the mass production of images of Sufi saints, whether imaginary portraits or photographs of living masters. All this publicization of Sufism occurred at precisely the time when Sufism was becoming an abstract subject, separated from Islam in Orientalist writings, and condemned by reformists as a non-Islamic innovation. The dissemination of Sufi books and recordings in Europe and America is a more elaborate version of what was happening in Muslim countries, although for a different kind of audience. While in Muslim countries Sufi publications functioned as apologetics, to keep in touch with distant followers, and as acts of piety, Sufi material in Europe and America has joined the shelf of New Age teachings, in a veritable marketplace of spirituality.

Another recent area of publicizing Sufism has occurred in relation to Sufi shrines and rituals, which governments increasingly view as sources of tourist revenue. The revival of the whirling dervish dance in Turkey in 1954 was permitted only on condition that it be a purely aesthetic and cultural performance rather than a religious event. Visitors to Turkey today are greeted by innumerable cassettes, posters, and kitsch statuettes relating to Mevlana Rumi and the dervishes (see Figure 5.1), with the annual festival of the anniversary of Rumi's death celebrated by the secular calendar on December 17 in Konya (formerly held in a gymnasium rather

Figure 5.1 Set of whirling dervishes and other ceramic products on sale at a roadside souvenir stall at Istiklal Caddesi in Istanbul, Turkey. Courtesy of iStockphoto.

than a Sufi lodge, but now in a specially built arena) as a major tourist draw. Music hall performances of the Whirling Dervishes in Turkey and in tours overseas are arranged by the Turkish Ministry of Culture, frequently in combination with concerts of classical Ottoman music. Yet the reception accorded the Whirling Dervishes is frequently at least as spiritual as it is aesthetic (Erguner 2006). Uzbekistan, having recently rediscovered its Islamic past after decades of official Soviet atheism, has taken to promoting pious pilgrimage to sites such as the tomb of Baha' al-Din Naqshband in Bukhara.

The production of items such as books and recordings is by no means the only form of technological change that has affected Sufism. While television remains under government control in Middle Eastern countries, and film has had only occasional use for purposes connected with Sufism, the internet boasts a robust Sufi presence, with dozens if not hundreds of websites representing Sufi traditions from all over the world. The apparent paradox of publicizing an esoteric tradition is nowhere more apparent than on the internet, where the open secret of mysticism must be reconfigured in terms of what are basically advertising paradigms. There are today a host of Sufi websites that proclaim themselves to interested internet surfers, offering everything from detailed textual materials online to boutiques of unusual products. Some of these are related to traditional Sufi orders, such as the Ni'matollahi, Naqshbandi, Rifa'i, and Chishti. Sometimes they appear to prolong and perpetuate the authority of the printed text, as one can see from the extensive devotional and spiritual treatises available online, in English translation, in the elaborate websites of the American Naqshbandi order led by Shaikh Hisham Kabbani (www.sunnah.org). This website also features extensive polemics directed against fundamentalist forms of Islam, and the name itself indicates an attempt to appropriate the key symbolic term of the Prophet's moral example (*sunnah*). Although many of the Sufi websites do have some interactive features, such as email addresses, in terms of their religious message they tend to be largely informational with a proselytizing touch. Increasingly, local Sufi shrines and orders are finding the internet to be a useful way both to keep in touch with their devotees, who are often scattered around the world as economic migrants, and to establish an online presence that may attract new seekers.

In contrast, the websites associated with Hazrat Inayat Khan in North America play much more fully into the internet sensibility. Pir Vilayat Inayat Khan, Sufi Sam, and other representatives of this Sufi tradition have a massive presence that is ramified in a number of parallel but distinct organizations as well as individual websites. These sites feature numerous interactive features including discussion groups, travel schedules of leaders, online classes, daily inspirational messages, audio files, and massive collections of links to sites on Sufism and other religions. Discussion groups associated with these sites have free-ranging and sometimes combative debates on topics such as the relationship between Sufism and Islam. This kind of website may truly be said to constitute a virtual community.

The variation in the kind of internet presence maintained by different Sufi groups can be understood in terms of some of the fundamental characteristics of modern communications media and technology. This new situation constitutes a challenge for groups that were traditionally defined by granting access to esoteric teachings reserved for a spiritual elite. I once asked the leader of a South Asian Sufi group whether or not he was interested in setting up a website (I posed this question on email, since he has access to this technology in his professional capacity as an engineer). He responded by quoting the words of a twentieth-century Sufi master from his lineage: "We are not vendors who hawk our wares in the bazaar; we are like Mahajans (wholesale merchants)— people come to us." Nevertheless, he indicated that he did find the idea interesting, and it turns out that Malaysian disciples of this order have in fact set up a website where English language publications of the leading masters of the order are offered for sale. And in another sign of Sufi presence on the internet, one can now take advantage of several Sufi blogs, including one (http://sufinews.blogspot.com/) maintained by an academic specialist on Sufism, Prof. Alan Godlas.

New Sufi-style teachings

For a citizen of the pre-modern Muslim ecumene, such as the fourteenth-century traveler Ibn Battuta, norms of piety and devotion were defined by spiritual intermediaries embodied in Sufi saints. Wherever he went, from Morocco to China, he took it for granted that these powerful exemplars of spirituality were key figures respected by everyone in Muslim society, from kings to peasants. That millennial tradition no longer holds today. The impact of reformism has brought a democratic spirit that is resistant to the spiritual elitism of Sufism. The parallel spread of secular learning has undermined the charismatic status and occult powers Sufi leaders claimed. Nevertheless, it is probably accurate to say that perhaps half the world's Muslim population preserves Sufi forms of piety and devotion, if only in the form of intense reverence for the Prophet Muhammad. Ritual practices such as the observance of the Prophet's birthday, and gestures of respect such as standing when his name is mentioned, are considered to be obligatory as well as deeply fulfilling emotionally by many Muslims, such as the followers of the Barelwi school in India. On the other hand, the contrary position of the Deoband school holds that these devotional practices are lamentable innovations that are probably based on non-Muslim practices found among Christians or Hindus.

Although these reform-driven debates have taken their toll on traditional Sufi orders and shrine organizations, this has not prevented the reformulation of Sufi-style spiritual teachings in new vocabularies that are more easily accepted by modern educated Muslims. To take a few examples, the Turkish scholar Said Nursi (d. 1960) is famous for his immense commentary on the Qur'an, the 6,000-page *Treatise of Light* (*Risala-i Nur*), which drew upon the language of modern science to refute materialism and show that Islam is a rational system of belief. A contemporary Turkish teacher in the same tradition is the influential US-based leader, Fethullah Gülen. His numerous followers have established an international network of centers and schools with a strong emphasis on interfaith dialogue and the ethics of service. Their enthusiastic activities have been met with suspicion particularly in secularist circles in Turkey, who fear the reintroduction of religious orthodoxy. These non-traditional modern Sufi teachers frequently invoke the teachings of the great Sufis of the past (particularly Rumi), but their followers are often drawn from the upwardly mobile and educated middle class rather than the rural populations formerly drawn to local shrines and teachers.

Women Sufi leaders

One of the other important developments of contemporary Sufism is the increasing prominence of women leaders. While there were in the past undoubtedly important women Sufis (such as the early mystic Rabi'a in the ninth century), biographical and literary information about them is scarce; it is clear that gender segregation and limited access to education restricted participation of women in Sufi practice at the elite level, although women of all classes have commonly been able to participate in shrine pilgrimage with few limitations. Nevertheless, there is historical evidence about the connection of upper-class women to Sufi orders, particularly as patrons, and there are examples of some notable Sufi women who were the teachers of men. But in recent times it is remarkable that prominent Sufi teachers from a number of traditions have been women. This is particularly true in the American extensions of Sufi orders from the Middle East and South Asia. Women play significant roles in the American branches of Turkish movements, such as the Halveti-Jerrahis, whose New York leader is an American woman, Shaykha Fariha al-Jerrahi. Likewise there is a branch of the Mevlevi order ("the Whirling Dervishes") headed by an American couple, Camille and Kabir Helminski. An Iranian-American woman, Dr. Nahid Angha, has established the Sufi Women Organization in connection with her movement, the International Association of Sufism. And in the American Sufi groups connected to Hazrat Inayat Khan there are quite a few women leaders. But the prominence of women in Sufism is not by any means restricted to the US. Women in Turkish Sufi circles have also come into their own in recent years, as for example in the Halveti Cerrahi charitable foundation in Istanbul. There is also a prominent circle of female Sufi teachers in the lineage of Turkish Sufi leader Kenan Rifai (d. 1950), including Samiha Ayverdi (d. 1993), founder of the Turkish Women's Cultural Organization. Her successor, Cemalnur Sargut, organizes numerous academic conferences and publications on Sufism. It is probably safe to say that the participation of women in Sufi orders is a subject that still remains relatively unexplored, but at the same time the changes in gender roles that are occurring worldwide are bound to have transformative effects on traditional Muslim societies where Sufism still flourishes.

US political interest in Sufism

Curiously enough, Sufism is also now attracting attention from potential foreign patrons such as the US government. Now that Islamic terrorism has replaced the Cold War as the most widely accepted international excuse for military activity (e.g., Russia against Chechnya, China against the Uighurs, and the generalized US war on terrorism), certain policymakers and think tanks have proposed to identify Sufism as a potential ally in this struggle. The right-wing Nixon Center published a report in 2004 on "Understanding Sufism and Its Potential Role in US Policy," suggesting that Sufism could assist the US in defeating terrorism. Likewise, the RAND Corporation (a think tank that often consults with the US government on political and military affairs) in 2007 proposed that Western governments could call on Sufism as an ally in the struggle against Muslim extremism. These manipulative scenarios, reminiscent of colonial policy at the high point of nineteenth-century imperialism, are unrealistic. For one thing, Sufi movements are decentralized, always being defined by diverse local traditions. It seems unlikely that foreign powers could successfully engage with the mass followings of Sufi saints for political purposes, and individual Sufi leaders generally have relatively circumscribed groups of followers. Still, it is striking to see that Sufism is still noticeable enough to come to the attention of American policymakers as a potential political force.

Summary

- Spiritual intermediaries play a key role in monotheism generally, and in Islam particularly, in the form of prophets, imams, and saints.
- Sufism, often defined as Islamic mysticism, is a spiritual and ethical tradition that has been institutionalized in Muslim societies in the form of master-disciple relations, royal patronage, and spiritual practices including pilgrimage to the tombs of saints.
- Criticism of Sufism as idolatrous arose in the late eighteenth century with the Wahhabi movement in Arabia. Later Muslim reformists as well as secular modernists also tended to reject Sufi practices as medieval superstition, although sometimes they retained its authority structure.
- European Orientalists believed that Sufism, which they admired, could not be connected to Islam, which they rejected. Their description of Sufism as un-Islamic coincides remarkably with the views of Muslim reformers, and may have influenced it.
- The advent of European colonialism aroused defensive Sufi resistance in some locations, while other Sufi leaders made accommodation with colonial rulers. Postcolonial states have attempted to either ban Sufi institutions outright or to control them through bureaucratic measures.
- Different majority-Muslim countries have distinctive histories of dealing with Sufism, which has varying degrees of support in urban and rural areas and among political rulers.
- The effect of globalization and communications technology (including the internet) has been to make the cultural products of Sufism, especially poetry and music, available to non-Muslim audiences, who often appreciate Sufism as a universal spirituality not necessarily connected to Islam.
- Despite reformist criticism of traditional Sufism, new forms of Sufi-style teachings stress the compatibility of Islam and science, offering a spirituality that is attractive to modern Muslims.

- Women have become increasingly prominent in contemporary Sufi circles in the US and Turkey.
- While there is some interest in US government circles in enrolling Sufis as allies against Muslim extremism, this seems an unlikely possibility.

Discussion points

- What are the reasons why Muslims have looked to spiritual intermediaries to connect them to God?
- What are some of the different ways that colonial and postcolonial states have related to Sufi establishments?
- What aspects of Sufi culture have non-Muslims found attractive? How is this affected by their attitudes toward Islam?
- What are the criticisms that have been directed at Sufism? To what extent do Muslim reformists, secular modernists, and European scholars agree in their assessments of Sufism?
- In what ways do Sufis use the internet and other modern forms of communication?

Further reading

Erguner, Kudsi (2006) *Journeys of a Sufi Musician*, London: Saqi Books.

The autobiography of an eminent Turkish musician who has witnessed the revival of the performances of the Whirling Dervishes.

Ernst, Carl W. (2011) *Sufism: An Introduction to the Mystical Tradition of Islam*, Boston: Shambhala Publications.

A contemporary survey of the origins, principles, practices, and contemporary manifestations of Islamic spirituality and mysticism.

Ernst, Carl W. and Bruce B. Lawrence (2002) *Sufi Martyrs of Love: Chishti Sufism in South Asia and Beyond*, New York: Palgrave Press.

A detailed study of the most prominent Sufi tradition in South Asia, from the perspective of religious studies. It offers a critique of the "golden age and decline" view of Sufism and rethinks the notion of what a Sufi order is.

Green, Nile (2012) *Sufism: A Global History*, Oxford: Wiley Blackwell.

The most comprehensive survey of Sufism to date, both in its geographical extent and its historical depth.

Kreiser, Klaus (1992) "The Dervish Living," in Raymond Lifchez (ed.) *The Dervish Lodge: Architecture, Art, and Sufism in Ottoman Turkey*, Comparative Studies on Muslim Societies, Berkeley: University of California Press, pp. 49–56.

A description of what life was like in Sufi lodges in the Ottoman Empire.

Schimmel, Annemarie (1975) *Mystical Dimensions of Islam*, Chapel Hill, NC: University of North Carolina Press.

A popular and enduring classical treatment of the subject, with a strong emphasis on mystical poetry.

References

Chodkiewicz, Michel (1993) *Seal of the Saints: Prophethood and Sainthood in the Doctrine of Ibn 'Arabi*, Cambridge: Islamic Texts Society.

Cornell, Vincent J. (1998) *Realm of the Saint: Power and Authority in Moroccan Sufism*, Austin: University of Texas Press.

De Jong, Fred and Berndt Radtke (eds) (1999) *Islamic Mysticism Contested: Thirteen Centuries of Controversies & Polemics*, Leiden: Brill.

Erguner, Kudsi (2006) *Journeys of a Sufi Musician*, London: Saqi Books.

Ernst, Carl W. (1996) *Ruzbihan Baqli: Mysticism and the Rhetoric of Sainthood in Persian Sufism*, Richmond: Curzon Press.

—— (1999) *Teachings of Sufism*, Boston: Shambhala Publications.

—— (2009) "Sufism, Islam, and Globalization in the Contemporary World: Methodological Reflections on a Changing Field of Study," In Memoriam: The 4th Victor Danner Memorial Lecture, Bloomington, IN: Department of Near Eastern Languages.

—— (2010) "Muhammad as the Pole of Existence," in Jonathan Brockopp (ed.) *The Cambridge Companion to Muhammad*, Cambridge: Cambridge University Press, pp. 123–38.

—— (2011) *Sufism: An Introduction to the Mystical Tradition of Islam*, 2nd edn, Boston: Shambhala.

Ernst, Carl W. and Bruce B. Lawrence (2002) *Sufi Martyrs of Love: Chishti Sufism in South Asia and Beyond*, New York: Palgrave Press.

Ewing, Katherine Pratt (1997) *Arguing Sainthood: Modernity, Psychoanalysis, and Islam*, Durham, NC: Duke University Press.

Friedlander, Shems (1992) *The Whirling Dervishes: Being an Account of the Sufi Order Known as the Mevlevis and its Founder the Poet and Mystic Mevlana Jalalu'ddin Rumi*, Albany, NY: State University of New York Press.

Hoffman, Valerie J. (1995) *Sufism, Mystics, and Saints in Modern Egypt*, Columbia, SC: University of South Carolina Press.

Homerin, Th. Emil (1994) *From Arab Poet to Muslim Saint: Ibn al-Farid, his Verse, and his Shrine*, Columbia, SC: University of South Carolina Press.

Karamustafa, Ahmet T. (1999) *God's Unruly Friends: Dervish Groups in the Islamic Middle Period 1200–1550*, Salt Lake City: University of Utah Press.

—— (2007) *Sufism: The Formative Period*, Edinburgh: Edinburgh University Press.

Kreiser, Klaus (1992) "The Dervish Living," in Raymond Lifchez (ed.) *The Dervish Lodge: Architecture, Art, and Sufism in Ottoman Turkey*, Comparative Studies on Muslim Societies, Berkeley: University of California Press, pp. 49–56.

Lewis, Franklin (2000) *Rumi: Past and Present, East and West*, London: Oneworld.

Lewisohn, Leonard (ed.) (1999) *The Heritage of Sufism*, 3 vols, London: Oneworld.

Massignon, Louis (1998) *Essay on the Origins of the Technical Language of Islamic Mysticism*, Notre Dame, IN: University of Notre Dame Press.

Nursi, Said (2008). *The Gleams: Reflections on Qur'anic Wisdom and Spirituality*, trans. Hüseyin Akarsu, Somerset, NJ: Tughra Books.

Sulami, Muhammad ibn al-Husayn (2000) *Early Sufi Women: Dhikr an-Niswa al-Muta`abbidat as-Sufiyyat*, trans. Rkia Cornell, Louisville, KY: Fons Vitae.

Taylor, Christopher Schurman (1998). *In the Vicinity of the Righteous: Ziyara and the Veneration of Muslim Saints in Late Medieval Egypt*, Leiden: Brill

Trimingham, J. Spencer (1971) *The Sufi Orders in Islam*, London: Oxford University Press.

Werbner, Pnina and Helene Basu (eds) (1998) *Embodying Charisma: Modernity, Locality, and Performance of Emotion in Sufi Cults*, London, New York: Routledge.

6

The multiple faces of Islamic education in a secular age

Malika Zeghal

Education in the Muslim world today is shaped in part by a history of modern contentions and debates around the respective definitions, values and roles of "secular" and "religious" knowledge. Theories of modernization make economic and political development contingent on the expansion of secular education and the corresponding reform and/or marginalization of religious education. In the twentieth century, secular mass education has developed at a rapid rate in Muslim majority countries as part of socio-economic development projects, albeit at different rhythms and through a diversity of national systems of education. Under the regulating power of the modern state, these national systems have developed compulsory primary and secondary education that have improved literacy rates for boys and girls, although disparities between countries can remain wide (Afghanistan vs. Tunisia for instance) and gender differences remain significant in most countries. In general, these systems have provided massive access to education, not only at the level of primary and secondary education, but also at the university level.

Up until the last decade of the twentieth century, there had been a tendency to analyze the evolution of educational systems in the Muslim world in terms of the diminishing importance of religious education. However, a recent renewal of scholarly interest has shown that religious education has remained significant and has in many cases thrived, in both the public and private sectors. Religious education in contemporary Muslim majority countries takes a variety of forms: from the traditional *madrasas* (literally "place of study"), also called the *ḥawza ʿilmiyya* (an "enclosure" devoted to knowledge, or a community of knowledge) in the Shi'i context, to the religious education imparted in private or public schools within an otherwise secular curriculum, and to the one-on-one teaching relationship between master and disciple in *tarīqas* (mystical structures of authority and worship). The respective roles of secular and religious education in Muslim majority societies, as well as their interaction, depend on these societies' specific histories of nation-building. Internal debates concerning education are usually embedded in discussions about national identity and religion. In particular, the place that Islam as a scriptural tradition and a set of sentiments and embodied practices plays in the institutions of education must be understood in combination with an examination of the extent and forms of regulation of education by state authorities.

The chapter will show that Western influences and colonization, together with state regulation of education, produced new forms of knowledge deemed more essential and efficient for social and economic development. These new forms of knowledge deeply transformed the modes of transmission of religious knowledge and the relationship between education and religion.

To better understand these dynamics in the contemporary Muslim world, one must first understand the general patterns of education in pre-modern times. After a brief review of pre-modern education, the chapter will examine how modern conceptions and practices of "religious education" evolved in the nineteenth and twentieth centuries alongside the development of secular mass education, which encroached upon older forms of transmission of knowledge centered on the Islamic tradition. The sheer diversity and number of cases that have been treated in the secondary literature does not allow for a comprehensive review. Therefore, the author of this chapter has made the choice of concentrating on a few cases and favoring comparisons and conceptualization over a comprehensive treatment of the subject.

The notion of education in the Islamic tradition: the pre-modern context

The Islamic tradition gives a central role to knowledge, or *'ilm* in Arabic, and with it the one who searches for knowledge (*ṭālib al-'ilm*) as well as those who possess knowledge and disseminate it: the scholars (*'ulamā* or "those who know"). As Franz Rosenthal wrote:

> *'ilm* is one of those concepts that have dominated Islam and given Muslim civilization its distinctive shape and complexion. In fact, there is no other concept that has been operative as a determinant of Muslim civilization in all its aspects to the same extent as *'ilm*.
>
> *(Rosenthal 2007: 2)*

The categories of learning (*ta'allum*) and teaching (*ta'līm*) are crucial parts of the conceptualization of Islamic knowledge, be it the knowledge of God, the afterlife (*ākhira*) or this life (*dunyā*). The search for knowledge and its transmission are often said to be related to the discovery or deepening of one's faith, and studying is considered a form of worship. In the Koran, God is the all-knowing (*'alīm*), and true knowledge of the worlds seen and unseen is the primary knowledge that God has. However, numerous hadiths underline the value that knowledge holds for humans as well, and describe the search for knowledge as a duty that produces rewards both in this life and in the hereafter. One should seek knowledge as far as China, to paraphrase a well-known hadith. The *'ulamā* hold a high status, and are often described as the inheritors of the prophets (*warathat al-anbiyā'*).

In his *Fātiḥat al-'ulūm,* Abu Hamid al-Ghazali (d. 1111), who reflected in diverse ways on questions of pedagogies and education, describes knowledge as a truly human endeavor, as an art and a profession (*ṣinā'a*) that can be classified according to the types of knowledge: what is known from the prophecy, what is known through reason (arithmetic), experimentation (medicine), or hearing (language); knowledge is also classified through a hierarchy of moral intentions and their interrelations. While the higher forms of knowledge were the domain of a small literate elite in pre-modern Muslim societies, "knowledge of practices and action" (*'ilm mu'āmalāt*) was incumbent upon each individual Muslim as a set of guidelines for virtuous behavior. The highest forms of learning in medieval times were that of the Koranic text, the study of hadiths, and the study of the law, in particular through the concept of *fiqh*, which refers to the process of "understanding" (*faqaha*) and to the set of juridical instantiations of the sharia (Berkey 1992).

These different kinds of knowledge are closely interrelated, but developed at different times as institutionalized pedagogical domains. In particular, the development of the madrasa in the eleventh century became institutionalized as the science of law became a central intellectual endeavor. George Makdisi distinguishes between three periods of development of institutions of learning, from the mosque to the madrasa. The madrasa was "the institution of learning *par excellence*," since it was devoted primarily to the study of Islamic law, "queen of the Islamic sciences" (Makdisi 1981: 9). As early as prophetic times, the learning circle (the *ḥalaqa*) in mosques was the locus for transmission of knowledge, and the *kuttāb* (the place of writing) developed in the first century of Islam as the place where elementary instruction was dispensed, often in a space adjacent to the mosque (Kadi 2006: 313). The emergence of the mosque-hostel-college took place later, between the tenth and the eleventh centuries, "at least a hundred years before their Western counterparts, the European universities" (Mottahedeh 1985: 89). They taught Islamic sciences—which were intended to foster the study of Islamic religious law—through a professional body of teachers, and were equipped with a structure for lodging their students. Their styles of teaching and contents have always been diverse and related to their context, as well as to interpretive traditions. For instance, the identity of the Shi'i *ḥawza* is grounded in the *disputatio*. Madrasas and *ḥawza*-s were most of the time sustained by a waqf (religious endowment) deed and therefore by individual or family patronage that could also be linked to the world of politics. Sultans, viziers and powerful elites as well as wealthy benefactors founded madrasas. Among them were some women, as in the case of the foundation of the Qarawiyyin of Fez in Morocco in 859 by Fatima al-Fihri, the educated daughter of a wealthy merchant. The madrasa was a central institution that mirrored the power of its founders through the reputation of its teachers and scholars, its architecture, its library, and all other elements that formed this institutional complex. Because deeds of endowments allowed the founders to specify the domains of instruction, the curricula of madrasas could vary. There was, however, a definite focus on the Islamic sciences. Other types of knowledge, such as Greek works, circulated in private homes and libraries or in the case of medical knowledge, in hospitals. In general, pre-modern Islamicate civilizations "made room for the efflorescence of the secular in the midst of the religious" (Kadi 2006: 312). However, the division between sciences was not rigid and did not reflect the existence of two entirely autonomous and separate worlds, the religious and the secular. For instance, philosophy could be taught by some 'ulamā under the rubric of hadith, as well as outside of the official curriculum (Makdisi 1981: 77–80).

These places for the transmission of knowledge catered to an elite of educated men, and more rarely women, and had different outlooks depending on the place and time. Jonathan Berkey has documented the extraordinary vitality of Muslim education in medieval Cairo and showed that Muslim education was as much an "informal affair" and a "dynamic network" as it was an institutional endeavor (Berkey 1992: 17, 20). Interpersonal instruction played a crucial role, in particular through the master-disciple relationship and the delivery of the ijāza, the written document that the master issued to his student to certify that he had transmitted to the student a number of prophetic traditions or that the student had studied a certain number of works under his tutelage.

The rupture of modern times: the distinction between secular and religious knowledge

In modern times, factors such as Western influence, direct occupation by foreign nation-states, or projects of broad social reform sustained by indigenous elites led to an institutionalized dichotomy between religious and secular knowledge. It became an objectified division, which was sustained by the birth of the new systems of education that gave priority to "modern sciences" (al-'ulūm al-ḥadītha) over religious knowledge. This new polarity led to tensions between traditional elites who taught in madrasas and representatives of the new educational institutions inspired by Western models. These tensions unsettled the authority and legitimacy of the traditional carriers of knowledge, and translated at the moral, social, and political levels. Under the pressure of European colonialism and under the influences of Western cultures, the existing networks of transmission of knowledge underwent a deep transformation that many historians have analyzed as a general decline of Islamic education, leading to its marginalization relative to newly emerging institutions of secular knowledge (Keddie 1972; Sayyid-Marsot 1972; Delanoue 1982). This process of marginalization is well documented, but more historical research would need to be done to understand the effects of the encroachment of secular education upon madrasa education on previous conceptions of knowledge and pedagogy. Nineteenth-century educators and intellectuals produced new narratives on education and underlined the need to reform it. Their diagnosis was that religious education was in decline and was becoming archaic in the context of the sweeping changes taking place in their societies. However, too much attention given to this paradigm of decline has obscured the transformations that took place more deeply in the epistemology of religious learning. The reformers' diagnosis disparaged what they evaluated as archaic methods in religious education and the incompetence they saw in most of the madrasa teachers (Hourani 1962). This added to the critiques articulated by representatives of the colonizing powers, and produced an extremely negative picture of the state of the madrasas that had also declined economically by the end of the eighteenth century and the early nineteenth century.

Reforming education: bringing Islam into the world

The modern reformers saw educational institutions as a channel to revitalize Islam within their broader projects of social and political reforms. Education was often crucial in reformist ideologies, because it was conceived as a pivotal instrument for change. As part of a project to revitalize and strengthen Islam by making it more relevant, reforms of the old madrasa system showed a desire to bring the sciences of religion (*'ulūm al-dīn*) closer to this world (*al-dunyā*) and to life (*al-ḥayāt*). Reform was meant to preserve Islamic education from decline, but not necessarily by isolating it from the influences of modern knowledge. Rather, since the aim was to endow religious knowledge with a new relevance for Muslims, reform had to make religious knowledge useful for life in this world, not only as correct practice, but also as sustaining knowledge of the secular world. This project of integrating religious knowledge with contemporary life implicated a transformation of the place of this knowledge in the general structures of teaching and learning and new conceptions of its transmission.

These reformist projects took different forms depending on the context. In India, for instance, where Muslims formed a minority, reformist *'ulamā* established new schools, such as the Farangi Mahall in Lucknow, in order to remedy the loss of patronage that came with the end of the Moghol Empire, and to preserve an Islamic heritage threatened by imperial assaults from the West. Schooling was based on the Dars I Nizami, a systematized curriculum that combined Arabic grammar, logic, philosophy, mathematics, rhetoric, fiqh and theology, and more marginally Koran and hadith (Metcalf 2005: 31). The British also established educational institutions, which combined features of the Muslim and British education systems, such as the Delhi College in 1825: there was an "English" track and an "Oriental" track, in which sciences were taught in Urdu. The Delhi College became the model on which the *'ulamā* later rebuilt their institutions of learning, clearly inspiring the structures of the modern madrasa. Barbara Metcalf's study of the Indian madrasas underlines a depoliticization of the *'ulamā* after the mutiny of 1857 and their shift toward a focus on internal reform and education projects. In particular, the establishment of the school of Deoband in 1867, financed by the public rather than by the rulers or the system of waqfs, provided a structured institution of education independent from the state and from the waqf system, that reappropriated the Dars I Nizami with a special focus on hadith, in order to train future reformers. Standardized examinations, a library, and a physical separation from the mosque made this new structure self-sufficient, explicitly institutionalizing education in a Muslim school that could efficiently cater to high numbers of students coming from all over the country.

A reverse process took place in the Ottoman state and its provinces in the nineteenth century. Whereas in India reforms of education sprung from the loss of state patronage, in Ottoman societies reform came from state-sponsored tanzimat (reforms), reflecting the new regulatory power of the modern state and announcing its authoritarian policies *vis-à-vis* education in general and religious education in particular.

During the nineteenth century, modern schools were established in the Ottoman provinces roughly following the model of the tanzimat. In general, these reforms were carried out by state authorities. These states were aiming to modernize their own administrations and produce new kinds of bureaucrats, as well as well-trained officers for their armies. They implemented reforms outside of the traditional system of education by circumventing it, which led to a dichotomy between the traditional and modern systems of education. In Egypt, Khedive Muhammad Ali (1805–49) and his successors opened up schools on the Western model. Schools training officers began opening in 1816, and a medical school was established in 1826. These schools contrasted with al-Azhar in both the form and the content of the knowledge transmitted. The new schools had a standardized curriculum and system of evaluation, organized according to the principles of Western pedagogies and disciplines (Mitchell 1991), whereas al-Azhar's teaching did not. Al-Azhar's classes were not organized by age, often took place inside the mosque or in the teacher's home, and were not based on a standardized curriculum. Rote learning and memorization were the most frequently used methods of learning, and the modern subjects taught in the new schools were often absent from the body of knowledge transmitted at al-Azhar. This contrast informed the diagnosis made by nineteenth- and twentieth-century Egyptian reformers who criticized the state of studies in institutions such as al-Azhar. This narrative was built on the comparison of the traditional and modern systems and based on the new dichotomy that separated schools for modern knowledge ('ulūm 'aṣriyya or ḥadītha) and schools for religious knowledge. However, in the language of the reformers, this "modern" knowledge was not necessarily dubbed "secular," or "a-religious," but rather understood as "new" or belonging to the present times. It is also worth underlining that this separation was not so clear cut in practice. Schools that disseminated scientific knowledge often recruited their students from the kuttabs and from al-Azhar, which necessitated the recruitment of translators to translate into Arabic the teaching offered by foreign instructors. "Middle range" schools were also established that took their subjects of instruction from both systems, such as Dar al-Ulum in Cairo, created in 1872, and the Sadiki college, created in 1875 in Tunis (Sraieb 1995). These middle range institutions transmitted religious knowledge, but in a way that explicitly differed from al-Azhar or the Zaytuna, even though they often recruited faculty from these traditional institutions. They taught a wider range of subjects than the traditional madrasas, from literature, history, and geography to sciences and foreign languages, and competed with al-Azhar and the Zaytuna in terms of quality of instruction, range of topics covered, and job opportunities for their graduates. State-imposed reforms of al-Azhar in the last quarter of the nineteenth century therefore aimed at reorganizing its administration and at clearly defining the status of the teaching body to bring it on par with modern institutions. New subjects were also introduced at al-Azhar between the end of the nineteenth century and the early twentieth century, such as algebra, geography, and history.

The crucial role of religious education in the wider reforms of education

It was in this context that in 1895, Muhammad 'Abduh (1849–1905), a graduate of and former teacher at al-Azhar, was given the task of reforming education at the largest institution of education in Egypt at that time. Al-Azhar offered education from the elementary level of the *kuttāb* to the highest degree, the *'ālimiyya*, which made its holder a scholar (*'ālim*). His proposals for reform were often resented by his more conservative colleagues who accused him of wanting to transform al-Azhar into "a school of philosophy and literary education that fights religion and wants to extinguish its light" (Von Kügelgen 2011). 'Abduh articulated a harsh critique of the *'ulamā* and of the curriculum at al-Azhar. In particular, he denounced the rigidity (*jumūd*) of the *'ulamā* as well as their aversion for "the contemporary sciences" (*al-'ulūm al-'aṣriyya*): "they gather their intellectual forces in order to focus on well known studies and ignore anything else to the point that it seems that they do not belong to this century and even worse: they do not belong to this world (*laysū min hādhihi al-dunyā*)" (Rida 1906–31: vol. 1, 411). While 'Abduh and other reformers severely criticized the methods of learning at al-Azhar and in particular the refusal of the *'ulamā* to engage with the modern sciences, they did not reflect on the fact that the conservative *'ulamā*'s position against reform was also related to their self-understanding as guardians of the Islamic tradition—a tradition which they perceived as threatened by modernization. They felt that engaging with the "contemporary sciences" carried the risk of marginalizing the tradition they were supposed to maintain and transmit.

This did not mean that 'Abduh and like-minded reformers were against the existence of religious education, but rather that they wanted to reform it in a way that would integrate all sciences, secular and religious, in order to maximize the benefits of education for Muslim students. For 'Abduh, this reform of education—in which religious instruction was central—was the channel through which society would be transformed and improved. Islam had to play a pivotal role in this reform. In a programmatic text dealing with the Nizamiyya primary and secondary schools in the Ottoman state, 'Abduh underlined that ignorance and immorality were tightly linked (Rida 1906–31: vol. 2, 505). In particular, he related what he saw as the catastrophic state of the Nizamiyya schools to the absence of religious education (ta'līm dīnī) and insisted on Koran education to be integrated in the curriculum: "the qur'ān is the secret of the success of Muslims" (Rida 1906–31: vol. 1, 414). In the same vein, he explained desertions in the army by the absence of religious education in military schools (Rida 1906–31: vol. 1, 415). The reformist narratives hence developed a project of mutual integration of religious and secular education, lamenting their isolation in separate domains. For 'Abduh, religious instruction (tarbiya or ta'līm) was the basis of all education. If used as a foundation it would strengthen morality and favor reasoning, leading to the next phases of instruction in modern scientific knowledge (Von Kügelgen 2011). Muhammad 'Abduh and Rashid Rida had great confidence in the power of education as a tool to shape their societies: "a reform of society (iṣlāḥ madanī) based on the Koran and the sunna" was what Muslim societies needed (Rida 1906–31: vol. 1, 415).

The loss of legitimacy and the transformation of Islamic education

Debates about the legitimacy and the methods of reform separated reformist 'ulamā at al-Azhar from those who refused to change their ways of teaching. These debates were not merely ideological, opposing modern to traditional conceptions of education. An important number of the 'ulamā resisted the reforms because they saw these modernizing projects as an assault on their own institutions, on their function of preserving the Islamic tradition and hence on their own authority. These debates were also related to economic questions, such as the growing vulnerability of graduates of traditional institutions of learning on the job market. Between the two World Wars, madrasa graduates could no longer compete with their counterparts from the modern schools. They were no longer forming the intellectual and professional elite of Egyptian society. Also, the emergence of political movements on a massive scale in the twentieth century, such as the Wafd Party or the Muslim Brotherhood, did place the effendis, the urban middle class that had little to do with the madrasa type of education, at the forefront of politics. The 'ulamā were being relegated to the periphery of Egyptian society, marginalized not only by the growing centrality of novel types of education, but also by emerging social and political movements.

It was in this context of a growing sense of marginalization among the 'ulamā that the law of 1911 regulated the processes for application, examination, and granting of degrees at al-Azhar. The mode of transmission of knowledge became less individual. At al-Azhar in the first part of the twentieth century, primary and secondary institutes, the *ma'had*s, started to replace the kuttabs, where children used to learn in a circle sitting on the floor, often in the mosque or in the house of the master. The institutes copied the school in its modern form, with chairs, tables, and a blackboard, in a building expressly designated for education. At the higher education level, three domains of learning were compartmentalized in different schools (*kulliyāt*): Arabic language, Sharia law, theology or "usūl al-dīn." Al-Azhar progressively shifted to a modernized structure for the transmission of religious knowledge that severed its links to the sacred space of the mosque and introduced a new spatial order for teaching.

While the forms of the madrasa and the modern university converged, the kuttabs never disappeared and the *ḥalaqa* (circle) as a form of transmission of knowledge did not cease to exist either. This speaks to the fact that while modernization transformed religious education in ways that somewhat severed its relation with the madrasa tradition, it also led to a diversity of forms of religious learning that persist to this day. In Egypt, North Africa, or Lebanon (Mervin 2000), to give only a few examples, the structures for the transmission of religious knowledge have become diverse, from the kuttabs, to more formal primary and secondary religious schools (the *madāris 'atīqa* in Morocco or the *ma'āhid azhariyya* in Egypt), to higher levels of education that cater to informal *ḥalaqāt* in mosques, to dissemination of knowledge within mystical communities, or to the modern university—such as the universities of Cairo and Damascus, which include schools of sharia. The *ḥawzas* of Najaf in Iraq and Qum in Iran are crucial locations of production and dissemination of Shi'i Islamic knowledge, and play a political and social role beyond the mere transmission of knowledge.

The transformation of contents and the expansion of religious education: a new hybrid?

The transformation of Islamic schooling in the twentieth century was not only one of forms and structures. The content of the knowledge transmitted and its presentation to students was also radically reshaped. For instance, changes to the legal system during the nineteenth century instigated curricular transformations in the domain of sharia. In the Arab world, the development of hybrid legal systems—based on European law but incorporating elements of the sharia—necessitated the training of lawyers and magistrates in Western positive law. New schools of law were created in the nineteenth century and the twentieth century, such as the Khedive Ismail school of law in 1868, the school of judges founded in Cairo in 1907, the *Centres d'études juridiques* founded by the French in Tunis in 1922 and in Rabat and Casablanca in 1927, or the school of law of Beirut in 1912. As described by Monique Cardinal, they taught positive law (*qānūn*) alongside sharia law, which led to the teaching of sharia in radically new forms (Cardinal 2005).

In the new schools of law, the classical treatises and *fiqh* compendia that used to inculcate legal knowledge in the traditional madrasa were no longer required to be read in their entirety by the students. In the twentieth century, new textbooks were written and published by scholars of sharia, themselves often graduates of traditional institutions, who specialized in teaching Islamic legal theory. These books mixed short excerpts from classical texts with concepts of positive law that became the framework for understanding legal theory. They also presented sharia in comparison with positive law, showing the possibility of a convergence between them (Cardinal 2005). This strategy might have been an attempt on the part of teachers of Islamic law to appeal to students in modern schools of law, as Cardinal has argued, but more fundamentally it was an attempt to present the law in terms that kept its linkage with tradition in a context where Western law had become hegemonic—nearly the only system through which law was legible. This new framework offered concepts through which it became possible to construct law through a narrative that made it markedly "Islamic." This integration of classical texts in textbooks that referred centrally to the vocabulary of Western positive law led to the fragmentation and marginalization of the classical tradition, as well as to a reinterpretation of sharia as "Islamic law" in comparison to positive law, or *qānūn*. This new narrative about Islamic law echoed and converged with the contemporaneous emergence of a vocabulary of political Islam that demanded the application of "Islamic law" and the foundation of an "Islamic state."

The fragmentation and near-effacement of the classical legal treatises did not exclusively take place in the modern schools of law. It also happened in colleges of sharia within traditional institutions of religious education such as al-Azhar in Egypt, the Qarawiyyin in Morocco or the Zaytuna in Tunisia. For instance, after the reform of 1961 at al-Azhar, the college of sharia (*kulliyyat al-sharīʿa*) became the college of "sharia and positive law" (*kulliyyat al-sharīʿa waʾl-qānūn*) and modern textbooks introducing excerpts of the classical literature were used in the curriculum of the school.

This combination of two references of unequal status—the texts of the Islamic tradition embedded in the Western paradigms of legal theory—did not only emerge as the product of pedagogical agendas produced in the new textbooks. It also originated from the projects devised by the newly independent Egyptian state that was attempting, with more or less success, to directly engage with and regulate religious knowledge, in order to control the potential political challenge from undomesticated religious authorities. The perfect illustration of this engagement with institutions of religious knowledge was the authoritarian reform of al-Azhar by Nasser's regime in 1961: law number 103 of 1961 made al-Azhar part of the administration of the state, reconfigured its administrative structure, and, most importantly for this argument, reformed the types of knowledge transmitted at al-Azhar. As a mosque (*jāmiʿ al-Azhar*), al-Azhar also officially gained the status of university (*jāmiʿat al-Azhar*). This echoed the status of Cairo University, which had been established in 1908 as the first Egyptian university. At the level of the primary and secondary institutes of al-Azhar, the curriculum was built on religious subjects as well as on the secular subjects taught in the system of public education. Young students acquired both types of knowledge and specialized afterwards in any of the schools of al-Azhar University. At the university level, the three schools remained (sharia and positive law, Arabic language, and theology), representing a "religious center," and new schools teaching secular subjects—from medicine to pharmacy, languages to biology—were built in the suburbs of Cairo, as well as in the provinces. The project reflected earlier reformist desires to integrate religious and secular knowledge in a way that would revitalize Islam and lead to the general progress of society. In that narrative, echoing 'Abduh's earlier observations about the isolation of the 'ulamā from the world around them, the carriers of religious knowledge had to be brought back into the world. The aim of the 1961 reforms was therefore to bring together religion and this world (dīn wa dunyā), and to make the 'ulamā and their knowledge "useful." The narratives justifying the 1961 reforms denied the 'ulamā the status of "men of religion," and insisted on the illegitimacy of a separation between the "science of religion" and the "science of this world," arguing that religion could not be a "profession" (ḥirfa) (Zeghal 1996).

This official narrative justifying the reform was deeply ambivalent, because it took a position defending "Islamic education" while at the same time diluting it with other subjects to preserve its relevance. The 'ulamā understood this ambivalence very well. They resented such a representation, because it denied them their specialization in the tradition as a specific domain of teaching. Indeed, the reforms radically reconfigured the 'ulamā as hybrids whose function was to bridge Islam and the world by becoming specialists of both domains. In fact, Nasser's reform echoed the project of the Muslim Brothers by conjoining the two orders constituted by "religion" and the "world" (dīn wa dunyā).

The most immediate practical result of this state-imposed reform of the early 1960s was to expand al-Azhar as a university. This was reflected in the increase of the number of students in the 1970s and 1980s, which in turn led to the proletarization of the university students. A significant number of 'ulamā who taught in the religious schools at the university hence expressed the desire to see al-Azhar recover its unique specialization in religion. They complained that the expansion of their university through the addition of modern subjects had produced graduates who excelled neither in the secular sciences nor in religious knowledge, and had strained the university's resources (Zeghal 1996). The combination of religious and secular knowledge in various educational contexts also created a commonality of epistemological conditions and worldviews between graduates of public secular schools and graduates of al-Azhar, since all students had access to a blend of secular and religious knowledge.

Some scholars have argued that it was precisely this combination of religious and secular concepts in the context of mass education after the 1960s that led to the development of political Islam (Kepel 1985). While this assertion is difficult to verify, it is nonetheless important to underline that religious knowledge was not necessarily marginalized, but rather deeply transformed by its combination with secular knowledge. This combination helped sustain the claim by Islamist ideologues that all knowledge, and scientific knowledge in particular, could be attained through Islam, and that Islam could be the foundation of all domains of life. Deepening the idea that a combination of secular and religious knowledge led to ideologies of Islamism, Olivier Roy has argued that Islamist students were more represented in scientific departments in universities of the Muslim world in the last quarter of the twentieth century than in other departments, precisely because they interpreted scientific knowledge as contained in the Islamic scriptures and verifiable through them (Roy 1990, 1996). The correlation between types of education and politicization is, however, difficult to verify: political Islam's ideology seems to be as much present among the graduates of secular scientific education as it is among the graduates of religious education (Zeghal 1996).

The desire to return to purer "religious roots" was often expressed by the *'ulamā* of al-Azhar—and was even realized in part, when, within the Faculty of Islamic Law and Positive Law, a program for the study of sharia was developed in the 1970s and a *kulliyyat al-da'wa* (school for the call to Islam) was established within the millenarian *jāmi'* (mosque where the Friday collective prayer is held) in the old center of Cairo. This desire is not to be interpreted as the expression of "Islamism" within an institution such as al-Azhar, but rather as a project to recenter knowledge on the Islamic tradition, and to make it less affected by the pressures of having to conform to the rules and constraints of secular domains of knowledge. The project to make al-Azhar conform more closely to the old madrasa system is also deeply linked to a desire for political independence from the state's administration. Projects to create a "private al-Azhar" under the Mubarak regime have been attempted unsuccessfully by some faculty members since the 1970s (Zeghal 1996). The aftermath of the 2011 Egyptian revolution might very well provide new opportunities for this enterprise of "liberation" of religious education from the grip of the state as well as from the constraints of secular "reform."

State reforms and the marginalization of Islamic education

While the 1961 reform of al-Azhar was an attempt on the part of the Egyptian state to modernize and domesticate the university, it also paradoxically led to its expansion in terms of the number of schools at all levels and in terms of the number of students. This reflected the high demand of Egyptian families for religious education in the second part of the twentieth century, as well as the use of al-Azhar by the government as a space in which to accommodate the overflow of high school graduates in search of a seat in a college. Al-Azhar's modern faculties in particular became the receptacle for lower performing high school graduates in the 1980s, leading to the transformation of al-Azhar into an institution for mass education.

Figure 6.1 al-Azhar University, Cairo. Courtesy of Lauren Kenney.

However, in the Arab Middle East, not all postcolonial reforms led to such an expansion of the religious education sector. In Morocco, the monarchy neglected its madrasas for a long time, leading to the weakening of the teaching institution of the Qarawiyin and the fragmentation of the networks of religious teaching into differentiated institutions (Eickelman 2007, Zeghal 2008).

In Tunisia, where state elites in the 1960s were strongly influenced by the Turkish model of secularism, state policies marginalized the traditional sector of education. The kuttabs were closed, along with the University of Zaytuna and its annexes in the provinces. Of the Zaytuna, only a small faculty of theology remained, which was integrated within the newly opened University of Letters of Tunis in 1960. While religious education remained in the curriculum in primary and secondary public schools under the name "religious and civic education" (*tarbiya dīniyya wa madaniyya*), at the higher level it was shrunk to a specialization until the Zaytuna was reinstated as a university in 1989. After 1989, President Ben Ali's authoritarian regime, faced with the expansion of the Islamist movement, undertook a radical reform of religious education. The textbooks for public schools were entirely rewritten under the authority of Minister of Education Mohamed Charfi (2009). The class of "religious and civic education" was divided into two separate classes: "religious education" and "civic education." The former was revamped to teach the basics of the tradition, as well as to transmit a modernist interpretation of the religious texts, presented in short excerpts. The latter insisted on the rationalist interpretation of reformist Islam in combination with texts from the European Enlightenment, in particular from the French tradition, transmitting the values of freedom and democracy. These new textbooks contrasted with previous teachings, which were more morally and politically conservative in tone and content. Because they inculcated human rights and democratic values, they were also strongly at odds with the increasing authoritarianism of the regime.

This textbook reform originated from the conviction on the part of the Ben Ali regime that Islamist ideologies posed a threat to the Tunisian state and society. The regime was particularly concerned that graduates of the Zaytuna, who had been teaching religious and civic education in secondary schools, and were allegedly immersed in Islamist ideologies, had thereby helped expand the reach of the Islamist movement in the younger generation (Zeghal 2009). It was on this basis that the Ministry of Education undertook to reduce the number of graduates from the Zaytuna after 1989, and to prevent them from teaching civic education, relegating them to teaching "religious education" only. This reform illustrates the power/knowledge nexus that is at play in any reform of educational institutions, showing how the state elites' understanding of political dangers can lead them to reform education in form and content. However, it is difficult to evaluate its effects on the evolution of Islamist movements in Tunisia.

It can be argued, nonetheless, that the striking contrast between the content of the new textbooks and the political reality of Tunisia in the last two decades of the twentieth century might shed significant light upon the revolutionary events of winter 2010–11 and the end of Ben Ali's authoritarian regime. The youth who were at the forefront of the uprisings were the very products of the educative reforms started by Ben Ali's regime in 1989, which disseminated ideals of democracy and human rights. During fieldwork in the summer of 2011 in Tunis, I had a conversation with a civic education teacher in a secondary school in the suburbs of Tunis that illuminated the contrast between the textbooks and the political reality of authoritarianism. I asked her if and how she was able to teach the democratic values inscribed in the civic education textbooks to her students in the authoritarian context before the revolution. She answered:

In schools, the politics of oppression (*qam'*) was rampant, even at the kindergarten level. Teachers would let the students speak about the texts, those texts about human rights, democracy, pluralism, etc., but would remain silent on them. The students would ask questions, but I would not respond. I knew there were also spies among the students. They would say, "The teacher is afraid. My father is silent. My grandfather is silent." This oppression has transformed bodies and minds into deprived bodies and minds (*maḥrūma*). Hence, the revolution was a revolution of bodies, not of reasons. And this is different from the revolution for our independence [the 1956 independence of Tunisia].

Her gripping analysis of the revolution and of her relationship with her young students reveals the tensions between a curriculum that expounded democratic values, and the political reality of authoritarianism. In this context, the desire for political change could not find a channel to express itself other than in the street. It expressed itself through street demonstrations that demanded the fall of the government, without articulating a new and clear political project. While the textbook reform had been praised for its "modern" contents (Béji 1997), it only had an effect "by default"—that is, by demonstrating the absence in everyday life of the principles these textbooks articulated.

The domestication of Islam and the quest for autonomy

Gregory Starrett has shown how religious education in Egyptian public schools "functionalized Islam," and how state reformers made education a channel for policies of social integration through Western sociological ideologies of progress. Islam was hence transformed from a set of practices to a set of values that promoted good citizenship and discipline (Starrett 1998). As in Tunisia, religious education was harnessed by the Egyptian state as a channel for moral indoctrination in its fight against political Islam. Contrary to the Tunisian case, the Egyptian state's strategy actually reinforced the Islamic "trend" in a context where printed and new media also deployed more content devoted to Islam in the last quarter of the twentieth century. Within the secular structure of public education, Islam gained a new objectified form that made it an attainable object that could be implemented in different domains. It was particularly legible as a political resource, as articulated by the slogan "Islam is the solution" (*al-islām huwwa al-ḥall*). This might be why the Egyptian state introduced a civic and moral program in the public school curriculum in 2001–2, separating religious from civic education as had been done in Tunisia in order to make Islam less "comprehensive" (Leirvik 2004: 233).

In contrast with the tight regulation and control of madrasa education in the Arab Sunni Muslim states, madrasa education in Pakistan, as well as in Iran and Iraq, has retained an important degree of independence from the state (Zaman 2002). For instance, in twentieth-century Iran, as in many countries of the Arab Middle East, the state extended control of the religious endowments, and the Iranian mullahs lost their administrative power over these sources of income even if they continued to finance the ḥawzas. More importantly and specific to many Shi'i madrasas, self-tithing financed the institutions of religious education, which ensured a certain level of independence in curricular choices. This contrasts greatly with the domestication of Sunni institutions of knowledge in the Arab world such as al-Azhar or the Zaytuna. As a consequence, Roy Mottahedeh remarked: "In their own view the mullahs of Iran have kept a great tradition of learning alive in its pure form; in the view of their Iranian critics they have kept their curriculum hermetically sealed against the modern world" (Mottahedeh 1985: 236). However, even in this case, this "hermetic sealing against the modern world" impinged on madrasa education, making it a more marked category, socially and politically, leading to the professionalization of religious specialists as well as to their politicization, as shown by the role of Khomeini in the Iranian revolution of 1979 (Mottahedeh 1985: 237).

The Islamic Republic reinforced the role of Islamic education at all levels of the schooling system, but was not able to enforce control on the great seminary of Qom. However, this control was easier to impose on seminaries such as Jāmi'at al-Zahra in Qom, a female ḥawza established in 1985 by the Iranian government. Like all other madrasas, the ḥawzas are dependent on the historical contingencies of politics. After the Iranian revolution, the Iranian ḥawzas of Qom gained more influence and religious authority, while Najaf in Iraq declined due to the repressive policy of Saddam Hussein. After the American invasion of 2003, the ḥawzas in Najaf regained more intellectual influence. Intellectual debates in the Shi'i ḥawzas have been particularly vigorous and creative in the early twenty-first century, in particular in Qom with the engagement of some of its religious authorities with the question of religion and politics, in opposition to Khomeini's doctrine of the vilayat al-faqih (guardianship of the jurist).

New religious authorities and the expansion of Islamic knowledge

The tensions between secular and religious education do not only express themselves at the level of state-sponsored national educational reforms. They can also be found at more diffuse levels, as with the attempts that have been made since the 1970s to reverse the encroachment of secular knowledge on Islamic knowledge and to remove the dichotomy between these two domains by making all modern academic disciplines "Islamic." Proponents of the Islamization of knowledge do not form a unified organization but rather operate in different countries of the Muslim world as well as in Europe and North America, either through universities or NGOs. A first conference to sustain the project was organized in Mecca in 1977, followed by other conferences around the Muslim world, and a book series called the "Islamic Education Series."

However, these efforts did not form a coherent and unified project, even if they sustained several individual careers (Abaza 2002). On the other hand, the proliferation of writings on Islam that inundated the book market in the last part of the twentieth century seems to have provided a diversified new supply of religious literature beyond formal curricula. This phenomenon is naturally related to the expansion of literacy and of mass education and to the growing access of Muslim populations to the written word. The old "yellow literature" (*al-kutub al-ṣafrā'*) that used to circulate among narrow networks of scholars gave way to mass-produced books about Islam, from the "pavement literature" (Gonzales-Quijano 1998) to more formal bookstores. The proliferation of booklets on devotional literature, the easy access to the Koran, as well as to all things "Islamic," from political pamphlets to more classical literature, has sustained the expansion of a public immersed in diverse religious narratives.

The effects of the printed religious literature have been further augmented by the development of satellite television programs since the mid-1990s, as well as by the new media, websites in particular. The development of print and new media has radically changed the world of Islamic knowledge: religious knowledge circulates more easily, it can be shared among large groups, and in particular it can easily circumvent the state-sponsored religious institutions. Thus religious knowledge can also be individually reappropriated, making it more open, freely used, and flexible. It has also become more fragmented, since religious authorities emerge in individualized forms.

Dale Eickelman has underlined that massive access to literacy has led to an "objectification" of Islam and to new forms of religious authority, that of modern Islamists in particular (Eickelman 1992b). At the same time, the fragmentation of religious authority has not led to the dilution of the social and symbolic capital that Islam has traditionally provided to intellectuals and educators (Eickelman 1985, 1992a). In particular, scholarly religious authorities use new media in ways that promote the printed word and their own networks of transmission of ideas, often intersecting with the world of politics. Shaykh Yusuf al-Qaradawi, himself an Azharite established in Qatar and an opponent of the Mubarak regime, uses the network of Al-Jazeera television, as well as his own website, to promote his ideas and books. He has built a large international audience and readership. States also promote the scholarly authorities that support state-sponsored policies and ideologies. This sponsorship, even when coming from authoritarian regimes, is not necessarily an obstacle to publicity and to the building of a large readership (as illustrated by the case of Said Ramadan al-Buti in Syria). This expanding world of self-styled religious authorities does not operate in a totally fluid and unconstrained way. Political and institutional constraints continue to shape this world, and allow only those who master them to emerge as recognized authorities. Madrasas reinforce their own transnational influences through the new media. It is therefore important to underline that religious curricula in schools are only one source of religious instruction, and perhaps not the most important, in broader contemporary national and transnational contexts. States are hence pushed not only to regulate their own school curricula but also to articulate their own conceptions of Islam with the help of individual authorities and of their own religious institutions. In other words, they are prompted to operate as religious authorities themselves, in competition with non-state authorities, and they play a role in the "systematization and explicitness of religious tradition" (Eickelman and Piscatori 1996: 39).

Islamic education's reputation after 9/11

A lot of attention has also focused on Islamic education since September 11, 2001, as pundits often relate the development of radical forms of Islamism to madrasa indoctrination, in Saudi Arabia and Pakistan in particular (Murphy 2011). In Saudi Arabia, the public education curriculum is heavily devoted to Islam as a living and embodied practice, which also reflects the interpretative bent of Wahhabism. Western and Arab media have underlined links between the narratives of the Saudi religious curriculum and the emergence of a radical interpretation of Islam. Allegations of such a link led to Saudi projects of revision of the public schools' Islam textbooks. The madrasas of Pakistan also came under scrutiny after 2001, since many of the Taliban in Afghanistan had graduated from Deobandi madrasas. However, the interpretations of Islam developed in madrasas at the end of the twentieth century and in the early twenty-first century vary enormously.

Islamist movements who aim to participate in legal politics and social work have been extremely attentive to education from their inception: for them, education in religious values will lead to the emergence of Muslim citizens and of an Islamic society. Their vision of education is therefore not only intended to provide religious instruction so that children can practice Islam properly, but also to express larger projects of social and political reform, not necessarily of a radical sort.

Islamic schools have also been developing in Muslim diasporas in the Western world, as sizable Muslim communities have settled there in the second half of the twentieth century. Where they have been authorized, they have usually started as "Sunday schools" in mosques and evolved into full-fledged schools on the model of the Catholic parish. They offer a mix of secular and religious curricula. There are also different models for Islamic higher education in the West. Some institutions attempt to recreate traditional forms of religious education based on the teachings of the traditional legal schools and the material forms of the halaqa—the Zaytuna Institute in California, for instance—often to counter forms of instruction that are assumed to sustain radical interpretations of Islam, and that do not consider the Islamic tradition in its historical and cultural depth. In some countries, where there is mounting opposition to a growing visibility of Islamic communities, the establishment of Islamic schools has become a difficult enterprise. This is the case in

France, where public authorities are reluctant to legalize and sponsor Islamic schools as they do other religious schools (Bowen 2010). As a question for future research, it will also be important to evaluate the impact of students migrating within and beyond the Muslim world to enroll in Islamic studies at the madrasas and universities themselves.

Islamic education has had an important presence in modern times: it has taken various forms and has stood in various relations to secular education. It has also become a politicized domain, since states see it both as an important stake that impinges on the formation of their citizenry and as a political resource that helps them situate their own identity as "Islamic," for instance in the way Islamic law is taught in universities or through religious and civic education in public schools. Islamic education is also a much contested domain, in which new actors, political and religious, expand their own symbolic and economic capital. Its modern forms are in tremendous debt both to the regulating power of the state and to the power of mass education, although these two phenomena are often in tension.

Summary

- The Islamic tradition gives a central role to knowledge and its dissemination. Since the eleventh century, establishments for the dissemination of knowledge developed, with the study of Islamic law and the sciences that it necessitated at their center. Different patterns of education developed, and in pre-modern times education was mainly a flexible and informal enterprise.
- In modern times education in the Muslim world has been inhabited by a tension between two types of education: the secular and the religious. Competition and mutual influences have marked the relationship between them. In particular, state-led reforms of Islamic education have brought religious knowledge into close interaction with secular projects and made "Islam" a common object of knowledge for students at all levels.
- Islamic education in modern history is marked by the impact (or the lack thereof) of the political control of the state. Two main patterns have emerged: the madrasas that have protected their autonomy from their states and those who have been domesticated by state authorities. However, more generally, in both cases, a revitalization of institutions of religious knowledge marks the end of the twentieth century and the early twenty-first century, and madrasas in the Muslim world have expanded numerically, helping absorb larger cohorts of students.
- The dissemination of secular knowledge, as well as new modes of dissemination such as the internet, are transforming the role and influence of madrasas. Migrations from and toward the Muslim world are also changing the makeup of the student population in Islamic institutions of education.

- In the end of the twentieth century, madrasas have experienced a revitalization process and some of them are witnessing important political and intellectual debates that may have an impact on politics. The recent reemergence of the madrasa as a significant institution playing political, educational and moral roles, should lead historians to explore further earlier tropes of "decline" and perhaps focus more on processes of reshaping of forms and contents of religious education rather than on tropes of decline and resurgence.

Discussion points

- In what sense is knowledge significant in the history of Islamic civilization? On what institutions was the dissemination of knowledge based?
- How did the religious systems of education transform in modern times? What problems did these changes create?
- How are states implicated in the reforms of religious education? Do religious education teachers accept state implication and control? What are the consequences of such a control?
- Under what conditions does religious education produce political radicalization?
- Does religious education favor socio-economic development?

Further reading

Doumato, E. and G. Starrett (eds) (2007) *Teaching Islam: Textbooks and Religion in the Middle East*, Boulder, CO and London: Lynne Rienner Publishers.

This book examines the content and role of religious textbooks in a diverse sample of Middle Eastern countries, including Jordan, Turkey, Syria, Saudi Arabia, and Iran.

Heffner R. and M.Q. Zaman (eds) (2007) *Schooling Islam: The Culture and Politics of Modern Muslim Education*, Princeton: Princeton University Press.

This collection of essays explores the cultural and political role of Muslim education in the Muslim world. It is particularly useful to get a sense of the latest academic debates on the subject.

References

Abaza, M. (2002) *Debates on Islam and Knowledge in Malaysia and Egypt: Shifting Worlds*, New York: Routledge Curzon.

Abu Hamid al-Ghazali, *Kitāb Fātiḥat al-'ulūm*, al-Maṭba 'a al-ḥusaynīya, Cairo, 1322 (1904 or 1905).

Béji, H. (1997) "La pédagogie des lumières, ou la réforme du système éducatif tunisien," in M. Chartouni-Dubarry, *Les Etats arabes face à la contestation islamique*, Paris: Travaux et Recherches de l'IFRI.

Berkey, J. (1992) *The Transmission of Knowledge in Medieval Cairo: A Social History of Islamic Education*, Princeton: Princeton University Press.

Bowen, J. (2010) *Can Islam be French? Pluralism and Pragmatism in a Secularist State*, Princeton: Princeton University Press.

Cardinal, M. (2005) "Islamic Legal Theory Curriculum: Are the Classics Taught Today?" *Islamic Law and Society*, 12(2): 224–72.

Charfi, M. (2009) *Mon combat pour les lumières*, Lunay, France: Zellige.

Delanoue, G. (1982) *Moralistes et politiques musulmans dans l'Egypte du 19ème siècle (1798-1882)*, Cairo: Institut Français d'Archéologie Orientale.

Eickelman, D. (1985) *Knowledge and Power in Morocco: The Education of a Twentieth Century Notable*, Princeton: Princeton University Press.

—— (1992a) "The Art of Memory: Islamic Education and its Social Reproduction," in J.R.I. Cole (ed.) *Comparing Muslim Societies: Knowledge and the State in a World Civilization*, Ann Arbor: University of Michigan Press.

—— (1992b) "Mass Higher Education and the Religious Imagination in Contemporary Arab Societies," *American Ethnologist*, 19(4): 643–55.

—— (2007) "Madrasas in Morocco: Their Vanishing Public Role," in R. W. Hefner (ed.) *Schooling Islam: The Culture and Politics of Modern Muslim Education*, Princeton: Princeton University Press, 131–48.

Eickelman, D. and J. Piscatori (1996) *Muslim Politics*, Princeton: Princeton University Press.

Gonzales-Quijano, Y. (1998) *Les gens du livre: Edition et champ intellectuel dans l'Egypte contemporaine*, Paris: CNRS Editions.

Hourani, A. (1962) *Arabic Thought in the Liberal Age: 1798-1939*, New York: Oxford University Press.

Kadi, W. (2006) "Education in Islam: Myths and Truths," *Comparative Education Review*, 50(3): 311–24.

Keddie, N. (ed.) (1972) *Scholars, Saints, and Sufis: Muslim Religious Institutions since 1500*, Berkeley: University of California Press.

Kepel, G. (1985) *The Prophet and the Pharaoh: Muslim Extremism in Egypt*, Berkeley: University of California Press.

Leirvik, O. (2004) "Religious Education, Communal Identity and National Politics in the Muslim World," *British Journal of Religious Education*, 26(3): 223–36.

Makdisi, G. (1981) *The Rise of Colleges: Institutions of Learning in Islam and the West*, Edinburgh: Edinburgh University Press.

Mervin, S. (2000) "The Clerics of Jabal 'Amil and the Reform of Religious Teaching in Najaf since the Beginning of the 20th Century," in R. Brunner and W. Ende (eds) *The Twelver Shia in Modern Times*, Boston and Koln: Brill.

Metcalf, B. (2005) *Islamic Revival in British India: Deoband, 1860-1900*, Oxford: Oxford University Press.

Mitchell, T. (1991) *Colonizing Egypt*, Berkeley: University of California Press.

Mottahedeh, R. (1985) *The Mantle of The Prophet. Religion and Politics in Iran*, New York: Simon and Schuster.

Murphy, C. (2011) "Post-Sept 11 Saudi Arabia Modernizing, Slowly," National Public Radio, www.npr.org/2011/09/07/140247658/post-sept-11-saudi-arabia-modernizing-slowly.

Rida, R. (1906-31) *Tārīkh al-ustādh al-Imām al-Shaykh Muḥammad 'Abduh*, Cairo: Matba'at al-Manār.

Rosenthal, F. (2007) *Knowledge Triumphant: The Concept of Knowledge in Medieval Islam*, Leiden and Boston: Brill.

Roy, O. (1990) "Les nouveaux intellectuels islamistes: Essai d'approche philosophique," in G. Kepel and Y. Richard (eds) *Intellectuels et militants de l'islam contemporain*, Paris: Seuil.

—— (1996) *The Failure of Political Islam*, Cambridge, MA: Harvard University Press.

Sayyid-Marsot, A.L. (1972) "The Ulama of Cairo in the Eighteenth and Nineteenth Centuries," in N. Keddie (ed.) *Scholars, Saints, and Sufis: Muslim Religious Institutions since 1500*, Berkeley: University of California Press.

Sraieb, N. (1995) *Le College Sadiki de Tunis (1875-1956): enseignement et nationalisme*, Paris: Editions du CNRS.

Starrett, G. (1998) *Putting Islam to Work: Education, Politics, and Religious Transformation in Egypt*, Berkeley: University of California Press.

Stenberg, L. (1996) *The Islamization of Science: Four Muslim Positions*, New York: Coronet.

Von Kügelgen, A. (2011) "'Abduh, Muhammad," in G. Krämer, D. Matringe, J. Nawas, and E. Rowson (eds) *The Encyclopedia of Islam*, 3rd edn, Brill Online.

Zaman, M.Q. (2002) *The Ulama in Contemporary Islam: Custodians of Change*, Princeton: Princeton University Press.

Zeghal, M. (1996) *Gardiens de l'Islam: Les oulémas d'al-Azhar dans l'Egypte contemporaine*, Paris: Presses de Sciences Po.

—— (2008) *Islamism in Morocco: Religion, Authoritarianism, and Electoral Politics*, Princeton: Markus Wiener.

—— (2009) "Public Institutions of Religious Education in Egypt and Tunisia: Contrasting the Post-colonial Reforms of al-Azhar and the Zaytuna," in U. Abi Mershed (ed.) *Trajectories of Education in the Arab World: Legacies and Challenges*, London: Routledge, 111–24.

Part II

Themes
and
trends

7 Women and gender in the Muslim world

Valentine M. Moghadam and
Namrata Mitra

Outline

- The Muslim world is too vast and differentiated for there to exist a homogeneous "Muslim woman." Muslim women are situated in diverse socio-political, economic, and cultural contexts.
- Women and gender constitute an integral part of the Muslim world's histories and movements, including modernity, nationalism, fundamentalism, legal reforms, and political change.
- The study of Islamic texts is not irrelevant to an understanding of the legal status of women in the Muslim world, and Muslim family law does exert influence on women's roles. Conservative Muslim family laws are increasingly challenged by new social forces, notably women's rights groups.

Since the 1980s, the issue of women and gender in the Muslim world has been tied to Islam's cultural and political reassertion, and particularly, the emergence of fundamentalist or politicized Islamist movements.[1] Critics and advocates of Islam hold sharply divergent views on this matter. Those identifying most with Islamic law are convinced that Islam provides all the necessary rights for humankind and womankind, and that Islamic states—such as the Islamic Republic of Iran—go the farthest in establishing those rights. Secular feminists have tended to describe adherence to Islamic norms and laws as the main impediment to women's advancement (e.g., the 1980s–1990s writings of Juliette Minces, Haleh Afshar, Mai Ghoussoub, and Haideh Moghissi). In contrast, Freda Hussein (1984) stressed "complementarity of the sexes" in Islam, distinguishing "authentic Islam" from "pseudo-Islam" and asserting that the former is emancipatory. She and other Muslim feminists—Asma Barlas (2002), Riffat Hassan, Azizah al-Hibri, and Amina Wadud, among others—emphasize the egalitarian and emancipatory content of the Qur'an, which they maintain has been hijacked by patriarchal interpretations since the early middle ages (see Badran 2009).

This emphasis on the status of women *in Islam* does little to satisfy a social science inquiry because Islam is experienced, practiced, and interpreted differently over time and space. As the Tunisian sociologist Abdelwahab Bouhdiba (1985) has shown, Islam is fundamentally "plastic" and there are varieties of Islam. One survey of attitudes toward religion and society in Egypt, Kazakhstan, Indonesia, and Pakistan showed significant variations in religiosity, ranging from extremely orthodox in Pakistan to syncretic and flexible in Indonesia, and to non-religiosity in most of Kazakhstan (Hassan 2002). Tunisia has long produced female lawyers, judges, parliamentarians, government officials, and political activists. In Senegal, the majority of women are not veiled and dress in the traditional African fashion. Malaysian women fully participate in their country's economic development and are employed in the export-manufacturing sector in large numbers. By contrast, Saudi women lack all these advantages. In short, whether the content of the Qur'an is inherently conservative and hostile toward women or egalitarian and emancipatory, although not irrelevant to a social science inquiry, is less central or problematical than is often assumed. Therefore, in order to understand Islam's social implications for the status of women, it is necessary to look at the broader sociopolitical and economic order within which these are realized.

The modern world of Islam has seen economic and social development, diverse political regimes, and a variety of social movements, including Islamist and women's rights movements. Given the geographic vastness of the Muslim world, its diversity, and rich histories, this essay can only touch on a number of salient issues, with a temporal focus on the twentieth and twenty-first centuries. We begin by locating the Muslim world in global terms and in a conceptual framework. We then turn our attention to "identity politics," with a focus on how women have figured symbolically, as well as physically, within nationalism, fundamentalism, and Muslim family law. We end with empirical presentations of women's political and economic participation across the Muslim world, and of women's campaigns for equality and change.

The analytical point of departure is that the Muslim world is located in a hierarchical world-system of states, economies, and cultures (Chase-Dunn 1998). Countries share common features (e.g., bureaucratic institutions and procedures, economic strategies, cultural values and norms inscribed in the international treaties that they have signed), but countries also have distinctive histories, resource endowments, and practices. The world-system and "world culture" (Boli and Thomas 1997) exert some influence over gender relations, but women's status is also shaped by the histories and institutions of particular nation-states. While social and gender inequalities are products of national and global processes alike, there are pressures at both domestic and global levels to improve gender relations and the status of women.

The Muslim world includes countries with different histories, political cultures, levels of development, and wealth. In modern times, many Muslim countries were subjected to Western colonialism, which often distorted their institutions and social structures and left bitter memories. Countries that escaped colonial rule include Afghanistan, Iran, and Turkey. In fact, Turkey was itself a colonial power, with the Ottoman Empire extending its rule across the Arab world and into Eastern Europe until the empire's collapse after the First World War. Before British colonial rule, the Mughal dynasty dominated the Indian subcontinent, and was one of three powerful Muslim empires (along with the Ottomans and Iran's Safavid dynasty). Western colonialism extended over Muslim-majority countries in Africa and Asia until the great independence movements of the mid-twentieth century. Thereafter, postcolonial countries found themselves with very different resources. The changing nature of international relations and the emergence of the Cold War saw Muslim-majority countries positioned differently; some allied themselves with the capitalist West (e.g., Iran, Lebanon, Pakistan, Senegal), others with the socialist bloc (e.g., Egypt, Syria, Iraq), and yet others helped form the Non-Aligned Movement (notably, Sukarno's Indonesia). The Soviet

Union included a number of Muslim-majority republics such as Azerbaijan, Tajikistan, and Uzbekistan. Development strategies and internal politics differed significantly across the Muslim world, with implications for women's participation and rights.

In addition to the study of the structural forces and factors that shape women's status, a body of feminist scholarship has analyzed the gendered nature of various movements—notably nationalist and fundamentalist movements—and their impact on women's legal status and social position (Jayawardena 1986; Chatterjee 1993; Yuval-Davis 1997). Key studies on the Muslim world (Badran 1995; Bodman and Tohidi 1998; Kandiyoti 1991; Joseph 2000; Moghadam 1993, 1995, 2013) have contributed to theory-building by elucidating the centrality of gender and "the woman question" in constructions of national, cultural, and religious identity. Women have been socially constructed as symbols of the nation-state, bearers of cultural identity, and repositories of religious values. More recently, the democracy movements in Iran in 2009 and Tunisia and Egypt in 2011 have shown that women can be major participants in such movements. As we shall see, however, the gender dynamics of political movements are not necessarily in favor of women's equality.

Nationalism and women

Nationalist movements have had positive and negative features. They may be expansive and inclusive or narrow and exclusionary. Nationalism may be imbued with concepts of inclusion and equality, modernity and progress, in which case it is often compatible with women's participation, advancement, and rights. Or it may be infused with cultural defensiveness and nostalgia for a bygone era or invented golden age, placing on women the burden of reproducing cultural values and traditions through prescribed dress and comportment. In some cases, nationalist movements grow violent and extremist, targeting the women of the opposing collectivity while also imposing ever tougher restrictions on their own women.

Jayawardena (1986) shows that for some Asian independence and liberation movements in the early twentieth century, women's emancipation was an explicit objective, inasmuch as it was a necessary component of the national goal of emancipation from feudalism, illiteracy, and backwardness. Women's activism in the anti-colonial movements was generally welcomed, and resulted in their inclusion in postcolonial state-building projects, the adoption and implementation of favorable legal frameworks and social policies, and state-sponsored education for women and girls. In Turkey, Egypt, and Iran, progress and modernity were equated with women's emancipation; and in the brief account of Afghanistan, Jayawardena notes the failed attempt at women's emancipation and modernization on the part of King Amanullah.

The movement for Indian nationalism was more complicated. Writers on colonial nationalism in undivided British India show how the idea of the new nation relied on specific constructions of Hindu or Muslim womanhood as "pure," embodiments of tradition, and repositories of communal honor (Didur 2006; Ray 2000; Mani 1990; Chatterjee 1993; Chakravarti 1990). Subsequently, "womanhood" became the site where competing nationalistic battles were enacted (Das 2006). But while Indian women's domesticity was elevated by many nationalists to a marker of cultural authenticity, some elite Bengali women, Muslim and Hindu alike, took exception to this image of the "ideal woman" and advocated for education and an end to *purdah*, or women's seclusion (Ray 2002). Rokeya Sakhawat Hossain, for example, stressed the importance of education of girls and women. Masuda Begum, a powerful voice in early twentieth-century Bengal, opposed male domination and called for better treatment of women. Kharunnessa Khatun, headmistress of a girl's school in North Bengal, wrote the following:

> It is not within our means to overcome the restrictions (placed on us by Islam), and it is illicit. We do not have unrestricted right to travel to other villages like Hindu women do. ... The first and main obstacle to the spread of education among Muslim women is that of appropriate schools which have to be established in each town and each village if necessary. ... The future of our society depends on girls, therefore we should educate them now.
>
> *(in Sarkar 2008: 113)*

Liberal nationalism in Egypt, Iran, Turkey, and Syria favored national integration via social and educational reforms, the promotion of a national language, and the establishment of a modern nation-state (Moaddel 2005). Yet feminist scholars of Middle Eastern social history have noted tensions between the goals of women's rights and of national liberation. In Lebanon, Syria, and Palestine, literary and philanthropic "ladies' societies" developed a political character as their activities increasingly served the nationalist struggle (Fleischman 1999). But at the first and second Eastern Women's Congresses (1930 in Damascus, 1932 in Tehran), the hostility of conservative male leaders to women's demands—e.g., for political rights and for equality within the family—forced the women leaders to retreat into the more acceptable minimalist demand for access to education. While nationalist leader Kemal Ataturk granted Turkish women the right to vote in 1930, this did not occur in Egypt, Iran, or Syria until much later. Even so, women's rights leaders remained loyal to the nationalist cause. In October 1938 in Cairo, Huda Shaarawi and the Egyptian Feminist Union sponsored the Eastern Women's Conference for the Defense of Palestine (Weber 2008).

In the wave of decolonization that took place in the mid-twentieth century, nationalism and socialism were embraced as paths to modernity and progress; for their part, women's rights leaders welcomed the nationalist cause as the pathway to their own liberation. In most postcolonial countries, political rights, including voting rights, were granted to women as well as to men.[2] As the newly independent states expanded, opportunities for women's participation were available in the sectors of education and health, and in public administration. Although most women remained in rural areas, working on family farms, some urban women were able to find work in the growing industrial sector. These were the heady days of Third World nationalism and modernization, which encompassed the Muslim world as well.

But nationalism has had a very destructive side as well. Partition of the Indian subcontinent into India and Pakistan—based on competing narratives of Hindu and Muslim nationalism—resulted in horrific violence on both sides, including mass rape and sexual violence against Muslim, Hindu, and Sikh women in regions where they constituted the minority communities. According to ethnographic research conducted with surviving families 50 years later, Hindu and Muslim families alike tried to preempt the possibility of dishonor and shame by encouraging female kin to end their lives (Menon and Bhasin 1998: 50–54). Other cases exist of ethnic or national rivalries in the Muslim world, with tragic results for women's human rights. The East Pakistan independence movement, which resulted in the creation of Bangladesh, entailed the mass rapes of Bengali women by Pakistani soldiers, as well as civilian men, in 1971 (Sobhan 1994). The 1980–88 war between Iran and Iraq—based in part on competing narratives of secular Arab nationalism (Baathist Iraq) and revolutionary Shiism (the Islamic Republic of Iran)—did not entail mass violations of women, but did reinforce hypermasculinity and the "protection," or control, of women in both countries. In the 1990s, the Serbian-Bosnian war saw the systematic rape of Bosnian Muslim women; during East Timor's independence struggle, numerous women were raped by Indonesian soldiers; and the Indonesian uprising against longtime President Suharto saw sexual assaults against Chinese women, who were regarded as part of an ethnic minority that had unfairly benefited from Suharto's rule (Primariantari 1999).

The violence of India's partition, as well as the gendered constructs of national identity, has been re-enacted in the ongoing nationalist contestation over Kashmir by India and Pakistan. Studies on women's lives in contemporary Kashmir show how nationalist resistance has been heightened due to the sexual assaults, displacements, and loss of life suffered by Kashmiri women, primarily at the hands of Indian security forces. Nyla Khan shows how supporters of different nationalisms in contemporary Kashmir have constructed Kashmiri womanhood as the "pure" repositories of Kashmiri tradition:

> [E]thno-nationalists assert that a native woman of Indian-administered J&K who marries a non-Kashmiri, non-Dogra, or non-Ladakhi loses her legal right to inherit, own, or buy immoveable property in the state. To them, by inhabiting the metaphoric inner domain, the native woman of J&K embodies the virginal purity of their culture and ethnicity, and these would get tainted by her stepping over the cultural threshold.
>
> *(Khan 2010: 127)*

Kashmiri women also have joined resistance movements, such as Dukhtaran-e-Millat (Daughters of the Nation). This organization identifies itself as an Islamic fundamentalist women's group and is a vocal and militant supporter of Kashmir being integrated within Pakistan. Swati Parashar (2009) comments on Dukhtaran-e-Millat's methods of enforcing codes of conduct and dress for women, which they claim are prescribed by Islam, such as banning beauty parlors, cinema halls, and wine shops, and carrying out attacks in cafés and restaurants that allow women to meet unrelated men. The Kashmir valley, which traditionally hosted a flourishing liberal-Sufi Islamic tradition, has seen backlashes in recent years by groups that police women's dress codes to the extent that "women have been sprayed with color paint or with acid or even shot in the legs for wearing Western dresses" (Parashar 2009: 248). Such forms of control over women, and violence against them, have been evident elsewhere, in similar conditions of a politicized and militant Islamist movement: Iran in the 1980s, Afghanistan and Algeria in the 1990s, and Somalia and northern Nigeria more recently.

Figure 7.1 After a lecture on the Quran from Asiya Andrabi (seen wearing white gloves), members of Dukhtaran-e-Millat leave their meeting in an illegal madrassa in Srinagar, Kashmir (2007). Courtesy of Veronique de Viguerie/Getty Images.

Women, Islamist movements, and family law

Until well into the 1980s, the Muslim world was arguably more diversified than it is today. The weakening and eventual break-up of the Soviet bloc coincided with the rise of religio-political movements and the emergence of a neoliberal global economy. Here we focus on the rise of Islamic fundamentalism and political Islam, which has had significant effects on Muslim women, who themselves have taken positions for or against these movements. In the 1980s and 1990s, Islamism spread across countries such as Afghanistan, Egypt, Sudan, Bangladesh, Pakistan, and Chechnya. In the early part of the new century, and in the context of a democratic transition following the overthrow of Suharto, Indonesia saw the growth of Islamism, with Aceh province instituting Sharia law (Rinaldo 2008, 2011). There have been important differences among Islamist movements; some have sought state power or have used violence while others have been satisfied to influence public policies or take part in governance non-violently. In most cases, however, Islamist movements have been preoccupied with cultural identity and authenticity, with implications for women's autonomy and rights. As discussed in the section on nationalism, women's crucial role in the socialization of the next generation makes them symbols of cultural values and traditions, and thus they are expected to behave and dress in prescribed ways. Some Muslim women regard this role as an exalted one, and they gladly assume it, becoming active participants, although rarely ideologues, in Islamist movements (see Afary 2001; Salime 2011). Other women find it an onerous burden; they resent restrictions on their individuality, mobility, and personal freedoms. Such non-conformist women may rebel in various ways; they may discreetly pursue alternative lifestyles; they may leave the country and settle elsewhere; they may join or form women's rights organizations. Yet other Muslim women have challenged political Islam through the intellectual and theological project known as "Islamic feminism" (Mirza 2006; Badran 2009).

The influence of fundamentalist movements and political Islam has generated polemics surrounding *hijab* (modest Islamic dress for women) in every country, and (re)veiling has spread since the 1980s. Fatima Mernissi (1987: iv) remarked that "if fundamentalists are calling for the return of the veil, it must be because women have been taking off the veil." In the new century, Indonesian women began to don the *jilbab* (headscarf covering hair, neck and shoulders), leading to discussions within women's rights groups about its meaning (Rinaldo 2008, 2011). Feminist scholars have tackled the conundrum in different ways. Some emphasize the personal choice and enhanced opportunities for mobility that veiling represents, especially for the women of the lower middle class and conservative families. Others stress its link to the appeal of fundamentalism and religious identity among women. Yet others point out that veiling is compulsory in some countries (notably Saudi Arabia and the Islamic Republic of Iran) and that elsewhere one observes social pressures on women to veil and thus achieve "respectability" or "authenticity." Such social pressures sometimes take the form of harassment and intimidation by self-styled male enforcers of correct religious behavior and public morality (Bennoune 1995; Moghadam 2003). Polemics on veiling have spread to Europe, with its growing population of Muslim immigrants from Africa and Asia. All in all, veiling can be regarded as an identity marker (of piety, of tradition, or of a distinct cultural or religious group), or it can be regarded as affiliation with the values and goals of political Islam.

Another outgrowth of fundamentalist movements and political Islam has been the contention around Muslim family law (MFL). Following Islamization in Iran after the 1979 revolution, MFL began to be strengthened or introduced across the Muslim world. Holdouts in the 1980s were the Democratic Republic of Afghanistan and the Central Asian republics of the Soviet Union, but that changed with the collapse of the communist bloc.

Despite differences in its application across the Muslim world, some common patterns of MFL may be identified (An-Naim 2002). Predicated on the principle of patrilineality, it confers privileges and authority to male kin. The highly formal Islamic marriage contract does require the consent of the wife, and in some countries women may insert stipulations into the contract, such as the condition that she be permitted to divorce should the husband take a second wife. Marriage, however, remains largely an agreement between two families rather than two individuals with equal rights and obligations. Moreover, marriage gives the husband the right of access to his wife's body, and marital rape is not recognized. Men may marry up to four wives simultaneously, and only men can divorce unilaterally and without cause. Children acquire citizenship and religious status through their fathers, not their mothers. Fathers or others in the male line are the guardians of children. Muslim women may not marry non-Muslim men.

Muslim family law also renders women as economic minors and denies them autonomy as economic agents. For example, although Islamic law gives women the right to own and dispose of property, they inherit less property than men do; brothers inherit more than sisters do, and a deceased man's brothers or uncles have a greater claim on his property than does his widow. The groom offers a *mahr* (dower) to the prospective bride and must provide for her; in turn, he expects obedience and child-bearing. There is no concept of shared matrimonial property and in the case of divorce the husband is liable only for the promised *mahr*. (What this means in practice is that unless a divorced woman has her own job and assets, or a rich family she can return to, she can become destitute.) Because male kin "maintain" women kin as well as children, the concept of male guardianship has evolved to mean that women are required to obtain the permission of father, husband, or other male guardian to undertake travel, including business travel, or to start a business. Although wives—at least those who are educated and politically aware—may stipulate in their marriage contracts the condition that they be allowed to work, many wives make no such stipulations, and courts have been known to side with the husband when the issue is contested (Sonbol 2003: 89–99). In some countries, certain occupations and professions, notably judges, are off-limits to women.

Strict application of Muslim family law has at least three disadvantages. First, it renders women second-class citizens and minors, dependent on male kin. Second, it could serve to deny women's political agency, thereby preventing their contributions to the country's political development. Third, inasmuch as women are "locked into" a patriarchal family unit, without the ability to contribute to economic development, MFL becomes economically and socially costly. Arguably these social effects are most striking in the Islamic "heartland"—the Middle East and North Africa, where the oil economy has similar effects (Karshenas and Moghadam 2001). It is here, too, where women's participation in formal politics is lowest, compared to other regions.

Unsurprisingly, many women across the Muslim world object to their legal status under MFL and have formed women's rights groups—within nation-states as well as transnationally—to counter it. In 1984, a group of women from Algeria, Pakistan, Bangladesh, Nigeria, Iran, and other countries where fundamentalist movements were growing and Sharia-based family laws were expanding formed Women Living Under Muslim Laws (WLUML). At around the same time, a legal case in India was revealing both the complexities of judicial action and the dilemmas faced by feminists in favor of a uniform civil code, especially in a context of communal contention: *Shah Bano vs. Ahmed Khan* (see Engineer 1985).

According to the Indian constitution, "secularism" means that the government recognizes that different communities are governed by different personal/family laws, and that it enables the law courts to practice different "personal laws" pertaining to different communities, should they wish it. (Muslims, in India, have the option of either marrying in a civil ceremony in court, or marrying in a religious ceremony and complying with the requirements of the Muslim Personal Law or MPL.) This practice was formally introduced in colonial India in 1937 by the British, who decided that it would be best if each community could be governed by its "own laws." After the violence of partition, the Indian government was reluctant to make changes to the laws of an already threatened minority community. While Hindu marriage laws were overhauled in the 1950s, the MPL was left untouched (Vatuk 2009: 353–54). This was so despite a directive principle in the constitution of India (Article 44), which declared that "[t]he State shall endeavour to secure for the citizens a uniform civil code throughout the territory of India."

Between 1978 and 1985, 60-year-old Shah Bano was caught up in a legal battle to receive compensation from her ex-husband, Ahmed Khan. She appealed at the level of the Supreme Court and won in 1985, but as Madhu Kishwar (1998), editor of the Indian feminist journal *Manushi*, pointed out, the Supreme Court judgment singled out Muslim men as whimsical, faithless, and backward, while implying that other faiths were somehow more progressive and egalitarian. As a result, Muslim women found themselves seemingly faced with two choices: either they could support a "progressive, anti-Muslim, pro-women's rights position" or they could support the "regressive, fundamentalist Muslim position." In the public furor that followed, and with the outbreaks of communal riots, Shah Bano rejected the Supreme Court judgment that she had won after her seven-year legal battle (Pathak and Sundar Rajan 1992).

In turn, the parliament passed the Muslim Women (Protection of Rights on Divorce) Act (1986). Here, a Muslim wife, once divorced, is required to be given a "reasonable and fair" amount of support by her husband to be made payable during the period of *iddat* (or iddah: the waiting period of usually three months before a divorced woman may remarry). If she needs any further support then the responsibility falls upon her children, and in case they are unable to support her or if she does not have children it is up to the local *wakf* (Islamic charitable) board to extend monetary support. The ironic legacy of the Shah Bano case is that the possibility of a divorced woman's appeal for state intervention has now become remote. In a context of growing Hindu communalism, Muslim fundamentalism, and state neoliberalism, feminist support for a Uniform Civil Code (UCC) in India faces the challenge of determining how the UCC will be formulated and implemented. Feminists in India are wary of handing over the formulation of a UCC to either the communities or the state (Sundar Rajan 2003: 116).

Elsewhere in the Muslim world, feminist strategies involve mobilizing grassroots and elite support for family law reform, drawing on either an "Islamic feminist" discourse (for example, the campaign for women's right to divorce in Egypt, which was won in 2000) or the UN-supported global women's rights agenda (adopted by feminists of the One Million Signatures Campaign, in Iran since 2006). In some cases both discourses are deployed, as in the Moroccan campaign for family law reform, which was won in 2003/4; in the ongoing Malaysian campaign led by Sisters in Islam; and in the activities of Indonesia's Solidaritas Perempuan. At the time of writing (2012), family law remains most conservative in Saudi Arabia, the Islamic Republic of Iran, Egypt, Jordan, Pakistan, Bangladesh, and Malaysia. It is most egalitarian in Kazakhstan and Tunisia, followed by Turkey and Morocco. The legal status of Algerian women improved with amendments to the Algerian family law in 2005. Family law reform has resulted from a variety of factors, including the influence of the UN-sponsored global women's rights agenda, feminist campaigns in the specific countries, and government action.

Campaigns around family law reform are but one example of Muslim women's advocacy and activism. The final sections provide more examples.

Patterns of women's social participation

Some scholars have argued that Muslim societies are the most resistant to gender equality, which has slowed their progress. David and Richard Landes (2001) attributed the Muslim world's lagging behind the West to the "slow evolution of Islamic societies' treatment of women." Ronald Inglehart and Pippa Norris (2003) believe that the cultural fault line dividing the West and the Islamic world relates to gender relations, the position of women, and attitudes toward sexuality. They maintain that on issues of gender and sexuality, "Muslim nations have remained the most traditional societies in the world." And yet, the Muslim world is hardly homogeneous, and what is more, considerable change has come about.

In the 1970s, Muslim societies were characterized by higher-than-average fertility and maternal mortality rates, and high rates of population growth (Weeks 1988). This was accompanied by high rates of illiteracy among the adult female population, gender disparity in education, and low rates of female labor force participation, especially in the MENA region and in South Asia. In 1980, women's share of the total labor force was the lowest in MENA (23 percent) and highest in the communist economies of Eastern Europe and the Soviet Union including Muslim Central Asian Republics. In 1990 women's participation in administrative/managerial jobs, clerical and service jobs, sales work, and production was lowest in South Asia, West Asia/Middle East, and North Africa. By the end of the century, women's share of the labor force in MENA had increased to about 27 percent, but it was still the lowest of any region in the world, including South Asia, where the female share was 33 percent (UN 2000). In 2000, adult female illiteracy and maternal mortality were the highest in Sub-Saharan Africa, South Asia, and the MENA region. A woman's estimated lifetime chance of dying in pregnancy or childbirth was 1 in 55 in MENA and 1 in 54 in South Asia but only 1 in 157 in Latin America and the Caribbean and 1 in 283 in East Asia and the Pacific (UNDP 2002: 27, 233).

Clearly, high rates of fertility, low literacy, high maternal mortality, and limited labor force participation in Muslim countries all point to the low status of women. But, as suggested at the beginning of this essay, the Muslim world is vast and includes very poor countries such as Chad, Mali, and Yemen; very rich oil economies such as the UAE, Qatar, and Kuwait; and more socially developed countries with diversified economies such as Iran, Malaysia, Tunisia, and Turkey. Gender gaps should be seen as a function of resource endowments, level of development, state policies, and class structure. Table 7.1 provides social and gender indicators for a sample of Muslim countries, organized by geographic region. Indeed, some regional patterns may be discerned. For example, the former Soviet bloc countries of Central Asia granted women the vote earliest, and they also have the highest female shares of non-agricultural paid employment. Indonesia and Malaysia have relatively low fertility rates and high rates of female participation in paid employment. The Muslim countries of Sub-Saharan Africa tend to be poorer, with the highest fertility rates and female illiteracy (not shown in the table); but at 23 percent, the female share of parliamentary seats in Senegal exceeds that of the United States (17 percent in 2010). In Bangladesh, the average age at first marriage is still 19, but the fertility rate has dropped to 2.3 children per woman, and the country's export-manufacturing development strategy has drawn a relatively large segment of the female economically active population out of the household and into the paid labor force.

Table 7.1: Social/gender indicators, Muslim-majority countries by region (2010)

	Total population (millions)	GDP ($US, billions)	Mean age of marriage (F, years)	Fertility rate	Female share, paid labor force	Female share, parliamentary seats	Year women receive vote
Eastern Europe							
Albania	3.14	5.66	23	1.9	33	16	1920
Central Asia/ Caucasus							
Azerbaijan	8.68	18.5	23	2.1	44	11	1918
Kazakhstan	15.67	37.27	23	2.3	50	18	1924, 1993
Kyrgyzstan	5.28	1.98	22	2.5	51	26	1918
Tajikistan	6.84	1.67	21	3.4	37	20	1924
Uzbekistan	—	—	—	—	—	22	—
South Asia							
Afghanistan	—	—	—	—	—	27.5	
Bangladesh	160	73.94	19	2.3	20	19	1935, 1972
Pakistan	166.11	108	23	4	13	22	1956
Sub-Saharan Africa							
Chad	10.91	3.02	18	6.2	6	5	1958
Eritrea	—	—	—	—	—	—	—
Mali	12.71	3.74	18	5.5	35	10	1956
Nigeria	151.21	74.18	21	5.3	21	7	1958
Senegal	12.21	6.55	21	5	11	23	1945
Southeast Asia							
Indonesia	227.35	247.23	23	2.2	32	18	1945, 2003
Malaysia	27.01	139.16	25	2.6	39	10	1957

Table 7.1: continued

	Total population (millions)	GDP ($US, billions)	Mean age of marriage (F, years)	Fertility rate	Female share, paid labor force	Female share, parliamentary seats	Year women receive vote
Middle East & North Africa							
Algeria	34.37	75.28	29	2.4	13	8	1962
Bahrain	0.78	13.16	26	2.3	10	3	2002
Egypt	81.53	145.59	23	2.9	19	2	1956
Iran	71.96	151.8	24	1.8	16	3	1963
Iraq	—	—	—	—	—	28	
Jordan	5.91	14.62	25	3.1	16	6.4	1974
Kuwait	2.73	61.4	27	2.2	23	8	2005
Lebanon	4.19	24.38	27	1.9	14	3	1952
Morocco	31.61	55.16	26	2.4	21	10	1959
Turkey	73.91	376.87	23	2.1	22	9	1930
Tunisia	10.33	28.34	27	1.9	25	28	1959
Oman	2.79	27.2	25	3.1	22	0	1994, 2003
Qatar	1.28	29.27	26	2.4	13	0	2003
Saudi Arabia	24.65	252.63	25	3.3	15	0	-
Syria	20.58	27.37	25	3.3	16	12	1949, 1953
Yemen	22.92	12.86	22	5.2	6	0	1967, 1970
UAE	4.48	113.77	24	1.9	20	23	2006

Source: Compiled by V. Moghadam from World Economic Forum, *Global Gender Gap Report 2010.* Data not available for Afghanistan, Bosnia, Eritrea, Iraq, Libya, Niger, Uzbekistan.

In MENA, the average age at first marriage for women has risen; meanwhile, fertility rates have declined dramatically and hover around replacement level in Iran, Lebanon, Turkey, Tunisia, and the UAE. What is more, women's share of university enrollments has exceeded those of men in most countries of the region (data not shown; see Moghadam and Decker 2010). But the region exhibits the smallest female shares of paid employment as well as parliamentary seats, and only Tunisia does well on both counts. Women's parliamentary participation ranges from the lows of Saudi Arabia (0 percent), Egypt (2 percent) and Iran (3 percent) to the respectable figure for Tunisia (28 percent), according to 2010 figures from the Inter-Parliamentary Union and as reported by the *Global Gender Gap Report 2010* (World Economic Forum 2010). It should be noted that the world average for female parliamentary representation is 19 percent. Thus Tunisia has surpassed the world average, but other countries in MENA have a long way to go. The generally low figures for the region may be explained at least in part by the fact that political rights were granted to women relatively recently, and mostly in the 1950s and 1960s. Jordanian women won the right to vote in 1974 and Kuwaiti women in 2005. Countries that have introduced parliamentary quotas include Jordan, Morocco, and Tunisia. But in most of the region—and even in Afghanistan and Iraq, where quotas have ensured a minimum 25 percent female representation—the levers of political power are almost exclusively in the hands of men, and this correlates with a high degree of authoritarianism and the persistence of patriarchal laws and norms. It is for this reason that another set of women's rights campaigns in the Muslim world revolves around political quotas to enhance women's political participation and representation.

Conclusions: women's rights campaigns in the Muslim world

That countries in the Muslim world are traditional and unchanging remains a powerful stereotype, and there appears to be much ignorance—in popular accounts as well as in many studies of the Muslim world or the Middle East—of the presence of dynamic feminist groups dedicated to women's empowerment, and of an array of women's organizations that engage with policy issues. Tables 7.2 and 7.3 provide summary information on selected women's organizations in Muslim-majority countries, their priority issues and campaigns, and the legal and policy changes that have ensued in recent years. As noted, change has occurred as a result of the efforts of the women's rights groups, often working with partners within civil society (e.g., human rights groups, trade unions, progressive political parties), with elite allies in and around the state, or with transnational advocacy networks. Feminist networks such as WLUML or the Women's Learning Partnership for Rights, Development and Peace (which consists of partner organizations from 20 countries, primarily Muslim-majority, and a secretariat in the US) provide solidarity, information dissemination, financial assistance, technical advice, or training.

Across the Muslim world, women's rights groups are among the chief proponents of democratic development and of its correlates of civil liberties, participation, and inclusion. When Turkey's civil society was still under tight military control in the 1980s, the new feminist movement helped to usher in democratization through campaigns and demands for women's rights, participation, and autonomy (Arat 1994).

Table 7.2: Women's organizations in selected Muslim-majority countries, and priority campaigns (c. 2010)

	Issues/priorities/campaigns
Afghanistan: AIL	Health and education needs of Afghan women, children, and communities; political awareness.
Bahrain Women Association for Human Development	Equal nationality rights for women (*Claiming Equal Citizenship: The Campaign for Arab Women's Right to Nationality*).
Bangladesh Women Lawyers' Association, and Ain o Salish Kendro (ASK—Centre for Human Rights Legal Aid)	Ending violence against women; child custody after divorce; lobbying for amendments to the Nari-O-Shishu Nirjatan Daman Ain 2000 (Law to End Violence Against Women and Children 2000).
Cameroon: CEDS	Advocacy campaign against forced early marriage
Egypt: FWID	Women's legal rights; ending gender violence; implementation of CEDAW.
Egypt: ECWR	Against sexual harassment; for more female political participation.
Egypt: ADEW	Legal literacy; economic empowerment; support for female-headed households.
Indonesia: Solidaritas Perempuan	Women's rights; ending human trafficking; rights for female labor migrants.
Iran: various women activists	Million Signatures Campaign for equal rights; ending violence against women; equal nationality rights for women; adopt CEDAW.
Jordan: SIGI/J	Equal nationality rights for women; lifting of CEDAW reservations; increasing women's political participation (e.g., raising the quota, committing political parties to minimum two women candidates endorsed by women's NGOs); ending violence and "honor crimes."
Kazakhstan: SWRC	Combat human trafficking and violence; help to the "vulnerable layers of society."*
Kyrgyzstan: CAC	Women's human rights; increasing women in parliament.
Lebanon: CRTD-A	Women's rights, Claiming Equal Citizenship: The Campaign for Arab Women's Right to Nationality; women's economic empowerment.
Malaysia: WDC	Ending violence against women; Women's Candidacy Initiative to improve women's political participation.
Mauritania: AFCF	Lift CEDAW reservations; equal nationality rights for women; women's human rights; increasing women's political power; women's literacy; ending FGM.
Morocco: ADFM	Lift reservations to CEDAW; joins "Spring of Dignity" coalition of 30 associations for penal code reform (e.g. address marital rape; reform abortion ban); consolidating democracy; empowering rural women.

	Issues/priorities/campaigns
Nigeria: BAOBAB	CEDAW, violence against women; women-friendly political candidates (has registered as an election monitor in 15–16 states for 2011 elections).
Pakistan: Aurat Foundation	Violence against women; women's political participation.
Palestine: WATC	Violence against women; CEDAW; women's participation in peace and security; support for SCR 1325.
Tunisia: ATFD	For women's equality in all areas, including inheritance; democracy and rights.
Tunisia: AFTURD	Full implementation of CEDAW; support for working women.
Turkey: Foundation for Support of Women's Work	Empowering low-income women and their cooperatives; women's human rights.
Yemen: Women's Forum for Research and Training	Legal literacy on women's rights in Islam; civic education.

*Focus on single women, single mothers, widows, poor, unemployed, as well as women invalids, women in need of retraining, and youth without professional education.
Source: WLP-I website and linked websites: www.learningpartnership.org; discussions and interviews at WLP Transnational Partners Meeting, Jakarta, April 10–11, 2010; personal communications.

After the collapse of the Soviet Union, women's groups in Uzbekistan tried to help consolidate democratization and citizens' rights by warning against the revival of Islamic laws and the overweening influence of market forces, and by calling for the preservation of "the equality of political and economic rights granted to women by Soviet power" (Tokhtakhodjaeva 1995: x). During the first Intifada, thousands of Palestinian women were arrested and thousands others provided important social services and logistical support. After the peace accords of the early 1990s, the three top priorities for women's rights advocates were changing the personal status laws, fighting domestic violence, and increasing women's political participation. The movement was identified as an agent for democracy "because of the *substance* of its goals—obtaining equal rights for half of Palestinian society—and because of the *process* it is using to accomplish its objectives" (Barron 2002).

The Moroccan feminist campaign for the reform of family laws, which began in the early 1990s and succeeded in 2003, should be regarded as a key factor in the country's gradual liberalization during that decade (Moghadam and Gheytanchi 2010). A press release issued by the Association of Tunisian Women for Research on Development (AFTURD) in 2008 declared that "no development, no democracy can be built without women's true participation and the respect of fundamental liberties for all, men and women". In Iran since 2006, the growing women's movement has become a highly

Table 7.3: Legal and policy changes in selected Muslim-majority countries (2006–11)

Country/date	Policy changes
Bahrain	
2009	The Council of Ministers approved a Claiming Equal Rights Citizenship reform that would extend free exemptions for public education and healthcare services to children of Bahraini women married to foreign nationals.
2010	Shaikha Sabika Award for Bahraini Women Empowerment by the Supreme Council for Women (SWC) is awarded to motivate employers to appoint women in executive and other important posts and motivate them to be involved in national development.
2011	Houda Ezra Ebrahim Noonoo appointed the first female ambassador from Bahrain to Washington. She is also Jewish.
Egypt	
2010	The government made efforts to combat female genital mutilation (FGM). These efforts included education, outreach, and the passage and enforcement of legislation criminalizing FGM. In addition, courts issued the first two convictions on sexual assault charges.
Jordan	
2008	Jordan removed its reservation to Article 15 of CEDAW, which grants women the right to travel freely and choose their place of residence.
2008	Minister of Political Development Musa Maaytah announced study to increase women's quota in the Lower House Parliament from six women to 12 or by 20 percent.
2010	New Domestic Violence Legislation was passed in 2008 prohibiting honor killings (Article 340 of penal code). "There are now 2 shelters for women victims of violence. Since Sept. 2009 there is a court that hears such cases, and since then no one has received a sentence of less than 10 years."
Kuwait	
2010	In the 2009 elections, four liberal-leaning women were elected to Kuwait's 50-seat parliament, since obtaining the right to vote in 2005.
Kyrgyzstan	
2009	Two women's rights activists elected as deputies in local elections.
Lebanon	
2009	Lebanon's Minister of the Interior urges issue of free, unconditional five-year residency permits to children and spouses of Lebanese women.

Country/date	Policy changes
2010	Lebanon's Cabinet approved an increase in women's quota to 20 percent for municipal elections.
Mauritania	
2006	20 percent Gender Quota Law adopted by government.
Morocco	
2007	The Claiming Equal Citizenship campaign achieved a success when Morocco changed its nationality code, allowing women who are married to foreign Muslim men to pass their nationality on their children.
2008	King Mohammed VI announced he would bring the country's domestic laws into compliance with CEDAW.
2009	A three-year campaign overturned century-old laws denying equal land rights to women of the Soulaliyates ethnic community to share, transfer, and benefit from 30 million acres of communally owned land.
Nigeria	
2009	A proposed bill to ban "indecent dress" was defeated.
Pakistan	
2009	Pakistan's Penal Code 509 amended to criminalize sexual harassment in the workplace.
Syria	
2009	A decree was passed granting children of Syrian women married to non-nationals equal rights to state subsidized higher education—indirectly acknowledging the mother's status as citizen.
Saudi Arabia	
2011	King Abdullah announces that Saudi women will be given the right to vote, beginning in 2015.
Tunisia	
2011	In August, the new transition government lifts remaining reservations on CEDAW.

Sources: Khaleej Times, "Bahraini Govt Will Reward Firms Empowering Women" (via email, 2008); Joseph Mayton, "Egypt Passes Law Banning Female Circumcision", All Headline News (2008), (www.allheadlinenews.com/articles/7011210977); personal communications; remarks by participants of the Women's Learning Partnership Transnational Partners Meeting, Jakarta, April 10–11, 2010; www.hrw.org/news/2011/09/06/tunisia-government-lifts-restrictions-women-s-rights-treaty.

visible force for change, initiating campaigns for women's equality and rights and staging public protests against arbitrary arrests that have huge social and political ramifications. For this, they have experienced state repression and many members have received prison sentences, but their cyberactivism continues.[3]

In Egypt, the Egyptian Center for Women's Rights (ECWR) has monitored the social realities of women's lives (e.g. lobbying against the problem of sexual harassment of women) while also integrating itself in the larger movement for democratization (e.g., election monitoring) and human rights.[4] The mass protests in Egypt of January and February 2011 saw participation by many Egyptian women, both veiled and unveiled. While Egypt's social movement for political change and democratization was very broad-based, it included a large movement that is patriarchal and socially conservative as well as highly organized and mobilized: the Muslim Brotherhood. In recent years, the Muslim Brothers have called for "the freedom of forming political parties" and "independence of the judiciary system," which are laudable goals, but they also advocate "conformity to Islamic Sharia Law," which is not conducive to gender equality or the equality of Muslim and non-Muslim citizens in all domains (Brown et al 2006). In August 2010, the ECWR issued a statement criticizing the Muslim Brotherhood for mock presidential elections held by its Youth Forum that denied the request by the Forum's Muslim Sisters' Group to be included in the nominations to the mock presidency (Komsan 2010a). The following November, the ECWR issued another press release protesting the parliament's overwhelming vote against the appointment of women judges (Komsan 2010b). In March 2011, the ECWR decried the absence of women from the committee drafting Egypt's new constitution. In contrast, Tunisia's transitional government promised gender parity while also upholding the country's Arab-Muslim identity. Tunisia's civil society organizations include very active human rights and women's rights organizations, as well as new political parties that took part in the successful elections of October 2011 (El-Amrani and Lindsey 2011). By all accounts, Tunisia's Islamic an-Nahda party is more attentive to women's rights than is Egypt's Muslim Brotherhood, even though Tunisian secular feminists have expressed concern (Goulding 2011; Tchaicha and Arfaoui 2011). The differences in the gender dynamics of the democracy movements in Egypt and Tunisia point to a central argument in this essay: broad-brush generalizations about the Muslim world must be avoided in favor of careful empirical research.

Summary

- Generalizations about the Muslim world must be avoided in favor of careful empirical research.
- Women and gender relations have been affected by economic and political forces such as nationalism, state-building, fundamentalisms, revolutions, and the gender policies of the state.

- Across countries and throughout modern history, women have been mobilized into male-dominated movements and political projects; they have also devised various forms of self-organization, notably women's rights movements and networks. Among the various strategies for women's rights, Islamic feminism seeks to attain women's rights by reclaiming Islam from patriarchal interpretations.

Discussion points

- In what ways does the construction of a nation rely on specific constructions of gender and religious identity? How would secular feminists, Muslim feminists, and Islamist women address this construction differently?
- How have women in the Muslim world responded to Islamic fundamentalist movements? What have been some of the reasons for their opposition to or support of such movements?
- How is women's access to political rights in the Middle East, South Asia, and North Africa regulated and legitimized through cultural constructions of Muslim womanhood? Put another way, how do cultural constructions of the nation influence the political functions of the state?
- The authors urge the readers to unpick developments in the Muslim world through careful socio-political analysis and empirical research. What is at stake in pursuing such an approach?
- The authors discuss the complex and varied relationships between nationalist movements and women's social and legal status within them through the course of the twentieth century. What would be some of the reasons for the development of these different forms of nationalisms?

Further reading

Ahmed, Leila (1992) *Women and Gender in Islam: Historical Roots of a Modern Debate*, New Haven, CT: Yale University Press.

This book traces the competing discourses on Muslim womanhood since ancient pre-Islamic Middle Eastern civilization until the late twentieth century, focusing on the political and cultural self-determination of Muslim women and providing a history of the diversity of religious and secular feminists in Muslim-majority countries.

Badran, Margot (2009) *Feminism in Islam: Secular and Religious Convergences*, Oxford: Oneworld.

Badran sets up a complex dialogue between Islamic and secular feminists in Egypt since the late nineteenth century until the twenty-first century, showing that while Islamic feminist approaches draw on the Qur'anic principles to dismantle fundamentalist religious approaches towards greater gender justice, secular feminists try to avoid giving religious texts the authority to determine social and political life.

Joseph, Suad (ed.) (2000) *Gender and Citizenship in the Middle East*, Syracuse, NY: Syracuse University Press.

Offering a feminist reading of citizenship in the Middle East, this collection critically examines the legal status and social positions of women, the rights and restrictions of women under family laws, and movements for legal reform.

Kandiyoti, Deniz (ed.) (1991) *Women, State and Islam*, New York: New York University Press.

The focus of this collection and its case studies is on the role of the state in women's subordination, including the state's complicity in the spread of fundamentalist movements and in the implementation of conservative family laws.

Marty, Martin E. and R. Scott Appleby (eds) (1993) *Fundamentalisms and the State: Remaking Polities, Economies, and Militance*, Chicago: University of Chicago Press.

Volume 3 of the editors' Fundamentalisms project examines the ways in which fundamentalist movements have been successful in remaking political structures, including states, political parties, legal-juridical institutions, and regional politics.

Menon, Ritu and Kamla Bhasin (1998) *Borders and Boundaries: Women in India's Partition*, New Delhi, Delhi: Kali for Women.

Nearly 50 years after the partition of British India into the independent nation states of India and Pakistan, Menon and Bhasin set out to interview the survivors of partition violence, with a focus on the widespread sexual violence carried out against Muslim, Hindu, and Sikh women especially in regions where they constituted a religious minority.

Mernissi, Fatima (1987) *Beyond the Veil: Male-Female Dynamics in a Muslim Society*, 2nd edn, Bloomington: Indiana University Press.

With a focus on Moroccan society and culture, the author argues that women's status has been shaped by patriarchal interpretations of the holy texts, socio-political dynamics, and national histories.

Moghadam, Valentine M. (2013) *Modernizing Women: Gender and Social Change in the Middle East*, 2nd edn, Boulder, CO: Lynne Rienner Publishers.

The book offers a sociological examination of the ways in which women and gender issues have figured in historical and social change processes, and the ways in which state policies, forms of national development, and social structure affect women's status and gender roles.

References

Afary, Janet (2001) "Portraits of Two Islamist Women: Escape from Freedom or from Tradition?" *Critique*, 19 (Fall): 47–77.

AFTURD (2008) "AFTURD's Declaration: Fighting Against Attempts of Regression," Tunis: Association of Tunisian Women for Research on Development (September 26), press release.

Al-Azm, Sadik (1993) "Islamic Fundamentalism Reconsidered: A Critical Outline of Problems, Ideas and Approaches," *South Asia Bulletin: Comparative Studies of South Asia, Africa, and the Middle East*, XIII(1–2): 93–121.

Anand, Som (1987) "Why Muslims Resist a Common Civil Code," in Asghar Ali Engineer (ed.) *The Shah Bano Controversy*, Hyderabad, Andra Pradesh, India: Orient Longman Ltd, 170–72.

An-Naim, Abdullahi (2002) *Islamic Family Law in a Changing World: A Global Resource Book*, London: Zed Books.

Arat, Yesim (1994) "Toward a Democratic Society: The Women's Movement in Turkey in the 1980s," *International Women's Studies Forum*, 17: 2/3, 241–48.

Badran, Margot (1995) *Feminists, Islam, and the Nation*, Princeton, NJ: Princeton University Press.

——(2009) *Feminism in Islam: Secular and Religious Convergences*, Oxford: Oneworld.

Barlas, Asma (2002) *Believing Women in Islam: Unreading Patriarchal Interpretations of the Qur'an*, Austin: University of Texas Press.

Barron, Andrea (2002) "The Palestinian Women's Movement: Agent of Democracy in a Future State?" *Middle East Critique*, 11(1): 71–90.

Bennoune, Karima (1995) "S.O.S. Algeria: Women's Human Rights Under Siege," in Mahnaz Afkhami (ed.) *Faith and Freedom: Women's Human Rights*, Syracuse, NY: Syracuse University Press.

Bodman, Herberi L. and Nayereh Tohidi (eds) (1998) *Women in Muslim Societies, Diversity Within Unity*, Boulder, CO: Lynne Rienner Publishers.

Boli, John and George M. Thomas (1997) "World Culture in the World Polity," *American Sociological Review*, 62(2): 171–90.

Bouhdiba, Abdelwahab (1985) *Sexuality in Islam*, London: Routledge and Kegan Paul.

Brown, Nathan, Amr Hamzawy, and Marina Ottaway (2006) "Islamist Movements and the Democratic Process in the Arab World: Exploring Gray Zones," Washington, DC: Carnegie Endowment for International Peace, Paper no. 67 (March), www.carnegieendowment.org/publications/index.cfm?fa=view&id=18095&prog=zgp&proj=zdrl,zme.

Butalia, Urvashi (1998) *The Other Side of Silence: Voices from the Partition of India*, New Delhi: Penguin.

Chakravarti, Uma (1990) "Whatever Happened to the Vedic *Dasi*? Orientalism, Nationalism and a Script for the Past," in Kumkum Sangari and Sudesh Vaid (eds) *Recasting Women: Essays in Indian Colonial History*, New Brunswick, NJ: Rutgers University Press, 27–88.

Chase-Dunn, Christopher (1998) *Global Formation: Structures of the World Economy*, 2nd edn, Totowa, NJ: Rowman and Littlefield.

Chatterjee, Partha (1993) *The Nation and Its Fragments: Colonial and Postcolonial Histories*, Princeton, NJ: Princeton University Press.

Das, Veena (2006) "Language and the Body: Transactions in the Construction of Pain," in *Life and Words: Violence and the Descent into the Ordinary*, Berkeley: University of California Press, 38–59.

Didur, Jill (2006). *Unsettling Partition. Literature, Gender, Memory*, Toronto: University of Toronto Press.

El-Amrani, Issandr and Ursula Lindsey (2011) "Tunisia Moves to the Next Stage," MERIP On-Line (November 8).

Engineer, Asghar Ali (ed.) (1985) *The Shah Bano Controversy*, Hyderabad, Andra Pradesh, India: Orient Longman Ltd.

Fleischman, Ellen (1999) "The Other 'Awakening': The Emergence of Women's Movements in the Modern Middle East, 1900–1940," in Margaret Meriwether and Judith Tucker (eds) *Social History of Women and Gender in the Modern Middle East*, Boulder, CO: Westview Press.

Goulding, Kristine (2011) "Tunisia: Women's Winter of Discontent," www.opendemocracy. net/5050/kristine-goulding/tunisia-feminist-fall (accessed October 25, 2011).

Hans, Asha (2000) "Women across Borders in Kashmir: The Continuum of Violence," *Canadian Women's Studies*, 19(4): 77–87.

Hassan, Riaz (2002) *Faithlines: Muslim Conceptions of Islam and Society*, Oxford: Oxford University Press.

Hussein, Freda (1984) (ed.) *Muslim Women*, London: Croom Helm.

Inglehart, Ronald and Pippa Norris (2003) "The True Clash of Civilizations," *Foreign Policy*, March–April.

Jayawardena, Kumari (1986) *Feminism and Nationalism in the Third World*, London: Zed Books.

Joseph, Suad (ed.) (2000) *Gender and Citizenship in the Middle East*, Syracuse, NY: Syracuse University Press.

Kandiyoti, Deniz (ed.) (1991) *Women, State and Islam*, New York: New York University Press.

Karshenas, Massoud and Valentine M. Moghadam (2001) "Female Labor Force Participation and Economic Adjustment in the MENA Region," in Mine Cinar (ed.) *The Economics of Women and Work in the Middle East and North Africa*, Greenwich, CT: JAI Press, 51–74.

Kepel, Gilles (2002) *Jihad: The Trail of Political Islam*, Cambridge, MA: Harvard University Press.

Khan, Nyla (2010) *Islam, Women and Violence in Kashmir: Between India and Pakistan*, New York: Palgrave Macmillan.

Khan, Yasmin (2007) *The Great Partition: The Making of India and Pakistan*, New Delhi, Delhi: Penguin.

Kishwar, Madhu (1998) "Pro-Women or Anti-Muslim," in *Religion at the Service of Nationalism and Other Essays*, Delhi: Oxford University Press, 206–24.

Komsan, Nehad Aboul (2010a) "The Muslim Brotherhood … . Returning Egypt to an Age without Law," press release issued by the Egyptian Center for Women's Rights, Cairo (August 25), available at www.ecwronline.org.

—— (2010b) "Who Judges the Judges? A Black Day in the History of Justice in Egypt," press release issued by the Egyptian Center for Women's Rights, Cairo (November 16), available at www.ecwronline.org.

Landes, David S. and Richard A. Landes (2001) "Girl Power: Do Fundamentalists Fear Our Women?" *New Republic* (September 29).

Mani, Lata (1990) "Contentious Traditions: The Debate on *Sati* in Colonial India," in Kumkum Sangari and Sudesh Vaid (eds) *Recasting Women: Essays in Indian Colonial History*, Piscataway, NJ: Rutgers University Press, 88–127.

Menon, Ritu and Kamla Bhasin (1998) *Borders and Boundaries: Women in India's Partition*, New Delhi, Delhi: Kali for Women.

Mernissi, Fatima (1987) *Beyond the Veil: Male-Female Dynamics in a Muslim Society*, 2nd edn, Bloomington: Indiana University Press.

Mirza, Qudsia (ed.) (2006) *Islamic Feminism and the Law*, London: Routledge.

Moaddel, Mansoor (2005) *Islamic Modernism, Nationalism, and Fundamentalism: Episode and Discourse*, Chicago: University of Chicago Press.

Moghadam, Valentine M. (ed.) (1993) *Identity Politics and Women: Cultural Reassertions and Feminisms in International Perspective*, Boulder, CO: Westview Press.

—— (ed.) (1995) *Gender and National Identity: Women and Politics in Muslim Societies*, London: Zed Books.

—— (2013) *Modernizing Women: Gender and Social Change in the Middle East*, Boulder, CO: Lynne Rienner Publishers.

Moghadam, Valentine M. and Tabitha Decker (2010) "Social Change in the Middle East," in Ellen Lust (ed.) *The Middle East*, 12th edn, Washington, DC: CQ Press/Sage, 65–98.

Moghadam, Valentine M. and Elham Gheytanchi (2010) "Political Opportunities and Strategic Choices: Comparing Feminist Campaigns in Morocco and Iran," *Mobilization: An International Quarterly of Social Movement Research*, 15(3): 267–88.

Pandey, Gyanendra (2001) *Remembering Partition: Violence, Nationalism and History of India*, New York: Cambridge University Press.

Parashar, Swati (2009) "Feminist International Relations and Women Militants: Case Studies From Sri Lanka and Kashmir," *Cambridge Review of International Affairs*, 22(2): 235–56.

Pathak, Zakia and Rajeshwari Sunder Rajan (1992) "Shah Bano," in Judith Butler and Joan W. Scott (eds) *Feminists Theorize the Political*, New York: Routledge, 257–79.

Primariantari, Rudiah (1999) "Women, Violence and Gang Rape in Indonesia," *Cardozo Journal of International and Comparative Law,* 7(2): 245–76.

Ray, Bharati (2002) *Early Feminists in Colonial India: Sarala Devi Chaudhurani and Rokeya Sakhawat Hossain*, New Delhi: Oxford University Press.

Ray, Sangeeta (2000) *En-gendering India: Woman and Nation in Colonial and Postcolonial Narratives*, Raleigh, NC: Duke University Press.

Reynolds, Jonathan T. (1998) "Islam, Politics, and Women's Rights," *Comparative Studies of South Asia, Africa, and the Middle East*, XVIII(1): 64–72.

Rinaldo, Rachel (2008) "Envisioning the Nation: Women Activists, Religion and the Public Sphere in Indonesia," *Social Forces*, 86(4): 1781–804.

—— (2011) "Muslim Women, Moral Visions: Globalization and Gender Controversies in Indonesia," *Qualitative Sociology*, 34(4): 539–60.

Salime, Zakia (2011) *Between Feminism and Islam: Human Rights and Sharia Law in Morocco*, Minneapolis: University of Minnesota Press.

Sarkar, Mahua (2008) *Visible Histories, Disappearing Women: Producing Muslim Womanhood in Late Colonial Bengal*, Durham, NC: Duke University Press.

Sobhan, Salma (1994) "National Identity, Fundamentalism and Women's Movement in Bangladesh," in V.M. Moghadam (ed.) *Gender and National Identity: Women and Politics in Muslim Societies*, London: Zed Books.

Sonbol, Amira al-Azhary (2003) *Women of Jordan: Islam, Labour, and the Law.* Syracuse, NY: Syracuse University Press.

Sundar Rajan, Rajeswari (2003) "Women Between Community and State: Some Implications of the Uniform Civil Code Debates," in *The Scandal of the State: Women, Law and Citizenship in Postcolonial India*, Durham, NC: Duke University Press, 147–73.

Tchaicha, Jane D. and Khedija Arfaoui (2011) "Tunisian Women in the Twenty-First Century: Past Achievements and Present Uncertainties in the Wake of the Jasmine Revolution," *The Journal of North African Studies,* available at http://dx.doi.org/10.1080/13629387.2011.630499 (accessed November 4, 2011).

Tokhtakhodjaeva, Marfua (1995) *Between the Slogans of Communism and the Laws of Islam*, Lahore: Shirkat Gah Women's Resource Center.

UN (2000) *The World's Women 2000: Trends and Statistic*, New York: United Nations.

UNDP (2002) *Human Development Report 2002*, New York: Oxford University Press.

Vatuk, Sylvia (2009) "A Rallying Cry for Muslim Personal Law: The Shah Bano Case and Its Aftermath," in Barbara D. Metcalf (ed.) *Islam in South Asia in Practice*, Princeton, NJ: Princeton University Press, 355–67.

Weber, Charlotte (2008) "Between Nationalism and Feminism: The Eastern Women's Congresses of 1930 and 1932," *Journal of Middle East Women's Studies*, 4(1): 83–106.

Weeks, John (1988) "The Demography of Islamic Nations," *Population Bulletin*, 43(4).

World Economic Forum (2010) *Global Gender Gap Report 2010*, World Economic Forum.

Yuval-Davis, Nira (1997) *Gender and Nation*, London: Sage Publications.

Notes

1 Syrian Marxist philosopher Sadik al-Azm has identified fundamentalism, whether Christian or Islamic, as the notion of inerrancy or infallibility of holy texts. Thus: "The Koran is absolutely infallible, without error in all matters pertaining to faith and practice, as well as in areas such as geography, science, history, etc." (Al-Azm 1993: 117). Political Islam refers to the movement and ideology of a state based on Islamic law, or Sharia as codified in one or another of the schools of jurisprudence (Kepel 2002). This essay uses "Islamism" to refer to movements and ideas predicated on the expressed goal of spreading Islamic laws and norms, whether through parliamentary means or violent means.

2 Although Nigerian women received the right to vote in 1958, the major Islamic party of the Muslim Northern Region, the Northern People's Congress, opposed female suffrage, "because of our religion" (cited in Reynolds 1998: 66). In contrast, the Northern Elements Progressive Union supported suffrage and indeed greater social participation for women.

3 See the following websites: End Stoning Forever Campaign: www.meydaan.com/English/aboutcamp.aspx?cid=46; Change for Equality Campaign: www.change4equality.com/english; Feminist School: http://feministschool.net/ and http://feministschool.net/campaign/.

4 See their website: www.ecwronline.org.

#Islam, social networking and the cloud

Gary R. Bunt

Outline

- The internet represents a significant channel of knowledge for (and about) Islam and Muslims in the contemporary world, and its impact continues to increase as the 'digital divide' diminishes in many contexts.
- Diverse forms of Muslim religious understanding, expression and authority can be found online – which are not necessarily complementary to one another. These can reflect a range of cultural, political and religious influences. Cyber-Islamic environments allow like-minded individuals and organisations to network on the internet through a variety of interfaces, in a way that might not be possible in 'analogue' contexts.
- Muslim religious expression online draws upon the latest technological innovations in a competitive information marketplace, reflecting sophisticated approaches to media production and distribution.

Approaching Islam and cyberspace

Understanding technological interfaces is increasingly important in developing a comprehension of contemporary Islamic issues and their dissemination. The continual evolution of interfaces, software and hardware must be accommodated within academic interpretations. Many of these are relatively recent innovations, which have been quickly adopted by users; consider the exponential growth in Facebook, YouTube and Twitter in the 2000s, and the impact of enhanced forms of internet access through mobile devices such as smart phones and tablets.

While clearly part of the spectrum in relation to Islam and the internet, there is a tendency for the 'jihadi' online zones to obscure the dynamic and vital aspects of everyday online Islamic activities. 'Mundane' religious practices, business, shopping, chat and social networking may fall under the radar of international headlines – but in many ways are equally significant as the jihadi sites that attract so much coverage in the contemporary media. While this chapter does look at online expressions of jihad, it also explores usage of the internet by Sufi 'mystical' groups, highlighting the impact of multimedia applications on religious authority. There is also a discussion related to the impact of social networking tools on the Arab Spring of 2011, when they were applied to organize and promote diverse activist agendas in various locations throughout the Middle East.

Increased net literacy and access – with a 'digital native' generation educated and brought up using the web – has had a profound impact on Muslim individuals and communities. These dramatic technological shifts are reflected in the chapter title, where the hashtag symbol (#) is a reference to social networking media, in particular hashtag use in Twitter to highlight trends, themes, concepts and keywords under discussion. 'The cloud' refers primarily to the reduced reliance on desk-bound computers, and the shift towards mobile devices where data are stored externally to the computer device, for example, on a server.[1]

The key element is to read this chapter with the internet on, in order to gain an active understanding of issues, content and contexts. Take time to check out the links and resources under discussion. However, it may be necessary to point out to readers that there are areas within this discussion – in particular relating to jihadi activity – where a degree of awareness is required when entering jihad forums and websites; there may be a susceptibility to being monitored in some contexts, for example, by content providers and/or security organisations. Caution should be exercised in downloading or copying such content, especially if it is on devices intended for transportation internationally, or if this transgresses terms of use from service providers or governments. Some institutions may have filtering software installed, even in some cases to restrict access to innocuous terms such as 'Muslim' or 'Islam'. Online content discussed in this chapter may have disappeared from the internet between the time of writing and publication, so selected screenshots have been archived and placed on www.virtuallyislamic.com.

The term 'cyber Islamic environments' refers to a variety of contexts, perspectives and applications of the media by those who define themselves as 'Muslims'. Cyber-Islamic environments contain elements of specific worldviews and notions of exclusivity, combined with regional and cultural understandings of the internet and its validity, and have demonstrated the ability to transform aspects of religious understanding and expression within Muslim contexts. A complex spectrum of access, dialogue, networking and application of the media associated with cyber-Islamic environments has emerged. The term's original definition, which I introduced in the late 1990s as an online internet space with an Islamic religious orientation, has evolved to incorporate elements of so-called 'Web 2.0' tools, as well as alternate interfaces such as web-enabled smart phones and televisions with net access. It can incorporate online services such as blogs, social networking sites, media distribution channels and interfaces in which the internet is integrated into 'traditional' media delivery (for example, media channels using online delivery in real time and storage modes) (Bunt 2000, 2003, 2009a).

Recording, analysing and studying Islam and Muslims on the internet has necessitated the development of new methodological approaches, which have evolved as the field has matured. The internet is never static, and technological shifts have required new responses to data-gathering, synthesized with a developed awareness of key sites, activities and responses to significant issues (Bunt 2008b). One should not separate the digital from the analogue, in terms of activities; while new networks and conceptual frameworks have emerged online, they may also connect directly at grassroots level to 'real world' activities and research. Islam is 'always on' technologically (and through 'traditional' channels), increasingly so through mobile phones, with little separation for those whose online activities and levels of net literacy integrate with their everyday life. Just as there can be different levels of determining religiosity and 'Islamic' activity, depending on the beholder, so the levels of Islamic activity and usage of online materials can vary. Different models could potentially be constructed, to indicate different typologies of 'Islamic' internet use.

For some, as with other aspects of everyday life, it is perfectly natural to consult the internet for a religious opinion, Islamic information or to interact with members of a network (informal and formal). The influence of 'Sheikh Google' has challenged traditional networks of authority, and raised concerns regarding influence and impact on communities and individuals (Al Hashemi and Ghazal 2012). As a channel of information distribution, the application of social networking tools provides immediacy in terms of connecting to followers, and a sense of identity for those participating. The reduced digital divide, particularly in relation to the expansion of mobile phone networks and broadband usage, reflects in this increasing influence of cyber-Islamic environments, while recognising that significant sectors still remain untouched – at least directly – from this discourse and participation.

Islamic ideas of the sacred manifest themselves in complex and diverse ways in cyberspace, reflecting the continuum of understandings located in the 'real world'. The world wide web, social networking resources, chat-rooms, photo upload sites, wikis, podcasts, blogs, mapping tools and video sites such as YouTube are typical resources that have been applied to represent aspects of Islam and Muslim expression (Bunt 2000: 66–103). Generic tools such as Flickr, YouTube, Google Maps, Twitter and Facebook have been increasingly integrated into cyber-Islamic environments. These offer a 'sticky' multimedia experience for users, who utilize a seamless multiplicity of interfaces and devices to access and interact with content – often located in the cloud.

Muslim expression in cyberspace

Diverse sectors of Muslim belief have recognised the need to go online, to meet demands of their communities or networks. These sectors represent a spectrum of Muslim perspectives, from transglobal Islamic political networks through to small community mosques; individual social media users may have a greater voice online within Islamic spheres than 'official' sites endorsed by traditional religious authorities.[2] Through creating attractive portals and online services, and keeping updated with software innovations and developments, various shades of the Islamic spectrum sought to channel their readers and 'manage' knowledge associated with their belief perspectives. English was a dominant language for cyber-Islamic expression during the internet's formative period. This includes the era prior to the development of browsers: there was still an element of 'Islamic' traffic online, for example when tools such as File Transfer Protocol (FTP) were used to transfer files (for example, the Qur'an). Usenet message boards, email lists and groups discussed Islam-related issues.

After the release of the early browsers Mosaic in 1993 and Netscape Navigator in 1994, diverse primarily English language Islam-related content emerged online, reflecting the educational background of software developers and content providers. Other Roman-based scripts were also to become significant within online Muslim constituencies, including European languages, Malay, Somali and Turkish. The development of non-Roman script software tools, combined with a reduction in the 'digital divide', was to lead to sustained growth in online Islamic expression in Arabic, Bengali, Farsi, Urdu and other languages utilized by Muslims. The twenty-first century has seen software tools and applications developed for and utilized in diverse linguistic markets – accessed on a variety of platforms and devices. While by no means universal, the rapid expansion of internet access and a developed digital literacy has had dramatic ramifications on general communication in Muslim contexts, and specifically on how information about Islam and Muslims is transmitted.

The model of an individual computer user rooted on a desktop has mutated, as alternate interfaces enabling mobile internet communication have evolved in many forms. While it is not the intention here to measure the impact numerically, it is possible to acquire awareness through statistics of key trends and developments in relation to social networking and Islam. There are degrees of separation between *Muslim*-specific internet use, and online participation *by Muslims.* The dramatic increase in Twitter use in 2011 in the Middle East and North Africa region, intensification of relevance of Facebook and associated platforms for social activism, and the application of tools for campaigning purposes were significant indicators. The expansion of smart phone use, through more competitive availability and increased digital awareness – and the integration of apps for platforms such as Android and iPhone – has had a substantial impact on the ways in which Muslims express themselves in everyday contexts, as well as changing the ways individuals and groups mobilize rapidly through networks that have been inherently difficult for authorities to control and censor.

Attention – particularly in Muslim contexts – was focused on the potential roles of social networking tools as an agent for mobilization and change in 2009, when activists in Iran drew upon resources such as YouTube, Google Maps, Twitter and Facebook to manage and promote protests throughout the country during the so-called 'Green Revolution' – a sequence of protests following Mahmoud Ahmadinejad's presidential election. In this context, perhaps the starkest application of Web 2.0 technologies was represented by the death on 20 June 2009 of Neda Agha-Soltan, a victim of Basiji militia gunfire. Agha-Soltan's death was captured on mobile phone footage, subsequently uploaded to YouTube; links were circulated on Twitter, and broadcast on media channels worldwide. Within 24 hours, tribute montages were also online, and '#Neda' was one of the most prominently trending topics on Twitter.

What was significant in the Iranian context was a recalibration of the application of social networking resources, to focus upon political-religious issues and discourse through a synthesis of various online resources and software. The internet was part of a natural discourse for 'digital natives' – there was no need to consider 'early adopters' of technology, or indeed interpreting this for any kind of novelty value. Immediacy was one significant element within the dynamics of any discussion on the scenario being played out in Iran. The ways in which, for example, protestors contributed to mobilization and the distribution of resources – including Twitter feeds and YouTube clips – may have made up for their lack of professional journalistic refinement with their immediacy and eyewitness qualities. Whether one describes the discourse as specifically 'Islamic' or not may be open to discussion: on- or offline, religion was clearly a key subtext and defining identity element in the Iranian context. Religious language was utilized as part of the dialogue of protest (Bunt 2009b). In part as a result of this sequence of events, the Iranian government announced in 2011 it would be setting up an Iran-only internet, separate from the international internet (Press TV 2011).

Mobile phones have been utilized to report and broadcast alternative perspectives on a range of events in Muslim contexts. This reflects the exponential growth in access, coupled with reduced costs: the use of mobile phone content is an adjunct to other Islam-related material presented elsewhere on the internet. In terms of their being used for internet access, surfing for 'Islamic' content is only a small strand of much wider online habits, embracing Web 2.0 applications, social networking and multimedia.

In contemporary contexts, all of these media forms can be said to be digital in many ways, and some would say there is no separation between the internet and other media. Rather, there is an integrated media, some of which is institutionalized, official and formal; some is within the private sector; some is unofficial and individual. There are points in between, and connectivity between these spheres. At times, it becomes difficult or unnecessary to distinguish between the virtual and non-virtual, as the forms of Islamic expression blur together, and new ways of Islamic interaction develop.

Accessing religious authority online

Many elements of Muslim religious life and activities can be observed online, with varying levels of potential participation. Religious knowledge transmission is an integral element of online activity. Computer programs provide prayer direction and timing. Qur'anic recitation comprises a central element of prayer. Exponents of recitation can be heard online, presenting different styles and choices from the Qur'an. A key element in cyber-Islamic environments, central to their development, has been the dissemination of the Qur'an. According to Islamic tradition, the Arabic

Qur'an is seen as immutable and fixed in time; the digital interfaces demonstrate imaginative ways to make the divine text accessible for a variety of users. Many sites contain a searchable database to facilitate the exploration of references to a key issue, while those Muslims seeking to learn different styles of recitation of the Qur'an can practice via the net. Online translations have become a 'competitive' area, with different players seeking to present their translations, commentaries and interpretations, attempting to expound the meaning of the text. Reproducing a print version of the Qur'an online may be insufficient. A Qur'an interface has to be user friendly, to maximise the benefit for the reader, and increasingly it must be available cross-platform. Phone apps are a further channel through which the Qur'an has been made accessible (Islamic Studies Pathways 2012).

*Khutbah*s or sermons from different imams and scholars are available online, often uploaded immediately after their initial presentation. These sermons, either transmitted 'live' or recorded and uploaded onto websites, have extended the audiences for numerous religious perspectives. Some organisations (and/or their followers) upload YouTube with regular sermons. Islamic branded outlets such as IslamicTube and HalalTube also present a variety of online materials, although it is recognized that generic channels such as YouTube may gain greater use levels even for Islamic-related content (http://islamictube.net; www.halaltube.com).

While these might not replace face-to-face activities and the obligations of attending congregational prayers, they are endorsed as a means of capturing and distributing religious moments, to be distributed to other followers (locally and globally), and to act as a narrative memory aid within the timeline of a religious institution. Sermons have also been produced specifically for web consumption, and these can have a range of formats, themes and religious perspectives: in the UK, StreetDawa uploads regular talks on Islamic issues, recorded as a means of engaging young audiences in Islamic issues (www.streetdawa.com). In the United States, Hamza Yusuf – a co-founder of Zaytuna College in Berkeley – features in numerous webcasts, video sermons and MP3 lectures that have been made available for download and distribution (Zaytuna Institute 2011). Imam Suhaib Webb became a prominent blogger and tweeter, integrating his online activities into his work as an imam in Boston (www.suhaibwebb.com).[3]

Some sites present pages that suggest that their authors, or those they represent, are 'authorities', even if they are not necessarily traditionally trained in Islamic sciences or regarded as traditional 'Islamic scholars'. The internet reflects a wider debate that was a precursor to the expansion of the medium, namely on the nature of religious authority, and on the control of mandate of power to interpret Islamic sources. An understanding of *ijtihad*, a term often (but not exclusively) associated with a striving for the pragmatic interpretation of Islamic primary sources in the light of contemporary conditions, has been a key to examining in detail the authority and processes associated with decision-making.[4] It is not assumed that all Muslim societies apply *ijtihad*, but the term can have some currency within analysis of 'Islamic law' and its historical development, especially in relation to understandings of the Qur'an and the scholarship surrounding various significant Islamic sources.

There is an established audience for Islamic opinion and interpretation via the internet, as well as the traditional articulation of religious values and understandings. Electronic *ijtihad*, or e-*ijtihad*, and/or electronic *fatwas* not only reproduce conventional processes of interpretation and reasoning to reach decisions or opinions; they are also created especially for the medium.[5] There can be a blurring between the two digital and 'conventional' sources. The extent to which a surfer will apply the knowledge acquired in cyberspace regarding Islam, and be influenced by pronouncements, is difficult to quantify. (Bunt 2003: 124–203; El-Nawawy and Khamis 2009).

Broad ranges of 'authoritative' Islamic opinions are located on the internet. Traditional scholars with international profiles, such as Yusuf al-Qaradawi and Ayatollah al-Sistani, extended and reinforced their spheres of influence through their opinions and profiles being promoted online (www.qaradawi.net; www.sistani.org; Skovgard-Petersen 2008; Bunt 2008a). Organisations behind popular preachers, including Amr Khaled, integrate multimedia and social networking into their online output, in conjunction with other media (for example, satellite television broadcasts) (www.amrkhaled.net; Mariani 2006).

The increase in the smart phone market, and developments in access, will mean over time that phone applications or apps become a significant part of user interfaces into Islamic and Muslim-related content. Of particular interest is the emergence of a number of Islam-related apps for mobile devices (Bunt 2004, 2009b; Malik 2010). Mobile devices have opened up access to the internet in a variety of Muslim contexts; for several years, Islam-oriented applications and programs have been devised for phones, and these have been enhanced with multimedia and flash elements as technology has further developed. The growth in mobile phone use in previously marginalized markets, such as sub-Saharan Africa and South Asia, has facilitated basic mobile phone access for many, including (for some) internet access. Many Muslim sectors have high mobile phone use and ownership (there is an implicit differential between the two), such as the United Arab Emirates, Saudi Arabia, Iran, Lebanon, Indonesia, Turkey and Malaysia (International Telecommunications Union 2010).

Whether all the key players within cyber-Islamic environments are responding effectively to this change in medium is open to question. As with the early growth of Islamic websites, there has been a vying for influence to promote Islamic apps and other programs to the mobile computing and smart phone markets, which may have the result of expanding influence on matters of religion. Some Islam-oriented websites were already user-friendly for mobile phones. Website design is critical, with many sites not always integrating content accessibility, bandwidth restraints, clarity and navigation for phones within their design.

Related to this is the emergence of iPads, tablets and other mobile devices. Apps for the iPad may be based on their iPhone siblings, although a range of Islamic apps developed specifically for the iPad and other platforms began to emerge (Bunt 2009b). Islamic apps focus on ease of access, clarity and user-friendly features. Apps provide a specific interface on a mobile phone, enabling quick access and implementing the specific multimedia features of a phone.[6] The early development phase was represented with apps offering *qibla* prayer direction, prayer times, Qur'an recitations and readings, hadith collections, and biographies of the Prophet Muhammad. Some of these were adaptations of content and tools that had been developed for other devices. The year 2011 saw the emergence of a hajj app for iPhones, incorporating location tracking and advice for each stage of the pilgrimage – together with an emergency button to request on-site assistance (*Economist* 2012; AMIR 2012). Such granulation of products will continue with the emergence of apps focusing on specific Muslim branches and affiliations, as well as particular requirements of Islam.

The impact of generic apps, such as those developed by Google, Twitter, Foursquare and Gowalla, are also significant – especially when they are applied as part of cyber-Islamic environments. Gowalla, for example, can be used to check in to various locations, and received substantial traffic for al-Masjid al-Haram in Mecca, indicating that users seemingly disregarding the edicts preventing the use of mobile phones in the holy sanctuary area (Gowalla 2011). Through their stimulation of discussion, mapping of mosques, and development of social networks, these and other apps form part of an intriguing integrated interface between mobile phone and personal computer. There is, increasingly, no need for an individual to have a personal computer in order to benefit from cloud computing, being able to access software and content through mobile devices.

Determining whether use of mobile devices for 'Islamic' purposes is appropriate has been a multifaceted subject of Muslim scholarly discussion. In Egypt in 2010, al-Azhar's Grand Mufti Sheikh Ali Gomaa presented a fatwa or religious opinion against the use of Qur'anic recitation recordings as 'phone tones', suggesting that they were disrespectful to the Divine Revelation (Meedan 2010). This context-specific ruling opinion determines that ringtones are seen as a disruption, and their Divine Message may not be imparted or contemplated in the format of a ringtone. Gomaa suggested that other Islam-related tones could be used instead, such as praises or chants derived from the secondary source of the hadith (traditions associated with the Prophet Muhammad and his companions) (Gomaa 2010).

Such issues associated with mobile devices increasingly became an issue of concern and debate, within diverse Muslim sectors. In Saudi Arabia, Sheikh Abdul Aziz al-Sheikh sought to ban camera-enabled phones on the grounds of their potential for immoral use (Dawn 2004). In India, the Deoband Darul Uloom Darul Ifta – a website representing a prominent and influential international Islamic movement based in

Deoband, India – noted the issue of the intrusion of phones into the mosque: 'One can have worldly or religious talks only as much as necessary by cell phone in a state of Etikaf (secluding oneself in mosque with the intention of worship)' (Deoband Darul Uloom Darul Ifta 2010). This opinion was also circulated to Deobandi institutions elsewhere within the movement's network of influence. For several years, in a number of contexts, there has been consternation in mosques when cell phones ring during prayer (Al-Munajjid n.d2). In South Africa, Mufti Ebrahim Desai provided a detailed breakdown on whether it was permissible to continue prayer if a mobile phone went off due to an individual's forgetfulness (Desai 2009). There have been mixed responses to the use of Islamic content on cell phones, with scholars debating their utility: IslamOnline's 'Ask the Scholar' feature included two opinions on the advantages and disadvantages of having the Qur'an available on a phone (al-Munajjid n.d1; al-Husaini 2004).

A variety of Islamic apps for the iPhone and other platforms emerged, offering Qur'anic texts and recitation, prayer orientation and other sources. Developments have come not just from the software industry, but from traditional centres of Islamic learning. Al-Azhar University in Cairo is a traditional centre of Sunni Islamic scholarship, with links to the Al-Azhar Mosque established in the tenth century. Al-Azhar's Grand Imam Mohamed Sayed Tantawi officially endorsed an Islamic Hotline phone resource – *el-Hatef el-Islami* – through which users could contact a religious scholar to obtain an opinion or advice (www.elhatef.com). While not as extensive as the opinions and answers to questions available on databases such as IslamOnline or Islam Q&A, the resource also contained listings of frequently asked questions, indicating a range of users' concerns: these were the same questions in Arabic and English. Family relations, sexual relationships and ritual dominated these listings, but this is no indication of the types of calls that are received on the Islamic Hotline, or the weight of traffic to the service. The key element within this present discussion is that this is a mobile phone enabled resource, established by a traditional centre of Islamic influence and scholarship. It sets a likely precedent for other related activities – which blur the distinction between religious authority, Islamic online interfaces and the phone.

Phone apps join the complex array of online services and portals that act as entry points to the exploration of Islam and Muslim issues, via diverse interfaces, digital configurations, and religious perspective. The intention of the next section is to provide focused case studies of how these dynamics of cyber-Islamic environments play out, in relation to specific and contrasting belief perspectives. There is no such thing as a representative sample in a brief chapter of this nature. It has to be stressed that this is a snapshot, offered to give a sense of online activities, and an approach which could be expanded through the reader's own exploration of Islam and the internet.

The final section of this chapter offers some brief case studies and profiles, to demonstrate some of the breadth of internet use from diverse perspectives within cyber-Islamic environments.

The multimedia Sufi

First, a multimedia web channel, centred on an 89-year-old spiritual leader of a branch of Sufism or Islamic 'mysticism', offers an insight into how cyber-Islamic environments have evolved – and how Islam *can* be represented in the modern world. In 2011, a series of animated videos emerged on YouTube that sought to satirise the differences between two Muslim perspectives – Salafis and Wahhabis – through a hypothetical exchange between two individuals, determining their points of agreement and the reaction when a difference emerged, essentially their judging of each other as 'unbelievers' for not worshiping in a particular mosque in a particular city. In another clip, a Sufi is confronted by a 'Wahhabi' who deigns him '*kafir*', an insulting term stressing a lack of Islamic religious beliefs. A few days after Osama bin Laden's death in May 2011, the site had uploaded a video response (from this particular Sufi perspective) on the perceived negative role of bin Laden in relation to Islamic interpretations of jihad (SufiLive 2011c, 2011d).

The YouTube content was generated by SufiLive, organised by followers of Mawlana Shaykh Nazim Adil Al-Haqqani (b. 1922) and the Naqshbandi-Haqqani Sufi Order (Allievi and Nielsen 2003; Draper et al 2006). The Naqshbandi-Haqqani Sufi Order is a reflection of the globalization of an Islamic movement, with centres and followers across the world: Al-Haqqani is based in Northern Cyprus; the SufiLive website is hosted in the United States. SufiLive describes itself as 'The Official Media Library of the Naqshbandi-Haqqani Sufi Order of America'. As with many other religious authorities, movements and leaders, on the internet there are no geographic barriers to networking and keeping in touch with the movement's activities. For example, within a week of the first 'Salafis vs. Wahhabis' video being uploaded, it had received several thousand views, and generated reaction from diverse perspectives via the YouTube comments. Some of this was negative. There was a suggestion that the clips were a cause of division within the ideal of the global Muslim community (*ummah*).

Some samples of the feedback follow. Technical terms have been explained by myself in parenthesis; original spellings, colloquialisms, typographical idiosyncrasies reflective of online dialogues, and terminology is maintained:

> Well done, for fueling the division amongst the Ummah. I wonder if the Prophet (sallAllahu 'alayhi wa sallam) [Peace and Blessings upon Him] would have approved of something like this? j4mila

SufiLive responded to this by attributing a division to 'Wahhabi' and 'Salafi' beliefs as being a cause of many problems relating to contemporary Islam and Muslims:

> @j4mila "Fueling the Division in the Ummah"! Amazing. which planet are you from! The_ Ummah is divided thanks to the Wahhabi and Salafi Doctrine and actions. I mean come on, according to the Wahhabi beliefs, three quarters of the Ummah are heretics and Kaafir. May Allah guide you, wake up.
>
> (SufiLive 2011d)

The dialogue and – in some places – arguments went on for several pages. The animated videos, emanating from Fenton, Michigan, formed part of the wider SufiLive site. It contained videos of Haqqani filmed in his base in Cyprus. In a one-month period, more than 40 videos had been uploaded: cameras had been recording the Shaykh's pronouncements, including during lunch with Shaykh Hisham Kabbani (who founded the Naqshbandi-Haqqani Sufi Order of America) and Shaykh Adnan Kabbani (based in Lebanon). There was a lack of self-consciousness over the plates of food, as the scholars discuss issues of government and religion, from their own particular Sufi worldview (SufiLive 2011a; Bunt 2003: 178).

Some videos were accompanied by English language transcriptions; each video could be downloaded for use offline; audio could also be downloaded, and other buttons offered multiplatform sharing and distribution options via social media. The main SufiLive page links to the complete multimedia libraries of Al-Haqqani and Kabbani. SufiLive could be followed on Twitter and Facebook, and pages were regularly updated; donations to the Sufi order (which can form part of religiously obligated charity) can be made via PayPal. Transcripts of (some) videos are provided in 15 languages. A live broadcast calendar indicates times for live streaming of sermons. SufiLive TV broadcasts live '24/7'. The site provides links to online shopping channels (themselves offering e-books and MP3s for download).

SufiLive connects in turn to eShaykh.com, an advice site providing responses to readers' questions. These are emailed in – together with requests for prayers, and dream interpretation. In one example, a question is placed from a person who had pledged affiliation to the Sufi order online – and had subsequently dreamt of the Grand Shaykh 'Abdullah al-Fa'iz ad-Daghestani:

> Plz 4give me if I lack proper manner but I want to know the interpretation of my dream.My bros [brothers] and I got online bayah 4m ure site.
>
> Dream:I saw that its nite time & a TV anchor is talking abt greatness of GrandShaykh (R) at the same time the sky is beautified with different colors, I think 2 myslf tht it(colors) is bcause of G.Shaykh.Me & my youngest bro go on our roof top to take pictures of sky & there some spiritual beings gather to wich

G.Shaykh Adresses,we get scared but G.Shaykh calls MSN & orders him sumthing,after they disappear the sky colors disappear 2;I tell my bros both young 2 me tht we shud do xikr of Kalima 2 bring back lite bt then we fear tht MSN might get angry so we leave 4 home.
  Plz tell me its meaning & thanks for reading
  JazakAllah [May Allah give you goodness].

(Siddiqui 2011)[7]

Here we have affiliation to the Order generated online – itself an innovation that is by no means universal – and the use of colloquial language and abbreviation in placing a religious question to an authority. Islamic terms such as xikr [*dhikr* – remembrance of the names of Allah], *kalima* ['words', reflecting phrases which are memorized as part of prayer] and *bayah* [a form of allegiance to a religious leader, such as a shaykh] comprise part of the dialogue. A traditional petition would probably have been couched in more formal language, perhaps face-to-face with a scholar or an associate. Online, an immediate response was generated in more measured tones by Taheer Siddiqui, a scholar and writer (with a science degree): 'This is a very good dream showing that Grandshaykh 'Abdullah al-Fa'iz ad-Daghestani (q) is sending guidance, lights and spiritual inspirations to your heart through his caliph Mawlana Shaykh Muhammad Nazim al-Haqqani (q)' (Siddiqui 2011).

There is no judgement as to the approach of the petitioner, who is courteously complemented and encouraged in his religious beliefs. This is a natural dialogue online, one of hundreds on the site, its answers available not just for the petitioner but for all readers. There is neither a gatekeeper on the site nor entry requirements, and payment is not required.

The use of question and answer pages such as eShaykh has been a major development within cyber-Islamic environments, across the Muslim spectrum of diverse interpretations and understandings.[8] The development of these pages has empowered some Muslims to search around for an opinion that suits their circumstances (a phenomena that predated the net) and has – in some contexts – introduced a practice that has subverted traditional roles of local religious scholars in analogue contexts.

The preponderance of online fatwas has raised concerns among scholars, their institutions and followers relating to notions of religious authority and legitimacy, within a competitive digital knowledge marketplace. The growing availability and flow of information – amplified by the increase in mobile technology and the integration of cloud computing on cheaper, faster and more accessible devices – could see an intensification of an intellectual and knowledge management battle between (and within) shades of Muslim opinion. New networks and affiliations have developed in relation to decision-making issues. The potential for scholars and authorities from non-traditional backgrounds to emerge online and present their opinions has, in some cases, challenged traditional religious values and understandings in relation to interpretation. It has ignited longstanding debates on who is qualified to present religious opinions, and opened up net users to opinions outside of their traditional religious cultural milieu. The fact that this searching for information can be confidential and anonymous adds another edge to the impact of online fatwas and religious opinions.

The purpose of discussing SufiLive here is to illustrate an evolution of development within cyber-Islamic environments. While such sites are innovative in their technological approach, they do not necessarily represent a mainstream of Islamic religious opinion. Their significance lies in their fusion of traditional Sufi values and outlook with cutting edge approaches to online activities, and a recognition that online activities in both global and local contexts have a role to play in promoting their interpretations and understandings of Islam. In this way, they present (not only with a positive reception) their Islamic worldview to other Muslims and to the wider world. They apply lighter approaches such as animation, and can draw the reader into denser religious debate online and more complex sources. There will be different levels of readership interest, in a competitive Islamic internet knowledge economy, where attention spans (as with other content) can be limited. Drawing site-users in through multimedia, offering podcasts, videos and a sense of affiliation represents classic marketing strategy, as well as a contemporary approach to religious propagation.

The SufiLive site and its Sufi affiliates show the way online networking is provided as a natural part of site activities, fully endorsed with the participation of senior religious figures. Such sites draw together disparately located Sufi individuals linked with the order, and introduces others to the specific religious beliefs in an accessible and user-friendly fashion. Full use of social networking media is applied, demonstrating a high level of net literacy among the organisation (and funding with which to engage in this kind of activity), together with a presumed net literacy among at least some of its readers. SufiLive demonstrates that there are multiple internet interfaces and platforms available through which to approach integrated material on these specific Muslim perspectives.

In the 1990s, the order's only online option was low-speed internet access (via a phone line); downloading a single photo could take an interminable time. In the 2000s, the progression to broadband and faster download/access times – together with a reduction in the digital divide – resulted in a progression of content. This ranged from (initially tentative) multimedia, including downloadable and streaming sermons (such as the SufiLive radio station). Greater levels of interactivity with the network(s) were facilitated though an increasing use of social media. The order's online identity was reinforced through branded URL domains. The wider accessibility and development of social networking tools and so-called 'Web 2.0', including elements such as Facebook, Twitter, live-streaming and YouTube, were further reflected and integrated into the al-Haqqani online network. Responsiveness to online trends was further indicated by the developed awareness that there was a shift in the ways content was accessed: away from desk-bound computers, towards mobile access by web-enabled smart phones and – more recently – other mobile devices such as tablets. At the time of writing there was no particular app associated with the order, but sermons could be obtained via podcast; content was fully accessible by cell phone.

This Sufi order's site is not necessarily 'typical' or representative of all Muslim platforms in its online activities. It is impossible to generalize, given the diversity of opinion, religious expression, cultural outlooks and linguistic differences on numerous online platforms. It does reflect how aspects of a particular Islamic outlook can be represented in multiple formats and languages, with immediacy, and presented for different levels of site users within a competitive and diverse internet knowledge marketplace.

Understanding that diversity also requires some exploration of the jihadi sphere – which can be viewed as very different in its orientation and approaches in the name of Islam and Muslims on the internet.

The networked e-jihadi

There is considerable multiplicity of interpretation and manifestations in relation to the term 'jihad', with references to lesser jihad (militaristic in nature) and greater jihad (relating to spiritual striving), within a number of approaches across history and through different religious perspectives. I apply the term e-jihad (electronic jihad) here – and elsewhere – as an umbrella term for online articulation of jihad with a militaristic emphasis in multiple digital electronic (e-) forms by proponents. There have been shifts in presentation as technology has changed: most recently, jihadi supporters have utilized YouTube, Twitter and Facebook for campaigns.

In conjunction with cheaper technology, greater digital literacy and an increase in bandwidth, jihad has been presented online as a central component of the strategies of organizations and individuals in a variety of contexts. Different formats have been applied – email, websites, multimedia, and magazines – to rapidly circulate information as part of an integrated approach to promoting jihad to supporters, 'the curious', and to national and world media. An increasing sophistication of output, combined with an aptitude for ensuring anonymity, has seen broadcast standard output frequently being drawn upon by international and local media channels as a primary news source.

The use of the web as a strategic 'jihadi' tool predates 9/11, with a relatively sustained level of activity – albeit among small groups, given lower levels of web literacy and access, across a variety of campaigns, not all of which applied the term 'jihad' in the same way. The internet was used to promote campaigns in and about the UK, Palestine, Lebanon, Saudi Arabia, Kashmir and Chechnya – with some efforts at connecting diverse jihad-oriented campaigns under single banners. Dialogues about jihad-oriented issues could be found online in the mid-1990s, primarily on mailing lists, FTP platforms and discussion groups. Files were small, text only – and often mass mailings. Early internet browsers led to the emergence of graphical interfaces presenting various Islamic perspectives, including online campaigns that had forms of jihadi discourse integrated into them.

While they might have lacked the sophistication of contemporary online content, these prototypes were significant, in setting models for further development, including: martyrs galleries, operational news services, fundraising campaigns, membership encouragement and networking development. Experimental platforms and gateways were important, in developing expertise and methodologies for the utilisation of the web in the name of 'jihad'. Primary readerships were English speaking Muslims with unrestricted (at the time) and relatively high levels of web access – for example, in North America and Europe.

There was a sustained expansion of e-jihadi activities in the years following 9/11. Al-Qaeda supporters and networks took advantage of expanding internet access and the increasing potential of online multimedia. Osama bin Laden's statements featured on channels such as al-Neda, while al-Sahab became the specific media distribution arm of al-Qaeda. Without the internet and its associated tools, al-Qaeda could not have functioned in the manner it did (Bunt 2003, 2009a). Digitally literate followers were able to evade filtering and censorship, in order to rapidly distribute their message. Osama bin Laden's speeches were first distributed as text files via mailing lists, then – as technology progressed – on websites, MP3s, and as videos with increasing audio-visual quality and production values. Graphics and translated subtitles augmented bin Laden's oratory skills, in which he evoked a specific interpretation of Qur'anic sources associated with jihad, combing it with commentaries upon and reactions to specific events. The videos were evidently well rehearsed, as videos of 'outtake rehearsals' emerged among the numerous computer files removed in 2011 from bin Laden's final hideout in Abbottabad, Pakistan (Associated Press 2011; ABC News 2011; Ackerman 2011).

A typical distribution pattern would involve a video being recorded and placed onto a memory stick or DVD; the video would be couriered to a secure place with internet access (such as a café) where it would be uploaded anonymously onto a file-sharing site, copied numerous times by followers onto other file-sharing sites, and the URLs circulated by emailing lists, websites and forums. They would also be publicized and played through media channels (leading to further downloads), and also circulated by specialized platforms seeking to observe and comment upon jihadi campaigns for political purposes. Some pro-Israel and right-wing platforms (the two are not necessarily synonymous) employed teams to collect and translate this output. It was also collected and commented upon by bloggers, journalists, academics and government organisations.

The technological shifts relating to the internet and computers in general have been reflected in the evolving nature of jihadi discourse. For example, the martyrdom pages of websites have technically evolved: from text only, to HTML (hypertext mark-up language) graphics, to poster-style photos, to MP3 audio statements, to slickly edited videos, to dedicated Facebook pages. Dominant traditional print and poster production of 'martyrs' was superseded by the generation of online materials, accessible through (and in some cases created through the use of) mobile phones. Increasingly emphasis was placed on the production of online manuals in downloadable PDF formats, as a means of propagation to nuanced audiences. This has also seen linguistic diversity, for example in the preponderance of English language manuals generated during 2010–11, prominently through *Inspire* magazine, and the activities of Anwar al-Awlaki – the focus of this present section.

Anwar al-Awlaki (1971–2011) and his followers utilized the internet to build a significant profile in jihadi contexts. Born in New Mexico of Yemeni heritage, al-Awlaki was a graduate of Colorado State University and the University of San Diego. He became an imam in the United States, where he was based until 2002, after which he spent several months in the United Kingdom (Gardham 2010). In 2004, al-Awlaki relocated again to Yemen. He was implicated in numerous al-Qaeda-related activities, in Yemen and in wider contexts.[9] Anwar al-Awlaki's role in al-Qaeda in the Arabian Peninsula, in particular the impact of his online sermons and other digital output, made him a focus for targeted assassination by US forces (Miller 2010). He acted as a channel for making al-Qaeda ideology more accessible for English language speakers, for example through translating and distributing the work of al-Qaeda ideologue Yusuf al-Ayiri (Al-Shishani 2010). Al-Awlaki's own output was also redistributed widely on jihadi forums, relating to different global campaigns. Various media channels interviewed him, and his supporters subsequently posted these dialogues online. Doubts emerged from some Muslim scholars as to al-Awlaki's own scholarly status and qualifications, which did not reflect a traditional paradigm of religious training (Temple-Raston 2010).

Al-Awlaki featured prominently in the output of *Inspire* magazine, an English language jihadi online publication, developed by Samir ibn Zafar Khan (1986–2011), a US citizen born in Saudi Arabia and resident in North Carolina who subsequently relocated to Yemen. Khan's online output via English language blogs and video posts supporting al-Qaeda and jihad captured a great deal of media attention prior to his re-emergence with *Inspire* magazine.

Inspire magazine had a 'glossy' format, with posters, graphics and photographs giving it a contemporary edge, together with its use of colloquial language. Their distribution patterns on jihadi forums and blogs, in easily downloadable formats, allowed for rapid and discrete circulation. By March 2011, five issues of *Inspire* had emerged. The first issue, published online in summer 2010, featured articles such as 'Make a Bomb in the Kitchen of Your Mom', 'What to Expect in Jihad', 'Sending and

Figure 8.1 Anwar Al-Awlaki. Courtesy of Reuters.

Receiving Encrypted Messages' and interviews with prominent jihadis.[10] Al-Awlaki contributed a 'Message to the American People and Muslims in the West'. Mukhtar Hassan's 'What to Expect in Jihad' article offered practical advice:

> 'The psychological state of mind one is required to have in jihad is far removed from what we see in jihadi videos. In simple language, it's not all about the shooting and ambushing of the enemy; rather it is much greater than this.'

The article discusses language barriers, what to bring on jihad, culture blending, and why 'having a friend makes a difference' when on jihad (al-Malahem Media 2010).

By the fifth issue, *Inspire* was offering reactions to (then) recent events in Palestine, Egypt and Libya; it gave a summary of critical comments and reviews of previous issues from analysts and experts. Readers were invited to submit questions by email to the magazine: the intention was to put these to Anwar al-Awlaki for use in a video interview. There was a focus on 'open source jihad', stressing it allowed training for Muslims 'at home' and that it was 'America's worst nightmare'. The magazine featured articles from several prominent jihadis, including the ideologue Abu Musa al-Suri, who had been influential in promoting a specific interpretation of jihad via the internet (Al-Malahem Media 2011; Lia 2007).

Although al-Awlaki did not manage, organize or produce all the content (that being the editorial responsibility of Samir Khan), *Inspire* was a formidable and high profile addition to al-Awlaki's media output and influence. Despite his targeted status and role in al-Qaeda, his lectures and sermons also remained widely available as MP3 downloads. Not all of these lectures were necessarily directly oriented towards jihad issues. The sites themselves pointed to generic file-sharing sites, with several broken links (islamfactory.com 2011; Imam Anwar al-Awlaki Lectures 2007).

Copies of al-Awlaki's original blog remained easily accessible in 2011, although the original URL has been taken down. Video sermons and other content remain on YouTube, IslamicTube and other channels.[11] Al-Awlaki's videos remained on these channels, despite United States governmental pressure to remove them after al-Awlaki had encouraged attacks on the United States (Ungerleider 2010). IslamicTube offered 312 videos relating to Anwar al-Awlaki, including lectures, interviews and Qur'an commentaries. Ultimately, it became easier for US interests to 'delete' Anwar al-Awlaki from life than remove his content from the internet. For even after he was killed (along with Samir Khan) in a US drone military strike in Yemen on 30 September 2011, his output continued to have a presence online.

The impact of this and other jihad-related online content has been multilayered; there is evidence, particularly from court cases, that it has influenced the recruitment and financing of some jihadi individuals; it has promoted campaigns outside of their traditional spheres of influence, and sought to develop specific allegiances and interpretations of a form of jihad – which has been applied in diverse contexts. It has provided a direct line for media channels to acquire information about al-Qaeda activities; internet output was integrated into campaigns and missions, for example through the production of 'martyrs' videos that were distributed in synch with operations. The output has had an impact on public perceptions of jihad, in Muslim and other contexts. For some, the presence of this content has fuelled anti-Muslim feeling, or acted as a means for legitimizing prejudice.

The negative stereotyping of Islam and Muslims in 'Western' contexts may have been increasingly influenced by online content generated by jihadi organisations – especially when online responses from Muslim organisations were muted, ignored or lacked the technical aptitude for distribution and production of al-Qaeda supporters. The victimization engendered by such videos may in turn become self-fulfilling, driving some vulnerable audience members towards a path of (self-) 'radicalisation'. Governments may also draw on this output, to justify military campaigns, expenditure on defence contracts, and monitoring of local Muslim communities. Its continued presence online may be linked to difficulties in controlling online content, although it could also be deemed a 'honeypot' trap for gathering intelligence on the activities and networking of online supporters. The net facilitated, for some, levels of membership and involvement; encryption and members-only networks facilitated participation that went beyond simply viewing a video, and enabled individuals to connect on a one-to-one level with recruiters.

The application of social networking tools such as Facebook and Twitter offers further stages of networking and participation in 'jihadi' activities: in 2011, the Taliban's supporters in Afghanistan and Pakistan used these channels as a means to promote their (separate) activities (Gwakh 2011). While this kind of online activity is but a small component within the cyber-Islamic spectrum, it is influential in terms of the attention it receives – including in academic circles – often at the expense of the everyday applications of the internet in relation to Islam and Muslims.

While jihad issues may dominate public perceptions of Islam, Muslims and the internet, many platforms and campaigns far beyond the jihadi sphere have applied the internet as a means to facilitate the promotion of agendas and coordination of activities. The most prominent example relates to the Arab Spring of 2011.

The online activists

The impact of a multimedia cross-platform information overload – given the sheer quantity of digital data relating to the study of Islam and Muslims that becomes available – was brought into sharp focus with the developments in the Middle East in 2010–11 and the 'Arab Spring', also referred to as the 'Facebook revolution' and/or 'Twitter revolution'. These and related terms are problematic (for example the latter two terms were also utilised in relation to protests in Iran in 2009), and make a number of assumptions that are not necessarily valid. The results in each context were very different, and not necessarily 'Islamic' in nature, although actors with Muslim identities participated in these dynamic and fluid events. It is also not necessarily helpful to generalise regarding 'Facebook revolution(s)' or similar epithets, given the combination of social, economic, cultural, religious and other factors.

There may be a danger in over emphasizing the importance of online elements within the Arab Spring, at the expense of other factors. However, social networking media were seen by commentators and participants as influential drivers for change in Tunisia, Egypt, Libya, Syria, Yemen, Bahrain and elsewhere. Demographics of social media usage have an impact in this regard.[12] Longstanding issues of regional economic and social deprivation, dissatisfaction with government and national leadership, (lack of) political accountability and representation, as well as human rights issues combined with the growing influence of diverse regional media to create a momentum of activism.

The 'exposure' through the uploading onto Wikileaks of sensitive US state documentation, including cables and emails from embassies discussing regional and local intelligence on specific countries, amplified regional discontent – particularly as these materials were discussed, edited and reposted by news media and through social networking sites (www.wikileaks.org). This coincided in turn with the intense growth in access to digital technology and broadcast media, and recognition of the potential of these tools to promote and mobilize campaigning.[13]

During the Arab Spring, coverage of relatively small protests received rapid coverage locally, nationally and internationally: this included 'conventional' domestic and satellite television broadcasts (such as al-Jazeera and al-Arabiya) and the reportage gathered from mobile phone clips and reports posted online. A symbiosis between these two sources meant that satellite broadcasters drew upon these alternative materials, rebroadcasting them on their own networks, while the grassroots activists also reposted and publicized broadcasters' reports. The reporting by satellite broadcasters had a profound effect on the Arab Spring sequence of events; the organization, mobilization and publicizing of protests was facilitated in a significant part through social networking tools such as Facebook, Twitter, YouTube, blogs and websites. These tools were mashed together and accessed at an unprecedented level online through mobile phone and computer use. This reflected a fusion of the technological knowledge of broadcasters and reporters, with that of certain activists and protestors.

While the events have their origins in the social and cultural histories of the region – with longstanding factors – the starting point in this sequence of events has been seen as the 'Jasmine Revolution' in Tunisia.[14] This developed from protests following the events on 17 December 2010, when street trader Mohamed Bouazizi (1984–2011) set himself on fire in the town of Sidi Bouzid. Bouazizi had apparently become frustrated at the lack of opportunity and the attitude of local authorities, following a conflict with a local official regarding trading permits. He had previously updated his Facebook status, with an oblique indication of his suicide plans (Arabcrunch.com 2011). The accounts of these events were disputed, but there is no doubt that the small protests in Tunisia rapidly gained a national momentum, as images of Bouazizi's death spread through the internet. They combined with concerns about food protests, the economy, and dissatisfaction with perceived government corruption.

Footage of a heavily bandaged Bouazizi being visited by President Zine El Abidine Ben Ali, apparently prior to Bouazizi's death on 4 January 2011, were followed by the uploading of clips showing Bouazizi's well-attended funeral, which the authorities had attempted to suppress. These were subsequently re-broadcast on satellite media, focusing international attention. Protests galvanised through the use of social networking tools by participants, and the uploading of phone clips online. Twitter hashtags such as #sidibouzid generated substantial traffic (Mourtada and Salem 2011b: 22). Its organisation could not be effectively suppressed or censored by state agencies, and contributed to the departure from office of President Zine El Abidine Ben Ali (b. 1936) in January 2011 (Anderson 2011; Lister 2011; Tsotsis 2011; Al-Atraqchi 2011).

Anonymity and collective approaches to activism mean that highlighting one individual in events may be seen as inappropriate. However, reference should be made to a most prominent online campaigner whose name emerged during protests in Egypt in 2011: Wael Ghonim (b. 1980), a Middle East executive for Google, who – in a personal capacity, initially anonymously – organized the 'We are all Khaled Said' Facebook page, which became the fulcrum for articulation of discontent and organization of protest in Egypt. Khaled Said (1982–2010) was murdered by security forces in Alexandria, Egypt, on 6 June 2010 after exposing police corruption and presenting it online (al-Masry al-Youm 2010). Photos of Said's body were posted on the internet, leading Ghonim and others into a flurry of protest. Ghonim's own participation combined digital media with appearances at demonstrations; he was arrested on 28 January 2011, and released ten days later. Ghonim was to address crowds at Tahrir Square in Cairo, the central protest point. Throughout the sequence of events in Egypt, Twitter was utilized, in particular through hashtags such as #Egypt, #Jan25 and #25Jan (Mourtada and Salem 2011b: 16).

These hashtags enabled Twitter users to keep pace with the thousands of tweets that emerged on Egyptian issues (Google RealTime 2011). This combined with dramatic phone footage posted on YouTube from the protests and re-broadcast worldwide. The role of broadcasts such as al-Jazeera, reporting from Cairo during this turbulent period, cannot be underestimated. Despite attempts at censorship by Egyptian authorities, internet users were able to circumnavigate restrictions, for example through posting audio reports by landline phone when online access was cut through services such as AliveInEgypt or Tweet2Speak (National Public Radio 2011; http://egypt.alive.in; http://twitter.com/#!/speak2tweet).

Bloggers and social networkers were aware of the implications of censorship and internet closure: 'While the Egyptian government believed that shutting down the Internet would quiet the protests, the exact opposite happened, said Tarek Amr, an Egyptian blogger and computer programmer. "The protests became bigger and bigger without the Internet."' *(Gross 2011)*

President Hosni El Sayed Mubarak's (b. 1928) departure on 10 February 2011 from office was heralded (on- and offline) by networks of opposition supporters in and outside of Egypt. Clips of Ghonim embracing Mrs Laila (Khaled Said's mother) in Tahrir Square emerged on YouTube and across social media sites of supporters (Egyptian Chronicles 2011; YouTube 2011a, 2011b). Feted by international media, Ghonim did not necessarily embrace this new status. Mubarak's departure from office did not end the problems for Egypt, with protests and activism continuing throughout 2011 and beyond, including on the internet. Protests against the interim governing Egyptian Supreme Council of the Armed Forces (SCAF) continued to be coordinated through the use of social media, such as further demonstrations in Tahrir Square.

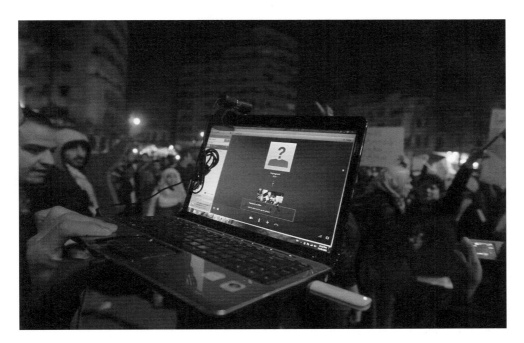

Figure 8.2 An Egyptian protester streams a demonstration via Skype in Cairo's Tahrir Square. Courtesy of Mohammed Abed/AFP/Getty Images.

One critical point within this sequence of events in Egypt is that these campaigns were not 'Islamic' in orientation, although some key participants had Muslim identities (on a number of levels), and the idiomatic expression of protest could incorporate language shaped by a Muslim milieu. Many participants would identify themselves as secular, agnostic or atheist. A number of participants were Coptic Christian. Some Muslim platforms held back from full involvement in that sequence of demonstrations. The Muslim Brotherhood in Egypt is a prominent example of this, although the organisation's infrastructure is web-literate, and it uses the internet to coordinate and publicise organisation activities. Facebook was also used to articulate internal disputes and quests for reform within the movement (IkhwanWeb 2011; Bar'el 2011). The Brotherhood was to benefit from the uprising (and their online presence) by winning, through its newly-formed Freedom and Justice Party, a majority in elections for a Egyptian legislature in January 2012.

As protests (and their suppression) continued in various forms in Libya, Bahrain, Syria and Yemen in 2011 and beyond, further layers of complexity were added. Conflicts were accompanied by extensive online activities. For example, the ousting of Libyan leader Colonel Muammar Gaddafi (1942–2011) and events surrounding his murder on 20 October 2011 in Sirte were captured through phone footage and rapidly broadcast worldwide. Protests in Yemen and Bahrain were coordinated and recorded through Facebook and Twitter pages. YouTube became a galvanizing force in Syria, recording the protests of citizens in Homs, Hama and elsewhere – and their violent suppression by President Bashar al-Assad (b. 1965) (Watson 2012).

What can be said, at this early stage, is that developing a comprehensive understanding of the role of the internet in social activism events such as the Arab Spring protests and their aftermath is a critical element within the study of Islam and Muslims in the modern world. While the actions were not predicated around Islam and Muslim issues, they clearly have a role in societal development, and have a mediating influence in the articulation of approaches towards contemporaneous religious issues in Islamic contexts.

Conclusions

The constructs presented within this chapter – of the multimedia Sufi, the networked e-jihadi, and online activists – represent a small element within the multiplicity of Islam-related (however obliquely) voices articulated online through a variety of interfaces. The modes and communications dynamics of scholars, opinion providers and petitioners (or consumers) are shifting in response to technological developments, while perhaps maintaining the essence of long-held traditions of religious authority and interpretation. As the digital divide reduces, and computer literacy increases with diverse Muslim contexts, following these trends will be a significant area for observers of Islam in the contemporary world. Profound changes in the dynamics of religious authority and networking have occurred in tandem with the shifts in society generated through the expansion of internet access.

Online articulation of religious values, and the use of internet tools as a natural means of acquiring data on a range of issues, has meant that cyber-Islamic environments increasingly dominate conversations about Islam by Muslims. They also act as a space where observation, as well as direct engagement, is possible between and within specific groups and interests. This conversation includes a range of beliefs and values, and can also include 'outsiders'. The marketplace for Islamic ideas online remains a competitive one, in which imagination and technological innovation is consistently applied. This does not necessarily mean a shift in traditional values of Islam, but a reframing of their articulation to accommodate the digital conduits of the twenty-first century – increasingly mobile and located in 'the cloud'.

Summary

- Cyber-Islamic expression has been integrated into everyday Muslim religious activities.
- Online multimedia is utilized by diverse organizations and religious perspectives to network with members and promote their worldviews, including through the adoption of technical innovations such as smart phones and tablets.
- The internet has been utilized to facilitate and propagate jihad agendas.
- Electronic media has an influential role within the social activism associated with events of the Arab Spring in 2011 (and beyond).

Discussion points

- How does the internet impact on the everyday religious lives of Muslims?
- How effective is the internet in developing knowledge transmission for religious world views?
- What are the advantages and disadvantages of seeking a religious opinion online?
- Should the internet be censored, in order that e-jihadi worldviews cannot be promulgated easily through the internet?
- How has social media influenced the organisation of activist platforms in Muslim contexts?

Further reading

Bunt, G.R. (2009) *iMuslims: Rewiring the House of Islam*, Chapel Hill: University of North Carolina Press.

The present writer's third book on Islam in cyberspace looks at the impact of Web 2.0 and social networking, as well as reviewing issues associated with religious authority and practice in relation to the internet. More information: www.virtuallyislamic.com.

Eickelman, D.F. and J.W. Anderson (2003) *New Media in the Muslim World: The Emerging Public Sphere*, 2nd edn, Bloomington: Indiana University Press.

This comprehensive study explored the significance of diverse media – including the internet – within a variety of Muslim contexts.

El-Nawawy, M. and A.S. Khamis (2009) *Islam Dot Com*, New York: Palgrave Macmillan, 2009.

This focuses on the importance of online fatwas with Muslim discourse, offering case studies and insights from a range of perspectives.

Ernst, C.W. (2005) 'Ideological and Technological Transformations of Contemporary Sufism', in M. Cooke and B.B. Lawrence (eds), *Muslim Networks from Hajj to Hip Hop*, Chapel Hill: University of North Carolina Press, 191–207.

This chapter includes reference to the impact on Sufi communities of 'new media'.

Ghonim, W. (2012) *Revolution 2.0*, London: HarperCollins.

Ghonim's pivotal role in the Arab Spring is discussed from his personal perspective, offering insights into how the internet played a significant role in Egyptian societal shifts in 2011.

Howard, P.N. (2010) *The Digital Origins of Dictatorship and Democracy: Information Technology and Political Islam*, Oxford: Oxford University Press.

This detailed study explores how Muslim political identities have been shaped through the application of digital media.

Larsson, G. (ed.) (2006) *Religious Communities on the Internet*, Stockholm: Swedish Science Press.

This edited volume includes chapters on jihadi cyberspace, Islamic knowledge online, identity issues, and Muslims and cyberspace in the UK.

Nunns, A. (2011) *Tweets from Tahrir: Egypt's Revolution as It Unfolded, in the Words of the People Who Made It*, New York: OR Books.

This volume collected tweets from participants in the first phase of the Arab Spring, as it related to Egypt. It provides an extensive survey of primary 'raw' data.

Arab Media and Society, www.arabmediasociety.com

Published by the The Kamal Adham Center for Television and Digital Journalism at the American University in Cairo, this online journal regularly features articles on issues associated with Islam, Muslims and electronic media.

CyberOrient, www.cyberorient.net

This open-access online journal contains articles and case-studies from a range of authors, discussing the use of electronic media in the 'virtual Middle East'.

References

ABC News (2011) 'Osama Bin Laden Videos Released by Government; Evidence Investigated', available at http://abcnews.go.com (accessed 8 May 2011).

Ackerman, S. (2011) 'Watch: Osama's Blooper Reel, Courtesy of Navy SEALs', *Wired*, available at www.wired.com/dangerroom (accessed 7 May 2011).

Al-Atraqchi, F. (2011) 'Tunisia's Revolution was Twitterized', *thedailynewsegypt.com*, available at www.thedailynewsegypt.com/columnists/tunisias-revolution-was-twitterized.html (accessed 16 January 2011).

Al Hashemi, B.A. and R. Ghazal (2012) 'Grand Mufti Calls for Dialogue about the Internet', *The National*, 20 February 2012, available at www.thenational.ae/news/uae-news/grand-mufti-calls-for-dialogue-about-the-internet (accessed 20 February 2012).

Al-Husaini, I.S. (2004) 'Words of Tawheed Appearing on a Mobile Screen', *IslamOnline*, available at www.islamonline.net/servlet/Satellite?pagename=IslamOnline-English-Ask_Scholar/FatwaE/FatwaE&cid=1119503545250 (accessed 24 September 2004).

Al-Malahem Media of al-Qaeda in the Arabian Peninsula (2010) *Inspire*, Issue 1.

—— (2011) *Inspire*, Issue 5.

Al-Masry Al-Youm (2010) 'Khaled Saeed Case Investigation', available at www.almasryalyoum. com/node/55686 (accessed 12 July 2010).

Al-Munajjid, M. S. (n.d1) 'Ask the Scholar, Entering Baths with Qur'an Recorded on Cell Phones', *IslamOnline*, available at www.islamonline.net/servlet/Satellite?pagename=IslamOnline-English-Ask_Scholar%2FFatwaE%2FFatwaEAskTheScholar&cid=1119503548124 (accessed 25 March 2004).

—— (n.d2) 'Fatwa 119636, Turning Off the Cell Phone During the Friday Khutbah – Does this Come Under the Heading of Idle Action that Invalidates the Reward of Jumu'ah?', *Islam Q&A*, available at www.islam-qa.com/en/ref/119636/cell%20phones (accessed 23 May 2011).

Al-Shishani, M.B. (2010) 'The Radical Source for Non-Arabic Speaking Muslims: Anwar al-Awlaki', *Terrorism Monitor,* 8(2), available at www.jamestown.org/single/?no_cache=1&tx_ttnews%5Btt_news%5D=35908 (accessed 16 February 2012).

Allievi, S. and J.S. Nielsen (2003) *Muslim Networks and Transnational Communities in and across Europe,* Leiden: Brill.

AMIR Personal Hajj Assistant for Men (2012) http://itunes.apple.com/ph/app/amir-personal-hajj-assistant/id473935680?mt=8 (accessed 15 February 2012).

Anderson, N. (2011) 'Tweeting Tyrants Out of Tunisia: Global Internet at Its Best', *Wired*, available at www.wired.com/threatlevel/2011/01/tunisia/all/1 (accessed 14 January 2011).

Arabcrunch.com (2011) 'The Last Facebook Status Update of Bouazizi Who Set him Self on Fire Starting the Tunisian Revolution', available at http://arabcrunch.com/2011/01/the-last-facebook-status-update-of-bouazizi-who-set-him-self-on-fire-marking-starting-the-tunisian-revolution.html (accessed 16 January 2011).

Associated Press (2011) 'Bin Laden was Logged Off, but not al-Qaida', available at www.npr.org/templates/story/story.php?storyId=136334743 (accessed 15 May 2011).

Bar'el, Z. (2011) 'Where is Egypt's Muslim Brotherhood Headed?', *Ha'aretz*, available at www.haaretz.com/print-edition/features/where-is-egypt-s-muslim-brotherhood-headed-1.354353 (accessed 7 April 2011).

Bunt, G.R. (2000) *Virtually Islamic: Computer-Mediated Communication and Cyber Islamic Environments*, Cardiff: University of Wales Press.

—— (2003) *Islam in the Digital Age: E-jihad, Online Fatwas and Cyber Islamic Environments*, London and Michigan: Pluto Press.

—— (2004) 'Rip. Burn. Pray: Islamic Expression Online', in D. E. Cowan and L. L. Dawson (eds) *Religion Online: Finding Faith on the Internet*, New York: Routledge, 123–34.

—— (2008a) 'Islam Online', in J. Esposito (ed.) *Oxford Encyclopedia of the Islamic World*, New York, Oxford University Press.

—— (2008b) 'Religion and the Internet', in P.B. Clarke (ed.) *The Oxford Handbook of the Sociology of Religion*, Oxford: Oxford University Press, 705–22.

—— (2009a) *iMuslims: Rewiring the House of Islam*, Chapel Hill: University of North Carolina Press.

—— (2009b) 'Gary Bunt on the 2009 Iranian Presidential Elections', *University of North Carolina Press Blog*, available at http://uncpressblog.com (accessed 22 June 2009).

—— (2009c) *A Diagrammatic Representation of Cyber Islamic Environments (CIES)*, available at http://virtuallyislamic.com/bibliography (accessed 23 April 2012).

—— (2010) 'Surfing the App Souq: Islamic Applications for Mobile Devices', *CyberOrient: Online Journal of the Virtual Middle East*, available at www.cyberorient.net/article.do?articleId=3817 (accessed 16 February 2012).

Daily Mail (2011) 'Sugar Hit: MI6 Brings Down Al Qaeda Website full of Bomb Making Instructions with Cup Cake Recipes', available at www.dailymail.co.uk/news/article-1393830/British-intelligence-crushed-al-Qaeda-website-containing-bomb-making-instructions-FAIRY-CAKE-RECIPE.html (accessed 3 June 2011).

Dawn (2004) 'Camera Cell Phones Termed un-Islamic', available at www.dawn.com/2004/09/30/int15.htm (accessed 30 September 2004).

Deoband Darul Uloom Darul Ifta (2010) 'Question 2757', available at http://darulifta-deoband.org/viewfatwa.jsp?ID=2757 (accessed 5 February 2010).

Desai, E. (2009) 'If anyone forget to switch off/silent mode to the mobile before proceeding the Salaah then, anyone called us during we are in the state of Salaah...', *Ask Imam*, available at www.askimam.org/fatwa/fatwa.php?askid=6266c74170547e4ae1330d1f2c543a38 (accessed 4 November 2009).

Draper, M., J.S. Nielsen and G. Yemelianova (2006) 'Transnational Sufism: The Haqqaniyya', in J. Malik and J. Hinnells (eds), *Sufism in the West*, London: Routledge.

Egyptian Chronicles (2011) 'The Photo of the Day: At Last They Met', available at http://egyptianchronicles.blogspot.com/2011/02/photo-of-day-at-last-they-met.html (accessed 8 February 2011).

Economist (2012) 'The Smart Way to Mecca', 13 February, www.economist.com/blogs/babbage/2012/02/helping-pilgrims (accessed 15 February 2012).

Eickelman, D.F. and J.W. Anderson (2003) *New Media in the Muslim world: The Emerging Public Sphere*, 2nd edn, Bloomington: Indiana University Press.

El-Nawawy, M. A. and S. Khamis (2009) *Islam Dot Com*, New York: Palgrave Macmillan.

Ernst. C.W. (2005) 'Ideological and Technological Transformations of Contemporary Sufism', in M. Cooke and B.B. Lawrence (eds), *Muslim Networks from Hajj to Hip Hop,* Chapel Hill: University of North Carolina Press, 191–207.

Gardham, D. (2010) 'Al-Qaeda Leader's Tour of Britain Revealed', *Daily Telegraph*, 5 November, available at www.telegraph.co.uk/news/uknews/terrorism-in-the-uk/8113977/Al-Qaeda-leaders-tour-of-Britain-revealed.html (accessed 5 November 2010).

Ghonim, W. (2012) *Revolution 2.0*, London: HarperCollins.

Gomaa, Ali (2010) 'Ask the Scholar: Setting Qur'anic Verses as Ringtones: Permissible?', *IslamOnline*, available at www.islamonline.net/servlet/Satellite?cid=1264249763406&pagename=IslamOnline-English-Ask_Scholar%2FFatwaE%2FFatwaEAskTheScholar (accessed 28 January 2010).

Google Blog (2011) 'Some Weekend Work that will [Hopefully] Enable more Egyptians to be Heard', available at http://googleblog.blogspot.com/2011/01/some-weekend-work-that-will-hopefully.html (accessed 31 January 2011).

Google Realtime (2011) 'Twitter Archive Search – Using Timeline', link deleted (accessed 2 February 2011).

Gowalla (2011) 'Al-Masjid Al-Haram', available at http://gowalla.com/spots/449885 (accessed 23 June 2011).

Gross, G. (2011) 'Egyptian Activist: Internet Shutdown Backfired', *IDG News/PCWorld Business Center*, available at www.pcworld.com/businesscenter/article/218630/egyptian_activist_ Internet_shutdown_backfired.html (accessed 3 February 2011).

Gwakh, B.A. (2011) 'Taliban Employs Modern Weapons In "War of Words"', *Radio Free Europe/ Radio Liberty*, available at www.rferl.org/articleprintview/2340644.html (accessed 16 March 2011).

Hegghammer, T. (2006) 'Global Jihadism After the Iraq War', *Middle East Journal*, 60(1).

Howard, P.N. (2010) *The Digital Origins of Dictatorship and Democracy: Information Technology and Political Islam*, Oxford: Oxford University Press.

IkhwanWeb (2011) 'Arab Youth – Changing Worldwide Perceptions', available at www. ikhwanweb.com/article.php?id=28411 (accessed 16 April 2011).

Imam Anwar al-Awlaki Lectures (2007) http://imamawlaki.blogspot.com/ (accessed 20 May 2011).

International Telecommunications Union (2010) 'Measuring the Information Society 2010', available at www.itu.int/ITU-D/ict/publications/idi/2010/index.html (accessed 12 May 2011).

Internet Haganah (2012) http://Internet-haganah.com/haganah/index.html (accessed 16 February 2012).

islamfactory.com (2011) 'Imam Anwar al-Awlaki MP3 Downloads', available at www. islamfactory.com/audio/talks/al-awlaki (accessed 25 May 2011).

Islamic Studies Pathways (2012) http://islamicstudies.tumblr.com (accessed 20 February 2012).

Jamestown Foundation (2012) www.jamestown.org (accessed 16 February 2012).

Jihadica (2012) www.jihadica.com (accessed 16 February 2012).

Kimmage, D. and K. Ridolfo (2007) *Iraqi Insurgency Media: The War of Images and Ideas*, Washington: Radio Free Europe/Radio Liberty, available at www.rferl.org/content/article/1077316.html (accessed 16 February 2012).

Kohlmann, E. (2004) 'Evan Kohlmann on al Qaeda & Saudi Arabia', *National Review Online*, February 9, available at http://old.nationalreview.com/comment/kohlmann200402090859.asp.

Lia, B. (2007) *Architect of Global Jihad: The Life of Al-Qaeda Strategist Abu Mu'sab Al-Suri*, London: C. Hurst & Co.

Mariani, E. (2006) 'The Production of Islamic Knowledge on the Internet and the Role of States and Markets: The Examples of Yussef al-Qaradawi and Amru Khaled', in G. Larsson (ed.) *Religious Communities on the Internet*, Stockholm: Swedish Science Press.

Lister, T. (2011) 'Tunisian Protests Fueled by Social Media Networks', *CNN*, available at http:// edition.cnn.com/2011/WORLD/africa/01/12/tunisia/ (accessed 13 January 2011).

Malik, S. (2010) '5 Must-Have Islamic Apps For The iPhone/iPod Touch', *Hilalspark.com*, available at www.hilalspark.com/blog-all/2010/01/14/4-5-must-have-islamic-apps-for-the-iphone-ipod-touch.html (accessed 14 January 2010).

Meedan (2010) 'Egypt's Grand Mufti Calls Time on Quran-based Ringtones', available at http:// beta.meedan.net/index.php?page=events&post_id=289934 (accessed 30 January 2010).

MEMRI (2012) www.memri.org (accessed 16 February 2012).

Miller, G. (2010) 'Muslim Cleric Aulaqi is 1st U.S. citizen on List of Those CIA is Allowed to Kill', *Washington Post*, available at www.washingtonpost.com (accessed 7 April 2010).

Mourtada, R. and F. Salem (2011a) 'Arab Social Media Report 1:1', *Dubai School of Government*, available at www.arabsocialmediareport.com (accessed 24 May 2011).

—— (2011b) 'Arab Social Media Report 1:2', *Dubai School of Government*, available at www.arabsocialmediareport.com (accessed 24 May 2011).

National Public Radio (2011) 'How Google Removed The Muzzle On Twitter In Egypt', available at www.npr.org/templates/story/story.php?storyId=133505503 (accessed 4 February 2011).

Northeast Intelligence Network (2012) www.homelandsecurityus.com (accessed 16 February 2012).

Nunns, A. (2011) *Tweets from Tahrir: Egypt's Revolution as It Unfolded, in the Words of the People Who Made It*, New York: OR Books.

Press TV (2011) 'Iran to test "National Internet"', available at www.presstv.com/detail/185831.html (accessed 22 June 2011).

Project for the Research of Islamist Movements (2012) www.e-prism.org (accessed 16 February 2012).

Roggio, B. (2010) 'US-Born Cleric Awlaki "Proud" to Have Taught al Qaeda Operatives', *The Long War Journal*, available at www.longwarjournal.org/archives/2010/04/usborn_cleric_awlaki.php (accessed 27 April 2010).

Siddiqui, T. (2011) 'Dream: Regarding Grand Shaykh Dagestani R.A.', *eshaykh.com*, available at http://eshaykh.com/dreams/regarding-grand-shaykh-dagestani-r-a/ (accessed 12 May 2011).

SITE Intelligence Group (2012) http://news.siteintelgroup.com (accessed 16 February 2012).

Skovgaard-Petersen, J. (2008) *The Global Mufti: the Phenomenon of Yusuf Al-Qaradawi*, London: C. Hurst & Co.

SufiLive (2011a) "Arsh Above 'Arsh: Precious Moments with Sultan ul-Awliya and Family', available at www.sufilive.com/_Arsh_Above_Arsh-3397.html (accessed 14 April 2011).

—— (2011b) 'Bin Laden and the Teachings of Islam', available at www.sufilive.com/Sufilive_Animation_Bin_Laden_and_the_Teachings_of_Islam-3452.html (accessed 9 May 2011).

—— (2011c) 'Wahhabi vs. Salafi: The Difference', available at www.sufilive.com/Sufilive_Animation_Wahhabi_vs_Salafi_The_Difference-3419.html (accessed 9 May 2011).

—— (2011d) 'Sunni vs Salafi – A Believer is His Brother's Mirror', available at www.youtube.com/watch?v=0dMAt7oAe5E (accessed 9 May 2011).

Temple-Raston, D. (2010) 'Officials: Cleric Had Role In Christmas Bomb Attempt', *National Public Radio*, 19 February, available at www.npr.org/templates/story/story.php?storyId=123894237 (accessed 23 February 2010).

Tsotsis, A. (2011) 'A Twitter Snapshot Of The Tunisian Revolution: Over 196K Mentions of Tunisia, Tweeted by over 50K Users', *TechCrunch*, available at http://techcrunch.com/2011/01/16/tunisia-2/ (accessed 17 January 2011.

Ungerleider, N. (2010) 'Despite Ban, YouTube Is Still a Hotbed of Terrorist Group Video Propaganda', *Fast Company*, available at www.fastcompany.com/1701383/youtube-terror-groups-jihad-anwar-al-awlaki (accessed 12 November 2010).

Views from the Occident (2012) http://occident.blogspot.com (accessed 16 February 2012).

VOA (2011) 'Egyptians Gain a Voice With Social Media Service Used by Stars', available at www.voanews.com/learningenglish/home/How-a-Social-Media-Service-Used-by-Stars-Gave-Egyptians-a-Voice-115430564.html (accessed 6 February 2011).

Watson, I. (2012) 'Syria's Media Rebels Lead Web Revolution', *CNN*, available at edition.cnn.com/video/?hpt=hp_c2#/video/world/2012/02/22/pkg-watson-syria-media-rebels.cnn (accessed 22 February 2012).

YouTube (2011a) 'Wael Ghonim is Free', available at www.youtube.com/watch?v=Cq2bFgvvtY E&feature=player_embedded (accessed 7 February 2011).

—— (2011b) 'Wael Ghonim's Speech in Tahrir Square', available at www.youtube.com/watch?v =jqESVmC1YI4&feature=player_embedded (accessed 8 February 2011).

Zaytuna Institute (2011) 'Hamza Yusuf', available at www.zaytuna.org/teacherMore.asp?id=9 (accessed 12 May 2011).

Notes

1 Coincidentally, the cloud(s) can also refer to *al-Sahab* ('the cloud'), the longstanding publicity arm and computer network established by al-Qaeda to promote and produce their multimedia output.

2 An extensive chart demonstrating this online diversity can be found on the Virtually Islamic site (Bunt 2009c).

3 It has to be said that all shades of religious perspective have taken advantage of this medium: thus, the online sermons and religious opinions of US born 'jihadi' Anwar al-Awlaki (discussed below) is a further example of the ways in which different types of Islamic dialogue can be propagated via the web.

4 The word *ijtihad* can be synonymous with 'renewal' and 'reform' within certain Islamic contexts although 're-evaluation' and 're-alignment' may be appropriate alternatives: the terms have several levels of meaning and relevance, depending on context.

5 A *fatwa* can be generally defined as a 'religious opinion'. There are variances in terms of the extent to which such opinions are followed, often dependent on the source, subject and context in which the fatwa emerged.

6 The term mobile phone is used here. It is recognised that not all mobile phones are smart phones with 3G/4G+ access, and that there are differentials in terms of access and service levels in and within diverse contexts.

7 The question is from an external source, and is answered by Siddiqui.

8 AskImam (www.askimam.org), Islamicity (www.islamicity.com), IslamOnline (www.islamonline. net), Islam Q&A (www.islam-qa.com) and OnIslam (www.onislam.net) are prominent examples of the developments of such services from different Muslim perspectives, drawing on traditional approaches to decision-making and knowledge acquisition, and providing searchable databases.

9 Anwar al-Awlaki's influence allegedly extended to the 9/11 hijackers, Umar Farouk Abdulmutallab (the 2009 Northwest Airlines Flight 253 'underwear bomber') and Nidal Hasan, the US Army major accused of the Fort Hood shootings in 2009 (Roggio 2010).

10 A version of the first edition was hacked by British Intelligence, and replaced with cake recipes. (*Daily Mail* 2011)

11 For example, on YouTube Anwar Al-Awlaki Audio (which claimed origins in Belgium), 14 videos had been uploaded (May 2011): it claimed 231 'friends', and 16,326 channel views in a 12-month period (www.youtube.com/user/AnwarAlAwlakiAudio).

12 For example, participation in Facebook is, according to statistical analysis by the *Arab Social Media Report*, primarily an activity undertaken by younger people between the ages of 15 and 29, comprising three quarters of Arab region Facebook users (Mourtada and Salem 2011a).

13 The use of internet tools in Iran during the 'Green Revolution' in 2009 provided a template of social networking practice, although the online campaigning itself did not elicit the substantial societal change or electoral reform desired by its participants.

14 Timelines of postings and links relating to the events discussed in this section can be found in the relevant archives (listed by date) of the *Virtually Islamic Blog*, http://virtuallyislamic.blogspot.com.

Islam: unbound and global

Bruce B. Lawrence

Outline

- Geography is necessary but not sufficient to explain the complexity, diversity and crucial importance of Islam in the twenty-first century.
- Asymmetric or uneven development in multiple regions of the world preceded 9/11, and its continued acceleration since 9/11 is at least as significant as 'Islam' in tracing responses of hostility, resistance or outright violence against the current global order.
- Journalists and pundits are often less informed, and certainly less humble, than high school students in assessing the ills of our time and our world.
- Two luminaries—one from Indonesia, the other from India-Qatar—point to the bright edges of tolerance and creativity that are marked as Muslim.

Background

One cannot talk about religion or Islam in the modern world without engaging in politics. Since the First World War, and in part due to the massive realignments occasioned by that event, political survival was impossible without representation in that form of governance known as the nation-state. In that sense, all Muslim polities, like their non-Muslim counterparts, had to be deployed as nation-states. But at another level, the similarity of Muslim nation-states to others—either to pre-existent others in Europe or to newly existent others in Africa and Latin America—was deceptive, for the experience of Muslim polities was shaped by two distinct factors: (1) their geographical clustering and (2) their ambivalent response to colonial rule. Both factors need to be scrutinized closely before one can understand the globalization of politics that has privileged capitalism and democracy as the twin carriers of modernity.

Geography needs to be foregrounded and stressed; it is too often overlooked or downplayed in the study of modern day Muslim polities. Muslim life is lived above all in Asia and Africa. To the extent that Islam embodies a culture, it is much more than a creed or a set of rituals or a corpus of law. Though these features do mark Islam as a religion and are fundamental to Islamic identity, they do not suffice to describe or interpret *the social reality of the Muslim world*. Islam, because it claims the allegiance of persons who inhabit those vast regions of the globe labeled Africa and Asia, projects an Afro-Asian civilizational tone. Glossing demography as geography, one can say that 95 percent of all Muslims live between Dakar (the capital of Senegal in W. Africa) and Jakarta (the capital of Indonesia in Southeast Asia).

If Asia and Africa provide the setting for Muslim self-expression, the nation-state has become the power container within which the political representation of Islam has been forged. All Muslims of Asia and Africa live in nation-states: even those who are refugees from one polity must eke out a marginal existence under the protection of another, neighboring polity. Most Afro-Asian Muslim polities have emerged only in the twentieth century. Frequently they have come into existence in the aftermath of colonial rule. No account of the contemporary Muslim world can ignore the colonial interlude, but at the same time what to make of that period remains a conceptual, interpretive problem that is as contested as it is insoluble.

Marx once declared that "men make history but they do not know the history they make." That applies to the history of nation-state-building in the Muslim world. It looks very different now than it did at the time that new nations of Africa and Asia, many with majority Muslim populations, were coming into being. Above all, the tragedy of 9/11 has caused many to rethink how unevenly Islam has become globalized since the end of the Cold War (1989).

Three trends need to be noted:

(1) Colonial rule elicited national movements organized in secular terms with mythical appeals, structural features, and institutional mechanisms that reflected, even when they did not imitate or replicate, the same instruments characteristic of the colonizers' country of origin.

(2) Islam as a rhetorical field was denied autonomy under colonial rule and also in postcolonial polities, and hence it became a symbolic resource, often couched in violent terms, seized upon by marginalized, dissident protestors. We cannot understand 9/11, or what is called Islamic radicalism, without acknowledging that long period of displacement for Islam as a central force in the public square and rhetorical field of Muslim nation-states.

(3) Islam is at once global and local. It is (a) global, since European norms of political rule, social and economic exchange, were introduced throughout Asia and Africa at the same time that they reflected changes going on in the New World, especially North America but it is also (b) local since the process was framed within and limited by indigenous factors, by specific Muslim responses to European norms. To the extent that we can depict a Muslim profile, it emerged after the First World War and exploded into prominence only after the Second World War. It was a profile that revealed a world turned inside out. Neither Muslim collectivities nor individual Afro-Asian Muslims could operate from a position of parity in the world-system. To the extent that they claimed to be either traditional or self-contained, they were, in the words of a noted Moroccan historian, embracing and fostering "historical retardation" (Laroui 1976: 174). All—whether by choice or by compulsion, whether explicitly adjusting or implicitly demurring—were reshaped by European norms and expectations. Precisely because their lives were under a constant stress, their identities were in flux, and Islam became a symbolic resource both shared and contested. Postcolonial reverberations were most evident in urban metropolitan centers, yet their impact also extended to rural or peripheral groups, even when these groups seemed not to be affected or represented by the momentous events occurring at the center.

Overview

It is against this background of asymmetric globalization or uneven development that we have to look at the horrific events of 9/11 and their aftermath. More than a decade has now passed since the World Trade Center and Pentagon attacks resulted in devastating loss of life and our own world turned upside down. How do we view Islam fairly? When I was interviewed for a Chicago-based Muslim TV program in June 2011, the first question I was asked was: how do you teach Islam post 9/11? Without hesitation, I responded: "Unlearn!" And then, as I recall, I added this commentary:

> Unlearn all the slogans about the red menace (communism) succeeded by the green menace (Islam), the axis of evil (mostly Muslim) overshadowing participatory democracy (almost never Muslim). Unlearn the words shari'a and jihad as catch-all categories for universal Islamic aspirations. Unlearn Islamic politics as the major reflex for Muslim social activists across the globe, whether Arab or Asian, Iranian or Turkish, African or American. In short, tell your listeners, as I have not ceased to tell my students: stop reading the headlines and the bylines that invoke Islam as the nemesis of all that is modern, Western and hopeful about the twenty-first century.

Of course, my response was partly tongue-in-cheek. I offered my interviewer the rhetorical equivalent of mission impossible: not just seasoned interviewers but also sympathetic onlookers to global trends as well as many "average" American Muslims have come to recognize that since 9/11 Islam has indeed been framed and renamed, framed as the "other," and renamed as the "enemy," for most non-Muslim Americans. Islam has been wrapped into the role of adversarial spoiler because the focus of the news is always on the present moment, and there is no dearth of public events, whether outright wars or threats of terror, which project Islam, individual Muslims, and/or Muslim polities, as pervasive obstacles rather than instruments for productive change.

How then can one even begin to talk about Islam as at once unbound and global? I advocate Islam unbound and global as the way forward, not just for Muslims but for all citizens of the twenty-first century. But that means that Islam must be unbound from stereotypes if it is to be projected as the global force that it truly and rightly is. One must first unlearn Islam as the caricature of a noble, piebald civilization now reduced to modern-day, postcolonial, and often ineffective nation-states. One must also see how major authorities, not just newscasters but also academics, have coupled the image of the Muslim "extremist" with the reality of the everyday Muslim next door, projecting all Muslims, and not just a renegade few, as threats to the future of humankind.

The negative process did not begin in 2001, but the tragedy of September 2001 became a benchmark accelerating its appeal and broadening its impact. To provide perspective, let me provide three anecdotes that transition from 2001 to 2006 to 2012. The first anecdote comes from fall 2001. Not long after the disastrous events of 9/11, I was participating in a weekend workshop with community college teachers. Our topic was religion and violence. I was attempting to demonstrate how in one part of the Muslim world, South Asia, religion is blamed for violence that also has systemic causes—political and economic, social and cultural—that have very little to do with religion, or at least with religion defined as the individual assent of belief, the collective observance of ritual, and the ceaseless negotiation, and renegotiation, of identity between this world and the next.

One of my co-panelists in the workshop objected. The issue has changed since September 11, she asserted. We are no longer talking about religion through the fine-grained lens of history. We are now confronting a deluge of stereotypes. All of them make us, Americans, out to be secular whatever our religious preference, and we therefore belong to an advanced, evolved species of the human race, while all others, especially Muslim Arabs, who make religion their passion, belong to a barbaric, uncivilized species of the human race. Never shall the twain meet. For the near future, and maybe into the distant future, they will hate us, and we will oppose them. The stereotype, dividing the world into two, allows for no peace between good and evil.

I thanked her for the commentary. While I voiced appreciation for her accent on the pervasive impact of stereotypes, I objected to her retreat from historical inquiry. To acknowledge the pervasiveness of stereotypes, I rejoined, is not a reason to abandon fine-grained history; instead, it makes our labor as historians even more critical. What other discipline but history provides tools to move beyond stereotypes? To her, and to others in this weekend seminar, I justified historical inquiry as more than just trivial pursuit played in the past tense. I held up history as the only sound way to interrogate the hard edges of stereotypes, to unravel their seamless classificatory logic, and to make all groups part of a common future that also has a shared past as well as a contested present.

Unfortunately, her query still reverberates more than ten years later. The situation post-September 11, more than earlier moments of crisis, has recalibrated public discourse about Islam and Muslims. Since September 11, professional historians have been drafted into the ranks of talking heads: they provide 'expert' footage for major journals or TV talk shows or online 24/7 news, blogs and even Facebook entries. Too many of them seem to have reinforced the very stereotypes that undercut historical nuance, even while enjoying their new stature as both good patriots and relevant intellectuals (Lawrence 2010b).

Indeed, many so-called Middle East experts, including one well-known historian, have abetted the fire-fighting penchant of journalists, making certain that one stereotype predominates over all others in Middle America's reflection on Islam. It is the stereotype of a backward Arab Muslim world opposing a progressive secular

American world. It ignores not just the long span of history but also the most recent period of colonial control of much of Africa and Asia, especially areas with large, majority Muslim populations. Rather than a stereotype, this contrast is presented as though it emerges logically, ineluctably from age-old historical patterns. It is a threefold message, with unflagging consistency: (1) Islam is not a peaceful religion in practice, (2) Arab Muslims are not democratic capitalists in tune with the modern world, and (3) because Islam is not peaceful and Arab Muslims are not democratic, they hate us. They hate us because we are so different from them. We do love peace; we are tolerant; we are also hard-working and therefore prosperous. We also elect our leaders and hold them accountable for their policies and actions.

It would be impossible to summarize the diverse, often sophisticated variants of this response that have appeared since September 11, 2001. They include Thomas Friedman, the noted *New York Times* columnist, who sees Islam and modernity as irreconcilable; Bernard Lewis, who imagines Islam as everywhere retrograde and political, except in Turkey; Samuel Huntington, who perceives a civilizational template that covers the entire globe and dictates its options as well as outcomes; and also one of Huntington's foremost students, Francis Fukuyama, who reckons that a liberal order guided by economics, politics and finally culture will reorder the world and consign Islam to the dustbin of history.

Friedman, Lewis, Huntington, and Fukuyama are not alone. With many others they purvey what average, middle of the road, middle class Americans, both male and female, have come to think about the rest of the world, including those parts, places and groups of Africa and Asia labeled Muslim. In a recent study Arshin Adib-Moghaddan displays how three binaries have influenced nearly all public discourse on Islam: the binary between the barbarian and civilization; between Christianity and Islam; and between the West and Islam, the last one having emerged with greater strength in the last two centuries (Adib-Moghaddan 2011).

Few policy pundits look beyond their own discourse bias to tackle directly the issue: why do Arab Muslims hate us so much? Fukuyama, to his credit, does look at how poverty, economic stagnation and authoritarian politics combine to make not just the Arab Muslim world but also a large stretch of the Central/South Asian Muslim world (including Uzbekistan, Afghanistan, and Pakistan) a hotbed for potential terrorists. He shares this concern with the best of the South Asian journalists writing on Central/South Asian Islamist movements, Ahmed Rashid, but unlike Rashid, Fukuyama blames faulty aid policies and corrupt regimes. He does not call into question current US foreign policy which, until the Arab Spring of 2011, had unblinkingly accepted the legitimacy of tyrannical military dictators; they were needed—or so it was supposed—as US allies in warring against other, equally tyrannical military dictators (Fukuyama 2011).

Even as commentators and politicians and academics are rushing to catch up with the Arab Spring, it is instructive how back in 2001 a North Carolina high school student had already grasped the problem and also provided a partial answer to its persistence. He asked the same question as others: why do they hate us so much? But he provided a different answer than did President Bush or mainstream popularizers, whether employed in the academy or the media.

To eliminate any problem (he noted in an email to me after a local event at his school where I spoke in fall 2001), one must look at the source of the problem. I have come up with two main reasons why this group of terrorists and other angry middle-eastern groups are so hostile to us.

One reason relates to their poverty and our wealth. Our government has already contributed to their poverty through funding and supporting the Taliban during the war of the Afghans against the Soviets. (The Taliban came to power after the Soviet period, of course, but many of its leaders were trained in US-supported initiatives, as was Osama bin Laden.) They, the Afghani people, see our wealth and how unfair it is that they have so little. If we could give them better support, the tension between our countries might be lessened.

The second reason relates to their lack of opportunity for democracy and our many opportunities to exercise democracy. These people need something to fight for and to believe in because they have nothing. Lacking education, they join the war against America. If we could find a way to inform them of alternatives to their current way of life, then they might think outside the circle, but not if we keep on supporting the Pakistani government. Right now, it suits us to support a non-democratic military regime. If history serves any lessons, though, it must be that we cannot win as long as Pakistan is seen as our ally. Once the war is over, either the US will abandon Pakistan because it no longer serves our purposes (to support them) or else the US will continue to support a dictatorship and thereby undermine all President Bush's rhetoric about Americans as a freedom loving people.

The bombings are neither reducing poverty nor building long-term alliances. Even if Osama bin Laden is the ultimate evil and the terrorist of the world, as President Bush says he is, the real truth is much bigger than Osama Bin Laden, and America is not helping solve the problem with these bombings. We have to move beyond the war against terrorism to the war against poverty and injustice and dictatorship.

Ten years later, with Bin Laden now dead after a US Navy Seal raid on his compound in Abbottabad, Pakistan, on 2 May 2011, the same questions have to be asked. Americans, more than a decade after 9/11, find themselves asking these questions, with rapt attention not to ideological agendas but to ground-level realities mostly absent in mainstream journalism, historical reflection, or political speculation about September 11.

And it is especially the decade-long Afghanistan campaign that underscores the need to look at other options. Even though American bombing in Afghanistan has driven the Taliban from power, reduced al-Qaeda to a network in shambles, and signaled to the entire world that US military might can exact a fearsome toll on any group that targets, attacks, and kills American citizens, has the war against terror succeeded? As that NC high school student noted back in 2001, the war on terrorism is more than a military exercise. It also requires a larger war, a war on poverty, injustice, and dictatorship, as well as a resistance to dyadic logic.

It is now clear that neither Islam nor the Arab mindset nor the Arab version of the modern nation-state can be blamed for the current level of global poverty or widespread despair. There is a huge deficit in human resources, job opportunities, quality of life, and education throughout much of Africa and Asia where Muslims predominate but the deficit is also huge in Latin America and Eastern Europe where Muslims are a minority. This was a central question before September 11, and it persists now ten years after September 11: how to mount a sustained attack on poverty across creedal, national, and geographic boundaries? Since September 11, and in part because of it, the question has become more urgent. Even though the actual terrorists were middle-class moderns in most respects, and Osama bin Laden a member of the richest non-royal family in Saudi Arabia, it is endemic poverty, as well as the gap between the very rich and the masses of poor and destitute Arab/Asian Muslims, which provides the breeding ground for discontent, the elementary school for terrorism.

Let us imagine that American strategists do succeed in their military campaign against the Taliban and their supporters in Afghanistan. Even after that success the USA, along with its allies, will have scarcely begun to chart the more massive, less defined but more crucial terrain of poverty. Poverty is economic but it is also elusive. It is not only how well, or badly, people live; it is also how they see themselves as citizens of the world. The poverty of the so-called Third World is mirrored by the poverty of imagination that leads us, citizens of the First World, too often to see all Muslims as Arab. We neglect the Asian difference because Arab actors and Arab nation-states dominate our headlines in print, TV, and online.

We need to see the Asian domain of the Muslim world with a sharper vision and a more persuasive insistence on change. Until the election of Barack Obama as President in 2008, very few Americans had thought much of Southeast Asia, except for the vague memory that it was the neighborhood where Vietnam is located and further to the east, the Philippines, once an American colony. But what about the modern day nation-state of Indonesia? It provides the context for my second anecdote. I spent spring of 2006 in Jakarta, the capital of Indonesia, along with my wife, Dr. Miriam Cooke, also like me an educator, and also like me a professor at Duke. We were both visiting Fulbright scholars at the leading Islamic university of Jakarta, UIN-JKT.

It was February 14, Valentine's Day. What do you do on Valentine's Day? You give your wife roses and take her out to dinner. In February 2006, I took my wife to an upscale restaurant in Jakarta. We ate a sumptuous six-course dinner. It lasted for almost three hours. Classical music piped in the background. A carafe of champagne was set by our linen table decked with a rose at each place. Waiters effortlessly glided by, as if on cue, to remove each empty plate, and then refill each near empty glass, asking us, always with a smile: "Is it okay? Are you enjoying the food? Are you ready for dessert?" When dessert did come, it was a rich chocolate mousse topped with lemon sorbet. It marked the perfect end to a perfect Valentine's Day dinner.

I did not have this memorable meal at Charlie Trotter's in Chicago, or at the 21 Club in New York, but in Jakarta at Huize van Wely, a Dutch restaurant that first opened its doors in 1922. Back then, Jakarta was not Jakarta but Batavia. It was the capital of a Dutch empire that extended from the Malay straits to Borneo. It was a rich jewel in the maritime overseas commerce that Holland had enjoyed since the early seventeenth century, when the Dutch bested the Portuguese, made truce with the British and became the European power controlling most of Southeast Asia.

Today Batavia has become Jakarta, the capital of an independent country, Indonesia. Indonesia is majority Muslim. With more than 230 million people, it is the fourth most populous country in the world. Only China, India, and the United States have more persons within national borders than Indonesia. Unlike China, India or the USA, most Indonesians (85 percent) are Muslims. That means 190–200 million Muslims, or almost one-fifth of all Muslims in the world, live in Indonesia. Not only is Indonesia the largest Muslim country but Java is the largest of Indonesia's 13,000 islands. Jakarta, its main city, extends for more than 15 miles in all directions, teeming with 13 million people, all but one million of whom are Muslims, so Jakarta is arguably the largest Muslim city in the largest Muslim country in the world.

Above all these superlatives, however, hangs a cloud. Indonesia is an ostensibly secular state yet its Muslims too have felt the ill-ease of being disempowered in post-independence Jakarta. One form of protest is through Islam, public Islam, the violent face of public Islam that is mirrored from around the world. What happens in the Middle East can, and does, make a difference in Southeast Asia. Even as my wife and I celebrated Valentine's Day, with gusto, at Huize van Wely, our conversation was about more than love and romance. Amid the roses and champagne we talked about the cartoon controversy. Everyone in Jakarta, it seemed, was talking about the cartoon controversy in February 2006. The controversy had begun a week earlier when a Danish newspaper published cartoons of Muhammad, the Prophet of Islam. The cartoons showed him to be a terrorist and a wife abuser. Riots erupted in many capitals of the Muslim world. In Jakarta protestors burned flags in front of the Danish embassy at the same time as they accused the West in general of having fueled this fire.

The dark undercurrent of violent Islam had erupted before on Valentine's Day. All of us remembered vividly September 11, 2001, but even earlier, back in 1989 on Valentine's Day there had also been a cloud. It came not from Denmark but from Iran. Instead of Copenhagen, it was Tehran that captured the headlines. On February 14, 1989 Ayatollah Khomeini was still the supreme leader of the Islamic Republic of Iran.

Ten years earlier he had returned from Paris, where he was in exile, to lead a successful revolution against the Shah. He was immediately caught up in a war with neighboring Iraq. Saddam Hussein had invaded Iran and, with American support, had fought for nine years to defeat Khomeini. By 1989 both sides were exhausted from a war that had cost over one million lives and countless billions of dollars. Yet Khomeini was adamant about his role as a spokesperson for all of Islam, not just Iran and not just Shi'ite Muslims. The previous year (1988) an Indian novelist living in England, Salman Rushdie, had published a novel, *The Satanic Verses*. In it Rushdie also had ridiculed the Prophet Muhammad, along with his wives, whom he provocatively depicted as women of pleasure or prostitutes.

Many Muslims had been incensed but Khomeini, wounded by the long war with Iraq, wanted to reaffirm his own authority as the Muslim spokesman. He issued a decree, or fatwa, that made of Rushdie not just a slanderous atheist but a renegade from Islam subject to the death penalty. The Ayatollah's fatwa carried a bounty of $1 million for the person able to carry out the decree. Killing the atheist Rushdie became a goal for many otherwise civil Muslims. Rushdie had to remain in hiding, always moving from place to place with an armed guard. I met him once in 1994. We both attended a literary conference in a remote Swedish palace. I came and left in a taxi. Rushdie came and left in an armored car, with guards protecting him at all times.

The world of public Islam almost always shows the violent face of Islam. In 1989 there were many Muslims who decried and opposed Khomeini's death decree against Salman Rushdie. Some of them were Asian voices, and they included voices from Southeast Asia and from the most populous Muslim country in the world, Indonesia. Indonesian voices were seldom heard, or if so, only as a background chorus to the main show which was the turbaned, menacing ayatollah justifying again and again his attack on the beleaguered novelist.

Yet in 2006 there were many Indonesian Muslims who did not approve of the cartoon controversy. Late in February I was speaking in Yogyakarta, the second capital of Indonesia, some would say the "intellectual" capital of Indonesia because of its numerous, highly acclaimed universities. The person speaking with me was Amien Rais, the leader of the second largest Muslim organization, known as the Muhammadiya. When asked about the cartoon furor, he replied: "Protest once—yes, but protest twice—no. Firmly but calmly, Muslims can, and should, protest against this insult to our Prophet. But do not protest twice, and never protest with violence. Those who do not feel the insult will only be further aggrieved at prolonged public outcries." Amien Rais was educated at Notre Dame and the University of Chicago. I joked with him afterwards about whether or not he had become too much a middle American after all his time in the Mid-West. No, he replied, with a smile, he had just learned that most Americans and most Indonesians share the same values, even if the media, like the American public, has never quite grasped this pervasive, important connection between the world's largest Muslim democracy and the world's only hyper-power, which is also a democracy!

The restraint of Amien Rais mirrors the need to look beyond the headlines to find other Muslim voices that also etch hope for a cosmopolitan future shared by Muslims as well as non-Muslims. If we look only at politics or political history, we miss an important element: cultural creativity. Often its exponents—artists, writers, poets and painters—have an impact that transcends and outlasts political dynasties as well as global conflicts. Among the most notable Muslim painters is the recently deceased Indian progressive, M.F. Husain. He is the subject of my third anecdote.

It was in September 2010 that Maqbool Fida Husain, aka M.F. Husain, celebrated his 95th birthday. He celebrated it by painting. He painted almost every day, from 4–9am. He had painted since he was 14. He painted big and small pictures, in acrylic and oil. Though he did individual frames, he preferred triptychs and large, multi-year projects. Constantly traveling, he still produced more than 30,000 works of art during his long, multilayered life. By the time he died in a London hospital on June 8, 2011, M.F. Husain had become arguably India's most famous, and certainly its most controversial, contemporary artist. His storyline belies the complexity of his legacy.

Figure 9.1 M.F. Husain poses in front of one of his paintings (London, 2007). Courtesy of Chris Jackson/Getty Images.

Husain was born in rural India in 1915. His mother died when he was but a child. His father wanted him to be a priest but he preferred to paint. He migrated to Mumbai (then Bombay), where he made a modest living doing street canvases. He wore no shoes then. He never did wear shoes, although in recent years he had begun to color his nails—toenails and fingernails. He lived in many parts of Europe, the UK, and the USA. He traveled to South America and to Southeast Asia. He won numerous prizes, he sold many paintings. He also inspired controversy, but always within the bounds of civility, till the mid-1990s when he was defined as a Muslim enemy by right-wing Hindu politicians. In 2006, after failing to assuage his critics or to find space to paint in his homeland, he moved first to Dubai, and then to Doha, at the invitation of the Qatari royal who also became his patron: Sheikha Mozah. His nonagenarian years assumed an annual pattern. Every spring he traveled to London, where had a studio, and part of the summer to Rome, where he had another studio, and to the USA, where he had no studio but an ongoing project. He divided his fall time between Dubai and Doha.

He not only painted but directed movies. He also produced some of his own books. One, *Poetry To Be Seen*, was privately published in 2006. It interspersed pages of poetry with charcoal sketches. At the end, he scrawled in a large black script: "When I begin to paint, hold the sky in your hands, as the stretch of my canvas is unknown to me."

I first met M.F. Husain in November 2008, and saw him frequently thereafter. In September 2010 when I had the chance to celebrate his 95th birthday in Doha at the I.M. Pei-designed Museum of Islamic Art, I convened a seminar of leading scholars on modern Indian art. Taking a cue from *Poetry To Be Seen*, we titled the event: The World Is His Canvas.

M.F. Husain embodied the fuzzy logic of an unbound Muslim cosmopolitanism. He combined many elements that he redefined: without denying their presence in him, or their impact in his life, he claimed their totality as a newness evoking wonder, awe, and celebration. All life, in his view, was to be celebrated. "Nothing in creation is useless," he once observed. "It is our duty to see how best to use it."

Nowhere was this more evident than in his relation to religion and to nation. He drew on resources that deny creedal finality even while acknowledging the appeal of revealed truth, and institutional patterns of liturgical observance. His series on Mahabharata was commissioned by the American collectors, Chester and Davida Herwitz, and many of its panels now reside in the Peabody Salem Museum. During the past four years, that is, after his 90th birthday, he began a series on Arab/Muslim civilization, featuring figures from Yemen, the Horn of Africa, along with desert Arabia, and the Abrahamic triumvirate—Jewish prophets, Christian bishops and Muslim sages.

There is also a canvas of the Last Supper, which makes of it a ritual exceeding the memory, the imagination and—for most—the plausibility of that most Christian of meals.

Mother Theresa also appears but always faceless. Why? "One sees in that empty face all the faces of those whom she has assisted." And so the empty space is not the lack of space but the encompassing of a greater space.

M.F. Husain was a cosmopolitan who happened to be Muslim. He resisted stereotypes and so is a fitting counterpoint to the narrowly etched images with which we began in the aftermath of 9/11. M.F. Husain brought together past and present, opposite moments in human history with connections that seem at once fantastic and farcical, irreverent as well as implausible, and yet suffused with joy and yes, evoking celebration.

One painting might qualify for center stage in reversing the tide of Islam as the shadowy enemy other to all that is new, and bright, and democratic in the West. It was inspired by Obama's election in 2008. Husain stayed up to listen to the results in Doha. He was so elated he could not sleep (at age 93), and so he devoted himself to a canvas of Bilal, the first Muezzin or prayer caller of Islam, a Habshi or Ethiopian, formerly a slave. The phrase Allahu Akbar is inscribed below, but one has to know the painter's story of its inspiration to guess that Obama is being depicted as the American counterpoint to Bilal. "It took America 200 years to do what Islam did at the outset: make a black man its major icon to the outside world," observed Husain. Bilal was, of course, not Muhammad, only the leader of ritual prayer and not the entire Muslim community, yet the comparison reflects the artist's dazzling ability to cross religion and politics enriching one with the other, and in this case it is seventh-century Islam that emblazoned the path now pursued by American democracy in the twenty-first century.

It is a picture to remember as one looks forward to that day when religion might herald a higher, more hopeful path for politics. Religion can too easily be trapped as ideology, no longer viewed as an instrument of divine purpose but rather a product of human connivance, furthering self or group interest at one time and in one place with blinders to other issues, concerns or outcomes. The life and the legacy of M.F. Husain stands as a beacon beyond that trap of religious boundedness, both against the Hindu extremists who ensnared him but also against all who look at Islam as a narrow political trajectory and not an unbounded cosmopolitan vision.

The new cohort of Muslim cosmopolitans

And there are others who, like Husain, labor to unbind Islam from its stereotypical invocation by many journalists and too many academics. Among the most significant is Ziauddin Sardar. Sardar is one of the most prolific cultural critics in the diasporic Muslim community of Britain. Sardar expresses himself as a Muslim intellectual, but a Muslim intellectual in sympathy with non-Muslim Asian others. Sardar, while critical of Islamic excesses, also sees a non-Western cultural alliance, above all, in art, which avoids the ills and evils of Western utopianism, aka modernity, or dystopianism, aka post-modernism (Lawrence 2010a: 260). In *Postmodernism and the Other: The New Imperialism of Western*

Culture, he also offers a strategy for surviving post-modernism, especially through art. It is not only about observing the present, it is also about recuperating the past and recognizing achievements previously slighted or misunderstood. He highlights Chinese paintings imitating Mughal miniatures. "What we witness in these paintings," observes Sardar, "is a thriving, dynamic culture ready to confront the problems of modernity and the nihilism of postmodernism: these parameters, as the paintings illustrate so breathtakingly, are common to both Islamic and Chinese traditions, and by corollary to all non-western traditions" (Sardar 1998: 273).

Rejecting the familiar elements of modernism to build structures, traits and attitudes that define and so homogenize large-scale collectivities, Sardar also rejects post-modernism with its insistent effort on unconnected localism.

On a practical level, the opposition to the West as the sole moral custodian of universal values is also challenged by other Muslims. Notable among them is the Malaysian activist, Chandra Muzaffar. Like Sardar, he is a prolific writer, and like Sardar, he speaks as a Muslim but on behalf of all Asians, non-Muslims together with Muslims, who reject the new World Order. In 1992 Muzaffar established the Just World Trust, an NGO with the goal of challenging Frances Fukuyama and all other West first advocates of global capitalism in the shadow, as well as under the influence, of the G9, or major industrialized economies. It was through Just World Trust that he published his most scathing critique of the linchpin of universalist ethics, human rights. In it he makes the argument that because a minority in the North, that is, the advanced capitalist economies, controls and dominates global politics, their leaders, acting independently but also through the United Nations, narrowed the meaning of human rights (Muzaffar 1993). They have restricted human rights to individual civil and political rights, ignoring other rights—social, cultural and economic—that affect the majority of humankind, above all, in Asia and Africa. Ancillary to this project is the distortion and demonization of Islam through images of Islam and Muslims that are projected through contemporary media, global politics, and cultural wars. The strategy of the Just World Trust and its numerous supporters is to produce an alternate form of knowledge that empowers individuals through revealing the distortions of dominant structures and offering the South another vision of the future.

That vision has been clearly mapped in an edited volume that brackets 14 major Muslim voices under the rubric *Progressive Muslims*. The editor is Omid Safi, an Iranian-American historian of religion, and in this remarkable volume, he tackles the themes of social justice, gender parity, and robust pluralism with ample critique of existing Islamic practices but also hope for another, better way forward for the collective body of Muslims, the *umma*. The final essay amounts to a manifesto from Farish Noor, one of Muzaffar's colleagues in the Just World Trust, and like him, a Malaysian activist. What is needed, pleads Noor, is "rejection of a dialectical approach to the Other," to be replaced with "a new chain of equivalences that equates universal concerns with Muslim concerns and universal problems with Muslim problems" (Noor 2003: 332).

Here is exactly the vista that needs to take shape if Islam is to be unbound and global. It needs theoretical support, and one of the strongest supporters for a Muslim cosmopolitan vision is Ebrahim Moosa. Moosa, a South African activist, turned critical thinker and ethicist, charts a way into Islam unbound that acknowledges indebtedness to European thinkers such as Kant, Weber, and Habermas but also provides a roll call of Muslim modernists. Moosa asks the crucial question that comes from a post-modernist perch: "Was modernism Islam's redeemer, nemesis, or perhaps a bit of both?" And then he answers his own question:

> What we do know is that some of the key figures of Muslim modernism, like Sir Sayyid Ahmad Khan, Shibli Nu'mani, and Muhammad Iqbal all from India, Muhammad Abduh, Rashid Rida, 'Ali Abd al-Raziq in Egypt as well as important figures in Turkey, Iran and elsewhere in the Muslim world, were tremendously impressed by both the ideals of realities of modernity. They truly believed that Muslim thought as they imagined it from its medieval incarnation had an almost natural tryst with modernity. Modernity and "Islam" were not mortal enemies, but rather, as many of them had suggested, Islam itself anticipated modernity.
>
> *(Moosa 2003: 117)*

In Moosa's view, modern day Muslims, like their modernist predecessors, can embrace innovation, openness, and pluralism as legitimate, natural dimensions of Muslim tradition or "orthodoxy." Reason and rationality are not the opposite of faith but its other face.

A further trajectory of the post-modern, post-Enlightenment, postcolonial Muslim mindset is post-patriarchal, opposing not just male dominated structures but also the language of a male god, Allah. The Islamic feminist Amina Wadud, while opting not to create "a new female-centered goddess tradition post-Islam," does wrestle with what she terms patriarchal interpretation. She also confronts the boundaries defining Muslim woman, apart from "personal or public insider aspects of identification," that is, Muslims who claim or project others as "authentic" Muslims because of their names, origins, or locations. She herself does not attempt to speak on behalf of the whole *umma*, or even in terms of a trajectory that sees West/non-West as ambiguous, and perhaps inherently conflictual, entities. Instead, she positions herself as one who imagines "such a thing as a post-Muslim" in order to raise the visibility of Muslim women scholars within Western academic circles and institutions (Wadud 2006: 80–86).

The difficulty facing Safi, Moosa, Wadud, and other pluralist Muslims is the unremitting efforts of certain public intellectuals to wage war against Islam on all fronts. The contradiction of the modern public square is its tolerance of all views, and its inability to monitor none. As a result, equal time is given to views that bugger the imagination, ignore counter evidence, and drill down deep to find every wisp of doubt, every echo of concern about Muslims, and then to make that narrative their platform.

These are the Islamophobes, and they are cited in media as the obverse of the Islamophiles, those who hold out hope, value and benefit from Muslims for a collective global future. In the final section we will examine how Islam unbound requires us to go beyond this further set of binaries, which, precisely because they are binary—excluding and precluding opposites—seem to demand equal attention in the twenty-first century public square.

Looking beyond a singular Islam: the punching bag of pundits and Islamophobes

The best source for understanding the pitfalls of an Islamophobia/Islamophilia dyad is an edited book of that title, *Islamophobia/Islamophilia: Beyond the Politics of Enemy and Friend* (Shryock 2010). Its editor, Andrew Shryock, who is a cultural anthropologist specializing in religious ethnography, engages the debate about what Islam is and what it is not. His collection of essays attempts to move beyond the dichotomization of Islam into bashers (Islamophobes) and admirers (Islamophiles). The goal of *Islamophobia/Islamophilia*, in his own words, is:

> [To] expose the tactical ignorance, malign and benign, that suffuses educated opinion on all things Muslim. Neither Islamophobia nor Islamophilia has cornered the market on mis/representation. [What is needed is] a deeper, more critical understanding of how patterns of anxiety and attraction are continually reinvented ... and how they relate to prevailing ideas—of race, gender, citizenship, secularism, human rights, tolerance, and pluralism—that are important to Muslims and non-Muslims alike.
>
> *(Shryock 2010: 21)*

The essays range from North America to Lebanon to France to Germany; their authors are as intent about urban renewal as they are about ethnic comedy. It is a collection at once serious and sensible in its scope, ambitions and outcome.

Shryock's volume requires the reader to shelve binaries long enough to consider the actual diversity within the Muslim community worldwide, as within the United States. Above all, he invites hard headed realists to look at the myths of Islamophobia. Consider, for instance, Ayaan Hirsi Ali. In a brilliant essay, Moustafa Bayoumi situates Hirsi Ali within a cohort that matches her own experience: Irshad Manji and Reza Aslan. All are immigrant Muslims to the United States. All attempt to explain Islam to others from their own experience of its excesses. Each draws "a singular narrative account of Islam, where the faith is both a singular system and a singular force in the world" (Bayoumi 2010: 84).

That grand narrative not only frames their life stories but, more importantly, it is used to explain history. Hirsi Ali's story, as recounted in her bestseller *Infidel*, and in its sequel, *Nomad,* invokes the trope of the slave narrative, and "like the slave narrative, hers is also one about achieving consciousness under a system of oppression" (Bayoumi 2010: 86). To achieve freedom she must escape slavery, not only her own but the slavery of all people "captivated" by Islam.

Just as the Bible has the power to move the spirit in the slave narrative (argues Bayoumi), so the *Atheist Manifesto* loaned to her by her boyfriend becomes Hirsi Ali's path to emancipation. But the emancipation she details is not hers alone, for what would it matter if one Muslim gives up her faith? Hers is instead a broad prescription for all her co-religionists, and by the end of her narrative it is clear that she is lecturing to all the Muslims of the world. If they are to enter modernity, they must give up God within their creed, not just individually but theologically. According to Hirsi Ali, Islam's salvation is atheism.

The notion of a singular Islam that must be invoked, and then defeated, permeates almost all the narratives and strategies of Islamophobia. The opposite stance informs Qasim Zaman's contribution in which the Princeton Islamicist sees a diffuse Islam, one that both requires and enjoys a complex intellectual engagement with the modern world.

Among Zaman's foremost subjects is no less a figure than Yusuf al-Qaradawi. Unlike Islamophobes, Zaman imputes subtlety and ambiguity to Qaradawi's thought. Indeed Zaman reviews Qaradawi's endeavors with sympathetic nuance. Why the sympathy? Because of Qaradawi's expansive effort to find a consensus among Muslims, not just scholars trained in madrasas, but also journalists, lawyers, and even Islamist leaders.

The effort to find such an unprecedented consensus in modern Islam has been channeled through the International Union for Muslim Scholars that Qaradawi helped found in 2004; it operates out of both London and (since 2008) Cairo. The real divide among this huge array of voices and perspectives is not between those calling for reform and those opposing it, but "rather between different kinds of reform—one genuine, because it is anchored in Islam, the other insidious, for serving anti-Islamic interests" (Zaman 2010: 120).

Though Qaradawi does strive for an Islamic religio-political order, he also projects a global Muslim consciousness as an alternate globalization, one charted in the face of what he deems to be the threat of Western neo-imperialist domination. Yet many of those in the Muslim Scholars Union do not agree with Qaradawi about where and how the line between genuine and insidious reform is to be drawn. After examining all available evidence, Zaman concludes that:

> there clearly is a broad and growing agreement within the ranks of the *ulama* [Muslim legal scholars] as well as between the ulama and other religious intellectuals that bridging the gulf between different intellectual traditions is

desirable and, indeed, a matter of great urgency. Yet there is no unanimity on what precisely is the gulf that most needs to be bridged and why the effort to do so is worth making. What does remain clear is the evolving arena of debate and contestation which... extends well beyond any dichotomous constructions.

(Zaman 2010: 133)

It is this messiness at the heart of contemporary Islam that needs to be highlighted even if it is less rhetorically gripping than a slavery-freedom narrative or has a less visceral appeal than an account of fatwas for or against public stoning for adultery. All of us—not just academics and Islam watchers—need to recognize the real face (or *faces*, more accurately) of the twenty-first-century Muslim world, which is no less diverse and complex, nor less baffling, bemusing, and ennobling than its Abrahamic counterparts who happen to be, or choose to be, Christian, Jewish, or even secular.

One can opt for Islamophobia or Islamophilia, but either option misses the actual drama of today's Muslim world, its enduring search for consensus and its multiple contestants for authority—both at home and abroad. And an instance of how that drama can change is provided by no less a figure than Francis Fukuyama. Rejecting his earlier espousal of the war on terrorism, he concluded five years ago that there was in fact no such war.

War is the wrong metaphor for the broader struggle, since wars are fought at full intensity and have clear beginnings and endings. Meeting the jihadist challenge is more of a 'long, twilight struggle' whose core is not a military campaign but a political contest for the hearts and minds of ordinary Muslims around the world.

(Fukuyama 2006).

Having made that intellectual switch, he then voted for Barack Obama in the 2008 US Presidential elections, and he is now hoping to show how liberal democracy can work in a post-Bush era and in other parts of the world than Western Europe and North America. Let us hope that he will reserve a chapter in his next book for what will turn out to be surprising developments in the Arab Spring, with portents for unbinding Islam and globalizing still further its potential for the good.

Conclusion

The challenge of seeing and pursuing Islam unbound cannot escape the challenge of modern politics. Not only social media but the entire canvas of human experience, in the view of one noted political observer, has shifted away from territorial to movable markers of identity, loyalty and labor. For the French political scientist, Olivier Roy, modern communications, combined with diasporic displacements, whether voluntary or (more often) involuntary, have produced a wholesale shift in contemporary Muslim identity. Muslims are at once deracinated and deterritorialized as never before. Civilization is itself simply part of the outdated vocabulary that no longer reflects the ground level reality of Muslim self-expression and group desire. Change not continuity is the harbinger for the future.

At a time when the territorial borders between the great civilizations are fading away, argues Roy, mental borders are being reinvented to give a second life to the ghost of lost civilizations: multiculturalism, minority groups, clash or dialogue of civilizations, etc. Ethnicity and religion are being marshaled to draw new borders between groups whose identity relies on a performative definition: we are who we say we are, or what others say we are. *These new ethnic and religious borders do not correspond to any geographical territory or area.* They work in minds, attitudes and discourses. They are more vocal than territorial, but all the more eagerly endorsed and defended because they have to be invented, and because they remain fragile and transitory. Deterritorialization of Islam leads to a quest for definition, because Islam is no longer embedded in territorial culture (Roy 2004: 20).

Roy has been cited at length because his argument, while sophisticated, overlooks a major point stressed in this essay: Muslims are like non-Muslims in many respects, and among the most basic similarity is that nearly all Muslims, like nearly all non-Muslims, must carry passports. That is to say, the globalized citizen is still the member of some territory. S/he is marked by that territorial, political location as distinct from others who are denied the privilege, as also the burden, of a particular nation-state identity. While politics is not limited to the state, and while civil society insures, or should insure, the plurality of group identities apart from the surveillant gaze of the state and its guardians, it is still majority Muslim nation-states who embrace the notion of a collective, homogeneous identity. It is they who advance themselves as the carriers of a distinctive Islamic(ate) civilization.

We do not have to share, or approve, the commitment of devout Muslims who are also national patriots to a supra-national identity, yet we cannot dismiss the boundaries and censuses, flags, and armies, that mark them as citizens of particular polities. The flags that fly in the United Nations are more than mere "secular" symbols of modern nation-states. They also convey a Muslim identity. While it has many parts, as well as disparate interpretations and divergent outcomes, it has been projected over space and time through a single, continuous vehicle: Islamicate civilization.

Yet Islamicate civilization is as much the model of diversity as the guarantor of uniformity. It is plural and conflicted, at once reactionary and progressive, but more the latter than the former. In short, Muslims unbound are global citizens like every other contemporary religious community, and the major difference is not a proclivity to violence but the search for a pattern of harmony not uniformity. That longing, which is also a belonging, is best glossed as cosmopolitanism. Not relativism or consumerism but cosmopolitan quests for justice, equity and compassion are the hallmarks of the new unbound Muslim citizen of the twenty-first century.

Summary

- Muslim cosmopolitans include some scholars of Islam. Among them are Omid Safi, Ebrahim Moosa, and Amina Wadud.
- The long-term debate about loving or hating Islam—known as Islamophilia versus Islamophobia—has just begun, and another academic Muslim, Qasim Zaman, points the way to think beyond narrow, and faulty, dyads.
- Despite the arguments of a major French intellectual, Olivier Roy, borders will not disappear in the Information Age, and Muslims will remain global citizens carrying passports, just like non-Muslims.

Discussion points

- Why do the media make Islam exceptional among world religions, often linking Islam and Muslims to notions of enmity, warfare, and terror?
- How have different groups responded to the crisis of a world where rich/poor are divided within and between countries, regions and religions?
- What are some of the best arguments linking Islam to modernity in a positive, constructive light?
- Who are the Muslim heroes and heroines of the twenty-first century? If you could have tea or supper with one of them, what would be your toughest question?
- Can cosmopolitans carry passports, or do passports characterize narrow, national identity, precluding any broad, expansive, and global outlook/agenda for those who carry them?

Further reading

Lawrence, Bruce B. (1989) *Shattering the Myth: Islam beyond Violence*, Princeton, NJ: Princeton University Press.

This book anticipated the Arab Spring by 20 years. It distinguishes different Islamic movements, from reform to revival to Islamist or fundamentalist. It examines pivotal countries such as Iran and Saudi Arabia but also Pakistan, Tunisia and Egypt, with a sidebar glance at the economic importance of Southeast Asia.

An-Na'im, Abdullahi (2008) *Islam and the Secular State: Negotiating the Future of Shari'a*, Cambridge, MA: Harvard University Press.

Can there be an overlapping consensus among believers and non-believers, Muslims and others, about the rights and responsibilities equivalent for all citizens in a liberal, secular democracy? That is a huge question, answered boldly and provocatively, in this major study by a pioneering Muslim scholar from the Sudan now teaching at Emory University School of Law.

March, Andrew F. (2010) *Islam and Liberal Citizenship: Search for an Overlapping Consensus*, New York: Oxford University Press.

This revised Oxford D.Phil dissertation examines the same question as the previous book, but does so from the perspective of comparative political ethics and with attention to distinctions between modernist and revivalist Muslim scholars on a range of daunting issues, from friendship with non-Muslims to service in the military forces of a non-Muslim nation (e.g. the USA) combatting majority Muslim nations (e.g. Iraq and Afghanistan).

Bayat, Asef (2010) *Life as Politics: How Ordinary People Change the Middle East*, Stanford: Stanford University Press.

An Iranian sociologist trained in the UK and teaching in the US, Bayat has produced a book that looks at social non-movements in a variety of Muslim contexts. He engages the politics of fun, as well as the everyday expressions of cosmopolitanism, with rapt attention to local detail and revealing anecdotes.

Bayat, Asef and L. Herrera (eds) (2010) *Being Young and Muslim: New Cultural Politics in the Global South and North*, New York: Oxford University Press.

Since the Arab Spring, many observers have alluded to the significant role of Muslim youth in the current, ongoing unrest. But what motivates, energizes and sustains these young people from diverse, seemingly unconnected backgrounds? No definitive answers, but lots of provocative observations, are to be found in this second book published within one year by the same prolific author.

References

Adib-Moghaddan, Arshin (2011) *Metahistory of the Clash of Civilisations: Us and Them beyond Orientalism*, London: Hurst.
Allawi, Ali (2009) *The Crisis of Islamic Civilization*, New Haven: Yale University Press.
Ayaan Hirsi Ali (2008) *Infidel*, New York: The Free Press.
—— (2010) *Nomad–From Islam to America: A Personal Journey Through the Clash of Civilizations*, New York: The Free Press.
Bayoumi, Moustafa (2010) "The God that Failed: The Neo-Orientalism of Today's Muslim Commentators," in A. Shryock (ed.) *Islamophobia/Islamophilia: Beyond the Politics of Enemy and Friend*, Bloomington and Indianapolis: Indiana University Press.
Bulliet, Richard (2004) *The Case for Islamo-Christian Civilization*, New York: Columbia University Press.
Ford, Glenn (2001) *Message to: Lawrence, B.* (email), October 19.

Fukuyama, Francis (2006) "After Neoconservatism," *New York Times Magazine*, February 19, available at www.nytimes.com/2006/02/19/magazine/neo.html?ex=1298005200&en=4126 fa38fefd80de&ei=5090&partner=rssuserland&emc=rss (accessed May 22, 2012).

—— (2011) *The Origins of Political Order: From Prehuman Times to the French Revolution*, New York: Farrar, Straus, Giroux.

Husain, M.F. (2010) Interview with B. Lawrence, September 23, 2010.

Katzenstein, Peter J. (2010) *Civilizations in World Politics; Plural and Pluralist Perspectives*, London and New York: Routledge.

Laroui, Abdallah (1976) *The Crisis of the Arab Intellectual - Traditionalism or Historicism?*, trans. Diarmid Cammell, Berkeley: University of California Press.

Lawrence, Bruce B. (2010a) "Modernity," in J. Elias (ed.) *Key Themes for the Study of Islam*, Oxford: Oneworld.

—— (2010b) "The Polite Islamophobia of the Intellectual," *Religion Dispatches*, June 1, available at www.religiondispatches.org/archive/politics/2635/the_polite_islamophobia_of_the_intellectual (accessed May 23, 2012).

Marx, Karl (1979) "The Eighteenth Brumaire of Louis Bonaparte, 1852," in Marx, Karl and Engels, Friedrick, *Collected Works*, New York: International Publishers.

Moosa, Ebrahim (2003) "The Debts and Burdens of Critical Islam," in O. Safi (ed.) *Progressive Muslims: On Justice, Gender, and Pluralism*, Oxford: Oneworld.

Muzaffar, Chandra (1993) *Human Rights and the New World Order*, Penang, Malaysia: Just World Trust.

Noor, Farish (2003) "What is the victory of Islam?" in O. Safi (ed.) *Progressive Muslims: On Justice, Gender, and Pluralism*, Oxford: Oneworld.

Ramaswamy, Sumathi (ed.) (2010/11) *Barefoot Across the Nation: Maqbool Fida Husain and the Idea of India*, London: Routledge; Delhi: Yoda Press.

Rashid, Ahmad (2000) *Taliban: Militant Islam, Oil and Fundamentalism in Central Asia*, New Haven, CT: Yale University Press.

—— (2002) *Jihad: The Rise of Militant Islam in Central Asia*, New Haven, CT: Yale University Press.

Roy, Olivier (2004) *Globalized Islam - the Search for a New Ummah*, New York: Columbia University Press.

Sardar, Ziauddin (1998) *Postmodernism and the Other: The New Imperialism of Western Culture*, London and Chicago: Pluto.

Shryock, Andrew (ed.) (2010) *Islamophobia/Islamophilia: Beyond the Politics of Enemy and Friend*, Bloomington and Indianapolis: Indiana University Press.

Wadud, Amina (2006) *Inside the Gender Jihad: Women's Reform in Islam*, Oxford: Oneworld.

Zaman, M. Qasim (2010) "Bridging Traditions: Madrasas and Their Internal Critics," in A. Shryock (ed.) *Islamophobia/Islamophilia: Beyond the Politics of Enemy and Friend*, Bloomington and Indianapolis: Indiana University Press.

10

Militant movements

William Shepard

Violence and terrorism: the "great reversal"

"Militant" does not necessarily mean "violent" but militant movements are often involved in violence in one way or another and this chapter will deal mainly with such movements in recent times. It will also consider the circumstances surrounding their violence. While these movements represent a minority of all Muslims they probably have a disproportionate influence and certainly receive disproportionate media attention. Violence here not only means "terrorism" and "suicide bombing," but also wars (especially guerrilla wars), pogroms, violent demonstrations, abductions, bombings, and assassinations. All of these may be considered "terrorism" by some people in some situations, since the definition of the term "terrorism" is far from uncontested and "one man's terrorist is another man's freedom fighter." I will therefore usually speak of "violence" rather than "terrorism." I shall also usually use the term "martyrdom operation" rather than "suicide bombing" because I prefer to use insiders' terms where possible. Only some of the many relevant movements will be presented here, a few in some detail and others more briefly. That the Arab world gets the most space is a function of my knowledge and (I think) the current state of scholarship more than of any lack of importance of other areas.

For perspective we must bear in mind that violence and terrorism are by no means limited to Muslims. For example, the Tamil Tigers have been responsible for more "martyrdom operations" in recent decades than any other group and the Peruvian Sendero Luminoso, a Maoist group, was responsible for some 30,000 deaths. We must also remember that those being targeted, e.g., states or foreign powers, usually engage in no less violence, albeit of a "legitimate" sort. Armies are no less violent than resistance movements and police may be as violent as "terrorists."

The general background to most of the ideologically based violence in contemporary Islam is what may be called the "great reversal." For 1,000 years Muslims had taken for granted, with some justification, that their civilization was the greatest, morally and materially, and that this was the will of God. Western domination in recent centuries, cultural as well as military and political, has severely challenged this and raised profoundly difficult questions. How is it that God's *umma* (community) has lost its pre-eminence? To what extent are Muslims responsible? What can be done? One response has been to fight back forcefully. Another has been to adopt Western ways in order to "catch up" to the West. Another is to try to purify Muslim belief and practice. Many do all of these.

Ideological responses to this crisis may be put into four very broad categories: traditionalist, secularist, (Islamic) modernist, and Islamist. Traditionalists prefer to keep to the old ways, including local customs, as much as possible. They may respond to the West with violence or by seeking some degree of isolation. Secularists generally embrace Western ways and adopt Western-derived ideologies such as nationalism and socialism. They reject the Shari'a as guidance for most or all areas of society but they usually see Islam as part of their national identity and the state usually supports and controls religious institutions. Islamic modernists adopt many Western ways but root them in Islamic sources, which they may reinterpret in radically different ways. Islamists stress the application of the Shari'a to all areas of society. They reinterpret it to some degree and adopt Western technology but strongly oppose Western social mores. They often call for an "Islamic state." Although Islamist violence receives more attention today, all of these groups may be violent for reasons labelled "Muslim" or "Islamic."

The violence we are considering is usually called *jihad* by its perpetrators. This word means "striving", and one who "strives" is called *mujahid*. In the Qur'an this does not always mean fighting but in the *hadith* (records of Muhammad's words and deeds) collections and in the books of *fiqh* (jurisprudence) it usually refers to warfare either to extend Muslim rule or to defend the *umma* from attack. In the former case participation is *fard kifaya* (obligatory for some in the community) and in the latter participation is *fard 'ayn* (obligatory for each individual). Activities supportive of fighting, such as providing funds and equipment, are included. Today fighting against Western imperialism, even under secular ideologies such as nationalism, is commonly called *jihad*. Some treat economic development as a form of *jihad*. Some say that only defensive fighting is *jihad* and some stress the "greater *jihad*," the struggle against the individual's lower self. Some Islamists say that all struggle against imperialism is defensive *jihad* and the greater *jihad* is spiritual preparation for fighting. Today those who call for violent *jihad* against the West are called *jihadis*. In this chapter the term *jihad* will refer to fighting unless otherwise indicated.

The Muslim Brothers and related groups

Muslim Brothers: Egypt

The first Islamist movement was the Society of the Muslim Brothers (*Al-ikhwan al-Muslimun*), founded in Egypt in 1928 by Hassan al-Banna (1906–49). Al-Banna was very much opposed to British colonialism and Christian missionary work and was concerned by what he saw as moral decline and religious laxity among Egyptians, as well as their imitation of Western ways. He called for an "Islamic Order," a society guided by the Shari'a. This would include government, but the primary role of his society was to educate the people. "When the people have been Islamized, a truly Muslim nation will naturally evolve" (Mitchell 1969: 308). Unfortunately the ultimately political nature of the society's goal and the circumstances of the time were to lead it into violence.

Al-Banna's leadership role as General Guide was central. His style was charismatic and authoritarian but also fatherly (the society was said to be like a family). The organizational structure was influenced by European fascism; al-Banna admired the fascist and Nazi forms of organization even though he disliked much of their ideology, especially their racism.

Figure 10.1 Hasan al-Banna. © Jamal Nasrallah/epa/Corbis.

The society developed a range of activities, including schools, clinics, social services, commercial ventures, and labor unions. In time it began to engage in political action, becoming a significant force by 1936 and probably the strongest popular political force by the late 1940s, although it did not declare itself a political party. If some other group would institute a government based on Islam, the Brothers would support it, al-Banna said. If not, the Brothers would seize power, by force if necessary, when they had the strength and their faith was perfected. The society's slogan was, "God is our goal, the Prophet is our leader, the Qur'an is our constitution, *jihad* is our way, death in the path of God is our highest desire, God is greatest, God is greatest (*Allahu akbar*)" (Mitchell 1969: 193–94, modified).

The society had a youth section that was affiliated to the Scouting movement but also had more activist tasks. Other parties had similar youth sections. Members of the society were encouraged to volunteer to fight in the war in Palestine in 1948. The greatest potential for violence was in the "Secret Apparatus," a unit created to defend the society from police and government threats.

The period following the end of the Second World War was chaotic and marked by violence on the part of all the major political actors including the Brothers. After the Prime Minister banned the Society, he was assassinated by one of the Brothers, in December of 1948, and al-Banna in turn was assassinated by government agents in February of 1949.

The society was made legal again in 1951 and initially supported the 1952 coup of the Free Officers, a number of whom had been in contact with it earlier. It moved into opposition, however, when it became evident that they were not willing to establish the Islamic Order it sought. When an (alleged) member of the Brothers attempted to assassinate Abdel Nasser in 1954, the Society was again banned, several of its leaders were executed and many members imprisoned for long terms.

Among those imprisoned was Sayyid Qutb (1906–66), who was to become a key figure in the development of the most radical Islamist ideologies. Until 1948 Qutb had been a secular literary critic and writer, but that year he adopted an Islamist position in his writings. He then spent two years in the United States, confirming his previous view of its materialism and moral bankruptcy. Sometime after his return in 1950 he joined the Brothers and soon became one of their main ideological spokespeople. He was released from prison in 1964 but was rearrested the next year and charged with conspiring against the government. He was executed in 1966. From about 1958, influenced partly by the harsh conditions the Brothers were experiencing in prison and partly by the ideas of the Indo-Pakistani writer Mawdudi (see below) and others, he developed some distinctive ideas about *jahiliyya* and *jihad*. Mawdudi had applied the term *jahiliyya*, conventionally used for the period of ignorance and barbarism before Muhammad, to later societies, arguing that even Muslim societies were partly *jahili*. Qutb took this a step further, arguing that all societies in his time, including those that called themselves "Muslim," were *jahili*, since they all failed in practice to recognize the sovereignty of God. He was, however, cautious about applying the label "unbeliever" (*kafir*) to individuals. *Jahiliyya* will not submit peacefully to Islam, he said, so sooner or later Muslims will be forced to engage in violent *jihad*, in effect interpreted by Qutb as revolution. Consistently with this he completely rejected nationalism. For him the only nation was the *umma* and the *umma* consisted of a small vanguard. The manner of his death, turning him into a martyr, added force to his ideas.

These ideas led to intense discussion among the Brothers, inside and outside of prison, and divided them. In the early 1970s the prisoners were released and the Society was allowed to resume its activities, though without legal recognition. It disavowed violence and rejected Qutb's views. It has continued its social and educational programs and has sought to take control of various professional syndicates. Candidates for parliament connected with the Brothers, but running under other labels, have contested almost every parliamentary election since 1984 and they have become the strongest opposition group there. The Society initially kept a low profile in the "Arab Spring" demonstrations in 2011.

Egypt: militant offshoots

Others have followed Qutb's radical ideas to a greater or lesser degree and we will consider three here that have engaged in violence. The first called itself The Group of Muslims (*Jama'at al-Muslimin*) and was led by Shukri Mustafa, who had been in prison with the Brothers. He took Qutb's idea of *jahiliyya* a step further, holding that the whole of society was *kafir* and that true Muslims, his group, should separate from it, living in "safehouses" in the cities until such time as they were strong enough to take control. They became known as *Takfir wa-Hijra* (declaring society to be *kafir* and making *hijra*, i.e. "emigration" from it). When some were arrested by the security forces they kidnapped a former government minister and then killed him when the government refused to release those arrested. The government then cracked down on the group and executed Shukri in 1978.

The other two groups, Egyptian Islamic Jihad (*Tanzim al-Jihad*) and the Islamic Group (*Al-Jamā'a al-Islāmiyya*) began among university students in the 1970s. The former was tightly organized and secretive while the latter has been loosely organized and relatively open in its activities. Egyptian Jihad organized the assassination of President Anwar al-Sadat in 1981, after he had made peace with Israel and then jailed a wide range of critics. The hope was to spark a revolt but this did not materialize. The best known defense of their position was provided by one of their leaders, Abd al-Salam Faraj in a tract, *The Forgotten Obligation* (Jansen 1986). It states that *jihad* to establish an Islamic state is an obligation and should be directed at the "near enemy," i.e. the *kafir* leadership of Egypt, before the "far enemy," i.e. Israel. He used the writings of Ibn Taymiyya about the Mongols to argue that a ruler who claims to be Muslim but does not rule according to the Shari'a is a *kafir*. He also reviewed the apparent alternatives to *jihad* claiming they would fail to achieve the goal of an Islamic state. The official authorities produced a lengthy rebuttal also drawn from the works of Ibn Taymiyya. Faraj was executed for his involvement in the assassination but most who were arrested were given relatively light sentences. Later Ayman al-Zawahiri reconstituted the group and eventually led much of it into union with al-Qaeda, as we shall see.

The most prominent leader of the Islamic Group is the charismatic preacher, Umar 'Abd al-Rahman, who was accused of involvement in the plot to kill the president but was acquitted. Later he was convicted in the US of involvement in the bombing of the World Trade Center in 1993. Its members come mainly from the southern part of Egypt and it has been suggested that this group is in part articulating grievances that southerners have against the dominant north. They have often clashed with the police and also with Copts (Egyptian Christians), though in the latter case the reasons may be rooted in longstanding rivalries. It is relevant to both groups that during the previous decades university education had been opened up for many, but enough suitable jobs had not been created. The resulting discontent has provided a fertile field for recruitment.

Both groups were engaged in violent actions in the late 1980s and 1990s. These included assassinations or attempted assassinations of political leaders and other prominent figures (including an attempt on the life of the president) and attacks on Copts and on tourists. The government, for its part, responded with considerable violence and many Islamists were killed. Attacks on tourists may reflect the fact that many tourists dress and act in a way that appears immoral to many Egyptians (not just Islamists) and also the fact that affluent tourists symbolize the dominance of the West. In the end, however, all the violence alienated the public and the leaders of the Islamic Group formally renounced it in 1999. In contrast to Sayyid Qutb's view that *jahiliyya* pervaded the whole of society, these groups believed that the people were fundamentally religious and only the leaders needed to be removed.

Jordan and Syria: Muslim Brothers

After the Second World War the Muslim Brothers spread to other Arab countries, with contrasting fates in Jordan and Syria. In Jordan they have had considerable support and have formed a political party that has sometimes done well in elections and once participated in government.

In Syria they competed with communists, Ba'thists and Nasserists. The radically secularist Ba'th party came to power in 1963 and in 1982 a period of violence involving the Brothers culminated in a revolt in the city of Hama, which the government brutally suppressed, destroying much of the city. The movement later revived, but in a much less radical form. In this case the issue was not just one of secularism versus Islamism but also one of urban against rural dwellers and one of Sunnis versus Alawis, a Shi'i sect that dominated the Ba'th party.

Palestine and Israel: Muslim Brothers and Hamas

During the British Mandate Palestinian resistance to both British rule and Jewish settlement took place under both nationalist and Islamic banners, culminating in the general strike and revolt of 1936, which received support from the Muslim Brothers in

Egypt. After the defeat of 1948 and the establishment of the State of Israel, *fida'iyyin* (self-sacrificers) undertook armed raids on Israel, usually attracting disproportionate retaliation, and engaged in some spectacular actions, such as the kidnapping and killing of Israeli athletes in Munich in 1972. These resistance groups were secular nationalist or Marxist in ideology, although Fatah, the largest of them, had a strongly Islamic orientation at the beginning (several of its founders were members of the Muslim Brothers). From 1964 they were loosely grouped together under the aegis of the Palestine Liberation Organization (PLO). The struggle was commonly described as *jihad*, though often a secular one. One Palestinian said, "I'm proud to be a Muslim and it is important to me, but *jihad* to me means to fight strongly for something—it isn't part of religion to me" (Johnson 1982: 76). The PLO initially called for the termination of the State of Israel but in 1986 it dropped this demand.

The Muslim Brothers in the West Bank after it came under Israeli control in 1967 continued to emphasize social and educational programs while seeking to win over the people and the same was true in Gaza, where it became very strong. As a result it was treated relatively favorably by the Israeli government, which viewed it as a counterbalance to the PLO and to communism.

Palestinians shared in the general "resurgence of Islam" in the 1970s and 1980s, at first in peaceful ways. In December 1987, frustrated by both Israeli intransigence and Arab ineffectiveness, the Palestinians mounted a popular uprising called the *intifada*. At this point two activist Islamic groups came to the fore, Hamas and Islamic Jihad, both with their roots in the Muslim Brothers and both influenced by the writings of Sayyid Qutb.

Islamic Jihad in Palestine is a small group formed in about 1983 by members of the Muslim Brothers who felt the Brothers were not sufficiently aggressive. It is committed to armed action to restore Palestinian rights and destroy the State of Israel, but it does not have an educational and social service network. Its first armed action was an attack on Israeli soldiers in 1986, before the *intifada*.

More important is Hamas (acronym for the Islamic Resistance Movement), which developed out of a branch of the Muslim Brothers and was founded in about 1978 by Shaykh Ahmad Yasin, who had created an "Islamic complex" with a mosque, clinic, primary school, and other services. With the advent of the *intifada* it took the name Hamas and began to circulate leaflets and call strikes, separately from the actions of the PLO. In August 1988 it published its charter, in which it stated its beliefs and objectives. In this it affirms its connection with the Muslim Brothers. It holds that the Caliph 'Umar made Palestine into a trust (*waqf*) for the Muslims for all time and therefore *jihad* to regain all of it is a duty of every Muslim (*fard 'ayn*). To participate in peace conferences is to make infidels arbiters over Muslims. It shows appreciation for the PLO but rejects its secularism. It states that in the past the crusaders and Mongols were repelled only by fighting, and it is only by fighting that their modern successors, imperialists and Zionists will be repelled. Hamas saw itself as taking up the struggle to regain all of Palestine that the PLO had abandoned.

The armed wing of Hamas is called Al-Qassam Brigades, named after 'Izz al-Din Qassam, who had led a short-lived action at the beginning of the 1936–39 revolt. There is debate about how closely connected the two wings of the movement are. Al-Qassam Brigades has engaged in the violent activities, such as bombings and abductions. The Israeli response to such violence, as earlier, has been no less violent. All told, far more Palestinians have been killed than Israelis. Hamas has expanded its educational and social service activities, often providing what other authorities cannot. This has gained it considerable popular support, especially since Hamas is considered to be free of the corruption that has marred the record of the PLO. It has received financial support from Iran, as well as from Arab sources.

In response to violent actions by Hamas the Israeli government in 1988 banned it and imprisoned Shaykh Yasin. In 1992, more than 400 Hamas activists were expelled to a camp in Lebanon, receiving widespread sympathy and also encouragement for "martyrdom operations" from Hizbullah (see below). Hamas rejected the 1993 Oslo peace accords, and its relationship with the Palestinian authority, which issued from these, has been complicated and fraught. Almost immediately "martyrdom operations" by Hamas and Islamic Jihad began. Nevertheless, Shaykh Yasin offered a truce if Israel would return to its 1948 boundaries. (Traditional *fiqh* allows for a truce of up to ten years if the enemy is too strong.) With the breakdown of the peace talks in 2000 the second *intifada* broke out and violence escalated, now including "martyrdom operations" by Al-Aqsa Martyrs Brigade, connected with the PLO, as well as Hamas and Islamic Jihad, and by women as well as men. The Israeli response included destruction of homes, building a wall to isolate the West Bank and assassinations of Hamas leaders, including Shaykh Yasin.

In 2005 Israel withdrew its troops and settlers from Gaza. The next year Hamas participated in the Palestinian Legislative Council elections and won. In 2007 it took control of Gaza by force from the Palestinian Authority, whereupon Israel (with Egyptian cooperation) virtually sealed off Gaza. Violence has continued on both sides, but statements by some leaders indicate that Hamas no longer seeks to destroy Israel.

In considering motivations for violence we may note that the Palestinian situation is an extreme case of the "great reversal." Here Westerners have not only dominated but also permanently settled on Muslim land. That it is Jews who have done this makes it harder, because the Qur'an is particularly critical of Jews and Jews have traditionally been viewed as weak. Add to this the difficulties of life in West Bank and Gaza and in refugee camps elsewhere. Many young people have few prospects and suffer regular humiliation at the hands of Israelis. This can lead to levels of despair and desire for revenge that can easily motivate a "martyrdom operation." There are also distinct personal factors in each case. Barbara Victor, in her book, *Army of Roses*, records a number of cases of women martyrs. One woman heard that her boyfriend had been killed by Israeli soldiers and wanted to follow him to paradise; another was divorced, unable to have children and thus a burden on her family.

Shi'i movements: Iran, Lebanon, Iraq

Iran: Revolution

Two important differences between Shi'is and Sunnis are relevant to Shi'i movements. One is the much greater influence of the *ulama* (religious scholars) among Shi'is, because every Shi'i is supposed to follow the *fiqh* rulings of a Grand Ayatollah, known as *marja'-i taqlid* (source of imitation), and also give donations for his institutions. Thus Shi'i movements are usually led by *ulama* while Sunni movements are often led by non-*ulama* and are often critical of the *ulama*. The other is the prominence of the account of Husayn and his death at Karbala. Husayn has traditionally been viewed as an intercessor and mourned in dramatic rituals but since the late 1960s a new interpretation has made him into a revolutionary martyr who sacrificed his life for justice.

Some of the Iranian *ulama* were politically active in the late nineteenth and early twentieth centuries but Reza Shah (r. 1925–1941) severely restricted them and his son, Muhammad Reza Shah (r. 1941–1979), attempted to do the same, though less thoroughly. During the period of relatively open politics from 1945 to 1953 the Fida'iyan-i Islam (Devotees of Islam), an Islamist group who had contact with the Muslim Brothers in Egypt, assassinated several prominent figures, including a prime minister. The larger political party of Ayatollah Kashani, the Mujahidin-i Islam, gave some support to the Fida'iyan.

As opposition to the Shah grew in 1970s, two guerrilla groups, the Feda'iyyin-i Khalq (People's Feda'iyyin) and the Mujahidin-i Khalq (People's Mujahidin), appeared, both engaging in violent confrontations with the government. The former was Marxist but the latter was Islamic modernist, holding to an Islamic reinterpretation of Marxism. During the period of revolutionary ferment from January 1978 to February 1979 it was the Shah's government mainly that engaged in violence while many demonstrators were killed and more risked death, seeing themselves as acting on the role of Husayn. Once the Islamic government was in power it also used violence against its opponents, particularly the Mujahidin-i Khalq, executing thousands of activists. The Mujahidin response was in kind, including the assassination of the president and prime minister. They, too, saw their sacrifices in the light of Husayn's martyrdom. In the war with Iraq the willingness of Iranian troops for martyrdom, especially the legions of boys who sacrificed their lives to clear minefields ahead of the regular troops, allowed Iran to hold its own against a better armed enemy. Iran has supported violent movements outside the country, such as Hamas and Lebanese Hizbullah, discussed below, as part of its effort to "export" its revolution.

Lebanon: Hizbullah

The Shi'is of Lebanon have been the poorest and most marginalized of the various religious-communal groups there, and the story of Hizbullah is very much bound up with their efforts to get a fairer share of the economic and political pie. It is also important to know that the *ulama* of Lebanon have been in contact with those of Iran since the sixteenth century.

In 1959, Sayyid Musa al-Sadr came from Iran to Lebanon and proved to be a charismatic figure whose modernist interpretation of Islam and efforts on behalf of the Shi'i community gained him a large following. He taught the revolutionary interpretation of Husayn and developed a "movement of the disinherited" for the poorer Shi'is. A Shi'i militia, Amal (Hope), was formed in about 1975, as Lebanon descended into civil war and Palestinian resistance to Israel brought devastation to the Shi'i villages of South Lebanon. In August 1978, al-Sadr vanished on a trip to Libya and was presumed dead, but his efforts had gained recognition for the Shi'is and had given them a new sense of identity.

His mantle was to some extent inherited by Sayyid Muhammad Husayn Fadlallah, who wrote that religion is a "call to strength" and that God loves the "pious strong man" (Ajami 1986: 215). He has had continuing influence on the Shi'i movements, although he has been somewhat marginalized politically.

The Revolution in Iran provided considerable encouragement for the militants among Sayyid Musa's followers and successors, and when the Israelis invaded in 1982 Iran sent a large contingent of Revolutionary Guards to Lebanon and many of the Lebanese *ulama* pledged allegiance to Khomeini as their *marja'-i taqlid*. This was the beginning of Hizbullah, although it did not openly declare its existence until 1985. Its military arm was called Islamic Resistance. Hizbullah accepts Khomeini's doctrine of *vilayat-i faqih* (political authority of the jurisprudent), recognizing Khomeini and later Khamane'i as its *marja'-i taqlid*. Amal has continued as the major secular political party of Shi'is, but in 1982 Islamic Amal split off from it and has been close to Hizbullah. Hizbullah's secretary general since 1992 and one of its main ideologues has been Sayyid Hasan Nasrallah.

The first "martyrdom operations" (carried out probably by groups related to Hizbullah) took place in November 1982 against an Israeli military headquarters and then in 1983 against the American embassy and the American and French barracks. These helped to induce these countries to abandon their "peace-keeping" missions. They were inspired by the example of the Iranians in the war with Iraq, and many more were to follow. Most Shi'is at first accepted the Israeli presence but an incident in October 1983 when Israeli soldiers drove through a crowd celebrating Ashura triggered a war of resistance, marked not only by "martyrdom operations" but also by ambushes, bombings, assassinations, and abductions by both sides, collective punishments by Israelis, and later on rocket attacks by Hizbullah and air strikes by Israelis. Islamic Resistance engaged in about 6,000 armed operations from 1985 until the Israeli withdrawal in 2000, far more than any other Arab group. It was also more disciplined and efficient. Hizbullah was probably implicated in the hijacking of two airplanes and the kidnapping of a number of Westerners, including Terry Waite. To maintain control of its areas it had confrontations with the Lebanese state, with Amal and with Syrian troops, although at other times it has cooperated with these.

While fighting Israel, Hizbullah's ultimate goal is to build an Islamic society and it has sought to apply the Shari'a as it interprets it in the areas it controls, although it also takes local customs into account. Hizbullah has a wide range of charitable and social services including education, health care, housing, and reconstruction programs, often more than the government would provide and often assisting Christians as well as Muslims. It has an agency, Jihad for Construction, presumably inspired by a similarly named agency in Iran. It is also represented in a number of trade unions and professional associations.

After 1989 the party, encouraged by Iran, adopted a more pragmatic approach to politics and began to participate in national and municipal government, considering this a "political *jihad*" (Hamzeh 2004: 112). It gained enough seats to form a bloc in parliament but did not accept a cabinet post until 2005, when it began to play a central role in the political system. Unlike other parties, however, it has refused to give up its arms as long as Israel exists. Since 2000 it has been involved in a limited number of clashes with Israeli military forces, one of which, in 2006, prompted an Israeli invasion that caused considerable destruction and loss of life. It was ended by UN mediation, but Nasrallah described it as "divine victory" (Dick 2010). It remains committed to its goals of terminating Israel and establishing an Islamic society but now is pursuing these by more indirect means and is partly coopted into the existing system.

Iraq: the Mahdi Army

It is not possible to deal with Iraq in any detail here, but we will consider one of the major Shi'i participants in the events following the American invasion in 2003. The Shi'is of Iraq have been ruled, and often oppressed, by Sunni-led governments since Ottoman times, and very much so during the regime of Saddam Hussein (1979–2003), even though they have been the majority of the population for a century or more. Nevertheless they have been largely loyal to the Iraqi state, even during the war with Iran from 1980 to 1988, though not without violent events at times. The regime murdered Muhammad Baqir al-Sadr, a leading Islamist thinker, and his sister in 1980 and Grand Ayatollah Sadiq al-Sadr, initiator of a populist movement, in 1999. The latter led to a brief uprising. An uprising in 1991 at the end of the first Gulf War, encouraged but then not supported by the Americans, was brutally put down. In 1982 with Iranian encouragement the Supreme Council for Islamic Revolution in Iraq (SCIRI) was formed and, based in Iran, engaged in various activities including guerrilla raids into Iraq.

The American invasion in 2003 removed Saddam Hussein's government and led to about four years of considerable turmoil and violence, including sectarian strife. Among the groups and parties contending for political power were secular groups led by former exiles and also SCIRI, which became a significant political force and whose Badr militia provided protection and aid for Shi'is.

The group with firmest local roots was the Mahdi Army, which was led by Muqtada al-Sadr, the son of Sadiq al-Sadr and son-in-law of Muhammad Baqr al-Sadr, who benefitted from their status as martyrs and to some extent inherited his father's following. The Army made its strongholds in the poorer Shi'i urban neighborhoods, especially "Sadr City" in Baghdad, and recruited particularly among often angry and desperate unemployed working class youth. It combined Islamism with Iraqi nationalism (thus anti-American on both scores) and undertook to provide services to its constituency and protect them from Sunnis, as well as participating in the "cleansing" of Sunnis from some areas. In 2004 it launched an insurrection against the occupation forces that was initially quite successful but soon faltered. When it attempted to take control of the shrine city, Najaf, it was soon hemmed in by American troops and was forced to stop fighting when the followers of Grand Ayatollah Sistani, the leading *marja'-i taqlid* of Iraq and opposed to the Mahdi Army's violence, marched peacefully on the shrine. After a couple of years discipline began to break down as some engaged in extortion and indiscriminate violence, causing a loss of popularity, and the Americans began hunting the top leaders. In 2007 al-Sadr declared a truce and the next year the Mahdi Army's strongholds were retaken by the government. Muqtada al-Sadr still retained considerable loyalty and shifted into a political mode. He had already joined a coalition of Shi'i parties approved by Ayatollah Sistani for the 2005 election and by 2010 had transformed his movement into a political party supporting the Shi'i-led government. It was, however, the previous militancy that gave him the prominence that allowed him to become a political force. (For an example of Sunni violence see Abu Mus'ab al-Zarqawi under al-Qaeda, below.)

Afghanistan: Taleban and al-Qaeda

Taleban

Afghanistan in the nineteenth century was the Muslim country that most successfully resisted Western imperialism. In the twentieth century some modernization took place in the cities and in the second half of the century Afghanistan was caught up in the pressures of the Cold War. In 1978 the Afghan communists seized power but factional infighting led the Soviets to send in troops in 1979. This triggered a massive *jihad* against them by ethnically and ideologically diverse groups, aided and abetted by the US and others. Most were Sunni but some were Shi'i. Some were traditionalists;

at least one group was secularist and several were Islamist, influenced by figures such as Qutb and Mawdudi. Many of the fighters had been in refugee camps or had studied in *madrasas* (religious school) in Pakistan. The Soviets were forced to withdraw in 1989. This had enormous repercussions throughout the Muslim world. For many it destroyed the "myth" of superpower invincibility. If the Soviet Union could be defeated, why not also the United States?

Unfortunately, the *mujahidin* groups could not form a stable government in Afghanistan after their victory. In reaction to their squabbling and corruption an ultra-traditionalist group known as the Taleban (the name refers to *madrasa* students) was formed by Mullah Omar in 1994. According to one account this happened after a local *mujahid* commander had abducted two teenage girls and Mullah Omar and his students rescued them, acquiring weapons in the process. After considerable fighting and with the support of the Pakistani Interservices Intelligence (ISI) they gained control of most of the country by 1996. At first they received popular support since they imposed order and made the country safer than it had been. They gave sanctuary to al-Qaeda and after its attack on the Twin Towers and the Pentagon on September 11, 2001 the Americans and their allies invaded Afghanistan and forced the Taleban to retreat to the mountains and to the adjacent areas of Pakistan, where many had been students. Since 2006 they have made a significant comeback in both Afghanistan and adjacent parts of Pakistan, where there are several Taleban groups.

The Taleban have a very conservative and "hard line" interpretation of the Shari'a and *pushtunwala* (the local customary law). Their harsh restrictions on women have received considerable international attention as has their destruction of the large statues of the Buddha in Bamiyan (idols to them). In later years, under the pressure of circumstances and the influence of al-Qaeda, they have become more international in their outlook and more "modern" in their methods. This includes the mounting of "martyrdom operations."

Al-Qaeda

The Afghan *mujahidin* were joined by many young men from elsewhere in the Muslim world who came to fight in the *jihad* and were called "Arab Afghans," although many were not Arabs. Some of them went on to fight in places such as Bosnia and Chechnya in the following decade, and others returned to their home countries, such as Egypt, Algeria, and Indonesia, to participate in violent Islamist activities there.

Among these "Arab Afghans" were Abdullah Azzam (1941–89), Osama bin Laden (1957–2011) and Ayman al-Zawahiri (b. 1951), leader of the Egyptian Islamic Jihad (see above). Azzam was a Palestinian and a passionate ideologue who preached that *jihad* is as important as *salat* (prayer) and is *fard 'ayn* so long as *kafirs* occupy or threaten Muslim lands. He was the mentor of bin Laden, who was a Saudi from a wealthy family of Yemeni origin. Together they gathered a small group of fighters, mostly Egyptian followers of al-Zawahiri, to form the group that would become known as al-Qaeda. After the Russian withdrawal, bin Laden returned to Saudi Arabia. When the Iraqis invaded Kuwait, he offered to organize a force of "Arab Afghans" to protect the kingdom but the royal family rejected this and opted for American troops, getting a *fatwa* from the leading Saudi *ulama* to justify their decision. This appears to have been crucial in deciding bin Laden's future direction. He went to the Sudan for several years and then, in 1996, returned to Afghanistan and reorganized al-Qaeda. The term may mean "base" (as in a military base), or "principle," or "foundation" in the sense of a "strong foundation (*qaeda*) for the expected victory" as Abdullah Azzam had termed it. Later al-Zawahiri wrote of *qaedat al-jihad*.

In February 1998, al-Zawahiri and bin Laden, along with others, issued a document entitled "World Islamic Front against Jews and Crusaders," attacking American activities. On August 7, 1998, "martyrdom operations" were carried out against the American embassies in Kenya and Tanzania, and on August 20 the Americans retaliated with missile attacks on targets in Afghanistan and the Sudan. The relationship between Mullah Omar and al-Qaeda was uneasy. As traditionalists the Taleban were rigid on matters of authority and interpretation and localized in their interests, while the radically Islamist al-Qaeda was global in its interests and more flexible in matters of authority and interpretation. Among other things, Mullah Omar felt that bin Laden, who is not one of the *ulama*, sometimes exceeded his authority. It is claimed that Mullah Omar was considering withdrawing his protection of al-Qaeda but was prompted by the American attacks to continue it.

Martyrdom operations continued in 2000 with an attack on the warship USS *Cole* by a small boat laden with explosives and on September 11, 2001, the best known operations took place when airplanes crashed into the Twin Towers of the World Trade Center in New York and the Pentagon in Washington, DC (9/11), giving bin Laden worldwide recognition. A number of later operations have been connected with, or ascribed to, al-Qaeda, including the bombing of a nightclub in Bali in 2002, the bombing of a commuter train in Madrid in 2004 and the bombings in London on July 7, 2005.

The level of al-Qaeda's involvement has varied, however, and often been uncertain. Al-Qaeda is loosely organized; it has an inner circle, then affiliated groups related to it in various ways, such as funding, and individuals recruited for specific operations, and then sympathizers who may act without being directly in contact with al-Qaeda. Most of the later operations have been carried out by affiliated groups or sympathizers. Those who carried out the Bali bombings, for example, may be considered an affiliated group. Richard Reid, who was caught with a bomb in his shoe during an airplane flight in December 2001, was an individual recruited by al-Qaeda. The London and Madrid bombers were influenced by al-Qaeda but not connected to it. Probably the most brutal affiliate was the one in Iraq led by Abu Mus'ab al-Zarqawi between 2004 and

2006, notable for its extreme anti-Shi'i violence and conscious intention to divide Sunnis and Shi'is. Al-Qaeda has become the prime symbol of terrorism and its name is regularly invoked where its influence at most indirect. Bin Laden, of course, contributed to this by his periodic appearance via videotapes. He was killed in Pakistan on May 2, 2011, in a hit by American special forces and was eventually replaced as leader by al-Zawahiri, but the effect of his death on al-Qaeda has yet to be seen.

As is common among radical Islamists, many connected with al-Qaeda come from middle class or higher backgrounds and have gone through higher education, especially in technical subjects. Ayman al-Zawahiri is a medical doctor. Muhammad Atta, the leader of the group that flew the airplanes into the Twin Towers, came from a family of professionals and had a degree in architectural engineering. Bin Laden himself studied business administration at university, although without completing a degree. On the other hand, Richard Reid came from a broken family and had a prison background.

Al-Qaeda represents a new stage in the globalization of Islamic militancy. Its geographical base has become problematic. Its leaders can appear everywhere by television and its participants communicate by cell phone and the internet. They come from many places including the Muslim diaspora in the West and many are highly mobile and lack firm roots anywhere. Their loyalty is less to a geographical nation or even to the Muslim *umma* as it is than to an ideal *umma* that exists mainly in their minds. Al-Qaeda also represents a progression in one thread of radical Islamist thinking. Abd al-Salam Faraj, one of the leaders of Egyptian Islamic Jihad, argued that they needed to attack the "near enemy," i.e. the local tyrant, before attacking the "far enemy," i.e. Israel. Bin Laden effectively argued that the further enemy, i.e. the US and other Western countries, should be attacked because they empowered the "near enemies."

Other groups and movements

Pakistan: Mawdudi and the Jama'at-i Islami

Abul A'la Mawdudi (1903–79) is important because he was the first and the most influential Islamist thinker (Banna was more of an activist than a thinker) and the organization he founded in 1941, Jama'at-i Islami, was the second Islamist organization. Mawdudi's ideology is well thought out and highly consistent. Islam is a "total scheme of life" including government, based firmly on God's Shari'a. The divine laws are not negotiable but in the administration of them a form of democracy should obtain. He also described Islam as a revolutionary ideology aiming to rebuild the social order of the world according to its ideals. In the context of the movement for the partition of India he rejected Jinnah's secularist Muslim nationalism, which envisaged a state run by and for Muslims but not necessarily run according to the Shari'a, but he moved to and supported the state of Pakistan in order to try to make it properly Islamic.

The Jama'at-Islami was created to be a disciplined vanguard that would work to educate and mobilize the masses. It became a political party and a force to be reckoned with but not a mass party. Its history has illustrated the difficulty of putting a consistent vision such as Mawdudi's into practice in the rough and tumble of politics. Mawdudi was imprisoned several times for pushing his ideological position too much. On the other hand, the Jama'at has regularly entered into alliances with other parties that do not fully share its ideology. In 1965 Mawdudi supported a woman for president, against his understanding of the Shari'a, but justified this as the lesser of two evils. The party came briefly into the corridors of power during the military rule of Zia ul-Haq (1977–88), who undertook an Islamization program, but distanced itself when it failed to get as much influence as it had expected and when it realized that association with the regime was costing it popular support. It supports the armed *jihad* in Kashmir and also has supported some of the Afghan *mujahidin* groups, especially that of Gulbudin Hekmatyar. A later leader has called bin Laden a "hero" (Stern 2003: 207) and some of its members are claimed to have contacts with al-Qaeda.

Pakistan: Lashkar-e Taiba

There are a number of other religiously based parties in Pakistan, generally connected with *ulama* groups. Since 1990 a number of violent groups have been formed mostly coming out of Deobandi tradition (originally a nineteenth-century conservative reform movement) and drawing on its *madrasas* (schools) but the largest and most prominent has been the Lashkar-e Taiba (The Army of the Pure), which derives from the Ahl-e Hadith, a stricter movement that is sometimes called "Wahhabi." The Lashkar-e Taiba was founded in Afghanistan about 1990. Its main concern has been *jihad* against the Indian occupation of Kashmir but it proclaims a larger aim of restoring Islamic rule to all of India. At least in its earlier stages it received help from the Pakistani army and intelligence agency (ISI). It has engaged in a number of guerrilla-type operations of which the most notorious was the attack on two hotels, a railway station, a café, and a Jewish center in Mumbai in 2008. It was officially banned in 2002 but has continued underground. Its political and social wing (some would say front), Jama'at-ud-Da'wa, was active in providing relief to flood victims in 2010. Polls in 2009 indicated that a quarter of Pakistanis had a favorable view of Lashkar-e Taiba (Burke 2011: 463)

Algeria

Algeria's war of independence from France from 1954 to 1962 was marked by atrocities on both sides and cost perhaps a million lives. Although the war was fought in the name of national liberation, Islam provided much of the symbolism and motivation. The one party government that took control after independence made Arab socialism its ideology along with a modernist form of Islam. The faltering of the development program and the example of Iran's Revolution, among other things, led to violent demonstrations by Islamist students. It was decided to hold multiparty elections in 1991, but after the first round the Islamic Salvation Front (FIS), a coalition of moderate and radical Islamists, was poised to win. The regime then cancelled the next round, banned FIS and imprisoned many of its members. Others, helped by returning "Arab Afghans," formed two guerrilla groups, the Islamic Salvation Army and the Armed Islamic Group. The latter, in particular, engaged in brutal actions and the government responded with comparable violence; by the late 1990s the government was largely in control. This weakened the enthusiasm for Islamism, but guerrilla activity has continued at a lower level in the form of an al-Qaeda affiliate, al-Qaeda in the Islamic Maghreb.

Chechnya

The Chechens have a history of *jihad* against Russian domination going back to the eighteenth century, often led by Sufis. More recently nationalism has also played a major role. Revolts in the 1940s led to the whole population being exiled to Siberia and Kazakhstan for more than a decade, with enormous loss of life. A monument to this has a Qur'an and a fist holding a sword and the inscription, "We shall not weep. We shall not weaken. We shall not forget" (Gammer 2006: 176). In 1991, as the Soviet Union was dissolving, the Chechens declared their independence, which was followed by a war in which Russian forces were first defeated (1996) but later regained control (1999). At first Islam in its traditional Chechen form was a mobilizing force but later "Arab Afghan" volunteers and Al-Qaeda support introduced a strict Islamism. As open resistance became harder, the Chechens increasingly resorted to "terrorism," including attacks on Russian soil, such as the attack on a school in the town of Beslan in 2003. Particularly notorious were "martyrdom operations" by women known as "Black Widows," often women who had lost family members to the Russians. The main effect of this violence, however, may have been to lose support in the outside world.

Indonesia

Indonesia has a deserved reputation for flexibility and tolerance in religious matters, but it also has been the scene of violent *jihad*. All of the violent struggles against Dutch imperialism, whether in the early days or in the war for independence (1945–50), were viewed as *jihad* by Indonesian Muslims. There were also the Dar al-Islam rebellions, separatist and Islamist, from 1945 to 1965, and a bloody pogrom of communists in 1965, after an attempted coup, that was considered a *jihad* by many Muslims. The most infamous recent actions are the "martyrdom" bombings in Bali and elsewhere between 2002 and 2005 carried out by the Jemaah Islamiya. While this group has received support and funds from al-Qaeda and some of its leaders had been in Afghanistan, its roots are Indonesian and its leaders had earlier been active in and imprisoned for Islamist activities. Communal conflict between Muslims and Christians can open the way for violent groups, such as Laskar Jihad, which was formed in 2000 in Maluku claiming to defend Muslims from *kafirs*.

Justifications for violence

The material presented here indicates how diverse the circumstances, forms and motivations of ideological violence in the Muslim world are, though it is clear that most of it is a response to Western violence (perceived or real). At this point it seems appropriate to review the reasons and justifications for Muslim violence, especially "terrorism" and "martyrdom operations."

All Islamic violence and especially martyrdom is meant to be for the sake of God, so it has value apart from any earthly effects. The primary reward of martyrdom is immediate entry to paradise. "Say not of those slain in the way of Allah that they are dead; in fact they are living, but you are unaware" (Qur'an 2:154). Moreover, many Muslims believe that God determines in advance the time of one's death, so one should not seek to avoid death but to seek the best death possible. Hasan al-Banna wrote, "God gives the *umma* that is skilled in the practice of death and that knows how to die a noble death, an exalted life in this world and eternal felicity in the next" (Wendell 1978: 156)

Does this apply to "suicide" operations? Many would say no because suicide is forbidden. Others would say with Muhammad Husayn Fadlallah, "oppression impels the subjugated to discover new weapons ... there is no difference between dying with a pistol in your hand or exploding yourself" (Euben and Zaman 2009: 392). They may still condemn the 9/11 operation as harming the *umma*.

Participation in *jihad* should also involve significant spiritual preparation. Sayyid Qutb says: "Before the Muslim enters the *jihad* of the battlefield he has already passed through the greater *jihad* within himself against Satan, his own desires and those of his tribe or nation" (Qutb 1978: 129). The document of advice for the 9/11 attack that was found in luggage deals almost entirely with spiritual and moral preparation.

Terrorism and other forms of violence sometimes work, as has been demonstrated in Lebanon, Iran, Afghanistan, and elsewhere. At the very least, they are seen as weakening the enemy. According to bin Laden, in the 9/11 attacks, a mere 19 *mujahids* "shook America's throne, struck its economy right in the heart, and dealt the biggest military power a mighty blow..." (Lawrence 2005: 149).

Terrorism is called the strategy of the weak. Often there is not much to choose between the "illegitimate" violence of guerrillas or terrorists and the "legitimate" violence of the state they oppose. One of the London "martyrs" said: "Until we feel secure you will be our targets. Until you stop the bombing, gassing, imprisonment and torture … we will not stop this fight. We are at war and I am a soldier" (Sadiq 2005).

Such operations are also intended to encourage the Muslims of the world by demonstrating US weakness, in spite of her apparent strength. Thus bin Laden wrote of the attack on the USS *Cole*:

> A destroyer, even the brave fear its might,
> It inspires horror in the harbour and in the open sea,
> She sails into the waves,
> Flanked by arrogance, haughtiness and false power,
> To her doom she moves slowly,
> A dinghy awaits her, riding the waves.

(Burke 2003: 191)

A frequent motive is revenge. Individual revenge is problematic. The 9/11 martyrs are advised not to seek revenge for themselves but to do what they do for God's sake. On the other hand, revenge may restore honor. Bin Laden said the 9/11 martyrs "erased the shame from the forehead of the *umma*" (Lawrence 2005: 155).

What about the killing of innocent people? According to many *fiqh* interpretations it is permissible to kill non-combatants under certain circumstances, such as when they are mixed in with combatants. Bin Laden has argued at length that the actions of 9/11 fall within these bounds. He has also stated that Americans are not innocent since they choose their leaders and approve their policies.

Some closing thoughts

Violence has its uses and its limits. The most extreme forms of violence seem destined to fail either because of the superior force of the state, or because of the alienation of those who are supposedly being helped, or because of divisions within or among the violent groups. The "great reversal," however, is still far from being reversed. The West is still immeasurably more powerful than the Muslim world militarily, politically, economically, and culturally and still dominates it in many ways. There is still plenty of evidence to support a proposition believed by many Muslims, that the West understands only force. Given this, we may expect violence to seem appropriate to many Muslims for the foreseeable future although we must also recognize that other more peaceful means of redressing the balance have been used and will be used by Muslims in the future.

Summary

- Ideologues justify violence by reference to the Qur'an and the Sunna, as well as by practical considerations.
- All of the ideological violence discussed in this chapter in some way aims at reversing the "great reversal."
- Violence also reflects particular local conditions and agendas.
- Islamists may or may not involve themselves in violence. The same is true of secularists.
- Violent groups also often engage in educational and social services that increase their acceptance by the people.
- The same group may be violent under some circumstances and not under others.
- Violence is often self-defeating since it attracts massive countermeasures from the state and eventually alienates the people.

Points for discussion

- How do particular movements discussed in this chapter relate to the "great reversal"?
- Are "martyrdom operations" justifiable by Islamic standards? Are they justifiable by any other standards?
- How would one assess the success of any violent action or movement (e.g. 9/11)?
- What kind of conditions conduce to ideological violence?
- Are some (Muslim) groups more prone to violence than others?
- How do Islamist and secularist violence differ from each other (if they do)?

Further reading

Burke, Jason (2003) *Al-Qaeda: Casting a Shadow of Terror*, London: I.B. Tauris.

An excellent study of al-Qaeda up to the time of its publication.

Burke, Jason (2011) *The 9/11 Wars*, London: Allen Lane.

Updates *Al-Qaeda* along with information on events in Afghanistan, Iraq, Pakistan and elsewhere.

Euben, Roxanne and Muhammad Qasim Zaman (eds) (2009) *Texts and Contexts from Al-Banna to Bin Laden*, Princeton, NJ and Oxford: Princeton University Press.

A good selection of texts by many of the figures mentioned in this chapter as well as others of interests.

Gammer, Moshe (2006) *The Lone Wolf and the Bear: Three Centuries of Chechen Defiance of Russian Rule*, London: C. Hurst & Co. Ltd.

Good on the historical background of the conflict.

Hamzeh, Ahmad Nizar (2004) *In the Path of Hizbullah*, Syracuse, NY: Syracuse University Press.

Thorough account and analysis of the movements, its leaders and structure.

Lawrence, Bruce (ed.) (2005) *Messages to the World: The Statements of Osama Bin Laden*, trans. James Howarth, London: Verso.

Bin Laden's major statements on a wide range of topics.

Mitchell, R.P. (1969) *The Society of the Muslim Brothers*, London: Oxford University Press.

The most thorough study of the Brothers, but carrying on only up to the 1950s.

Oxford Islamic Studies Online, www.oxfordislamicstudies.com.

Short entries and longer articles on a number of relevant topics. Some items are free but individual or institutional subscription required for most.

Qutb, Sayyid (1978) *Milestones*, trans. S. Badrul Hasan, Beirut: Holy Koran Publishing House, 1978. Also revised translation with a forward by Ahmad Zaki Hamad, Indianapolis: American Trust Publications, 1990.

Qutb's best known and most radical work. Translations are acceptable.

Stern, Jessica (2003) *Terror in the Name of God: Why Religious Militants Kill*, New York: HarperCollins.

A very informative study.

References

Ajami, Fuad (1986) *The Vanished Imam: Musa al-Sadr and the Shia of Lebanon*, Ithaca, NY: Cornell University Press.

Burke, Jason (2003) *Al-Qaeda: Casting a Shadow of Terror*, London: I.B. Tauris.

—— (2011) *The 9/11 Wars*, London: Allen Lane.

Dick, Marlin (2010) "Hizballah's Domestic Growing Pains," *Middle East Report*, September 13, available at www.merip.org/mero/mero091310.html (accessed September 15, 2010).

Euben, Roxanne and Muhammad Qasim Zaman (eds) (2009) *Texts and Contexts from Al-Banna to Bin Laden*, Princeton, NJ and Oxford: Princeton University Press.

Gammer, Moshe (2006) *The Lone Wolf and the Bear: Three Centuries of Chechen Defiance of Russian Rule*, London: C. Hurst & Co. Ltd.

Hamzeh, Ahmad Nizar (2004) *In the Path of Hizbullah*, Syracuse, NY: Syracuse University Press.

Jansen, J.J.G. (1986) *The Neglected Duty: The Creed of Sadat's Assassins and Islamic Resurgence in the Middle East*, New York: Macmillan.

Johnson, Nels (1982) *Islam and the Politics of Meaning in Palestinian Nationalism*, London: Kegan Paul.

Lawrence, Bruce (ed.) (2005) *Messages to the World: The Statements of Osama Bin Laden*, trans. James Howarth, London: Verso.

Mitchell, R.P. (1969) *The Society of the Muslim Brothers*, London: Oxford University Press.

Qutb, Sayyid (1978) *Milestones*, Beirut: Holy Koran Publishing House.

Sadiq (2005) "London Suicide Bomber Before 'Entering Gardens of Paradise,' and Ayman Al-Zawahiri's Threats of More Bombings in the West," MEMRI Special Dispatch Series 979, available at http://memri.org/bin/articles.cgi?Page=archives&A rea=sd&ID=SP97905 (accessed October 27, 2008).

Stern, Jessica (2003) *Terror in the Name of God: Why Religious Militants Kill*, New York: HarperCollins.

Victor, Barbara (2003) *Army of Roses: Inside the World of Palestinian Women Suicide Bombers*, Emmaus, PA: Rodale.

Wendell, C. (ed. & trans.) (1978) *Five Tracts of Hasan al-Banna*, Berkeley: University of California Press.

11

Secularization and the search for an authentic Muslim modern

Jeffrey T. Kenney

Introduction

To modernize is to Westernize, and to Westernize is to secularize. Such was the underlying assumption of most theories of development advanced in the nineteenth and twentieth centuries, and global patterns of development seemed to prove the assumption correct. These patterns extended to the Muslim world and had taken firm root by the midpoint of the twentieth century when many Muslim peoples gained their independence and entered a phase of nation-building. Muslim majority countries as far removed and culturally diverse as Turkey, Pakistan, and Malaysia set themselves on a course of political, social, and economic modernization that explicitly mirrored Western models; and these changes were often framed in secular terms. Indeed, embracing secularization was a way for political leaders and the cultural elite to demonstrate their commitment to ending age-old practices and lifestyles that were thought to hold their societies back. Islam, at least the Islam exhibited by traditional scholars and institutions, was viewed as stagnant and mired in the past. Secularization, by contrast, was seen as progressive and future-oriented. By the end of the twentieth century, however, enthusiasm in Muslim societies for secular modernism had waned dramatically; and in some places, the idea of the secular was under full attack.

Why did attitudes toward the secular shift in the Muslim world? One common answer that unites some Muslim thinkers and Western skeptics of a modern (-izable) Islam is that Islam fuses religion and state, and thus is not compatible with secularization. Those who hold this view tend to believe that Islam has an essential nature—one that is unchanging and that requires Islam to dominate public and private life. Another explanation, actually more of a confessional observation, is that our understanding of secularization has been flawed all along; and the evidence for this misunderstanding is the global religious resurgence that has been identified throughout the world and across religious traditions, including those in the West. Peter L. Berger, a sociologist who contributed to secularization theory in the 1960s, has labeled this resurgence "desecularization," claiming that "the assumption that we live in a secularized world is false" (1999: 2). The modern world, as it turns out, is awash in religiosity—and conservative religiosity at that; and those scholars who predicted a correlation between modernization and religious decline got it wrong, Berger included. Like many students of religion, Berger was surprised by signs of global religious resurgence in the second half of the twentieth century, including the 1979 Iranian Revolution, the growth of Islamist movements throughout the Muslim world, the prominence of the Religious Right in American politics in the 1980s, and the spread of Evangelicalism in Latin America.[1]

Only two paragraphs deep into this chapter and already the secular has appeared on the modern historical stage and then disappeared like a phantom. And all this before a definition of the secular has even been offered. So, has secularization occurred in the Muslim world or not? Are Muslim societies capable of secularization or not? Is the modern world secular or not?

The story of secularization is not easy to tell because it is still unfolding and how this story is told has also become a subject of debate among scholars and developing world peoples for whom the secular is more than an abstract academic interest. Sorting out this story, and its variant versions, is key to understanding the Muslim experience of modernity and the very notion of what it means to be modern in a globalized world.

Roots of the secular and secularization

Three interconnected terms require clarification: secular, secularization, and secularism. The modern word "secular" derives from a (Christian) Latin root that means of or related to the world as opposed to the Church. It was often used to distinguish the affairs of religion and Church from temporal, lay, or civil matters. The cognate word "secularization" designated the process or act of converting an ecclesiastical or Church-related person or place into a secular one. "Secularism," by linguistic and historical extension, came to mean a belief in or ideological commitment to the separation of religion and this-worldly affairs.

An important early example of secularization occurred with the Protestant Reformation (1517) and the resulting theological and political tensions that it set loose throughout Europe. These tensions led to the Thirty Years' War or religious wars, which pitted Protestant princes against Catholic princes who were allied with the Holy Roman Empire. The resulting peace, the Treaty of Westphalia (1648), removed land previously under Church control, transferring it to civic political authorities, and gave rise to the modern European state system and an emphasis on religious tolerance.

The Enlightenment, which followed the Thirty Years' War, added further impetus to secular thinking and the secularization process in Europe. An eighteenth-century intellectual trend, the Enlightenment challenged traditional ideas and institutions, especially established religion, and emphasized critical reason as a means of scientific, political, and social progress. In France, the birthplace of the Enlightenment, strong anti-clericalism created a sense that reason and revelation were incompatible. In Europe as a whole, enlightenment thinking had a reforming effect on religion, giving rise to rational forms such as Deism. Among the masses, belief in God did not decline during this period. Among an emergent body of intellectuals, however, the groundwork was laid for secular, this-worldly explanations of the human condition that undermined the divine framework fostered by religious authorities (Chadwick 1975).

These historic challenges to Church power and authority paralleled other signs of progress in the West, such as the scientific and industrial revolutions, centralized bureaucracy, system of world trade, the university, and democratic politics. Taken together, they comprise the Western narrative of modernity, the story that is told to account for the rise of the West. Of course, it was the very rise of Western powers, along with their capacity and will to project themselves around the world, that made the West's path to modernity a compelling model. Thus the assumption about development cited at the outset—to modernize is to Westernize, and to Westernize is to secularize—had a certain logic to it.

The logic, however, also contained a problematic expectation: that developing peoples in Asia, Africa, and the Middle East would travel not just the same material path of progress as the West but the same secular cultural path as well. This same expectation influenced sociology, the very field of study in the Western academy that identified secularization as part of modernization. Case in point is Peter Berger's original, often-quoted definition of secularization: "the process by which sectors of society and culture are removed from the domination of religious institutions and symbols" (1967: 107). Like many sociologists, Berger believed that secularization was a universal phenomenon, something that occurred in every modernizing society. But the evidence for secularization, like the evidence for modernization itself, was drawn from historical developments that occurred first in the West.

In the West, however, the material and the cultural factors that gave rise to modernization were historically intertwined. In the Muslim world, by contrast, the first flowerings of modernization were largely material—industry, science, and technology. Cultural considerations of identity and values came later; and when they did emerge, they initially raised questions about the legitimacy and relevance of Islamic history and tradition. Were Muslim peoples supposed to experience the same tensions and confrontations with religious authority and power as Westerners had? Was Islam compatible with modernity? Was the Islamic tradition in need of its own Martin Luther, the intellectual catalyst of the Protestant Reformation, or its own Spinoza, an Enlightenment critic of religious tradition? Such comparative references were common among Muslims and non-Muslims who sought to locate the key to modernization in Muslim societies. In some cases, these comparisons reflected a deep understanding of both Western and Islamic civilizations. For example, the nineteenth-century reformer Jamal al-Din al-Afghani (1839–97) often referred to Martin Luther and the Protestant Reformation in his writings, presenting them as models worthy of emulation; and he is said to have wanted to play a Luther-like role in the Islamic tradition (Keddie 1983: 82–83). The Egyptian philosopher Hasan Hanafi (b. 1935) looked to Western philosophers, particularly Spinoza, to push for intellectual reform in Islamic thought, and he came to advocate a tolerant, liberation-theology reading of Islam reflective of Spinoza's ideas (Kersten 2011: 114, 156, 168). In other cases, the comparison takes the form of a passing remark, such as the one made to a reporter by an Iranian woman frustrated with the intolerant aftereffects of the 1979 revolution: "We need a Spinoza in Iran."[2] When adopted in Western sources, the question of whether someone such as Tariq Ramadan, a Swiss-born academic who has written extensively about Islam and Muslims in the West, is the Muslim Martin Luther might be an innocent, although misguided, attempt to help Western readers understand the intellectual importance of someone in a different religious tradition.[3] Or such a comparison might be an attempt to demonstrate the unlikelihood of Muslims modernizing like people in the West have, such as the conservative columnist Marc Gerecht's observation that democracy among Muslims in not likely to succeed because as "the history of democratic Christendom" has shown, "you don't get to arrive at Thomas Jefferson unless you first pass through Martin Luther."[4] What all these references demonstrate is the extent to which the West's historical experience has become the standard point of reference.

By the time such comparisons were being made, however, the Islamic world had already embarked on a series of dramatic social and economic transformations. These transformations marked the dawn of secular influence, both real and perceived, in Muslim societies.

Modernization, social change, and cultural reform

Modernity arrived in the Islamic world on a wave of Western expansion that took many forms, including colonialism. Flush with scientific and technological prowess, economic strength, and a sense of cultural superiority, Western powers—primarily the British, French, and Dutch—pushed into Africa, the Middle East, and Asia. Their impact was dramatic, laying the basis for a modern world system. This system established economic, political, and cultural connections still in effect today. It also led to an asymmetric transfer of knowledge, from the West to the rest, that transformed what came to be known as the "developing world."

The first wave of Western expansion was economic, reflecting a desire for cheap resources and new markets. As early as 1600, the British had established trading interests in India, which at the time was ruled by the Mughals, an Indian-Persian Muslim elite whose empire extended from Afghanistan to the subcontinent. The British East India Company built and ran factories in several cities to produce cloth and other materials for export. By the end of the century, the East India Company had formed its own "government" to organize and control its interests. Remnants of the waning Mughal Empire challenged British influence in the region, as did the French who sought to stake their own claim in the subcontinent. But the British emerged the dominant power in India by the end of the eighteenth century, laying the foundation of an empire that would last until the end of the Second World War. To cement its colonial hold on the country and facilitate commercial development, the British built roads, railways, and telegraphs. British colonial governance reflected home rule, at least in its structural outlines; and a new legal system, again based on that of the British, was established. Over time, a body of Indian bureaucrats emerged, reflecting the extent to which colonial governance depended on the colonized for its maintenance. New schools to train bureaucrats and other functionaries eventually gave rise to a complete system of education based on the British model.

A similar pattern of European commercial expansion followed by colonial rule occurred in Muslim Southeast Asia. Throughout the 1600s and 1700s, first the Portuguese and then the Dutch struggled for control over trade in pepper, spices, tin, and opium. The Dutch eventually won out but were later challenged by the British who gained a foothold in Singapore and the Malay states in the late eighteenth century. While technically the British regarded the Malay states as a protectorate, not a colony, the control they exercised there—over the economy, society, and politics— made the region seem of a piece with British colonial rule elsewhere.

In the Middle East, European powers vied for commercial interests in an Ottoman Empire already weakened by territorial loss and administrative failure. The frontline Islamic power on Europe's border, the Ottomans had witnessed first-hand the growing power of and threat from their old Christian nemesis. Intent on staving off decline, the Ottomans implemented a series of military, economic, bureaucratic, and social reforms, many of which were based on European models and implemented with the assistance of European advisors. In the mid-nineteenth century, these reforms, known as the Tanzimat, undermined traditional religious authorities (ulama), replaced Islamic law with a European system, revamped state organization and ministries, and made improvements in industry, commerce, and banking. Technical innovations, such as railways, telegraphs, and steamships, were also introduced (Lewis 1968). In the end, these top-down attempts to reinvigorate a fading empire failed, but they did put in place modern structures that, in the next century, facilitated the emergence of the Turkish nation-state. Egypt, an autonomous land within the greater Ottoman Empire, followed a course of modernization similar to that of its Ottoman compatriots. Drawing on British expertise and loans, Muhammad Ali, the Khedive of Egypt, and later his son Ismail, instituted reforms in the military, education, industry, and land usage. Scientific and technical developments entered the country at a rapid pace, exposing Egyptians to new ideas, inventions, and ways of life. Tensions over economic policy and loan repayments led the British to recall their loans and eventually take control of Egypt, in 1882, to ensure their investments. Like India, Egypt would not win its independence from Britain until the mid-twentieth century.

While each of the countries reviewed above—India, Malay states (later Malaysia), Ottoman Empire (later Turkey), and Egypt—had its own unique path toward modernization, shared patterns are evident. Clearly, modernization was linked with exposure to Western powers and their scientific and technological knowledge. Modernization also entailed the importation, either voluntarily out of self-interest or through colonial force, of new ways of thinking and living; and these new ways contrasted dramatically with existing society. As a result, traditional societies began to see themselves as "traditional" and "developing" because of the changes in industry, commerce, communication, education, and social organization.[5]

At first glance, these wide-ranging changes do not appear to be secular. Certainly Muslims did not need to possess a secular outlook to accommodate the changes happening around them. Indeed, the very idea of the secular or secularization remained foreign to most Muslims until the late twentieth century, when a conscious discourse on secularization began to take hold in places such as Egypt.[6] Structurally, however, Muslim societies were becoming more complex: job specialization was increasing, as was the training necessary to perform new tasks and to work with modern technology; social institutions such as law, education, and commerce also developed higher levels of complexity to facilitate the integration of Muslim societies into the modern world system; and centralizing states sought to bring heretofore isolated regions and autonomous groups (tribes, ethnicities, minorities) into a more organized and productive whole. Sociologists call this growing structural complexity "social differentiation" and regard it as one of the defining features of modernization. Differentiated societies are ones with different spheres: the secular spheres of politics, science, and economy; and the religious-cultural sphere. Indeed, modernity also brought a secular distinction into culture, which was no longer solely reflective of religious expression. These separate spheres are governed by autonomous rules, norms, and practices that are sometimes in conflict, and that require a more complex balancing act on the part of individuals who operate in them. Having multiple spheres entails having multiple identities or, at least, richer and more segmented identities—all of which means that individuals find themselves pulled in new directions and self-conscious about this modern condition.

In Europe, as sociologist José Casanova has pointed out, social differentiation was part of a larger pattern of secularization that included a decline of religious beliefs and practices and the privatization of religion (Casanova 1994: 20–39). Evidence for such a social reality can be found in a number of modern European nations (for example, France, Denmark, and Sweden), where public displays of religion and religiosity became rare and largely rejected, and where church attendance and belief in God waned dramatically. But not all nations with a secular sphere came to exclude religion from public spaces or experienced a decline in religious belief. In the United States, religion has historically played an active part in public life and the vast majority of Americans has always adhered to some belief in God or the sacred. According to polling data gathered by Gallup in 2009 and 2010, for example, a significantly higher percentage of people in the United States believe that religion is an important part of their daily lives than people in most Western European nations.[7] Thus secularization developed in different ways in different places.[8]

In Muslim societies, secularization in the form of social differentiation was embedded in a web of modernizing trends and structures introduced from the outside and imposed from the top down.[9] To be sure, state leaders in Muslim societies were not thinking in terms of "social differentiation" or "secular spheres" when they implemented reforms. Their goal was simply to foster development, to bring their people into the modern world and make them competitive. But such a goal necessarily entailed shaping new institutions and attitudes, and challenging old ones; and religious institutions and attitudes were a clear-cut target of concern. When state leaders established new systems of education based on Western models, they marginalized traditional Islamic learning and leadership. And they limited potential challenges by confiscating the holdings of Islamic foundations and bringing their operation under government bureaucratic control. By the mid- to late nineteenth century, a number of Muslim reformers had emerged—such as Jamal al-Din al-Afghani (1839–97) and Muhammad 'Abduh (1849–1905) in Egypt and Sayyid Ahmad Khan (1817–98) in India—who criticized existing Islamic leadership and provided new Islamic legitimacy for the changes already underway (Schulze 2002: 14–59). These reformers were part of a larger modernizing elite, many of whom had studied in Western nations and developed a familiarity with the differences between Western and Muslim societies and cultures.

Perhaps no figure better captures the reformist spirit than Jamal al-Din al-Afghani. His career as a journalist and writer-activist took him to a variety of regions—India, Egypt, Persia, and Istanbul—where he witnessed the challenges facing Muslim societies and tried to advocate authentic solutions. Al-Afghani, like many reformers, was a harsh and unflinching critic of the modern Muslim condition, which he regarded as weak and woefully unprepared for the future that lay ahead. For far too long, he argued, Muslims had neglected reason and science—twinned elements of a philosophic tradition that contributed to Islam's golden age. Islam was once a great civilization, according to al-Afghani, a beacon of knowledge in the arts and sciences that cast its light upon the entire world. This glorious past, however, was now lost, and Muslims were forced to seek science from Europe, its new abode. For al-Afghani, looking to the West for scientific knowledge and understanding was a completely logical move and a necessary one if Muslims hoped to progress and prevent further Western incursions. In al-Afghani's analysis, science and the progress of civilizations went hand-in-hand. By turning toward the West, then, Muslims were turning toward civilization; and once the supremacy of science and reason had been restored among Muslims, Islamic civilization could be restored.

Al-Afghani blamed the backward state of affairs in Muslim societies on Islam itself or more precisely on the Islam of the traditional scholars (ulama). After reaching the pinnacle of learning in the classical period, he claimed, Muslim scholars grew complacent and failed to seek new knowledge and integrate it into their understanding. Satisfied with their narrow religious sciences, they ignored the practical sciences that developed in Europe. Indeed, many scholars rejected the modern, Western sciences as unimportant, if not un-Islamic. Al-Afghani regarded such a dismissive attitude toward science as a betrayal of the highest qualities of true Islam and as proof of how out of touch Muslim scholars were with the world in which they lived and with the religion they purported to teach. "The Islamic religion," he wrote, "is the closest of religions to science and knowledge, and there is no incompatibility between science and the foundations of the Islamic faith..." (Donohue and Esposito 1982: 19).

Similar arguments about Islam's scientific and rational spirit were made by other reformers intent on demonstrating to Muslim populations the importance of adopting Western science and the relevance of Islam to living and participating in the modern world. In a very real sense, reformers were engaging in a cultural defensive modernization that paralleled the material defensive modernization of state leaders. But the reformers faced imposing challenges. First, they needed to reconnect Muslims with their essential Islamic origins, a method of cultural argumentation common among religious reformers everywhere, and they had to do so at the very time that traditional Islam came under severe criticism, even by reformers themselves. The result was a highly nuanced Islam versus Islam discourse that would multiply dramatically over the next century and come to include many Muslim intellectuals with no formal training in the Islamic sciences (Hourani 1983: 103–92). Second, they had to encourage Muslims to learn from the West, studying Western sciences and languages, even to live in Western countries, while rejecting the West's cultural conflict with religion and remaining obedient to Islamic tradition, rightly understood. This led to debates about what aspects of Western society and values were compatible with Islam. And reformists themselves were split on the issue.

An informative example of such a split occurred between al-Afghani and the Indian Muslim reformer Sayyid Ahmad Khan. An original thinker with a passion for introducing Western ideas and education in India, Khan wrote extensively on how and why Muslims must modernize. In one essay, he took to task Muslim scholars who, in his opinion, mindlessly applied traditional methods and interpretations to new phenomena; without using their own intellect or any modern knowledge, these scholars simply repeated classical insights as if the world had stood still. New kinds of knowledge acquisition had emerged in the West, in particular those related to the natural sciences, according to Khan, and Muslims must be prepared to integrate them into their theological outlook, instead of relying solely on past precedents. Khan himself thought that Islam must be explored in much the same way as nature is explored by the natural sciences; and if this human reason-based approach is followed, a clear truth about God's creative genius would be reached: "Islam is nature and nature is Islam" (Donohue and Esposito 1982: 43). For al-Afghani, such reasoning was tantamount to heresy, because it undermined foundational Islamic teachings about God, creation, and the worshipful response required of humans; it also made humans or human reason the measure of all things. While al-Afghani recognized the power and importance of Western science, he was not prepared to take Muslim thought in the direction of a this-worldly materialism that had, in his estimation, undermined previous civilizations and was then dominant in Europe. Moreover, al-Afghani believed that the materialist philosophy adopted by Khan reflected a British plan to undermine Muslim faith and the unity of the Muslim community, so getting the philosophy/theology right was essential to an effective anti-imperialist stance (Hourani 1983: 124–26; Keddie 1983: 65–73).

What this dispute reveals is the extent to which Western ideas had penetrated intellectual circles in Muslim societies and influenced the way Muslims thought about a range of modern concerns, religion included. The masses were unaware of such disputes and could not follow the cross-civilizational exchange at work. But modernizing trends from the West were apparent on the streets and were beginning to be felt in homes. The rulers of Egypt and Persia, for example, "were so impressed by late-nineteenth century Paris that they rebuilt parts of their capitals in imitation, with wide boulevards, public parks, and landscaped roads" (Gelvin 2005: 108). And upper-class households began to mimic the décor and pastimes of European society. Reformers often framed these trends, at least the intellectual and institutional ones, in Islamic terms, making them culturally legitimate and easing the stresses on individual and group consciousness. This legitimacy also facilitated the social differentiation that had taken root, and the secular sphere that was emerging. Clear evidence of secular attitudes and mindsets would not be apparent until the early decades of the twentieth century, when nationalism and nation-state-building occupied Muslim populations. Reformers, however, laid the groundwork for a secular Muslim modernity by wrapping this new reality in a mantle of Islamic identity discourse.

Muslim identity and the politics of the nation-state

The impact of secularization on Muslim societies was strongest and most obvious in political thought and institutions. As early as the late nineteenth century, reformers such as Rifa'a al-Tahtawi (1801–73) of Egypt were arguing for the compatibility of Islam and modern political ideals found in Europe: democracy, freedom of thought, and equality. In India, Chiragh Ali (1844–95) claimed that Islam was capable of progress, especially political progress, because Muhammad, contrary to popular Muslim opinion, never combined religion and state. These attitudes reflect the extent to which Western political thought had found a home in the modern Muslim imagination. And the more Western political ideas took root, the less feasible traditional Islamic politics seemed. Nowhere was this more apparent than in the crisis surrounding the abolition of the caliphate, the leadership office of the successor of the Prophet Muhammad.

Founded in CE 632, immediately following the death of the Prophet Muhammad, the caliphate had long served as a symbol of Islamic political legitimacy and Muslim unity, even after its actual power had significantly diminished. With the break-up of the Ottoman Empire and the emergence of modern Turkey, the country's new leader, Mustapha Kemal Ataturk (1881–1938), took the dramatic step of abolishing the caliphate in 1924. Ataturk intended to secularize Turkey (more on this later), and the caliphate created one of the greatest impediments to this end since the institution directly linked Turkey's modern politics with an Islamic past. Justifications for the abolition, which interwove religious and secular political thinking, need not detain us here. More important is the reaction the abolition provoked, or rather the lack of serious reaction, in the wider Muslim world. The initial shock generated by the announcement led to isolated voices of protest in Turkey, the Middle East, and elsewhere. Indian Muslims proved to be the most upset over the issue, primarily because their own claims for self-rule rested on their supposed (political and spiritual) allegiance to the caliph. A movement to restore the caliphate and the Ottoman Empire drew popular support among Indian Muslims, but it was short-lived. While most Muslims had sentimental attachments to the caliphate as a symbol of past Islamic strength and glory, their more immediate political concerns at the time centered on independence from colonial rule and nation-state-building. Restoration of the caliphate conjured up images of an archaic political system that the vast majority of Muslims had already put behind them.

To foster unity and modern political consciousness, nationalists in Muslim societies drew upon the same standard elements as European nationalists: people, land, language, common history, and religious culture. Some Muslims, those who became known as Islamists (see below), viewed nationalism as a false political ideology, one rooted in secular Europe and foreign to Muslim history and culture; most, however, embraced it and found ways to integrate it with their Muslim identity. In fact, Muslims not only found nationalism compatible with Islam, but they also viewed secular political ideologies (socialism, capitalism, and even communism) and governing structures (presidency, parliament, congress) that defined nation-states as fully in line with Islam (Zubaida 1993).

The precise nature of Islam-state relations in newly emergent Muslim nation-states depended on a variety of factors. Just like the nationalist movements that presaged their creation, however, nation-states in the Islamic world sought Islamic legitimacy. This was true even for the most blatantly secular of Muslim nations, Turkey. Ataturk became president (for life) of the Republic of Turkey in 1923, and set a course for fast-paced economic and cultural modernization. Changing the way Turks thought about and practiced Islam was central to Ataturk's vision of modern Turkey—a Turkey integrated economically and culturally with the West, not the Islamic world. He instituted a number of policies over time to reorient Turkish identity: abolishing the caliphate; declaring Sufi mystical orders illegal because their esoteric practices were thought to interfere with modernization; prohibiting the fez (traditional head covering for men associated with prayer because it had no brim and thus allowed men to touch their heads to the ground in prostration); replacing the Arabic-Turkish script with a Latin one, and eliminating Arabic and Persian roots from the language; and adopting a Western system of law to replace Islamic law (shari'a). At the same time he was removing traditional expressions and symbols of Islam from the public/secular sphere, Ataturk also sought to harness a much-diminished Islam for the state. A ministry of religious affairs was created to ensure that a secular-friendly (apolitical and privatized, following the French model) Islam was taught in schools and mosques (Lewis 1968).

Ataturk's policies toward Islam and development in general—top-down, with little regard for popular opinion—reflect the kind of authoritarian rule that became the norm in many Muslim societies in the first half of the twentieth century. Not all state leaders of Muslim countries were as overtly aggressive toward Islamic institutions and eager to sing the praises of secular governance and society as Ataturk, for doing so risked angering the pious masses. While most leaders were themselves part of the modernizing-secularizing elite, they adopted a nuanced religious politics, one that glossed the secular nature of the state and its policies with an aura of Islamic sanctity. This was accomplished by a combination of media propaganda, limited civil society, and state control over Islamic institutions and voices of Islamic authority. A case in point is the religious politics of Gamal Abdel Nasser (1918–70), the first president of modern Egypt.

Nasser came to power following the 1952 revolution, which brought an end to the monarchy and, in short order, an already-declining British colonial rule. Like Turkey, Egypt also became a presidential republic and a one-party state. The ideological glue holding the Nasserist state together was Arab socialism, and al-Azhar (university), the oldest institutional center of Islamic learning in the Muslim world, lent its support to the new regime and its socialist plans for the nation's future progress. Nasser ensured this support by bringing the Islamic university under government control, appointing its leaders, and transforming Muslim scholars into state functionaries. With their livelihood dependent on state largesse, al-Azhar scholars tended to become complacent, if not enthusiastic, advocates of government policies. Nasser instituted a policy of nationalization that brought much of the country's assets under state control: banks, utilities, transportation, and media. Religion/Islam was just another asset, another potential source of power and authority on which to capitalize and to manage for the good of the nation. But there was also more to state control of Islam than simple socialist collectivism, for Islam had gained a political resonance in Egypt that went beyond the usual religious politics to which all nationalist movements contributed prior to the revolution. In 1928, during a period of heated anti-colonial activism and nationalist debates, the Society of Muslim Brothers (hereafter Muslim Brothers) was founded, the first organized expression of Islamism.

The founder of the Muslim Brothers, Hassan al-Banna (1906–49), advanced an alternative path of political and cultural modernization to that of the secular elite. Rejecting Western systems of politics, al-Banna called for the formation of an Islamic state, one which would unite Muslims everywhere and implement Islamic law. Like the reformers before him, al-Banna recognized the need to "borrow" from the West, but he drew a strict line between Western contributions to practical sciences and those to society and culture, including political culture. The Qur'an, for al-Banna, provided the foundation for modern Muslim society, just as it had at the time of the Prophet Muhammad. While he regarded nationalism as a threat to Muslims, because it established borders between them and undermined the unity of the community of believers (umma), he also recognized that it might be a necessary first stage of organization, given the modern political reality. But for al-Banna, the only nationalism worth considering was a religious nationalism in which Islam played a foundational role in the political and everyday life; secular nationalism imposed a false consciousness upon Muslims, alienating them from their tradition and its divinely established social order (Mitchell 1969: 264–67).

By the 1950s, the Muslim Brothers had grown into a multilayered movement, with branches throughout the country and a range of preaching, charitable, and business projects. After the 1952 revolution, Nasser banned all political parties, except for the Muslim Brothers who were allowed to continue their public outreach efforts. The movement's impressive membership rolls and organizational structure made it an attractive target for Nasser's regime. State attempts to coopt it, however, proved fruitless once the Muslim Brothers realized that the regime had no intention of taking Islamists or their understanding of Islam seriously. A Muslim Brother's assassination attempt against Nasser in 1954 led to a government crackdown and the movement was declared illegal. Operating underground, both in and out of prison, the Muslim Brothers continued to advocate an Islamist alternative modernity for Egyptians (and Muslims everywhere) and to challenge the religious and political legitimacy of Nasser's secular state.

Secular nationalism and the secular nation-state, then, did not go unquestioned. But in the heady days of independence and national pride, the masses in Muslim societies placed their hopes in the progressive rhetoric and development policies of leaders such as Nasser. And the authoritarian style of such leaders created an environment where hope seemed rational and obligatory. Aside from Islamists such as the Muslim Brothers, no one thought Muslim society and culture were under threat from secularization. When Muslim peoples envisioned their future in the aftermath of independence and the early days of nation-state-building, they saw a bright, prosperous one; and the religious establishment assured people that the new features of Muslim life—modernization, nationalism, industrialism, socialism—were fully in line with Islamic teachings (Hourani 1983). Thus, at the time, Islam's compatibility with Western, secular forms of development was not a matter of concern.

Tensions between secular and Islamic national identity were more pronounced in countries that either relied more heavily on Islamic identity politics at the time of founding or had a significant non-Muslim minority population. An example of the former is Pakistan, which came into existence in 1947 with the division of India. Islam had factored into modern Indian Muslim consciousness in a way that it did not, or did not need to, in other Muslim majority countries. British divide-and-rule policies in India played on religious differences, pitting Hindus and Muslims (and Sikhs) against one another; and while Indian Muslims worked to achieve independence alongside their Hindu counterparts, they had serious concerns about their status, politically and culturally, in an independent, Hindu-majority India. As a result, the Muslim secular elite in India, represented by the Muslim League, found themselves playing on many of the same Islamic cultural themes as the main Indian Islamist movement, Jama'at-i Islami. At independence, a secular government emerged to lead Pakistan, but much of the nation's post-independence politics, domestic and foreign, has been fraught with debates about what it means to be an Islamic state. Thus, despite the secular state structure and policies at its core, Pakistan has remained a nation searching for a stable modern identity.

In the Malay states (later Malaysia), minority issues shaped the Islamic politics of the secular state. Foreign laborers from China and India had immigrated to the Malay states in the eighteenth and nineteenth centuries to take advantage of the trade promoted by Dutch and later British colonists. Native Malays, the majority Muslim population, found themselves under a dual threat: their economic status was threatened by immigrants whose entrepreneurial spirit was better suited to the globalizing economy, and their existing system of hereditary politics (the sultanates) was weakened by British policies. As in other developing Muslim societies, the Malay states produced different responses to the challenges of modernization—reformers, modernizers, and traditionalists—and Islam was a prominent feature of each response. And also like other Muslim societies, secular modernizers emerged as leaders at the time of independence, in 1957. This leadership, however, reflected the ethnic diversity of Malay society, and the constitution reflected the compromises necessary to create a workable society. Islam was made the official religion, but freedom of religion was guaranteed to all citizens. Native Malays, the so-called Bumiputra, were granted special advantages in education and government positions, but minority rights and economic interests were also confirmed. Post-independence party politics has reflected the challenge of a Malay majority dealing with sizable and economically powerful minorities. The largest and most successful party, the United Malays National Organization (UMNO), has negotiated the minefield of national politics by promoting three, sometimes conflicting, values: ethnic diversity, Malay-Islamic culture, and the global economy. UMNO's major competitor, the Pan-Malayan Islamic Party (popularly known as PAS), has advanced an Islamic platform, which includes implementing Islamic law and curtailing the strength of non-Muslim minorities. While PAS has had success in regional elections, in conservative states like Kelantan, its policies have not won national consensus (Mutalib 1993). The secular status quo, then, has been maintained by mainstream Muslim interests fusing with those of minorities in a democratic, or largely democratic, setting.

Discontent with modernity and the secular

In the last quarter of the twentieth century, Muslim societies witnessed rising discontent with modernity and the secular values and institutions with which it was associated. A variety of factors contributed to this discontent: slow economic progress, lack of social justice and responsible politics, restrictive civil societies, corrupt governments, and growing disillusionment with Western modernity and the West's interventionist policies in the Muslim world. These factors themselves came to be viewed by the Muslim masses as signs of the failure of modern economic and political systems to perform as advertised by their Westernized, secular leaders. Starting in the nineteenth century, Muslim states, on behalf of their populations, had placed their faith in the capacity of Western-style development, and newly formed nations in the twentieth century followed the same pattern. When the highly vaunted benefits of this development failed to materialize quickly enough or to spread equally across populations, Muslims began to reassess the narrative of modernity they had embraced, and to create a new one that drew more explicitly on Islamic culture and values and eschewed those associated with the secular West.

Historical events, not abstract theorizing, fueled the discontent with modernity. An event that reverberated loudly in the Middle East and beyond was the 1967 war between Israel and surrounding Arab countries (Egypt, Jordan, and Syria). In Egypt, the staggering loss of life, land, and equipment in six short days stunned the nation and gave rise to a collective crisis of identity, both spiritual and political. Egyptians asked themselves why God had abandoned them, allowing them to be punished by their ancient Jewish enemy. They also, given the backdrop of a stagnant economy, raised angry questions about Nasser's leadership and development strategy. Egyptians, like other Muslims in developing nations, had reached a tacit agreement with their secular leaders: the sacrifice of political freedoms to empower the state to grow the economy and society uncontested by political opposition. For many, mild authoritarianism was a small price to pay for becoming a player on the global political and economic stage. But 1967 brought home to Egyptians the underlying reality of their Faustian bargain: Egypt remained an underdeveloped nation, with insufficient technological capacity to defend itself, too few jobs to sustain its citizens, and a political apparatus that ruled through jingoism and force, not the will of its people.

Over the next several decades, Egypt witnessed a rising tide of personal religiosity, Islamist activism, and public debates about the meaning and place of Islam in Egyptian society (Abdo 2000). While a segment of the population continued to espouse a secular ideal for Egypt's future, the argument became more difficult to maintain in the face of widespread appeals to Islamic heritage. And successive governments contributed to the trend by manipulating Islam for their own political purposes. Anwar Sadat (1918–81), who came to power after Nasser's death in 1970, freed imprisoned Islamists to create a bulwark against socialist forces (Nasserists) who opposed him; he also cast himself as the believing president. Adopting the same authoritarian style as Nasser, Sadat took the country in new directions, without concern for popular sentiment: he made peace with Israel and, in the process, established strong political and economic ties with the United States. His so-called "open door" policy, because it opened Egypt to foreign trade, ushered in an experiment with free market capitalism, after the failed socialism under Nasser. In 1981, angered over Sadat's peace with Israel, a militant band of Islamists, the Jihad group, assassinated him. Sadat's successor, Hosni Mubarak (b. 1928), maintained his predecessor's economic policies and political agreements. But in an era of global economic downturn, the Egyptian state, like many around the world, found itself unable to make good on the basic benefits promised by previous governments. So, at the same time that the divide between rich and poor became more pronounced due to the capitalist-inspired open door policy, the state began to retreat from its social commitments. For many struggling Egyptians, it seemed that both socialism and capitalism had failed them—a sentiment that was reinforced by Islamist anti-secular, back-to-Islam preaching.

In 1979, another dramatic event challenged the viability of secularism in Muslim societies and lent support for a Muslim-defined modernity: the Iranian Revolution. Iran had, starting in the early decades of the twentieth century, experienced fast-paced development, and secularization, under Reza Shah Pahlavi (1878–1944). Possessing vast oil reserves and strategic access to the Persian Gulf, the nation had long attracted the interest of Western powers. World War II heightened Western concern for the free flow of oil, and in 1941, a combined British-Soviet invasion deposed Reza Shah, who had established close relations with Germany, and placed his son, Muhammad Reza Shah (1919–80), on the throne. Muhammad Reza Shah's hold on power and relations with the West were threatened when a popular political coalition, led by Muhammad Mosaddeq (1882–1967), nationalized Iranian oil, for which the British had won development rights. A coup in 1953, organized by the CIA, sent Mosaddeq into political retirement and restored Muhammad Reza Shah's power. Once back on the throne the Shah pushed through modernizing-secularizing policies, much like Ataturk, and established close economic, social, military, and political ties with the United States. The next several decades brought dramatic changes and growing dissatisfaction with the Shah's rule from a range of economic classes and ideological factions. Merchants, workers, students, communists, and others came together under the symbolic leadership of Ayatollah Khomeini (1902–89), one of Iran's most respected religious scholars and a vocal critic of the Shah. Widespread public demonstrations brought a violent backlash from the Shah's secret police, Savak, but the Shah was eventually driven from the country. Khomeini, the hero of the Revolution, quickly emerged as the nation's leader and declared Iran an Islamic republic to be ruled by an Islamic government.

After more than a century of modernization in the Muslim world following Western models, the Iranian Revolution shocked Western governments and leaders of Muslim nations. The shock came, in part, from the twin assumptions that informed development theory in the first-half of the twentieth century: that secular leadership in Muslim societies was well entrenched and that Islam, while widely practiced, had little to offer the masses as a political force. And the viability of an Islamist-led government was also dismissed by development theorists as improbable, as Manfred Halpern made clear in his assessment of social change in the Middle East:

> When traditional Islam reacts by transforming itself into a religio-political totalitarian party, it can safely be challenged as a novel ideology rather than as a hallowed way of life. There will still be battles, but this particular war is over in the great majority of Middle Eastern states.
>
> *(Halpern 1963: 130)*

Islam, then, like religions elsewhere, was viewed as a spent political force, something that nations had moved beyond, relying on it only to influence the uneducated masses. The idea that a secular, Western-friendly leader could be pushed aside by a religious revolution to install clerical rule seemed like a throwback to a previous era and suggested that Westernization was not as firmly entrenched in Muslim societies as many had come to believe. Khomeini claimed that Iran's Revolution would be a model for the world's downtrodden, Muslims and non-Muslims. But it was primarily Islamist movements and oppressed Shi'a minorities in Persian Gulf countries who found direct inspiration in the Revolution. Most Iranians had participated in, or at least supported, the Revolution to make basic improvements in their everyday lives: to ensure social, economic, and political justice. And Khomeini had won popular support by publically advocating these pragmatic concerns in the face of the Shah's oppressive regime and by situating the concerns within the framework of Islamic justice.

The growing appeal of Islamic values and ideals in Iran and Egypt emerged in a context of increasing disappointment with both the substance and style of secular-oriented ruling elites. This disappointment extended to Western nations, especially the United States, because of their support for corrupt dictators in the Muslim world and their failure to uphold the democratic values that they espoused. For many

Muslims, the West seemed all too ready to compromise its ideals—of open societies, tolerance, and freedom—when dealing with Muslim leaders in order to maintain political stability, ensure the flow of oil, and undermine Islamists. In Algeria, for example, after Islamists won a decisive victory in parliamentary elections in 1991, the West stood silent as the ruling National Liberation Front nullified the democratic results and maintained its hold on power. For Western nations, friendly autocratic governments appeared to be more desirable political partners than democratically elected Islamist ones. This became even more apparent after the terrorist attacks of September 11, 2001, when Western fears of global militant Islam led to military intervention in Afghanistan and Iraq. For many Westerners, good Muslims were those who supported the war on terror, even as it devastated Muslim societies and threatened a new era of colonialism. For Muslims, however, the war on terror made the Muslim world, if not Islam itself, the enemy. And such suspicions found resonance in Western rhetoric, which, following the fall of the Soviet Union, emphasized the possibilities of a clash of civilizations and Muslims as the new cold war enemy (Mamdani 2004).

Taken together, these developments contributed to a backlash against the West and Western values among Muslims, and a parallel reinforcement of Islamic heritage and identity. In this context, Muslims began to see the secular in a negative light, as something that was incompatible with, if not antagonistic to, Islam and Muslim society. It is important to note that this was a perception, not a sociological understanding along the lines outlined earlier, and this perception was rooted in an emerging global environment in which cultural identities, while often loudly proclaimed, were blurred and shifting phenomena. Two recent examples of the secular in action and in dispute provide insight into the way modernization and secularization are evolving in Muslim thought and life.

In twenty-first-century Europe, Muslim citizens, mostly immigrants and their descendants, have found themselves on the defensive as states and organizations have challenged Muslims' ability to adapt to secular society. Historically, European societies have relegated religion to the private sphere—to home and church—but an increasing Muslim population has brought new signs of religiosity and religious culture into the public eye. This has taken the visible form of headscarves and mosques, but these are mere symbols of a deeper cultural transformation at work, a transformation that is raising questions about the political ideals of secular states and the implications of a fading Christian identity. If European societies are tolerant and free, Muslims and others argue, then surely Muslims should be able to believe and practice as they see fit. So, why should France ban the headscarf in public schools, as it did in 2004? And why should Switzerland ban the construction of minarets (architectural towers typically attached to mosques) in 2009, when there were only four in the country? Societies, however, operate not just by laws but also by communal assumptions and consensus; and Muslims have, unintentionally, challenged these assumptions and the consensus about European culture. As a result, some Europeans see Islam as a threat because Muslims are seemingly unable, or unwilling, to live according to the norms of secular society. For others, however, the real problem in Europe lies elsewhere: "Islam is a mirror in which the West projects its own identity crisis" (Roy 2007: xiii).

In January 2011, major street protests broke out in Tunisia and then Egypt, leading to the eventual downfall of two longstanding autocratic, secular regimes and raising questions about the political future of the two nations. The protests were organized, in both countries, by tech-savvy youth whose political inclinations and goals were democratic and secular. The people pouring into the streets had basic complaints and demands, as one chant heard in Cairo's now famous Tahrir or Liberation Square nicely communicates: "Bread, freedom, social justice."

But tensions quickly emerged between secular-minded organizers and Muslim Brothers, who despite coming late to the protests brought a level of discipline and commitment that proved critical to the success of the uprisings. Secularists in Tunisia and Egypt expressed fears that Islamist fundamentalists bent on creating a theocratic state would hijack the progressive direction of the so-called Arab Spring. Women and minorities were especially worried. What became clear, as the street protests quieted

Figure 11.1 Tahrir Square, Cairo. Courtesy of Jonathan Rashad/Getty Images.

and political maneuvering began, is that secularists do not enjoy popular support outside a narrow class of educated urbanites. The Muslim masses simply do not resonate with secular-based values and discourse, even when they agree on the endpoint of those values and discourse: freedom, participatory politics, social justice, and jobs. This became all too clear when, in the aftermath of the Arab Spring, Islamist parties in both Tunisia and Egypt won impressive victories in parliamentary elections, demonstrating their organizational strength and popularity. Put simply, the political message of secularists must contend with the failed history of secularism in the region, with the negative associations that have accumulated against secular governments and policies in the West, and with the popular notion that Islamic values are an unrivaled bulwark of a good society.

Conclusion

The idea of a good society brings this exploration full circle, back to the very goal of modernization and secularization. Creating a good society, whether in the Muslim world or beyond, is a balancing act between addressing the fundamental needs of citizens—the bread, freedom, and social justice expressed by Egyptians in Tahrir Square—and finding a means for citizens to debate about these needs and negotiate their fulfillment. Muslim societies have secularized structurally in terms of social differentiation, but they have not, with notable exceptions such as Turkey, adopted secular values and ideals as the language of modernization. Indeed, despite the secular leadership that has emerged in most Muslim countries, the language of public political debate has always been infused with religious ideas, principles, and values. Modernization itself was nurtured with such religiously infused language, and even Turkey is currently experiencing a revived debate about the role of Islam in public life, sparked by a sense that Ataturk's secular reforms went too far.

In a very real sense, there is no dispute over whether Muslim societies are capable of secularization. The only real issue is how they have secularized, how they have negotiated the dislocating effects of the universal processes of capitalism, industrialization, monetized labor, and differentiated spheres. These global processes have tended to flatten out cultural differences, reducing peoples around the world to producers and consumers. At the same time, these processes have also created avenues for religious cultures to reassert themselves, either as interpretive instruments that integrate tradition and modernity or as reservoirs of traditional values that critique and, potentially, reform modernity's ill effects.

Thus the study of secularization and the secular in Muslims societies is actually a study of the transformations—both material and cultural—that have affected all peoples in the modern era. It is an ongoing story, with different narrative turns, but it is a story that binds us all together, despite our religious and cultural differences.

Summary

- Secularization is a multifaceted concept and process that is often linked to modernization.
- Modernization and secularization became linked in theory because of their fusion in the Western historical experience.
- Secularization has both a structural/institutional aspect and a cultural one.
- Structural/institutional secularization is readily evident in Muslim societies but cultural secularization has largely been rejected as inauthentic, if not un-Islamic, by many Muslims.
- Analysis of the usage of the word secularization in Western and Muslim societies brings out cultural differences about what it means to be modern and why, along with judgments about how "others" have modernized.

Discussion points

- How would you define/describe secularization?
- Is there a difference between secularization and modernization? If not, how are they similar? If so, how are they different?
- Does secularization necessitate a decline in religious faith?
- Have Muslim societies secularized? If not, why not? If so, how?
- Why has so much confusion and debate arisen about secularization in Muslim societies?

Further reading

Secularism and Muslim societies/Islam

An-Na'im, Abdullahi Ahmed (2008) *Islam and the Secular State: Negotiating the Future of Shari'a*, Cambridge, MA: Harvard University Press.

Argument for the need of a secular state in modern Muslim societies, based on a comparative analysis of the interaction of state, society and religion in India, Turkey, and Indonesia.

Esposito, John L. and Azzam Tamimi (eds) (2000) *Islam and Secularism in the Middle East*, New York: New York University Press.

Collection of essays that explore the history, theory and practices of secularization and secularism in the Middle East.

Yared, Nazik Saba (2002) *Secularism and the Arab World*, London: Saqi Books.

Highly readable overview of the impact of secular thinking in the modern Arab world, in fields such as politics, education, law, and literature.

Comparative studies of secularism

Kuru, Ahmet T. (2009) *Secularism and State Policies Toward Religion: The United States, France, and Turkey*, Cambridge: Cambridge University Press.

Comparative study of styles of secularization (passive and assertive) as they have developed in three nations and the impact of these styles on state policies and cultural assumptions.

Norris, Pippa and Ronald Inglehart (2004) *Sacred and Secular: Religion and Politics Worldwide.* Cambridge: Cambridge University Press.

Analysis of global patterns of secularization based on data from the World Values Survey.

Secularization theory

Asad, Talal (2003) *Formations of the Secular: Christianity, Islam, Modernity*, Stanford, CA: Stanford University Press.

Critical, anthropological interpretation of the way in which secularism has been used to frame differences between the European and Middle Eastern experience of modernity.

Taylor, Charles (2007) *A Secular Age*, Cambridge: The Belknap Press.

New reading of Western intellectual history that challenges standard secularization theory and provides a unique insight into the place of religion and virtue in modern Western societies.

References

Abdo, Geneive (2000) *No God But God: Egypt and the Triumph of Islam*, New York: Oxford University Press.

al-Qaradawi, Yusuf (1990) *al-Islam wa'l-ilmaniyya..wajh li-wajh*, Cairo: al-Risala.

Anderson, Jon Lee (2010) "After the Crackdown," *The New Yorker*, August 16 & 23.

Berger, Peter L. (1967) *The Sacred Canopy*, Garden City, NY: Doubleday.

—— (ed.) (1999) *The Desecularization of the World: Religious Resurgence and World Politics*, Grand Rapids, MI: William B. Eerdmans Publishing Company.

Casanova, José (1994) *Public Religions in the Modern World*, Chicago: University of Chicago Press.

Chadwick, Owen (1975) *The Secularization of the European Mind in the 19th Century*, Cambridge: Cambridge University Press.

Donohue, John J. and John L. Esposito (1982) *Islam in Transition: Muslim Perspectives*, New York: Oxford University Press.

Gelvin, James L. (2005) *The Modern Middle East: A History*, New York: Oxford University Press.

Gerecht, Marc (2005) "In the Middle East, the Democratic Genie is Out of the Bottle," *The Weekly Standard*, March 14.

Halpern, Manfred (1963) *The Politics of Social Change in the Middle East and North Africa*, Princeton, NJ: Princeton University Press.

Hourani, Albert (1983) *Arabic Thought in the Liberal Age 1798-1939*, Cambridge: Cambridge University Press.

Keddie, Nikki R. (1983) *An Islamic Response to Imperialism: Political and Religious Writings of Sayyid Jamal ad-Din al-Afghani*, Berkeley: University of California Press.

Kersten, Carool (2011) *Cosmopolitans and Heretics: New Muslim Intellectuals and the Study of Islam*, New York: Columbia University Press.

Kuru, Ahmet T. (2009) *Secularism and State Policies Toward Religion: The United States, France, and Turkey*, Cambridge: Cambridge University Press.

Lewis, Bernard (1968) *The Emergence of Modern Turkey*, 2nd edn, London: Oxford University Press.

Mamdani, Mahmood (2004) *Good Muslims, Bad Muslims: America, the Cold War, and the Roots of Terror*, New York: Pantheon Books.

Mutalib, Hussin (1993) *Islam in Malaysia: From Revivalism to Islamic State*, Singapore: Singapore University Press.

Mitchell, Richard P. (1969) *The Society of Muslim Brothers*, London: Oxford University Press.

Norris, Pippa and Ronald Inglehart (2004) *Sacred and Secular: Religion and Politics Worldwide.* Cambridge: Cambridge University Press.

Roy, Olivier (2007) *Secularism Confronts Islam*, trans. George Holoch, New York: Columbia University Press.

Schulze, Reinhard (2002) *A Modern History of the Islamic World*, trans. Azizeh Azodi, Washington Square, NY: New York University Press.

Zubaida, Sami (1993) *Islam, the People and the State*, London: I.B. Tauris.

Notes

1 The signs of global religious resurgence identified by Berger are addressed in a more systematic manner by José Casanova (1994).

2 See Anderson (2010: 62).

3 See the *Salon* article of February 15, 2002; www.salon.com/2002/02/15/ramadan_2/.

4 See Gerecht (2005).

5 For a sense of the self-conscious attempt to develop and move beyond traditional society, even while trying to maintain cultural authenticity, see Lewis (1968) and Hourani (1983).

6 This discourse was largely driven by Islamists bent on proving that secularization and secular society were direct threats to Islam and Muslim well-being; see, for example, al-Qaradawi (1990).

7 See www.gallup.com/poll/128210/Gallup-Global-Reports.aspx. For another global assessment of religiosity, see Norris and Inglehardt (2004).

8 For an insightful comparative analysis of secularization in three modern countries, see Kuru (2009).

9 Scholars have rightly noted that differentiation in the sense of a separation of religious and political leadership was long a part of Muslim society. Such a separation in the classical period, however, should not be confused with the exponential complexity of differentiation that occurred in the modern period, nor should it be confused with modern secularization.

12 Islam and popular culture

Mark Sedgwick

Outline

- Contemporary Muslim popular culture differs from earlier Muslim popular culture because of globalization and modernity.
- The West has had a significant impact on Muslim popular culture, but this impact has been uneven.
- Adoption of Western culture has sometimes meant that cultural practices have become less connected to Islam, and sometimes Western culture has been Islamized.
- The idea of authenticity is important.
- Many local cultural practices are dying out because of the influence of new interpretations of Islam.
- There has always been an Islamic consumer culture, but it has recently become more globalized and commercial.
- Important parts of Islamic consumer culture are goods such as food, clothing, and toys, and services such as travel.
- Islamic consumer finance is the most commercially important part of Islamic consumer culture.
- Islamic media include Islamic alternatives to standard print and audio media and address varied audiences.

Introduction

Islam plays a major role in the popular culture of the Muslim world, as it does in the popular culture of Muslims living as minorities in non-Muslim countries, a group that has grown dramatically in size and importance since the end of the Second World War, as discussed in Chapter 15. Muslim popular culture today differs from earlier models in three important ways. One is that it no longer reflects just the normative Islam developed in ancient institutions such as mosques and madrasas (place of study), or even in modern institutions such as universities and government ministries, discussed in Chapters 6 and 11. Muslim popular culture is now also in part a product of another sort of modern institution, informal but still important: the "public sphere." A public sphere is an intellectual space that is independent of both the institutions of the state and of the institutions of established religious authority, and it has been argued that a public sphere is actually more important for modernity than are classic "modern" institutions, since what happens in the public sphere is the origin of the cultural and intellectual attitudes and assumptions that underlie the formal institutions of modernity (Wittrock 2000).

The second way in which contemporary Muslim popular culture differs from earlier models is that, although still very diverse, it has become less diverse than it was. This partial standardization is a consequence of globalization and of the spread of education. Globalization has affected Muslim popular culture in two, somewhat contradictory, ways. On the one hand, globalization has meant the flow of ideas and practices from the West into the Muslim world, and of Muslims into the West, bringing some aspects of Muslim popular culture into line with norms and practices that are not Islamic, originating as they do outside the Muslim world. On the other hand, globalization has facilitated flows of ideas and practices within the Muslim world itself, bringing certain aspects of popular culture into line with norms that are seen as more Islamic, and that are certainly more uniform. Despite this, much popular culture remains very local, and much remains unconnected to Islam. Islam is only one influence among many on popular culture, and it is a classic methodological error to seek to explain everything that is done by a person or society that happens to be Muslim in terms of Islam. That Muslim men in Tunisia place jasmine flowers behind their ears when they go out for a walk in the evening has nothing to do with Islam, and neither does the way in which some young, unemployed Muslim men in France periodically set fire to parked cars.

The third and final way in which contemporary Muslim popular culture differs from earlier models is that Islamic "consumer culture" is now part of it. This, too, reflects globalization, and Islamic consumer culture is as globalized as are other modern economic phenomena. The development of Islamic consumer culture also reflects modernity, since a third candidate among theorists for what constitutes the essence of modernity, along with modern institutions and a public sphere, is the world market economy.

The Muslim public sphere

Globalization is relevant to all three ways in which contemporary Muslim popular culture differs from earlier models, since many of the ideas that flowed into the Muslim public sphere, and thence into Muslim popular culture and consumer culture, did so as a result of globalization.

The Muslim world and the West have been in contact for at least 1,000 years, but during the nineteenth century these long-established contacts changed both in kind and intensity, with major consequences for the popular culture of the Muslim world. Originally, the Muslim world and the West were two separate "systems" that mostly operated independently of each other, just as China and Africa operated independently of each other. During the nineteenth century, however, the Muslim world and the West became part of a new world system, as one single system replaced previous multiple regional systems (Beaujard 2005). This was the beginning of the globalization of the Muslim world, a process that is still accelerating. The places the Muslim world and the West occupied in the new world system were unequal: the West was at the center, and the Muslim world at the periphery. The Muslim world was weaker, economically, diplomatically, and militarily—as was demonstrated by the increasing number of Muslim countries falling under direct Western control between the 1820s and 1920s. As a result of these unequal positions, as is normal in relations between center and periphery, ideas and practices generally flowed from the West to the Muslim world, although some ideas and practices did also flow in the opposite direction, from the Muslim world to the West. Among the ideas that flowed from the West to the Muslim world were new conceptions of society, the community, and the individual (Wittrock 2000). Among the practices that flowed from the West were new forms of architecture, new social habits, and new fashions in female clothing.

These new ideas and practices were not adopted uniformly across the Muslim world. The new practices were to be found especially in great cities and major towns, and the ideas were to be found in what the German sociologist Jürgen Habermas calls the "public sphere" (1991). Outside the control of the formal institutions of state and religious authority, the public sphere in the Muslim world has received, developed, and transmitted new ideas about religion and society. This development was as significant for understandings of Islam as was the establishment of the institutions of Islamic religious authority in the first place, more than 1,000 years before, and is a topic that much of this book deals with, in one way or another. It was also important for its direct and indirect impact on Muslim popular culture.

Among the new ideas received in the public sphere were those central to nineteenth-century European social science, notably the concepts of "society" and of the "individual" as we understand them today. With the modern concept of "society" come ideals such as "social justice," ideals that have since been identified as Islamic, but that in reality cannot be found in earlier texts, for the simple reason that the concepts did not then exist. This, of course, does not mean that they cannot be "read into" earlier texts, and they have been, as by Sayyid Qutb (1949). Modern ideals such as social justice are as a result now part of Muslim popular culture, widely if not universally accepted. They may not have been Islamic in origin, but they are Islamic now, since many Muslims consider them to be Islamic. They are an example of how a global ideal may take a local Islamic form.

With the modern concept of society also comes the idea of the national community, and thus also the concepts of national culture. These concepts have been especially useful during a period in which previous understandings of the community have been challenged, both by urbanization and by increased contact between the Muslim world and the West. As urbanization progressed in the Muslim world, more and more people found themselves living in conditions in which there was no natural community. The village, being small, constitutes a natural community. Even if not everyone knows everyone, most people know most people. The same is not true of the town, and is even less true of the city. This was one reason why a new community had to be "imagined," in the sense in which that word is used by Benedict Anderson, the great theorist of nationalism. For Anderson, the nation is an "imagined community" (1983). Starting in the nineteenth century in a process continuing today, increasing numbers of Muslims began to understand themselves as members of nations, although it was not always clear what defined the nation: language, religion, or geography. In the end, a mixture of language and geography won out in much of the Muslim world, but religion was never forgotten, and remains especially important in countries such as Pakistan, now set to replace Indonesia as the single largest Muslim country, and in the Arab world. The old concept of the *umma* came increasingly to be understood as an "Islamic nation," with "nation" understood in its modern sense (Saunders 2008). Just as modern ideals such as social justice have passed into Muslim popular culture, then, so have nationalist ideals, an imagined Islamic nation, with an imagined Islamic culture to go with it. "Imagined" does not, in this context, mean the same as "imaginary," it does not mean that an Islamic nation and Islamic culture do not exist. It means, rather, that they exist primarily because people think they exist.

As well as responding to needs created by urbanization, the imagining of an Islamic nation and an Islamic culture responded to the flow of new practices into the Muslim world—what many saw, and many still see, as the Westernization of the Muslim world. One reaction to this perceived Westernization was a preoccupation with authenticity, with identifying and promoting that which is authentically "Islamic." This preoccupation, and the related preoccupation with identity that came with the imagination of the Islamic nation and of Islamic culture, underlie much that has happened since in Muslim popular culture.

"Authenticity" was itself a new and modern conception, and also one that preoccupied the nineteenth-century West. In the West, the nineteenth century saw the discovery and formalization of national culture, both at the level of the building of museums, galleries, and monuments, and at the level of the collection of folk tales and folklore. In the great cities of the Muslim world, museums, galleries, and monuments also came into being, both an example of the adoption of Western practices and a reaction against that process. Among the earliest "Islamic" museums were those in Cairo, where a collection was opened to the public in 1881 and a purpose-built museum completed in 1903, and in Istanbul, where an Islamic museum opened in 1913. Among the most recent are the Islamic museums in Kuala Lumpur, opened in 1998, and in Doha, Qatar, opened in 2008. The Turkish museum was housed in a sixteenth-century palace, but the other three museums were purpose-built in "Islamic" styles. As well as Islamic museums, and "Islamic art" to fill them, "Islamic architecture" came into being.

These were new conceptions. Something that might be called Islamic art had previously existed, as some of the objects that the new Islamic museums contained, such as beautifully calligraphed Qurans or the decorated key to Mecca's Kaaba that was displayed in Cairo, had indeed been made for religious purposes. Many of the objects displayed had been created for other purposes, however. Plates, glasses, carpets, and illuminated poetic manuscripts, for example, had been made to adorn the houses of the rich and powerful, and although they sometimes used Quranic verses for decorative purposes, they also sometimes incorporated pictures and even sculpture that was religiously problematic. They were in fact Islamic only indirectly, in the sense that they originated from societies that were made up mostly of Muslims. The same was true of Islamic architecture. There had been architects who built mosques, and mosque architecture could thus be described as Islamic in the same way that a calligraphed Quran could be, but much of what came to be conceived of as Islamic architecture had actually been intended for domestic rather than religious purposes, such as the former palace in which the Istanbul Islamic museum was installed. Again, these architectural styles were Islamic only indirectly, in the sense that they originated from societies that were made up mostly of Muslims. And those societies had been very different from each other. Ceramics, like architectural styles, are normally classified by scholars working on them in terms of place and period, as Seljuk or early Mughal or late Ottoman, not as "Islamic." The coming into existence of Islamic museums of Islamic art, and of Islamic architecture, however, created one single unified concept out of many different ages and regions. Modern Islamic art and architecture are eclectic, mixing together different countries and centuries. However ancient the individual objects and buildings now classified as Islamic art and Islamic architecture may be, then, understanding them as "Islamic" is actually very modern.

As well as the modern concept of "society," the new Muslim public sphere received and developed the modern concept of the "individual," and thus ideals such as individual rights and individuality. These, like the national community and national culture, are considered by many scholars to be quintessentially modern. At a religious level, the ideal of individuality is thought to have two main consequences: an interest in self-realization, and the individualization of religious belief and practice (Fadil 2005). Some form of self-realization is found in almost all religious practice, but when combined with individuality the emphasis shifts from the other-worldly to the this-worldly, self-realization comes to be measured partly in terms of satisfaction, and even success. Individualization of religious belief and practice is often understood by reference to the supermarket: an individual assembles his or her own personal basket of beliefs and practices from those on offer. This may involve transgressing the boundaries that separate one religion from another. These boundaries have always been more visible to the theologian or the scholar of religions than they have to the ordinary follower of a religion, and a certain amount of borrowing has always gone on across religious lines, especially in areas where different religions live side by side. Particular places, for example, may be sacred to more than one religion, whether major sites such as Jerusalem's Temple Mount or minor sites such as a saint's tomb visited by Muslims and Christians in Egypt or Muslims and Hindus in India. With modernity, however, borrowings have become more dramatic. The Hindu concept of karma, for example, is informally accepted by many Western Christians, as is the Hindu practice of yoga. Despite periodic warnings from some members of the ulama (religious scholars) that yoga is not Islamic, and so is forbidden, Muslim popular culture too has absorbed yoga, though not to the same extent that Western culture has, save perhaps in Iran. Yoga is typically Islamized by replacing the Hindu sacred syllable "Om" with "Allah." As well as Islamic yoga, there is Islamic reiki, this time of Buddhist origin, and again condemned by some members of the ulama. The concept of karma has made little progress, but—although the extent and penetration are hard to judge—religious individualization is now found in Muslim popular culture.

The public sphere, then, is the space within which many ideas and practices characteristic of modernity have been received and developed, and is itself an important characteristic of modernity, as a space outside the control of state and religious authority where new ideas and assumptions can be developed, as well as an important route for new ideas to enter Muslim popular culture. The public sphere does not produce uniform views, and is not the same as Muslim society as a whole, being inhabited chiefly by the urbanized and the educated, and being more globalized than Muslim society as a whole. It is, however, an important source of contemporary Muslim popular culture, as it is of contemporary Islam.

Cultural practices

As has been said, much popular culture in the Muslim world and of Muslims elsewhere has nothing to do with Islam, and it would be a serious mistake to try to explain all aspects of Muslim popular culture in terms of religion. Much popular culture, however, is saturated with Islam, notably when it comes to relations between men and women. Gender roles and relations are probably the area in which Islam in the modern world differs most from earlier Islam, partly because of globalization and because of ideas passing from the Muslim public sphere into popular culture, and partly because of increased female education, urbanization, and perhaps above all economics. Women and gender, however, have been discussed in Chapter 7, and this important aspect of modern Muslim popular culture will not be discussed in this chapter.

Some practices of Western origin that have flowed into Muslim popular culture as a result of globalization have made that culture less Islamic. One example is the use of the knife and fork. Muslim conceptions of good manners, including table manners, are molded by Islam. It is virtuous (*mustahabb*), for example, to wash one's hands before eating, and to eat only with the right hand. Until the nineteenth century, Muslims from Morocco in the far west through India to Indonesia in the far east followed the recommendations of Islam in these two respects, both as a religious practice and as a part of popular culture. Washing one's hands before eating presents no problems in the modern world, and has even been facilitated by modern plumbing, which makes water more easily available. Eating with one's right hand, however, does present a problem, because the use of the knife and fork is one of those practices that have spread from the West as the global center to become very general, and involves placing food in the mouth with the left hand, as this is the hand that commonly holds the fork.

Approaches to this problem vary from person to person, and also vary by social class: the cultural as well as the economic differences between different social classes remain far greater in most of the Muslim world than in developed economies such as the United States, and even greater than in the social-democratic economies of some parts of Western Europe. In much of the Muslim world, knives and forks are not to be found in the houses of the poor or in the cooked-food shops they use, so the link between Islam and good manners persists. In the homes of the prosperous, however, and in smarter restaurants, knives and forks have often become the norm. For most of those who live in such homes and use such restaurants, or live in the West, a very basic aspect of culture has thus lost its link with Islam, corresponding instead to the modern global norm. There are, however, some devout Muslims who maintain the link, putting down their knives and shifting their forks to their right hands before placing food in their mouths. There are also Muslims who are left-handed, of course, which solves the problem.

Knives and forks do not play a part in the lives of all Muslims, but calendars do. The use of the Gregorian calendar, dating from the date conventionally ascribed to the birth of Jesus, is one of the Western practices that have spread most widely. Most Muslim countries have adopted the use of the Gregorian calendar, with Saudi Arabia and Iran among the few exceptions that still insist on using the *hijri* calendar, dating from the migration of the first Muslims from Mecca to Medina. Other countries sometimes use both calendars simultaneously for official purposes, but generally use the Gregorian calendar in business and in private arrangements. An important link between Islam and the structure of the year has thus been lost.

The weekend falling on Saturday and Sunday has been adopted less widely than the Gregorian calendar, because its use involves making Friday a working day. There is no religious requirement for Muslims to rest on Fridays, but there is a requirement for male Muslims to attend communal prayers at midday, and these and associated activities cannot easily be fitted into a break in the working day. As a result, some Muslim countries place the weekend on Thursday and Friday, and some on Friday and Saturday, despite the disruption this causes to international business, thus maintaining the link between Islam and the structure of the week. Only such determinedly "secular" countries such as Turkey and Indonesia follow global practice and place the weekend on Saturday and Sunday.

Knives and forks and the Gregorian calendar both represent ways in which Muslim popular culture has become less Islamic, more globalized, and less diverse. The contrary trend, most visible on the peripheries of the Muslim world, is for diversity to be reduced by the extinction of local practices that contravene newly adopted religious norms. This, too, is a result of globalization, since improved communications, both physical and electronic, has facilitated flows of ideas and practices within the Muslim world as well as from the West into the Muslim world. It is also a result of the spread of education.

Ideas and practices have always flowed within the Muslim world. This is why it makes sense to speak of a Muslim world in the first place. Until the nineteenth century, however, they flowed slowly and with difficulty. Some traders, officials, and members of the ulama traveled long distances, but travel was expensive, slow, and dangerous. Villages were isolated, both physically and intellectually. They were hard to travel to or from, and if a villager was literate, there was little to read. This has now changed. Travel within the Muslim world is much cheaper and easier, and although for economic reasons Muslims on average still travel less than Westerners, the number of future members of the ulama studying outside their countries of origin has increased enormously. Many villages are now connected to towns by roads, and towns are connected to cities. Literacy has increased dramatically, and there is much more to read, whether in printed form or on the internet. As a result, ideas and practices flow much more easily than they once did. As usual, they flow more easily from the center to the periphery than the other way round. The Muslim world has no single center, but one center that has become increasingly important for training the future ulama who matter for the transmission of ideas that can impact practices, and also important as a destination for the migrant workers who on their return home to the periphery often transmit the practices of the center, is Saudi Arabia. The ideas and practices that have recently flowed within the Muslim world, then, often reflect strict, Saudi interpretations of Islam.

Because ideas now flow more easily, local practices that were once unquestioned can now be seen to be different from those elsewhere, and are questioned and often condemned as un-Islamic. Many of the local practices that have been replaced by newly adopted Islamic norms have to do with gender. Female clothing is increasingly uniform within the Muslim world, and unusual local practices regarding women are being replaced by standard Islamic ones. The rule of *pushtunwali*, the customary law of much of Afghanistan, that forbids inheritance by females, for example, is now under attack as un-Islamic. In the opposite direction, the customary law that once permitted inheritance of land only in the female line in some parts of Indonesia and Malaysia has now been generally replaced by standard Islamic practice. Gender, however, is the topic of Chapter 7, and will be discussed no further in this chapter.

Other local practices that have been or are being displaced by standard Islamic norms, being local, vary greatly from place to place. In northern Malaysia it is puppet theater that is condemned as un-Islamic, and in the western Sudan it is slightly alcoholic beer. One set of local practices that has been disappearing since the nineteenth century, however, is common to most parts of the Muslim world: practices relating to the tombs of saints. These were once of enormous importance in local popular culture, as is indicated by the way that villages and urban districts across the Muslim world are often named after local saints. Tombs were visited in search of divine blessings for spiritual or—more often—mundane purposes. Miraculous cures were sought and, apparently, granted. The annual celebration of saints' anniversaries was one of the major local festivals of the year, if not the major local festival. Activities associated with these festivals were often peculiar to particular localities: in Luxor, Egypt, for example, a boat formed the centerpiece of a procession that showed signs of Pharaonic origins. These very diverse elements of local popular culture have been in decline everywhere since the end of the nineteenth century. Some tombs are no longer visited, or are visited only by the old; some festivals are no longer celebrated, or are celebrated only by the poor and uneducated.

Muslim popular culture, then, has changed with modernity most of all with regard to gender roles and relations, and also in becoming less diverse, either as a result of the adoption of global practices of Western origin, or as a result of the displacement of local practices by new Islamic norms, often of Saudi origin. Muslim popular culture has also changed as a result of new concepts and ideals that have been received from the Muslim public sphere, and with the increasing role of consumer culture, to which we now turn.

Islamic consumer culture

Some theorists of modernity emphasize not so much the public sphere as the development of, and participation in, a world market economy. To varying degrees, Muslim countries have been integrated into the world market economy since the nineteenth century, and the wealth that this has generated (often spread rather unevenly) has contributed to the growth of urbanization and of education, and so to the creation of a Muslim public sphere and to the standardization of popular culture just discussed. It has also meant the development of a variety of new goods and services.

Religion and economics have always been connected, in the case of Islam as in the case of other religions. For centuries, providing various services to pilgrims was the mainstay of the economy of the Hejaz, the area around Mecca and Medina, and craftsmen produced goods for religious use, notably Qurans, prayer mats, and *sibhas* (rosary-like prayer beads), some of the finer examples of which are now found in Islamic museums. These ancient goods and services are still produced, though the Hejaz is now part of Saudi Arabia and depends much more on oil than on pilgrims, and many prayer mats are now made in China, as are so many other consumer goods. Prayer mats and services to pilgrims have been joined by a wide range of other goods and services specially developed for the Islamic consumer, and often produced and consumed globally.

The products that supply Islamic consumer culture fall into three categories: goods, services, and media. Starting with goods, there is Islamic food, Islamic fashion, and even Islamic toys. There always was Islamic food, of course, in the sense that the raw materials and cooked meals sold in Muslim-majority countries complied with the requirements of the Sharia. Animals were slaughtered according to the Sharia, making their meat *halal* (permitted). If *haram* (forbidden) pork and alcohol were on sale, which they sometimes were, they had their own special and separate outlets, patronized by non-Muslim minorities and sometimes, at least in the case of alcohol, by less devout Muslims. This is still the case for locally produced products in the Muslim world, save that in some countries alcohol in drinkable forms has crept onto supermarket shelves.

Food has become an issue partly because the numbers of Muslims living as minorities in non-Muslim countries has increased, and partly because much food today is not locally produced, and contains long lists of ingredients, some of which can be problematic. Gelatin, for example, is widely used in manufacturing ice cream, and is of animal origin, as is lipase, used in making some cheeses and baked goods. The inclusion of such animal products raises questions over how the animal in question was slaughtered—according to the requirements of the Sharia, so that the product that contains it is *halal*, or not? This does not worry all Muslims, many of whom are content with avoiding what is obviously pork, and who prefer to know as little as possible about the details of ice cream manufacturing. Devout Muslims in non-Muslim countries, however, and food importers in Muslim countries, do have to concern themselves with how ice cream is made. Many Muslims in non-Muslim countries, even if they do not worry about ice cream, avoid not only pork but also any other meat they do not actually know to be *halal*.

These are the problems that the Islamic food industry addresses. For internationally traded foods, there are a range of (competing) *halal* certification authorities. Major meat producers in the West and in Latin America ensure that their slaughtering processes are *halal*, and major multinational manufacturers such as Nestlé produce *halal* versions of some of their products. In non-Muslim countries where there are significant Muslim minorities, there are specialist *halal* butcher's shops and *halal* restaurants. All KFC's French restaurants are *halal* certified, as are some in America. Many national supermarket chains in France and England sell and produce *halal* goods for their Muslim customers, as does one Walmart in Michigan. American manufacturers of kosher foods, which conform closely enough to the requirements of the Sharia to satisfy many, sell some 15 percent of their produce to Muslims.

This *halal* food industry confronts and addresses issues raised by globalization. In some cases, it also addresses issues of identity and authenticity. For Muslim minorities, *halal* food helps create communities. Some food products also address issues of authenticity, notably Mecca Cola, invented in France and now available elsewhere.

Figure 12.1 Halal food store, Japan. © Emran Kassim.

Like the Islamic food industry, the Islamic fashion industry is a product of globalization. Once, just as all food in the Muslim world automatically fulfilled the requirements of the Sharia, so did the clothing industry—until the arrival of French fashions during the nineteenth century, as part of the flow of practices from the center to the periphery of the new global system. As that century drew to an end, women's clothes in cities such as Istanbul and Cairo became more revealing, and the face-veil grew thinner and thinner until it finally vanished, followed by the headscarf. By the 1960s, fashions of Western origin predominated in much of the Muslim world, and "traditional" clothing had often become the mark of the poor. With the Islamic revival of the 1970s came a need for female clothing that was both Islamic (and, incidentally, authentic) and fashionable: loose rather than revealing, incorporating a headscarf, but not drab or poorly made. This need was met by increasing numbers of manufacturers, stores, and even fashion shows. What started as a consequence and expression of new piety became increasingly standard, to the extent that in many cities today Islamic fashion is the norm, worn by the less devout as well as by the devout. Islamic fashion is aimed principally at females, but a market for male Islamic clothing is now beginning to develop, led by loose and non-revealing swimwear, which joins the so-called "burqini," Sharia-compliant female swimwear. Islamic fashion allows its buyers to conform to their interpretations of the Sharia, and also addresses questions of identity, to which clothing is always closely related.

The best known Islamic toy, Fulla, is a reflection of Islamic fashion and, again, a response to globalization. Fulla is modeled closely on Barbie, but with a more restrained anatomy, clothes that follow Islamic rather than Western fashion, and no hint of a boyfriend. She has dark rather than blonde hair, and can be bought with her own prayer mat. She also comes as a dentist, a teacher, and a hair stylist—occupations generally considered unproblematic for a female, even in more conservative parts of the Muslim world. Fulla is available in specialist toy stores in the US, as well as throughout the Arab world and in some other countries. Boys, too, are catered to, with a variety of educational games suitable for both genders. A British toymaker, for example, produces an "Animals in the Quran" snap game, as well as books such as *Zaynab and Zakariya Learn to Recycle*, which aims to provide an Islamic perspective on a range of contemporary issues. A company in Hong Kong produces "My Mosque," a battery-powered plastic toy that names parts of the mosque when they are pressed. Toys such as "My Mosque" are normally bought by more devout parents, but Fulla may also be bought by any parent concerned with issues of authenticity and identity.

Figure 12.2 Islamic fashion store, Canada. © Muhammad Ghouri.

Islamic goods, then, are an important part of Muslim popular culture, and also a significant business sector. Islamic services, however, are even bigger business. Pilgrimage remains important to the travel industry. That industry is also now seeing a new trend, the development of luxury Islamic hotels. These are aimed by marketing executives primarily at the growing tourist trade from wealthy Arab Gulf countries. An Islamic hotel serves *halal* food and does not sell alcohol or offer problematic movies on its television. It has convenient facilities in its bathrooms for performing pre-prayer ablutions, showcases Islamic art and architecture, and markets itself as family-friendly and as heir to centuries of legendary Arab hospitality—one aspect of the imagined (but not necessarily imaginary) Arab national culture. Several such chains are currently under development, one in partnership with the Swiss Kempinski group, owners of such outstanding European hotels as Berlin's Adlon and London's Stafford. As with KFC in France, though aiming at a different income bracket, the participation of the Kempinski group is an example of how non-Muslim multinational businesses supply Islamic consumer culture. Islamic popular culture provides an important market that many multinationals feel they cannot afford to ignore.

The single most important Islamic service sector is Islamic finance. The Sharia has very detailed rules relating to financial transactions, and all but the most creatively liberal interpretations of these rules class not only interest-bearing deposits as forbidden, but also such commonplace transactions as the use of credit cards, buying a house with a mortgage, or taking out life insurance. Despite this, standard international financial transactions are routinely carried out in most Muslim countries, and many Muslims bow to necessity and use the same banks and financial instruments as non-Muslims do. Other Muslims, especially in some parts of the Muslim world, are simply too poor to be concerned with bank accounts or mortgages, which lie beyond their reach. Cash is much more widely used in the Muslim world than it now is in the West. Some devout Muslims, however, are both wealthy and scrupulous in financial matters, especially in the Arab Gulf countries that are the hoped-for source of visits to the new luxury Islamic hotels. Devout Muslims in the West, where cash is not much used and where houses need to be bought somehow, are also users of Islamic finance, even if they are not always wealthy.

Islamic finance aims to provide essentially the same services that Western finance provides, building on ancient financial models sanctioned by the Sharia, and adapting these to contemporary needs. Islamic banks provide Islamic checking accounts, deposits, and loans to individuals, and also provide a variety of Islamic financial products such as bonds to businesses. There is also *takaful*, an Islamic alternative to insurance. The largest Islamic banks are based in the Gulf, Saudi Arabia and Iran, with Malaysia and Indonesia also having very significant Islamic banking sectors. Other Islamic banks are based in countries with significant Muslim minorities, notably Britain. Many major international banks, such as JP Chase Morgan and HSBC, have Islamic banking subsidiaries.

In all cases, one objective is to provide financial products that compete directly with those offered by standard banks, and can be marketed in much the same way. The other objective is to avoid anything that is clearly interest, as well as investments in businesses or assets which might not be *halal.* An Islamic bank, or the Islamic banking division of an international bank, will not trade with a business that involves the sale of alcohol, for example, and may even avoid financing meat-processing equipment. In this respect, Islamic banks have something in common with standard "ethical banking." Islamic hotels are financed through Islamic banks.

As well as Islamic goods and Islamic services, the Islamic consumer sector produces Islamic media. These include the television preachers discussed in Chapter 13, and the internet services discussed in Chapter 8. There are also Islamic print and audio media, of which print media are the oldest, dating back almost to the first introduction of printing in the Muslim world in the nineteenth century. The first ever international Islamic newspaper, *Al-Manar*, was launched in 1898, and there are now great numbers of Islamic newspapers, magazines, publishers, and bookstores. Like French KFC and Islamic hotels or Islamic banks, many Islamic media aim to provide an Islamic alternative to the standard product. The Turkish newspaper *Zaman*, for example, is in most ways a regular newspaper, and differs from other Turkish newspapers principally in its editorial line, and also in not printing certain sorts of photograph. There are Islamic women's magazines that feature Islamic fashion, again an alternative to the standard product. There are also magazines that focus entirely on Islamic issues, as there are books that deal exclusively with Islamic issues—as there are books that deal with issues specific to any other religion, of course. These books are extremely popular, sold and read very widely.

Islamic audio media have developed considerably in recent years. Once consisting largely of cassette-tape recordings of Quran reciters and popular preachers, sometimes homemade, Islamic audio media today include everything from downloadable Islamic ring tones for cell phones, including a neat iPhone app that plays the Call to Prayer at appropriate times, to Islamic pop stars. Many pop stars in Muslim countries record songs with Islamic themes alongside more standard music, but given that standard pop music often deals with themes and uses instruments that more devout Muslims find problematic, there are also singers who focus on exclusively Islamic themes, often using only male voices and using percussion rather than stringed or brass instruments, a style known as *nasheed*, and considered *halal* by almost all Muslims. *Nasheed* fuses traditional Eastern and contemporary Western musical modes, often using electronic modification of the original *halal* instruments to achieve complex effects. The most internationally famous *nasheed* singer is at present Sami Yusuf, a British Muslim whose songs generally start in English and end in Arabic or, more rarely, in Persian or Turkish. The lyrics of his songs are religious and austere, but at the same time simple, as in one of the most popular, "Al-Mu'allim" ("the Teacher," that is, the Prophet Muhammad):

We once had a Teacher
The Teacher of teachers,
He changed the world for the better
And made us better creatures,
Oh Allah we've shamed ourselves
We've strayed from Al-Mu'allim,
Surely we've wronged ourselves
What will we say in front of him?

In contrast, the music videos that accompany these lyrics are extremely glossy, featuring luxurious residences and designer lifestyles as well as prayer and famous mosques. The overall message is the combination of simple religious devotion and worldly success that has also been identified in the preaching of Amr Khaled, discussed in Chapter 13, and has been associated with the modern ideal of self-realization. Another part of the overall message is authenticity. In the words of Suma Din, writing in the British Muslim magazine *Q-News*, *nasheed* "has provided a soundtrack for the emergence of a distinctly religious cultural identity."

The American hip-hop group Native Deen, in contrast, focuses on the harsh realities of life as Muslim in the West. One of their most popular songs, "Not Afraid to Stand Alone," features a single mother who converts to Islam, puts on a headscarf, and is told after a job interview "You got the job, but you gotta lose the outfit." Rather than a designer lifestyle, the accompanying music video features the lead singer as a school janitor, complete with wet floor and mop. The message here is more of struggle and resistance than of self-realization.

At the furthest extreme from Sami Yusuf are groups such as the American punk group The Taqwacores or the British hip-hop techno group Fun-Da-Mental, both of which have toured in Pakistan, but are firmly rooted in Western Muslim youth subcultures. The Taqwacores have made their story into a movie (2010), and are famous among other things for infiltrating a talent show at the annual convention of the Islamic Society of North America (ISNA). When the organizers called the police to remove them, they began to chant "Pigs are haram in Islam." The British group Fun-Da-Mental is known for their album "All Is War (The Benefits of G-Had)," and especially for one track "Cookbook DIY," which describes the do-it-yourself manufacture of explosives for a suicide bomb.

Fun-Da-Mental and Sami Yusuf, it goes without saying, have very different followings. Sami Yusuf is popular worldwide, while Fun-Da-Mental is appreciated principally in restricted circles in Britain and Pakistan. Fun-Da-Mental intends to shock, and succeeds in doing so. Sami Yusuf seeks to inspire, and also succeeds in doing so. Both, along with Islamic goods and services, are part of Islamic consumer culture, and so of contemporary Muslim popular culture.

Muslim popular culture in the twenty-first century

The popular culture of the Muslim world is, like popular culture everywhere in the modern world, being more globalized and more standardized. Purely local popular culture is on the retreat, whether because it is being replaced by global popular culture, or because it is no longer seen as Islamic, as is most notably the case when it comes to anything related to the celebration of saints' anniversaries. Some Islamic elements in Muslim popular culture, such as the use of the right hand in eating, are also on the retreat, but sometimes global popular culture is being Islamized, producing products such as Fulla, services such as the Islamic hotel, and media such as the Islamic women's magazine. *Nasheed* music can be seen either as something spreading from Islam into a space created by globalization, or as an Islamic alternative to something already existing (pop music).

As well as practices, products, and services, there are ideals such as social justice and concepts such as authenticity that are global and modern in origin but local and Islamic in impact. In the case of social justice, the ideal has been Islamized, and in the case of authenticity, the idea has fed into Muslim consumer culture, producing Mecca Cola, but also everything from *nasheed* music to "Islamic" architecture, which before was only the architecture of a particular time and of a particular place within the Muslim world.

Despite this, some elements of Muslim popular culture of course remain as they have been for centuries, including elements that are local and unconnected to Islam, like jasmine flowers in Tunisia. Muslim popular culture today, then, is a mixture: old and new, local and global, unconnected with religion, Islamic and Islamized. It is within the context of this popular culture that Muslims experience Islam, as religion and also as culture and identity, categories that are so hard to disentangle that some scholars hold that they should not be separated. Islam is accepting the unity of God and the prophethood of Muhammad, but it is also reading an Islamic newspaper. Islam is prayer, but may be prayer using a prayer-mat made in China, and includes listening to Sami Yusuf. Islam is fasting, but Islam is also buying *halal* food at a French supermarket. Islam is giving alms, but it is also giving Fulla dolls. Islam is pilgrimage, but it is also staying in an Islamic hotel. Islam is the ulama, but it is also the public sphere.

Much of this book deals with Islam as it is experienced by the very devout—those who pray five times a day, for example. Not all Muslims pray five times a day, however. Conclusive statistics on this do not exist, but it seems clear that at least in certain places today the majority of Muslims do not actually pray five times a day. Almost everywhere, attendance at Friday prayers increases considerably during Ramadan: there are a lot of people, then, who do not go to Friday prayers when it is not Ramadan. Those who only go to Friday prayers during Ramadan are still Muslims, however, as are other less devout Muslims. And all participate, to one degree or another, in Muslim popular culture, and in the meanings and identities that it generates.

Summary

- Not all aspects of the popular culture of Muslims can be explained in terms of religion, but much popular culture is related to Islam.
- Contemporary Muslim popular culture differs from earlier models because of the growth of the public sphere, a decrease in diversity, and the increased importance of consumer culture.
- Since the nineteenth century, the Muslim world has been on the global periphery, and so has tended to import culture from the global centers, although the impact of this has been very uneven.
- Sometimes the importation of Western culture has moved popular culture away from Islam, and sometimes imported culture has been Islamized.
- Authenticity is important, and "Islamic" art and architecture are modern creations that supply authenticity.
- Such cultural practices as eating and reckoning time have often become less connected to Islam as a result of Westernization.
- Local cultural practices such as those connected with the tombs of saints have often declined as a result of globalization and the related influence of Saudi Arabian interpretations of Islam.
- Islamic consumer culture has always existed, but has become more important under conditions of modernity and globalization.
- Islamic food and clothing are now important commercial sectors.
- Islamic hotels are now joining Islamic travel (pilgrimage) as a significant sector.
- Islamic consumer finance, the most commercially important part of Islamic consumer culture, attempts to replicate standard finance without contravening the Sharia.
- Islamic print media offer Islamic alternatives to standard consumer media.
- Islamic audio media attempt to avoid contravening the sharia and differ according to their market.

Discussion points

- Why has Muslim popular culture become less diverse?
- What aspects of Muslim popular culture are most connected to Islam?
- What is Islamic art?
- Should multinational companies promote Islamic products?
- How Islamic are Sami Yusuf and the Taqwacores?

Further reading

Armbrust, W. (ed.) (2005) *Culture Wars: The Arabic Music Video Controversy*, Cairo: AUC Press.

This collection of essays is not just about music videos, and covers a wide variety of topics relating to transnational and national broadcasting and other media.

El-Gamal, M.A. (2006) *Islamic Finance: Law, Economics, and Practice*, New York: Cambridge University Press.

This is an academic work on Islamic finance, going into much detail in terms of sharia, history, and practice.

Iqbal, Z. and A. Mirakhor (2007) *An Introduction to Islamic Finance: Theory and Practice*, Singapore: John Wiley.

This is a more practically oriented textbook on Islamic finance, with an emphasis on financial aspects, but also covering theoretical aspects,

Pink, J. (ed.) (2009) *Muslim Societies in the Age of Mass Consumption: Politics, Culture and Identity Between the Local and Global*, Newcastle-upon-Tyne, UK: Cambridge Scholars.

This is a collection covering many aspects of contemporary Islamic consumer culture, with a focus on the Arab world and Turkey but also covering Europe and Indonesia.

Singerman, D. and P. Amar (eds) (2009) *Cairo Cosmopolitan: Politics, Culture, and Urban Space in the New Globalized Middle East*, Cairo: AUC Press.

As the title says, this collection covers only Cairo, but it covers a range of topics from cafés and coffee shops through cinemas to housing developments.

Temporal, P. (2011) *Islamic Branding and Marketing: Creating a Global Islamic Business*, Singapore: John Wiley.

This is a practically oriented textbook on Islamic consumer culture, covering markets, brands, and sectors from travel to the internet. Aimed at the practitioner more than the scholar, but interesting to both.

Wittrock, B. (2000) "Modernity: One, None, or Many? European Origins and Modernity as a Global Condition," *Daedalus*, 129(1): 31–60.

This is a thought-provoking article about the question of what "modernity" might mean, providing a good introduction to an important topic of broad relevance to many of the issues discussed in this chapter.

Further viewing

Check out Sami Yusuf and the groups mentioned in this chapter on YouTube.

References

Anderson, B. (1983) *Imagined Communities: Reflections on the Origin and Spread of Nationalism*, London: Verso.

Beaujard, P. (2005) "The Indian Ocean in Eurasian and African World-Systems Before the Sixteenth Century," *Journal of World History*, 16: 411–65.

Din, S. (2006) "The Day the Music Died," *Q-News*, 336: 34–36.

Fadil, N. (2005) "Individualizing Faith, Individualizing Identity: Islam and Young Muslim Women in Belgium," in J. Cesari and S. McLoughlin (eds) *European Muslims and the Secular State*, London: Ashgate, 134–54.

Habermas, J. (1991) *The Structural Transformation of the Public Sphere: An Inquiry into a Category of Bourgeois Society*, Cambridge, MA: MIT Press.

Qutb, S. (1949/2000) *Social Justice in Islam*, Cairo, 1949; recent English translation by John B. Hardie, Oneonta, NY: Islamic Publications International.

Saunders, R.A. (2008) "The Ummah as Nation: A Reappraisal in the Wake of the 'Cartoons Affair,'" *Nations and Nationalism*, 14: 303–21.

Wittrock, B. (2000) "Modernity: One, None, or Many? European Origins and Modernity as a Global Condition," *Daedalus*, 129(1): 31–60.

Part III

Case studies of tradition and change

13

The emergence of media preachers: Yusuf al-Qaradawi

Marcia Hermansen

New forms and technologies of Islamic discussions and authority

In February 2011, Shaykh Yusuf al-Qaradawi, in the light of the uprisings in Libya against that country's despot, Muammar al-Qadhdhafi, whose forces were mowing down unarmed civilians in several Libyan cities, announced on al-Jazeera television: "I hereby issue a ruling (fatwa) that anyone in the Libyan armed forces who is able to fire a shot at al-Qadhdhafi and kill him in order to relieve the people from his evil should do so." How is it possible for a Muslim religious preacher to gain so much authority and issue a revolutionary fatwa that would be controversial and have direct implications for geopolitics and armed resistance? We will discuss how such preachers have come to be accorded mass popularity and whether their new modes of exercising authority may threaten both the traditional ulama and repressive governments across the Muslim world.

Recent decades have seen important changes, not only in religious leadership in Muslim societies, but in the very nature of religious authority and how the message and teachings of Islam are communicated and received by a mass audience. One aspect of that change is in the population itself. Most Muslim majority nation-states that emerged in the postcolonial era promoted government supported mass education up to the university level. For the first time such state education became accessible to males and females from diverse class backgrounds, raising both rates of literacy and expectations for meaningful employment on the part of graduates.

This increase in literacy was exponential, allowing individual Muslims to independently consult religious texts and sources in ways never before possible. According to some analysts, this development parallels the rise of vernacular literacy in Europe on the eve of the Protestant Reformation in 1453. This inspired some observers to anticipate a similar Islamic reformation, coupled with searches for a figure to be dubbed the Muslim Martin Luther. However, Islam, whether Sunni or Shi'a, is not Protestantism, although similar struggles pitting traditional authority guarded by its custodians, the ulama, against the ability of individual Muslims to resort directly to the scriptural word—have certainly increased. While the new focus on higher education was avowedly secular, the public's increased interest in debates about how to be properly "Muslim" amid rapidly changing social and material circumstances, and in strategies to Islamicize the private as well as the public sphere, created a space where custodians of authentic Islamic knowledge, joined by those who could articulate the relevance of Islam in today's world, were welcome voices.

In the twentieth-century Muslim world, more than literacy rates and educational access were changing. If the medium of communication is considered to be a major element of the message itself, then a shift of epic proportions was taking place on a global scale with the proliferation of new technologies for delivering data and the multiplication of channels or sources conveying that information.

In many parts of the Muslim world, the same nation-states that had only recently achieved independence or been constituted in the wake of colonialism sought to dominate the information received by their citizens. Some monarchies or dictatorships followed a Soviet-style top-down monopoly over institutions and organs of communication, while others used tight censorship in the name of Islam to repel outside influences or mute dissident voices. Some of the first examples of media preachers who appeared on state television were therefore perceived as being aligned with government policy, a notable example being Shaykh Muhammad Mitawalli Sha'rawi (1915–98) in Egypt. Sha'rawi was a graduate of the prestigious al-Azhar Islamic University, held important government posts in religious affairs, and also was closely associated with Saudi Arabian interests. Sha'rawi cultivated a media presence that was both folksy and authoritative, conducting most of his session in Egyptian colloquial Arabic delivered in expressive and colorful style, while remaining in control of a selected studio audience listening with rapt attention.

New formulations of Islam as an alternative political response that could address the moral and material shortcomings of this world had been formulated by activists from outside of the traditional ranks of the ulama such as Hassan al-Banna (1906–49) and Sayyid Qutb (1906–66) of the Egyptian Muslim Brotherhood and Syed Maududi (1903–79), founder of the South Asian Jamaat-e Islami. Yet these movements primarily appealed to a more narrow vanguard of individuals who felt that the Islamization of society would best be implemented through a top-down process. The works of these figures were primarily disseminated in print, with newspapers and pamphlets beginning to play an important role, alongside more formal book projects. The circulation and translation of such works across languages such as Arabic, Urdu, and English, also reflected a new kind of Islamic internationalism.

The 1970s was the era of cheap cassette technology that dispersed, along with music and entertainment, sermons and preaching by a new type of Muslim preacher. Such tapes could be produced and transported inexpensively and were often associated with oppositional trends in Muslim societies, for example, the case of Ayatollah Khomeini's sermons being sent back to Iran from France while he was in exile. Similarly in Egypt the Islamist preacher Shaykh Kishk criticized social and political trends under the regimes of Nasser, Sadat, and Mubarak and achieved pan-Arab popularity.

In the Muslim world, new television networks were potential sites of the propaganda battles in the Cold War between the capitalist West and the Soviet bloc that was being fought by proxy in the developing nations of Latin America, the Middle East, Africa, and Asia. While the non-aligned movement of the 1970s was dominated by progressive or left-leaning leaders of developing nations, at the popular level calls for a return to Islamic values and practice had begun to find a receptive audience.

The emergence of the media preacher in the Muslim world, then, is a striking development that occurred due to the confluence of new technologies, a rise in transnational Islamic consciousness and presence, and a more individualized, emotive, and mass oriented response to Islamic authority and discourse. The 1990s was the era of the spread of internet connections and satellite channels through which the information carried by these new communication technologies became global and universal. Increasingly English, along with the traditional Arabic, became an international language of Islamic discourse, and the presence of growing numbers of Muslims in Europe and the United States made long-distance communication and interaction more common.

The story of Yusuf al-Qaradawi

Biography

Yusuf al-Qaradawi is perhaps the most well-known and prolific Muslim preacher in the world today. His books and pamphlets, numbering into the hundreds, are translated into many languages; his television programs on al-Jazeera satellite network are viewed throughout the Middle East; and his online legal/moral advice is sought by Muslims everywhere.

Figure 13.1 Yusuf al-Qaradawi. Courtesy of Fayez Nureldine/AFP/Getty Images.

Al-Qaradawi draws his authority both from traditional sources and institutions and from new media to engage, interpret, and communicate with changing generations in an evolving global context. His triumphal return to Egypt to preach to millions from Tahrir Square in February 2011 symbolizes the confluence of religious, moral, political, and charismatic authority that he, among all Islamic media preachers, epitomizes most effectively.

The sacred language of Islamic tradition is Arabic, and al-Qaradawi comes from Egypt, the country whose media production, dominance in publishing, and large population gave it cultural preeminence in the Arab world in the twentieth century. Yet it was al-Qaradawi's departure from Egypt and its hierarchical state system of ulama bound to government approval and patronage that gave him the freedom and flexibility to think and act outside the box represented by such a system.

Born in 1926, al-Qaradawi came from a small, unremarkable village and family in the Nile delta region of northern Egypt. From childhood, his intellectual interests lay in religion and on the basis of merit he was admitted and supported in pursuing advanced studies at al-Azhar, the most prestigious institute in the Sunni Muslim world for training religious scholars.

Al-Azhar, established by the Fatimid dynasty in CE 969, has been described as a combination of the authority and functions of the Vatican, with those of the US Supreme Court and the Congress. Students traditionally came from all corners of the Sunni world to spend years studying the Islamic religious sciences there. During the 1960s, al-Azhar, under government mandate, undertook a series of internal reforms to modernize and broaden its curriculum, adding secular subjects such as medicine and engineering. This reform was viewed by some observers as a move to weaken and diffuse its authority and rigor and as an indication of the marginalization of the influence of traditional Muslim scholars (ulama) in the face of new systems of authoritative knowledge in modern and technical fields.

Al-Qaradawi joined the Muslim Brotherhood movement in the late 1940s and later became their leading representative at al-Azhar. This relationship has continued, with al-Qaradawi being offered the leadership of the movement at several points during his later career, an offer that he preferred to decline. He graduated from al-Azhar with an undergraduate degree in the Fundamentals of Religion (Usul-al-Din) in 1953. His graduate study was finally concluded in 1973 with a PhD on "Zakat and its effect on solving social problems" having been interrupted and delayed by political persecution, imprisonment, and self-imposed exile. In fact, al-Qaradawi spent a few years in prison in Egypt during the early Nasser regime, a common fate of many Muslim activists during that period.

In 1962 al-Qaradawi moved to Qatar where he worked to establish the new educational system in this small sheikhdom in the Gulf. He became a confidant of the ruler, Shaykh Khalifa bin Hamad (b. 1932), who patronized his activities. While supported by the

Qatari ruler, al-Qaradawi has been considered an oppositional figure in most other Arab countries because of his links to the Muslim Brotherhood. Coincidentally, al-Qaradawi's relocating in Qatar coincided with the economic rise of the small oil-producing nations of the Gulf where, subsequent to the dramatic boost in oil revenues in the wake of the 1973 OPEC embargo on oil exports to the West, the newly wealthy Gulf States began to exercise their strategic and financial weight in the world.

Qatar, a small island state, became notable for its sponsorship of the popular satellite television station, al-Jazeera, launched in 1996 with the support of Hamad bin Khalifa II (b. 1952) who had deposed his father as ruler in 1995. Al-Jazeera rapidly became popular among Arab viewers across the Middle East due to its allowing controversial social and political topics to be openly debated, in contrast to the censorship prevalent in most government-controlled channels across the region. Despite pressure from conservative Arab regimes and the United States, this station achieved great popularity and a reputation for covering the news in a manner independent from Western governments and their official and commercial media outlets.

"Shari'a and Life": a program and a concept

In January 1997 al-Jazeera launched "Shari'a and Life," a program that showcased al-Qaradawi as a media preacher and a general authority on the shari'a as well as on specific issues in Islamic law. On this program, moderated by a non-expert, al-Qaradawi represented the authoritative voice of the Islamic scholar interpreting the shari'a in response to questions drawn from the everyday life experiences of viewers. This show featured debates over contemporary issues evaluated in the light of the principles of Islamic law. In a process of instant *ifta*—requesting legal opinions on a variety of issues—Muslims were able to call in live from around the world.

It may be wondered why Islam is such an interesting subject in the pan-Arab media. One factor is that Islam constitutes an important part of the identity of most people living in the Arab world. Opinions on how to be a Muslim and navigate changing social circumstances are contested and spark lively interest. Such issues include women's roles or moral dilemmas raised by new medical technologies. Featuring explicitly Islamic content in programming also resonates with the idea that the independent Arab media provides an oppositional forum, distinct from the content and messages distributed from the West.

In his successful media preaching, al-Qaradawi has been able to engage three new elements of the global Islamic audience: women, youth, and Muslims living abroad in the so-called "diaspora." In terms of the female audience, despite his relatively conservative stance, al-Qaradawi has proven adaptable in some of his rulings on gender issues, in contrast to many of the more traditional ulama. For example, he has supported not only female suffrage, but also the political rights of women to themselves run for office as candidates. His own daughters pursued higher professional degrees abroad and subsequent careers.

One illustration of his position on the issue of Muslim women's dress being more liberal than some, but certainly remaining conservative, is drawn from the following 2010 interview.

Niqab in Europe and the fiqh of Muslim minorities

Al-Qaradawi was asked in an Online Islam interview about the niqab (full-face veil) that some Muslim women wear being outlawed in France. He replied:

> My opinion about the niqab is well-known, which is that the niqab is not obligatory; however, I respect the opinion saying it is. And I do not agree with some sheikhs who regard it as an innovation or tradition that has no basis in Islam. …
>
> If a Muslim woman is convinced that wearing the niqab is obligatory and the face is 'awrah, we have to respect her choice and avoid being an obstacle to her religious commitment.
>
> Online Islam: What should a Muslim woman do if the country where she lives bans the niqab, while she believes that it is obligatory?
>
> Sheikh al-Qaradawi: … I told them [Muslims in France] to wear hijab outside the school and to put it off when they arrive at the school gate to enter. Such a case is governed by two rules:
>
> The first rule: Necessities make what is forbidden permissible. The need can be regarded as a necessity. Accordingly, if wearing the niqab is confronted with the necessity of education or the necessity of work, while the woman needs it, in this case she is permitted to give up the niqab.
>
> The second rule: Necessities should be weighed accurately and honestly. In other words, once a Muslim woman leaves work or school, where the hijab is banned, she has to put it on again; and the same applies to the niqab.
>
> (al-Qaradawi 2010)

The new youth audience attracted by al-Qaradawi is important because of its dynamism and participation in Islamic revival movements and the 2011 Arab Spring uprisings. It is also increasingly influential in the light of demographic trends in much of the Muslim world where the percentage of the population under 20 years of age is much higher than in Western nations. It has been stated that the role of Muslim ulama as the "heirs of the Prophet" should be to forge a bond with the youth and guide them. In the West, as in the traditional Muslim world, the search for authenticity and Islamic identity movements among young Muslims make them particularly attracted to the sources of traditional Muslim authority embodied by figures such as al-Qaradawi.

During his triumphal Friday sermon delivered in Tahrir Square in Cairo, in February 2011, al-Qaradawi specifically addressed youth as follows:

> This is why these youth from all regions in Egypt, from all social classes, rich and poor, educated and illiterate, workers and cultured—though the majority were cultured and educated people—we saw altruism increase among them. They became, they fused into, one melting-pot: Muslims and Christians, radicals and conservatives, rightists and leftists, men and women, old and young, all of them became one, all of them acting for Egypt, in order to liberate Egypt from injustice (*zulm*) and tyranny (*taghut*). It was inevitable that Egypt be liberated, because these youth willed it, and when the youth will, their will participates in the will of God.

In terms of the broader diaspora audience, al-Qaradawi has had important outreach to European Muslims. A prominent example is his role in the establishment of the European Council for Fatwa and Research in 1997 in London to coordinate ulama in Europe. Over time, however, European perceptions of al-Qaradawi changed and some of his fatwas, such as those allowing Palestinian "martyrdom" operations as well as certain illiberal pronouncements made in his work, *The Permitted and the Forbidden in Islam*, on issues such as gay rights, led to his being banned from visiting a number of European countries, and he has also been barred from entering the United States since 1999.

These developments epitomize some of the tensions implicit in al-Qaradawi's positions and in their reception among diverse publics. We may take as an example one of his works that has been translated into many languages and found popular acceptance among diaspora Muslim communities. This is the previously mentioned book on the permitted and forbidden according to Islamic law. The idea of rulings designating permitted (halal) and forbidden (haram) is certainly well-known in Islamic law and enshrined in a hadith (saying of the Prophet) to the effect that, "The permitted is clear and the forbidden is clear and between them are many dubious/ambiguous things that should be avoided." Al-Qaradawi's volume on this topic is presented in the form of a manual of rulings on everyday situations that any Muslim can follow. While the very polarity of *halal* and *haram* suggests a black-and-white view of the world, it also resonates with the Islamist project of a comprehensive Islamic approach to all aspects of everyday life conceived as a total system. Furthermore, it functions as a means for the re-enchantment of modern life experience by bringing everything into relationship with the divine mandate. While some perceive this project as a positive source for inculcating and clarifying Islamic norms, others find the concept to be simplistic and stultifying. One expert characterizes the new production of such manuals and their pronouncements as "journalistic," in contrast to classical Islamic legal and religious argumentation that was heavily intertextual and layered in sophisticated prose that needed to be read by specialized experts (Skovgaard-Petersen 2009). This new genre is omniscient and straightforward, eschewing nuance and ambiguity, while presenting itself as a primer or "operator's manual" for the modern, technologically minded, Muslim.

A critical concept invoked by al-Qaradawi to characterize his positions is "wasatiyya" (the middle way or moderation)—thereby denoting a centrist position. While al-Qaradawi is not exclusive in using this term, it establishes him as being a balanced alternative or mediating element between opposed extremes, for example, in being positioned between the secular, non-observant Muslim and the militant fundamentalist, or in the case of his juristic opinions, it suggests that he favors pragmatic solutions grounded in revealed sources that are neither excessively rigid nor compromised by liberalism. In the sphere of political Islam, the "moderate" label signals a rejection of extremism. His mediation of various spheres of cultural life and Islamic norms is further viewed as making space for art and a new Islamic consumerism. It also finds its place in the contemporary discourse of Islam that is shifting to address personal and social identity issues rather than debating ideal forms of politics and governance (Skovgaard-Petersen 2009).

In classical Islamic political theory, the focus was on the legitimacy and qualifications of the ruler and his (being male was often cited as a qualification) implementation of the shari'a. In al-Qaradawi's socio-political thought we find greater attention being given to considerations of public welfare and social justice, for which the classical Islamic legal concept of *maslaha* (taking public interest into account) is elaborated as a way to move the rulings of the law forward.

In addition to his public role on al-Jazeera, al-Qaradawi's internet website, Islam Online, has become the largest Islamic portal in the world. It provides coverage of world news from an Islamic perspective, while another important and popular feature of the site is his dispensing online fatwas as part of the "global mufti" phenomenon. A mufti is an Islamic scholar who issues opinions as to the Islamic status of diverse actions or doctrines. Over the past 150 years, fatwas, now broadly disseminated, have achieved greater significance in shaping Muslim life and public opinion. The traditional process of scholars' deriving their rulings within one of the four Sunni schools (madhahib) was known as *taqlid*, or accepting the traditional authority of the legal schools in upholding their decisions on issues that had been ruled on by the great scholars of the past.

Increasingly, beginning in the late 1700s, some Muslim scholars called for a revival of the process of *ijtihad* (independent legal reasoning), returning to the revealed sources of the religion in search of answers for new questions that had come up or in response to changed perceptions about issues that had been ruled on in the past. *Ijtihad* was advocated both by certain literalist movements such as the Wahhabis, and at the same time offered as a principle of movement and creativity within the religion by thinkers who were inclined to liberal attitudes and advocated the modernization of society as being compatible with the spirit of the Qur'an. The sort of new lifestyle and technology issues addressed by Muslim preachers such as Qaradawi provide the ability to exercise ijtihad in a less radical "reinventing the wheel" way since the novel circumstances themselves demand a response and traditional sources and authority do not need to be directly interrogated by the process.

With the formation of new nation-states in the twentieth century, many governments in the Muslim world realized the moral authority, as well as the social and political benefits, of appointing fatwa committees composed of Islamic scholars to rule on issues significant to official policy that needed to be accepted by the public. One striking example is the debate over the nature and permissibility of birth control, often framed less controversially as "family planning." In countries such as Egypt, having Islamic scholars declare in fatwas that Islam sanctioned contraception proved strategic in garnering public compliance. However, participating scholars could be subjected to the criticism that they had allowed themselves to be coerced by government patronage.

Standing outside of the reach of any one government has allowed Qaradawi to rule on a number of issues that are controversial and prominent. Examples of these are his rulings justifying suicide bombings by Palestinians, or his endorsing the choice of Muslim Americans who signed up to fight in the US armed forces. Most recently, Qaradawi sanctioned uprisings against autocratic regimes such as those in Libya or Egypt, whereas many local jurists promoted quietism for either religious or pragmatic reasons.

Muslim preachers: a global phenomenon?

When we look at other media preachers in diverse local Islamic contexts, we note how their new media presence has challenged some traditional concepts of Islamic authority, while observing that there are significantly distinct ways in which such individuals engage media and the modern components of the role. Let us take several other examples to compare with the al-Qaradawi phenomenon: a fellow Egyptian, an Indonesian, and two Pakistanis.

Amr Khaled (Egypt and the Arab world)

The foil for al-Qaradawi has often been his compatriot, Amr Khaled (b. 1967). Khaled is from a significantly younger cohort and lacks both the background in the traditional Islamic sciences and the mantle of authority bestowed through being a formally trained scholar (*'alim*). He rather defines himself as a *da'iyya*, one who "calls to Islam" through invitation (da'wa) (Rock 2010: 18). Trained as an accountant, he began preaching in mosques in 1990 while still working in his regular profession. Khaled's increasingly popular lectures were broadcast on the IQRA channel via the NILESAT satellites, and distributed over the internet and on audio and videocassette tapes. In 1998, Khaled embarked on a full-time preaching career, primarily on satellite television with popular series such as "Words from the Heart" (2001) and "Life Makers" (Sunna' al-Hayat).

Amr Khaled has proven himself to be charismatic. He usually preaches dressed in stylish Western suits and has been compared to American personalities such as Billy Graham and Dr. Phil. In fact, Christian televangelists and their programs were studied and emulated by Khaled and his production team. His programs have attracted a large youth following, especially among the upper middle class, ultimately bringing him under government scrutiny and threat that led him to move to the United Kingdom between 2002 and 2007 (Rock 2010: 16).

Khaled's preaching notably emphasizes self-help and forming networks of like-minded youth to undertake projects of moral and social rectification. This has created a sense of community among viewers who then organize grassroots social projects in their own neighborhoods.

Media scholar Lindsay Wise observes:

> *Sunna' al-Hayat* is part self-help psychology—an emotional and positive twelve-step program to a better Islamic life—part spiritual experience, and part televised call for social reform and grassroots organization. This tactic helps create a sense of achievement, identity, and community among his viewers...
>
> Since he doesn't have the authority to issue *fatwas*, there is very little finger-wagging discussion of exactly what is *haram* or *halal*. Instead, Khaled offers practical moral advice, such as urging his audience to avoid listening to songs with sexy or provocative lyrics, even encouraging them to write protest letters to music channels. But he doesn't ask them to give up music all together. In fact, he goes so far as to offer an alternative to what he refers to as sappy, empty-headed pop music.
>
> On college campuses and community centers, students sell t-shirts, key chains, and stickers bearing the *Sunna' al-Hayat* logo and motto "Together We Build Life" in both English and Arabic to raise money for their philanthropic clubs. These trendy (and fairly expensive) commodities are reminiscent of the virginity promise rings and "What Would Jesus Do" bracelets so popular among born-again Christian youth in America. On the internet, Khaled's own high-tech Arabic webpage, *www.amrkhaled.net*, offers live "dialogues" with the preacher himself, as well as e-books, cartoons, songs, MP3 recordings of his sermons, web broadcasts, and translations in eight languages.

(Wise 2004)

It could also be claimed that Khaled's message projects a "prosperity gospel" that appeals to the upwardly mobile, and he has been characterized as the "richest Islamic preacher" by *Forbes Arabia* (Rock 2010: 21). The strength of his global profile is such that *Time* magazine has numbered him among the 100 most influential people in the world (2007).

K.H. Abdullah Gymnastiar (Gym) (Indonesia)

A media preacher from beyond the Arab world is K.H. Abdullah Gymnastiar (Gym) (b. 1962) from Indonesia. Gym attracted a large audience of Indonesian youth, as well as middle-aged and middle-class admirers in the open, pluralistic, and moderate environment that followed the fall of the dictator Suharto in 1998. His preaching was distinctive in incorporating relationship issues into a homiletic genre that he termed "managing the heart." He dealt with topics such as how to have an ideal family life in the Islamic mode, while following the consistent theme of how to apply Muslim practice and values in everyday situations. At the height of his popularity millions of viewers watched Gym's weekly television shows; hundreds of thousands made pilgrimages to his Islamic school; and politicians of all leanings lined up for photo-ops during campaign season. He managed his image by telling his fans to call him "older brother," suggesting a more intimate and approachable identity than that of a traditional religious teacher. Further "branding" contributed to extensive commercial and popular success, casting Gym as a modern religious scholar who ran several businesses, went sky-diving with the Indonesian special forces, and flew fighter jets with the air force—all while wearing a turban (Hoesterey 2007).

Gym's style is reminiscent of the "self-help" and "how to succeed" genres in the West, for example, one of his slogans describes three "beginnings"—"begin with yourself, begin with small things, and begin now." He also drew inspiration from Sufi tales and dream spirituality, which resonate with Indonesian Muslim culture. Gym is said to have lost a lot of his popular following when he married a second wife in 2007, in particular since his first wife, mother of his seven children, had been presented as a role model and object of his devotion.

> Heartbroken and betrayed, his followers staged a backlash and the event became a national scandal. Infotainment shows and gossip magazines circulated stories of female followers who shredded his pictures, boycotted his television shows, and cancelled weekend pilgrimages to his Islamic school and 'spiritual tourism' complex, Daarut Tauhiid (DT). Pressured by hundreds of protest text messages, SBY [Susilo Bambang Yudhoyono—the President of Indonesia] ordered a review of the national marriage law. Gymnastiar lost his pending television contracts; his business empire started to crumble, and DT became a ghost town.
>
> *(Hoesterey 2007)*

Gym has since attempted to draw a new audience by reinventing himself in a more traditionally Islamic mode, upgrading his religious knowledge by taking madrasa-type courses and altering the tone of his discourse toward religious conservatism. For a time his newly expanded family projected polygamy as an acceptable option with mixed success, but by 2011 he had divorced his first wife, Ninih Mutmainah, only to remarry her in 2012.

Moving between popular media such as film, television, and the music world into Islamic preaching and missionary outreach (da'wa) seems to be a global trend. For example, in Egypt, the trope of popular actresses abandoning secular screens and donning Islamic dress (the hijab) has been characterized as a movement of repentance (tawba). Ultimately the media itself is not the enemy, since many of these figures return to the public stage in proper Islamic roles and dress (van Nieuwkerk 2008).

Junaid Jamshed (Pakistan)

In Pakistan the case of "repentant" rock star Junaid Jamshed bears instructive parallels to developments in the Arab world. Jamshed (b. 1964) was formerly a lead singer for a popular Pakistani rock band of the 1980s, Vital Signs. His attraction to Islam, and in particular, his involvement with the conservative international Islamic piety movement, Tablighi Jama'at, led him to hang up his guitar in 2002 and to grow a long beard, along with other manifestations of embracing a pious Islamic lifestyle.

Currently Jamshed operates a national Pakistani chain of exclusive clothing boutiques for males and females. Such ventures characterize other contemporary trends among pious Muslim figures and social movements who embrace religious fervor and revival and yet conform to, and even facilitate, popular aspirations to consume quality goods in a modern, affluent mode. Junaid Jamshed does not concentrate on media preaching, however, and in general Tablighis have eschewed, not only electronic, but even print media to communicate their message. Jamshed is still seen from time to time on Pakistani TV, reciting na't—poems in praise of the Prophet Muhammad—without any instrumentation, in conformity with perceived Islamic strictures on musical performance. In fact videos of some of his lectures are readily available on internet sites and indicate that he tours internationally presenting lectures and fundraising for Muslim Centers and activities.

Farhat Hashmi (Pakistan/Canada)

Farhat Hashmi is a female Pakistani preacher with a strong television and internet presence. Her program, broadcast on Pakistan's GEO satellite network, features a seated Hashmi looking at the camera dressed in full face veil or niqab while reading from the screen of her computer—an image that projects the confluence of pious traditionalism and media-savvy prosperity. Hashmi, who holds a PhD in Islamic Studies from the University of Glasgow, Scotland, has been spearheading a religious revival among the Pakistan "begamat"—(primarily) upper class females—for some 15 years. She left a position as a professor at the International Islamic University in Islamabad to allow herself more independent scope and interpretation of Islam that yet remains conservative. Her lectures and website feature advice for women in dealing with everyday topics including relationship issues and household management (Ahmad 2008). At the same time Hashmi developed an intensive two-year course of almost daily lessons that inculcates basic teachings of Qur'an and hadith studies along with Islamic ritual law. Established in 1994, this al-Huda course is franchised across Pakistan and operated locally by females who have been her students. Scholarly views and public opinion differ as to whether Hashmi is an empowering innovator for female Muslims or a regressive force. In 2004 Hashmi relocated to Toronto, Canada, where since 2005 she has operated the al-Huda Institute to train diaspora South Asian women in her educational method and interpretations. Here they follow a 20-month course called Taleem ul-Quran, paying a nominal fee of $60 a month, and attending classes four days a week for five hours a day. Meanwhile Hashmi's global media presence continues to expand through her prerecorded television broadcasts and active internet and publishing outreach.

Conclusion

In summarizing the rise of media preachers, Yusuf al-Qaradawi's position as a global mufti and popular celebrity illustrates the confluence of several important trends in the contemporary Muslim world. Among the figures we considered here, Qaradawi is the prime example of a combination of traditional scholarly authority with a contemporary media presence. His positions on Islamic rulings as well as on contemporary social and political affairs resonate with an increasingly globalized Muslim youth culture struggling to carve an alternative path between religious extremism and disillusionment with state-controlled clerics.

  This confirms Lindsay Wise's conclusions that:

> As demonstrated by the growing popularity of everything from "dial-a-sheikh" telephone services that charge by the minute and online "*fatwa* sessions" that invite Internet users to submit religious questions by e-mail, there is a growing mass market catering to Muslims seeking spiritual guidance, both moral and mundane: Should teenagers be allowed to date? Is masturbation against Islamic law? How should Muslim women dress at the beach? Is it a sin to play football on a Friday? Are suicide bombers martyrs or murderers? Is kidnapping un-Islamic? In the search for answers, people no longer look only to their neighborhood

sheikh or local mosque, but to all forms of media, including audiotapes, DVDs, broadcast television, telephone hotlines and the World Wide Web.

(Wise 2004)

Many of the examples given in this chapter suggest that preoccupation with personal and social identity issues such as a renegotiation of gender roles, coupled with a new Muslim consumerism, are elements of primary concern to the new publics addressed by media religious teachers. It should also be noted that there are serious collective and political consequences to the larger roles accorded to them. For example, in the public sphere the preachers' new forms of authority and teachings regarding daily life have implications that may potentially mobilize Muslim youth and women in ways not previously seen. Each of the cases of current media preachers cited in this chapter confirm how religious challenges to existing political systems in the Muslim world are increasingly "not based only on personal reputation and knowledge of texts but also on a demonstrated grasp of society and the ability to share with audiences a grasp of their daily challenges" (Eickelman and Anderson 2003: 13).

Among the global cases of Islamic media preachers that we have profiled here, we find those who, like al-Qaradawi, project an Islamic message through popular media and appeal to the same youth and female demographic. Yet none of these others is in the same position of actually ruling authoritatively on matters of Islam law in the sense of being an authorized 'alim or mufti. Therefore, we may conclude that al-Qaradawi is unique in his role, but that his popularity has blazed the trail for a new cohort of Muslim media preachers who, on the whole, primarily connect with the personal "life"-style element of Islamic preaching, rather than the textually based "shari'a" one.

Summary

- This chapter explored the rise of Muslim media preachers, providing context and causes for their emergence and popularity, and considering the importance of such phenomena for Islamic authority.
- Significant background historical developments that laid the foundation for the emergence of popular media preachers in the Muslim world include:
  - the development of new technologies from cassettes to satellite television stations, that limit state control of media messages;
  - mass education and a new interest and public debate about Islamic topics;
  - Islamic revivalist movements that often focused on issues under the control of individuals when making personal lifestyle choices.
- Al-Qaradawi as the "global mufti" is the prime example of such a "media preacher." The chapter reviewed his biography including his humble origins, study at al-Azhar, achieving credentials for traditional scholarly authority as one of the ulema, his

participation in the Muslim Brotherhood movement, and transformation from scholar to media presence.

- The reach of his message is broadened both by satellite and internet connections and appeal to new audiences: women, youth, and the Muslim diaspora in the West.
- A survey of some other media preachers suggests how personal style and appeal combines with Islamic preaching and teaching in a range of local contexts:
  - Amr Khaled (Egypt): lacks traditional scholarly credentials, but has a pan-Arab appeal, especially to youth who network in projects for social activism;
  - K.H. Abdullah Gymnastiar (Gym) (Indonesia): appeals to lifestyle and relationship issues, but became discredited due to turmoil in his own family life;
  - Junaid Jamshed (Pakistan): represents the case of a "repentant" rock star;
  - Farhat Hashmi (Pakistan/Canada): a female preacher who developed courses on Qur'an and hadith; networking and franchising her instructional method across Pakistan and now globally, her program has a particular appeal in addressing lifestyle issues for contemporary Muslim women.

Discussion points

- What might an Islamic Reformation look like? How would an Islamic Reformation both resemble and be distinctive from the Protestant counterpart?
- What are some of the factors contributing to the emergence of the media preacher phenomenon in the Muslim world?
- How are the messages of these media preachers distinctive from traditional forms of religious argumentation and discourse? Why do you think these changes are taking place?
- Discuss how questions of gender play out in the lives and opinions of the new media preachers?
- Do the categories of "liberal," "conservative," "extremist," "moderate" make sense when we try to apply them to the opinions and rulings given by Muslim media preachers?

Further reading

Ahmad, Sadaf (2009) *Transforming Faith: The Story of al-Huda and Islamic Revivalism Among Urban Pakistani Women*, Syracuse, NY: Syracuse University Press.

A participant-observation based study of Farhat Hashmi's al-Hoda Islamic courses in Pakistan.

Eickelman, Dale and Jon W. Anderson (2003) *New Media in the Muslim World: The Emerging Public Sphere*, Bloomington: Indiana University Press.

An edited volume that pioneered the study of how new technologies and genres were globally impacting Islamic discourses and authority.

Hirschkind, Charles (2009) *The Ethical Soundscape: Cassette Sermons and Islamic Counterpublics*, New York: Columbia University Press.

An exploration of the role of cassette sermons in impacting the genre of popular preaching and Islamic authority in contemporary Egypt.

Larsson, Goran (2011) *Muslims and the New Media*, Farnham, UK: Ashgate.

A discussion of how Muslim scholars have responded to new technologies from print, to the telephone, film, and the internet. Provides a useful historical and doctrinal context for understanding the emergence of Muslim media preachers.

Moll, Yasmin (2010) "Islamic Televangelism: Religion, Media and Visuality in Contemporary Egypt," *Arab Media and Society*, 10 (spring), available at www.arabmediasociety.com/?article=732, (accessed May 14, 2012).

Concentrates on the role of television as a medium in shaping the nature of contemporary Islamic preaching in Egypt.

Wise, Leslie (2003) "Words from the Heart: New Forms of Islamic Preaching in Egypt," MA Thesis, Oxford, available at http://users.ox.ac.uk/~metheses/Wise.html (accessed April 27, 2012).

The most detailed study of Amr Khaled from a scholar of media and communication theory. This and her other writings are particularly astute in understanding his appeal and the role that media and audience play in shaping his message.

Zaman, Muhammad Qasim (2007) *The Ulama in Contemporary Islam: Custodians of Change*, Princeton, NJ: Princeton University Press.

Zaman presents a detailed historical overview and analysis of how Islamic scholars and their institutions are responding to social change and challenges to traditional authority in both the Arab world and South Asia.

www.onislam.net/english/shariah/contemporary-issues/

This website has replaced Islam Online as a repository for al-Qaradawi's opinions available in English translation.

http://wp.farhathashmi.com/

Farhat Hashmi and al-Huda materials, videos, etc.

www.jjamshed.com/

Junaid Jamshed audio and video

References

Ahmad, Sadaf (2008) "Identity Matters, Culture Wars: An Account of Al-Huda (Re) Defining Identity and Reconfiguring Culture in Pakistan," *Culture and Religion*, 9(1): 63–80.

al-Qaradawi, Yusuf (1980) *The Lawful and the Prohibited in Islam*, available online at various sites, www.witness-pioneer.org/vil/Books/Q_LP.

—— (2010) "Sheikh Qaradawi's First Interview with Onislam.net," www.onislam.net/english/ shariah/contemporary-issues/interviews-reviews-and-events/449388-sheikh-qaradawis-first-interview-withonislamnet.html?Events= (accessed November 4, 2012).

Eickelman, Dale and Jon W. Anderson (2003) *New Media in the Muslim World: The Emerging Public Sphere*, Bloomington: Indiana University Press.

Gräf, Bettina and Jakob Skovgaard-Petersen (eds) (2009) *The Global Mufti: The Phenomenon of Yusuf al-Qaradawi*, New York: Columbia University Press.

Hoesterey, James B. (2007) "The Rise, Fall, and Re-branding of a Celebrity Preacher," *Inside Indonesia*, 90 (Oct–Dec), available at www.insideindonesia.org/weekly-articles/aa-gym (accessed October 16, 2011).

—— (2008) "Marketing Morality: The Rise, Fall and Rebranding of Aa Gym," in Greg Fealy and Sally White (eds) *Expressing Islam: Religious Life and Politics in Indonesia*, Singapore: Institute of Southeast Asian Studies, 95–114.

Rock, Aaron (2010) "Amr Khaled: From Da'wa to Political and Religious Leadership," *British Journal of Middle Eastern Studies*, 37(1): 15–37.

Skovgaard-Petersen, Jakob (2009) "In Defense of Muhammad: 'Ulama', Da'iya and the New Islamic Internationalism," in Meir Hatina (ed.) *Guardians of Faith in Modern Times: 'Ulama' in the Middle East*, Leiden: E.J. Brill, 291–309.

van Nieuwkerk, Karin (2008) "Piety, Penitence and Gender: The Case of Repentant Artists in Egypt," *Journal for Islamic Studies*, 28(1), 37–65.

Wise, Lindsay (2004) "Amr Khaled: Broadcasting the Nahda," *Transnational Broadcasting Studies Journal*, 13 (fall), available at www.tbsjournal.com/Archives/Fall04/wiseamrkhaled.html.

14 Assertive secularism, Islam and democracy in Turkey

Ahmet T. Kuru[1]

Outline

- Turkey is neither the only democracy, nor the only secular state in the Muslim world. Of the 49 Muslim-majority countries, 11 are democratic, and 23 of these 49 are secular states.
- French-type assertive secularism, which requires the state to play an assertive role to exclude religion from the public sphere, was the dominant ideology in Turkey since its foundation.
- As part of recent democratization, Turkey began to embrace American-type passive secularism, which demands the state to play a passive role by allowing public visibility of religion.

Islam, secularism, and democracy

In the 1950s and 1960s, modernization theorists regarded Turkey as a model country that dropped its Islamic tradition to reach modernity (Lerner 1958; Lerner and Robinson 1960). More recently some scholars depicted Turkey as almost a unique example to show that democracy was possible in a Muslim-majority country as long as the secular state kept Islam under control. In the words of Samuel Huntington: "The one Islamic country that sustained even intermittent democracy after World War II was Turkey, which had, under Mustapha Kemal, explicitly rejected its Islamic tradition and defined itself as a secular republic" (1984: 208). Bernard Lewis also shared this perspective: "Some observers, especially among those who see in Islam an obstacle to democratic development, point to secularism as the crucial difference between Turkey and the rest of the Muslim world" (1994: 45).

Beyond academia, this perception was also reflected in court decisions. While (re) imposing the headscarf ban at universities three times in two decades, the Turkish Constitutional Court repeatedly argued that Islam, unlike Christianity, had particular characteristics that needed to be controlled by strict secularism and such secularism was the guarantor of democracy in Turkey (March 7, 1989, decision no. 1989/12; June 5, 2008, decision no. 2008/116). The European Court of Human Rights upheld Turkey's headscarf ban arguing that a particular "notion of secularism," which bans headscarves at universities, "may be considered necessary to protect the democratic system in Turkey," which faces the Islamist threat (November 10, 2005, *Leyla Şahin v. Turkey*: 28, 46).

This perception has three main problems. First, Turkey is neither the only democracy nor the only secular state in the Muslim world. The Freedom House's 2011 list of electoral democracies includes ten other Muslim-majority countries besides Turkey. Although Turkey was the first Muslim-majority country with a secular state, it is no longer the only one. The table below lists democracies and autocracies among Muslim-majority countries in addition to categorizing them with three types—Islamic states, states with

Islam as the official religion, and secular states. In the first type, the constitution defines the state as "Islamic;" in the second type, it declares Islam as the official religion without defining the state as Islamic; and in the third type, the constitution does not establish any religion. Out of 49 Muslim-majority countries, only 11 have Islamic states, 15 have states with Islam as the official religion, and 23 are secular states.

The second problem is about the relationship between secularism and democracy. Table 14.1 shows that secularism is neither a necessary nor a sufficient condition for a Muslim-majority country to become democratic. About two-thirds (16/23) of Muslim-majority secular states are authoritarian, while only a third (7/23) are democracies. Although the majority of democracies in the table are secular states, more than a third (4/11) are not.

The table also indicates that all Islamic states, except one, are authoritarian. This is not surprising given the fact that Islamist regimes have generally violated basic principles of democracy, such as people's sovereignty. They have institutions, e.g., Supreme Leader and supreme Sharia councils, which are unaccountable to the people and over the elected bodies. Thus, even though secularism is not a *sine qua non* for a Muslim-majority democracy, the lack of religious hegemony over the political and legal system is. In other words, a Muslim-majority country can be democratic while merely recognizing Islam as the official religion, but it cannot be democratic if religious institutions supersede elected institutions.

The third problem of this perception is its definition of secularism as a monolithic ideology that always keeps religion under control. Secularism, in fact, has two main types, and only one can be linked to the idea of keeping religion under the state control. "Assertive secularism," demands that the state play an assertive role in confining religion to the private domain. It has been the dominant ideology in countries such as France and Mexico. "Passive secularism," on the other hand, requires the state to play a passive role, by allowing public visibility of religion. It has been dominant in the United States and India (Kuru 2009: 11–14, 31–34). Due to its aim to exclude religion from the public sphere, assertive secularism employs state control over religion in various degrees. For example, although both France and Turkey have embraced assertive secularism, the latter has imposed a much deeper level of state control over religion than the former. Turkey has had a governmental agency, the Diyanet, which pays the salaries of imams, appoints them to mosques, and centrally coordinates their sermons.

A state that aims to exclude religion from the public sphere would need a certain level of control over religion if an important segment of society prefers to publically express their religiosity. Such an exclusionary policy is unlikely to exist, at least to become successful, in a consolidated democracy. That is why Turkish democracy has suffered a tension between assertive secularist policies of the state elite and religious demands of its people for decades (see Göle 1997: 48).

Table 14.1: State-religion regimes and democracy in 49 Muslim-majority countries

Islamic states (11)	*States with Islam as the official religion (15)*	*Secular states (23)*
Autocracies (38)		
1. Afghanistan	1. Algeria	1. Azerbaijan
2. Bahrain	2. Djibouti	2. Burkina Faso
3. Brunei	3. Egypt	3. Chad
4. Iran	4. Iraq	4. Eritrea
5. Mauritania	5. Jordan	5. Gambia
6. Oman	6. Kuwait	6. Guinea
7. Pakistan	7. Libya	7. Guinea-Buisseau
8. Saudi Arabia	8. Malaysia	8. Kazakhstan
9. Sudan	9. Morocco	9. Kosovo
10. Yemen	10. Qatar	10. Kyrgyzstan
	11. Somalia	11. Lebanon
	12. U.A.E.	12. Nigeria
		13. Syria
		14. Tajikistan
		15. Turkmenistan
		16. Uzbekistan
Democracies (11)		
1. Maldives	1. Bangladesh	1. Albania
	2. Comoros	2. Indonesia
	3. Tunisia	3. Mali
		4. Niger
		5. Senegal
		6. Sierra Leone
		7. Turkey

Source: Kuru 2009: 7-8, 259; Freedom House (www.freedomhouse.org); US Department of State, International Religious Freedom Reports (www.state.gov/j/drl/rls/irf/).

Recently, Turkey has become democratized despite, not because of, assertive secularism. Turkey's 60-year history of democratization is full of several back-and-forths between democratization and de-democratization. As Table 14.2 summarizes, the main authoritarian force behind the de-democratization cycles has been the military—the guardian of assertive secularism. In its direct or indirect interventions to democracy, the Turkish military has received support from its assertive secularist allies in political parties, the media, and the judiciary (Kuru 2012).

In its depiction of democratization and de-democratization cycles, Table 14.2 primarily refers to the procedural aspects of democracy, such as (a) free, fair, and competitive elections with universal suffrage, and (b) the elected civilians' control over the military or any other non-elected body (see Linz and Stepan 1996: 3). In Turkey and elsewhere, political actors are mostly "contingent democrats" (Bellin 2000). In other words, both Islamic and secularist actors support democracy or authoritarianism based on their conceptualization and calculation of particular interests. Assertive secularists are more likely to become authoritarian in a country where the majority of society is religious and thus resists the assertive secularist state policies.

Turkish society is highly religious given the ratios of being affiliated with Islam (99 percent) and regular religious observance (69 percent)—the weekly Friday prayer for men and daily prayer for women (Survey of *Milliyet* and A&G, *Milliyet*, May 31, 2003).

Table 14.2: Periods of democratization and de-democratization in Turkey

Period	Regime type
1925–46	Single party rule
1946–60	Democratization
1960–61	Military regime
1961–65	Semi-military regime
1965–71	Democratization
1971–73	Semi-military regime
1973–80	Democratization
1980–83	Military regime
1983–97	Democratization
1997–2002	Semi-military regime
2002–	Democratization

Therefore, the Turkish society largely opposes assertive secularist policies, such as the state ban on headscarves in educational institutions and the discrimination against the public Islamic Imam-Hatip schools' graduates in the nationwide university admission exam. According to surveys, the opponents of these two state policies constitute 78 percent and 85 percent of Turkish society, respectively (Çarkoğlu and Toprak 2006: 55, 58, 71; Survey of *Milliyet* and Konda, *Milliyet*, December 3–4, 2007). In this regard, it is not surprising that the main supporter of these unpopular policies, the assertive secularist leftist parties, especially the Republican People's Party, have never received the majority seats in Turkish Parliament. Their total vote shares have been not only limited but also largely declining in recent parliamentary elections: 1987 (33 percent), 1991 (32 percent), 1995 (25 percent), 1999 (31 percent), 2002 (21 percent), 2007 (21 percent), and 2011 (26 percent). Being constantly disappointed by electoral failures, many assertive secularist actors supported various military or judicial interventions to Turkish democracy.

To elaborate these general points, the rest of the chapter will examine specific actors and summarize relevant events in Turkish political history. The following sections, therefore, will analyze assertive secularists and their rivals in three historical stages. In the first period (1924–94), center-right parties struggled with assertive secularists. Between 1994 and 2002, moderate Islamists became the major rivals of assertive secularists. In the third stage, from 2002 to the present, passive secularists, i.e., the pro-Islamic conservatives and the liberals, have weakened assertive secularism.

Assertive secularists vs. the center-right

A year after the foundation of the Republic in 1923, the framers of modern Turkey were divided into two competing parties—the ruling Republican People's Party (RPP) and the opposition Progressive Republican Party. The opposition differed itself from the RPP by stressing in its program that it was "respectful to religious thoughts and beliefs." A year later, the RPP leaders, including President Mustafa Kemal Atatürk and Prime Minister İsmet İnönü, closed down the opposition party, as well as taking all newspapers and other sources of opposition under strict governmental control. Then they imposed assertive secularist policies in an authoritarian manner.

The assertive secularist reforms in the 1920s and 1930s could be categorized in two groups. One set of reforms, such as the adoption of European laws, replacement of the Arabic-Ottoman script with the Latin alphabet, and enforcement of wearing the top hat, aimed for socio-cultural Westernization. The other group of reforms sought the marginalization and control of Islam in the public life. It included the closure of madrasas, ban on the Arabic calls to prayer, and prohibition of all Islamic (both Sunni and Alevi) groups, titles, and places. Mosques remained as the only legal Islamic places and were strictly controlled by the Diyanet, which was under the prime

Figure 14.1 Turkish flag and statue of Atatürk. Courtesy of Image Source/Getty Images.

minister's office. From 1933 to 1949, all institutions for Islamic education were shut down, aside from few Qur'an courses in some villages. Islamic groups, such as the Nakşibendi and Kadiri tariqas (Sufi orders) and the followers of Bediüzzaman Said Nursi, faced state oppression, even if they were exclusively focusing on mysticism and religious education.

These groups did not react to state policies with violence except in some rare cases that mixed Islamic opposition with Kurdish nationalism. Because Islamic groups became illegal, they had to either go underground or find some legal covers, such as corporations and cultural centers, to be publically visible.

In 1946, the RPP allowed competing political parties. A major reason for this decision was Turkey's need to be part of the "Free World" led by the United States against the threatening Soviet Union. The first truly democratic elections took place in 1950, in which the center-right Democratic Party (DP) won a landslide victory and its leader Adnan Menderes became prime minister. The DP, which pursued more liberal policies toward Islamic groups and Islamic education than the RPP, ruled Turkey throughout the 1950s by winning all national elections. The RPP criticized Menderes and the DP for compromising the Islamic reactionaries at the expense of secularism (Azak 2010: 61–138). A group of junior officers staged a coup in 1960, which resulted in the closure of the DP and the execution of Menderes together with his two cabinet members. In addition to the RPP, the assertive secularists within the judiciary and academia supported the coup. The coup makers allowed multiparty elections only after redesigning the political system with military and judicial tutelage mechanisms over democracy. New institutions they framed, such as the Senate (in which some coup stagers became permanent members), the Constitutional Court, and National Security Council, were meant to limit the efficacy of the elected parliamentarians.

The closure of the DP did not mean the end of the struggle between assertive secularists and center-right politicians. RPP's new rival, Süleyman Demirel and his center-right party, won a victory in the 1965 elections. Demirel followed Menderes' legacy of pursuing liberal policies toward Islamic associations and education. From 1950 to 1970, Islamic groups were not publicly visible political players except for being important sources of votes for Menderes and Demirel. In 1970, however, Necmettin Erbakan founded the first explicitly Islamist party of Turkey. Some Islamic groups supported Erbakan's party, while others continued to vote for Demirel. In 1971, the military issued a memorandum arguing that the Demirel government was unable to maintain political order and to reach the level of "the modern civilization." Demirel resigned and the military took control, this time without abolishing Parliament. Although the coup stagers were primarily anti-communist, they also targeted Islamic actors. During the semi-military rule, the Constitutional Court closed down Erbakan's party. Later, Erbakan founded a new party and became vice-prime minister in three different coalition governments in the 1970s.

In 1980, when Demirel was again prime minister, the military staged another coup. The coup targeted all groups in Turkey's ideological spectrum in a brutal way and closed down all political parties. The generals had ambivalent policies toward Islam. They wanted to use it as a bulwark against communism. Thus, they added obligatory religious instruction in schools in the 1982 Constitution. Yet they also imposed the headscarf ban at universities and closed down several Qur'an courses mostly belonging to the Süleymancı community.

In 1983, Turgut Özal's center-right party, the generals' least favored, won the first elections after the coup. Özal became the prime minister (1983–89) and then president (1989–93) of Turkey by receiving support from different segments of society, including several Islamic groups. Özal struggled with assertive secularists through his attempts to lift the headscarf ban at universities, sympathy toward Islamic groups, and appointments of passive secularist bureaucrats. Özal also initiated several liberalization reforms, such as the abolishment of three articles of the Penal Code that had resulted in the imprisonment of socialist and Islamic activists, the transformation of the economy from import-substituting to export-oriented, and the permission of private universities and TV channels.

Özal's liberalization policies provided Islamic groups, especially the movement initiated by Fethullah Gülen, with the opportunity to set up their own educational, media, and economic institutions (Kuru 2005). Economic liberalization helped the emergence of a new pro-Islamic bourgeoisie with their own business associations, such as MÜSİAD and TUSKON (Demiralp 2009), as alternatives to TÜSİAD, which represented the biggest and mostly assertive secularist industrialists in Istanbul. Socio-economic strengthening of the Islamic groups also resulted in a bigger political might.

Assertive secularists vs. Islamists

Following Özal's death in 1993, Prime Minister Demirel became the president and left party politics. The absence of these two leaders created a vacuum in center-right political parties, which was at least partially filled by Erbakan's moderate Islamist party. It was hard to define Erbakan's "Islamism" because he never openly sought for the implementation of the Islamic law. His Islamist rhetoric mostly focused on such issues as founding an Islamic union (as an alternative to the European Union), issuing an Islamic currency, and establishing a "just order." In the 1994 local elections, Erbakan's party won the mayor's seats in Istanbul and Ankara. A year later, it became the first Islamist party in Turkish history that won the plurality in Parliament.

Assertive secularists led by the military initiated a campaign against Prime Minister Erbakan. The National Security Council meeting of February 28, 1997, in which the generals dictated certain demands to Erbakan, turned into a "soft coup." It was "soft" because the coup was an indirect military intervention supported by assertive secularists in the judiciary, the media, and political parties. Following the coup, Turkey experienced a semi-military rule that was called the "February 28 process." This process was a clear example of the authoritarian implications of assertive secularism. During this period, Erbakan was forced to resign, he was banned from politics, and his party was closed down. Tayyip Erdoğan, the mayor of Istanbul from Erbakan's party, was imprisoned because of reciting a poem. Other assertive secularist policies during this process included the strict imposition of the headscarf ban in all educational institutions; the prohibition of teaching the Qur'an to children under 12 years old; and the closure of the Imam-Hatip schools' secondary sections and discrimination of their graduates in the nationwide university admission exam by calculating their scores with a much lower coefficient. Also during this process, the military discharged its allegedly Islamist (avowedly pious) officers.

The Gülen movement, whose leader was forced into a voluntary exile in the United States, responded to the February 28 process by emphasizing toleration, dialogue, and democracy (Gülen 2001), as well as searching for new ways of engagement with secular civil society and state actors (Turam 2006; Agai 2003). A major example of the movement's such attempts are the Abant meetings it has organized since 1998. These annual meetings have brought together academics, politicians, and journalists from sharply different ideological backgrounds (Islamists, agnostics, liberals, socialists, nationalists, etc.) to head off socio-political polarization. The meetings discuss broad issues such as Islam and secularism, state-society relations, democracy and the rule of law, pluralism, and Turkey's membership of the European Union (EU).

Similar to the Gülen movement, the young generation in Erbakan's party also experienced an intellectual transformation. In 2001, the leader of the young generation, Erdoğan, broke up with Erbakan and founded his own Justice and Development Party (JDP). Beyond leadership, the JDP ideologically differed from Erbakan's Islamist parties with its keen support for Turkey's membership of the EU, positive attitude toward the secular state, and self-definition as "conservative democrat," instead of Islamist (Akdoğan 2006). The JDP also differed from assertive secularists by defending passive secularism.

In the 2002 elections, the JDP received 34 percent of the votes and about two-thirds of seats in Parliament. Erdoğan became the prime minister. The debate between the JDP and assertive secularists has not been a struggle between Islamism and secularism, but rather a wrangling between passive and assertive types of secularism.

Assertive secularists vs. passive secularists

Assertive secularists and the JDP cooperating for the EU reforms

From 2003 to 2005, the JDP pursued important democratization reforms as part of the EU membership process. These reforms were supported by a large coalition including Islamic groups and pro-EU assertive secularists such as the RPP. This period experienced important reforms, particularly in civil-military relations, women's rights, and minority rights. Before these reforms, the National Security Council had included the president, prime minister, and several ministers and been dominated by five top generals. In 2003, Parliament turned the Council into a genuine advisory body, removing its influence over the civilian bureaucracy. In 2004, the State Security Courts, which had included both military and civilian judges, were also abolished. That reform empowered civilian courts to prosecute military officers.

In 2004, the Turkish Parliament amended the Constitution by adding the following line to Article 10: "Women and men have equal rights. The state is responsible for the realization of this equality." In the same year, it passed a new penal code that categorized female sexuality as a matter of individual rights, instead of social morality or family honor. Moreover, the JDP government initiated new programs to prevent domestic violence and improve girls' access to education (European Stability Initiative 2007). Some reforms also promoted the rights of religious minorities. The word "mosque" in the law concerning religious places was replaced with "place of worship," for permitting religions other than Islam to open temples. The JDP government cancelled the state surveillance over non-Muslims citizens by abolishing the Subcommittee for Minorities, which had been monitoring them for 42 years.

De-democratization attempt: the e-coup

Political considerations changed in 2006 because of the upcoming presidential election a year later. The presidency was crucial for the preservation of the status quo based on the co-habitation of the popularly elected passive secularist government with the assertive secularist president elected by Parliament. Since assertive secularist parties only had around 20–30 percent of the popular vote and roughly that ratio of parliamentary seats, the assertive secularists had various strategies, including military interventions, to get a president of their political disposition to be elected. The president shaped the bureaucracy by having the final signature in the appointment of generals, top civilian bureaucrats, high court judges, and university presidents. Assertive secularists opposed the possible election of a JDP member as the new president.

On April 27, 2011, a few hours after the first round of presidential elections in Parliament, the military posted an ultimatum on its website, which meant an "e-coup." The ultimatum referred to the attempts to reinterpret secularism, Qur'an recitation competitions, and celebrations of the birthday of the Prophet as anti-secular activities. It also targeted Kurds, noting "all those who oppose the statement of the founder of our Republic, Great Leader Atatürk, 'How happy is he who says "I am a Turk"' are enemies of the Turkish Republic and will remain as such." The RPP already applied to the Constitutional Court for the cancellation of the presidential election for a technical claim. In a few days, the court upheld the RPP's application (Özbudun 2012: 159).

Failing to elect the president, Parliament had to go for a new parliamentary election. The JDP became the winner of the July 2011 elections by increasing its vote share to 47 percent. The new Parliament elected the JDP's candidate Abdullah Gül as president. A few months later, a constitutional amendment package, which turned future presidential elections into popular votes, received 69 percent of the votes. This annulled the military's strategy to control presidential elections by pressing parliamentarians.

De-democratization attempt: the judicial coup

Following the parliamentary elections, the JDP group passed several reform laws regarding religious and ethnic issues. In 2006, they had legislated a bill that recognized the legal status and property rights of Christian and Jewish foundations. Then President Necdet Sezer, a leading assertive secularist, had vetoed the bill arguing that it would expand economic activities and social status of religious foundations. In 2008, the JDP group got the bill passed again and new President Gül signed it into law. Yet two main opposition parties, the RPP and the Nationalist Action Party (NAP), strongly contested this law (Kılınç, 2008: 297–303). The NAP's opposition was linked to its nationalism, which did not sufficiently respect ethnic and religious minorities. The RPP's resistance was primarily associated with its assertive secularism, which aimed to exclude not only Islam, but also all other religions, from the public sphere. Assertive secularists have been concerned about the expansion of non-Muslim minorities' rights in Turkey, which would create similar demands by the Muslim majority. On some other issues, the RPP and NAP also agreed in opposing the JDP's reforms due to their shared understanding of nationalism. For example, they both opposed the JDP group's limitation of the law no. 301 that had been used for the censorship and prosecution of writers/speakers by the alleged accusation of "insulting Turkishness." Similarly, when the JDP initiated the public TV channel (TRT Şeş) for broadcasting exclusively in Kurdish, both RPP and NAP opposed its inception.

Major disagreement between the RPP and NAP occurred during Parliament's attempt to lift the headscarf ban at universities. The headscarf ban affected a large segment of society since about two-thirds of women in Turkey were wearing headscarves and the ban went beyond universities, covering public institutions and elected posts (Akbulut 2011). During Özal's premiership and subsequent presidency, Parliament had lifted the ban twice by passing laws, but the Constitutional Court had declared the first legislation as unconstitutional and re-interpreted the second one in a non-liberating way. Therefore, in 2008, the NAP and the JDP amended the Constitution to lift the ban for university students with a very favorable vote (411 to 103). A group of parliamentarians led by the RPP applied to the Constitutional Court for unconstitutionality. As explicitly mentioned in Article 142 of the Constitution, the court had no authority to cancel a constitutional amendment by reviewing its content. Yet, it still struck down the amendment referring to the principle of secularism (June 5, 2008; decision no. 2008/116).

The opponents of the JDP tried a "judicial coup" using the headscarf debate. The chief prosecutor of the High Court of Appeals opened a case at the Constitutional Court for the closure of the party and the imposition of five-year political bans to President Gül, Prime Minister Erdoğan, and 70 other leading JDP politicians. Six of the 11 Constitutional Court judges voted for the closure of the party; it was one vote less than the required seven (July 30, 2008; no. 2008/2). This meant the failure of the judicial coup attempt.

The conservative-liberal cooperation: de-militarization

The two main groups that have defended passive secularism as an alternative to assertive secularism in Turkey are the pro-Islamic conservatives, such as the JDP and the Gülen movement, and the liberals, who are secular academics and journalists defending democratization and liberalization. The conservatives have a substantial capacity to shape the majority of the electorate by their grassroots organizations and increasing influence over the media outlets. The liberals lack such popular influence yet they are effective with their intellectually rich democratic discourse.

The conservative-liberal coalition has played an important role in making the Ergenekon case a major source of the de-militarization of Turkish politics. In 2006, the

Council of State, the highest administrative court of appeal, decided that it was inappropriate for a teacher to wear a headscarf even on the street. Later, an assassin shot the judges who made the decision, attacking the Council's building, and killed one of them. The assertive secularists presented the incident as an assault against secularism and accused the JDP for encouraging it by having criticized the Council's decision. Then the police found out evidence that allegedly linked the assassin to a "deep-state," ultra-nationalist, and secularist organization (Ergenekon) led by retired military officers. Several cases have been opened against Ergenekon for allegedly plotting assassinations to prepare conditions for a military coup. This and other related cases have resulted in the detainment and prosecution of about 60 generals/admirals, more than 200 other military officers, and around 300 civilians. Although the verdicts in these cases have yet to be made, they have already destroyed the military's untouchable image and limited the possibility of a direct military intervention in Turkey.

The conservative-liberal coalition also ended the assertive secularist domination in the judicial system. In the September 2010 referendum, 24 constitutional amendments were approved by 58 percent of the votes. The amendments restructured top judicial institutions and this led to the weakening of the assertive secularist influence. The declining power of assertive secularists within the military and judiciary, in addition to the JDP victory in the 2011 parliamentary elections with 50 percent of the votes, started the replacement of assertive secularism with passive secularism in Turkey. The Council of Higher Education, which was redesigned by President Gül and the JDP government's appointments, has played a major role in this transformation. Recently, the Council led to the lifting of the headscarf ban in most of the universities and ended the discrimination against the Imam-Hatip graduates. As part of the transition to passive secularism, the JDP government also issued a circular that returned or compensated several properties belonging to Christian and Jewish foundations, which were confiscated throughout a long process that started with the foundation of the Republic.

Conclusion

The relationship between Islam, secularism, and democracy is a complex issue. The idea that the secular state should keep Islam under control for the sake of democracy misses this complexity. In fact, assertive secularism may become a barrier against democratization with its ambition to exclude religion from the public sphere and to impose state control over religions. The Turkish democratization experience shows the problematic relationship between assertive secularism and democracy, especially in a country where the majority would like to express their religiosity in the public domain. The assertive secularist elite in Turkey, comprising mainly the military, judiciary, and RPP, allowed multiparty elections as long as the dominance of assertive secularism was not challenged by the religiously conservative masses. Otherwise, they either supported a coup or strengthened the military and judicial tutelage over democracy.

The recent conservative-liberal alliance to replace assertive secularism with passive secularism, as well as to end the military and judicial tutelage, has played a crucial role in democratization. There are still major challenges to the consolidation of Turkish democracy, such as finding a democratic and peaceful solution to the Kurdish question and writing a new, more liberal constitution. Moreover, it remains to be seen whether the Islamic actors will produce liberal discourses, which are deeply rooted in their religious principles, instead of pragmatic and rhetorical statements, about democracy and civil rights. This would convince the skeptics that Turkey will not face an assertive Islamism, after ending the dominance of assertive secularism.

The Turkish case may inspire comparative analyses with its rich debates on the role of the assertive secularist and Islamic actors in the democratization process. The idea of Turkish exceptionalism, which is based on the misleading perception of Turkey as the only democratic and secular state in the Muslim world, should not distract scholars from such comparative analyses.

Summary

- The perception of Turkey as a unique example, where democracy is possible if the secular state keeps Islam under control, is misleading.
- Turkey has become democratic not because of assertive secularism, but despite it.
- Recently, the alliance between the pro-Islamic conservatives (especially the JDP and the Gülen movement) and the liberals has replaced assertive secularism with passive secularism in Turkey.

Discussion points

- What are the differences between passive and assertive secularism?
- Why was there a tension between the military and most of the elected governments in Turkish political history?
- Why and how did conservatives and liberals support the adoption of passive secularism in Turkey?
- Discuss the impacts of the 2002, 2007, and 2011 parliamentary elections on Turkish politics.
- Although Turkey is a parliamentary regime (where the prime minister is more effective than the president), the election of the president led to a major crisis in 2007. Why?

Further reading

Hale, William and Ergun Özbudun (2009) *Islamism, Democracy, and Liberalism in Turkey: The Case of the AKP*, London: Routledge.

This book analyzes the origin, policies, and impacts of the JDP, covering various issues from civil-military relations to secularism and Islamism.

Kasaba, Reşat (ed.) (2008) *The Cambridge History of Turkey: Vol. 4, Turkey in the Modern World*, New York: Cambridge University Press.

This volume covers the periods from the Tanzimat Reforms (1839) to the present. Chapters analyze political parties, economic development, migration, the military, Kurds, Islamic movements, women's rights, architecture, and literature.

Kuru, Ahmet T. and Alfred Stepan (eds) (2012) *Democracy, Islam, and Secularism in Turkey*, New York: Columbia University Press.

This edited book examines contemporary Turkish politics. Chapters explore Ottoman diversity, Kemalism and its homogenizing policies, multiple secularisms, civil-military relations, constitutional crisis, and the EU membership process.

Kuru, Ahmet T. (2009) *Secularism and State Policies Toward Religion: The United States, France, and Turkey*, New York: Cambridge University Press.

This is a comparative analysis of passive secularism in the United States and assertive secularism in France and Turkey. It analyzes their historical roots regarding the *ancien régime* based on the alliance between monarchy and hegemonic religion.

Turam, Berna (2007) *Between Islam and the State: The Politics of Engagement*, Stanford, CA: Stanford University Press.

This book examines the new ways of engagements between the state agents and pro-Islamic conservatives (the JDP and the Gülen movement) in Turkey.

References

Agai, Bekim (2003) "The Gülen Movement's Islamic Ethic of Education," in M. Hakan Yavuz and John L. Esposito (eds) *Turkish Islam and the Secular State: The Gülen Movement*, Syracuse, NY: Syracuse University Press.

Akbulut, Zeynep (2011) "Banning Headscarves and Women's Subjectivity in Turkey," PhD Dissertation, University of Washington.

Akdoğan, Yalçın (2006) "The Meaning of Conservative Democratic Political Identity," in M. Hakan Yavuz (ed.) *The Emergence of a New Turkey: Democracy and the AK Parti*, Salt Lake City: University of Utah Press.

Azak, Umut (2010) *Islam and Secularism in Turkey: Kemalism, Religion, and the Nation State*, New York: I.B. Tauris.

Bellin, Eva Rana (2000) "Contingent Democrats: Industrialists, Labor, and Democratization in Late-Developing Countries," *World Politics*, 52(2): 175–205.

Çarkoğlu, Ali and Binnaz Toprak (2006) *Değişen Türkiye'de Din, Toplum ve Siyaset*, Istanbul: TESEV.

Demiralp, Seda (2009) "The Rise of Islamic Capital and the Decline of Islamic Radicalism in Turkey," *Comparative Politics*, 41(3): 315–35.

European Stability Initiative (2007) "Sex and Power in Turkey: Feminism, Islam and the Maturing of Turkish Democracy," Berlin, June 2, 2007, www.esiweb.org/pdf/esi_document_id_90.pdf.

Göle, Nilüfer (1997) "Secularism and Islamism in Turkey: The Making of Elites and Counter-Elites," *Middle East Journal*, 51(1): 46–58.

Gülen, Fethullah (2001) "A Comparative Approach to Islam and Democracy," *SAIS Review*, 21(2): 133–38.

Huntington, Samuel P. (1984) "Will More Countries Become Democratic?" *Political Science Quarterly*, 99(2): 193–218.

Kılınç, Ramazan (2008) "History, International Norms, and Domestic Institutional Change: State-Religion Relations In France and Turkey," PhD Dissertation, Arizona State University.

Kuru, Ahmet T. (2005) "Globalization and Diversification of Islamic Movements: Three Turkish Cases," *Political Science Quarterly*, 120(2): 253–74.

—— (2009) *Secularism and State Policies Toward Religion: The United States, France, and Turkey*, New York: Cambridge University Press.

—— (2012) "The Rise and Fall of Military Tutelage in Turkey: Fears of Islamism, Kurdism, and Communism," *Insight Turkey*, 14(2): 37–57.

Lerner, Daniel (1958) *The Passing of Traditional Society: Modernizing the Middle East*, New York: The Free Press.

Lerner, Daniel and Richard D. Robinson (1960) "Swords and Ploughshares: The Turkish Army as a Modernizing Force," *World Politics*, 13(1): 19–44.

Lewis, Bernard (1994) "Why Turkey is the only Muslim Democracy?" *Middle East Quarterly*, 1(1): 41–49.

Linz, Juan J. and Alfred Stepan (1996) *Problems of Democratic Transition and Consolidation: Southern Europe, South America, and Post-Communist Europe*, Baltimore: Johns Hopkins University Press.

Özbudun, Ergun (2012) "The Turkish Constitutional Court and Political Crisis," in Ahmet T. Kuru and Alfred Stepan (eds) *Democracy, Islam, and Secularism in Turkey*, New York: Columbia University Press.

Turam, Berna (2006) *Between Islam and the State: The Politics of Engagement*, Stanford, CA: Stanford University Press.

Note

1   I would like to thank Alfred Stepan and Etga Uğur for their helpful comments.

15

The new
Muslim Europe

Jørgen S. Nielsen

Outline

- The Muslim presence in Europe can be traced back to the early days of Islam, and Muslims have been living in Eastern Europe for centuries. More recent is the arrival of labor immigrants and refugees into Western Europe. Most of the discussion about Muslims in Europe is focused on the immigrants and their descendants.
- The process of settlement has obliged both Muslims and the traditional structures of European states to adapt to a new situation of religious diversity.
- International developments since the 1990s and a focus on security after 9/11 has been a dominant factor in the environment in which new generations of Muslims are navigating.

Immigration and settlement

Very soon after the rise of Islam 1,400 years ago, the first Muslims appeared in Europe, some as individual traders or craftsmen and others in military encounters. The Arabs first laid siege to Constantinople in the 670s. Of longer-lasting effect was the Arab-Berber expedition which crossed into Spain in 711 and laid the foundations of a Muslim presence of almost eight centuries. While this period, together with the shorter Arab rule of Sicily and parts of southern Italy from the ninth till the eleventh century, left behind significant cultural and intellectual traces it did not lead to permanent Muslim settlement, unlike the two later major episodes. The thirteenth century saw the first of several Mongol expansions from the steppes of east Asia into central and west Asia, establishing a number of successor states, most of which in due course became Muslim in character. Their successors, known as Tatars, governed and settled in the Volga river valley and around the northern coast of the Black Sea. When their kingdoms gradually fell to Russian expansion, concluding in the sixteenth century, the Tatars became a permanent part of the Russian population. In the early fifteenth century Tatar soldiers entered the service of the Grand Duchies of Lithuania and Poland and settled in the area of today's Poland, Belarus, the Ukraine and Lithuania. Only slightly later than the Mongol invasions the Ottoman clan gradually asserted its power in what is today Turkey. From there, its rule spread across the Aegean Sea into southeastern Europe. In 1453 the remains of the Byzantine Empire with its capital Constantinople fell. Twice, in 1527 and 1683, the Ottomans besieged Vienna but after that their power declined until only the modern state of Turkey remained at the end of the First World War. But by then well-established Muslim communities, Turkish, Slavic, and Albanian-speaking, were to be found across southeastern Europe, particularly in today's Albania, Bulgaria, and the republics of the former Yugoslavia, especially Bosnia-Herzegovina (Maréchal et al 2003: xvii–xxvii; and Nielsen 2004: 1-7, for the history).

In western Europe, Muslim traders, diplomats and prisoners of war were not uncommon in the major capitals. In central Europe—Vienna, Munich, Berlin, for example—this flowed from the direct contact with the Ottoman state. In southern Europe—Venice, Pisa, Genoa, Marseille, Malaga, etc.—the main cause was continuing Mediterranean trade. In northwestern Europe—London, Amsterdam, Paris—it was linked to the commercial and imperial expansions of the seventeenth to nineteenth centuries. But they were not yet of sufficient numbers to have a major public impact. That only started after 1945 when post-war European reconstruction and economic development quickly needed to look beyond the bounds of the continent for labor. The most natural sources were the regions with which connections already existed: the empire for the British and the French and, for Germany, its very close economic and historical relationship with the late Ottoman Empire. So British labor migration came especially from the Caribbean and South Asia and the French from north Africa. The smaller north European countries followed suit. In some cases the flow was governed by formal labor supply agreements with the countries of origin, in other cases recruiting companies operated independently, while in other cases again it was the migrants themselves who organized their moves. Characteristic of the major proportions of this immigration was that it originated in the much larger migration from the countryside to the cities which was taking off at that time throughout Asia and Africa. Most of the immigrants were therefore not highly educated, and among the women there was a high rate of illiteracy. They found work as unskilled or semi-skilled workers in industries—especially coal, steel, and heavy engineering—where serious unemployment took hold later in the 1980s. This is a major point of difference with the Muslim immigration experience of North America (Castles and Kosack 1985).

In the early 1970s (a decade earlier in Britain) a combination of economic circumstances and political debates led to a gradual closing of labor migration into western Europe. But the doors were left open for fiancées, wives, and children as a result of which a major immigration flow continued but now one that established families and communities, and temporary gradually became permanent. This combination of family reunion and longer-term expectations brought with it a conscious focus on religious needs, especially facilities for worship and basic religious instruction. As the opportunities for migration for labor were increasingly restricted, much of the movement to western Europe from parts of the Muslim world shifted to refugees and asylum seekers, especially as instability in parts of the Muslim world grew during the 1980s, from the Iranian Revolution (1979), the long Lebanese civil war (1975–90), the collapse of Somalia (from 1991), wars in Bosnia and Algeria (early 1990s), wars and subsequent unrest in Iraq (1990 and 2003) to continuing problems in Palestine.

Statistics in this field are notoriously unreliable and are usually derived from figures (often also estimates) based on nationality or ethnicity. They also become part of sometimes very heated political arguments which tempts the various parties to accept either exaggerated or undercounted totals (Spielhaus 2011). But best estimates indicate a total of about 15 million people of Muslim cultural background in the countries of western Europe out of a total population of about 385 million, which is a bit less than 4 percent (Nielsen et al 2011).

The character of Muslim communities in western Europe is one which is in a continuous process of transition from immigration and settlement to becoming native, as the children of the immigrants—and increasingly also their grandchildren—grow up and seek ways of living in urban and often sharply secular urban environments, a process which also raises challenges to the local and national contexts and contributes to a European debate about national identities which has become more vocal since the turn of the 1990s.

Organization

Such firm data as exist indicate convincingly that Muslims began to organize around mosque projects as a direct consequence of the family reunion process starting after the gates of labor migration were first closed. It was clearly the process of family reunion which brought with it the need for cultural and religious facilities. Generally mosque projects were local and initially limited to acquiring premises which could be turned into places where prayers could take place and where children could get basic religious instruction, usually not much more than some reading of the Qur'an—memorized phonetically if they did not know Arabic—and essential knowledge of rituals. Only slowly did some of the communities through the 1980s and 1990s build up sufficient resources to start building new mosques, often in face of resistance from the local majority communities. Occasionally an enterprising community leadership with connections was able to raise funds for mosque-building abroad, especially from oil-rich countries after the oil price rises of the early to mid-1970s, but the importance of this funding route has often been exaggerated. On the other hand, however, there were organizations from the countries of origin that followed these new communities in their migration. There was an interest in maintaining and extending the impact of the organization, but there was also a sense of offering their services to communities which found themselves isolated from the larger Muslim environments in which they had lived before migrating. In parallel a small number of Islamic organizations and governments with claims to represent Islam internationally took part in this process, especially from Saudi Arabia, but also Libya, Egypt, and Iran. So-called Islamic cultural centers, an institution with little precedent in the Muslim world, have usually come out of this latter process (Shadid and van Koningsveld 1991).

From the mid- to late 1970s, local community organizations and transnational organizations began to link up, and national networks began to appear. One factor in this process was the concern among the governments of the sending countries to keep some kind of influence over their emigrés. Among Turks, the Directorate of Religious Affairs of the Turkish prime minister's office, commonly called the *Diyanet*, significantly expanded its influence after the military coup of September 1980, and today it still plays the major role among Turks in Germany, the Netherlands, Belgium, and the Scandinavian countries. In France the *Grand Mosquée de Paris* is generally regarded as representing the Algerian government, while the *Fédération Nationale des Musulmans de France* (FNMF) is close to the Moroccan government. Links between Pakistani authorities and their diaspora in the United Kingdom are rather looser, as power in Pakistan has been much more fluid. The main contest for influence here has been between the Sufi-oriented Brelwi movement and the more puritanical Deobandi movement. The latter is particularly known for its colleges of which there are several in Britain.

On the other hand, important organizations independent of, and sometimes opposed to the 'sending' government have also set root. The Sufi-oriented Süleymanci movement and the more Salafi-inclined Milli Görüş, widely active among Turks in Europe, have both at various times had difficult relations with the Turkish authorities. Over the last 10–15 years a new Turkish movement, led by Fethullah Gülen, a businessman disciple of the Sufi Nurcu movement, has attained a major influence through networks of community associations, schools and colleges, and associations for interreligious dialogue wherever there are communities of Turkish origin. The movement is said to be on amicable terms with the governing Justice and Development Party (AKP) in Ankara. Among Arabs, including North Africans, the main movements to contest the claims of the government-sponsored networks are those which have grown out of the Muslim Brotherhood (*al-Ikhwan al-Muslimun*), in France gathered mostly in the *Union des Organisations Musulmanes de France* (UOIF) (Maréchal 2008). More broadly linked in ethnic and national terms is the *Tablighi-jamaat*, a pietistic usually apolitical movement known especially for its tradition of sending its members on preaching missions for a few months at a time. With its origins in India as an offshoot of the Deobandi movement it has spread throughout the Muslim world; in France it is known as *Foi et pratique*.

Less noticed but becoming more public during the last decade are the many Sufi networks, whose growing visibility may, at least in part, be a reaction against the high public profile of Islamic political movements, whether associated with the Muslim Brotherhood, the Saudi-oriented Salafis, or the more radical and extremist groups associated in the public mind with "Islamic terrorism." Some of these Sufi networks are the heirs of traditional orders, such as the Naqshabandis, which can be found across both the west and the east of the region, Tijanis and Mourides among West Africans, and Alawis from North Africa. Among Turks the Alevis (not be confused either with the North African Alawis or their namesake in Syria) have in some countries distanced themselves visibly from the Turkish majority. As such they have achieved a large degree of recognition in Germany and are seeking separate recognition in Austria (Malik and Hinnells 2006; Massicard 2012).

Smaller Shi'ite communities can be found among the large Sunni majority. While most are of Iranian, Iraqi, or Lebanese origin, there are small but very active groups also of South Asian origin. This includes Ismailis of Gujarati origin who have often moved to Europe after some generations in east or southern Africa. Under the leadership of the Aga Khan, the Ismailis often have a well-resourced infrastructure with regional centers in Geneva and London. Among the Ithna'ashari majority the transnational links are mainly to Iran but there are important Iraqi or Lebanese centers too, including the Khoei Foundation in London, of Iraqi origin.

Recognition

As parts of the immigrant communities began to organize under the label "Islam" they very quickly found themselves having to maneuver in an environment that was heavily influenced by national and regional histories, above all by the inherited relations between state and Church. This was not just a matter of laws and legally sanctioned institutions but often also a matter closely related to national identities (Fetzer and Soper 2005). Since before the Reformation in the sixteenth century, one of the main themes of European history was the struggle for supremacy between king and Church. Strong kings were able to impose their will on the Church in their domains, especially if the pope was weak, and strong popes could make even the German emperor submit. The Churches that grew out of the Reformation (Lutheran, Calvinist, and Anglican, as well as Catholic) were much more closely identified with the domains of the kings, who at the Treaty of Westphalia in 1648 had confirmed their right to determine the confessional identity of the population living in their lands. This identification with a particular religion was reinforced as political power moved from kings and aristocracy to the people with the appearance of democratic nation-states in the nineteenth century. In England even today the default response on forms asking for religion is "Church of England," as is Lutheran in the Scandinavian countries. Even in formally secular states, like France where Church and state were separated in 1905, the public space is strongly colored by the ongoing contest between political secularism and a dominant Catholic tradition.

Very broadly, after centuries of often violent contestation about the place of religion/Church in the political system, the countries of Europe can be divided into three categories:

> Those Roman Catholic countries (e.g. Italy, Spain, Portugal) which until quite recently functioned on the basis of a concordat with the Vatican that gave the Catholic Church a privileged position, especially in education, in the formalization

of marriages, and in certain, usually family-related, ethical questions (e.g., divorce, contraception, abortion). This category has been disappearing in recent years as concordats have been replaced by forms of recognition in the third category below.

Countries that had instituted a complete break between church/religion and state—France is the main example but this also covers certain Swiss cantons such as Geneva. In fact, the break is often not as complete as is argued, thus in France there is a form of financial recognition in that the state is responsible for the maintenance of Catholic Church buildings that existed before 1905.

Countries that have some kind of system of recognition whereby particular religious communities are accorded certain privileges, often in the field of education or access to state-owned radio and television. In most cases the law has established a general category of recognition, and religious communities can apply to be added to the list. In a few cases, most notably England, certain religious communities are governed by their own particular legislation but there is no general status of "recognition."

(Ferrari and Bradney 2000)

A word needs to be said about the concept of a "state" or "established" Church. In England the Church of England (Anglican) holds a historically privileged position in relation to parliament and government, and the monarch is formally the head of the Church, but the Church receives no financial assistance from the state. In Denmark the "national" Church (Lutheran) is administered by the state, and the monarch is obliged to be a member of the Church. It is financed by a "church tax" collected and administered by the state. In Germany the state also collects a "church tax," which is passed on to the Churches to administer. But in both cases other religions also have historically had access to legal privileges.

Across all of these categories the arrival of new religions has been a challenge both to the legal-political tradition and to the newly arrived religious communities. In a number of countries the Jewish community had been incorporated in a variety of ways but this was only seldom a useful precedent for Muslims. Austria was fortunate in that it had a ready-made model available. The Austrian-Hungarian dual monarchy had taken control of Bosnia-Herzegovina from the Ottoman Empire in 1878, and in 1912 a law was passed adding the "Islamic community of Hanefite rite" to the list of recognized religious communities, a category first established in 1867. The law fell into disuse after the break-up of the dual monarchy at the end of the First World War, but the Islamic community established out of the immigration of the 1960s and 1970s was able to negotiate its revival in 1979. As a consequence, Muslims now have access to public broadcasting and Islamic religious education in schools, which means that the University of Vienna has opened a unit to train the teachers of the subject. Less fortunate was the Belgian decision five years previously to add Islam to the list of recognized religious communities. The recognition was granted to the then Saudi-led Islamic Cultural Centre in Brussels, and the mainly Moroccan and Turkish mosque networks refused to cooperate. Only by the late 1990s was anything approaching a publicly funded system of Islamic religious education in place, and to this day it has been impossible to implement that part of the recognized status which would allow the state to pay the salaries of Muslim clergy. In 1992 Spain recognized Islam, a status whose main practical effect is that marriages formalized in an approved Islamic setting have civil validity (see relevant country entries in Nielsen et al 2011).

The search for recognition is driven by both practical necessities and by the deeper and in many ways more important, but at the same time vaguer desire to be recognized as co-citizens with an equal voice in the public space, recognition that is more cultural and political than it is legal. This latter dimension of recognition lies at the core of the issues to be discussed in later sections of this chapter. The practical necessities are the primary short-term driver of the process, and these necessities include the facility to conduct aspects of family life in an Islamic fashion. As mentioned, it is possible to formalize a legally valid marriage in an Islamic setting in Spain. This possibility also exists in Britain, where the official registrars of birth, deaths and marriages can delegate their functions to recognized clergy of any religion (the clergy of the Church of England, the Roman Catholics, the Quakers, and the Jews have the right automatically, each under their own specific legislation). In Denmark the state has taken to "acknowledging" religious communities, including more than 20 Islamic ones at the end of 2010, which gives the right to conduct valid marriages. In most countries only marriages formalized by the civil authorities are valid, and in many it is illegal to conduct a religious wedding ceremony before the civil wedding has taken place.

More importantly, the search for recognition has obliged Muslims, as they have developed organizations at the national level, to develop forms that fit into the particular existing legal-political frameworks (Fetzer and Soper 2005). In most of the countries of origin, the state took care of the formal national Islamic organization. In many places the state's ministry of *waqf* (religious endowments) had taken over the administration of the bulk of traditional religious endowments and used them to finance a network of publicly sponsored mosques and their imams, preachers, and other officials. This usually did not prevent privately funded networks from building their own local mosques or pious foundations with their own personnel. But in Europe, this latter option was the only one, and funding has often been a problem, which is one reason why many have established links with wealthy foreign sponsors. In some larger cities "Islamic Cultural Centers"—a concept previously unknown in Islamic tradition—have been set up, in some cases with significant funding and prestigious buildings. It is clear that some of these centers have seen themselves or been seen by others, including government authorities, as possible national representatives of the Muslim community. The long delays in implementing the terms of the 1974 Belgian recognition can substantially be attributed to misunderstandings about its role on the part of the Belgian government, and the fact that the Center itself and the representatives of the resident Muslim communities had very different views of who should play the role of official representation, roles which in the Churches and the Jewish community were played by the bishops and the chief rabbi respectively. In France, it is the government which has put on pressure for the establishment of a Muslim body that could represent all the Muslim community. The current *Conseil Français du Culte Musulman*, founded in 2002, was the third attempt since the early 1990s to establish such a body. The German situation is more complicated because religion is within the competence of the various federal states (*länder*), but to avoid individual states varying too widely they coordinate. For many years one of the main arguments given by the authorities why Muslim organizations could not be given public law status was that Muslims did not show evidence of permanency. This argument could no longer be upheld when the federal government in the late 1990s finally accepted that Germany was a country of immigration (rather than temporary guest workers). Since then two states have recognized two named communities as "religious" opening the way for them to provide Islamic religious education. But none have yet admitted a Muslim organization to the public law status which would give them access to extensive tax advantages (Laurence 2012).

Laws of association in Britain have in the past been more permissive than elsewhere in Europe, and so there has been a proliferation of associations, so much so that at one point many were not much more than one person and a letterhead. That has been significantly tightened up since the turn of the century, driven in part by security consideration after September 11, 2001. But the general picture remains much less structured than elsewhere. There have been various claims over the decades on the part of one or other association to the status of a national representative, going back to the Union of Muslim Organisations of the UK and Eire established in 1970 but now essentially irrelevant. Arising out of the protests against Salman Rushdie's *The Satanic Verses* in 1988–89, the UK Action Committee on Islamic Affairs was founded (Lewis 1994). The organizations involved built on their experience to inaugurate in 1997 the Muslim Council of Britain (MCB). For some years the New Labour government, after coming to power later the same year, regarded the MCB as its first contact for Muslim affairs but the relationship became problematical after the outbreak of the Second Gulf War in March 2003. Since then national umbrella organizations, or organizations claiming some form of national representativity, have been in constantly changing relations with each other and with the government (Ansari 2004).

Changing generations

In Britain during the early 1980s one began to see the first signs of the children of the immigrants pushing their own priorities. This found expression, for example, in youth culture, but it was still expressed mostly in race and ethnic terms. Thus clashes between youth groups and the police or between different youth groups in 1981 and 1985 were usually talked of as "race riots," usually involving Afro-Caribbeans and South Asians. This changed in 1989 when protests grew against Salman Rushdie's novel *The Satanic Verses*. The "Rushdie affair" early in the year was followed in September by the first French "headscarves affair," when a secondary school in a Paris suburb excluded three teenage girls for insisting on wearing headscarves (usually *hijab* in Arabic or *foulard* in French) to school. On both occasions the protests were explicitly termed Muslim/Islamic both by the protesters and by the media and politicians trying to explain or understand. This was the first time that young people who had come to Europe very young or had been born there expressed themselves publicly as Muslims. Certainly in the British case, and to an extent also in the French, there was an expression here of frustrated expectations. In both countries the children of immigrants had easy access to the full rights of citizenship, at least in law. They had been taught to expect to be able to exercise these rights—in Britain it was not unusual for both parents and mosque leaders to tell young people that it was their Muslim duty to participate in and contribute to their country. But they were now coming out of school in growing numbers and finding their prospects in employment restricted because of an severe economic downturn at the time which was exacerbated by racial discrimination in the job market.

The Rushdie affair was internationalized by the intervention of the leader of the Iranian Islamic republic, Ayatollah Khomeini, when he issued a death sentence against the author. The "affairs" were followed in quick order by the First Gulf War against Iraq's invasion of Kuwait and then by the wars in Algeria and the collapsing state of Yugoslavia, where fighting between Muslim Bosnians on the one hand and Christian Croats and Serbs on the other served to strengthen the focus on religious, and especially Islamic identities. During the 1990s the world was seeking to adjust to the collapse of the Soviet system and the end of the Cold War. A growing focus on Islam and the Muslim world had both political and military overtones with loose talk of "Islam the new enemy" seemingly underpinned by the idea of a "clash of civilizations" propagated first by Samuel Huntington in an article and then a book of the same title. As the 1990s progressed Islam became more often a subject discussed with security undertones, a development which culminated in the terrorist attacks on New York on September 11, 2001—9/11 (Akbarzadeh and Mansouri 2007; Abbas 2011).

These developments were the context, and sometimes the pretext for major new trends among Muslims and in the European environment generally—and it is worth noting that, as the countries of Eastern Europe emerged from beneath the communist system, experiences there began to resemble those of the western half of the region ever more closely. Growing senses of insecurity, more culturally and politically than physically—although terrorist attacks on Madrid in March 2003 and on London in July 2005 were frightening—tempted politicians and voters to move towards more openly nationalist policies that particularly targeted immigrants and immigration. A number of countries made the gradual change from being among the most open, especially to refugees, to becoming among the most closed.

The Muslim responses to this changing environment have been mixed. Many parts of the communities of immigrant Muslim ethnic origin remained on the social margins characterized by high unemployment and low levels of success in education. Among the younger generation educational failure has often continued, although the proportion of success in further and higher education is often higher than in the general population, especially among young women. While the Islamic organizations and networks established by the immigrant generation continue to play a significant role, new associations are being founded with a larger variety of specialist interests. New Muslim networks with weaker connections to the countries of origin have also become more prominent. Both Salafi and Sufi networks have grown and become more visible, while groups with explicit political agendas, both in domestic and foreign policy, have also appeared. In most countries individuals of Muslim background have become active in political parties and been elected to national parliaments, some with an explicitly Muslim dimension to their electoral image.

The violent events of the last decade, and more localized events such as the Danish cartoons crisis in the winter of 2005–6 and the rise of anti-Islamic politics in a number of countries, among them the Netherlands, France, and Switzerland, have encouraged some Muslim groups to take a public stand against these phenomena. While campaigning against a proposal to ban headscarves in French schools, the main French Muslim organizations also sharply condemned the kidnapping of French aid workers by an Islamic terror group in Iraq. UK Muslims who had been active in the campaign against British involvement in the March 2003 Iraq invasion revived their slogan "Not in our name" to condemn the London bombings two years later. However, there was also a serious concern, shared by many among the non-Muslim majority that the political and security authorities were being tempted to view the Muslim communities as a whole as a security problem. Some Muslims responded by lowering the profile of their "Islamicness" while others felt provoked to raise it, a move which could be used by the political right and nationalist tendencies to strengthen their claims for further tightening of immigration law and integration policies.

In some ways Islam has become a lightning rod (or possibly scapegoat), common to a broad range of European countries, for broader and deeper European uncertainties about national identity—can one be Muslim *and* German or French etc?— and fears of globalization—the supranational powers of the European Union, the economic threats

Figure 15.1 Prayer in Paris, France. Courtesy of Miguel Media/AFP/Getty Images.

of emerging economies such as Brazil and India and, above all, China—in short a sense that things are changing too fast and outside the control of ordinary people. Having said that, it is also worth noting the broad experience that has been built up over several decades of various kinds of local regional and national cooperation in which Muslims have been active partners. Local government has in many places encouraged and sponsored local activities across ethnic and religious boundaries. Massive amounts of research and development have taken place in the education systems of Europe in what has variously been called multicultural or intercultural education. In most countries, except those such as France where religious education in publicly funded schools is prohibited, religious education has in varying degrees become multireligious in content, quite explicitly in the United Kingdom and in Norway but also in countries where Christianity remains the core focus. Dialogue with Islam and Muslims has developed from small beginnings in the 1970s to the point where, today, most churches are in some form of dialogue with Muslims at the national and international levels.

Overall, therefore, the situation of Muslims in western Europe in 2012 is one that shows both positive and negative elements. Aspects of the public debate and selected readings of international affairs places them under pressure. Much local experience and the strength of formal and informal networks and organizations, both among

Muslims and with the wider society, provides an environment conducive to those forces which seek a constructive participation in society—call it integration. The gradually broadening experience of individuals, especially young people, working together in schools, associations, and the workplace is also one that has contributed and will continue to contribute to the breaking down of barriers. In sum, it can be suggested that the only generalization applicable to the situation of Muslims in western Europe is that no generalization is valid.

Summary

- There have been permanent Muslim populations in some parts of Europe for more than 1,000 years.
- Immigration from Muslim regions into western Europe is linked to European imperial history.
- Post-1945 labor migration became family settlement when labor migration was sharply restricted. Much new immigration since then has been of refugees.
- Following family reunion communities started organizing, initially around mosques and Qur'an schools.
- National networks then appeared and were often encouraged from the countries of origin.
- Different theological-legal and religious-political trends are to be found among Muslim organizations, and ethnic origins continue to be an important factor.
- Islamic organizations have had to adapt their structures and programs in each country to be able to work with the very different national contexts.
- In a few countries this has led to formal recognition parallel to existing religious communities, usually the major churches.
- The children (and increasingly grandchildren) of the immigrants have started to develop forms of organization, activities, and thinking more relevant to their European environments.
- Political and security crises involving Islam, especially since 2000, have focused public attention on Muslims and contributed to a growth of the nationalist right.
- At the same time, local communities have developed practical experience of living with diversity in which Muslims are participants.

Discussion points

- Look at ways in which Europe's imperial past may have influenced Muslim immigration to Europe in the twentieth century.
- Assess the continuing impact of the countries of origin on European Islam.

- How have existing Church-state relations affected the development of Islamic organizations?
- To what extent might events in 1989 and in 2011 be regarded as crucial to the modern history of Islam in Europe?
- Consider how new generations of Muslims might be adapting to being European Muslims.

Further reading

A comprehensive collection of up-to-date data is Jørgen S. Nielsen, Samim Akgönül, Ahmet Alibašić and Egdūnas Račius (eds) (2012) *Yearbook of Muslims in Europe*, Vol. 4, Leiden: Brill.

The most recent attempt to provide a thematic analysis of the whole region is Brigitte Maréchal, Stefano Allievi, Felice Dassetto, and Jørgen Nielsen (eds) (2003) *Muslims in the Enlarged Europe: Religion and Society*, Leiden: Brill.

Joel S. Fetzer and J. Christopher Soper (2005) *Muslims and the State in Britain, France, and Germany*, Cambridge: Cambridge University Press, discusses how Muslim collective integration has been framed by existing church-state relations.

The Open Society Institute's "At Home in Europe Project" (2010) has sought to evaluate experience and past and future policy options in *Muslim Europe: A Report on 11 EU Cities*, London: Open Society Institute.

References

Abbas, Tahir (ed.) (2011) *Islamic Radicalism and Multicultural Politics: The British Experience*, London: Routledge.

Akbarzadeh, Shahram and Fethi Mansouri (eds) (2007) *Islam and Political Violence: Muslim Diaspora and Radicalism in the West*, London: I.B. Tauris.

Ansari, Humayun (2004) *The Infidel Within: Muslims in Britain since 1800*, London: Hurst.

Castles, Stephen and Godula Kosak (1985) *Immigrant Workers and Class Structures in Western Europe*, 2nd edn, Oxford: Oxford University Press.

Ferrari, Silvio and Anthony Bradney (eds) (2000) *Islam and European Legal Systems*, Aldershot, UK: Ashgate.

Fetzer, Joel S. and J. Christopher Soper (2005) *Muslims and the State in Britain, France, and Germany*, Cambridge: Cambridge University Press.

Huntington, Samuel P. (1993) "The Clash of Civilizations?" *Foreign Affairs*, 22–49.

—— (1996) *The Clash of Civilizations and the Remaking of World Order*, New York: Simon & Schuster.

Laurence, Jonathan (2012) *The Emancipation of Europe's Muslims: The State's Role in Minority Integration*, Princeton, NJ: Princeton University Press.

Lewis, Philip (1994) *Islamic Britain: Religion, Politics and Identity among British Muslims*, London: I.B. Tauris.

Malik, Jamal and John Hinnells (eds) (2006) *Sufism in the West*, London: Routledge.

Maréchal, Brigitte (2008) *The Muslim Brothers in Europe: Roots and Discourse*, Leiden: Brill.

Maréchal, Brigitte, Stefano Allievi, Felice Dassetto, and Jørgen Nielsen (eds) (2003) *Muslims in the Enlarged Europe: Religion and Society*, Leiden: Brill.

Massicard, Elise (2012) *The Alevis in Turkey and Europe: Identity and Managing Territorial Diversity*, London: Routledge.

Nielsen, Jørgen (2004) *Muslims in Western Europe*, 3rd edn, Edinburgh: Edinburgh University Press.

Nielsen, Jørgen S., Samim Akgönül, Ahmet Alibašić and Egdūnas Račius (eds) (2012) *Yearbook of Muslims in Europe*, vol. 4, Leiden: Brill.

Shadid, W.A.R. and P.S. van Koningsveld (eds) (1991) *The Integration of Islam and Hinduism in Western Europe*, Kampen, the Netherlands: Kok Pharos.

Spielhaus, Riem (2011) "Measuring the Muslim: About Statistical Obsessions, Categorizations and the Quantification of Religion," in Jørgen S. Nielsen, Samim Akgönül, Ahmet Alibašić, Hugh Goddard and Brigitte Maréchal (eds) *Yearbook of Muslims in Europe*, vol. 3, Leiden: Brill, 695–715.

16 Routinizing the Iranian Revolution

Mohsen Kadivar[1]

Outline

- Revolution lays foundations of new Iranian state and Constitution.
- Charismatic leadership and Shi'i political theology gave birth to the Islamic Republic of Iran.
- Constitutional values undermined by a context of political threats to Iran.
- Expedient secular values adopted by charismatic religious leadership erodes values of constitution and religion.

The dramatic developments in 1979 shook the world. Popular uprisings forced Iran's despotic monarch, Muhammad Reza Shah Pahlavi (1919–80) into exile. He was replaced by a charismatic cleric Ayatollah Ruhollah Khomeini (1902–89). Khomeini touched down at Tehran's Mehrabad airport on February 4, 1979, back from his temporary exile in France. In the wake of the heady events of the Revolution he was instantly catapulted into the role of the leader of the Revolution much to the surprise of the other political players. Since that day, the Islamic Republic of Iran has continued to unfold into one of the most dramatic stories in modern religion and politics. What defines the Islamic Republic of Iran is the story of a charismatic figure who inserted a revolutionary Shi'i political theology into a modern nation-state (Enayat 2008). The current Iranian government has both withstood international efforts to undermine its revolutionary impact and also resisted internal dissent. Whether it will be able to withstand the new waves of discontent sweeping the Middle East remains a poignant political question (Keddie 1988).

Islamic Revolution of 1979

Continuous uprisings began in January 1978 in the city of Qom, seat of some of the most important institutions of learning in Iran where more than 100 seminary students and inhabitants were killed by the security forces. Forty days later, a protest in Tabriz, meant to memorialize the martyrs of Qom, turned into a bloody event as security force brutality triggered a nationwide chain of memorials. In what became known as Black Friday, security forces murdered hundreds of peaceful protesters in Tehran. By September 1978 the Pahlavi regime's days were numbered. The government officially transferred rule to the military, but the uprisings continued. Many soldiers and officers deserted their command in support of the protests. In the largest demonstration on 'Ashoura, commemorating the martyrdom of the Prophet Muhammad's grandson, Husayn, more than two million protestors took to the streets.

Mosques and other religious centers became the heart of the revolution. All people, regardless of religion, gender, language, or social status, participated in the demonstrations. But the Shi'i clergy had a distinguished role. In every village, town, city, and region the presence of the clergy was unmistakable and the clerical fraternity functioned like a political party. Declarations and speeches made by Ayatollah Khomeini circulated through the underground (Algar 1981). Khomeini had challenged the monarchy 15 years earlier, and spent time and gained popularity during his exile in Turkey, Iraq and France.

Although some revolutionary writers, students and militant groups were secular and even communists, the great majority of participants in the Revolution were folk with some form of religious convictions. No one could compete with Ayatollah Khomeini in stature and influence. The people trusted him and his plan for the future of their country. Most of the senior Ayatollahs in Qom supported him. Khomeini's leadership was based on a consensus among oppositional parties. High school and university students, women, laborers, teachers, businessmen, and clergy all followed him.

The protests were expressed in the form of demands announced through slogans, placards, sayings, and underground pamphleteering and information distribution networks. The demands of the protestors are important for several reasons. They formed the core demands of the Revolution and continue to inform Iran's national identity. To grasp these demands is to also understand the revolutionary generation of Iran and the country's conduct both domestically and on the national stage.

First: uncompromising independence and sovereignty

Public opinion held that Iran should be managed by a national plan, based on protecting its public interests. Income generated by the oil industry should be channeled into the country's national treasury in order to improve the lives of its citizens. The monarch, government, and army commanders should put the interests of Iran ahead of the interests of international powers and oil companies. In privileging the interests of foreign companies, Iranians believed that the monarch and his supporters were violating the sovereignty of Iran in plundering the resources for their personal gain.

The real ruler of the country, they charged, was the American Ambassador in Tehran, not the Shah. Iran's most important allies were the United States and Israel. After a CIA coup against liberal prime minister Muhammad Musaddiq in 1953, who nationalized the Iranian oil industry, US foreign policy emasculated Iran's priorities via the monarch Muhammad Reza Shah. The Shah oppressed all national movements in the Middle East, especially in the Persian Gulf, as a US proxy. Iranians hated the Shah because of his absolute obedience to US foreign policy and unconditional support for Israel irrespective of Israeli policies towards Palestinians.

The revolution was not only against imperialism; it was also staunchly anti-communist. The Soviet Union and China, like the US, were not ideal exemplars for Iran.

As the Soviet Union was Iran's northern neighbor, Iranians had a unique view of the political events in that country. Iranians were strongly disappointed by communist policy. The Iranian Communist Party (*Tudeh*) became known as the foreign policy wing of another superpower. A major slogan of the revolution was "No to the East (Soviet Union, China, and communism), no to the West (US, Europe, capitalism and imperialism)."

Diverse Iranian groups supported national sovereignty. Religious groups grounded their critique in Qur'anic principles. The religious authority denounced dependence on foreign powers as a sign of illegitimacy. Leftist intellectuals and socialists also called for an independent Iran. Many communists maintained loyalty to the Soviet Union but joined in denouncing imperialism and the US. The national businessmen and the trader markets, called the *bazar*, supported it too (Ashraf 1988); their aim was to establish a national economy based on the interest and investment of Iranians. Ayatollah Khomeini banged loudly on the drum of independence. First and foremost, the Revolution of 1979 was an expression of the quest for independence (Rajaee 2007).

Second: the right to rebel against injustice, discrimination, and corruption

Social justice was also a powerful demand of the Revolution. Due to skyrocketing oil prices in the 1970s, huge amounts of money flowed into the country. But the Pahlavi administration did nothing to distribute this wealth. A large part of the money was wired directly to the royal family's personal accounts in Western banks. National money was also used to line the pockets of loyalists, who Iranians dubbed the "thousand families." These families, along with the royal family, held a monopoly on the import of Western goods.

The poor became poorer and the rich became richer. Pressure was mounting on the lower classes. The average income in Iran increased in the 1970s, but the gap between the rich minority and the majority was gaping. Middle- and lower-class citizens made up the majority of the opposition. Their demands were for social justice and ending discrimination.[2]

Injustice was also manifest in the judiciary. Corrupt judges never failed to side with a party that boasted connections to power. If the case was political, the scales were even more weighted in favor of the rulers.

Religious authorities, leftists, and elites sounded the call for reform. The masses felt these injustices in their skin and bones. Ayatollah Khomeini called the Shah an "unjust ruler." Religiously, these words alone could strip his administration of its legitimacy. Demands for equity and justice rang through Iran. The Revolution of 1979 was the voice of justice. It was an egalitarian revolution.

Third: a quest for freedom and the right to rebel against oppression, censorship, and coercion

In the 1970s and throughout the Pahlavi period, Iran was a closed society. Criticizing the king and his office was tantamount to apostasy. The government choked out any independent media that might have provided space for free expression. Opposition parties were prohibited. Prisons were filled with political activists. Any mention of human rights in the constitution was seemingly erased. Human rights were violated, political prisoners were tortured. Books, films, theaters, and all cultural products were placed under harsh censorship. Jimmy Carter's election in 1976 as US President and his emphasis on human rights allowed the international media to highlight the crisis of human rights violations in Iran as well as other countries.

The elites led the call for freedom and liberty. The religious authority supported them, buttressing these demands with Qur'anic exegesis and by proffering examples of governance furnished by the Prophet Muhammad and Imam 'Ali. Writers, intellectuals, academicians, teachers, students, journalists, artists, and political activists threw in their support. Political freedom was one of the major goals of the revolution.

Fourth: the call for the end of autocratic monarchy and secular dictatorship

Iran had a long history of civilization. But this was a history supported by kingdom, autocracy, and monarchy. The Pahlavis made crucial adjustments to this historic model.

Both of the Pahlavis came to power thanks to foreign support. Reza Shah (1878–1944) was propped up by Britain in 1925, as was his son, before the US also came to his aid (1941 and 1953). In all of Iranian history, Muhammad Ali Shah Qajar (1872–1925) had been the only previous Iranian ruler to accept aid from foreign powers (1907–9). He was in the service of Russia.

The Pahlavis were also unique in their stance against religion. As radical secularists they tried to expunge Islam from the public sphere. They drew a tight line around Shi'i seminaries and Shi'i authorities and gave short shrift to religious teachings. The Pahlavis' "modernization" was closely linked to Westernization. The monarchist program of Westernization led to severe restriction on Islam as a public faith while expanding Western forms of life in Iran.

This secularizing project elicited a particularly strong reaction from religious people and Shi'i authorities. They identified the Shah as the enemy of Islam. But religious and secular citizens alike agreed that his government spouted a pack of lies. "Death to Shah" was another major slogan on the lips of the revolutionaries.

Ayatollah Khomeini demanded that the Shah step down. He sought to end Iran's long-dominant method of governance, 25 centuries of monarchical rule. Iranians welcomed this goal. Their demands would be met in 1979, which marked the last year of monarchical rule in Iran. But did dictatorship die with the official death of the monarchy? That is the questions that many Iranians ask today.

Fifth: the demand for Islamic teachings in the public domain

More than 98 percent of Iranians are Muslims and more than 90 percent of them are Shi'i. Clearly, most citizens felt strongly about their religious practice. Following Muslim tradition meant that Friday should be an official holiday and the Hijri calendar should organize the country's official year. Restrictions on religious affairs in the public sphere ran contrary to these social facts and attested to the secular leaders' strong-arm tactics. But, as would become clear, Muslim civil society in the 1970s was strong.

The majority of protesters called for the respect of Islamic norms, creed, and faith. They pursued the protection of Islamic ethics and rituals as enshrined in Islamic rules (*Shari'a*). There were two approaches to *Shari'a*: traditional/conservative and reformist/modern. But, being as there was no experience in implementing *Shari'a* during that time, the protesters did not make this distinction. Their call was simply one of respect for Islamic teachings.

While the secular and non-practicing minority did not support this pursuit, they apparently did not reject its demands. The Revolution was called "Islamic" for many reasons: first, the call for the implementation of Islamic norms was among the major demands of the Revolution; second, the Shi'i authority was the revolutionary vanguard; third, mosques and religious institutions were organizational conduits for revolutionaries; fourth, the clergy had a distinguished role in the Revolution.

Ayatollah Khomeini: spiritual architect of the Islamic Republic of Iran

Ayatollah Khomeini's most dramatic intervention was to link the doctrine of the "guardianship of the jurist" (*wilayat al-faqih*) with modern Islamic political thought. Khomeini's political ideas evolved over time during his exile in Iraq and France. He developed them systematically, drawing on older precedents in Shi'i political thought; they stemmed from a reconstruction and critique of several doctrines.

First, Khomeini constructed the idea of an Islamic revolution from the Islamic teaching that every believer was obliged to "command the good and to prohibit the evil." In his view, of all the evils in the world, oppression by an unjust ruler was the worst. Khomeini held that the optimum and lawful manner of "commanding the good" was to form an Islamic government.

Second, he argued, the learned in religion, those who were expert in ethical and moral teachings—known as the *faqih* (pl. *fuqaha*) translated as "jurists" in modern parlance—had a special responsibility and duty in Islam. Theirs was a special calling.

In his view, it was the unqualified duty of Muslim jurists, the *fuqaha* and *ulama*, to do everything in their power to prosecute political evil and injustice as the repositories of moral conscience in Islam. More pragmatic religious scholars believed it was not an unqualified duty to resist political injustice. One should resist evil only when there was a high probability that an intervention would successfully make a difference. (Khomeini 1961: 472–83) Khomeini disagreed with this view. He was critical of those Iranian clerics who adopted political quietism. Such self-serving pragmatism, he argued, was in defiance of the commandments of the Qur'an and the prophetic teachings that taught the need to resist and revolt against evil.

The commandment to do good in Islam, he argued, was first and foremost addressed to the *faqih*, the jurist. It is the just jurist who is addressed by God, the supreme legislator. In turn, the lay people or ordinary believers are urged to support the leadership of the just jurist in all ethical and moral matters. In fact, Khomeini made the explicit argument that the just jurist possessed the same custodial powers in moral and ethical matters as did the Prophet Muhammad and the Shi'i Imams (Khomeini 1971: 461, 472). He made his case stronger by citing authority. According to some teachings of the sixth Shi'i Imam, Ja'far al-Sadiq, and other custodial religious leaders (imams), he said, the jurists are the successors of the Imam.[3] As such, they are the designated rulers of the community. Therefore, in Khomeini's view, *Shari'a* or *fiqh* (Islamic jurisprudence), provided a template for expanding justice in society.

Background of custodial rule of the jurist (wilayat al-faqih)

The doctrine of the custodial role of the jurist goes back to the early nineteenth century of Qajar rule in Iran. The weak Qajar monarchs were pitted against powerful religious authorities. In order for the Qajar monarchs to wage war, jihad, against external enemies they needed the religious validation of their actions from the Shi'i religious authorities. It was in that context that a prominent Shi'i scholar and jurist, Mulla Ahmad Naraqi (d. 1829) stated for the first time that jurists have a custodial role or moral guardianship not only in religious affairs, but also in temporal political affairs. In other words, according to this view, the jurists were the disguised sovereigns of both the religious and secular realms. Naraqi's claim did not go unchallenged. His distinguished student, Shaikh Murtada Ansari (1781–1864) challenged his teacher for expanding the power of the jurists in this manner.

This very idea played out somewhat differently in the early twentieth century when Iranians experimented with constitutional government. Shi'ite clerics were divided about the legitimacy of constitutional government. The majority of the Shi'i authorities at the learning centers in Najaf in Iraq and those in Tehran, Tabriz, and other cities supported the idea of constitutionalism. They found juristic and theological arguments to restrict the monarchy and appealed to justice. In doing so they validated the rule of law, equality of all citizens before the law, freedom of the citizens, and the responsibility and the accountability of the ruler. The most significant point they made was that the power of the ruler was limited in religious terms.

Among the most distinguished authorities who supported this division of powers and limitation of the right of secular rulers were Akhund Mulla Muhammad Kazim Khorasani (1839–1911) and Mirza Husain Na'ini (1850–1936) (Ha'eri 1977). Khorasani was the spiritual leader of the movement (Kadivar 2005); Na'ini wrote the most important theoretical book on governance in Islam (Na'ini 2010). They began the process of reconciling Islam and the modern state. Khorasani made one significant point that would later resonate in twentieth-century Iran: the religious jurists do not have powers of guardianship and custodial authority. The administration of the country should devolve to Parliament.

But during the constitutional movement there were also hardline clerics who opposed the separation of secular and religious powers. In some way they channeled the views of Naraqi and opposed the restriction of political power. So therefore they opposed the idea of constitutional rule, arguing that it was antithetical to Islam and Shi'i thought. But effectively they were monarchists who gave absolute power and authority to the monarch. Foremost among them was the famous jurist Sheikh Fadlullah Nouri (d. 1909). He believed that freedom, equality, and civil law all were antithetical to Islam and he despised any attempt to restrict the power of the ruler.

Khomeini's ideas evolved amid these complicated debates among the Shi`i clergy (Enayat 1983). In his early writings he supported constitutional rule, the form favored by Na'ini (Khomeini 1943: 222). Prior to 1978 he used the term "Islamic governance" when describing the future for Iran that he envisioned. Then in October 1978 he first used the phrase "Islamic Republic" when he was in Paris. What did he mean by these two terms? Was this a new vision or was it merely a reflection of an older and broader Shi'i sentiment?

A few months before victory of Islamic Revolution, Khomeini began promoting his ideas for Iran's future. Iran would be an "Islamic Republic," he said, acknowledging that the government should represent its citizens. The people, he said, must directly elect the president of Iran. On the other hand, the clergy or jurists like himself would not hold governmental positions. Their role should be purely and transparently advisory. At the time he did not mention the theory of "guardianship of the jurist" (*wilayat al-faqih*) in any of his Paris speeches or writings. He appealed to freedom of expression for all political players and opposition parties, including Marxists. But Parliament, he said, should apply *Shari'a* and take serious the views of the Muslim jurists (Kadivar 1999: 160–203).

In his first speech made after his return to Iran, Khomeini expressed the right of each generation to choose its own destiny. He appointed Mehdi Bazargan (1907–95) as the prime minister of the revolutionary regime. Bazargan was a liberal Muslim, an intellectual, and the leader of the Freedom Movement Party (Chehabi 1985). Bazargan had three assignments: to hold a referendum in favor of regime change; to prepare a draft constitution; and to elect an assembly of experts (*majlis-e mu'assesan*) to design the final constitution.

Figure 16.1 Ayatollah Khomeini is greeted by his supporters during his return to Iran after 15 years in exile (Tehran, 1979). Courtesy of Gabriel Duval/AFP/Getty Images.

While Ayatollah Khomeini called the new regime the "Islamic Republic of Iran", Bazargan preferred the name of "Islamic Democratic Republic of Iran." The Leader of the Revolution argued that Islam is perfect in itself and therefore the term "democratic" was unnecessary. When Bazargan held the referendum in favor of the Islamic Republic, yes or no, there were several objections. Some secular intellectuals criticized the idea for three reasons. First, they said, the phrase "Islamic Republic" is ambiguous. Second, the role of *Shari'a*, the jurists and their role in determining what were the national interests were all unclear. Third, they proposed that other models of governance, such as "republic" and "democratic republic," be put in the referendum alongside the choice of an "Islamic republic."[4]

In April 1979, 98.2 percent of the voters affirmed the idea of an "Islamic Republic." The Bazargan cabinet published the first draft of the constitution of the Islamic Republic in June 1979. This draft bore many resemblances to both Western European countries' constitutions and Iran's constitution of 1905. The president of the Islamic Republic was to be the commander in wartime, the leader in peacetime, and the highest official in the country at all times. This constitution did not make any provisions for *wilayat al-faqih* or for the special rights of the clergy. For the most part, the Shi'i authorities approved the draft. Neither did the Ayatollah Khomeini decry the absence of *wilayat al-faqih*.

Iranians selected the assembly of experts for the final review of the constitution. The assembly was largely composed of the clergy. It made deep revisions to the draft constitution or rewrote it. The most significant addition was the clause instituting the guardianship of the jurist, *wilayat al-faqih*. The final constitutional draft gave to the guardian jurist (*wali-e faqih*) the three powers that were given to the president, namely commander in wartime, leader in peacetime, and the highest official in the country. In addition, the guardian jurist had the power to appoint all key figures to the government, including the judiciary, army, and the guardianship council. The appointed guardian jurists had the right to veto parliamentary rules, disqualify candidates in all elections, and were vested with the exclusive right to interpret the constitution. The guardianship council was the most powerful institution in this constitution. It was a complete coup conducted by the authors of the final constitution.

Only eight members of Iran's assembly of experts objected to the article providing for *wilayat al-faqih*. Among them were Izatullah Sahabi (1930–2011), a member of the revolutionary committee, Ali Golzadeh Ghafiuri (1923–2009), an open-minded clergyman, and Abul-Hasan Bani-Sadr (b. 1933), a liberal Muslim who would later become the first president of the Islamic Republic. The distinguished leader of Friday prayer in Tehran, Ayatollah Sayyied Mahmoud Taleqani (1911–79) who passed away one month before this event, voiced his disagreement to a special committee of the assembly of experts.

The most influential opposition to the guardianship of the jurist, *wilayat al-faqih*, and the constitution was expressed by Ayatollan Sayyid Muhammad Kazem Shariatmadari (1905–86), the main rival of Ayatollah Khomeini for more than 50 years. Shariatmadari voiced his opposition to the guardianship of the jurist *wilayat al-faqih* in a declaration that was not broadcast by government radio and television. He believed that articles 5 and 110 of the constitution were in violation of national sovereignty that is the basis of the constitution. Shariatmadari called for a boycott of the vote to ratify the constitution. His followers in Tabriz took to rioting and took over the city for several days and protested against the new constitution and the central government (Chehabi 1991).

Secular opposition to the new regime said that *wilayat al-faqih* was tantamount to dictatorship. The turban worn by the clerics had simply replaced the crown of the deposed Shah (Amir Arjomand 1989). Ayatollah Khomeini broke his silence on this matter and welcomed the guardianship of the jurist as a divine gift. He called *wilayat al-faqih* the guarantee of Islam and the protector of the country. Governance of the jurist, *wilayat al-faqih* was the very opposite of dictatorship, he claimed.

Iranians ratified the constitution in the referendum of December 1979. Only 75 percent of participants that took part in the first referendum came out for the second. In November 1979 student followers of Imam Khomeini occupied the US Embassy in Tehran. The occupiers took the US staff as hostages. Bazargan and his ministers resigned in objection to this event after nine months. The prime minister was accused of being too shallow and non-revolutionary, and Ayatollah Khomeini became the leader of an energetic revolution. The time of hardliners had begun.

Hardliner domination

Several factors led to the rise of the hardliners. First, anti-clerical terrorist groups assassinated several religious figures and army commanders in the early aftermath of the revolution. Second, militant organizations, such as the People's Mujahedin (Abrahamian 1989), a Muslim-Marxist organization, and the Marxist People's Party made demands to share governance. Third, border provinces largely made up of ethnic minorities such as Kurds, Baluchs, Turkamans, Arabs, and Azaris tried to secede from the central state. Militant Marxist groups with foreign help supported these secessionist demands. Fourth, Saddam Hussein and the Iraqi Army attacked Iran in October 1980. Fifth, the US and European countries supported all internal and external opposition movements. Sixth, the violated interpretation of *Shari'a* of some of the revolutionary forces including the office of Ayatollah Khomeini himself (Moin 2005) also contributed.

The new Islamic regime quickly sent shockwaves through the Middle East region. Revolutionary slogans announced the desire to see revolution worldwide, a universal jihad against monarchy and dictatorship, the destruction of Israel, international unity against imperialism and capitalism, and the dawn of a new Muslim awakening. When the US announced that it was to end ties with Iran, Khomeini welcomed the news.

From the early days of the Islamic Republic the courts and judicial authorities eagerly enforced the regime's injustice. Many of the previous regime's agents and army commanders, including the last prime minister, were put to death after summary show trials. Such cynical and speedy justice could at first be ascribed to early revolutionary fervor. But over time it became the norm. The government established a special "revolutionary court" where all political and security cases, including cases involving the press, were referred. While the constitution mandated an open trial by jury and the right of the defendant to choose a lawyer all cases were heard behind closed doors and without the advocacy of independent lawyers.

Political prisoners, especially militants and separatists, were tortured despite the practice being constitutionally outlawed. The death penalty was meted out frequently and without due process to adversaries of the regime (Abrahamian 1999). Most of the revolutionary court judges did not attend law school. They generally studied *fiqh* in the seminaries of Qom and other cities for a few years, not enough time required to attain the qualified status as an independent jurist (*mujtahid*).

Vocal criticism of the revolutionary courts and the implementation of *Shari'a* instead of penal codes increased, including the opposition of Bazargan. One political party, the National Front, called the use of Islamic penal codes as "medieval." Ayatollah Khomeini responded harshly, denouncing members of the National Front as apostates. To criticize the use of *Shari'a* in his view was tantamount to attacking Islam. Many grand Ayatollahs too denounced the revolutionary courts for not complying with their standards of *Shari'a*.

The war with Iraq and internal civil skirmishes were used to muzzle the media despite the fact that Iranians, including Ayatollah Khomeini himself, had made freedom of expression one of their loudest revolutionary rallying cries. Khomeini accused critical media of receiving support from the West. Revolutionary elements took over the offices of some non-governmental newspapers. The public prosecutor of the revolutionary court banned all non-governmental media. Radio and TV production was placed under the office of the leader.

Political parties were also restricted. Marxist parties were banned immediately. Most of them were pro-Soviet, pro-China, militant or separatists. In the second round of restrictions, the People's Mujahedin, the National Front and Ayatollah Shariatmadari's Azari Party were outlawed. Finally, the Freedom Movement was banned. The Islamic Republic Party held a monopoly on politics. Five grand Ayatollahs were placed under house arrest or restriction in the 1980s.[5] Most of them criticized Khomeini for not having thoroughly implemented *Shari'a*.

Two months after the Revolution, the assassination of government officials began. The first trigger was pulled on Ayatollah Murtada Mutahhari (1920–79), one of the most distinguished students of Khomeini. The People's Mujahedin managed the second round of terror. An office of the Islamic Republic Party was bombed, which killed more than 70 party members, Ayatollah Dr. Muhammad Beheshti (1928–81), the head of judiciary, among them. Two months later, the same wave of terror killed President Raja'i (1933–81) and Prime Minister Bahonar (1933–81). These acts only furthered the restrictions on domestic freedoms. The government began censoring books, films, theater and music. The first president, Abul-Hassan Bani-Sadr, fled to Paris less than two years after he took office.

The clergy-run government could not endure pluralism and diversity. The constitution only guaranteed clergymen roles in leadership and the guardianship council. After a few years clergy dominated parliament, the judiciary, the ministry of security, the army office of security and the revolutionary guard. The Islamic Republic *became* a Republic of the Clerics.

Ayatollah Khomeini: a complex revolutionary cleric

Ayatollah Khomeini was one of the more progressive grand Ayatollahs. His religious interpretations removed bans on music, on women artists on television and in cinema, on the right of women to work outside of the house. His views on the chador were comparatively liberal in that he ruled that if a woman covered her hair and body it sufficed as religious dress. A wife could initiate divorce from her husband if she stipulated this in her marriage contract. Husbands needed the permission of their wives if they wished to enter a polygamous marriage. He advocated women's suffrage. He removed restrictions on playing chess if it did not involve gambling. And he permitted sex-change surgery.

He was the first Shi'i jurist who acknowledged the concept of the modern state in his jurisprudence. He thought that *Shari'a* was the best source of governance in the political, social, financial, cultural, and militarily spheres. Later he increasingly found the historical interpretations of the *Shari'a* incompatible with the modern state. Thus he increasingly relied on the rule of necessity and argued that what was expedient and in the public interest should take precedence over religious rules.

This trend marked a turning point in more than 12 centuries of Shi'i jurisprudence. It marked the secularization of Shi'i *fiqh* (Matsuanga 2009). He established a new organization called the Expediency Council. This council was placed above the guardianship council, the main representative of *Shari'a*. This new hierarchy put "regime expedience" above the *Shari'a*-oriented guardianship council that oversaw parliament. Ayatollah Khomeini might not have been familiar with the work of Thomas Hobbes, but if we were to replace the absolute power of the state with the power of the "guardian jurist" formulated by Khomeini there would be striking resemblances.

After a UN-brokered ceasefire between Iran and Iraq, the militant People's Mujahedin attacked Iran with the support of the Iraqi Air Force. Even though the Revolutionary Guards finally defeated them, thousands of Iranians were killed. In this atmosphere, Khomeini issued an order to question each Mujahedin prisoner as well as other political prisoners, even if he or she was not in the battlefield, to either denounce the group or face the death penalty. Almost 3,000 prisoners in Tehran, many of who had only been sentenced to a few years in jail, were put to death. The event remains one of the blackest moments on the record of the Islamic Republic.

Ayatollah Hussein-Ali Montazeri (1922–2009), identified as Ayatollah Khomeini's successor, opposed the execution of the regime's opposition (Akhavi 2008). Taking the life of one innocent human being was the same as murdering all of humanity, Montazeri wrote in a critical letter to Khomeini. Ayatollah Montazeri resigned as Khomeini's deputy less than three months before Khomeini's death. Ayatollah Khomeini wrote to Montazeri that leadership was more complicated than Montazeri's simple temperament could bear and stripped him of his title.

Khomeini was neither reformist nor fundamentalist, neither liberal nor a monarchist, neither open-minded nor a hardliner. He was a unique figure. He was Khomeini. He established a new style of politics in the Middle East and in the world. He increased the self-confidence of citizens, showed independence in promoting the authority of Islam and disregarding the superpowers of both capitalism and communism. He decried Zionism and promoted the compatibility of Islam with progress and development. He believed in Islamic theocracy as the required condition of implementation of *Shari'a* and saw secularism, democracy and human rights as the political tools of the Western enemy to attack the Islamic world.

Although he established the Islamic Republic with *Shari'a* he soon accepted secularization by increasing the role of the notion of public interest or regime expediency. In that sense Khomeini's experiment is a learning moment for all those who wish to pursue *Shari'a*-based politics.

After Khomeini

Ali Khamenei has followed in Khomeini's footsteps but lacks his charisma, stature, and credibility (Ashraf 1990; Amir-Arjomand 2009). Khamenei has maintained the trajectories of industrial modernization, health planning, and social welfare. He has increased educational and work opportunities for women as well as enhanced national literacy rates. Yet accountability, the rule of law, democracy, freedom, human rights, transparency, and justice have all suffered under his watch. Most of Khomeini's supporters now oppose Khamenei.

Khamenei's most vocal opponent was Ayatollah Montazeri. The latter was both an advocate of the guardianship of the jurist (*wilayat al-faqih*) and wrote a seminal book on

Figure 16.2 Billboards with Ayatollah Khamenei (current spiritual leader of Iran) and Ayatollah Khomeini (previous leader and force behind the 1979 Revolution). © dbimages/Alamy.

the topic. Yet he later revised his earlier views and criticized the absolute authority of the guardianship of the clerics (Kadivar 2011). Citizens should elect the president and jurists do not have any guardianship or religious authority on the executive power. Montazeri believed in governance with the consent of the citizenry and was a mortal opponent of authoritarian rule. His final statement, made a few months prior to his death in 2009 was, "This regime is neither Islamic nor a Republic" (Sadri and Sadri 2010).

Key figures once involved in government have joined the opposition. All of the former presidents, Abul-Hasan Bani-Sadr, Akbar Hashemi Rafsanjani (b. 1934), and Muhammad Khatami (b. 1943), the former foreign policy minister Ebrahim Yazdi (b. 1931), the former prime minister Mir-Hussein Mousavi (b. 1942), and the former parliament spokesman Mahdi Karroubi (b. 1937) all are vocal opponents of the regime of leader Khamenei and President Ahmadinejad (b. 1956). Mousavi and Karroubi have been under house arrest since February 2011.

Today, the Islamic Republic is in the grip of a power triangle: the office of the guardian jurist, commanders of revolutionary guards, and President Mahmoud Ahmadinejad and his team. Dictatorship, corruption and misadministration dominate policy. Most Shi'i authorities do not support Khamenei. Among the grand Ayatollahs, supporters of the regime are a small minority. But, while some Shi'i authorities have openly criticized the regime, most are quiet. The opposition believes that they are a majority. The Green Movement, begun in the aftermath of fraudulent presidential elections in 2009, is taking a strong stand in favor of democracy. Another generation of Iranians now weaned off the Islamic Republic is taking to the streets. On their lips are calls for a secular democratic state and a compassionate form of Islam.

Summary

- Diverse protesters united around a set of core demands during the Iranian Revolution of 1979. These demands included:
  - A call for uncompromising independence and sovereignty;
  - The right to rebel against injustice, discrimination, and corruption;
  - End to censorship and coercion under the Shah's autocratic monarchy;
  - Islamic teachings in the public domain.
- The charismatic figure Ayatollah Khomeini took root and inserted a revolutionary Shi'i political theology into the nation-state of Iran.
- Iran has been branded as an "Islamic Republic" since then.
- After the Revolution factions began to appear. A group of clergy monopolized all rights and inscribed their power and authority into the Constitution. Other clergymen and secularists protested. Amid this tumult, the religious hardliners gained the edge.
- In contemporary Iran, a new generation is calling for a secular democratic state and a compassionate form of Islam.

Discussion points

- What were the core demands of the Islamic revolution of 1979?
- What were the main characteristics of Khomeini?
- Did Iran request a theocratic regime or guardianship of the jurist in their revolution? Which factors made the Islamic Republic as it is?
- What factors dominated hardliners in Islamic Republic? What is the role of the US?
- What would be the demand of revolution (in 1979) if Iran had had the experience of three decades of Islamic Republic?

Further reading

Abrahamian, Ervand (1982) *Iran Between Two Revolutions*, Princeton, NJ: Princeton University Press.
Amir Arjomand, Said (1989) *The Turban for the Crown: The Islamic Revolution in Iran*, Oxford: Oxford University Press.

Bakhash, Shaul (1991) *Reign of the Ayatollahs: Iran and the Islamic Revolution*, New York: Basic Books.
Kurzman, Charles (2004) *The Unthinkable Revolution in Iran*, Cambridge, MA: Harvard University Press.
Mottahedeh, Roy (2008) *The Mantle of the Prophet: Religion and Politics in Iran*, Oxford: Oneworld.
Rajaee, Farhang (2007) *Islamism and Modernism: The Changing Discourse in Iran*, Austin: University of Texas Press.

References

Abrahamian, Ervand (1989) *The Iranian Mojahedin*, New Haven, CT: Yale University Press.
—— (1999) *Tortured Confessions: Prisons and Public Recantations in Modern Iran*, Berkeley: University of California Press.
Akhavi, Shahrough (2008) "The Thought and Role of Ayatollah H.A. Montazeri in the Politics of Post-1979 Iran," *Iranian Studies*, 41(5): 645–66.
Algar, Hamed (trans. and annotated) (1981) *Islam and Revolution: Writings and Declarations of Imam Khomeini (1941-1980)*, Berkeley, CA: Mizan Press.
Amir Arjomand, Said (1989) *The Turban for the Crown: The Islamic Revolution in Iran*, Oxford: Oxford University Press.
—— (2009) *After Khomeini: Iran Under His Successors*, Oxford: Oxford University Press.
Ashraf, Ahmad (1988) "Bazaar-Mosque Alliance: The Social Basis of Revolts and Revolutions," *International Journal of Politics, Culture, and Society*, 1(4): 538–67.
—— (1990) "Theocracy and Charisma: New Men of Power in Iran," *International Journal of Politics, Culture, and Society*, 4(1): 113–21.
Chehabi, H.E. (1985) "Society and State in Islamic Liberalism," *State, Culture, and Society*, 1(3): 85–101.
—— (1991) "Religion and Politics in Iran: How Theocratic Is the Islamic Republic?" *Daedalus*, 120(3): 69–91.
Enayat, Hamid (1983) "Khumaini's Concept of Guardianship of Jurist-Consult," in James P. Piscatori (ed.) *Islam in Political Process*, Cambridge: Cambridge University Press.
—— (2008) *Modern Islamic Political Thought*, Austin: University of Texas Press.
Ha'eri, Abdul-Hadi (1977) *Shi'ism and Constitutionalism in Iran: A Study of the Role Played by the Persian Residents of Iraq in Iranian Politics*, Leiden: Brill.
Kadivar, Mohsen (1999) *Hokumat-e Wela'i* (Government as Guardianship), Tehran: Nashre-Ney.
—— (2005) "Political Innovative Ideas and Influences of Molla Muhammad Kazim Khorasani," *Annals of Japan Association for Middle East Studies (AJAMES)*, 21(1): 59–73.
—— (2011) "Wilayat al-Faqih and Democracy," in Asma Afsaraddin (ed.) *Islam, the State and Political Authority: Medieval Issues and Modern Concerns*, Basingstoke, UK: Palgrave Macmillan.
Keddie, Nikki R. (1988) "Iranian Revolutions in Comparative Perspective," in Edmund Burke III and Ira M. Lapidus (eds) *Islam, Politics and Social Movement*, Berkeley: University of California Press, 298–314.
Khomeini, Ruhollah Mousavi (1943) *Kashf al-Asrar* (Revealing the Secret), Qom.
—— (1961) *Tahrir al-Wasilah*, vol.1, Qom.
—— (1971) Book on "Sales" (al-bay'), vol.2, Qom.

Matsuanga, Yasuyuki (2009) "The Secularization of a *Faqih*-headed Revolutionary Islamic State of Iran: Its Mechanisms, Processes, and Prospects," *Comparative Studies of South Asia, Africa and the Middle East*, 29(3): 468–82.

Moin, Baghir (2005) "Khomeini's Search for Perfection: Theory and Reality," in Ali Rahnema (ed.) *Pioneers of Islamic Revival*, London: Zed Books, 64–97.

Na'ini, Muhammad Hossein and M. Taleqani (2010) *Governance from the Perspective of Islam*, trans. L. Khanji and M. Nafissi, Edinburgh: Edinburgh University Press.

Rajaee, Farhang (2007) *Islamism and Modernism: The Changing Discourse in Iran*, Austin: University of Texas Press.

Sadri, Ahmad and Mahmoud Sadri (2010) "Delegitimizing the Islamic Republic of Iran with a Fatwa: The Significance of Ayatollah Montazeri's Post-Election Legal Ruling of July 2009," in Nader Hashemi and Danny Postel (eds) *The People Reloaded*, Hoboken, NJ: Melville House.

Notes

1 I wish to thank Sam Kigar and the editors of this volume for editorial suggestions and comments.

2 Ali-Asghar Haj-Sayyed-Javadi, a secular writer, wrote two open analectic critical letters in fall 1978 on this issue that were published largely underground.

3 The majority of Shi'i jurists believe that this hadith is about judiciary not ruling.

4 Mustafa Rahimi, a secular writer, published his famous open letter to Ayatollah Khomeini in daily *Ayandigan* in December 31, 1978: "Why do I disagree with the Islamic Republic?"

5 Sayyed Kazem Shari'atmadari (1906–86), Sayyed Mohammad Husseini Rohani (1920–97), Sayyed Muhammad Husseini Shirazi (1928–2001), Sayyed Hasan Tabatabi'i Qomi (1911–2007) and Sayyed Muhammad Sadiq Husseini Rohani (b. 1926).

17 Muslim advocacy in America

Kathleen M. Moore

Introduction

The first months of 2011 gave the American public a sense of how deep-seated Islamophobia may be and how it can be used in the rough and tumble world of electoral politics to dishonor one's opponents. Upon becoming the new Chair of the House Committee on Homeland Security in January, US Representative Peter King (R-NY) launched a congressional inquiry into the radicalization of Muslim Americans. This climaxed in March in a public hearing on Capitol Hill. The event generated a lot of heat as people objected to King's rationale for the inquiry. Standing by remarks he made in 2004—that the vast majority of Muslim American community leaders are "an enemy living amongst us"—and in 2007—there are "too many" mosques in America— King cautioned the media not to give too much credence to what Muslim American organizations had to say about the extent of radicalization within their own community. After the hearings were over, King said in a CNN interview that "the only reason there's any chance for propaganda coming out of the hearing" can be attributed solely to the "many professional hard-core Muslim organizations attacking" him and the congressional committee (CNN 2011).

It is not surprising to find such rhetorical jousting in almost any partisan discussion of Islam in the last ten years. There are certain moral categories that political leaders and ordinary citizens apply to themselves and the social world they occupy which command our attention. Warnings about the dangers presented by "Islamofascism," "sleeper cells." and "creeping Shari'a" have become commonplace—and are generally unchallenged—in current political communication. In depicting his critics as "professional hard-core" Muslim organizations, as King does, he suggests strongly that they are menacing, perhaps even pathological, and attached to an extreme ("hard-core") ideology. By asserting they are the sole source of rumors, propaganda, and attacks, King not only discredits Muslim American advocacy; he maps his interpretation of the world around him and his overt belief that Islam plays an intrinsic part in the creation of extremist ideologies. For these and other reasons, in light of our present political landscape, the need to know about the diversity, number, and scope of Muslim American groups organizing for Islam in Washington, DC, has never been greater.

Against this background of mounting anxiety in the general political culture, religious diversity and in particular the presence of Muslims in the United States are seen as a significant challenge. The link in the social imaginary between Islam and terrorism predates 9/11 but it has been heightened by the attacks on the United States in 2001 and the climate of increased suspicion of and hostility toward Muslims and Islam. A *Newsweek* poll in the summer of 2008, at the height of the presidential election campaign, showed that nearly half the American public would not vote for a Muslim for president (Gilbert and Harder 2008). This leaves us to ask the question, what role is religion, and in particular Islam, permitted to play in government-civil society relations? This chapter is about organizing for Muslim advocacy in America. It examines the emergence of an American Muslim civic engagement at a critical historical moment when we find the dominant American political culture plagued by security fears. In what follows I relate how important American Muslim organizations have grown, built capacities, and advocated for their constituencies in the public policy field, all while living under exceptional circumstances (Moore 2010). The chapter is arranged into three parts, covering in turn the politics of organized religious groups; the growth of Muslim American associational life; and contemporary Muslim American advocacy organizations in Washington, DC. What key cultural codes and rules become internalized or contested in the process of organizing for Islam in America?

The evolution of national religious advocacy in politics

When sociologists refer to the "management" of religion in public life they are addressing the modern state's response to the so-called "depersonalization" of religious practice (Casanova 1994). In this instance, the specific issues surrounding

Figure 17.1 Imam Feisal Abdul Rauf during a rally in Times Square against the House of Representatives hearings on "Radicalization of American Muslims" chaired by Peter King (New York, March 2011). Demonstrators and religious leaders who spoke to the crowd saw the hearings as divisive and racist. Courtesy of Robert Nickelsberg/Getty Images.

Peter King's congressional hearing can be seen as an illustration of the larger problem of state and religion in late modernity. In spite of the constitutional separation of church and state, the government finds itself formulating policies relating to religion, however implicit, in order to deal with the tensions and anxieties endemic to a religiously and culturally diverse society.

Furthermore, American political culture is accepting of the political activism of religious individuals and groups. Religious activism is as old as the Republic, and although at first this was restricted to the state and local levels, religious activists were drawn more and more into national campaigns regarding issues important to religious people, such as slavery, child welfare, poverty, illiteracy, and prohibition. The common pattern from the nineteenth through the beginning of the twentieth century was for religious groups to form temporary coalitions to shape public policy on religion-related issues when these issues arose, whether in the local, state, or national arena.

Religious activism and advocacy in political channels is constantly evolving. It has grown dramatically over time, with the appearance of more and different kinds of groups as the nation has become more diverse. Early groups included the United Methodist Church, which established a Washington office in 1916 to promote prohibition; the National Catholic Welfare Conference, established in 1919; and the Quakers, who opened the first full-time registered religious lobby in 1943 to protect conscientious objector status (Fowler et al 2010: 121). By the mid-century, Jewish and Baptist organizations joined the scene, primarily to litigate church-state issues. A study released in 1950 showed that at least 16 national religious groups had offices in Washington, DC, representing Protestant, Catholic, and Jewish constituencies (Fowler et al 2010).

Since 1950 that number grew dramatically. The Pew Forum on Religion and Public Life published a study in 2011 that identified more than 200 national religious organizations engaging in public policy advocacy at least occasionally if not often. Among these are several mainline Protestant, evangelical, African American Protestant, Catholic, and Jewish interest groups. But also included in this number are many organizations from other religious communities, including Muslims, Baha'is, Hindus, Tibetan Buddhists, Sikhs, and so on. As a whole, currently religious advocacy organizations employ at least 1,000 people in the Washington, DC, area and spend over $390 million a year on influencing national public policy (Pew 2011).

Additionally, as the reach and prominence of the federal government increased over the course of the twentieth century, so too have the policy areas in which religious advocacy organizations are involved. There are many reasons for this. First, the changing modern role of federal government, with its size and scope of responsibility expanding, has acted as a catalyst for the growth of religious advocacy organizations. Many groups have been set up to monitor the impact of public policy on their religious freedom generally and, more specifically, their institutions, such as hospitals, schools, charities, and social service agencies. Second, the growth in religious pluralism and

Table 17.1: Pew Forum Report, "Lobbying for the Faithful: Religious Advocacy in Washington, DC"

Name (arranged alphabetically)	D.C. Arrival Date
Ahmadiyya Movement in Islam, USA	1948
American Islamic Congress	2006
Center for Islamic Pluralism	2005
Center for the Study of Islam and Democracy	1999
Council on American-Islamic Relations (CAIR)	1994
Free Muslims Coalition	2004
International Quranic Center	2007
International Uyghur Human Rights and Democracy Foundation	2005
ISNA, Office for Interfaith and Community Alliance	2006
Karamah: Muslim Women Lawyers for Human Rights	1993
Kashmiri American Council	1990
Minaret of Freedom Institute	1993
Muslim American Society	1993
Muslim Public Affairs Council (MPAC)	1997
National Committee of Women for a Democratic Iran	1990
Uyghur American Association	2004
World Organization for Resource Development & Education	2000

In late 2011, the Pew Forum on Religion and Public Life released a major study of religious advocacy organizations in Washington, DC—who they are, what they do, and how they do it. It charts the growth in diversity of groups. Of the 212 organizations identified in the study, 17 self-report as Muslim. A list of these organizations is provided with the date each set up offices in the Washington, DC, area.

Note: This list is limited to those organizations the IRS considers lobbyists, strictly defined as attempting to influence, or urging the public to influence, specific legislation, whether the legislation is before a legislative body, such as the US Congress or any state legislature, or before the public as a referendum, a ballot initiative, a constitutional amendment, or a similar measure. It also includes those organizations that aim their efforts at the White House, federal agencies, the courts, or educating and/or mobilizing religious constituencies on particular issues.

Source: The study may be found on the Pew Forum's website, www.pewforum.org.

the associated sense that such pluralism leads to greater competition among religious groups to promote their collective interests has created an imperative for religious groups to organize (Fowler et al 2010). Some watch one another as, for instance, in the case of groups, including but not limited to Muslims, who wish to respond to the impact that Jewish groups conventionally have had on decisions regarding US assistance in the Middle East. Third, for one reason or another, an increasing number of people of faith have determined that it is time to get organized and enter the political fray in order to defend or promote traditional values that are important to them. This finding is consistent with the greater emphasis on moral values since the 1960s, when religious activism in the civil rights movement and against the Vietnam War was pivotal; it is also consistent with the phenomenon of the "values voter"—hyped in the analysis of the 2004 national elections—who turned out to vote in record number in states and regions where issues of gay rights or abortion were on the ballot. Fourth, the changing global role of the United States as a superpower after World War II encouraged advocacy organizations to address questions of foreign aid and military intervention. To take just one small example, the national Kashmiri organization, the Kashmiri-American Council, has regularly petitioned lawmakers on Capitol Hill to support the Kashmiri people in their struggle for self-determination, and to encourage the US government to take an active role in the peace process. Other groups seek American support for their persecuted co-religionists abroad.

These are at least some of the explanations for the recent growth in religious advocacy in American politics. For theorists of modernity—as opposed to the activists and advocates on the contemporary political scene—religion is not so much about personal expressions of piety, or even about a religion's theology, as it is an important marker of individual and group identity in the public sphere. Seen through the prism of the public, then, religion has increasing salience in the general hierarchy of value. Increasingly it is understood as a symbol of identity and an arbiter of status, or in other words, as an important variable in the politics of recognition in which claims are asserted for a place at the table for distinctive perspectives in a "difference-friendly" world. These are the sort of claims that some political philosophers have placed at the center of a new paradigm for justice (e.g., Kymlicka and Banting 2006; Appiah 2005). This salience of religion in identity politics is true no more so for Muslims than for Christian evangelicals and other religious actors who work hard to mobilize their membership lists and shape public opinion, influence lawmakers, and litigate key issues of the day.

Landmark studies of prominent advocacy organizations of the mid-twentieth century—the NAACP (Vose 1973 [1959]), the American Indian Movement (Nagel 1996), and La Raza (Delgado and Stefancic 1998), to name just a few—have indicated the ways in which racial identities are fluid and can change. Racial identities have been created and re-created as activists have struggled to gain official recognition for their constituencies and to achieve the redistribution of resources in a way that would alleviate their marginalization. Many of these same studies show us that advocacy through formal organizations has been met with suspicion in the public policy arena, because it is considered to be disruptive of the social, cultural, economic, and political interests of other constituencies or groups. Thus by its very nature, the political process through which interest groups define their mission and hone their skills can be expected to draw them more than their fair share of criticism and hyperbole.

At the heart of the legislative process, whether in Congress or state houses, lies the art of compromise. While compromise might seem a dubious prospect for religious activists, legislators view it as the key to action, and advocates must accept it as a necessity (Fowler et al 2010: 127). Coalition-building is essential to reaching political goals. While religious advocacy organizations have grown in number and size, they are still miniscule when compared to the giants of the major secular lobbies, such as the National Educational Association, the American Association of Retired Persons, and a multitude of political action committees (PACS). With more than 17,000 lobbyists registered to operate in the District of Columbia alone, religious advocacy organizations are a mere drop in the bucket. That said, however, even modest political influence on Capitol Hill counts heavily on specific issues, and coalitions can be effective because of their array of expertise. In other words, a coalition of advocacy groups can be effective in an issue area because of their credibility or special expertise in that area. For instance, Quakers might lead a coalition on nuclear proliferation because of their doctrine of non-violence but Baptists would do so on religious liberty issues. Sometimes temporary coalitions develop around a single issue, such that organizations sharing a position on a particular bill in Congress might make common cause even if they tend to disagree on other matters. Or on other issues, long-time allies might part ways over particular policies. For example, liberal mainline Protestant groups have parted ways at times with their Jewish counterparts over Israeli policies regarding Jewish settlements in the Occupied Territories because the Protestants see these as unjust to Palestinians (Fowler et al 2010: 128).

Religious advocacy can be a formidable factor in politics when groups across the theological and ideological spectrum cooperate. Examples of this are evident in judicial politics. When organizations sign onto an amicus brief in a lawsuit bearing on someone's rights and freedoms, they coalesce to stake a position on constitutional values. This can be very powerful in the context of a modern pluralist America.

This overview would be incomplete without a discussion of the impact of the rapidly advancing changes in the ways we communicate, which is changing the world of political advocacy in unexpected ways. Virtually all religious advocacy groups are using new media to mobilize constituents, pressure lawmakers, and generally get their message out. Email communications with thousands of supporters, lobbying software that can monitor which constituents send emails to which members of

Congress, and social networking modalities such as Twitter and Facebook connect advocates, lay members, and politicians in an increasingly interactive web. Thus the most effective communications are those that "go viral," where, for example, not just Muslims but friends of Muslims who are removed from Muslim American advocacy organizations by two or three degrees of separation, are activated by a national campaign. We can see how this has occurred dozens if not hundreds of times since 9/11 when non-Muslim supporters have felt compelled to respond to something noxious. As this is being written, founder of the hip-hop record label Def Jam, Russell Simmons, has stepped forward in response to the decision by Lowe's Home Improvement Stores to pull advertising from the Learning Channel's reality TV show *All American Muslim* after the Florida Family Association—an evangelical organization that, according to the *New York Times*, is run by a single individual, David Caton—urged its members to email the show's advertisers (Freedman 2011). Simmons met the shortfall created by pulled advertisements by purchasing the remaining advertising spots on the show. Thus we can see the power of the internet to amplify the voice of one man (Caton) to tap into a significant groundswell of anti-Muslim bigotry, as well as the success of another individual (Simmons) to counteract the deleterious effect of Caton's actions because of what he had read about the controversy on Twitter. The most astute leaders of religious advocacy organizations will need to ride the wave of this new media, to great effect, for their communities.

Associational life

The public representation of Muslims in the United States has undergone a major transformation since the 1990s. As Table 17.1 demonstrates, most of the Muslim American advocacy organizations in our nation's capital have arrived there since the 1990s. The rising level of civic engagement and associational life among Muslims in the United States is an indication of rapid change and requires explanation. Some organizations have been around for a long time, performing services and providing community networks for their members, and staking a position on political issues from time to time but not defining themselves primarily as interest groups or lobbyists. Others are of more recent vintage. Nearly all by now have included collective political advocacy in their repertoire, in large part as a result of the more general protest movement activism (e.g., civil rights, antiwar movements) in the United States at mid-twentieth century. That is, organizations that existed prior to the "protest cycle" of the 1960s were typically service-oriented, performing important lifecycle functions such as marriages and burials, and providing members with specific types of information and education as well as a platform from which to socialize and form a base for solidarity. In contrast, political advocacy objectives became more important from the second half of the 1960s onward, once advocacy in general became an accepted part of associational life in the United States. The move toward collective political advocacy—staging events to garner public attention for claims and concerns, working political channels, and coalescing with other groups—is also explained in part by the trajectory of the development of Muslim American life from consisting of relatively small, ethnically defined and detached enclaves into a maturing, nationally networked constituency.

Early years

In the early years associational life revolved around the mosque or masjid, the house of worship for Muslim Americans. Many Muslims who immigrated to the United States early in the twentieth century showed little overt interest in participating in Islamic functions or even in identifying primarily with Islam rather than ethnicity or national origins. From what little data we have (from court records, immigration reports, etc.), we can surmise that in the period between the two world wars, ethnicity or national origins was given salience over religious modes of self-identification (GhaneaBassiri 2010: 171; Moore 1995). According to Kambiz GhaneaBassiri, aside from a small number of foreign-sponsored missionaries and Black Muslim movements, few Muslims prior to World War II thought about establishing Islam nationally in the United States. Rather, the practice of Islam was either individualistic or limited to one's immediate community (GhaneaBassiri 2010: 178). But because of the frustration in not finding social acceptance from other Americans, and the satisfaction gained by sharing experiences they had in common with other Muslims, over the years progressively more were drawn to participate more openly in religiously-based activities. These Muslims created forums for collective worship, to observe Friday prayer, and other activities that facilitated their performance of Islam.

The earliest mosques were built in the 1920s and 1930s and the mosque movement gained momentum by the mid-century. The founders of the mosque built in Cedar Rapids, Iowa, in 1934 called themselves a "league," resembling the numerous fraternal orders and benevolent societies of the day whose purpose was to perform "benevolent duties" (GhaneaBassiri 2010: 184). In Cedar Rapids, most grocery stores owned by Muslims could not afford to lose business by closing at noon for *jumu'ah* prayer on Fridays, so they held their congregational prayers on Thursday nights, and followed it with some socializing and a lecture or reading from the Qur'an (GhaneaBassiri 2010: 184). In 1936, an article in the *Cedar Rapids Gazette* reported that two sons of the community's founding families, Abdallah Igram and Hussein Sheronick, were said to be "the first in the United States to achieve a reading knowledge of the Koran in a temple class, practically all study of this type having been heretofore conducted privately" (cited in GhaneaBassiri 2010: 190). According to ethnographers of the first half of the twentieth century, mosques were built as places to socialize. When the

Cedar Rapids mosque was opened, it was suggested it be called a *nadi* (or club) so that its use would not be restricted to prayer. Other forms of associational life took hold as well; for instance in 1918 Syrian and Turkish Muslims formed the Association of Islamic Union of Cleveland (Ohio) in order to "foster social relations and solidarity among Moslems" (cited in GhaneaBassiri 2010: 185) and, in 1919, South Asian Muslims in the Sacramento area formed the Moslem Association of America in order to establish proper burial grounds in California (GhaneaBassiri 2010: 186). The Muslim community in Michigan City, Indiana, reportedly numbered 200 families in 1925 when it founded the Society of the New Era and bought a cemetery and two buildings—one for the First World War veterans and the other for social gatherings. Then in 1934 the association bought another building to use as a mosque, and divided it in two, using one half for prayers and the other for socializing.

Before the establishment of mosques in America, many early immigrants felt simultaneously isolated and empowered to practice their religion as they saw fit. If at all, they prayed in their homes and improvised ways to keep their observances. Aspects of the religion were selectively observed; many would avoid alcohol and pig products but would not perform ritual activities such as daily prayer or the fast of Ramadan. An observant member of the early Palestinian Muslim community in Chicago had this to say about his largely non-observant co-religionists:

> The Arabs in Chicago behave more like Kafir [sic] [or non-believers] rather than Muslims. They don't make the salat [or ritual prayer], they have forgotten the shahada [the confession of faith], drink like they were from Dublin, and eat ham sandwiches as if they were food from paradise. All they have on their minds is women.
> *(Cited in GhaneaBassiri 2010: 188)*

More than anything, the frustration expressed in this anecdote attests to how lonely it must have been to be an observant Muslim in the 1920s and 1930s. Generally Muslims of a wide range of ethnic backgrounds tended to downplay the differences performed through rituals and emphasized what they held in common with Americans, whether Muslim or not.

When the Islamic Center of Washington, DC, opened in 1957, it signaled that Islam was being recognized by Islamic countries as a permanent presence in the American religious landscape. The Islamic Center was built as a cooperative venture between the American Muslims and Islamic governments. The idea for building this mosque was to serve the growing number of diplomats and their families from Muslim countries, and reportedly dates back as early as 1944 when the Turkish ambassador passed away in Washington, DC, and there was no suitable site to hold a memorial service. Following this, American Muslims cooperated with a number of diplomats to raise money to build the mosque and 14 Muslim countries contributed. According to

GhaneaBassiri, it was the first of its kind to be built in the "architectural vocabulary" of the mosques in the Muslim world, incorporating motifs from various Islamic civilizations (2010: 255). President Eisenhower spoke at its opening ceremony, saying that "thousands of Americans" live, work, "and grow in understanding" among Muslim people in the United States, and that "under the American Constitution, this Center, this place of worship, is as welcome as any similar edifice of any religion" (GhaneaBassiri 2010: 256). This official endorsement of the Islamic Center not only brought national attention, it rhetorically named religion—aspirationally—as the medium for understanding and cooperation.

Later years

There have been significant changes in the demographics of the Muslim American population in five decades since the Islamic Center of Washington, DC, opened, which help to explain the pronounced changes we see in the collective representation of Muslim American interests. To understand this, we need to take into account that the immigration history of Muslim Americans is divided into three waves, the last of which brought the overwhelming majority of Muslims to the United States beginning in the mid-1960s, when US immigration policy changed. Until the 1960s, the size of Muslim communities in the United States was limited, and communication among them, even more so. In 1965, the US Congress passed an immigration reform law that removed national origins quotas that had been an obstacle to extensive immigration from non-European countries including those in the Islamic world, and replaced them with specific preferences for family reunification, professional and occupational skills, and humanitarian ends. With this turning point in immigration policy, a steady upward trend in the number of immigrants admitted from the so-called "Third World" sending countries meant that hundreds of thousands of new arrivals from Arab, African, South Asian, and East Asian countries (many of them Muslim majority) came to the United States. While earlier waves of Muslim skilled laborers had found jobs in industry (such as automobile manufacturing) and agriculture, this new wave contained many professionals and graduate students bound for graduate schools across the United States. Students were not confined by immigration provisions, since they came to the United States on non-immigrant student visas. Many began to arrive in the United States under the auspices of the Fulbright Program established by Congress in 1946. Between 1948 and 1965 the number of students from Muslim countries increased fivefold; some belonged to Islamist movements, inspired by ideologues such as Sayyid Qutb (Egypt) and Ala' al-Mawdudi (India/Pakistan). Thus inspired, these students had a significant impact on the subsequent organizing for Islam in America. In 1963, they founded a national organization, the Muslim Students Association of the United States and Canada (MSA), at the University of Illinois Urbana-Champaign, to serve the needs of this new wave of sojourners. Within five years of its founding, the Muslim Students Association assumed the responsibility of coordinating annual conventions and various other community events including the two Eid holidays and the observance of Ramadan, the month of fasting (Haddad 1986).

In the following two decades, the MSA became the most successful national organization of Muslim Americans founded by immigrants. When it formed in 1963 it had ten affiliates at various colleges and universities. By 1968, it already had 105 local associations across the US and Canada, and began printing books and pamphlets on Islam for both Muslims and non-Muslims. It published a magazine called *Al-Ittihad*; established a charitable fund; gave lectures on Islam to local Muslim and non-Muslim organizations; and made prison visits. It had no center for its operations until 1973 when it founded its headquarters in Gary, Indiana. Later this was relocated to its permanent headquarters in Plainfield, Indiana. The students who founded the MSA did so in part because they were dispersed throughout the country, and the organization sought to strengthen "fraternal bonds" among Muslim students (GhaneaBassiri 2010: 266). For MSA activists, adherence to Islamic beliefs was not only a religious duty but a means to practice a comprehensive way of life in the modern world that would transcend ethnic and racial barriers. In many of the MSA publications, Sayyid Qutb is cited to affirm that the faith of Islam is "divinely ordained" and to propagate a utopian understanding that soon became emblematic of the MSA: "Islam is the solution" for humanity's problems (cited in GhaneaBassiri 2010: 267). Within the pluralistic context of the United States, the MSA realized the unique opportunity to advocate a pan-Islamic, complete way of life that displaces cultural, ethnic, or linguistic specificity. In other words, the novelty of the MSA was in the normative vision of its leadership that Islam is the universal bond among a diverse population of Muslims in the United States.

Social scientists have indicated the way new organizational practices reconstitute both the objects and the subjects of practice. In various domains, major shifts in practice are tied to ontological changes in the meaning of particular objects as well as creating and being carried by new subject positions closely associated with those practices (Friedland 2009: 53). In the domain of associational life, the meaning assigned to Islam—whether normative or descriptive, individualistic or communitarian—does not solely produce the specific patterns of social life but combines with the larger institutional environment to structure collective action. Within that larger environment, there are practical consequences; associations provide substantive guides for collective action and are durable to the extent that they are reinforced through interaction or legitimation. The interactive process between an association and its larger institutional environment is one in which "the moral becomes factual" and the question of how social arrangements and beliefs come to be taken for granted resonates with political theorists' conception of a "third level" of power: "the means through which power influences, shapes or determines conceptions of the necessities, possibilities and strategies of challenge in situations of latent conflict" (Clemens and Cook 1999: 446). Regular patterns of social action may be constrained by external forces, produced by internalized beliefs, or a combination of the two. But what is most clear is that with respect to religious associations, the regularity of these patterns will be strengthened when the two (external and internal) sources coincide and reinforce each other. This we will see in the following section, when we look at how contemporary Muslim American advocacy organizations are building a reasonable degree of political effectiveness.

Contemporary Muslim American organizations

Currently approximately eight in ten young Muslim Americans, between the ages of 18 and 29, say that religion plays an important part in their daily lives, and this translates into increased civic engagement and support for Muslim American organizations (Gallup Center for Muslim Studies 2011). The local mosque remains the central institution of religious and cultural life for Muslim Americans, young and old. But a relatively recent phenomenon, the rise of political organizations to advocate for Muslim American interests, is also notable. In this section I provide brief profiles of selected Muslim American organizations in the United States representing the diverse histories, orientations, and missions found among these organizations. These provide a basic history of the organizations' origins and purposes. I do not try to cover the full spectrum of Muslim American organizations. For instance, I do not include any of the several social service providers or the governing councils of masjids or Islamic centers. These types of organizations tend to be local institutions that deliver their services to a local constituency and interact with other agencies within their specific locations and areas of expertise. Additionally, the vastly important area of African American Islam is beyond the scope of this chapter, which concentrates on the advocacy organizations established by immigrants and their children, which to some degree may also represent African American Muslims but are not established or run by them. Rather, here the primary focus is on organizations claiming a national constituency dealing with matters that affect national policy or potentially impact Muslim Americans across the country. This is *not* to say that the national organizations that are discussed here do not help Muslim communities with day-to-day religious issues, improving education, and encouraging personal piety. They pursue these goals as well, in particular, through their regional chapters. But primarily these organizations strive to determine which concerns receive attention as a "Muslim issue" in the media, in government circles, and in the broader public debates in the United States. In recent years, these organizations have become proficient at responding to negative portrayals of Muslims and Islam in local and national media outlets, and have developed political channels to purse a range of policy agendas. For instance, the Muslim Public Affairs Council, the Center for Global Understanding, and the Muslim Public Service Network are just a few examples of organizations that offer Washington, DC, internship programs for college students with the objective of encouraging career paths in public, non-profit, and government institutions. They advocate working within the civic, legal and political institutions across the nation and build coalitions with other non-Muslim organizations and make grassroots efforts to address pressing issues in their regional and national communities.

Several Muslim American organizations embrace the tools provided by new media to reach their members. Social networking through Twitter, Facebook, blogs, and online videos is common. Web destinations such as YouTube are filled with content from Muslim American organizations. Increasingly these organizations' messages are designed to appeal to young Muslims raised in the United States. Thus the internet and other new technologies have made it easier for Muslim organizations in the United States to reach a younger generation of Muslims and are now a permanent feature.

Several government agencies have played a pivotal role in classifying advocacy organizations from several disparate communities as a unified whole and, in the process of securitizing the nation-state against future terrorism, have effectively given a singular, racialized identity to all Muslims and those who resemble Muslims (Love 2011a). For instance, the US Department of Justice has convened "Middle Eastern American" meetings with representatives from a range of advocacy organizations in order to address problems of national security and civil liberties.

Surprisingly few women have served as top executives of Muslim American organizations, especially given that when many of these organizations came into being, civil rights laws had already been enacted to promote non-discrimination on the basis of race, color, sex, national origins, and creed (Love 2011b). Notable exceptions include Ingrid Mattson, the president of the Islamic Society of North America from 2006 to 2010; Hadia Mubarak, the former president of the Muslim Students Association, and the first US-born person to be elected to that position; Dr. Azizah al-Hibri, the founding executive director of the organization Karamah: Muslim Women Lawyers for Human Rights; and Farhana Khera, the founding Executive Director of Muslim Advocates.

Islamic Society of North America (ISNA)

The Islamic Society of North America (ISNA), founded in 1983 as an outgrowth of the Muslim Students Association (established 1963), functions as a broad-based organization that holds annual conventions attended by Muslims of a wide range of backgrounds and orientations. It is an umbrella organization representing more than

Table 17.2: Major Muslim American advocacy organizations and the dates they were founded

Name	Date Founded
Muslim Students Association	1963
Islamic Society of North America (ISNA)	1982
Muslim Public Affairs Council (MPAC)	1988
American Muslim Alliance/American Muslim Taskforce	1989
Karamah: Muslim Women Lawyers for Human Rights	1993
Council on American Islamic Relations (CAIR)	1994
National Association of Muslim Lawyers (NAML)	2000
South Asian Americans Leading Together	2000
Institute for Social Policy Understanding (ISPU)	2002
Muslim Advocates	2005
Assembly of Turkic American Federations (ATAF)	2011

Note: This list of organizations is different from the one provided by the Pew Forum in Table 17.1, and in some instances, the founding dates are different from those provided by the Pew Forum. This is because the information provided here pertains to the life of each organization, whether or not they advocate on public policy or try to influence public opinion on a political matter. In contrast, the Pew Forum study provides information about the registration of organizations as bona fide political lobbyists, according to criteria established by the IRS.

2,000 mosques and Islamic centers in the United States and Canada. Recently much attention has been paid to tracing the origins of the Islamic Society of North America (ISNA) and its predecessor, the Muslim Students Association (MSA)—as well as the Muslim American Society (MAS) and the Council on American-Islamic Relations (CAIR), organizations founded in the 1990s—to the Muslim Brotherhood (Pew 2010). However, regardless of any (unfounded) past affiliation with the Muslim Brotherhood movement, the current leadership of all three organizations have renounced any ties and have concentrated their activities on advocacy and civil rights and educational issues within the United States.

The ISNA has long been a service organization that has periodically taken a position on policy. More recently, in the past decade, it has established a lobbying arm in Washington, DC, which it calls ISNA, Office of Interfaith and Community Alliances. On

February 19, 2011, in light of the congressional inquiry into the radicalization of Muslim Americans conducted by Congressman Peter King, ISNA held an Interfaith and Government Forum in Crystal City, Virginia, to strategize what Americans can do to counteract anti-Muslim bigotry.

The Fiqh Council of North America, an affiliate of ISNA, is a prominent network of religious scholars from the United States and Canada which offers Islamic legal advice on the application of religious principles.

The Muslim Youth of North America (MYNA) is also sponsored by ISNA and plays an important role in staging conferences and events with an Islamic focus. Divided into four regions covering Canada and the eastern, central, and western United States, MYNA provides occasions for young people to talk about issues of common concern and to develop leadership skills.

Muslim Public Affairs Council (MPAC)

Founded in 1988 by the Islamic Center of Southern California, MPAC quickly became a national organization that aims to inform and shape public opinion regarding issues of importance to the nation. It also places considerable resources behind a multifaceted program of education for young leaders to encourage careers in public service, and works with law enforcement agencies to insure the protection of Muslim Americans' civil liberties. This organization has an affiliate, the Muslim Women's League, which promotes women's rights.

Council on American Islamic Relations (CAIR)

Founded in 1994, CAIR emerged at a time when certain pundits were bringing public attention to the problem of "militant Islam." In the same year, PBS aired a Steve Emerson documentary called *Jihad in America*, which advanced the idea that some ill-defined Islamist ideologies and organizations represented a credible threat to "the West," which was similar to what the communist threat had been during the Cold War. CAIR's mission is to educate the American public about Islam, to challenge defamatory representations of Islam and Muslims, to protect the civil liberties of Muslim Americans, and to lobby on behalf of Muslim American interests. Soon after its founding, CAIR was baptized by fire, gaining national attention for its advocacy for Muslim Americans in the aftermath of the Oklahoma City bombing on April 19, 1995. It published a report, *A Rush to Judgment*, which documented more than 200 incidents of harassment and hate crimes against Muslim Americans in the days following the bombing. Since then CAIR has regularly published reports about backlash discrimination, and is considered by many to be the premier Muslim American advocacy group.

National Association of Muslim Lawyers/Muslim Advocates

The National Association of Muslim Lawyers (NAML), founded in 2000, and joined by its sister organization, Muslim Advocates, in 2005, is a national legal advocacy and educational organization that promotes the protection of freedom, justice, and equality regardless of faith. It uses the tools of legal advocacy, policy engagement, and education to meet its aims. In its mission statement this organization states that it endorses the founding principles of American constitutionalism, and believes that these principles can be fulfilled without compromising the nation's security. Since its founding in 2005, Muslim Advocates has established itself as a networking agent among the nation's leading lawyers, community and mosque leaders, government officials, the media, and allies in the human rights and national security fields. In addition to its advocacy efforts, Muslim Advocates has provided technical assistance to Muslim charities to help them be in legal compliance.

Assembly of Turkic American Federations (ATAF)

The Assembly of Turkic American Federations (ATAF) opened in 2011 in Washington, DC, to serve as an umbrella organization to coordinate the various activities of six regional "dialogue" associations of the Hizmet Movement in the United States (Hendrick 2012). The Hizmet Movement—associated with the retired Turkish Islamic preacher and writer, M. Fethullah Gulen, living in self-imposed exile in Pennsylvania since 1998—also funds several Gulen-inspired private schools in the United States, including the Pinnacle Academy in suburban Washington, DC, aimed primarily at Turkish-American communities. Additionally, members of the Hizmet Movement have opened several dozen public charter schools that cater to non-Muslims, offering a rigorous science- and technology-based curriculum primarily in low-income neighborhoods. They also run a satellite cable television station called Ebru TV, which broadcasts a range of family-oriented educational and lifestyle programs.

Conclusion

Civil society, a seedbed for civic virtues and competence, consists of the myriad associations and institutions that point citizens away from isolation and toward their shared interests with others. Religious institutions as a whole, including places of worship, faith based institutions such as hospitals, schools, and service organizations as well as advocacy organizations, represent the single largest component of civil society. Historically, religious institutions have played an important role in generating civic engagement. More than half of the volunteer activity in the United States takes place within religious settings, nearly 60 percent of Americans are members of a house of worship, and more than one third are associated with religious groups other than houses of worship. Thus religious institutions are bound to have a significant impact on the civic life and, in turn, on the abilities of American Muslim leaders to influence politics.

Associations themselves become conduits of moral and behavioral codes, rules of conduct and ritual guidelines. The argument is that people are more likely to participate in politics, and to be more effective participants, when they have experience doing a variety of things that occur frequently in their places of worship, such as organizing meetings, electing governing boards, writing letters, and speaking in public. The assumption is that basic civic skills are transferable, and what is learned in one venue can be put to use in another. Houses of worship and other religious associations are important for building skills because they provide opportunities that participants might not otherwise have.

The time period covered in this chapter has witnessed an ever greater diversity of voices competing to be heard and to get their agenda on the table of the national discussion. Instances like the congressional hearing on the "radicalization of American Muslims" have led to what many consider a confusion of the tongues. What are we to believe from all of the bombast? Many Muslim American groups have emerged with the purpose of providing reliable and accurate information, and this has led to increased coalition building among religious groups and between political parties and religious groups. We can reasonably expect this pattern to continue.

Another inescapable conclusion is the resilience and adaptability of pluralism in the United States. For all its diversity, the nation appears to be in a strong position to allow both religious and political perspectives to coexist. Of course, it is inevitable that viewpoints will clash, and that is why the legal relationship between religion and politics is so important.

Summary

- Generally, political activism by religious individuals and groups has been a longstanding tradition in the United States, notwithstanding the principle of separation of church and state.
- In the case of Muslim Americans, civic engagement and associational life have grown dramatically since the 1960s.
- Much of this growth has happened in a political landscape characterized by reductionist generalizations about alleged connections between terrorism and Islam.

Discussion points

- Discuss religious activism in American politics, and how moral values can motivate individuals and groups to become involved in political causes.

- What events of the 1960s were of particular importance for the relationship of politics and religion?
- Discuss the role of religion in the early mosque movement in the United States.
- What impact did the arrival of foreign students have in the organization of Islam in the United States? What impact did changes in immigration law in the 1960s have on the growth of Muslim American communities and their representative advocacy organizations?
- How do events such as the Peter King congressional inquiry into the "radicalization" of Muslim Americans present a particular challenge?

Further reading

Haddad, Yvonne Yazbeck, Jane I. Smith, and Kathleen M. Moore (2011 [2006]) *Muslim Women in America: The Challenge of Islamic Identity Today*, New York and Oxford: Oxford University Press.

This book represents the diversity of Muslim women in the United States and the roles of Muslim American women in public and private lives.

Nadam, Ajil (2006) *Portrait of a Giving Community: Philanthropy by the Pakistani-American Diaspora*, Cambridge, MA: Harvard University Press.

Based on the giving habits of Pakistani-Americans, this book studies the history, demography, and institutional geography of Pakistani-Americans and looks at how charitable giving and volunteerism are tools to navigate multiple identities.

Nimer, Mohamed (2002) *The North American Resource Guide: Muslim Community Life in the United States and Canada*, New York: Routledge.

This book provides a synthesis of Muslim values and institutions in the two countries and contains a directory of schools, mosques, and other organizations.

Peek, Lori (2011) *Behind the Backlash: Muslim Americans after 9/11*, Philadelphia: Temple University Press.

This book provides personal narratives of Muslim American men and women who experienced discrimination before and after 9/11 and the ways they have adapted since the terrorist attacks.

Sinno, Abdulkadr H. (ed.) (2009) *Muslims in Western Politics*, Bloomington, IN: Indiana University Press.

This collection of papers examine questions of political representation, identity politics, civil liberties, immigration, and security issues in North American and Western European societies.

References

Appiah, Kwame Anthony (2005) *The Ethics of Identity*, Princeton, NJ: Princeton University Press.
Casanova, Jose (1994) *Public Religion in the Modern World*, Chicago: University of Chicago Press.

Clemens, Elizabeth S. and James M. Cook (1999) "Politics and Institutionalism: Explaining Durability and Change," *Annual Review of Sociology*, 25: 441–66.

CNN (2011) "Interview with New York Congressman Peter King," March 10, available at www.lexisnexis.com.proxy.library.ucsb.edu:2048/hottopics/lnacademic/? (accessed August 26, 2011).

Delgado, Richard and Jean Stefancic (1998) *The Latino/a Condition: A Critical Reader*, New York: New York University Press.

Fowler, Robert Booth, Allen D. Hertzke, Laura R. Olson, and Kevin R. den Dulk (2010) *Religion and Politics in America: Faith, Culture, and Strategic Choices*, 4th edn, Boulder, CO: Westview Press.

Freedman, Samuel G. (2011) "Waging a One-Man War on American Muslims," *New York Times*, December 16, available at www.nytimes.com/2011/12/17/us/on-religion-a-one-man-war-on-american-muslims.html?_r=1&src=tp&smid=fb-share (accessed December 16, 2011).

Friedland, Roger (2009) "Institution, Practice, and Ontology: Toward a Religious Sociology," in Renate E. Meyer et al (eds), *Institutions and Ideology*, Bingley, UK: Emerald Books, 45–84.

Gallup Center for Muslim Studies (2011) "Muslim Americans: Faith, Freedom, and the Future," available at www.gallup.com/se/ms/153611/REPORT-Muslim-Americans-Faith-Freedom-Future.aspx (accessed January 24, 2011).

GhaneaBassiri, Kambiz (2010) *A History of Islam in America*, London: Cambridge University Press.

Gilbert, Mary and Amy Harder (2008) "Religion and the Race," *The National Journal*, July, available at www.nationaljournal.com/njonline/religion-and-the-race-20080714 (accessed January 24, 2011).

Haddad, Yvonne Yazbeck (1986) *A Century of Islam in America*, Washington, DC: American Institute for Islamic Affairs.

Hendrick, Joshua D. (2012) *The Community: Globalization and Post-Islamism in Turkey*, New York: New York University Press.

Kymlicka, Will and Keith G. Banting (2006) *Multiculturalism and the Welfare State: Recognition and Redistribution in Contemporary Democracies*, Oxford: Oxford University Press.

Love, Erik (2011a) "Confronting Islamophobia: Civil Rights Advocacy in the United States," doctoral dissertation thesis, UC Santa Barbara, submitted March 2011.

—— (2011b) "Gendered Work in Confronting Islamophobia and Anti-Arab Racism," in Michael Suleiman and Suad Joseph (eds) *Arab American Women*, Syracuse, NY: Syracuse University Press.

Moore, Kathleen M. (1995) *Al-Mughtaribun: American Law and the Transformation of Muslim Life in the United States*, Albany, NY: SUNY Press.

—— (2010) *The Unfamiliar Abode: Islamic Law in the United States and Britain*, New York: Oxford University Press.

Nagel, Joane (1996) *American Indian Ethnic Renewal: Red Power and the Resurgence of Identity and Culture*, London and New York: Oxford University Press.

Pew Forum on Religion and Public Life (2010) "Muslim Networks and Movements in Western Europe," September, available at http://pewforum.org/Muslim/Muslim-Networks-and-Movements-in-Western-Europe.aspx (accessed January 24, 2011).

—— (2011) "Lobbying for the Faithful: Religious Advocacy Groups in Washington, DC," November, available at www.pewforum.org/lobbying-religious-advocacy-groups-in-washington-dc.aspx (accessed December 9, 2011).

Vose, Clement E. (1973 [1959]) *Caucasians Only: The Supreme Court, the NAACP, and Restrictive Covenants*, Berkeley: University of California Press.

18 Women and Islamic law in Bangladesh: finding a space for the fatwa

Tiffany A. Hodge

Introduction

In January 2001, the High Court of Bangladesh ruled it illegal to pronounce *fatwas* (opinions on a point of law), after hearing a case in which a Muslim woman was forced, by edict of a local religious authority, to marry her ex-husband's cousin. Shahida did not want to divorce her husband; nor did her husband want to divorce her, despite his pronunciation of *talak* (divorce) in anger. They continued to live together as a married couple and even had a child. But their neighbor, many months later, issued a *fatwa* that their marriage had been dissolved by the *talak*; if Shahida wanted to stay with her husband, she would have to marry another man before she could re-marry her husband. This type of arrangement, called *hilla/hila* in Bangladesh (*tahlīl* marriage), allows a woman to return to her husband—if both so desire it—after *talak* has been pronounced, but requires her to marry another person, consummate the marriage, and divorce before returning to her first husband. Having followed the directive, however, Shahida was left to face a husband who no longer wanted her. The High Court took up the case *suo moto* (on its own initiative), with two human rights organizations arguing against the use of *fatwas* (*Editor* vs. *District Magistrate* 2002: 228–32).[1]

The legal battle did not stop there, although it took ten years before the Supreme Court ruled in May 2011 that *fatwas* were not of themselves illegal but could not be used to punish anyone. High-profile Islamic scholars have accepted the judgment as satisfactory, women's rights activists are less pleased. While related cases might be brought forward in the future, it seems that, for now, the Bangladeshi legal system has arrived at a momentous decision in dealing with legal pluralism in a modern, Muslim-majority nation-state. In the ten years since the initial ruling, a number of questions have been raised that highlight the tensions between those who want official status for Islamic law in the country and those who believe Islamic law cannot conform to standards for human rights and women's rights. The cases raise a number of questions related to larger concerns in Bangladesh: What are *fatwas*? Who should be allowed to give them? And, most important, what is the place of Islamic law within the modern nation-state?

Shari'a (Islamic law) continues to be very important for Muslims today, but what it means to follow Islamic law—and which competing legal systems vie for authority—depends on the context. Bangladesh, like many Muslim-majority countries, has retained aspects of *shari'a* in only one area: family law. Women's rights activists are well aware that many of the key provisions in the legal code meant to protect women from unilateral decisions made by their husbands are not followed. Islamists insist that the family law code is not "pure" *shari'a*.

Family law is not, however, only enforced through the state courts. Bangladeshi Muslims face competing legal systems. A weak state and rampant corruption in the legal system ensure that other, non-state legal forums continue to thrive. Legal pluralism does not necessarily provide for equitable distribution of justice, but non-state options are often cheaper and more time-efficient than the state courts. As conflicts and disputes arise in their daily lives, many Bangladeshis choose to go to legal forums not associated with the state. Other authorities—including religious scholars and community leaders—are called upon to solve problems and answer questions. The informal, community court (*salish*) to which Bangladeshis often take their disputes has deep roots in pre-colonial structures of adjudication in rural areas, but it has also been the site of horrific violence against women, through an instrument called a *fatwa*.

Examining the discourse surrounding the *fatwa* provides insight into the religious and legal complexities facing Bangladeshi Muslims today. Bangladesh has often been portrayed as a country struggling to decide between two options: Bengali cultural nationalism (associated with secularism) and religious fundamentalism.[2] The situation for individual Muslims is obviously far more complex, particularly for poor women and their families, who rarely make decisions based solely on their position on this ideological schism.[3] From the state's perspective, the proliferation of authority presents a problem, but it is often left to legal activists to compel the judiciary to act on behalf of women and the marginalized. This chapter explores the legal and religious challenges faced by the Bangladeshi government, as well as rights activists, in the attempt to balance the demands of Muslim scholars, a public with varied views on how to live as a Muslim, and the standards of equality for women.

"Fanatics with wrong views"

The nation-state of Bangladesh gained independence in 1971. Prior to the 1971 Liberation War, the area was known as East Pakistan, separated from its western wing (today's Pakistan) by the wide expanse of India. The population of East Pakistan was majority Muslim, but differed in ethnic, cultural, and linguistic background from its western Pakistani counterparts. Pakistan as an independent country was built upon the notion of a "Muslim homeland" for the Muslims of colonial India. This Muslim homeland did not necessarily mean an Islamic state; the constitution and laws of independent Pakistan were not purposefully based upon the Qur'an and *sunna*. Relations between the wings steadily deteriorated, however, as West Pakistan treated East Pakistan as a colony of its own. Economic development occurred at a significantly faster rate in the western wing, which served as the seat of governmental power. In addition to the enforced economic hierarchy, the West Pakistani leaders considered East Pakistanis, with their Bengali culture, as not "Muslim" enough. One of the primary languages of West Pakistan, Urdu, was set as the language of the state, while Bengali (Bangla) was devalued; this action was undertaken despite the numerical majority enjoyed by Bengali speakers.

As an independent nation, Bangladesh has struggled to overcome a number of obstacles. While the nation was established as a secular democracy, successive governments have sought to emphasize the Muslim character of the nation and strengthen ties to other Muslim-majority countries. In the 1980s, Islam was declared the state religion and the constitution was amended to include religious phrasing. Because of the ambiguous positions taken by the government on the subject of religion and the state—in addition to the state's inability (or disinterest) to protect vulnerable citizens and deliver legal justice—it is not at all uncommon for Bangladeshis to take their concerns to community leaders not authorized or monitored by the government. It is within these informal, local spheres that the *fatwa* has generated so much national attention.

Over the past two decades in Bangladesh, the term *fatwa* has been used publicly to refer to coercive, corporal punishments meted out against (mostly) poor women for alleged sexual indiscretions.[4] One of the earliest, media-covered cases involved a young woman accused of adultery named Nurjahan, who was buried up to her waist and stoned. She later committed suicide. Until the incident was reported in the news media, the police did not investigate or charge anyone with a crime. In the years following this case, researchers have documented many more incidences, although most believe the number is far higher than reported.[5] Deena Nargis and Faustina Pereira, well-known human rights activists in Dhaka, note that the punishments from *fatwa*s range from inhumane treatment such as "shaving their victims' heads, or parading them around the village, or ostracizing them" to "physical mutilation or even death" (Nargis and Pereira 2002: 216). The brutality involved, and the fact that the violence is most often directed at women and justified as *shari'a,* has concerned many secularists and women's rights activists who fear the possibility of Islamic law gaining greater influence in the country.

It was in response to this rise in *fatwa*-induced violence that, in late 2000, two High Court judges decided to take up the case of Shahida, despite the fact that no one involved in the situation had approached the courts for a ruling. After reading about her plight in a newspaper, *The Daily Bangla Patrika*, the judges issued a show cause ruling against the district magistrate in her area, asking why nothing had been done either to protect Shahida or arrest the perpetrators. The lack of police involvement during or after the forced marriage is not unusual in Bangladesh. Even in more public, physically violent cases of *fatwa* punishments, the police rarely intervene and suits are seldom brought against those responsible.

The judges ruled that, not only had the district magistrate failed to punish the perpetrators of this particular *fatwa*, but that *fatwa*s in general were illegal. The judges explained in this case, however, that they disagreed even with the pronouncement of the *fatwa* against Shahida on the question of *talak*. In arguing this point, they utilized Qur'anic verses (in particular, 4:4 and 2:231), *hadith* (reported speech or action of the Prophet Muhammad), and state law, in the form of the Muslim Family Law Ordinance (discussed below). They disparaged those who would support the tradition of instant divorce, saying that such men, who receive their education from *madrasas* (religious schools), "are becoming fanatics with wrong views. They must be defect [sic] in their education and their attitude" (*Editor* 2002: 231).

Figure 18.1 Female activists shout slogans during a protest against the public caning of women in Dhaka (June 2009). A spike in harsh punishments raised concerns among women's and human rights activists. Courtesy of Munir Uz Zaman/AFP/Getty Images.

While many human rights activists cheered the decision, the Supreme Court issued a stay on the ruling. The court did not take up this particular case again until March 2011. In the ten years between the two proceedings, the right-of-center Bangladesh National Party (BNP) gained power in the 2001 election season that included a number of incidences of violence against women and minorities. From 2006 to 2008, the country then experienced two years of a "caretaker" government backed by the military.[6] In 2008, the left-leaning Awami League took power in a landslide election. Throughout this decade, newspapers continued to publish reports of *fatwa*-induced violence, but it was not until 2010 that another major case on *fatwas* came before the High Court. This writ petition, filed by five human rights organizations, including the Bangladesh Mahila Parishad and Ain-o-Salish Kendra, covered a number of incidences of extra-judicial violence carried out following *fatwas*.

The judges in this case were clear in stating that they were not ruling on the validity of *issuing fatwas*; rather, their case was "concerned with the question of imposition of extra-judicial punishments including those in the name of execution of Fatwa" (Hossain 2001: 20). The judiciary thus left open the possibility that Islamic law, through *fatwa* pronouncements, could still be lawful, so long as the pronouncers did not impose punishment. The May 2011 judgment supports this ruling.

Table 18.1 Court cases and judgments

Court cases	Judgments
2001, on the issue of *hilla*	Fatwas deemed illegal, in presumably all cases
2010, variety of instances, including several assaults	Fatwa punishments cannot contravene Bangladeshi law
2011, revisiting *hilla* case	Fatwas legal, so long as they do not contravene Bangladeshi law, particularly with regard to punishment

From *shari'a* to code

While there are those in Bangladesh—including scholars and lay-people—who speak of the need to have *shari'a* as the state law, it is not entirely clear what they mean. *Shari'a,* as is often noted by Islamic Studies scholars, refers to the whole of divine guidance from God. As Bernard Weiss describes it, this "right path ... constitutes an entire way of life" (Weiss 2006: 18). Despite the ways in which the term is often used, *shari'a* does not refer to a body of rules, collected in an easily disseminated form. Rather, it is the totality of God's directives for human action, and it exists fully only with God. This conception of "the law" means that humans can only *attempt* to discern God's will.

The attempt at understanding, or *fiqh,* is carried out by highly trained scholars. These scholars, the jurists (*fuqaha*), have played an important role in Islamic legal history; those who have surpassed the highest levels of education are eligible to engage in the interpretation of the Qur'an and *hadith.* The jurist may have a number of roles within the Muslim community: as a teacher or professor, as a judge (*kazi,* or Arabic *qadi*), or as a jurisconsult (*mufti*). The *kazi* has often been associated with the ruling power. As *mufti,* the scholar provides learned opinions (*fatwas*) to questions on Islamic law and may or not be affiliated in any way with the state.

Scholars of Islamic legal history describe the *fatwa* as a non-binding opinion, given in response to a question by a petitioner. Muhammad Khalid Masud calls it the "most enduring form of guidance in Muslim society" (2009: 339). In Bangladesh, this conception of a *fatwa* is still practiced by *muftis.* Not unlike their historic predecessors, they hear petitioners' requests for a learned opinion on a legal problem. *Muftis* in the region where I have conducted fieldwork note that, while family law figures prominently in the requests by petitioners, many supplicants come to ask for learned opinions on *zakat* (alms), *namaz* (prayer), and *roza* (fasting).

The process by which *muftis* give *fatwas* to their petitioners has been a part of South Asian Muslim life for centuries. It has served as a means through which laypersons could gain advice on how to live piously or correctly. *Muftis* still engage in this endeavor today, but the influence and role of religious scholars, and particularly that of the *kazi*, in society changed significantly in the eighteenth century. I will only briefly note here the history of Islamic law in South Asia, as a number of scholars have written on this topic.[7]

With the increasing reach of the British in the subcontinent in the eighteenth century came a focus on "discovering" the law in such a way that it could be administered by the new colonial power. The personal (family) laws[8] of the various religious communities under their rule became a major focus for colonial authorities as they instituted what John Griffiths calls legal pluralism in the 'juristic sense' (Merry 1988: 871, citing Griffiths). In order to create a legal system consisting of "different bodies of law for different groups of the population varying by ... religion," (Merry 1988: 871), the British authorities relied upon translated religious texts. Sir William Jones, colonialist and philologist, was prominent among those who insisted that the authentic and authoritative Muslim (or Hindu) laws to govern the population could be found in the oldest legal texts, if only one could find and translate them into English (Cohn 1996: 69). Often referred to as Anglo-Muhammadan law, this construction had become something quite other than *shari'a,* or even *fiqh,* by the very act of attempting to codify and fix it in time.

The colonial courts depended on indigenous *kazis* who "served as mechanisms of inquiry, while the classical religious-legal texts, whatever their genuine relevance, were taken as the key to understanding colonized cultures and societies" (Anderson 1993: 172). So, for example, a legal text such as *al-Hidaya,*[9] despite being only one of many legal texts used by pre-colonial *kazis* and *muftis,* served as the foundation for the formulation of Islamic law in the subcontinent. *Al-Hidaya,* translated into English by Charles Hamilton in 1791, was followed by the translation of *al-Sirajiyya*, a treatise on inheritance, and *Fatawa Alamgiri,* a compendium of Muslim law assembled under the Mughal Emperor Aurangzeb. While Jones often consulted Muslim legal scholars early in his career as in India, he had a profound distrust of the "fallible and seemingly overly susceptible" religious scholars whose "interpretations and knowledge had to be found or reconstituted" (Cohn 1996: 69). Gradually the *kazis* lost their influence, and Jones embarked on a project to create a complete digest of Muslim law based only upon a few medieval legal texts.

The use of texts without reference to social situations ignored the actual flexibility of Islamic law. Gregory Kozlowski has argued that the colonial process produced a modern state which "has given Muslims a Personal Law with rules clearer and more rigorously enforced than in any previous epoch" (Kozlowski 1993: 77). Such a focus on texts also served to hypostasize Muslim law and fix it in time: the British understanding of Muslim law was based upon a few historical texts that were taken as the final word on law, thus "presenting the *sharī'a* as something it had never been: a fixed body of immutable rules beyond the realm of interpretation and judicial discretion" (Anderson 1993: 176).

The actions of the British served as a foundation for Muslim personal law in the subcontinent long after their colonial rule ended. The creation of a domain of "personal law" ignored the fact that "both Hindu and Muslim 'world-views' considered all aspects of life [to be] equally subject to religious rules," thus producing "a religious/private sphere and a secular/political sphere" (Lemons 2010: 8; quoting Parashar and Dhanda 2008: *xi*). This dichotomy was reproduced in the Muslim Family Law Ordinance of 1961, even as the legislation attempted to "modernize" Islamic law as practiced in South Asia.

Islamic law in Bangladesh

MFLO, 1961

The issue of *hilla* that persuaded the High Court to declare *fatwa*s illegal was addressed, if only briefly, in the Muslim Family Law Ordinance (MFLO), 1961, the most comprehensive legislation with regard to collective personal (family) law in independent Pakistan, and, subsequently, in Bangladesh. It is the only part of contemporary Bangladeshi law that can be termed "Islamic." The Commission on Marriage and Family Laws which advocated the reforms later instituted in the MFLO included only one member of the *ulama* (plural of *alim*, a learned, knowledgeable person; the scholars), Maulana Ihtishām-ul-Huq Thanvi. This member was the only dissenting member of the commission, and he produced his own minority report.[10] In the majority report, however, it is clear that the commission viewed the reform of Muslim family laws as necessary and obligatory. The majority report applauded those scholars and legal experts who were "progressive enough to believe that the reconstruction and fresh adaptation of the basic injunctions of Islam are urgently needed to remedy the evils and remove the hurdles caused by unsalutary traditions and customs masquerading in the garb of religion" (Donohue and Esposito 1982 [1956]: 203). The new laws were introduced in order to reduce the injustices suffered by women and children and perceived to be prevalent in Pakistani society.

These laws, although they did not introduce full equality for women in the legal sphere, were intended to provide protection for women from traditionally employed marriage and divorce methods, such as the *tin talak* (saying "I divorce you" three times in one sitting, after which the wife is divorced and often cast out of the house).[11] Those supporting the laws hoped that it would be possible to lessen the hardships faced by women due to sudden divorce, polygamy, and *hilla*. It was not possible, however, or perhaps even desirable, to institute reforms that had no relation to Islamic law as it was understood in the subcontinent. Instead, the majority opinion in the Commission justified the decision to alter the traditionally accepted laws and customs through an appeal to the Qur'an and *sunna* of the Prophet. Indeed, they argued that *ijtihad* (independent reasoning) such as their own is necessary in the modern world because the Prophet Muhammad could not "comprehend the infinite variety of human relations for all occasions and for all epochs" (Donohue and Esposito 1982 [1956]: 201).

The MFLO remained in effect once Bangladesh received its independence from Pakistan in 1971. It is still the most important legislation with respect to family law in Bangladesh, despite the lack of enforcement. Section 7, for example, covers the types of divorce on the husband's initiative permissible under state law. Following the declaration of *talak*, a husband must give notice to the union chairman (Section 7(1)) and then wait 90 days before the divorce is in effect. During this time, the union chairman is to convene an arbitration council to attempt to bring about reconciliation. Section 7(6) of the MFLO states that "[n]othing shall debar a wife whose marriage has been terminated by talaq effective under this section from re-marrying the same husband, without an intervening marriage with a third-person, unless such termination is for the third time so effective." While some legal scholars have argued that this law only discourages *hilla,* the judges in the High Court's 2010 decision write that, "hilla marriage is also an offence as it is contrary to the existing law of the country" (*Bangladesh Legal Aid and Services Trust* vs. *Government of Bangladesh* 2010: 12).

Many Islamists and their supporters[12] have argued, with Maulana Ihstishām-ul-Haq Thanvi, that the "arbitrary *ijtihād* of the Commission" was born out of an "inferiority complex" (Donohue and Esposito 1982 [1956]: 205, 207) with respect to Western countries. The restriction of polygamy, in particular, was a sign of acquiescence to cultural norms that instead permit adultery. Abu-l-'Ala Mawdudi (d. 1979), the ideological spokesman for Jamaat-i-Islami, insisted that laws making polygamy more difficult were contrary to the rights given to men by the Qur'an and would "simply encourage [men] to take up 'mistresses' and 'girlfriends'" (Shehabuddin 2008: 60, citing Mumtaz and Shaheed 1987: 59). Beyond issues of gender, opponents argue that the benefits given to orphan children under the MFLO are in opposition to Qur'anic verses about inheritance. Yet ironically, Islamists in contemporary Bangladesh have accepted the premise of Anglo-Muhammadan law: that *shari'a* is not only completely discernible, it is codifiable.

The perspective of women's rights activists

Although the MFLO was meant to improve the lives of women, it did not attempt to make men and women equal in matters related to family law. Many activists contend that even if the laws are properly followed, they are still unequal because men have the right to unilaterally end the marriage, while women do not. Men can initiate *talak* without sufficient cause. Women can only initiate the divorce in three situations: if they asked for such a right in the pre-nuptial agreement, if the couple agrees upon an acceptable exchange (i.e. the dower is returned to the man), or by taking the case to the court (Huda 1994: 139, 143–45). Such laws, argue activists, are not conducive to the goal of raising women's social, economic, and political status. Instead, they argue for a uniform personal law framework in which women of all religious backgrounds are given rights equal to those of men.

Activists arguing for a uniform personal code in Bangladesh often point to universal human rights documents such as the United Nations Convention for the Elimination of Discrimination Against Women (CEDAW) as the basis for changing personal laws. A number of areas within traditional Muslim personal law and in the MFLO directly conflict with CEDAW, including inheritance rules, marriage and divorce, and custody of children. Muslim personal law as practiced in South Asia thus "stands in the way of unreserved acceptance of article 16 [of CEDAW]" (Connors 1996: 365). Article 16 of CEDAW states that countries will "take all appropriate measures to eliminate discrimination against women in all matters relating to marriage and family relations."[13] Perhaps not surprisingly, Bangladesh has standing reservations against Articles 2, 13(a), 16(c) and (f).

Sultana Kamal, well-known lawyer and legal rights activist, has written extensively on the issue of religious personal laws in Bangladesh. In her view, personal laws are maintained because "Third World countries ... are caught up in the web of military, despotic, undemocratic, and fundamentalist rules [that] sidetrack issues on women's rights by falling back on various excuses like religious morality, national integrity, social harmony, internal security, [and] political stability" (Kamal 2001: 13). Whatever the reasons may be, it appears that the Bangladeshi state is unwilling to institutionalize reforms that might generate further hostile criticism from Islamists and their supporters, even as it assures international bodies of its commitment to women's rights. The government will continue to make contradictory decisions as long as it "regards the issue of women's rights—and of Islam itself—in essentially instrumentalist terms" (Kabeer 1991: 52).

For many women's rights activists, despite what is often a quite contentious relationship with the state administration, the modern state must be the "final arbiter and adjudicator in matters having legal consequences" (Nargis and Pereira 2002: 218). These activists therefore focus their efforts primarily on changing state policy. The MFLO is, at least, an identifiable piece of legislation that activists can appeal either in court or through legislation. The *fatwa,* however, represents an unregulated sphere of authority, in which religious scholars can potentially offer advice counter to the outlook of the state or contrary to human rights standards. The stakes are raised even higher when police collude to conceal and thus perpetuate violence against women.

Competing legal forums

Salish and fatwa

Although Bangladesh has laws such as the MFLO to cover family issues, families often do not approach the state to adjudicate when disputes arise. Instead, they seek out other venues, including informal community courts called *salish*, in which local community members give rulings on disputes. Informal dispute resolution has a long history in the rural areas of South Asia. The *panchayat* (as it is often known in northern India) preceded the British and served as a way to resolve both criminal and civil disputes among villagers. The British left the *panchayat* system largely intact, until the Village Government Act of 1919; village courts were supposed to take over the functions of the *panchayat/salish*. At the same time, the union level of government was created, over which elected officials—chairmen—would preside.[14] While union chairmen continue to be elected in contemporary Bangladesh and serve as the primary government officials for villages, the village court is largely defunct. But the *salish*, which does not have any legal standing and whose "resolutions are non-binding to parties involved in the mediation process" (Riaz 2005: 176) continues to be practiced. Here, by non-binding, Ali Riaz refers to its lack of backing by the state. It is, however, binding upon those who do not have the social or economic power to circumvent the decision of the *salish*.

When a dispute occurs, the parties involved may decide against going to the state-run courts because of the time and money involved in the court process. It is well-known that cases in such courts usually proceed at a snail's pace and only with substantial bribes. The parties instead agree to a *salish* committee, consisting of an odd number of members, which hears both sides and makes a decision. Yet it is only since the 1990s that the term *fatwa* has been used to describe these judgments, thus giving the *salish* a religious significance that it had not had historically.

Regulation by the state

In the landmark 2001 case, the judges note:

> Fatwa means legal opinion, which, therefore, means legal opinion of a lawful person or authority. Legal system of Bangladesh empowers only the Courts to decide all questions related to legal opinion on the Muslim and other Laws as in force. We, therefore, hold that any fatwa including the instant one are all unauthorised and illegal.
>
> (*Editor* 2001: 231)

The judges appear to condemn the giving of *any fatwa*, regardless of whether or not the *fatwa* calls for punishment that is illegal under Bangladeshi law. It seemed that even a *fatwa* given on a question of, for example, the correct amount of yearly alms, would be illegal following this judgment.

This was the complaint of religious leaders in Dhaka; thus, well-known scholars such as Obaidul Haq (d. 2007), the then-*khatib* (person who delivers the "sermon" during Friday prayers; in this case, also the highest-ranking official) at the Baitul Mukarram

National Mosque, publicly called for *fatwas* to be legal. Perhaps overshadowing this particular concern, however, was the eruption of violence on the streets following the judgment, as Islamists demonstrated more generally against the ruling and its perceived attack on the status of Islam in Bangladesh. The judges were labeled *murtads*, or apostates. The Supreme Court stay on the ban on *fatwas* was in direct response to unrest.

In the most recent Supreme Court case, decided in May 2011, the judges finally grappled with the dual nature of the *fatwa* in the Bangladeshi context: is a *fatwa* a non-binding opinion on Islamic law? Or is it a final judgment, complete with prescribed punishment for supposed transgressions? The judges ruled that religious experts may give *fatwas*, so long as they do not force the petitioner to engage in otherwise illegal activities or prescribe illegal punishments. But then the question becomes: who qualifies as an expert?

The concern over the qualifications of those giving *fatwas* was apparent even in the 2001 case, as the judges condemned "fanatics with wrong views." The 2011 court heard arguments on this issue, with both sides denouncing the sentencing of punishment by uneducated "quacks." Islamic scholars, chosen by the Islamic Foundation Bangladesh to give statements in this case, argued that the pronouncement of *fatwas* is integral to Islamic life, yet agreed that only those highly trained in Islamic jurisprudence should be allowed to engage in this activity.

Underlying this criticism of the education level of the *fatwa*-givers is anxiety over the relative lack of regulation of *madrasas* (religious schools) by the state. At least three million students in Bangladesh receive their education in *madrasas*; these schools vary widely in the level of governmental control, with a large number operating with no oversight at all. The judges in the 2001 case called for a unified educational system; the judges in 2010 asked that the government disseminate educational materials to all schools on the laws of Bangladesh. The rulings display a concern that goes beyond the educational level of those giving *fatwas*: it questions the very nature of the *madrasa* system of education in the modern state.

Concluding remarks

The May 2011 verdict is certainly not the last word on *fatwas* in Bangladesh. Even given the current acceptance by high-profile Islamic scholars that illegal punishments should not be carried out through *fatwas*, the question over the role of Islamic law in the nation remains. Political parties—most prominently Jamaat-i-Islami—continue to work through the political system to institute Islamic law as *the* law of the country.[15]

But given their support of the ban on all *fatwas*, will women's rights activists always be at odds with initiatives encouraging Islamic law? At least in Bangladesh, the answer appears to be 'yes.' While at least one prominent activist has offered an alternative that includes an Islamic legal strategy called *talfiq* ('mixing' Islamic legal school principles), most are adamant that women can only be protected through state law based on international standards of equality for men and women: not on the Qu'ran, *hadith,* or *fiqh.* The non-binding *fatwas* and the *muftis* who give them have a space in communities across Bangladesh for now but one that is increasingly uncertain, scrutinized, and contested.

Summary

- In 2001, the Bangladesh High Court declared the giving of *fatwas* illegal. Religious leaders immediately took issue with the verdict, saying that it jeopardized centuries of tradition in Islam. The verdict was then stayed for ten years.
- When the courts took up the issue again, judges had to grapple with a number of questions including who can give *fatwas* and what kind of *fatwas* should be legal. The final verdict in 2011 does not set guidelines for the qualifications of those who provide *fatwas*, but does insist on the supremacy of state law over the judgments of religious or community leaders.
- Women's rights activists in Bangladesh have taken on religious law and ideology a number of times over the past 40 years, often through the court system. Although many believe that the Muslim Family Law Ordinance, 1961, does not go far enough in protecting women's rights, the ordinance remains the most comprehensive piece of family law reform in force in Bangladesh.
- Some of these activists believe that Bangladesh can uphold the equal rights of women only if laws are based on the United Nations Convention on the Elimination of Discrimination Against Women (CEDAW) and other international documents. Islamic law would, in such a case, play no role in determining the laws of the country, unless the provisions aligned with CEDAW.
- The legal situation is complicated by the continued use of traditional, informal "courts" in lieu of state-run courts. These courts may or may not adhere to Bangladesh law. Legal pluralism is not unique to Bangladesh, but the lack of confidence in the legal system is significant; especially when the police fail to intervene in clearly unjust (and illegal) punishments, these local courts can serve as sites for the virtually unmitigated use of power against vulnerable groups.

Discussion points

- What is the popular understanding of the *fatwa* of Bangladesh today? How is it different from the traditional definition?
- How did the government choose to regulate religious authority in this situation? Should the government be involved in making such decisions?
- What is the difference between *shari'a* and *fiqh*? Why is this distinction significant?

- The Majority Report for the Commission on Marriage and Family Laws could be understood as a "modernist" position, while that of the dissenting member might be viewed as "traditionalist." What is the difference between these views? What does it mean to perform *ijtihad* in this situation?
- Can community courts truly provide justice for disputants, especially those from marginalized or otherwise vulnerable populations?

Further reading

Pereira, Faustina (2002) *The Fractured Scales: The Search for a Uniform Personal Code*, Calcutta: STREE.

Pereira, a well-known activist and scholar in Bangladesh, lays out the negative consequences of a legal system that allows for separate personal (family) codes and the need for a uniform personal code in the country. She also provides a path for reform. Whether or not one agrees with the call for a uniform personal code, the text can be helpful in understanding what is at stake in making (or not making) decisions about family law reform.

Shehabuddin, Elora (2008) *Reshaping the Holy: Democracy, Development, and Muslim Women in Bangladesh*, New York: Columbia University.

Shehabuddin's fieldwork in Bangladesh reveals the complex relationship between rural women, Islamist political parties, and non-governmental organizations. Instead of placing women in the role of victims of Islamist politics, Shehabuddin shows that women carefully negotiate and respond to the particular power dynamics of their communities. Her analysis of women's words and actions is not completely on the functional level, however; she also takes seriously their religious commitments and piety.

Uddin, Sufia (2006) *Constructing Bangladesh: Religion, Ethnicity, and Language in an Islamic Nation*, Chapel Hill: University of North Carolina.

Bangladesh has a rich history, despite its relatively young status as an independent country; in this text, Uddin focuses on the last two centuries of religious and cultural debate and discussion, with special emphasis on language. Throughout, she argues for the mutual construction of Bengali and Muslim identities in the region.

References

Ahmed, Mumtaz (2004) "Madrassa Education in Pakistan and Bangladesh," in R.G.W. Satu, B. Limaye, and Mohan Malik (eds) *Religious Radicalism and Security in South Asia*, Honolulu, Asia-Pacific Center for Security Studies.

Anderson, Michael (1993) "Islamic Law and the Colonial Encounter in British India," in David Arnold and Peter Robb (eds) *Institutions and Ideologies: A SOAS South Asia Reader*, Richmond, UK: Curzon Press.

Bangladesh Legal Aid and Services Trust and others vs. *Government of Bangladesh and others*, 8 July 2010.

Cohn, Bernard (1996) *Colonialism and Its Forms of Knowledge: The British in India*, Princeton, NJ: Princeton University Press.

Connors, Jane (1996) "The Women's Convention in the Muslim World," in Mai Yamani (eds) *Feminism and Islam: Legal and Literary Perspectives*, Reading, UK: Ithaca Press.

Donohue, John J. and John Esposito (1982 [1956]) "The Modernist Majority Report," in *Islam in Transition: Muslim Perspectives*, New York: Oxford University Press, 1982.

Editor, The Daily Banglabazar Patrika and others vs. *District Magistrate and Deputy Commissioner, Naogaon*, in *Daily Star*, Law Report, 7 January 2001. Reproduced in *Interventions* 4(2) (2002): 228–32.

Hossain, Sara (2001) "High Court Nails Fatwa," *Holiday*, January 5. Reprinted in *Interventions* 4 (2) (2002): 220–23.

Huda, Shahnaz (1994) "Untying the Knot: Muslim Women's Right of Divorce and Other Incidental Rights in Bangladesh," *The Dhaka University Studies, Part F, Journal of the Faculty of Law*, V(1): 133–57.

Kabeer, Naila (1991) "The Quest for National Identity: Women, Islam, and the State of Bangladesh," in Deniz Kandiyoti (ed.) *Women, Islam, and the State,* London: Macmillan.

Kamal, Sultana (2001) *Her Unfearing Mind: Women and Statement of Responsibility*, Dhaka: Ain o Salish Kendro.

Khan, Zillur Rahman (1985) "Islam and Bengali Nationalism," *Asian Survey* 25 (8): 834–51.

Kozlowski, Gregory (1993) "Muslim Personal Law," in Robert D. Baird (ed.) *Religion and Law in Independent India*, New Delhi: Manohar.

Kugle, Scott (2001) "Framed, Blamed and Renamed: The Recasting of Islamic Jurisprudence in Colonial South Asia," *Modern Asian Studies*, 35(2): 257–313.

Lemons, Katherine (2010) "At the Margins of the Law: Adjudicating Muslim Families in Contemporary Delhi," unpublished dissertation, University of California, Berkeley.

Masud, Muhammad Khalid (2009) "Fatwa Advice on Proper Muslim Names," in Barbara Metcalf (ed.) *Islam in South Asia in Practice*, Princeton, NJ: Princeton University Press, 339–51.

Merry, Sally Engle (1988) "Legal Pluralism," *Law and Society Review*, 22(5): 869–96.

Nargis, Deena and Faustina Pereira (2000) "Taking Cognizance of Illegal Fatwa," *The Daily Star*, December 31. Reproduced in *Interventions*, 4(2) (2002): 215–19.

Riaz, Ali (2005) "Traditional Institutions as Tools of Political Islam in Bangladesh," *Journal of African and Asian Studies*, 40(3): 171–96.

Sarkar, Ashutosh (2001) "Fatwa Legal, Not to be Imposed," *The Daily Star*, May 13.

Shehabuddin, Elora (2008) *Reshaping the Holy: Democracy, Development, and Muslim Women in Bangladesh*, New York: Columbia University.

Weiss, Bernard (2006) *The Spirit of Islamic Law*, Athens, GA: University of Georgia.

Notes

1　*Editor, The Daily Bangla Patrika* vs. *District Magistrate and Deputy Commissioner, Naogaon*. Ruling reproduced in *Daily Star*, Law Report, January 7, 2001. Also reproduced as "The Fatwa in Question is Wrong," in *Interventions*, 4(2): 228–32. Justice Mohammad Golam Rabbani and Justice Nazmun Ara Sultana presided.

2　See, for example, Khan (1985).

3 Elora Shehabuddin has written persuasively on the challenges that poor Muslim women in Bangladesh must negotiate, particularly with respect to the Islamist parties and the state. See Shehabuddin (2008).

4 With a few major exceptions, such as the *fatwa* pronounced against feminist and writer, Taslima Nasreen, calling for her execution because she was an "apostate." This notion of a *fatwa* is not unlike the one made by Ayatollah Khomeini against writer Salman Rushdie. Several instances of *fatwas* against poor men and women involved with non-governmental organizations have also been reported.

5 See, for example, the statistics cited by Nargis and Pereira (2002: 217).

6 Although the process is, as of 2011, under review by the current Awami League government, Bangladesh has had, for two decades, a system in which a caretaker government takes over between elected governments, to ensure that parliamentary elections are free and fair.

7 See, recently, Katherine Lemons' unpublished dissertation, "At the Margins of Law: Adjudicating Muslim Families in Contemporary Delhi" (Lemons 2010). Also Kugle (2001).

8 By the nineteenth century, the British had introduced their own criminal laws in the subcontinent.

9 Also spelled "Hedaya," this text was written by the Central Asian Hanafī jurist, Burhan al-din Abu 'l Hasan 'Ali b. 'Abd al-Jalal Farghani al-Marghīnānī (d. 1197), as a commentary on his own *Kitāb Bidāyat al-mubtadī.*

10 The member made it quite clear in his minority report that he viewed the other members as unqualified to take on the issue of reform and *ijtihād,* as they were not scholars or legal experts of Islam. According to his perspective, only members of the *ulama* should be permitted to work on such topics.

11 *Tin talak* is still viewed as valid by many in South Asia, including religious leaders.

12 I use this term with caution. The wide variety of people who agree with this perspective do not necessarily approve of the particular positions of Islamist political parties such as Jamaat-i-Islami or of the militant actions of extremist groups.

13 To see the entire text of the convention, see www.un.org/womenwatch/daw/cedaw/text/econvention.htm.

14 A union, in contemporary Bangladesh, is the lowest tier of government.

15 Jamaat-i-Islami is not the only Islamist party active in Bangladesh today, although it certainly is the largest, with the most political authority. Other groups include the Islamic Oikya Jote, Khalifat Majlish, Ahl-e-Hadith, Islamic Chatra Sena, Jamiatul Modarassin, and other, illegal groups. Many of these groups, in the aftermath of the Taslima Nasreen incident, demanded that blasphemy laws be passed, that Ahmadiyyas be declared non-Muslim, and that atheists, *murtads,* and those writing against Islam be punished. Some groups, including the outlawed Jamatul Mujahideen, have been implicated in bombing attacks against governmental offices, holy shrines, and NGOs.

19

Far from Mecca: modern Islam in Indonesia and Malaysia

Muhamad Ali[1]

Outline

- In Southeast Asia, the process of Islamization is deemed unfinished. Rulers and the people have been open to new ideas, Islamic, Western, or otherwise, and appropriated these within their local cultures. Responding to colonial modernity and Islamic reform, many formed either modernist or traditionalist organizations and networks.
- Being colonized by the Dutch for centuries, Indonesia is not an Islamic state, nor a secular state, but a state based on *Pancasila*, or five pillars. Muhammadiyah and *Nahdlatul Ulama,* including the progressive youth among them, support Pancasila and promote democracy and pluralism, although a few groups among the Islamists reject all of these. In their diversity, however, Muslim activists use modern means.
- Being colonized by the British, Malaysia is a constitutional monarchy with Islam as the official religion, and so with the state pillars (*rukunegara*) it comprises kingship as well as the Constitution. Both reformist and conservative Malay Muslims—the United Malays National Organization (UMNO) and the Pan-Malaysian Islamic Party (PAS)—have been engaging with Islam and modernity in Malay terms. Progressives, such as Sisters in Islam*,* are critical of the government and Islamist politics of Islamization in the country.

Unfinished Islamization process

Max Weber and other modernization theorists have argued that the pursuit of modern science and technology would lead to a decline in religion, which was associated with traditionalism, spiritualism, magic, superstition, and other-worldliness (Rostow 1971; Black 1975; Bentley 2003: 8–11). These theorists believed that Western nations came to dominate the world because they adopted science and technology and dispensed with religion as an organizing narrative. They thought that the rest of the world could only be modern if they too followed the same path.

Other scholars, however, have argued that modernization does not weaken religion, nor render it irrelevant, nor cause it to go private (Casanova 1994; Hefner 2000). Muslim scholars such as Fazlur Rahman and Seyyed Hossein Nasr, among others, contended that Islam persists in the modern world, either because of its intellectual capability to adjust to modern circumstances or because of its rich spiritual vitality, which serves as an antidote to the more poisonous aspects of modern Western culture (Rahman 1984; Nasr 2011). They believed that being modern does not necessarily mean being Westernized. Western colonialism, however, elicited a response to Western modernity from colonized societies. In this chapter, which focuses on Indonesia and Malaysia, I demonstrate that Islamization and modernization can mutually reinforce each other. Many scholars and networks in these two neighboring countries in Southeast Asia have actively engaged with Islam and modernity from within their local circumstances.

Southeast Asia, home to approximately 600 million people, is a crossroads of world religions. In distinctive ways, the world's major religions—Hinduism, Buddhism, Islam, and Christianity—intersect with local beliefs and practices and other ideologies in order to form unique constellations of faith. According to the Pew Forum on Religion and Public Life report in 2009, Southeast Asia is home to about 231 million Muslims, representing about 20 percent of the world's estimated 1.57 billion Muslims. More Muslims live in Indonesia (88 percent of the total population of 234 million, or 15.6 percent of the world's Muslims) than in any country of the world. Indonesia today is the largest Muslim-majority country in the world. Malaysia is about 50 percent Muslim; Brunei is 67 percent; Singapore is 14.9 percent; about 5 percent of the predominantly Catholic Philippines are Muslim; and the Muslim population makes up less than 4 percent of the predominantly Buddhist nations of Thailand, Cambodia, Laos, and Burma (Pew 2009). These statistics suggest that rulers and people in Southeast Asia have been open to outside ideas and practices that they view as attractive, relevant, and useful in spiritual, moral, economic and/or political terms. More qualitative studies show how these ideas are appropriated within local contexts. In Southeast Asia, being modern can be said to be "paradoxically global and local" (Andaya 1997: 409).

The Arabic-speaking world has a special status within and beyond Islam. As Islam's birthplace, it is an important node in networks of learning and scholarship. More recently the Arabian Gulf region gained prestige for its trade, commerce, and opportunities for labor, attracting millions of people, especially Muslims, from across the globe. Muslim scholars (ulama) established religious-intellectual networks between the Middle East (particularly Mecca and Egypt) and Southeast Asia centuries before the arrival of European colonialism in the sixteenth century CE. They maintained their spiritual, intellectual, and often physical connection to the centers through the hajj (pilgrimage) and educational travel (thalab al-ilm). Many Arab, Indian, and Chinese Muslims, including mystical (Sufi) and legal scholars, penetrated into the region in a peaceful manner. However, there were also several wars of "conversion" in the islands of Sumatra, Java, and Sulawesi. Some newly converted kings used force to convert neighboring kings. In this period, it was common then that subjects would emulate the religion of their kings. During the colonial and postcolonial periods, Southeast Asian networks developed and expanded to include India, Pakistan, Europe, and the United States; they often span geographical, ethnic, and class boundaries.

Southeast Asia has been held up as a model of a peaceful and Sufi Islam, which emphasizes the spiritual, mystical dimension, rather than the ritualistic, legalistic, political one. Indeed, Sufism has flourished and contributed to the diversity and complexity of Islam in the region; but, in Southeast Asia, as in much of the Islamic world, the normative legal practices (shari'a and its specific form of fiqh) have remained a benchmark in Muslim life (Azra 2004; Laffan 2011). Across the diverse terrain of Islam, we find Muslims adjusting to new developments in science and technology. The place of politics, education, and culture are crucial concerns for many in the region; and the matrix of opinions, affiliations, and allegiances form diverse identities and contribute to the polarization of Muslims. The creation of an ecumenical Islamic community (*umma*) remains an ideal that Muslims aspire to achieve through propagation (*da'wah*), education (*tarbiyah*), and to a varying and changing degree, through politics (*siyasah*) locally, nationally, and even globally. Therefore, the process of Islamization has taken old and new forms, ranging from trade and inter-marriage to preaching, teaching, and writing. Political organization is now taking shape along lines provided by mass media, mass education, and virtual networks. Islamization has never been final or singular.

Today it is not unusual to encounter Southeast Asian Muslims listening to recitations of the Qur'an in Arabic on their cell phones. With a few finger swipes they load Indonesian or English translations of the same verse. Sufis, wearing distinctive dress, drive luxury cars, speak Javanese or Indonesian, and maintain robust Facebook and Twitter accounts. Even a casual observer will note a sense of present-mindedness in the region; yet connection to the past has never withered. Despite many tensions, Muslim elites boast multilayered identities where religious, nationalist, ethnic, and global features jostle cheek by jowl.

Traditionalist and modernist Muslims

For some Muslims the alleged opposition between Islam and modernity seemed stark when they encountered European colonialism and Christian missions concurrently with reformist (*tajdid*) Muslim ideas, particularly from Egypt. The Portuguese, Dutch, British, Spanish, and later the Japanese brought their ideas and modern institutions to many people in Southeast Asia who responded in a variety of ways. In the East Indies (Indonesia) and British Malaya (Malaysia), we can divide Muslims into traditionalists and modernists based on their responses to colonial modernity.

Modernist Muslims adopted and adapted to modern science and technology, educational systems, and legal, political, and economic organization believing them to be important in the attainment of a prosperous Muslim community. The modernists were inspired by the reformist ideas of Jamaluddin al-Afghani (1838–97) and Muhammad Abduh (1849–1905). They relied on the fundamental doctrines of the Qur'an and the Prophet's tradition (*sunna*), rather than the authority of the medieval religious scholars (*ulama*), as the primary sources of inspiration for being up-to-date Muslims. They sought to carry out *ijtihad* (independent reasoning) in solving social problems. They borrowed Western, or Christian institutions: classroom, curriculum, exam, and certificate. After their country's independence, they established more modern institutions, including universities, hospitals, orphanages, banks, political parties, and public administration, all of which were considered to be beneficial in the furthering of their objective of building a prosperous and just society.

The traditionalist Muslims saw little problem with adapting to modern ideas and institutions, but they preferred to maintain the medieval style of scholarship in interpreting the Qur'an and the Prophet's tradition. They did not teach modern science, nor did they adopt a modern educational system, or embrace modern modes of organization. For them, medieval scholasticism provided sufficient answers to the questions of life. In education, they preserved the system of *pesantren* (from Sanskrit word *santri* meaning pupil), or *pondok* (meaning hut, a local term for Arabic *ma'had*), a community-based boarding school, which emphasized the teaching of classical and medieval texts in Arabic. Students lived in a complex with a mosque and the house of the religious teacher (*kiyai* or *tokguru*). Pedagogically, teachers emphasized memorization and internalization of Arabic and Islamic knowledge.

Theologically, the traditionalist Muslims tended to emphasize predetermination and God's blessings, whereas the modernist Muslims emphasized hard work and self-determination. The traditionalist group held that there was religious significance to all aspects of human behavior: whereas the modernist group tended towards a narrower definition of religion and emphasized the boundary between the sacred and the secular. It is perhaps surprising that the traditionalist group tended to be less concerned with the purity of Islam. More than the modernists, they were hospitable to local beliefs and practices. The modernist group, on the other hand, emphasized a purified form of Islam (Geertz 1960: 149–50). Indeed, many among the modernist Muslims could be regarded as religiously conservative in the sense that they endorsed a strict and puritan theology and rejected many aspects of local beliefs and practices. Conversely, many among the traditionalist Muslims could be considered progressive in the sense that they integrated medieval scholarship and the Qur'an and the Prophet's tradition with modern philosophies and institutions. An increased access to knowledge and information, mass education, and globalization, contributed to both diversifying and homogenizing tendencies. Thus, progressive Muslim youth, who will be discussed below, come from both traditionalist and modernist educational backgrounds.

In contemporary Indonesia and Malaysia, modernist and traditionalist Muslims share common values and practices: to a varying degree, they accept democratic institutions such as the state's constitution and laws, the electoral systems, and forms of education that combine religious and secular sciences. Both groups aim to live well in this world (*dunya*) and in the hereafter (*akhira*). While the distinction between the modernist and the traditionalist is contingent and fluid, many contemporary Muslims still use the modernist and traditionalist categories when they need to identify mainstream religious orientations (Ali 2007).

Muhammadiyah, NU, and Islamists in the Pancasila state

After several centuries of Dutch colonization and almost three years of Japanese rule, Indonesia emerged as an independent state. Its nascent state ideology was called *Pancasila* (a Sanskrit phrase meaning five pillars): belief in one God, just and civilized humanity, national unity, democracy led by wisdom through deliberation and

tion, and social justice for all the people. Born in 1945, Pancasila was an eclectic philosophy drawn from monotheism, humanism, nationalism, democracy, and socialism. The founding fathers, who were predominantly Muslim, considered two models when developing these principles. The concept of the Islamic state and the secular state formed competing poles in this debate. Pancasila compromised between these two. Many introduced a motto *Bhineka Tunggal Ika,* a Sanskrit phrase for unity in diversity. From then onward, Indonesian leaders have stated in their speeches that Indonesia is not an Islamic state, nor a secular state, but a Pancasila state. This does not mean that there is no tension at all between those who want Indonesia to be more Islamic and those who want Indonesia to be more secular. For the overwhelming majority throughout Indonesian history, however, the idea of the Pancasila state has remained triumphant.

In 1912 the modernist Muhammadiyah organization, meaning the followers of Muhammad, was founded by a Javanese teacher named Ahmad Dahlan (d. 1923), who returned from Mecca to Yogyakarta. In colonial times, the Muhammadiyah aimed to "promote the teaching and learning of Islam in the Netherlands Indies and to fashion a Muslim life in accordance with the will of Islam" (*Verslag Moehammadijah di Hindia Timoer ke -X* 1923: 9). Since colonial times the organization has spread to other parts of Indonesia. The Muhammadiyah seeks to purify Islamic belief in oneness of God (*tauhid*). They are also focused on good action (*amal shalih*) through propagation, education, charity, health services, and social work. Operating predominantly in cities, the Muhammadiyah adopt modern systems of education, utilizing classrooms, curricula, and modern clothing for teachers and students. Together with their autonomous branches—including women's (*Aisyiyah*), youth (*Pemuda Muhammadiyah*), and student (*Ikatan Mahasiswa Muhammadiyah*) groups—the Muhammadiyah own and manage universities, hospitals, businesses and entrepreneurships, and humanitarian units, which work on disaster relief and environmental issues.

More recently, in response to global terrorism and ethno-religious violence in parts of Indonesia, Muhammadiyah leaders and activists promote the idea of *jihad fi sabilillah* (struggle in the path of God). This use of "jihad" eschews war and the use of force and promotes social and educational struggle. In response to the rise of transnational Islamic movements and local religious and socio-political issues, Muhammadiyah activists are generally divided into conservative and progressive groups. Being associated with Islamic modernism, the conservatives seek to maintain its emphasis on faith and the purification character, allowing change and reform only in the affairs considered mundane (*dunya*), such as economic and political affairs. The progressives, on the other hand, seek to formulate a new Islamic theology that is compatible with modern life. Their interpretations are influenced by and seek to promote liberation theology, multiculturalism, religious pluralism, civilizational dialogue, gender equity, and a vibrant civil society (Ghazali et al 2007; Tim Penyusun 2010).

The *Nahdlatul Ulama* (the Awakening of the Islamic Scholars, NU) is thought to be representative of traditionalist Islam. It was established by Hasyim Asy'ari (d. 1947) in 1926 in response to the abolition of the Caliphate system in Turkey and the rise of *Wahhabi* attacks in Mecca. The NU was also founded in response to the emergence of Muhammadiyah, which the NU scorned for disregarding traditional Islamic boarding schools (*pesantren*) in villages. Unlike the Muhammadiyah, the NU stresses the importance of outward religious practice, such as loud recitation of one's intention to pray and the audible recitation of the Qur'an and the *tahlil* (the declaration of the unity of God) before the dead. The NU also supports visitations to the graves of saints (*wali*) in order to seek their blessings (*baraka*). In this regard, NU is more accommodative toward local practices than Muhammadiyah.

Unlike the Muhammadiyah, the NU operated as a political party from 1955 to 1984. In their relations with the nation and the state, NU leaders do not resist or challenge Pancasila (Bush 2009, 164). Ahmad Siddiq's trilogy of Islamic solidarity, national solidarity, and human solidarity has been popular and inspiring. The late Abdurrahman Wahid (d. 2009), a former NU leader, went on to become the President of Indonesia. He promoted the "domestication of Islam" against "Arabization" as well as reform within the *pesantren* tradition in Indonesia. The current President Susilo Bambang Yudhoyono views him as the "father of pluralism" for his defense of the rights of religious and ethnic minorities in Indonesia.

Initially, the NU maintained "traditional" modes of pedagogy in the *pesantren*. Gradually they incorporated modern organization, modern schooling, health and development programs for males and females. In 2006, for example, the *Muslimat NU*, the Female Muslims organization associated with the NU, established *pesantrens* for women in Aceh, which focused on family health and nutrition.

The relationship between Islam and political modernity has taken different forms. With the collapse of the Soeharto regime in 1998, along with the old political parties (the Faction of Work, or *Golongan Karya* of the Soeharto period, the Muslim Party of Unity and Development, or PPP, and the Party of Indonesian Democracy, or PDI), new Islamic political parties emerged. Some placed the stress on Islam rather than the Pancasila, yet they all worked out within the framework of the representative democracy (the fourth pillar of the Pancasila).

Islamist parties like the Party of Justice and Prosperity (*Partai Keadilan Sejahtera*, PKS), which was inspired by the Egyptian Muslim Brotherhood and figures such as Yusuf al-Qaradawi, articulate an Islamic agenda to combat corruption and social injustice without promoting the idea of an Islamic state. Their political model is a social contract (*mithaq*) patterned on the one implemented by the Prophet Muhammad in Medina between different faith communities. The PKS and other Islamist political parties, such as the Party of the Crescent and Star (*Partai Bulan Bintang*, PBB) are vocal critics of Western forms of democracy and economic development. They frequently denounce the US occupation of Afghanistan and Iraq and its double standard vis-à-vis the Israel-Palestine conflict. Western modernity, they point out, perpetuates "moral excesses" such as pornography, moral decadence, and limitless freedom, while, at the same time, inhibiting civic freedom and diversity. Islamists enthusiastically participate in democratic politics.

Outside political parties, a few Muslim groups have taken a hardline path, such as the Front of Defenders of Islam (*Front Pembela Islam*, FPI), The Council of Indonesian Jihadists (*Majlis Mujahidin Indonesia*, MMI), the transnational Party of Liberation, Indonesia (*Hizbut Tahrir Indonesia*, HTI) and the underground terrorist *Jama'ah Islamiyah* (JI). Two of these, the FPI and the HTI, have small memberships, but nonetheless voice their aspirations in street demonstrations, mass media, websites, publications, and social media. They reject Western ideologies, such as democracy and capitalism; but they use modern forms of organization and technology to broadcast their messages (Barton 2005; Jahroni in Sukma and Joewono 2007; Rosadi 2008).

Progressive Muslims in Indonesia

Progressive ideas and movements have flourished in a democratic Indonesia. The Institute for Islamic and Social Studies (*Lembaga Kajian Islam dan Sosial*, LKiS), the Progressive Islam Network (*Jaringan Islam Progresif*), the Liberal Islam Network (*Jaringan Islam Liberal*, JIL), and the Muhammadiyah Young Intellectual Network (*Jaringan Intelektual Muda Muhammadiyah*, JIMM), all seek to reform Islam. They are inspired by international activists and scholars such as the modernist Muhammad Abduh, as well as contemporary thinkers like Muhammad Abid Al-Jabiri of Morocco, Fazlur Rahman of Pakistan, as well as US-based scholars such as Abdullahi An-Nai'm, Amina Wadud, and Farid Esack of South Africa. Local scholars, such as the late Nurcholish Madjid and Abdurrahman Wahid, were immensely influential. Progressives are less interested in Islamizing science and democracy. Their main emphasis is on contextualizing the Qur'an and the Prophet Muhammad's tradition in a bid to emphasize the substantive values of justice, equality, peace, and human rights in both national and global contexts. In newly created "epistemic communities," these scholar-activists have expanded their discourses to include interfaith dialogue and pluralism, the emancipation of women, religious freedom, and secularism. They remain engaged with the Islamic heritage of exegesis (*tafsir*), philosophy (*falsafa*), and mysticism (*tasawwuf*), but they attempt to find new ways to interpret and apply the tradition in a digital world. In NU circles, the liberal youth activists have been empowered by progressive ideas. They challenge Islamist hardliners and ideologues by creating both face-to-face and virtual spaces to address a variety of modern issues including Islamic liberalism, secularism, and pluralism.

The progressives hold that the current position of the Muhammadiyah and the NU are not progressive enough to face pressing modern challenges or to counter what they view as growing Islamic conservatism. They remain engaged with the Islamic heritage (*turath*) such as scriptural interpretation (*tafsir*), jurisprudence (*fiqh*) and theological discourse (*kalam*), but they attempt to contextualize these sciences; and they seek new ways of interpreting and applying them to modern societies. For example, the Muhammadiyah young activists attempted to contextualize the Qur'anic concept of the downtrodden or the abased on earth (*mustadh'afin*), by including all those people marginalized and powerless. They name them the "new *mustadh'afin*."

> The new *mustadh'afin* are individuals and groups who are economically, politically, socially, and culturally weakened and exploited by the global structures of state, market, and mass media. The new *mustadh'afin* can include woman laborers, minority groups, farmer workers, migrant laborers, and many more. The Muhammadiyah, of course, cannot deal with all these groups, but can make the most realistic and immediate decisions to address some of them.
>
> *(Boy et al 2008: 58–59)*

These liberal Muslim activists hold that in order to address these issues, they have to revive the spirit of independent reasoning (*ijtihad*). By interpreting the religious texts contextually, they support liberalism, secularism and pluralism, including an interfaith marriage, between Muslims and non-Muslims:

> Due to its position as a law based on *ijtihad*, it is possible to create a new opinion that Muslim women are allowed to marry with non-Muslim men. This opinion is derived from the spirit of the Qur'an. First, religious pluralism is the law of God (*sunnatullah*) ... Second, the objective of marriage is to create love (*mawaddah*) and mercy (*rahmah*) ... And third, the spirit of Islamic message is liberation, not enchainment.
>
> *(Sirry 2005: 164–65)*

One of these progressive Muslims groups calls itself the *Liberal Islam Network* (*Jaringan Islam Liberal*, JIL). This network of young activists promotes liberal Islamic thinking through its discussion list, websites, interviews, radio and television talk shows, and periodicals. "Islam does not oppose secularism as long as it does not mean a total rejection of religion," the co-founder of the network, Ulil Abshar Abdalla said. He and others engage the teachings of the medieval Maliki jurist Imam al-Shatibi (d. 1388). Shatibi advocated the application of the objectives of the Islamic law (*maqasid al-shari'a*), which involve preserving religion, reason, life, property, and family. They do not see any problem when a Muslim converts to Christianity and vice versa, because Islam protects such freedom.

A similar reinterpretation of the objectives of Islamic law was elaborated by another group of the NU progressive young activists, the Institute for the Study of Islam and Society (LKiS), in the following way:

Hifdz al-din: the right of Muslims to practice their religion, extended to mean the right of others to practice their own religions, thus religious tolerance.

Hifdz al-nafs wa al-irdl, the right to life, described as the right to the basic necessities of life, the right to freedom, and the right to justice.

Hifdz al-'aql: the right to intellectual expression and activity, extended to include the right to free speech and the right to one's own opinion.

Hifdz al-nasl: reproductive rights and the right to ensure the future of one's descendents, including the right to a profession, expressed as the right to individual privacy

Hifdz al-mal: the right to own property, and by extension a prohibition against harming someone else's property, including through corruption, theft, and monopolies.

(in Bush 2009: 96)

Younger adherents of the Muhammadiyah also advocate teachings that keep pace with "the spirit of the time" (*semangat zaman*). They promote the Sunni–Shi'a, interfaith, and inter-civilizational dialogues, as well as non-violence, scientific development, human rights, gender equality, a vibrant civil society, and multiculturalism (Ali 2005). A greater emphasis on the humanities and social sciences is viewed as the pathway to reforming knowledge. Progressive activist-intellectuals reiterate an argument that it is better "to retain the worthy part of the vintage tradition combined with the enhanced modern" (*al-muhafaza 'ala al-qadim al-salih wa al-akhz bi al-jadid al-aslah*).

Contemporary Islam has found a colorful outlet in the popular media, including television and the internet (see Fealy and White 2008). Male and female Muslim preachers such as Yusuf Mansur and Mamah Dedeh and university professors such as Muhammad Quraish Shihab and Musdah Mulia have become part of a growing popular religious culture. Even Sufism, which is commonly perceived as a quietist and traditional, is actively promoted by preachers and professors on television shows. Different forms of knowledge and varieties of Islamic piety now reach the public through modern technology. The meaning of Islam and its role in society is robustly debated in the digital sphere. Thus modern technology shapes the process of Islamization and diversifies religious authority. At the same time there is a great deal of boundary crossing and hybridity between traditionalist and modernist versions of Islam.

Malay Muslims in the Islamic federal state of Malaysia

Historically conditioned by the British intervention in "secular" matters and non-intervention in "religious and customary matters," Islam in Malaysia has become largely bureaucratized by the state and by the *ulama* associated with it.

British colonial documents classified a Malay as "any person belonging to the Malayan race," "who spoke Malay or any other Malayan language" and "who professed

Islam" (Andaya and Andaya 2001: 183). The postcolonial Malaysian government kept the definition. Malaysia's constitution stipulates that Islam is the state's religion although it recognizes religious plurality and multiculturalism.

Although Islam and local culture were for centuries embedded among Malays, Islam has gained greater prominence since the beginning of the New Economic Policy (NEP) in the 1970s. This was a response to domestic socio-economic circumstances and ethnic tensions between Malays and Chinese. It also mirrored a worldwide resurgence of Islam. Islam and Malay ethno-nationalism remain a salient point of public discourse. The government continued to combine Islam and Malay in inexorable ways. While Malaysia did not take an extremist path, ethnic prejudices and exclusionary feelings remained present between the Malays, the Chinese, and the Indians. In May of 1969, the killing of a Chinese man in Kuala Lumpur resulted in riots. In the next election, Chinese opposition parties campaigned for rights for the non-Malay population. The riots caused the ruling government to proclaim a new ideology, *Rukunegara* (articles of faith of the state): belief in God, loyalty to king and country, sanctity of the Constitution, rule of law, and good behavior and morality (Andaya and Andaya 2001: 297–99).

Malaysia's articles of faith resemble Indonesia's Pancasila, but they differ in some respects. The Malaysian's state philosophy has a monotheistic dimension to it, but emphasizes both kingship and nation, along with the Constitution, rule of law, and morality. Indonesia's Pancasila imbricates humanism, democracy, and social justice, but it does not embrace kingship. The Malaysia's *Rukunegara* was conditioned by racial tensions and economic battles between groups; whereas *Pancasila* served as a philosophical compromise between those Muslims who wanted to make the new Indonesia an Islamic state and those who wanted to make her a secular state. Although Malaysia is only 50 percent Muslim, Islam is the official religion; whereas Indonesia, which is 88 percent Muslim, does not call Islam an official religion. The idea of democracy is embraced by both nation-states, but it is applied in different ways.

Conservative and reformist ulama

Rural schools remain bastions of Islamic traditionalism and conservatism. Malays use the term *pondok,* instead of *pesantren,* to describe these schools. In *pondok*s, education is organized in a simple manner. It is characterized by an informal, hierarchical relationship between teachers and pupils, the centrality of the mosque, an emphasis on memorization, and the use of Arabic (*jawi*), or Malay in Arabic script. An increasing number of *pondok*s are reforming and modernizing aspects of their education, by introducing English and some modern sciences. The modern *pondok*s teach both traditional Islamic knowledge and modern sciences. Schools such as Ma'had Muhammady and Madrasah Muhammady, in the state of Kelantan, offer Malay and English instruction (Ali 2006). Apart from the traditional *pondok* and modern *pondok* or *madrasah,* there are many Malay schools and English schools. In the 1970s, Islamic and secular colleges and universities began to emerge. Regardless of some efforts at combining and integrating the religious and the secular sciences, educational dualism (between the traditional and the modern) remains intact in Malaysia.

The religious scholars (*ulama*), who usually identify with the religious schools, are divided into the old faction (*Kaum Tua*) and the young faction (*Kaum Muda*). These groups publish a range of journals that address Islamic issues as well as "Malay problems:" backwardness and illiteracy, criticism of "superstitious beliefs" such as witchcraft and black magic, and support for reform and hard work. The reformist authors are concerned with Malay education, work ethics, Malay language, history, and politics. On the other hand, the old faction of *ulama* maintains their established religious authority, which is linked to the sultans.

Being part of the global Islamic resurgence, there have been revivalist movements from the 1970s onward in campuses. These movements work through means of Islamic propagation (*da'wah*). For example, the Malaysian Islamic Youth Organization (*Angkatan Belia Islam Malaysia,* ABIM) uses a popular slogan, "Islam First, Malay Second" (Mutalib 1993: 1–2). This youth organization has continued to be among the most active players in the culture and politics of Islamization in contemporary Malaysia.

UMNO, PAS, and politics of Islamization

The tension between forms of Islam and interpretations of modernity in Malaysia is demonstrated by the struggle between the government, which is controlled by the National Front or the United Malay National Organization (UMNO) and the opposition parties. The Pan-Malaysian Islamic Party (PAS) represents the opposition and more recently the Party of Justice has also joined those ranks. UMNO and PAS activists have struggled for power through political mobilization. Both groups claim to be the true agents of Islamization in Malaysia. The UMNO and the PAS leaders have charged each other with "politicizing Islam" for their own interests. The PAS leaders have tried to implement "Islamic criminal law" (*hudud*), which is commonly associated with cutting off a thief's hand or stoning adulterers to death; but they have failed, partly because the federal government, controlled by the UMNO, has always blocked the move.

Apart from the *hudud* debate in Malaysian politics, PAS leaders and *ulama* seek to challenge the perception that they are anti-science. The PAS spiritual leader of the state of Kelantan, Nik Aziz Nik Mat, gave the following speech to correct the popular image of his party:

> Although religious people, like myself, have been labeled as anti-science and anti-technology, I come here to correct this false image. Before the fall of Islam, Islamic scholars were famous scientists. Their sciences became reference in the West.

The false image comes from the science-church conflict in the West. Islam is not the same. Islam and Western science are different in their foundation. For Islam, this universe is created, whereas for the West, this universe is not created ... Islam fears no scientific facts. Allah has created this universe and its law as well as the Qur'an. The Qur'an and science support each other and both increase faith in the glory of Allah.

(in Wan Jusoh 1999: 51)

In Nik Aziz Nik Mat's statement there is a partial and simplistic picture of the science-church relationship in the West. There is also the assertion that Islam does not object to scientific development. For him and for most people in Malaysia, Islam and modern science are not in conflict. The question, however, is: to what extent did PAS work for scientific development when it was in power?

UMNO leaders have also sought to promote a modernist vision of Islam. Abdullah Ahmad Badawi, the then prime minister, promoted a progressive, civilizational Islam (*Islam Hadhari*) in 2000 until his end of the office in 2009. Badawi defined *Islam Hadhari* as "an approach that emphasizes development, consistence with Islam, and which focuses on the enhancement of the quality of life." He says it is not a new religion, not a new school of thought (*madhhab*), but an approach that is "rational, tolerant, inclusive, and progressive."

For Badawi, it is a pragmatic approach to Islam in order to increase Malays' competitiveness and the national prosperity. He formulated ten principles, including faith and piety in God, just and trustworthy government, free and independent people, a vigorous pursuit and mastery of knowledge, and a balanced and comprehensive economic development. Badawi argued that a change in the Malay mindset would require encompassing, drastic, and systematic action, which also maintained the concept that life should be in the service of God. Inspired by medieval formulations of the objectives of the *shari'a,* centered on the idea of public good (*maslahah 'ammah*), Badawi and the advocates of *Islam Hadhari* constructed an Islamic form of modernity based on *ijtihad*, independent reasoning.

Today we must encourage reform and renewal. I have always believed that by opening up discursive space in the Muslim world, we enrich our intellectual tradition and directly challenge the extremist doctrines, which have become synonymous with Islam over the last few years. Muslim political leaders, scholars, and intellectuals, must be courageous enough to encourage—and not stifle—the voices of moderation and reason. Where one refers to these voices as those of "modernist Islam," or "progressive Islam," or even "liberal Islam," I believe they have an important contribution to make toward the renewal of Islamic thought. Islam must not be ossified and fossilized by blind imitation of traditional thought and opinion. Rigid obscurantism, exclusively literalist doctrines and atavistic notions of a past ideal, prevents Islam from being a religion for all time as intended by Allah

(Badawi 2006: 4–5)

The PAS leaders, such as Abdul Hadi Awang and Nik Aziz Nik Mat, rejected the idea of *Islam Hadhari,* saying that it represented the manipulation of Islam for their political gain. Abdul Hadi Awang commented in response to *Islam Hadhari,* "If Islam has an attribute civilized, then there should be another part of Islam that is uncivilized. Islam itself is a complete civilization." Instead, he introduced what he calls Islamic civilization (*Hadhara Islamiyya*) (Awang 2005). Awang believed that *Islam Hadhari* failed to take the Qur'an and hadith as the primary basis of the state. The leaders of UMNO, Abdul Hadi Awang continued to argue, "are using the law of human creation and are forcing people to obey them as the leaders even though they disobey Allah" (Awang 2005). For Awang, Islamic civilization could only take place under an Islamic State (*Negara Islam*), first exemplified by Muhammad through the Constitution of Medina and as subsequently demonstrated by Muslim caliphs and sultans. "If Islam gains power, the country will be safe; if the ḥudūd law and qiṣāṣ are enacted, criminals will be afraid; the Islamic state is the solution to [our] problems. What is prevailing today is not based on the Qur'an" Awang conceives of Islamic comprehensiveness in terms of the formalization of the Islamic state in its fullest, judicial sense. On the other hand, UMNO leaders and scholars maintain Malaysia's Constitutionalism, stating that although Malaysia regards Islam as the official religion, it has to recognize all other religions. The same contract (*mithaq*) of Medina is interpreted by UMNO as an inspiring model for "a just and trustworthy government," and "religious freedom" within a multi-religious and racial country.

The construction and contestation of *Islam Hadhari* by UMNO and PAS leaders discussed above demonstrates an unfinished project of Islamization and modernization among Malays in modern Malaysia. Nobody wants to merely connect to the past and not to see the present and the future. *Islam Hadhari* was an approach reconciling piety and pragmatism; a tool for gaining or maintaining power amid competing players; an identity and image restoration of Islam as a complete and perfect civilization; and a response to Western dominance and an effort to rehabilitate the golden age of Islam at a time of crisis facing modern Muslims (Ali 2011).

Progressive Muslims in Malaysia

Farish Noor, identifying himself as a progressive Muslim activist, has been an advocate for Malaysia to become a real progressive Muslim country.

Now, more than ever, the truly progressive and moderate face of Islam must show itself. In the Malaysian context, this would mean developing a new voice of Islam

Figure 19.1 Petronas Towers and Masjid al-Syakirin Mosque in Kuala Lumpur, Malaysia. Courtesy of iStockphoto.

that is committed to universalist and humanitarian principles that would critique the abuse of power both at home and abroad. It would mean a school of Islamic thought that is prepared to take up issues and concerns like democracy, civil society, gender politics, and economic justice under its wing. ... The first thing it has to do is turn itself into a real democracy, to show that Islam is indeed compatible with the values of a progressive, liberal, and pluralist age

(Noor 2002: 176)

Women have become agents for Islamic modernization in Malaysia, such as Sisters in Islam (SIS), founded in 1987 by Zainah Anwar. SIS has opposed the introduction or enactment of the *hudud* (meaning criminal law) legislation in the states of Kelantan and Trengganu. In one of her writings on women and *shari'a*, Zainah Anwar said:

It's as if in Islam, women don't have any rights at all. One woman was asked, if the house were on fire, would she then have to seek her husband's permission to flee! Women cannot even use their common sense to save their (own) lives. This cannot be Islam. God is just. Islam is just.

(www.sistersinislam.org.my)

On polygamy, Anwar continues:

> The Qur'an says: "If you fear that you cannot treat them the same, then marry just the one." That was a moment of epiphany. It was that kind of questioning that made us want to read the Qur'an with a new lens. It was a liberating process understanding that the Qur'an speaks to women and is lifting and empowering.
>
> *(www.sistersinislam.org.my)*

Zainah Anwar and SIS resist the traditionalist *ulama*'s monopoly on religious interpretation. On the whole, the Malaysian government has remained tolerant towards SIS, preferring to allow them to enhance Malaysia's international image as a progressive, modernist, and moderate Muslim country (Hassan in Weiss and Hassan 2003: 108–9).

Today in Malaysia there is "the ongoing interaction of global knowledge, Western and Islamic, and local knowledge, both indigenous and indigenized" (Samsul in Hefner and Horvatich 1997: 224). The contest has been to define not only what is authentically Islamic, but more importantly what is modern and beneficial for the well-being of Malay Muslims in a multi-ethnic country. Ethnicity, religion, capitalism, national citizenship, and globalization are now closely linked (Peletz 2002; Fischer 2008; Frisk 2009). Modern Muslims in Malaysia, as in Indonesia, are striking a difficult balance between local and global forces, between textual interpretations and contextual considerations. They become modern in diverse and dynamic ways.

Conclusion

Being Muslim and modern are identities that mutually reinforce each other in Southeast Asia. Muslim scholars and activists in this region have actively engaged with both Islam and modernity from within and from without. Even though Muslims in this region continue to respond to ideas and influences from the West, they have primarily drawn their ideas and practices from Islamic and local traditions. They are defining and contesting what Islam and modernity mean. Being a modern Muslim means a constant engagement with the past, but within changing intellectual, cultural, and socio-political forces; but, more importantly in Southeast Asia globalizing economic forces. Colonial histories, ethnic and demographic composition, socio-religious networks, educational systems, national politics, economic development, and globalization have shaped the dynamic ways in which Muslims define and contest Islam and modernity in local and global contexts. There is no monolithic way to be a modern Muslim in Indonesia, Malaysia and other similar regions of Southeast Asia.

Summary

- Islamization is deemed an unfinished process, although the overwhelming majority of Muslims in Southeast Asia are of Sunni theology and of Shafi'i legal school of thought. Depending on their response to Islamic reform, Western modernity, and local beliefs and practices, Muslims are in general either traditionalist or modernist.
- In Indonesia, the modernist and the traditionalist Islamic organizations (Muhammadiyah and *Nahdlatul Ulama*) emerged in a response to Dutch colonial modernity, but have operated in response to each other, and to changing socio-political conditions. Both maintained their support for the state ideology of Pancasila, and the progressive activists from among them take a further step in reforming Islam. The Islamists, moderate and radical, sought to undermine it. In their diversity, Muslim activists use modern technology to disseminate their ideas and conduct their activities.
- In Malaysia, being colonized by the British, the reformist and the conservative Malay Muslims (represented by the ruling party of United Malays National Organization and the Pan-Malaysian Islamic Party) have demonstrated their politics of Islamization, including the idea of *Islam Hadhari* and the idea of *Hadharah Islamiyyah*. The progressive associations and activists have been critical of both parties, emphasizing substantive values such as equality and justice rather than formal politics. Being diverse politically, they accept the assumption that modernized Islam would help improve the condition of the Malays as well as non-Malay citizens.

Discussion points

- To what extent is the theory of modernization helpful in explaining Muslims responses to Western modernity?
- Identify and explain who the modernist Muslims, the traditionalist Muslims, and the progressive Muslims? Do they share some ideas and practices in common?
- What is Pancasila? Having Pancasila as the state ideology, is Indonesia closer to an Islamic state or to a secular state? First define what you mean by Islamic state and secular state and then discuss the position of Indonesia accordingly.
- Why did *Rukunegara* emerge in Malaysia? Discuss *Rukunegara* in relation to the Malaysian Constitution that stipulates Islam as the official religion of the state, but recognizes religious freedom. How is it possible for the Malaysian state to be tolerant toward other religions, adhered by Chinese, Indian, and others?
- Could you compare and contrast between Indonesia and Malaysia in terms of their politics and culture of Islamization and modernization? Do they become Muslim and modern in similar ways?

Further reading

Greg Fealy and Virginia Hooker (eds) (2006) *Voices of Islam in Southeast Asia: A Contemporary Sourcebook*, Singapore: Institute of Southeast Asian Studies.

This is a sourcebook to present a wide selection of contemporary materials on Islam in Southeast Asia, covering six broad themes: personal expressions of faith; Islamic law; state and governance; women and family; *jihad*; and interactions with non-Muslims and the wider Muslim world. The book looks at the ideological and doctrinal content of Islam in Southeast Asia in all its facets, while also exploring the motivations underlying different interpretations and viewpoints.

Robert. W. Hefner (ed.) (2009) *Making Modern Muslims: The Politics of Islamic Education in Southeast Asia*, Honolulu: University of Hawaii Press.

This is a collection of essays on Islamic education and modernization in Southeast Asia, with a good overview by Hefner in the introduction, and with separate chapters on Indonesia, Malaysia, Southern Thailand, Cambodia, and the Philippines. The book argues that modernist and traditionalist Muslim educational systems have to face modernization.

Michael G. Peletz (2002) *Islamic Modern: Cultural Politics in Malaysia*, Princeton, NJ: Princeton University Press.

This ethnographic work focuses on the tension and compromise between Islamic courts and the modern legal system in Malaysia. The book discusses modern notions of law, identity, Asian values, and civil society within the Islamic and Malay contexts.

Rizal Sukma and Clara Joewono (eds) (2007) *Islamic Thought and Movements in Contemporary Indonesia*, Jakarta: Centre for Strategic and International Studies.

The authors, all Indonesian scholars, write about contemporary Islamic ideas such as the Islamic State, Islamic society, and Islamic movements such as the Salafi, the mainstream, the moderate, the Sufi, and women's movements.

Andrew N. Weintraub (ed.) (2011) *Islam and Popular Culture in Indonesia and Malaysia*, London and New York: Routledge.

This is the first book that analyzes various aspects of Islam, popular culture, and modernities in Indonesia and Malaysia. The authors discuss Muslim expressions in mass media, art, cinema, music, the internet, magazines, films, and literature.

References

Ali, Muhamad (2005) "The Rise of the Liberal Islam Network (JIL) in Contemporary Indonesia," *The American Journal of Islamic Social Sciences*, 22(1): 1–27.

—— (2006) "Transmission of Islamic Knowledge in Kelantan," *Journal of the Malaysian Branch of the Royal Asiatic Society*, 79(2): 39–58.

—— (2007) "Categorizing Muslims in Postcolonial Indonesia," *Moussons*, 11: 33–42.

—— (2011) "Eclecticism of Modern Islam: Islam Hadhari in Malaysia," *Studia Islamika: Indonesian Journal for Islamic Studies*, 18(1): 1–27.

Andaya, Barbara W. (1997) "Historicising 'Modernity' in Southeast Asia," *Journal of the Economic and Social History of the Orient*, 40(4): 391–409.

Andaya, Barbara W. and Leonard Y. Andaya (2001) *A History of Malaysia*, Honolulu: University of Hawaii Press.

Anwar, M. Syafi'i (1995) *Pemikiran dan Aksi Islam Indonesia: Sebuah Kajian tentang Cendekiawan Muslim Orde Baru*, Jakarta: Paramadina.

Awang, Abdul Hadi (2005) *Hadharah Islamiyyah Bukan Islam Hadhari*, Kuala Lumpur: Nufair Street Sdn Bhd.

Azra, Azyumardi (2004) *The Origins of Islamic Reformism in Southeast Asia: Networks of Malay-Indonesian and Middle Eastern 'Ulama' in the Seventeenth and Eighteenth Centuries*, Crows Nest, Australia: Asian Studies Association of Australia in association with Allen & Unwin; Honolulu: University of Hawaii Press.

Badawi, Abdullah Ahmad (2006) *Islam Hadhari: A Model for Development and Progress*, Selangor, Malaysia: MPH Group Publishing.

Barton, Greg (2005) *Jemaah Islamiyah: Radical Islamism in Indonesia*, Singapore: Singapore University Press.

Bentley, Jerry H. (2003) *Shapes of World History in Twentieth-Century Scholarship*, Washington, DC: American Historical Association.

Black, C.E. (1975) *The Dynamics of Modernization*, New York: Harper & Row.

Boy, Pradana et al (eds) (2008) *Era Baru Gerakan Muhammadiyah*, Malang, Indonesia: Penerbitan Universitas Muhammadiyah Malang.

Bruinessen, Martin van and Julia Day Howell (eds) (2007) *Sufism and the 'Modern' in Islam*, London: I.B. Tauris.

Bush, Robin (2009) *Nahdlatul Lama and the Struggle for Power within Islam and Politics in Indonesia*, Singapore: Institute of Southeast Asian Studies.

Casanova, José (1994) *Public Religions in the Modern World*, Chicago: University of Chicago Press.

Fealy, Greg and Sally White (eds) (2008) *Expressing Islam: Religious Life and Politics in Indonesia*, Singapore: Institute of Southeast Asian Studies, 2008.

Fischer, Johan (2008) *Proper Islamic Consumption: Shopping among the Malays in Modern Malaysia*, Copenhagen, Denmark: NIAS Press.

Frisk, Sylvia (2009) *Submitting to God: Women and Islam in Urban Malaysia*, Copenhagen: NIAS Press.

Geertz, Clifford (1960) *Religion of Java*, Chicago and London: University of Chicago Press.

Gerth, Hans H. and C. Wright Mills (eds) (1946) *From Max Weber: Essays in Sociology*, New York: Oxford University Press.

Ghazali, Abd Rohim et al (2007) *Muhammadiyah Progresif: Manifesto Pemikiran Kaum Muda*, Jakarta: Jaringan Intelektual Muda Muhammadiyah and Lembaga Studi Filsafat Islam.

Guan, Lee Hock (ed.) (2004) *Civil Society in Southeast Asia*, Singapore: Institute of Southeast Asian Studies.

Hamka (1991) *Tasawuf Modern*, Jakarta: Pustaka Panjimas.

Hefner, Robert W. (2000) *Civil Islam: Muslims and Democratization in Indonesia*, Princeton, NJ: Princeton University.

Hefner, Robert W. and Horvatich, Patricia (eds) (1997) *Islam in an Era of Nation-States*, Honolulu: University of Hawaii Press.

Laffan, Michael (2011) *The Makings of Indonesian Islam: Orientalism and the Narration of a Sufi Past*, Princeton, NJ: Princeton University Press.

Mutalib, Hussin (1993) *Islam in Malaysia: From Revivalism to Islamic State*, Singapore: Singapore University Press.

Nasr, Seyyed Hossein (2011) *Islam in the Modern World: Challenged by the West, Threatened by Fundamentalism, Keeping Faith with Tradition*, New York: HarperOne.

Noor, Farish A. (2002) *The Other Malaysia: Writings on Malaysia's Subaltern History*, Kuala Lumpur: Silverfishbooks.

Peletz, Michael G. (2002) *Islamic Modern: Religious Courts and Cultural Politics in Malaysia*, Princeton, NJ: Princeton University Press.

Pew Forum on Religion and Public Life (2009) "Mapping the Global Muslim Population," available at http://pewforum.org/Mapping-the-Global-Muslim-Population.aspx.

Pimpinan Pusat Muhammadiyah (2000) *Pedoman Hidup Warga Muhammadiyah*, Jogjakarta, Indonesia: Suara Muhammadiyah.

Rahman, Fazlur (1984) *Islam and Modernity*, Chicago: University of Chicago Press.

Roff, William R. (ed.) (1974) *Kelantan: Religion, Society and Politics*, Oxford: Oxford University Press.

Rosadi, Andri (2008) *Hitam Putih FPI (Front Pembela Islam)*, Jakarta: Nun Publisher.

Rostow, W.W. (1971) *Politics and the Stages of Growth*, Cambridge: Cambridge University Press.

Sirry, Mun'im A. (ed.) (2005) *Fiqih Lintas Agama: Membangun Masyarakat Inklusif-Pluralis*, Jakarta: Yayasan Wakaf Paramadina and the Asia Foundation.

Sukma, Rizal and Clara Joewono (eds) (2007) *Gerakan & Pemikiran Islam Indonesia Kontemporer*, Jakarta: Centre for Strategic and International Studies.

Tim Penyusun (2010) *1 Abad Muhammadiyah: Gagasan Pembaharuan Sosial Keagamaan*, Jakarta: Kompas.

Wan Jusoh, Wan Ismail bin (ed.) (1999) *Koleksi Ucapan Rasmi Yab Tuan Guru Datp' Haji Nik Abdul Aziz bin Haji Nik Mat Menteri Besar Kelantan*, Kota Bharu, Malaysia: Dian Darulnaim.

Weintraub, Andrew N. (ed) (2011) *Islam and Popular Culture in Indonesia and Malaysia*, London and New York: Routledge.

Weiss, Meredith L. and Saliha Hassan (eds) (2003) *Social Movements in Malaysia: From Moral Communities to NGOs*, London and New York: Routledge Curzon.

Journals and websites

Pengasuh, no.1, July 11, 1918; no.13, January 3, 1919; no.309, December 21, 1930.
Verslag Moehammadijah di Hindia Timoer ke –X, 1923.
http://islamlib.com/en/pages/about.
www.sistersinislam.org.my.

Note

1   I would like to thank Professors Ebrahim Moosa and Jeffrey Kenney as well as Sam Kigar and Jillian D'Urso for their editorial suggestions and improvisations to this text. All errors remain mine.

20 Politics and Islamization in African public spheres

Abdulkader Tayob

Outline

- The revival of religion in Africa and elsewhere poses a challenge to understanding modern societies.
- Two concepts in the study of Islam, public Islam and Muslim publics, have suggested how new groups are formed and ideas debated.
- In Africa, these new publics may be recognized since colonialism, and continue in postcolonial contexts.
- This article suggests that three major issues have been identified in recent research: identity politics, Islamization of the public and critical debates on Islam.
- The article concludes that Islam in the public spheres of African societies grapples with a new politics of religion.

Islamist politics in North Africa, the extension of *shari'a* in northern Nigerian in 1999, and the constitutional review process in Kenya from the late 1990s to 2010 are some prominent examples that show how Muslim debates have formed an important part of African political life. Public life debates are not, however, restricted to politics. In non-political spheres, the presence of symbols in mosques, schools, personal dress and faith-based social services cannot be missed. Notwithstanding this great diversity, some patterns and key preoccupations of public life are noticeable. This essay identifies some distinct sites and expressions of Islamic public life in Africa from the beginning of the period of liberation and emancipation in the 1950s until the present. The expressions reflect the changing political conditions inaugurated by colonialism, and continued by postcolonial states in African societies. Muslim publics in Africa range from those that are clearly concerned with politics, those concerned with civil society issues and those that are very specifically focused on the production and reproduction of good Muslim believers. They include deliberations and competition over the state, as well as other more non-political and even apolitical dimensions of public life.

Public Islam and Muslim publics

The public sphere has been one of the dominant frameworks for understanding the modern revival of religion. After the initial scramble to come to terms with secularization theories that had predicted the end of the public role of religion, the idea of the public sphere provided a useful framework for understanding the impact of religions in their complexity and variety. The role of religion in the public sphere was first identified in Latin America, Eastern Europe and then extended to other countries. Casanova called it another wave of democracy led by Catholicism in Latin American and Eastern Europe (Casanova 1994, 2001; Ellis and ter Haar 1998). The role of religion in public life seemed a more productive approach to a complex and sensitive phenomenon.

Scholars of Islam have also developed the concept of religion in the public sphere to understand developments in Muslim societies. Eickelman and Salvatore have written extensively, and brought a number of scholars together to reflect and write on 'public Islam' and 'Muslim publics'. Public Islam referred to

> [...] highly diverse invocations of Islam as ideas and practices that religious scholars, self-ascribed religious authorities, secular intellectuals, Sufi orders, mothers, students, workers, engineers, and many others make to civic debate and public life. In this 'public' capacity, 'Islam' makes a difference in configuring the politics and social life of large parts of the globe, and not just for self-ascribed religious authorities.
>
> *(Salvatore and Eickelman 2004b: xii)*

Public Islam referred to articulations and claims made on the meaning of Islam. Such articulations were by definition not restricted to a particular class of leaders (*ulama*). In contrast to public Islam, a Muslim public was a discursive space created by these articulations. Drawing on the ideas of Dewey, Salvatore and Eickelman defined Muslim publics as discursive spaces enabled by shared standards of anticipation (Salvatore and Eickelman 2004a: 16). The role of new media technologies and the entry of non-specialists were crucial in the definition of Muslim publics and public Islam.

Studies on public Islam and Muslim publics have been useful concepts for thinking about how technologies of communication created new possibilities for the meaning and articulation of Islam. However, in order to assess patterns of engagement, one has to be more specific about the political contexts in which these publics are formed and located. The role and meaning of religion in a state, laws regulating dress codes and moral actions, and the freedom enjoyed by or restrictions imposed on opposition movements, are guided and shaped by concrete political contexts. Public Islam and Muslim publics are part of the broader public sphere, which by definition is located between private and official spheres within a modern state. This article seeks to identify patterns of such public engagement in African countries.

Postcolonial public spheres and Islam

Soares' study of Islam in French West Africa is a useful starting point for understanding public Islam and Muslim publics in African public spheres. He pointed out how colonial policies created new spaces for Muslim political and social activities (Soares 2005). Islam lost its independent political capital at the court, but retained its relevance when prominent religious leaders were actively promoted to grant legitimacy to colonial rule. Colonial policies did not only lead to accommodative practices among Muslims. They also favoured, implicitly and explicitly, the practice of Islam that was not overtly political. Islamic cultural practices and scholarly relations thrived and spread to parts of Africa that had only nominal contact, or none at all, with Islam and Muslims. New theological and religious movements propelled these developments. Sufi orders such as the Muridiyya and Tijaniyya in West Africa thrived, or older ones like the Qadiriyya rejuvenated in East Africa among the newly urbanized in Dar-es-Salaam (Stewart 1990). Moreover, modern forms of associational life such as charity foundations, brigades, newspapers, *daw'a* (propagation) movements, youth movements and also nascent political movements proliferated (Brenner 1993). Muslims thrived especially in the new cities: from Cape Town to Nairobi to Bamako to Lagos to St. Louis (Trimingham 1980). In the colonial context, then, religion was differently employed than before, balanced between legitimacy to rulers and active engagement in public life.

National liberation movements achieved independence from colonial powers, beginning immediately after the Second World War and continuing up to the end of apartheid in 1994. Within this new political context, three dominant preoccupations and expressions may be identified in Muslim publics. I will call the first a 'politics of identity' that captured the desire of Muslims to give shape and expression to national public life. This ranged from North African countries where Islam became a state religion, to countries such as Nigeria, Kenya and Tanzania where Muslims formed a significant percentage of the population. In these latter societies, Islamic identity politics dominated public life in competition with Christian groups. The second public manifestation of Islam was a continuing preoccupation with defining orthodoxy and orthopraxis for Muslim social life. In the postcolonial contexts, such concerns included the formation of *ulama* bodies, the proliferation of schools and mosques, and the adoption of public practices derived from the normative, textual sources of Islam. A small but widely dispersed critical discourse on Islamic law was a third expression of public Islam. Critical discourse first appeared in national politics, as Muslims throughout Africa participated in liberation movements and post-independence reconstructive programmes. These have ranged from the elaborate political philosophy of Mahmud Muhammad Taha (executed 1983) to activism against apartheid in the 1980s (Mahmoud 2000; Jack 1959; Esack 1988). This progressive trend has recently taken a legal shape when more liberal political changes were inaugurated in a number of African countries, and Islamic law introduced in national debates and legislatures. Critical debates and movements have emerged against an uncritical application of Islamic law. Relatively marginal and much smaller in number, a critical discourse over Islamic law is an equally prominent expression in African public spheres. Each of these expressions is directly related to a particular political context in which they have emerged and thrived, but there are some similarities across regions, and across the continent.

Politics of identity

I begin this exploration on identity with the idea of religious nationalism that has played an important role in public sphere debates and discussions, and also conflicts in several African countries. Religious nationalism refers to a nationalist ideology in which symbols, narratives and concepts have played a significant role first in Europe and then later in the postcolonial contexts of the Third World. The overtly secular framing of nationalism has been brought into question, pointing out how central a role religious discourse has played in the imagination of nations (Hastings 1997). It is this entanglement between religion and nation-state that is present in African politics and Muslim public debates as well.

North Africa is the obvious place to begin to examine the place of a Muslim nationalist discourse in Africa. From the Moroccan king to Egypt's socialist, democratic republic, Islam was declared the state religion, and each of the countries pursued a path of modernization and state-building that included a reformist discourse of Islam (Brown 1964; Christelow 1987). The roots of this reformist/nationalist discourse can be traced to the nineteenth century. Personalities such as Amīr ʿAbd al-Qādir al-Jazāʾirī (d. 1883) and Khayr al-Dīn al-Tunisī (d. 1890) loomed large in a nineteenth-century Islamist reformist tradition that resisted European colonialism and imperialism. They were followed by others in the twentieth century, centred around the vast influence of Egyptian modernist Muḥammad ʿAbduh (d. 1905). Reformist Islam in these countries was a familiar trope of returning to the original teaching of Islam, but unique in one important sense. This particular reformism also claimed that Islam in essence was compatible with modernization (and not Westernization) as inaugurated in Europe (Abu Zeid 1999). After independence, this particular reformist understanding of Islam was absorbed into the national identity of the new states. Reformist Islam provided a strong foundation for the states, allowing them also to monopolize the definition of religion, and explicitly proscribe and limit non-state political parties and movements founded in the name of Islam.

Islamist movements from the 1970s challenged the legitimacy of these states precisely on their religious foundations. The most widely studied of these movements has been the Muslim Brothers in Egypt, and the most successful at the polls was the *Projet de Programme du Front Islamique du Salut* (FIS) coalition of Islamic parties and movements that won the first round of national elections in Algeria in 1990. The Islamists (National Islamic Front) in the Sudan, under the leadership of Hasan al-Turabi, supported the military coup of Omar al-Bashir in 1989 and wielded enormous power which it used to Islamize state and society (Shahin 1997). In general, Islamists offered a new form of politics and public life, one that, in their view, was more committed to the traditions of Islam. They charged that the postcolonial states were not wholly committed to Islam, deriving their models and inspiration from European ideas. In their view, postcolonial states were enforcing and promoting public life practices in flagrant contradiction with the society's cultural traditions. Moreover, in the absence of efficient or non-existent social services by the state, they often also provided medical help and economic relief in distinctively religious idioms. By the time the Arab revolutions swept across North Africa and the Middle East in 2011, Islamist groups emerged as the most prominent political and public groups in Tunisia, Egypt and possibly other countries. Towards these goals, the place of Islam in state and society was debated among newly emergent literate classes. Issues of identity and authenticity were the central preoccupations of this public discourse.

Religious nationalism in the form of an explicit state ideology did not play such a dominant role in all African societies. Muslim-majority countries in sub-Saharan Africa created generally more secular states with sufficient co-optation of and legitimacy from religious leadership. These included countries such as Mali, Senegal, Niger and Chad that inherited secularism (*laïcité*) from the French, and also Somalia with a history of Italian colonialism. Countries that had emerged from British colonial rule were not as decisive on secularism, even though they did not develop explicitly religious states. In some of these countries, Muslims and Christians engaged in a battle over the symbolic identity of the state. Such politics included a close watch over the religious identities of those in power, a dominant religious identity among citizens, and intra- and inter-religious conflict and competition. The public sphere dimension of this contestation may be clarified when we look at some examples.

In Nigeria, the ruling aristocracy, nurtured and protected by the British through indirect rule, transformed itself into political players in the new state. Ahmadu Bello, governor of northern Nigeria from 1959 to 1966, played a dominant role in laying the foundation of such a transformation in post-independent Nigerian politics. His political ambition was closely connected to the construction of a particular Nigerian Muslim identity. As head of the Northern People's Congress, he wanted the support of Nigerian Muslims in one political party with a history linked to the Islamic state of Uthman dan Fodio in the eighteenth and nineteen centuries. Bello formed a national body Jamaat Nasr al-Islam (Society for the Support (Victory) of Islam), headed by himself and key northern leaders. Bello also tried to found a new Sufi order, Usmaniyya, to supersede or bring together rival Sufi groups of the Tijaniyya and Qadariyya. More significantly, he supported a rising Islamic preacher, Abu Bakr Gumi, who would dominate Islamic debate and discourse in Nigeria until his death in 1992. Gumi was appointed Grand Kadi, and invited to present a series of sermons in the Sultan Bello Mosque (Gumi and Tsiga 2001). Bello himself was assassinated in 1965, but the search for both Muslim unity and hegemony on the national front did not die with him (Hunwick 1992; Loimeier 1997). His politics laid the foundation of a dominant politics of identity in Nigeria that continued long after him. They may become much clearer when compared with those of another prominent politician who had a different perspective on the role of Islam and its traditional leaders in Northern Nigeria.

Figure 20.1 Crowd outside the mosque in Kano, Nigeria. Courtesy of Aminu Abubakar/AFP/ Getty Images.

Aminu Kano (1920–83) was born in a religious scholarly family, became a school teacher, and then went on to lead the Northern Elements Progressive Union. He opposed the indirect rule pursued in Northern Nigeria, and also the local aristocracy that benefited from a hierarchical social order (Jack 1959). Values of social justice, development and equality were more important than the prominence of religious symbols in public life.

In comparison with Nigeria, Muslim identity has had a more equivocal and complex place in East African public life. Prior to independence, the island of Zanzibar witnessed the emergence of Swahili nationalism with a strong Muslim identity. But the contradictions were too deep between the different classes and ethnicities that constituted Swahili identity, and the general current in the region tended toward secular nationalist leadership, led mainly by mission-educated Christians. Moreover, Islam was associated with slavery and Zanzibari Arab colonialism within nationalist circles. The Zanzibari revolution of 1964 put an end to any ambition of Islamic identity in the body politic of East African states (Lofchie 1965).

While a secular politic was jealously guarded, religion was not completely banished. Political leaders in the region, both Muslims and Christians, openly sought support from religious establishments. On occasion, politicians adopted religious symbolism in their political rhetoric. Alamin Mazrui has argued that Daniel Arap Moi of Kenya (r. 1978–2002) employed an idiosyncratic Christian symbolism to inscribe the nation. In this national imagination, according to Mazrui, religious minorities could not be fully accommodated (Mazrui 1993). More generally, the relationship between government and Muslims was expressed through state-recognized bodies. Islam's counterpart to the Church were state-sponsored and state-supported national bodies in each of the countries: Kenya's Supreme Council of Kenya Muslims (SUPKEM) (est. 1973), Tanzania's Baraza Kuu la Waislamu (Higher Islamic Council), Uganda's National Association for the Advancement of Muslims (est. 1964) and National Muslim Council (1965), and the Muslim Association in Malawi. These organizations worked with ruling governments and parties, irrespective of their political philosophies and ideologies (Constantin 1995; Haynes 2006).

This approach to politics has been questioned since the 1990s when a more assertive politics emerged in East Africa. In Kenya, Oded studied the rise and fall of the Islamic Party of Kenya (IPK), tracing its inspiration from religious scholars trained outside Kenya. The latter offered a more challenging approach to politics for Kenyan Muslims who felt deeply aggrieved by their marginalization. Refused registration by the Moi government, supporters of the Islamic Party took their frustrations to the streets of Mombasa, where they were quickly quashed. The Islamic Party of Kenya was part of a wider public engagement of Muslims in the region that had deeper implications for public life. At the political level, such Muslims contested the representation of the national bodies. They created alternative organizations (often quickly closed by states), and promoted alternative forms of religious and social life. These groups tended to form Islamist and Salafi oriented groups (Turner 2009; Loimeier 2011; O'Brien 2003; Oded 1996).

The politics of identity in the public sphere, then, is one of the distinct expressions of African Muslim publics. It ranges from the place of a modernist reformist discourse in North African state ideologies, to the contestations over the representation of Muslims in the national politics of East Africa. Public debates were preoccupied with the place and meaning of religion in politics and statecraft. Alternative Muslim discourses emerged to challenge agreed settlements in this sphere. Islamists in North Africa challenged what they called the secularist and Western frameworks of the status quo, whilst activists in East Africa challenged the national representation models established in the 1960s and 1970s. A politics of identity has been regularly inserted by Muslims into the public and political spheres in Africa.

Islamization of the public sphere

Gumi did not only serve Bello's political interests; he was also influential on the greater representation of Islam in the public sphere. Like other reformists, he campaigned for Muslim public practices to be reformed in terms of the Qur'an and *sunna* of the Prophet. In the Nigerian context, such reformist ideas were directed against the vast influence of Tijaniyya and Qadiriyya Sufi networks (Loimeier 1997). Similar challenges to the status quo in East Africa came from Salafi teachers and students who had studied abroad (Turner 2009). Religious scholars, Sufi Shaykhs, *mallams* and *ulama*, were also organizing themselves in various ways, and advocating some religious reform or another. And, without exception, they have become prominent in almost every African country. Not unexpectedly, this redefinition and reclamation included contestations among competing groups. Again, some examples from African societies will locate these general trends, and show how public life was targeted by diverse movements of Islamization.

Vahed and Moosa have documented and studied the Islamization of the public sphere in the minority context of South African Muslims of South Asian origin (Moosa 1997; Vahed 2003). At the height of repression practiced by the apartheid state in the 1960s and 1970s, Islamic public life was being slowly transformed. This change was led mainly by religious leaders who graduated from the seminaries of India, and returned to take over the control of mosques and ritual spaces in the country (Tayob 1999). Islamization took root within sectarian conflicts between Deobandis and Barelvis. Deobandis criticized the folk and family traditions inherited from India with regard to marriage rites, prophetic celebration rituals, funeral traditions and traditional practices. Moreover, the Tablighi Jamaat, as a close ally of the Deobandis, popularized these changes through an effective mass movement. The Barelvis defended themselves against these charges, and mounted their own attacks on theological grounds (Vahed 2003; Moosa 2000). This contest laid the foundation for extensive public teaching, the proliferation of texts and later extensive use of media (radio) to increase awareness of Islamic religious obligation. The sectarian conflicts led to increased devotion to religious rituals and adoption of symbols on both personal and communal levels.

Janson has studied the Islamization of the public sphere in the Gambia, which gives a different perspective to reform in a majoritarian Muslim society. She notes the very explicit support given to Islamic debates by the president of the country, President Yahya Jammeh, since 1994. A reformist understanding of Islam took shape against a Sufi-oriented epistemology which included claims to an esoteric access to knowledge, and support for traditional practices at graveyards and commemoration sites. Janson argues that the two approaches did not apparently lead to any single dominating approach (Janson 2006). She has documented the rise of the Tablighi Jamaat, with strong support from South Africa, among young unemployed men and women (Janson 2005). Reformist groups seem diverse, but they all seem to succeed in promoting public religious observance in societies. More populist, folk and esoteric traditions and cultures were pushed to the margins or the background.

Educational institutions have played a significant role in the Islamization of the public sphere. Scholarly networks continued transmitting the traditions of Islam from one generation to the next, through teacher-pupil relations and also through newly established colleges and madrasahs. The scholarly traditions in West Africa around Malikism, and in East Africa around Shafi'ism, have played a significant role in the ubiquity and strength of Islamization in the public sphere. The Hanafis and Shafi'is in South Africa have also founded Dar al-ʿUlūm modelled on Indian traditions (Sayed 2010; Reetz 2011). These scholarly traditions have been preserved within mystical orders as in Senegal, or without them as in Kenya. Often, as in Nigeria, Kenya and Zanzibar, such traditions are maintained through a legally sanctioned system of Qadhi and *shari'a* courts. And most of them maintain a continuous link with their counterparts outside Africa through educational sojourns, mystical lineages and book transfers. The teachers and scholars run basic schooling for children all over African Muslim communities. They also provide the basic knowledge base of religious education for new Muslim schools that have combined modern scientific education and religious socialization (Islamic schools). The vitality and success of these scholarly networks and schools has promoted greater adherence to the textual traditions of Islam.

Islamic schools have been founded by both governments and religious communities to promote some form of modern education among Muslims. Muslims had at first resisted these due to their association with colonialism or Christianity. Later, however, some Muslims themselves introduced new kinds of schools when they recognized the importance and value of modern education. The Yoruba were probably the first Nigerian Muslims who took this approach and still maintained their leadership in this regard. In some countries, modernization was significantly enhanced when independent countries embarked on massive programmes of universal education in order to create new citizens, professionals and leaders for emerging states. Such contexts became the breeding ground for a strong sense of religious identity, often in an attempt to replicate or oppose Christians (Reichmuth 1997; Starret 1998; Tayob et al 2011). Brenner has studied these highly organized schools in Mali where the secular state's refusal to provide for religious education prompted students of Arabic to found their own schools. In such a way, the promulgation of Islamic norms and mores continues in spite of the secular ideology of the state (Brenner 2000).

Figure 20.2 Boy going to Islamic school in Cape Town, South Africa. Courtesy of Shaamielah Davids.

These and other movements for Islamization throughout Africa indicate greater access to the sources of Islam, and thus conformity to the textual traditions of Islam. On the surface, it seems that this process of greater Islamization has been going on for a long time, and bears testimony to what Sanneh and Fisher have called an internal logic within Islamic tradition. As the texts and sources of Islam are made available to

Muslims, there is a slow but inexorable trend to greater conformity (Sanneh 1994; Fisher 1985). Folk traditions are thereby marginalized as the reformist discourse and logic holds sway. In the context of Africa, so-called African traditions are identified for removal from the public sphere (Rosander 1997).

This range of acceptable and consensual *public* practice conceals more complex changes within the societies, two of which will be mentioned here. Writing on reformist trends in Kenya and the East African coast since the nineteenth century, Seeseman has shown how the content of what is identified and thus targeted as African has changed. In particular, the *mawlid* celebrations in honour of the birth of the Prophet are attacked as steeped in African customs and traditions. And yet, these practices were introduced into Africa in the nineteenth century from the Yemen (Seeseman 2006). Similarly, spirit possession cults in both East and West Africa are thoroughly interwoven within Islamic cosmology and ritual. Lewis has described their integration into a pan-Islamic fabric of Islamic life over many generations:

> religious phenomena that existed before Islam entered a given region, and which are there authentically 'pre-Islamic', become after their diffusion to other Islamic areas post- and sometimes even pan-Islamic.
>
> *(Lewis 1986: 105)*

Recent studies on spirit possession practices in East and West Africa point to their continued vitality and demand (Larsen 2001). In an ironic reversal of puritan traditions originating from Saudi Arabia, O'Brien has pointed to their great demand in the Arabian peninsula (O'Brien 1999). Soares suggests that they find support from some modern states, such as Mali, that want to protect their secular tradition against a demanding public Islam (Soares 1999). It seems that the public practice of Islam simply forces alternative and marginalized traditions to continue in less public ways.

The Islamization of the public sphere is a process where Muslims in modern publics are accessing the texts of Islam in diverse ways. Through educational movements, critical argumentation over orthodoxy and orthopraxis, Muslims actors are adopting what they consider to be the original meaning of Islam. Their answers are diverse, but they seem to be agreeing on a framework which elevates the text above experience, the book over the person, and form over essence. A closer look at Islamization reveals some complex formations, and further studies should pay attention to what is occuring at these apparently marginalized dimensions.

Islamic law and critical activism

Critical activism is exactly one of the shades of Islamization that merits reflection as a distinct expression of public Islam.

Since the 1990s, Islamic law has become the site for critical activists, men and women, to challenge some of the effects of Islamization. Supported by 'traditional' leaders, Islamists demanded that the *shari'a* be the sole or primary source of state legislation. Moreover, advocates of Islamization have not lost any opportunity to impose Islamic legal norms on society when they have attained power (the Sudan, and northern Nigeria in Africa). Critical activism emerged in response to these developments, challenging the dominant interpretation in radical ways. Abdullahi an-Na'im is one of the few Muslim intellectuals to propose that Muslims fully accept a secular state wherein religion does not play any role, while the public space becomes a space free for the articulation of religious values (Na'im 1990). In general, however, critical activists have interrogated the meaning and implications of Islamic law, particularly with regard to women's rights. They have advocated Islamic legal reforms in diverse ways.

The democratic dispensation inaugurated at the end of apartheid in South Africa ratified one of the most progressive constitutions in the world. It included numerous cultural rights, one of them being the right to marriage systems in terms of a cultural tradition. However, it also insisted that such rights would be governed by the general principles of the constitution (the Bill of Rights). Clause 3 or Article 15 (Chapter 2) of the Constitution of South Africa 1996 read as follows:

> This section does not prevent legislation recognising
>> marriages concluded under any tradition, or a system of religious, personal or family law; or
>> systems of personal and family law under any tradition, or adhered to by persons professing a particular religion.
>
> Recognition in terms of paragraph (a) must be consistent with this section and the other provisions of the Constitution.
>> (www.info.gov.za/documents/constitution/1996/96cons2.htm#15, accessed 21 June 2011)

South African Muslims have debated the particular content and form of legislation proposed by the Constitution. The contentious point has revolved around the compatibility between Muslim personal law and the Bill of Rights. The majority of Muslims seemed to believe that a compromise with the Constitution was inherently impossible. In contrast with the human construction of the Constitution, some argued, Muslim Personal Law was divine in origin. Its provisions, they insisted, would not be subject to compromise and historical conditioning (see wwwserver. law.wits.ac.za/salc/salc.html, accessed 24 August 2007). Women's interest groups and progressive Islamic organization disagreed, and insisted that Islamic law was always a product of interpretation. They argued that the particular article in the

Constitution should be read in its entirety. For them, the crux of the constitutional provision was subject to 'other provisions of the Constitution' (Clause 15 (3) (b)). This constitutional clause would ensure an interpretation of Islamic law that would not be disadvantageous to women.

The leading and most articulate spokesperson for this new interpretation of Muslim Personal Law was Ebrahim Moosa. In both academic and newspaper articles, he argued that many traditional provisions in the *shari'a* should be regarded as *fiqh* (positive law), mainly produced by a history of male scholarship whose interpretations need no longer be valid (Moosa 1996). Making a distinction between a divine and idealized *shari'a* and humanly constructed *fiqh*, Moosa argued that the latter could be reconstructed in terms of the constitution. Moosa taught and inspired students and activists to revisit traditional issues in Islamic law. With Moosa in the lead, a strong voice emerged for a significant reformulation of Islamic law. Even when Moosa moved to the United States, this critical activist voice remained vigilant and creative, and was eventually taken over by a number of Muslim lawyers and feminist activists. Under pressure from the Women's Legal Centre, the Minister of Justice presented a proposed Bill in 2009, which reopened a critical debate over the meaning and purpose of Islamic family law in public life among South Africans. In this way, a critical voice on Islamic law has become part of the South African Muslim public (Tayob 2011).

Critical Islamic voices have been mobilized and galvanized in other contexts. They have been heard in the extension of *shari'a* in northern Nigerian states since 1999. Judgments passed by courts in cases of adultery have been challenged in higher courts, but also within Muslim public debates (Imam 2003). In Egypt, the parliament passed the so-called Khul^c Law in 2000, which basically gave women the right to apply for a no-fault divorce without the consent of their husband (Arabi 2001). Importantly, the new law was supported by legal activists and women's groups in Cairo. In 2004, Morocco passed a Reformed Family Code after years of intense public debate. Human rights activists demanded more rights for women in Moroccan marriages, whilst opponents saw the 1956 Family Code as the centrepiece of a nationalist tradition (Dieste 2009). The Moroccan example clearly illustrates the difference between a national Islamic identity conflicting with a critical voice.

Critical discussions on Islamic law have challenged the received wisdom on the shape and meaning of Islamic law in contemporary contexts. Such a discourse has generally appealed to the greater objectives (*maqāṣid*) of the *shari'a* more than its specific rules. African Muslims have been part of, if not taken the lead in, these debates on a global level (Johnston 2007). They have pointed repeatedly to the changing context of contemporary social relations in which Muslims live. As a result, they have argued that *shari'a* rules, even if derived directly from the foundation texts, should be open to revision. Such critical voices do not always enjoy a great deal of popular support. However, as these few examples show, they are part of a vibrant public debate, and are effective in being heard within societies and political and legal circles. Some of these critical discussions have even made an impact within Islamist movements in Tunisia, Egypt and South Africa (Akhavi 2003; Lee 2008; Tayob 2004). And they may make a bigger one still in the wake of the Arab Spring revolutions of 2011.

Conclusion

Muslim publics debating or competing over politics are firmly located in the public sphere, even though they have not accepted the classic Western distinction between political and public spheres. At the very least, the modern state in Africa created such conditions. In this review of Islam in African public spheres, I have identified three expressions of Muslim publics. The first, a politics of identity, represents a desire to find some kind of Islamic representation in the political sphere. Whether directly focused on the nature of the state or the symbolic trappings of the president and the ruling classes, Muslims publics in Africa have pursued various forms of identity politics. This expression demonstrates that Muslims are not entirely in agreement over the nature of the postcolonial state. Secondly, Islamization of the public represents a second theme of African publics surveyed in this article. It is a sphere that it is inherited from the past since political and religious authority was bifurcated during the early Abbasid period (Hurvitz 2002). Although religion and politics were ideally indistinguishable in the model bequeathed by the Prophet, religious and political authority functioned in distinct, but mutually supportive ways. In the modern context, Muslims have taken advantage of new social formations and new technologies to Islamize public life in terms of the normative, textual traditions of the Qur'an and *hadith*. Associations, schools and mass media have created new identities and new opportunities to bring Islam to every corner of the globe. Greater Islamization has clearly been very successful, but it has also opened up the gates of new interpretations. Much of this interpretation takes place within a consensual public sphere. However, there is clearly on the horizon a critical public discourse which I have identified as the third expression. This critical voice has focussed particularly on the interpretation of Islamic law, and the need for radical rethinking for modern states and modern social conditions.

The three expressions are distinct, but their relation with each other merits some comment. Critical activism is undoubtedly a reaction and challenge to the first and second expressions of public Islam, particularly where they are engaged in the Islamization of the state and society. However, the publics are not simply reactions and responses to each other. They pursue different objectives and goals. Muslim publics facing contentious issues do not coalesce around common values and goods. They sometimes combine with broader national civil society projects, as much as they contribute to social fragmentation. Some Muslim publics support the accumulation of social and symbolic capital on the margins of society. Ethnicities, language and class create multiple Muslim publics. Others pursue entirely apolitical and trans-national objectives. Muslim publics hardly become one Muslim public.

The three expressions clearly suggest diverse Muslim politics in African societies. The politics of identity is very clear, and so is the critical activism committed to the kind of secular state clearly advocated by an-Na'im. However, Islamization of the public sphere is more difficult to classify. Within this expression, there is a deep-seated hostility to the secular state, but also a large measure of indifference or convenient accommodation. While the two expressions may not be ignored, it is this middle ground that draws on the long history of Islamic values in the public sphere. It seems that this inherited model is being adapted for the specific conditions of the modern state. Public Islam seems most successful in this expression. However, as I have indicated, this space is as settled as it is open to challenge.

Summary

- Public Islam and Muslim publics emerged in modern colonial contexts, when religion and politics were redefined for Muslims.
- Public Islam is characterized by increased access for Muslims to the foundational texts of Islam, and to new media in which new views may be articulated.
- Although Muslim publics are diverse, at least three main expressions may be identified across the continent of Africa.
- Muslim publics are preoccupied by a politics of identity, the Islamization of the public sphere, and critical debates on Islamic law.
- Muslim publics delineate a new politics for Muslims in postcolonial states, even as most activities are directed at non-political goals.

Discussion points

- What is the difference between public Islam and Muslim publics?
- How has technology made an impact on the public expression of Islam?
- Why do political questions dominate many Muslim publics?
- What form of politics is most likely to emerge from Muslim Publics?
- What are the prospects of democracy and/or liberalism from public Islam and Muslim publics?

Further reading

Brenner, Louis (ed.) (1993) *Muslim Identity and Social Change in Sub-Saharan Africa*, Bloomington: Indiana University Press.

An earlier insightful collection of essays on Muslim societies in modern African nation-states. Brenner's introduction presents a very good overview on identity and associations in African Muslim societies.

Robinson, David (2004) *Muslim Societies in African History: New Approaches to African History*, Cambridge: Cambridge University Press.

A good introductory text on themes in diverse African countries. Includes North Africa, and provides a concise history of the regions as well.

Seeseman, Rudiger and Roman Loimeier (eds) (2006) *The Global Worlds of the Swahili: Interfaces of Islam, Identity and Space in 19th and 20th-Century East Africa*, Berlin: Lit Verlag.

This collection provides some contextual and theoretical reflections on studying Islam in Africa in general; a standard for the study of Islam in East Africa.

Soares, Benjamin F. (ed.) (2006) *Muslim-Christian Encounters in Africa: Vol. 6, Islam in Africa*, Leiden: Brill.

One of the few studies that examines developments in Christian and Muslim societies and communities.

Tayob, Abdulkader (ed.) (2007) *Islam and African Muslim Publics: Vol. 27, Journal for Islamic Studies*, Cape Town: Centre for Contemporary Islam.

A collection of case studies on Islam, politics and the public spheres in modern contexts.

References

Abu Zeid, N.H. (1999) 'The Modernisation of Islam or the Islamisation of Modernity', in R. Meijer (ed.) *Cosmopolitanism, Identity and Authenticity in the Middle East,* Richmond, UK: Curzon, 71–86.

Akhavi, S. (2003) 'Sunni Modernist Theories of Social Contract in Contemporary Egypt', *International Journal of Middle East Studies*, 35: 1, 23–49.

Arabi, O. (2001) 'The Dawning of the Third Millennium on Shari'a: Egypt's Law no. 1 of 2000, or Women May Divorce at Will', *Arab Law Quarterly*, 16: 1, 2–21.

Brenner, L. (1993) 'Introduction: Muslim Representations of Unity and Difference in the African Discourse', in L. Brenner (ed.) *Muslim Identity and Social Change in Sub-Saharan Africa*, Bloomington: Indiana University Press, 1–20.

—— (2000) *Controlling Knowledge: Religion, Power and Schooling in a West African Muslim Society*, London: Hurst & Company.

Brown, L.C. (1964) 'The Islamic Reformist Movement in North Africa', *The Journal of Modern African Studies*, 2: 1, 55–63.

Casanova, J. (1994) *Public Religions in the Modern World*, Chicago and London: University of Chicago Press.

—— (2001) 'Civil Society and Religion: Retrospective Reflections on Catholicism and Prospective Reflections on Islam', *Social Research*, 68: 4, 1041–80.

Christelow, A. (1987) 'Ritual, Culture and Politics of Islamic Reformism in Algeria', *Middle Eastern Studies*, 23: 3, 255–74.

Constantin, F. (1995) 'Muslims and Politics: The Attempts to Create Muslim National Organisations in Tanzania, Uganda and Kenya', in H.B. Hansen and M. Twaddle (eds) *Religion and Politics in East Africa: The Period Since Independence*, London: James Curry, 19–31.

Dieste, J.L.M. (2009) '"Demonstrating Islam": The Conflict of Text and the *Mudawwana* Reform in Morocco', *The Muslim World*, 99: 1, 134–54.

Ellis, S. and G. ter Haar (1998) 'Religion and Politics in Sub-Saharan Africa', *The Journal of Modern African Studies*, 36: 2, 175–201.

Esack, F. (1988) 'Three Islamic Strands in the South Africa Struggle for Justice', *Third World Quarterly*, 10: 2, 473–98.

Fisher, H.J. (1985) 'The Juggernaut's Apologia: Conversion to Islam in Black Africa', *Africa: Journal of the International African Institute*, 55: 2, 153–73.

Gumi, S.A. and I.A. Tsiga (2001) *Where I Stand?* Ibadan, Nigeria: Spectrum Books.

Hastings, A. (1997) *The Construction of Nationhood: Ethnicity, Religion and Nationalism*, Cambridge: Cambridge University Press.

Haynes, J. (2006) 'Islam and Democracy in East Africa', *Democratization*, 13: 3, 490–507.

Hunwick, J.O. (1992) 'An African Case Study of Political Islam', *Annals of the American Academy of Political and Social Science*, 524: 143–55.

Hurvitz, N. (2002) 'The *Mihnah* (Inquisition) and the Public Sphere', in M. Hoexter, S.N. Eisenstadt, and N. Levtzion (eds) *The Public Sphere in Muslim Societies*, Albany: State University of New York, 17–29.

Imam, A. (2003) *Please Stop the International Amina Lawal Protest Letter Campaigns.*

Jack, H.A. (1959) 'Malam Aminu Kano: A Profile', *African Today*, 6: 4, 6–10.

Janson, M. (2005) 'Roaming About For God's Sake: The Upsurge of the Tabligh Jama'at in the Gambia', *Journal of Religion in Africa*, 35: 4, 450–81.

——(2006) '"We Are All the Same, Because We All Worship God": The Controversial Case of a Female Saint in the Gambia', *Africa*, 76: 4, 502–25.

Johnston, D.L. (2007) 'Maqāṣid al-sharīa: Epistemology and Hermeneutics of Muslim Theologies of Human Rights', *Die Welt des Islams*, 47: 2, 149–87.

Larsen, K. (2001) 'Spirit Possession as Oral History: Negotiating Islam and Social Status. The Case of Zanzibar', in B.S. Amoretti (ed.) *Islam in East Africa: New Sources*, Rome: Herder Editrice le Libreria, 275–96.

Lee, R.D. (2008) 'Tunisian Intellectuals: Responses to Islamism', *Journal of North African Studies*, 13: 2, 157–73.

Lewis, I.M. (1986) *Religion in Context: Cults and Charisma*, Cambridge: Cambridge University Press.

Lofchie, M.F. (1965) *Zanzibar: Background to Revolution*, Princeton: Princeton University Press.

Loimeier, R. (1997) 'Islamic Reform and Political Change: The Example of Abubakar Gumi and the Yan Izala Movement in Northern Nigeria', in E.E. Rosander and D. Westerlund (eds) *African Islam and Islam in Africa*, London: Hurst and Company, 286–307.

—— (2011) 'Zanzibar's Geography of Evil: The Moral Discourse of the Anṣār al-sunna in Contemporary Zanzibar', *Journal for Islamic Studies*, 31: 4–28.

Mahmoud, M. (2000) 'Mahmud Muhammad Taha's Second Message of Islam and His Modernist Project', in J. Cooper, R. Nettler, and M. Mahmoud (eds) *Islam and Modernity: Muslim Intellectuals Respond*, London: I.B. Taurus, 105–28.

Mazrui, A. (1993) 'Ethnicity and Pluralism: The Politicization of Religion in Kenya', *Journal of Muslim Minority Affairs*, 14: 191–201.

Moosa, E. (1996) 'Prospects of Muslim Law in South Africa: A History and Recent Developments', in E. Cotran and C. Mattat (eds) *Yearbook of Islamic and Middle Eastern Law: Volume 3*, London: Kluwer Law International, 130–55.

—— (1997) 'Worlds "Apart": Tablighi Jama'at in South Africa Under Apartheid, 1963–1993', *Journal for Islamic Studies*, 17: 28–48.

—— (2000) 'Worlds "Apart": Tablighi Jama'at in South Africa Under Apartheid, 1963–1993', in M.K. Masud (ed.) *Travellers in Faith: Studies of the Tablighi Jama'at as a Transnational Islamic Movement for Faith Renewal*, Leiden: Brill; Boston: Koln, 206–21.

Na'im an-, A.A. (1990) *Toward an Islamic Reformation: Civil Liberties, Human Rights, and International Law*, Syracuse, NY: Syracuse University Press.

O'Brien, D.B.C. (2003) *Symbolic Confrontations: Muslims Imagining the State in Africa*, London: Hurst & Company.

O'Brien, S. (1999) 'Pilgrimage, Power and Identity: The Role of the Hajj in the Lives of Nigerian Hausa Bori Adepts', *Africa Today*, 46: 11–40.

Oded, A. (1996) 'Islamic Extremism in Kenya: The Rise and Fall of Sheikh Khalid Balala', *Journal of Religion in Africa*, 26: 406–15.

Reetz, D. (2011) 'Introduction', in A.I. Tayob, I. Niehaus, and W. Weisse (eds) *Muslim Schools and Education in South Africa and Europe*, Münster, Germany: Waxmann Verlag, 85–104.

Reichmuth, S. (1997) 'A Regional Centre of Islamic Learning in Nigeria: Ilorin and its Influence on Yoruba Islam', in N. Grandin and M. Gaborieu (eds) *Madrasa: La Transmission du Savoir dans le Monde Musulman*, Paris: XP Editions Arguments, 229–45.

Rosander, E.E. (1997) 'Introduction: The Islamization of "Tradition"and "Modernity"', in D. Westerlund and E.E. Rosander (eds) *African Islam and Islam in Africa: Encounters between Sufis and Islamists*, London: Hurst and Company in co-operation with the Nordic Africa Institute Uppsala Sweden, 1–27.

Salvatore, A. and D.E. Eickelman (2004a) 'Muslim Publics', in A. Salvatore and D.E. Eickelman (eds) *Public Islam and the Common Good*, Leiden: Brill, 3–27.

—— (2004b) 'Preface: Public Islam and the Common Good', in A. Salvatore and D.E. Eickelman (eds) *Public Islam and the Common Good*, Leiden: Brill, xi–xxv.

Sanneh, L. (1994) 'Translatability in Islam and in Christianity in Africa: A Thematic Approach', in T.D. Blakely, W.E.A. van Beek, and D.L. Thomson (eds) *Religion in Africa: Experience and Expression*, London: James Curry, 22–45.

Sayed, M.K. (2010) *The Shifting World of South African Madrasahs, 1973-2008*, MA thesis, University of Cape Town.

Seeseman, R. (2006) 'African Islam or Islam in Africa? Evidence from Kenya', in R. Seeseman and R. Loimeier (eds) *The Global Worlds of the Swahili: Interfaces of Islam, Identity and Space in 19th and 20th-century East Africa*, Berlin: Lit Verlag, 229–50.

Shahin, E.E. (1997) *Political Ascent: Contemporary Islamic Movements in North Africa*, Boulder, CO: Westview Press.

Soares, B.F. (1999) 'Muslim Proselytization as Purification', in A.A. an-Na'im (ed.) *Proselytization and Communal Self-Determination in Africa*, Maryknoll, NY: Orbis Books, 228–45.

—— (2005) *Islam and the Prayer Economy: History and Authority in a Malian Town*, Edinburgh: Edinburgh University Press; Ann Arbor: University of Michigan Press for the International African Institute.

Starret, G. (1998) *Putting Islam to Work: Education, Politics, and Religious Transformation in Egypt*, Berkeley: University of California Press.

Stewart, C.C. (1990) 'Islam', in A.D. Roberts (ed.) *The Colonial Moment in Africa: Essays on the Movement of Minds and Materials, 1900-1940*, Cambridge: Cambridge University Press, 191–222.

Tayob, A. (1999) *Islam in South Africa: Mosques, Imams and Sermons*, Gainesville: University of South Florida Press.

—— (2004) 'Race, Ideology, and Islam in Contemporary South Africa', in R.M. Feener (ed.) *Islam in World Cultures: Comparative Perspectives*, Santa Barbara, CA: ABC CLIO, 253–82.

—— (ed.) (2011) *Muslim Marriages in South Africa: From Constitution to Legislation: Papers presented at Muslim Marriages Workshop, Saturday 22 May 2010, Capetonian Hotel*, Cape Town: Centre for Contemporary Islam.

Tayob, A., I. Niehaus and W. Weisse (eds) (2011) *Muslim Schools and Education in South Africa and Europe*, Münster, Germany: Waxmann.

Trimingham, J.S. (1980) *The Influence of Islam upon Africa*, London: Longman.

Turner, S. (2009) '"These Young Men Show No Respect for Local Customs" – Globalization and Islamic Revival in Zanzibar', *Journal of Religion in Africa*, 39: 3, 237–61.

Vahed, G. (2003) 'Contesting "Orthodoxy": The Tablighi-Sunni Conflict Among South African Muslims in the 1970s and 1980s', *Journal of Muslim Minority Affairs*, 23: 2, 313–34.

Appendix: maps and tables

Map A Distribution of Muslim population by country and territory*

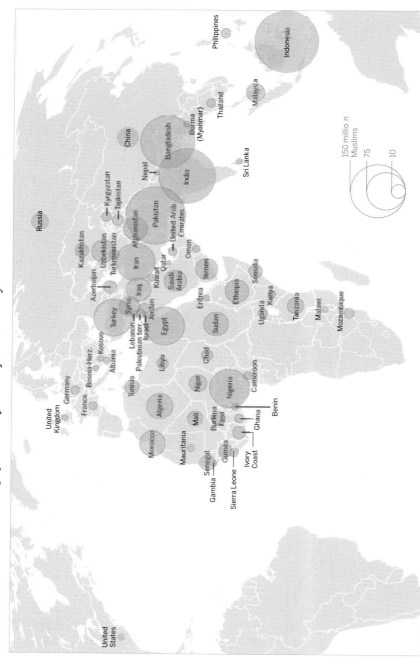

*only countries with more than one million Muslims are shown

Source: Pew Research Center's Forum on Religion and Public Life: Mapping the Global Muslim Population, 2009. Used with permission. www.pewforum. org/Muslim/Mapping-the-Global-Muslim-Population.aspx

Map B World distribution of Muslim population

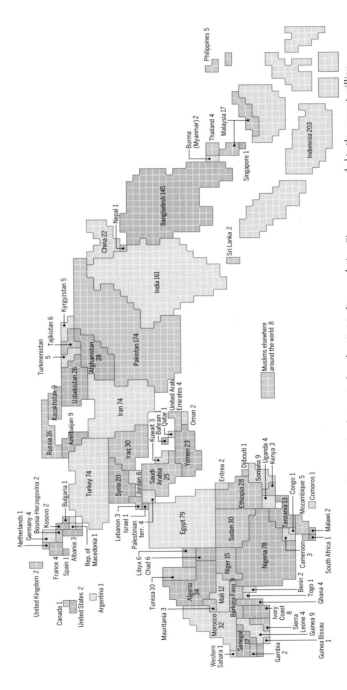

World Population 6.8 billion

Muslim Population 1.57 billion

Canada 1
United States 12
Argentina 1

United Kingdom 2
Netherlands 1
Germany 4
Bosnia-Herzegovina 2
Kosovo 2
France 4
Albania 3
Spain 1
Bulgaria 1
Rep. of Macedonia 1
Turkey 74
Russia 16
Azerbaijan 9
Kazakhstan 9
Turkmenistan 5
Tajikistan 6
Kyrgyzstan 5
Uzbekistan 9
Afghanistan 28
Iran 74
Pakistan 174
China 22
Nepal 1
Bangladesh 145
India 161
Sri Lanka 2

Burma (Myanmar) 2
Thailand 4
Malaysia 17
Singapore 1
Philippines 5
Indonesia 203

Lebanon 3
Israel 1
Palestinian terr. 4
Syria 20
Jordan 6
Iraq 30
Saudi Arabia 25
Kuwait 3
Bahrain 1
Qatar 1
United Arab Emirates 4
Yemen 23
Oman 2

Muslims elsewhere around the world 8

Western Sahara 1
Mauritania 3
Morocco 32
Tunisia 10
Algeria 34
Libya 6
Chad 6
Egypt 79
Mali 12
Niger 15
Sudan 30
Senegal 12
Burkina Faso 9
Nigeria 78
Gambia 2
Guinea Bissau 1
Guinea 9
Sierra Leone 4
Ivory Coast 8
Ghana 4
Togo 1
Benin 2
Cameroon 3
Congo 1
Ethiopia 28
Eritrea 2
Djibouti 1
Somalia 9
Uganda 4
Kenya 3
Tanzania 13
Mozambique 5
Malawi 1
Comoros 1
South Africa 1

This 'weighted' map of the world shows each country's relative size based on its Muslim population. Figures are rounded to the nearest million.

Source: Pew Research Center's Forum on Religion and Public Life: Mapping the Global Muslim Population, 2009. Used with permission. www.pewforum.org/Muslim/Mapping-the-Global-Muslim-Population.aspx

Table A Muslim population by region

	Estimated 2009 Muslim population	Percentage of population that is Muslim	Percentage of world Muslim population
Asia-Pacific	972,537,000	24.1%	61.9%
Middle East-North Africa	315,322,000	91.2%	20.1%
Sub-Saharan Africa	240,632,000	30.1%	15.3%
Europe	38,112,000	5.2%	2.4%
Americas	4,596,000	0.5%	0.3%
World Total	1,571,198,000	22.9%	100%

Source: Pew Research Center's Forum on Religion and Public Life: Mapping the Global Muslim Population, 2009. www.pewforum.org/Muslim/Mapping-the-Global-Muslim-Population.aspx

Table B Countries with the largest number of Muslims

	Estimated 2009 Muslim population	Percentage of population that is Muslim	Percentage of world Muslim population
Indonesia	202,867,000	88.2%	12.9%
Pakistan	174,082,000	96.3%	11.1%
India	160,945,000	13.4%	10.3%
Bangladesh	145,312,000	89.6%	9.3%
Egypt	78,513,000	94.6%	5.0%
Nigeria	78,056,000	50.4%	5.0%
Iran	73,777,000	99.4%	4.7%
Turkey*	73,619,000	98%	4.7%
Algeria	34,199,000	98.0%	2.2%
Morocco*	31,993,000	99%	-2%

*Data for Turkey and Morocco comes primarily from general population surveys, which are less reliable than censuses or large-scale demographic and health surveys for estimating minority-majority ratios. As a result, the percentage of the population that is Muslim in these two countries is rounded to the nearest integer.
Source: Pew Research Center's Forum on Religion and Public Life: Mapping the Global Muslim Population, 2009. www.pewforum.org/Muslim/Mapping-the-Global-Muslim-Population.aspx

Table C Countries with the largest number of Muslims living as minorities

	Estimated 2009 Muslim population	Percentage of population that is Muslim	Percentage of world Muslim population
India	160,945,000	13.4%	10.3%
Ethiopia	28,063,000	33.9%	1.8%
China	21,667,000	1.6%	1.4%
Russia	16,482,000	11.7%	1.0%
Tanzania	13,218,000	30.2%	0.8%
Ivory Coast	7,745,000	36.7%	0.5%
Mozambique	5,224,000	22.8%	0.3%
Philippines	4,654,000	5.1%	0.3%
Germany*	4,026,000	5%	<1%
Uganda	3,958,000	12.1%	0.3%

*Data for Germany comes in part from general population surveys, which are less reliable than censuses or large-scale demographic and health surveys for estimating minority-majority ratios. As a result, the percentage of the population that is Muslim in Germany is rounded to the nearest integer.
Source: Pew Research Center's Forum on Religion and Public Life: Mapping the Global Muslim Population, 2009. www.pewforum.org/Muslim/Mapping-the-Global-Muslim-Population.aspx.

*I*ndex